W9-AXV-756

Across Cultures

A READER FOR WRITERS

Second Edition

Sheena Gillespie

Robert Singleton

Queensborough Community College
City University of New York

ALLYN and BACON

BOSTON   LONDON   TORONTO   SYDNEY   TOKYO   SINGAPORE

*To Ruth, Flo, and Helen; to Jay Ford; and to the Memory of
Rachel Maria Asrelsky, a Victim of Pan Am Flight 103,
December 21, 1988—Advocates of Crossing Cultures*

Executive Editor: Joseph Opiela
Series Editorial Assistant: Brenda Conaway
Production Administrator: Rowena Dores
Editorial-Production Service: York Production Services
Cover Administrator: Linda Dickinson
Composition Buyer: Linda Cox
Manufacturing Buyer: Megan Cochran

Copyright © 1993, 1991 by Allyn and Bacon
A Division of Simon & Schuster, Inc.
160 Gould Street
Needham Heights, Massachusetts 02194

All rights reserved. No part of the material protected by this copyright notice may be reproduced
or utilized in any form or by any means, electronic or mechanical, including photocopying,
recording, or by any information storage and retrieval system, without written permission from
the copyright owner.

Library of Congress Cataloging-in-Publication Data
Gillespie, Sheena, date
    Across cultures : a reader for writers / Sheena Gillespie, Robert
Singleton. — 2nd ed.
        p.   cm.
    ISBN 0-205-14577-9 (acid-free paper)
    1. College readers. 2. Pluralism (Social sciences)—Problems,
exercises, etc. 3. Readers—Pluralism (Social sciences)
4. Culture—Problems, exercises, etc. 5. English language-
—Rhetoric. 6. Readers—Culture. I. Singleton, Robert. II. Title.
PE1417.G48   1993
808'.0427—dc20   92-21758
                                                              CIP

This textbook is printed on
recycled, acid-free paper.

Credits
Pages 6–7 From *The Beginning: Creation Myths around the World* by Maria Leach. Copyright ©
1956 by Funk & Wagnalls Co. Renewed 1984 by Macdonald Leach. Reprinted by permission of
HarperCollins Publishers.

Credits continued on page 582, which constitutes an extension of the copyright page.

Printed in the United States of America
10 9 8 7 6 5 4 3   97 96 95 94 93

CONTENTS

CHAPTER 3.   Education   191

CHAPTER 5.   Interactions

CHAPTER 7.   Aspirations   507

*Student essay.

RHETORICAL CONTENTS

Narration

Description

Definition

Comparison and Contrast

Cause and Effect

Persuasion

PREFACE FOR THE TEACHER

Across Cultures is a reader that invites students to look beyond their own society and culture. The title embodies our guiding image of a reaching out—moving beyond the immediate and the parochial to an acknowledgment and acceptance of pluralism and diversity within and among cultures. In our usage, such reaching out does not mean blending or blurring or assimilating (or hybridizing, in the biological sense). The outreach we mean may be found first, in the selection of readings by authors from and about many countries: by North Americans writing about other cultures and about United States culture and subcultures; by members of ethnic subcultures in the United States, such as immigrants or their children, African-Americans, or American Indians, writing about the United States; and by persons from other cultures writing about those cultures. Second, this reaching out is encouraged by the text's apparatus, in aids to the student. "Perspectives" (quotations); chapter introductions; selection headnotes; the end-of-lesson trio "Interpretations," "Correspondences," "Applications"; and "Additional Writing Topics" are found in every chapter.

The second edition of *Across Cultures* includes two student essays per chapter, reinforcing our conviction that students do examine their own cultural interactions and are open to new ones. In Chapter 1, for example, Andrew Rein and Yael Yarimi recall mourning rituals for a family relative, while Brian Delancy and Juliet Wright evaluate their experiences with vastly different cultures. We have also included three additional selections in each chapter on topics suggested by users of the first edition.

The outreach implied by the title *Across Cultures* is an outgrowth of our understanding of the term *culture*. To define culture is a task not to be limited to a mere dictionary definition. Distinguished anthropologists A. L. Kroeber and Clyde Kluckhohn have devoted a sizable volume, *Culture: A Critical Review of Concepts and Definitions,* to this topic. Their effort continues whenever anthropologists communicate. In assembling this textbook, we have found Bronislaw Malinowski's essay on culture in the *Encyclopedia of the Social Sciences* (vol. IV), and Kluckhohn's 1962 essay, "The Concept of Culture," particularly useful. In those works these definitions appear: Culture is the "artificial, secondary environment" that human beings superimpose on the natural, and (from Kluckhohn)

> Culture, then, is . . . that part [of human life] which is learned by
> people as the result of belonging to some particular group, and
> is that part of learned behavior which is shared with others. It is
> our social legacy, as contrasted with our organic heredity. It is
> the main factor which permits us to live together in a society,
> giving us ready-made solutions to our problems, helping us to
> predict the behavior of others, and permitting others to know
> what to expect of us.

From these definitions, then, these characteristics of culture follow:
Culture is social, it is a human achievement, and human achievements are
designed to serve an end or good; that is, the good of human beings. The
world of culture is a world of values. Although the good may be immate-
rial—truth, beauty, honor, glory—cultural good must be realized in tem-
poral and material form. Culture consists as much in conserving values as
in realizing them. And finally, culture is pluralistic. It is society's attempt
to realize a large number of values, some of them highly complex.

Today, travel across boundaries and continents—physical meeting of
people from different cultures—is going on at a rapid rate. The rate of
immigration to America approaches that at the turn of the century. "With
an annual influx of 90,000 or more legal immigrants and an additional
40,000 or so undocumented aliens arriving each year, the proportion of
foreign-born New Yorkers may pass the historic 1910 high of 40 percent
within a decade," writes Sam Roberts in *The New York Times* of July 22,
1989. "The latest group of immigrants is considerably more diverse na-
tionally," he says. These numbers and this diversity are reflected in our
schools, especially those in New York, Los Angeles, Miami, San Antonio,
and other cities, but also in smaller towns across the country.

When we look up from our daily newspapers and around at the faces
of our students, we can see that this immigration is reflected in our
students' diverse racial, ethnic, national, and cultural backgrounds—
blacks, whites, Native Americans, Asians, Africans, and Hispanics. If ever
a group of people faced the world's variety, it is today's teachers and
students. As Mike Rose, associate director of Writing Programs at the
University of California at Los Angeles and author of *Lives on the Boundary: The Struggles and Achievements of America's Underprepared* (1989),
writes:

> Diversity. A word much in the news. A single word used to
> represent many kinds of students who are not from mainstream
> America: ethnic minority students, immigrant students, older
> students, students from the white working class. Both the popu-
> lar media and our professional literature tell us about the prob-
> lems and challenges a diverse student population presents to

colleges—to our professional training, our curricula, our institutional procedures.*

And Ronald Takaki, professor of ethnic studies at the University of California at Berkeley, writes in the same *Chronicle* (March 8, 1989), p. 15:

> The need to open the American mind to greater cultural diversity will not go away. We can resist it by ignoring the changing ethnic composition of our student bodies and the larger society, or we can realize how it offers colleges and universities a timely and exciting opportunity to revitalize the social sciences and humanities, giving both a new sense of purpose and a more inclusive definition of knowledge.

In the last few years we have heard much about cultural literacy. Without engaging in the debate about whether E. D. Hirsch overemphasizes education as information, we simply point out that Hirsch sees no conflict in cultural literacy and *multi*cultural literacy: a large percentage of the items in Hirsch's own "Appendix: What Literate Americans Should Know"† relate to non-American or American minority cultures. Abraham and Isaac, Achilles, Africa, Afghanistan, the Alamo, Algiers, Allah, Ankara, Apaches, apartheid, and Aztecs are just a few of the A items.

Advocates of both cultural and multicultural literacy may complain that Hirsch's list is arbitrary, but who would wish it monocultural? The goal of this volume is to provide a sampler of today's vast cultural diversity. In doing so, we hope to promote an attitude of acceptance, even celebration, of that diversity and to suggest ways of probing correspondences, relationships, and mutual benefits therein. We do not attempt to—we cannot—hide the difficulties and suffering sometimes caused by cultural diversity, but we do believe these difficulties can be reduced when people know more about others and therefore are more accepting of them.

The selections we offer in *Across Cultures* cover a much greater variety of cultural trends than the table of contents indicates. For example, traditions, the subject of Chapter 1, naturally lead to questions of family life, the roles of women and men, the influence of feminism, class differences, and rituals and ceremonies of all kinds. Work, the subject of Chapter 4, leads to such related subjects as affirmative action, immigration, cultural displacement, family narratives, and definitions of success.

---

*"Non-Traditional Students Often Excel in College and Can Offer Many Benefits to Their Institutions," *Chronicle of Higher Education* (Oct. 11, 1989), p. B2.
†*Cultural Literacy* (1987), pp. 152–215.

The chapter on aspirations (Chapter 7) deals with many of these same subtopics, but seen from a different angle; it also focuses on the relationship between the individual and the group, mentors, and role models. The chapters are also interconnected in ways that the table of contents cannot indicate. For example, "work" exists within a matrix of traditions, relationships, education, choices, and aspirations. Hence our inclusion of "Correspondences" throughout the book. These questions ask students to make connections and draw comparisons between the "Perspectives" (brief quotations at the beginning of each chapter) and the selections in that chapter, between the selections within the chapter, and between the selections in different chapters.

Each chapter begins, as we have said, with "Perspectives," brief provocative quotations that stimulate thought and discussion on the chapter topic. Next come the selections—myths, folk tales, essays, and short stories. Whereas many of the essays and stories reflect the seemingly endless—often tumultuous—changes in current events, our rationale for including myths and folk tales is to show culture in its conserving role. Although *Across Cultures* probably pays more attention to shifts in population and to political and economic changes around the world, these changes occur against backgrounds of centuries of history and tradition, of treasured stories of origins and beginnings that give direction to the current shifting allegiances. Such stories may actually revive and sustain some cultures.

The opening selections of each chapter are myths and folk tales that remind us of how culture sustains us. These stories are regarded as holy, as scripture, as culturally indispensable; they link time and the timeless. As N. Scott Momaday says of the storyteller in American Indian tradition: "[He] creates himself and his listeners through the power of his perception, his imagination, his expression, his devotion to important details. He is a holy man; his function is sacred."

Helen Vendler, distinguished critic, professor of English at Harvard University, and past president of the Modern Language Association, pleads in her Presidential Address of 1980 for the implicit value of studying "myth, legend, and parable":

> It is not within our power to reform the primary and secondary schools, even if we have a sense of how that reform might begin. We do have it within our power, I believe, to reform ourselves, to make it our own first task to give, especially to our beginning students, that rich web of associations, lodged in the tales of majority and minority culture alike, by which they could begin to understand themselves as individuals and as social beings. We must give them some examples of literature, suited to their level of reading, in which these tales have an indisputable literary embodiment. All freshman English courses, to my mind, should

devote at least half their time to the reading of myth, legend, and parable; and beginning language courses should do the same. [*PMLA*, Vol. 96, no. 3, p. 350]

Cultural commentary in our text is direct and explicit. Each chapter includes one section on general American culture by an American writer, two or three selections by writers from diverse ethnic groups within the United States writing either on the experience of those groups or on individuals within them, and about five selections by writers from cultures elsewhere in the world.

A "Geographical Index" at the back of the book indicates the world-wide scope of these selections, the better to place American culture and its own diversity in a world context for comparison. Comparison or cross-examination is the purpose of the questions called Correspondences, which follow each selection. The Applications section provides writing and discussion topics and follows each group of "Perspectives" and each selection.

These activities call on the student to analyze cross-cultural similarities and differences and sometimes to place themselves at crossroads. Each selection is preceded by a biographical/cultural headnote and is followed by questions—Interpretations—which provoke thinking and discussion, probe comprehension, call attention to important rhetorical features, and help the reader relate the selection to the chapter topic.

We are again grateful to Joe Opiela, our editor, who enthusiastically supported the inclusion of student essays. Our special thanks to the following faculty at Queensborough who offered incisive criticisms and suggestions and assisted in obtaining student texts: Mary Bernardez, Virginia Cleary, Jean Darcy, Terezinha Fonseca, Gretchen Haynes, Allen Lanner, Elizabeth McGrath, Helene O'Connor, Tony Pipolo, and Barbara Witenko. We acknowledge our gratitude to Margaret Cavanaugh, Kathy Howard, and Marge Caronna for their generous assistance in the preparation of the manuscript.

We would like to thank the following reviewers for their helpful comments and suggestions: Margot Banks, Kean College of New Jersey; Vivian R. Brown, Laredo Junior College; Kathleen Shine Cain, Merrimack College; Barbara Carr, Stephen F. Austin State University; Ian Cruikshank, Florrisant Valley Community College; Jean English, Tallahassee Community College; Sallyanne H. Fitzgerald, University of Missouri-St. Louis; Christopher Gould, University of North Carolina; Alan Heineman, University of San Francisco; Carol Hovanec, Ramapo College; Keith Miller, Arizona State University; Joyce M. Pair, Dekalb College; Victor Villanueva, Northern Arizona University; Gary Waller, Carnegie-Mellon University; John R. Williams, Southeastern Louisiana University.

PREFACE FOR THE STUDENT

This book points toward possibilities hardly imagined in the world of your parents. Through business travel, tourism, governmental foreign aid, immigration, and an explosion in all kinds of communication, cultural interactions are occurring at a greater rate than ever before.

Old cultures, and even some not so old, like that of the United States, like to think, "We are the world." But once cultures cross—whether such meetings add to or subtract from the sum of their parts—they are never again the same: they can never again claim absoluteness, exclusivity, or monopoly. To promote such meetings, or crossings, is the purpose of *Across Cultures: A Reader for Writers.*

Whenever you read a newspaper or watch television, you are reminded that every aspect of your life—from politics and economics to music, the movies, fashion, sports, and education—is affected by developments around the globe. A tunnel is built under the English Channel from Dover to Calais and people in Gloucestershire pubs feel less like islanders. The Berlin Wall falls and Washington talks of a peace dividend. The U.S.S.R. has been replaced by the Commonwealth of Independent States (C.I.S.). The NATO and European Community countries must adapt to a non-Communist Eastern Europe and a united Germany. Tiananmen Square explodes and London steps up its attempts to evacuate a shaky Hong Kong. Only thirty-five years after the Civil Rights sit-ins in Montgomery, Alabama, approximately 7,000 African Americans hold public office in the United States, one of them the first black governor. The New World reverberates in the Old. Nelson Mandela walks out of prison in Capetown and credits world-wide sanctions with bringing hope to anti-apartheid forces in South Africa. Change begets change. Immigration to New York City approaches again its historic 1910 high of 40 percent. How do we meet such changes? Preparation for the redefinition of an educated person: An educated person is one who is culturally literate and appreciates, understands, and is tolerant of intercultural relationships.

Cultural meetings can occur in many ways. By culture we mean that "artificial, secondary environment" (Malinowski) which human beings superimpose on the natural environment. Wherever people make their mark on nature, they are creating a culture; a great deal of effort goes into a "creative conversation" about the value of these marks. A society expends a great deal of effort in attempting to conserve what it deems to be most valuable. Our first chapter, "Traditions," deals with such efforts. The remaining six chapters suggest some of the many ways in which cultural meetings can occur: in the family and other relationships, in education, in our work, interactions, choices, and aspirations.

At the center of each chapter are readings on a common subject or meeting ground, but you are introduced to the chapter through a group of brief quotations ("Perspectives") to stimulate personal responses in journal entries and collaborative explorations in group projects. Each selection is introduced with a biographical headnote that places the author in a particular historical-geographical context. After each selection are two sets of questions: "Interpretations," to provoke thinking and discussion and to call attention to specific rhetorical features, and "Correspondences," to encourage comparisons of cultures. Accordingly, you will often be asked to compare selections within, between, and among chapters.

The first one or two selections in each chapter are myths or folktales. These stories show culture in its conserving role. The stories purport to explain a people's origin or trace their values to earliest times. Each chapter also has selections by authors from and about a variety of countries: by North Americans writing on other cultures or about United States culture and subcultures; by members of ethnic subcultures within the United States, writing about themselves (often as outsiders); and by foreigners writing about their native cultures. At least two selections in each chapter are short stories.

Several features of the book will help you to apply the readings to your study of writing. The "Perspectives" section can be used to stimulate journal writing. "Applications" questions provide structured opportunities for you to convey what you have learned to a wider audience than just your peers through more structured writing and discussion activities. The "Additional Writing Topics" at the end of each chapter require you to conduct interviews, engage in debate, take positions, or reach conclusions. And a "Rhetorical Glossary" defines terminology essential to any writing class.

When you look around your classes and your campus, you probably see a student body diverse in its many countries, classes, and ages. When *this* inclusive group says, or sings, "We are the world," they are right. This is the world of *Across Cultures*.

CHAPTER 1

Traditions

The idea of tradition or heritage is inherent in most definitions of culture. For example, the anthropologist Edward Sapir says that "culture is . . . the socially inherited assemblage of practices and beliefs that determines the texture of our lives" (*Language*, 1921, p. 221). J. L. Myers asserts, "culture, then, is what remains of men's past, working on their present, to shape their future" (*Political Ideas of the Greeks,* 1927, p. 16).

Although conservation of traditional values is characteristic of all cultures, some honor it more than do others. "Rejection of tradition," writes Paula Gunn Allen in *Who is Your Mother? Red Roots of White Feminism* (p. 14), a leading Native American writer and anthologist, "constitutes one of the major features of American life." Americans, continues Allen, can and should learn from Native Americans to value tradition: "The Native-American view, which highly values maintenance of traditional customs, values, and perspectives . . . has the advantage of providing a solid sense of identity and lowered levels of psychological and interpersonal conflict."

Robert Bellah qualifies this line of argument. He feels that the tendency of Americans to reject tradition does not necessarily eliminate its influence: "In our forward-facing society, we are more apt to talk about the future than the past . . . yet even in the debate about our future, our cultural tradition in its several strands, is still very much present, . . . (*Habits of the Heart: Individualism and Commitment in American Life,* 1985, p. 27). Thus it is no surprise that our attitude toward tradition is ambivalent. (We want it, but we want to be free of it; we love part of the tradition but also hate part of it.) Tradition is both past and future, both history and destiny: "So long as it is vital, the cultural tradition of a people—its symbols, ideas, and ways of feeling—is always *an argument about the meaning of the destiny its members share. Cultures are dramatic conversations* about things that matter to their participants, and American culture is no exception" (italics ours). Americans need to learn to participate in such conversations about our own traditions and those of other, older cultures. It is no accident that almost every selection in this chapter comes out of a very old culture—Bantu, Mayan, Native American, Egyptian, Persian (Iranian), Chinese, and Polish.

Our purpose in this chapter is to explore the significance of these traditions—both our own and those of others. These opening selections demonstrate the universal importance of traditions but also celebrate their diversity. They show that the "dramatic conversations about things that matter" are continuous and may lead to a number of conclusions. They suggest an astonishing variety of tradition in its "several strands": rituals, ceremonies, customs, "symbols, ideals, and ways of feeling." Little wonder, then, that *intra*-cultural (and, less wonder, *inter*cultural) conversation is sometimes argument.

We can see such argument variously in progress, whether in Russell Baker's and N. Scott Momaday's reflections on the importance of their family origins or in Jehan Sadat's visit back in time to her husband's village and her subsequent reassessment of her assumption "How miserable the [traditional Egyptian] women must be." On a lighter note, Michael Kaufman explains and defends handkissing's contribution to Polish morale.

In "The Water-Faucet Vision," Gish Jen gives a spirited child's-eye view of Chinese-Americans in California, juxtaposing childhood encounters with Catholic Christians and adult encounters with fundamentalist Christians. In "The Wedding," Shusha Guppy shows the happy side of arranged marriage in the pre-Iran Persia of her parents' generation.

In "Seven Days of Mourning" and "Taxidermist's Funeral" student writers Yael Yarimi and Andrew Rein describe traditions surrounding death in their different Jewish cultures.

When "dramatic conversation" stops—when tradition is unquestioningly accepted or revered—it can stifle, maim, or kill. So, at least, suggests John King Fairbank as he looks at footbinding, a thousand-year-old custom that ended only in this century. In "The Lottery," a cautionary tale set in a New England village, Shirley Jackson also suggests that blind adherence to custom can be deadly.

Let us hope that the overheard conversations in this chapter will convince you that "answering" our heritage(s) is preferable to silence.

PERSPECTIVES

I was born a thousand years ago, born in the culture of bows and arrows . . . born in an age when people loved the things of nature, and spoke to it as though it had a soul.
                                                                    Chief Dan George

When you are in the presence of sorrow, you are in a holy place.

                                                                    George Santayana

But in order to speak about all to all, one has to speak of what all know and the reality common to all. The sea, the rain, necessity, desire, and the struggle against death—these are the things that unite us all.
                                                                    Albert Camus

I have found that life persists in the midst of destruction, and therefore, there must be a higher law than that of destruction.
                                                                    Mohandas K. (Mahatma) Gandhi

When there is pain, there are no words; all pain is the same.

                                                                    Toni Morrison

The position of women in a society provides an exact measure of the development of that society.

                                                                    Gustav Geiger

Memory is the diary that we all carry about with us.
                                                                    Oscar Wilde

Tradition is a guide and not a jailor.
                                                                    W. Somerset Maugham

To everything there is a season, and a time to every purpose under the heaven: a time to be born, and a time to die; a time to plant, and a time to pluck up that

*which is planted; a time to kill, and a time to heal; a
time to break down, and a time to build up; a time to
weep, and a time to laugh; a time to mourn, and a time
to dance; a time to cast away stones, and a time to
gather stones together; a time to embrace, and a time to
refrain from embracing; a time to get, and a time to
lose; a time to keep, and a time to cast away; a time to
rend, and a time to sew; a time to keep silence, and a
time to speak; a time to love, and a time to hate; a time
of war, and a time of peace. What profit hath he that
worketh in that wherein he laboreth?*

Ecclesiastes 3: 1–10

We do not remember days, we remember moments.

Cesare Pavese

*We have to do with the past only as we can make it
useful to the present and the future.*

Frederick Douglass

*We want to remain curious, startled, provoked,
mystified, and uplifted. We want to glare, gaze, gawk,
behold, and stare. We want to be given opportunities to
change, and ultimately we want to be told that we can
become kings and queens, or lords of our own destinies.
We remember wonder tales and fairy tales to keep our
sense of wonderment alive and to nurture our hope that
we can seize possibilities and opportunities to transform
ourselves and our worlds.*

Jack Zipes

*Memory is something we reconstruct, something we
create. Memory is a story we make up from snatches of
the past.*

Lynne Sharon Schwartz

Myths are public dreams, dreams are private myths.

Joseph Campbell

*And poetry is a marvelous lightning,
A rain of silent words,
A forest of throbbings and hopes,
The songs of oppressed peoples,
The new songs of liberated peoples.*

Javier Heraud

Applications

1. Wilde and Schwartz comment on the relationship between memory and identity as well as its importance in the rituals of storytelling. Freewrite on their perspectives. How might writing in your journal enhance your memories? To what extent is it true that we all have stories to tell?

2. Analyze the points of view expressed in these perspectives on aspects of traditions. On what functions of traditions do they focus? What do they suggest about the roles of traditions? Do you agree that our attitude toward tradition is ambivalent? Explain your answer.

In the Beginning
Bantu Creation Story

African Legend

Here are two different stories about how the world was created. The first is a legend from the Bantu, a diverse black people inhabiting a large part of southern Africa south of the Congo and speaking many languages (including Zulu and Swahili) and dialects. The second is the opening of the Popol Vuh, *the sacred saga of the Quiché, a branch of the great Mayan civilization. The Quiché Maya live in what is now western Guatemala.*

IN THE BEGINNING, in the dark, there was nothing but water. And Bumba was alone.

One day Bumba was in terrible pain. He retched and strained and vomited up the sun. After that light spread over everything. The heat of the sun dried up the water until the black edges of the world began to show. Black sandbanks and reefs could be seen. But there were no living things.

Bumba vomited up the moon and then the stars, and after that the night had its light also.

Still Bumba was in pain. He strained again and nine living creatures came forth: the leopard named Koy Bumba, and Pongo Bumba the crested eagle, the crocodile, Ganda Bumba, and one little fish named Yo; next, old Kono Bumba, the tortoise, and Tsetse, the lightning, swift, deadly, beautiful like the leopard; then the white heron, Nyanyi Bumba, also one beetle, and the goat named Budi.

Last of all came forth men. There were many men, but only one was white like Bumba. His name was Loko Yima.

The creatures themselves then created all the creatures. The heron created all the birds of the air except the kite. He did not make the kite. The crocodile made serpents and the iguana. The goat produced every beast with horns. Yo, the small fish, brought forth all the fish of all the seas and waters. The beetle created insects.

Then the serpents in their turn made grasshoppers, and the iguana made the creatures without horns.

Then the three sons of Bumba said they would finish the world. The first, Nyonye Ngana, made the white ants; but he was not equal to the task, and died of it. The ants, however, thankful for life and being, went searching for black earth in the depths of the world and covered the barren sands to bury and honour their creator.

Chonganda, the second son, brought forth a marvellous living plant from which all the trees and grasses and flowers and plants in the world have sprung. The third son, Chedi Bumba, wanted something different, but for all his trying made only the bird called the kite.

Of all the creatures, Tsetse, lightning, was the only troublemaker. She stirred up so much trouble that Bumba chased her into the sky. Then mankind was without fire until Bumba showed the people how to draw fire out of trees." There is fire in every tree," he told them, and showed them how to make the firedrill and liberate it. Sometimes today Tsetse still leaps down and strikes the earth and causes damage.

When at last the work of creation was finished, Bumba walked through the peaceful villages and said to the people, "Behold these wonders. They belong to you." Thus from Bumba, the Creator, the First Ancestor, came forth all the wonders that we see and hold and use, and all the brotherhood of beasts and man.

Quiché-Mayan Creation Story

Quiché-Mayan Legend

BEFORE THE WORLD was created, Calm and Silence were the great kings that ruled. Nothing existed, there was nothing. Things had not yet been drawn together, the face of the earth was unseen. There was only motionless sea, and a great emptiness of sky. There were no men anywhere, or animals, no birds or fish, no crabs. Trees, stones, caves, grass, forests, none of these existed yet. There was nothing that could roar or run, nothing that could tremble or cry in the air. Flatness and emptiness, only the sea, alone and breathless. It was night; silence stood in the dark.

In this darkness the Creators waited, the Maker, Tepeu, Gucumatz, the Forefathers. They were there in this emptiness, hidden under green and blue feathers, alone and surrounded with light. They are the same as wisdom. They are the ones who can conceive and bring forth a child from nothingness. And the time had come. The Creators were bent deep around talk in the darkness. They argued, worried, sighed over what was to be. They planned the growth of the thickets, how things would crawl and jump, the birth of man. They planned the whole creation, arguing each point until their words and thoughts crystallized and became the same thing. Heart of Heaven was there, and in the darkness the creation was planned.

Then let the emptiness fill! they said. Let the water weave its way downward so the earth can show its face! Let the light break on the ridges, let the sky fill up with the yellow light of dawn! Let our glory be a man walking on a path through the trees! "Earth!" the Creators called. They called only once, and it was there, from a mist, from a cloud of dust, the mountains appeared instantly. At this single word the groves of cypresses and pines sent out shoots, rivulets ran freely between the round hills. The Creators were struck by the beauty and exclaimed, "It will be a creation that will mount the darkness!"

Interpretations

1. In the Bantu story "The creatures themselves then created all the creatures": fish produced fish, birds produced birds (except for the predatory kite), and so on. How "scientific" is this explanation?

2. Why is there almost no explanation of Bumba's identity (other than his being white and "the Creator, the First Ancestor") or of his sickness? Are such details better omitted? Can you supply the missing explanation?

3. In the Bantu story what purpose does the retching incident serve? (What tone does it set?)

4. What is the purpose of the Bantu story?

5. How important in the Quiché creation story is language?

6. In the Quiché story what are the creators' main attributes? How are they demonstrated in the story?

7. What seems to be the Creators' main motive in creating "a man" in the Quiché story?

8. Interpret the last sentence of the Quiché story. What explanation does it provide for the Creation?

9. Compare the tones and meanings of the two creation stories.

Correspondences

1. Review the quotation *Ecclesiastes* (pages 3–4). Compare the creation concepts in Ecclesiastes with those in the Bantu and Quiché stories. Which account do you prefer? How do they differ in implication?

2. We are accustomed to thinking of time as segments of past, present, and future. Compare your concept of time with those implied in Ecclesiastes 3:1–10 and the two creation stories.

Applications

1. Working in your group, discuss the roles and function of creation texts. Why is it important to become aware of different cultural explanations of the origins of the natural world?

2. Myths or folk tales link the timebound and the timeless. Analyze the significance of the motifs of light and darkness in both creation stories. What do they suggest about the nature of good and evil?

from Morrisonville

Russell Baker

Russell Baker (b. 1925) was born in Morrisonville, Virginia. He is a regular columnist for The New York Times. *He began his career in journalism with the* Baltimore Sun, *and in 1954 joined the Washington Bureau of the* Times. *His books include* An American In Washington *(1961),* All Things Considered *(1965),* Poor Russell's Almanac *(1972), and two autobiographies,* Growing Up *(1982) and* The Good Times *(1989).*

In "Morrisonville," a selection from The Good Times, *Baker shares childhood memories about the delight of growing up nineteenth-century style, but adds that it was a poor time in which to prepare for the twentieth century. As you read this selection, focus on what Baker has to say about the memories triggered at his mother's funeral and about family traditions.*

WHEN MY MOTHER died in 1984 we went back to the Virginia churchyard where my father and Herb were buried. It was a bitterly cold January day, and the wind off the Short Hill Mountain scattered the preacher's words down the valley and made us cling tight to each other against the icy blasts of winter and death.

"They'll never get me back up there in those sticks," she used to say in the bad old Depression days after she had taken Doris and me out of Virginia and made us city people in New Jersey.

"Back up there in those sticks." She made it sound so forlorn, such a Godforsaken backwater out beyond Nowhere. She said it so often—"back up there in those sticks"—that it became my memory of the place. For years I never wanted to go back. Sometimes I even told people, "They'll never get me back up there in those sticks."

She was talking of Morrisonville, the village where I was born. It lay in the Loudoun Valley of northern Virginia, a long sweep of fat, rich Piedmont farmland cradled between mountains that parallel the Blue Ridge into the Potomac River. Four miles to the north was the New Jerusalem Lutheran Church where Morrisonville worshiped and buried its dead. I remembered going there in a long procession of black cars for my father's funeral on a golden November day in 1930.

"This is the biggest funeral there's ever been in the Lutheran church," an old gentleman told my mother that day, trying to make her feel honored, I guess.

A few weeks later my mother, Doris, and I were gone from Morrison-ville. Gone for good, to hear her tell it. "Never get me back up there in those sticks."

She had been brave then. Maybe the bravest of all the brave things she did was giving Audrey, her baby, only ten months old, for adoption by my uncle Tom and aunt Goldie. Uncle Tom, one of my father's brothers, had a good job with the B&O Railroad and could give Audrey a comfortable life, not the kind of adventure my mother was in for as she headed off to New Jersey with Doris and me, off to patching those worn-out smocks in the A&P laundry.

"Never get me back up there in those sticks."

Maybe it was only bravado, which was lost on a boy, but I was in middle age and had seen half the world before I came back to Morrison-ville one day and gazed at it in wonder, thinking, *My God, this is one of the most beautiful places I have ever seen.*

Until then, I had never thought of it longingly with love, though it was my birthplace and my father's, too, and had been home to my father's family for two hundred and fifty years. For me it had always been a shabby, mean place "back up there in those sticks" which I had been lucky to escape.

So bringing her back at the end was not a vengeful attempt to have the last word in the lifelong argument between us. It was done out of a sense that a family is many generations closely woven; that though generations die, they endure as part of the fabric of the family; and that a burying ground is a good place to remind the living that they have debts to the past. This churchyard was where she belonged. It was full of her life.

The grave was beside Herb's. He had died in 1962. My father was a short stroll southward down the slope, beside his mother, Ida Rebecca. Ida Rebecca and my mother had once been bitter competitors in the passionate matter of which one would rule my father. A short stroll westward was Uncle Tom, a good and gentle man who had been a loving father to Audrey.

Down the hillside a few yards from Ida Rebecca and my father were Uncle Irvey and his wife, Aunt Orra. Uncle Irvey was Ida Rebecca's oldest boy, the solemn one, the responsible one. My mother never liked Uncle Irvey, although he and Orra had taken her and my father to live with them at Morrisonville when they were first married and too poor to afford their own place, and though I had been born in Uncle Irvey's house. Maybe she could never forgive Uncle Irvey for having once needed his charity; still, she had dearly loved Aunt Orra.

There was far more of Morrisonville in the graveyard than there was in Morrisonville. Here was my uncle Edgar, one of Ida Rebecca's twin boys, who used to manage the Morrisonville baseball team. Here was my father's youngest brother, Uncle Lewis, who used to put me on a board on his barber chair and cut my hair with artistic scissor flourishes, then douse it with Jeris or Lucky Tiger when my father took me to his barbershop.

Nearby were the husband and wife with whom my mother boarded when she first came to Loudoun County as a young schoolteacher in the 1920s. And the preacher whose Sunday sermons she had attended. The teacher who taught the upper grades in the two-room schoolhouse they shared. Students she had taught in the second grade.

That day's ceremony was not among the biggest funerals ever held there. She was in her eighty-seventh year. Except for children, grandchildren, and great-grandchildren, most of her world had passed by. Doris, Audrey, Mary Leslie, and I huddled together under a canvas canopy crackling in the wind. The people we had married stood close behind with some of our children and three or four of our cousins from nearby Lovettsville who remembered her from long ago.

Our sorrow that day was tempered by relief. After six years of the nursing home, of watching her change into somebody else, and then into nobody at all, death seemed not unwelcome. It had been heartbreaking to see her mind run down, fading slowly at first, then swiftly emptying out almost everything but a few old memories that had got wedged in the crevices and the primordial instinct not to give up, not to quit, not to let life beat you, not to die.

"Don't be a quitter, Russell," she used to tell me. "If there's one thing I hate, it's a quitter."

Toward the end, sitting by the bed, holding her hand, I had silently told her, "It's not worth fighting for anymore. Give it up. Let go. It's all right to quit now."

For three days we argued the point in absolute silence. I don't think I won that argument. I don't think she finally quit there at the end. She was just overwhelmed by superior power.

Afterward, I felt bad about having broken the faith. Maybe I had let her down at the end. This was romantic nonsense, of course, because for all practical purposes she had been gone for years, and, in any case, that silent argument over the final three days had not been an argument at all, but only my own mind privately doubting the values she had hammered into me in childhood. Still, even in death, she retained the power to make me dissatisfied with myself by dwelling on the failures.

There was my failure to become the next Edwin James, for instance. Hadn't I disappointed her there? Never mind that I lacked the temperament, the desire, and the talent to run a big bureaucracy like the *Times*'s news operation. Maybe I could have overcome those drawbacks if I hadn't given in to Old Devil Laziness. Or so I told myself when the memory of her battle cries rattled my peace of mind.

"If at first you don't succeed . . ."

"For God's sake, Russell, show a little gumption for once in your life. . . ."

To be sure, the column had been successful enough. I had been writing it nearly twenty-two years by the time she died. It was not a column meant to convey news, but a writer's column commenting on the news by using different literary forms: essay devices, satire, burlesque, sometimes even fiction. It was proof that she had been absolutely right when she sized me up early in life, guessed I'd been born with the word gene, and steered me toward literature, believing that writing might be the way I could make something of myself, could amount to something.

The column had got its share of the medals American newspaper people give themselves, including a Pulitzer Prize in 1979. My mother never knew about that. The circuitry of her brain had collapsed the year before, and she was in the nursing home, out of touch with life forevermore, with the world of ambition, success, prizes, and vanity.

I could only guess how the woman she used to be might have responded to the news of the Pulitzer, but the guessing wasn't hard. I'm pretty sure she would have said, "That's nice, Buddy. It shows if you buckle down and work hard you'll be able to make something of yourself one of these days."

In training me to pass hard judgments on myself, she finally led me to pass hard judgments on the values by which she lived. Long before she died, even before her mind collapsed, I had begun to have a bad conscience about the constant hunger for success that had consumed those good, early years in the business.

Things had come my way too easily. Hadn't I repaid Buck Dorsey shabbily, considering how much he seemed a father to me? I hadn't even been involved in the great stories of my era, as the earlier generation of World War Two reporters had been. Reston, Phil Potter, Bill Lawrence, Price Day, Bill White, Gerry Fay, Eric Sevareid, Harrison Salisbury—tempered by their experience of the war, they all seemed to have a depth of character, a passion for their calling, and a sense that there were things even more important than success, another raise, a promotion, a gaudy title, and a prize citation to hang on the wall.

Well, of course, in my time as a reporter, which was from 1947 to 1962, there were not many great stories to broaden a newsman and deepen the character. Those were the good times, from the summer I started at the *Sun* in 1947 to Dallas in 1963, at least compared to what had gone before and what came afterward. They were especially good times if you were young, ambitious, energetic, and American. Being young makes all times better; being American in that brief moment that was America's golden age of empire made it the best of any time that ever was or will be. Provided you were white.

Good times, though, are not the best times for a reporter. When the country began to pull apart in the 1960s and 1970s, I felt melancholy about being left out as a new bunch of reporters went off to cover the demonstrations, riots, wars, and assassinations; to challenge the integrity of the government my generation had believed in; and, eventually, to change the entire character of American journalism, and change it for the better, too.

Part of the upheaval of that time was an attack on the values my mother had preached and I had lived by. The attack on ambition and striving for success was especially heavy. People who admitted to wanting to amount to something were put down as materialists idiotically wasting their lives in the "rat race." The word "gumption" vanished from the language.

Our children were adolescents now. They brought the fever for change into the house. Not wanting to be the dead hand of the corrupt past, I tried to roll with the new age. I decided not to drive my children as my mother had driven me with those corrupt old demands that they amount to something.

Materialism, ambition, and success were out the window. The new age exalted love, self-gratification, mystical religious experience, and passive Asian philosophies that aimed to help people resign themselves peaceably to the status quo. Much of this seemed preposterous to me, but I conceded that my mother might have turned me into a coarse materialist, so kept my heretical suspicions to myself while trying to go along with the prevalent theory, enunciated best by The Beatles, that "love is all you need."

And then I broke. The trouble was that too many people were not playing the love game. Too many people were still playing my mother's gumption game, and playing it very hard. Gradually I saw that these people were quietly preparing themselves to take over the country. Slowly, I began to fear that our three children—Kathleen, Allen, Michael—were not going to be members of the take-over class. I started preaching the ambition gospel to them.

It was silly, of course. Adolescence is too late to start hearing about gumption. Still, something had to be done. The schools were sending home alarming report cards. Reading that progression of grim report cards, I reached a shameful conclusion: I had failed to fire my children with ambition.

This was a time when, despite the new age, parents talked about getting their children into Harvard the way old folks once talked about getting into Heaven. It was the old rat race. Still going on. And plenty of children not too love-besotted to run the course. Everywhere I saw adults transforming their children into barracuda, pressuring tots for grades that would get them into elite colleges, which would get them elite jobs, where they would eat life's losers.

My children's report cards read like early warning signals. I panicked. Were my lovely children destined to feed the barracuda because I had failed them?

One evening at dinner, when the report cards had been as bad as usual, I heard myself shouting, "Don't you want to amount to something?"

The children looked blank. Amount to something? What a strange expression. The antique idea of life as a challenge to "make something of yourself" meant nothing to them because I had never taught it to them.

I had been at the martinis before dinner.

"Don't you want to make something of yourselves?" I roared.

The children studied their plates with eloquent faces. I could see their thoughts.

That isn't Dad yelling, they were thinking. *That's those martinis.*

They were only partly right. It wasn't the gin that was shouting loudest. It was my mother. The martinis had freed me to preach her old-time religion. The gin only gave me the courage to announce that yes, by God, I had always believed in people trying to make something of themselves, had always believed in success, had always believed that without hard work and self-discipline you could never amount to anything, and didn't deserve to.

In gin's awful grip, I was renouncing the faith of the new age in the power of gentleness, love, and understanding. I was reverting to the primitive faith of my mother. She had embedded it in my marrow, bone, and blood. There, anchored beyond reason's power to crush, it would keep me always restless, discontented, always slightly guilty for not amounting to something a little bit more.

In those days it led me into misunderstanding the children. The bleak report cards did not forebode failure, but a refusal to march to the drumbeat of the ordinary, which should have made me proud. Now they were grown people with children of their own, and we liked each other and had good times when we were together.

One defect of my mother's code was the value it placed on money and position. The children never cared a lot for that. To care, I suppose, you had to have been there with her during the Depression.

The ceremony in the churchyard was briefer than it might have been, because of the icy wind off the mountain, and afterward we went to a house in Morrisonville for food and the warmth of oak logs burning in a stone fireplace.

A house of primitive log construction, it was maybe a hundred and seventy years old, maybe more. Nobody could tell for sure. Some long-dead forebears of mine, names lost to the twentieth century, had probably helped dig the foundation, raise the logs, or mix the chinking. The family had been in those parts since 1730, but they had not been a people who wrote things down, except for an occasional ancient tombstone inscription here and there around the county.

The house was filled with a sense of timelessness that afternoon. Doris, Audrey, Mary Leslie, and I were children of the twentieth century. Up the road a short distance, I had been babied and spoiled by my grandmother, Ida Rebecca, who was born in the time of the Civil War.

My mother, whose death had brought us there, back up there in those sticks, had spent childhood in the age of the horse, buggy, and Teddy Roosevelt.

Two of Audrey's eight children had come down from New England with her, and Mimi's and my three children were also there. These were the children of America in the good times, born in the middle of the twentieth century, destined most likely to know what the twenty-first holds.

And two of our granddaughters were there, Mimi's and mine, born in the 1980s, who would, all going well, reach far into the next century. I was aware of my life stretching across a great expanse of time, of reaching across some two hundred years inside this old house and connecting Ida Rebecca's Civil War America with whatever America might be in the middle of the twenty-first century.

My father's funeral procession had set out from another house just up the road from this one. Thirty-three he was at death. And now my daughter Kathy was thirty-two, my son Allen thirty-one, my son Michael twenty-nine.

Looking at them grouped with Audrey's children around the fireplace, I realized that if my father were mysteriously compelled to join us this day, he would gravitate naturally to my children for the companionship of his own kind. If he noticed me staring too curiously at him, he might turn to Kathy or Allen or Michael and whisper, asking, "Who's the old man in the high-priced suit?"

I was now old enough to be his father.

So it is with a family. We carry the dead generations within us and pass them on to the future aboard our children. This keeps the people of the past alive long after we have taken them to the churchyard.

"If there's one thing I can't stand, Russell, it's a quitter."

Lord, I can hear her still.

Interpretations

1. What purpose(s) does repetition serve? Is Baker's use of it successful? Why or why not?

2. If Morrisonville was, in his mother's view, the hated "sticks," why did Baker bring her body back there for burial?

3. How can funerals serve tradition? Can funerals do so more effectively than weddings or other anniversaries? Why or why not?

4. Baker's grandmother Ida Rebecca and his mother "had once been bitter competitors in the passionate matter of which one would rule [his] father." What is the tone of the phrase "the passionate matter"?

Why would Baker now want (or be able) to take an objective second view of this once "passionate matter"?

5. What portrait of Baker's deceased mother emerges? Consider such phrases as "Maybe the bravest of all the brave things she did was giving Audrey, her baby, only ten months old, for adoption by my uncle Tom and aunt Goldie" and "Maybe she could never forgive Uncle Irvey for having once needed his charity" and, of course, "[They'll] Never get me back up there in those sticks."

6. Does the pervading American culture cause or fuel conflict between mothers and daughters-in-law over who bosses the son/husband, or has it developed some way of establishing harmony? (Is there a single dominant culture in such matters?)

Correspondences

Review the Perspectives on pages 3–5.

1. How does the Camus quotation apply to Baker's memories of his mother's struggles, values, and influence on his life? To what extent do his insights about the family tradition go beyond the personal?

2. Review the last section of Baker's essay, beginning with "The ceremony in the churchyard. . . ." What does he experience there? How does the "sense of timelessness" here compare with that in Ecclesiastes 3:1–10?

Applications

1. Write a paragraph defining the mother–son relationship in Russell Baker's "Morrisonville."

2. Write a journal entry on the significance of or necessity for memoirs, both public and private.

Footbinding

John King Fairbank

John King Fairbank (1907–1991) was born in South Dakota and received degrees from Harvard and Oxford universities. He was the director emeritus of Harvard's East Asian Research Center and enjoyed a distinguished career in the field of Asian studies. His numerous books on China include Modern China: A Bibliographical Guide to Chinese Works, 1898–1937 *(1950);* The United States and China *(1971); and* Chinabound: A Fifty-Year Memoir *(1983).*

China, one of the world's oldest civilizations (dating at least to 5000 B.C.) with a fifth of the world's population (about a billion inhabitants), has had a tumultuous history, especially in the last two centuries. For thousands of years, beginning with the Shang Dynasty (about 1500–1000 B.C.), a succession of dynasties ruled China and expanded Chinese political and cultural domination of East Asia. In 1644 a foreign invader, the Manchus, established the Ch'ing Dynasty without destroying the underlying culture. The nineteenth century was a time of increasing stagnation and rebellion. European powers took advantage of internal strife to take control of large parts of the country. The country became a republic in 1912 but lost much of its territory to the Japanese, both before and during World War II. The People's Republic of China was declared in 1949 under the leadership of Mao Zedong by which time footbinding—but not its effects—had vanished. In the excerpt that follows, Fairbank describes the rise of the custom of footbinding in the tenth century, details its mechanics and its influence on domestic life, and advances reasons for its longevity.

OF ALL THE MANY unexplored facets of China's ancient history, the subjection of women has been the least studied. Women were fitted into the social and cosmic order (which were a continuum) by invoking the principles of Yang and Yin. All things bright, warm, active, male, and dominant were Yang while all things dark, cold, passive, female, and yielding were Yin. This dualism, seen in the alternation of night and day or the contrast of the sun and moon, was a ready-made matrix in which women could be confined. The subjection of women was thus a sophisticated and perfected institution like the other Chinese achievements, not a mere accident of male biceps or female childbearing as might be more obviously the case in a primitive tribe. The inequality between the sexes was buttressed with philosophical underpinnings and long-continued social practices. Symbolic of woman's secondary status was her bridal night: she expected to be deflowered by a stranger, a husband selected by her family whom she had never seen before. Even though the facts may often have been less stark, the theory was hard-boiled.

Out of all this complex of theory and custom by which the Chinese world was given an enduring and stable order, the most neglected aspect is the institution of footbinding. This custom arose at court in the tenth century during the late T'ang and spread gradually among the upper class during the succeeding Sung period. By the Ming and Ch'ing eras after 1368 it had penetrated the mass of the Han Chinese population. It became so widespread that Western observers in the nineteenth century found it almost universal, not only among the upper class but throughout the farming population.

Footbinding spread as a mark of gentility and upper-class status. Small feet became a prestige item to such an extent that a girl without them could not achieve a good marriage arrangement and was subjected to the disrespect and taunts of the community. In short, bound feet became *de rigueur,* the only right-thinking thing to do for a daughter, an obligation on the part of a mother who cared about her daughter's eventual marriage and success in life. The bound foot was a must. Only tribal peoples and exceptional groups like the Manchu conquerors or the Hakka Chinese migrant groups in South China or finally the mean people, that lowest and rather small group who were below the social norms of civility, could avoid binding their daughters' feet.

The small foot was called a "golden lotus" or "golden lily" *(chin-lien)* and was much celebrated in poems and essays by male enthusiasts. Here is the early Sung poet Su Tung-p'o (1036–1101):

Anointed with fragrance, she takes lotus steps;
Though often sad, she steps with swift lightness.
She dances like the wind, leaving no physical trace.
Another stealthily but happily tries on the palace style,
But feels such distress when she tries to walk!
Look at them in the palms of your hands, so wondrously small
that they defy description.

The Sung philosophers stressed women's inferiority as a basic element of the social order. The great Chu Hsi (1130–1200) codified the cosmology of China as magistrally as his near contemporary Thomas Aquinas (d. 1274) codified that of Western Christendom. When he was a magistrate in Fukien province, Chu Hsi promoted footbinding to preserve female chastity and as "a means of spreading Chinese culture and teaching the separation of men and women."

By the Ming period the overwhelming majority of Han Chinese women all over the country had artificially small feet. The Manchu emperors many times inveighed against it in hortatory edicts, but to no avail. Male romanticizing on the subject continued unabated as in this poem of the fourteenth century:

> Lotus blossoms in shoes most tight,
> As if she could stand on autumnal waters!
> Her shoe tips do not peek beyond the skirt,
> Fearful lest the tiny embroideries be seen.[1]

There can be no doubt that footbinding was powered by a sexual fetish. Chinese love manuals are very specific about the use of bound feet as erogenous areas. All the different ways of taking hold of the foot, rubbing it with the hands, and using the mouth, tongue, and lips are explicitly catalogued. Many cases are recorded with the verisimilitude of high-class pornography. Meanwhile, the aesthetic attractiveness of the small shoes with their bright embroidered colors was praised in literature, while the tottering gait of a bound-foot woman was considered very fetching as a symbol of feminine frailty, which indeed it was. In fact, of course, bound feet were a guarantee of chastity because they kept women within the household and unable to venture far abroad. Lily feet, once formed, could not be unlocked like a chastity belt. By leaving only men able-bodied, they ensured male domination in a very concrete way.

Thus the prevalence of footbinding down to the 1920s, while the movement against it began only in the 1890s, vividly index the speed and scope of China's modern social revolution. This may be less comprehensible to white American males than to white women, or especially to black Americans, for Chinese women within the present century have had an emancipation from veritable slavery.

While footbinding is mentioned in so many foreign books about China, it is usually passed by as a curious detail. I don't think it was. It was a major erotic invention, still another achievement in Chinese social engineering. Girls painfully deformed themselves throughout their adolescence in order to attract desirable husbands who, on their part, subscribed to a folklore of self-fulfilling beliefs: for example, that footbinding made a vagina more narrow and muscular and that lotus feet were major foci of erotic sensitivity, true erogenous zones, a net addition of 50

---

[1]Howard Levy, *Chinese Footbinding: The History of a Curious Erotic Custom* (New York: Walton Rawls, 1966), p. 47.

percent to the female equipment. Normal feet, we are now told by purveyors of sexual comfort, are an underdeveloped area sensually, but one must admit they are a bit hard to handle—whereas small lotus feet could be grasped, rubbed, licked, sucked, nibbled, and bitten. The garrulous Jesuit Father Ripa, who spent a decade at the court of K'ang-hsi in the early 1700s, reported that "Their taste is perverted to such an extraordinary degree that I knew a physician who lived with a woman with whom he had no other intercourse but that of viewing and fondling her feet."[2] Having compacted all their nerve endings in a smaller area, golden lilies were far more sensitive than, for example, the back of the neck that used to bewitch Japanese samurai. After all, they had been created especially for male appreciation. When every proper girl did it, what bride would say that her sacrifice, suffering, and inconvenience were not worth it? A bride without small feet in the old China was like a new house in today's America without utilities—who would want it? Consequently in the 1930s and '40s one still saw women on farms stumping about on their heels as they worked, victims of this old custom.

A girl's foot was made small, preferably only three inches long, by pressing the four smaller toes under the sole or ball of the foot (plantar) in order to make it narrower. At the same time it was made shorter by forcing the big toe and heel closer together so that the arch rose in a bowed shape. As a result the arch was broken and the foot could bear no weight except on the heel. If this process was begun at age five, the experience was less severe than if a little girl, perhaps in a peasant household, had been left with normal feet until age eight or ten so that she could be of more use in the household.

> When I was seven [said one woman to Ida Pruitt], my mother . . . washed and placed alum on my feet and cut the toenails. She then bent my toes toward the plantar with a binding cloth ten feet long and two inches wide, doing the right foot first and then the left. She . . . ordered me to walk but when I did the pain proved unbearable. That night . . . my feet felt on fire and I couldn't sleep; mother struck me for crying. On the following days, I tried to hide but was forced to walk on my feet . . . after several months all toes but the big one were pressed against the inner surface . . . mother would remove the bindings and wipe the blood and pus which dripped from my feet. She told me that only with removal of the flesh could my feet become slender . . . every two weeks I changed to new shoes. Each new pair was one-to-two-tenths of an inch smaller than the previous one. . . . In summer my feet smelled offensively because of pus

[2]Fortunato Prandi, ed. and trans., *Memoirs of Father Ripa* (London: John Murray, 1855), p. 58.

and blood; in winter my feet felt cold because of lack of circulation . . . four of the toes were curled in like so many dead caterpillars . . . it took two years to achieve the three-inch model . . . my shanks were thin, my feet became humped, ugly and odoriferous.[3]

After the first two years the pain lessened. But constricting the feet to a three-inch size was only the beginning of trouble. By this time they were very private parts indeed and required daily care, washing and manicuring at the same time that they had to be kept constantly bound and shod night and day. Unmanicured nails could cut into the instep, bindings could destroy circulation, blood poisoning or gangrene could result. Massage and applications of hot and cold water were used to palliate the discomfort, but walking any distance remained difficult. It also produced corns on the bent-under toes, which had to be pared with a knife. Once deformed to taste, bound feet were of little use to stand on. Since weight was carried entirely on the heels, it had to be constantly shifted back and forth. Since the bound foot lacked the resilience of a normal foot, it was a tiring and unsteady support.

Footbinding, in short, had begun as an ostentatious luxury, which made a girl less useful in family work and more dependent on help from others. Yet, once the custom had spread among the populace, lotus feet were considered essential in order to get a good husband. Marriages, of course, were arranged between families and often by professional matchmakers, in whose trade the length of the lily foot was rated more important than beauty of face or person. When the anti-footbinding movement began at the end of the nineteenth century, many mothers and daughters, too, stubbornly clung to it to avoid the public shame of having large feet. The smallness of the foot, in short, was a source of social pride both to the family and to the victim. First and last one may guess that at least a billion Chinese girls during the thousand-year currency of this social custom suffered the agony of footbinding and reaped its rewards of pride and ecstasy, such as they were.

There are three remarkable things about footbinding. First, that it should have been invented at all—it was such a feat of physio-psycho-sociological engineering. Second, that once invented it should have spread so pervasively and lasted so long among a generally humane and practical-minded farming population. We are just at the beginning of understanding this phenomenon. The fact that an upper-class erotic luxury permeated the peasantry of Old China, for whom it could only lower

---

[3]Ida Pruitt, *A Daughter of Han: The Autobiography of a Chinese Working Woman* (Yale University Press, 1945), p. 22.

productivity, suggests that the old society was extraordinarily homogeneous.

Finally, it was certainly ingenious how men trapped women into mutilating themselves for an ostensibly sexual purpose that had the effect of perpetuating male domination. Brides left their own homes and entered their husband's family in the lowest status, servants of their mothers-in-law. Husbands were chosen for them sight unseen, and might find romance in extra-marital adventures or, if they could afford it, bring in secondary wives. But a woman once betrothed, if her husband-to-be died even as a child, was expected to remain a chaste widow thereafter. Mao remarked that "women hold up half the sky," but in the old China they were not supposed to lift their heads. The talent that one sees in Chinese women today had little chance to grow and express itself. This made a weak foundation for a modern society.

Interpretations

1. What is Fairbank's purpose in describing "the principles of Yang and Yin"? How does this relate to the topic of footbinding? Does the intellectual theory (Yang-Yin) really explain any important aspects of Chinese behavior? (or is it a rationalization? a pretext? an emblem?)

2. The (non-Chinese) Manchu Dynasty did not practice or condone footbinding; indeed, it tried to eradicate the practice. Why, according to Fairbank, did they fail? How was the end of footbinding like emancipation from slavery?

3. What examples can you give of elaborate psychological or other theories in contemporary America that have the aura of science or intellect but really explain very little? Do these theories affect our society for good or for ill, or do they simply remain in the realm of theory? If you find they have practical effects on people's behavior, what effects?

Correspondences

1. Review the Douglass quotation on traditions (page 4). How does it apply to the selection by Fairbank? (To what extent was footbinding "useful" in the culture of its day?)

2. Review the Geiger quotation (page 3). How does it apply to "Footbinding"? To which other selections in this chapter is it also relevant? In what way?

Applications

1. Fairbank estimates that "at least a billion Chinese girls during the thousand-year currency of this social custom suffered the agony of footbinding . . . ." What does this estimate suggest about the need to re-examine custom?

2. What is the general relationship between tradition and individual desires? For example, are the traditional ethnic or tribal costumes you are familiar with calculated to promote individual beauty (or sex appeal) or the beliefs and values of the tribe or collective?

Cinderella

Jacob and Wilhelm Grimm

*Jacob and Wilhelm Grimm (1785–1863 and 1786–1859) col-
lected their stories—known as* Grimm's Fairy Tales *(1812–1815),
the most popular collection of European folk tales—from simple
folk of the farms and villages around Kassel, in Hesse, western
Germany. They recorded what their informants told them without the manipulation and distortion of earlier collectors, and
they were impressed with the care and consistency with which
these tales were remembered and recited.*

THE WIFE OF a rich man fell sick, and as she felt that her end was drawing
near, she called her only daughter to her bedside and said: "Dear child,
be good and pious, and then the good God will always protect you, and
I will look down on you from heaven and be near you." Thereupon she
closed her eyes and departed. Every day the maiden went out to her
mother's grave and wept, and she remained pious and good. When
winter came the snow spread a white sheet over the grave, and by the
time the spring sun had drawn it off again, the man had taken another
wife.

The woman had brought with her into the house two daughters, who
were beautiful and fair of face, but vile and black of heart. Now began a
bad time for the poor step-child. "Is the stupid goose to sit in the parlor
with us?" they said. "He who wants to eat bread must earn it; out with the
kitchen-wench." They took her pretty clothes away from her, put an old
grey bedgown on her, and gave her wooden shoes. "Just look at the
proud princess, how decked out she it!" they cried and laughed, and led
her into the kitchen. There she had to do hard work from morning till
night, get up before daybreak, carry water, light fires, cook and wash.
Besides this, the sisters did her every imaginable injury—they mocked
her and emptied her peas and lentils into the ashes, so that she was forced
to sit and pick them out again. In the evening when she had worked till
she was weary she had no bed to go to, but had to sleep by the hearth in
the cinders. And as on that account she always looked dusty and dirty,
they called her Cinderella.

It happened that the father was once going to the fair, and he asked
his two step-daughters what he should bring back for them. "Beautiful
dresses," said one, "pearls and jewels," said the second. "And you,
Cinderella," said he, "what will you have?" "Father, break off for me the

first branch which knocks against your hat on your way home." So he brought beautiful dresses, pearls and jewels for his two step-daughters, and on his way home, as he was riding through a green thicket, a hazel twig brushed against him and knocked off his hat. Then he broke off the branch and took it with him. When he reached home he gave his step-daughters the things which they had wished for, and to Cinderella he gave the branch from the hazel-bush. Cinderella thanked him, went to her mother's grave and planted the branch on it, and wept so much that the tears fell down on it and watered it. And it grew and became a handsome tree. Thrice a day Cinderella went and sat beneath it, and wept and prayed, and a little white bird always came on the tree, and if Cinderella expressed a wish, the bird threw down to her what she had wished for.

It happened, however, that the King gave orders for a festival which was to last three days, and to which all the beautiful young girls in the country were invited, in order that his son might choose himself a bride. When the two step-sisters heard that they too were to appear among the number, they were delighted, called Cinderella and said: "Comb our hair for us, brush our shoes and fasten our buckles, for we are going to the wedding at the King's palace." Cinderella obeyed, but wept, because she too would have liked to go with them to the dance, and begged her step-mother to allow her to do so. "You go, Cinderella!" said she; "covered in dust and dirt as you are, and would go to the festival? You have no clothes and shoes, and yet would dance!" As, however, Cinderella went on asking, the step-mother said at last: "I have emptied a dish of lentils into the ashes for you, if you have picked them out again in two hours, you shall go with us." The maiden went through the back-door into the garden, and called: "You tame pigeons, you turtle-doves, and all you birds beneath the sky, come and help me to pick

> The good into the pot,
> The bad into the crop."

Then two white pigeons came in by the kitchen-window, and afterwards the turtle-doves, and at last all the birds beneath the sky, came whirring and crowding in, and alighted amongst the ashes. And the pigeons nodded with their heads and began pick, pick, pick, pick, and the rest began also pick, pick, pick, pick, and gathered all the good grains into the dish. Hardly had one hour passed before they had finished, and all flew out again. Then the girl took the dish to her step-mother, and was glad, and believed that now she would be allowed to go with them to the festival. But the step-mother said: "No, Cinderella, you have no clothes and you cannot dance; you would only be laughed at." And as Cinderella wept at this, the step-mother said: "If you can pick two dishes of lentils out of the ashes for me in one hour, you shall go with us." And she thought to herself: "That she most certainly cannot do again." When the step-mother had emptied the two dishes of lentils among the ashes, the maiden went through the back-door into the garden and cried: "You tame pigeons, you turtle-doves, and all you birds beneath the sky, come and help me to pick

> The good into the pot,
> The bad into the crop."

Then two white pigeons came in by the kitchen-window, and afterwards the turtle-doves, and at last all the birds beneath the sky, came whirring and crowding in, and alighted among the ashes. And the pigeons nodded with their heads and began pick, pick, pick, pick, and the others began also pick, pick, pick, pick, and gathered all the good grains into the dishes, and before half an hour was over they had already finished, and all flew out again. Then the maiden carried the dishes to the step-mother and was delighted, and believed that she might now go with them to the wedding. But the step-mother said: "All this will not help; you cannot go with us, for you have no clothes and can not dance; we should be ashamed of you!" On this she turned her back on Cinderella, and hurried away with her two proud daughters.

As no one was now at home, Cinderella went to her mother's grave beneath the hazel-tree, and cried:

> "Shiver and quiver, little tree,
> Silver and gold throw down over me."

Then the bird threw a gold and silver dress down to her, and slippers embroidered with silk and silver. She put on the dress with all speed, and went to the wedding. Her step-sisters and the step-mother however did not know her, and thought she must be a foreign princess, for she looked so beautiful in the golden dress. They never once thought of Cinderella, and believed that she was sitting at home in the dirt, picking lentils out of the ashes. The prince approached her, took her by the hand and danced with her. He would dance with no other maiden, and never let loose of her hand, and if any one else came to invite her, he said: "This is my partner."

She danced till it was evening, and then she wanted to go home. But the King's son said: "I will go with you and bear you company," for he wished to see to whom the beautiful maiden belonged. She escaped from him, however, and sprang into the pigeon-house. The King's son waited until her father came, and then he told him that the unknown maiden had leapt into the pigeon-house. The old man thought: "Can it be Cinderella?" and they had to bring him an axe and a pickaxe that he might hew the pigeon-house to pieces, but no one was inside it. And when they got home Cinderella lay in her dirty clothes among the ashes, and a dim little oil-lamp was burning on the mantle-piece, for Cinderella had jumped quickly down from the back of the pigeon-house and had run to the little hazel-tree, and there she had taken off her beautiful clothes and laid them on the grave, and the bird had taken them away again, and then she had seated herself in the kitchen among the ashes in her grey gown.

Next day when the festival began afresh, and her parents and the step-sisters had gone once more, Cinderella went to the hazel-tree and said:

"Shiver and quiver, little tree,
Silver and gold throw down over me."

Then the bird threw down a much more beautiful dress than on the preceding day. And when Cinderella appeared at the wedding in this dress, every one was astonished at her beauty. The King's son had waited until she came, and instantly took her by the hand and danced with no one but her. When others came and invited her, he said: "This is my partner." When evening came she wished to leave, and the King's son followed her and wanted to see into which house she went. But she sprang away from him, and into the garden behind the house. Therein stood a beautiful tall tree on which hung the most magnificent pears. She clambered so nimbly between the branches like a squirrel that the King's son did not known where she was gone. He waited until her father came, and said to him: "The unknown maiden has escaped from me, and I believe she has climbed up the pear-tree." The father thought: "Can it be Cinderella?" and had an axe brought and cut the tree down, but no one was on it. And when they got into the kitchen, Cinderella lay there among the ashes, as usual, for she had jumped down on the other side of the tree, had taken the beautiful dress to the bird on the little hazel-tree, and put on her grey gown.

On the third day, when the parents and sisters had gone away, Cinderella went once more to her mother's grave and said to the little tree:

"Shiver and quiver, little tree,
Silver and gold throw down over me."

And now the bird threw down to her a dress which was more splendid and magnificent than any she had yet had, and the slippers were golden. And when she went to the festival in the dress, no one knew how to speak for astonishment. The King's son danced with her only, and if any one invited her to dance, he said: "This is my partner."

When evening came, Cinderella wished to leave, and the King's son was anxious to go with her, but she escaped from him so quickly that he could not follow her. The King's son, however, had employed a ruse, and had caused the whole staircase to be smeared with pitch, and there, when she ran down, had the maiden's left slipper remained stuck. The King's son picked it up, and it was small and dainty, and all golden. Next morning, he went with it to the father, and said to him: "No one shall be my wife but she whose foot this golden slipper fits." Then were the two sisters glad, for they had pretty feet. The eldest went with the shoe into her room and wanted to try it on, and her mother stood by. But she could not get her big toe into it, and the shoe was too small for her. Then her mother gave her a knife and said: "Cut the toe off; when you are Queen you will have no more need to go on foot." The maiden cut the toe off, forced the foot into the shoe, swallowed the pain, and went out to the King's son. Then he took her on his horse as his bride and rode away with her. They were obliged, however, to pass the grave, and there, on the hazel-tree, sat the two pigeons and cried:

> "Turn and peep, turn and peep,
> There's blood within the shoe,
> The shoe it is too small for her,
> The true bride waits for you."

Then he looked at her foot and saw how the blood was trickling from it. He turned his horse round and took the false bride home again, and said she was not the true one, and that the other sister was to put the shoe on. Then this one went into her chamber and got her toes safely into the shoe, but her heel was too large. So her mother gave her a knife and said: "Cut a bit off your heel; when you are Queen you will have no more need to go on foot." The maiden cut a bit off her heel, forced her foot into the shoe, swallowed the pain, and went out to the King's son. He took her on his horse as his bride, and rode away with her, but when they passed by the hazel-tree, the two little pigeons sat on it and cried:

> "Turn and peep, turn and peep,
> There's blood within the shoe,
> The shoe it is too small for her,
> The true bride waits for you."

He looked down at her foot and saw how the blood was running out of her shoe, and how it had stained her white stocking quite red. Then he turned his horse and took the false bride home again. "This also is not the right one," said he, "have you no other daughters?" "No," said the man, "there is still a little stunted kitchen-wench which my late wife left behind her, but she cannot possibly be the bride." The King's son said he was to send her to him; but the mother answered: "Oh no, she is much too dirty, she cannot show herself!" But he absolutely insisted on it, and Cinderella had to be called. She first washed her hands and face clean, and then went and bowed down before the King's son, who gave her the golden shoe. Then she seated herself on a stool, drew her foot out of the heavy wooden shoe, and put it into the slipper, which fitted like a glove. And when she rose up and the King's son looked at her face he recognized the beautiful maiden who had danced with him and cried: "This is the true bride!" The step-mother and the two sisters were horrified and became pale with rage; he, however, took Cinderella on his horse and rode away with her. As they passed by the hazel-tree, the two white doves cried:

> "Turn and peep, turn and peep,
> No blood is in the shoe,
> The shoe is not too small for her,
> The true bride rides with you,"

and when they had cried that, the two came flying down and placed themselves on Cinderella's shoulders, one on the right, the other on the left, and remained sitting there.

When the wedding with the King's son was to be celebrated, the two false sisters came and wanted to get into favor with Cinderella and share her good fortune. When the betrothed couple went to church, the elder was at the right side and the younger at the left, and the pigeons pecked out one eye from each of them. Afterwards as they came back, the elder was at the left, and the younger at the right, and then the pigeons pecked out the other eye from each. And thus, for their wickedness and false-hood, they were punished with blindness all their days.

Interpretations

1. What is indicated by Cinderella's repeated efforts to pass her step-mother's tests with the lentils?

2. What does Cinderella's good relationship with various birds indicate about her? What relationship do you see between the birds—espe-cially the ones who peck out the step-daughters' eyes—and Cin-derella's own natural mother?

3. The step-mother says to her daughter, "Cut the toe off; when you are Queen you will have no more need go on foot." Comment on the mother's values implied here and their influence on the daughter's behavior and values.

4. Artificially small feet are no match for Cinderella's own feet. Do you think this story aims simply to entertain, or to teach young readers an important truth about human nature? If the latter, what truth?

Correspondences

1. Review Campbell's perspective (page 4). To what extent does it apply to Grimm's version of the Cinderella story? What examples can you think of to support his thesis that "dreams are private myths."

2. What parallels exist between the Cinderella story and Fairbank's "Footbinding"? How do you account for the story's popularity in cultures as diverse as the United States, Germany, and China?

Applications

1. Read poet Anne Sexton's version of "Cinderella" in her book *Transformations*. What criticism of the fairy tale does Sexton make? To what extent do you agree or disagree with her point of view?

2. Write a journal entry on your memory of a favorite childhood fairy tale. Then reread the story and write a second entry describing your adult response. How do you account for the differences? What insights did you gain?

The Algonquin Cinderella

Native American Myth

The small Algonquin tribe of Canada was one of the first with whom the French formed alliances. Because of their mingling with whites, little remains of Algonquin culture. Their name, however, came to be used to designate other nearby tribes, and their language family (known as Algonquian) is one of the most widespread of all North American Indian languages, extending from New Brunswick to the Rocky Mountains. Among Indian languages in the Algonquian stock are the Arapaho, the Cheyenne, the Blackfoot, the Potawatami, the Ottawa, the Passamaquoddy, the Penobscot, the Delaware, and the Cree.

THERE WAS ONCE a large village of the MicMac Indians of the Eastern Algonquins, built beside a lake. At the far end of the settlement stood a lodge, and in it lived a being who was always invisible. He had a sister who looked after him, and everyone knew that any girl who could see him might marry him. For that reason there were very few girls who did not try, but it was very long before anyone succeeded.

This is the way the test of sight was carried out: at evening-time, when the Invisible One was due to be returning home, his sister would walk with any girl who might come down to the lakeshore. She, of course, could see her brother, since he was always visible to her. As soon as she saw him, she would say to the girls:

"Do you see my brother?"

"Yes," they would generally reply—though some of them did say "No."

To those who said that they could indeed see him, the sister would say:

"Of what is his shoulder strap made?" Some people say that she would enquire:

"What is his moose-runner's haul?" or "With what does he draw his sled?"

And they would answer:

"A strip of rawhide" or "a green flexible branch," or something of that kind.

Then she, knowing that they had not told the truth, would say:

"Very well, let us return to the wigwam!"

When they had gone in, she would tell them not to sit in a certain place, because it belonged to the Invisible One. Then, after they had helped to cook the supper, they would wait with great curiosity, to see him eat. They could be sure that he was a real person, for when he took off his moccasins they became visible, and his sister hung them up. But beyond this they saw nothing of him, not even when they stayed in the place all the night, as many of them did.

Now there lived in the village an old man who was a widower, and his three daughters. The youngest girl was very small, weak and often ill: and yet her sisters, especially the elder, treated her cruelly. The second daughter was kinder, and sometimes took her side: but the wicked sister would burn her hands and feet with hot cinders, and she was covered with scars from this treatment. She was so marked that people called her *Oochigeaskw,* the Rough-Faced-Girl.

When her father came home and asked her why she had such burns, the bad sister would at once say that it was her own fault, for she had disobeyed orders and gone near the fire and fallen into it.

These two elder sisters decided one day to try their luck at seeing the Invisible One. So they dressed themselves in their finest clothes, and tried to look their prettiest. They found the Invisible One's sister and took the usual walk by the water.

When he came, and when they were asked if they could see him, they answered: "Of course." And when asked about the shoulder strap or sled cord, they answered: "A piece of rawhide."

But of course they were lying like the others, and they got nothing for their pains.

The next afternoon, when the father returned home, he brought with him many of the pretty little shells from which wampum was made, and they set to work to string them.

That day, poor Little Oochigeaskw, who had always gone barefoot, got a pair of her father's moccasins, old ones, and put them into water to soften them so that she could wear them. Then she begged her sisters for a few wampum shells. The elder called her a "little pest", but the younger one gave her some. Now, with no other clothes than her usual rags, the poor little thing went into the woods and got herself some sheets of birch bark, from which she made a dress, and put marks on it for decoration, in the style of long ago. She made a petticoat and a loose gown, a cap, leggings and a handkerchief. She put on her father's large old moccasins, which were far too big for her, and went forth to try her luck. She would try, she thought, to discover whether she could see the Invisible One.

She did not begin very well. As she set off, her sisters shouted and hooted, hissed and yelled, and tried to make her stay. And the loafers around the village, seeing the strange little creature, called out "Shame!"

The poor little girl in her strange clothes, with her face all scarred, was an awful sight, but she was kindly received by the sister of the

Invisible One. And this was, of course, because this noble lady understood far more about things than simply the mere outside which all the rest of the world knows. As the brown of the evening sky turned to black, the lady took her down to the lake.

"Do you see him?" the Invisible One's sister asked.

"I do, indeed—and he is wonderful!" said Oochigeaskw.

The sister asked:

"And what is his sled-string?"

The little girl said:

"It is the Rainbow."

"And, my sister, what is his bow-string?"

"It is the Spirit's Road—the Milky Way."

"So you *have* seen him," said his sister. She took the girl home with her and bathed her. As she did so, all the scars disappeared from her body. Her hair grew again, as it was combed, long, like a blackbird's wing. Her eyes were not like stars; in all the world there was no other such beauty. Then, from her treasures, the lady gave her a wedding garment, and adorned her.

Then she told Oochigeaskw to take the *wife's* seat in the wigwam; the one next to where the Invisible One sat, beside the entrance. And when he came in, terrible and beautiful, he smiled and said:

"So we are found out!"

"Yes," said his sister. And so Oochigeaskw became his wife.

Interpretations

1. Why does Oochigeaskw succeed where her sisters failed?

2. What explanation does the story offer or imply for Oochigeaskw's ability to see the Invisible One? How is this ability related to Oochigeaskw's persecuted position in the family?

3. How do the clothes Oochigeaskw makes or assembles for herself indicate a reverence for tradition? What effect do you think this reverence might have on her success in winning the Invisible One?

4. What part do moccasins play in the story?

Correspondences

1. Compare the Native American version of the Cinderella story with that of the Grimms. What motifs do they have in common? How do their main themes differ?

2. How do the thematic differences in the two versions of the story reflect the social and cultural values of their communities? Which version do you find more appealing?

Applications

1. Write a contemporary version of a favorite childhood fairy tale and analyze the significance of your changes. To what extent do they reflect your values?

2. Using the Cinderella story, discuss how fairy tales might be used as a tool for teaching children to respect individual versions.

The Way to Rainy Mountain

N. Scott Momaday

N(atachee) Scott Momaday (b. 1934), is a native of Oklahoma and a member of the Kiowa tribe. His writings include a novel The House Made of Dawn *(1968), a story of a man caught between cultures (for which he won the 1969 Pulitzer) and* The Way to Rainy Mountain *(1969), a collection of Kiowa legends and folktales. Recently he has chosen poetry as a vehicle to re-create the often poignant legends of his people.*

In the following excerpt from The Way to Rainy Mountain, *Momaday traces the migration of his tribe, from their origins in Montana to Oklahoma. He chronicles alliances of the Kiowas with other tribes (the Comanches and the Crows) and their subjugation by the U.S. Army. Notice how Momaday uses the memories of his grandmother's death to evoke the importance of preserving tribal traditions.*

After 1840 the Kiowas, occupying the Arkansas River region of western Oklahoma, allied with the Comanches and others against Eastern tribes that had moved west. This provoked the U.S. Army to move against both groups. By 1874 the Kiowa were devastated; their horses had been killed, and their leaders had been deported to Florida. They surrendered at Fort Sill. By 1879 most of the tribe had been moved to a reservation in southwest Oklahoma, between Fort Sill and the Washita River—the very landscape Momaday describes so dramatically here.

A SINGLE KNOLL rises out of the plain in Oklahoma, north and west of the Wichita Range. For my people, the Kiowas, it is an old landmark, and they gave it the name Rainy Mountain. The hardest weather in the world is there. Winter brings blizzards, hot tornadic winds arise in the spring, and in summer the prairie is an anvil's edge. The grass turns brittle and brown, and it cracks beneath your feet. There are green belts along the rivers and creeks, linear groves of hickory and pecan, willow and witch hazel. At a distance in July or August the steaming foliage seems almost to writhe in fire. Great green-and-yellow grasshoppers are everywhere in the tall grass, popping up like corn to sting the flesh, and tortoises crawl about on the red earth, going nowhere in the plenty of time. Loneliness is an aspect of the land. All things in the plain are isolate; there is no confusion of objects in the eye, but *one* hill or *one* tree or *one* man. To look upon that landscape in the early morning, with the sun at your back, is to lose the sense of proportion. Your imagination comes to life, and this, you think, is where Creation was begun.

I returned to Rainy Mountain in July. My grandmother had died in the spring, and I wanted to be at her grave. She had lived to be very old and at last infirm. Her only living daughter was with her when she died, and I was told that in death her face was that of a child.

I like to think of her as a child. When she was born, the Kiowas were living that last great moment of their history. For more than a hundred years they had controlled the open range from the Smoky Hill River to the Red, from the headwaters of the Canadian to the fork of the Arkansas and Cimarron. In alliance with the Comanches, they had ruled the whole of the southern Plains. War was their sacred business, and they were among the finest horsemen the world has ever known. But warfare for the Kiowas was preeminently a matter of disposition rather than of survival, and they never understood the grim, unrelenting advance of the U.S. Cavalry. When at last, divided and ill-provisioned, they were driven onto the Staked Plains in the cold rains of autumn, they fell into panic. In Palo Duro Canyon they abandoned their crucial stores to pillage and had nothing then but their lives. In order to save themselves, they surrendered to the soldiers at Fort Sill and were imprisoned in the old stone corral that now stands as a military museum. My grandmother was spared the humiliation of those high gray walls by eight or ten years, but she must have known from birth the affliction of defeat, the dark brooding of old warriors.

Her name was Aho, and she belonged to the last culture to evolve in North America. Her forebears came down from the high country in western Montana nearly three centuries ago. They were a mountain people, a mysterious tribe of hunters whose language has never been positively classified in any major group. In the late seventeenth century they began a long migration to the south and east. It was a long journey toward the dawn, and it led to a golden age. Along the way the Kiowas were befriended by the Crows, who gave them the culture and religion of the Plains. They acquired horses, and their ancient nomadic spirit was suddenly free of the ground. They acquired Tai-me, the sacred Sun Dance doll, from that moment the object and symbol of their worship, and so shared in the divinity of the sun. Not least, they acquired the sense of destiny, therefore courage and pride. When they entered upon the southern Plains, they had been transformed. No longer were they slaves to the simple necessity of survival; they were a lordly and dangerous society of fighters and thieves, hunters and priests of the sun. According to their origin myth, they entered the world through a hollow log. From one point of view, their migration was the fruit of an old prophecy, for indeed they emerged from a sunless world.

Although my grandmother lived out her long life in the shadow of Rainy Mountain, the immense landscape of the continental interior lay like memory in her blood. She could tell of the Crows, whom she had never seen, and of the Black Hills, where she had never been. I wanted to see in reality what she had seen more perfectly in the mind's eye, and traveled fifteen hundred miles to begin my pilgrimage.

Yellowstone, it seemed to me, was the top of the world, a region of deep lakes and dark timber, canyons and waterfalls. But, beautiful as it is, one might have the sense of confinement there. The skyline in all directions is close at hand, the high wall of the woods and deep cleavages of shade. There is a perfect freedom in the mountains, but it belongs to the eagle and the elk, the badger and the bear. The Kiowas reckoned their stature by the distance they could see, and they were bent and blind in the wilderness.

Descending eastward, the highland meadows are a stairway to the plain. In July the inland slope of the Rockies is luxuriant with flax and buckwheat, stonecrop and larkspur. The earth unfolds and the limit of the land recedes. Clusters of trees and animals grazing far in the distance cause the vision to reach away and wonder to build upon the mind. The sun follows a longer course in the day, and the sky is immense beyond all comparison. The great billowing clouds that sail upon it are shadows that move upon the grain like water, dividing light. Farther down, in the land of the Crows and Blackfeet, the plain is yellow. Sweet clover takes hold of the hills and bends upon itself to cover and seal the soil. There the Kiowas paused on their way; they had come to the place where they must change their lives. The sun is at home on the plains. Precisely there does it have the certain character of a god. When the Kiowas came to the land of the Crows, they could see the dark lees of the hills at dawn across the Bighorn River, the profusion of light on the grain shelves, the oldest deity ranging after the solstices. Not yet would they veer southward to the caldron of the land that lay below; they must wean their blood from the northern winter and hold the mountains a while longer in their view. They bore Tai-me in procession to the east.

A dark mist lay over the Black Hills, and the land was like iron. At the top of a ridge I caught sight of Devil's Tower upthrust against the gray sky as if in the birth of time the core of the earth had broken through its crust and the motion of the world was begun. There are things in nature that engender an awful quiet in the heart of man; Devil's Tower is one of them. Two centuries ago, because they could not do otherwise, the Kiowas made a legend at the base of the rock. My grandmother said:

Eight children were there at play, seven sisters and their brother. Suddenly the boy was struck dumb; he trembled and began to run upon his hands and feet. His fingers became claws, and his body was covered with fur. Directly there was a bear where the boy had been. The sisters were terrified; they ran, and the bear after them. They came to the stump of a great tree, and the tree spoke to them. It bade them climb upon it, and as they did so, it began to rise into the air. The bear came to kill them, but they were just beyond its reach. It reared against the tree and scored the bark all around with its claws. The seven sisters were borne into the sky, and they became the stars of the Big Dipper.

From that moment, and so long as the legend lives, the Kiowas have kinsmen in the night sky. Whatever they were in the mountains, they could be no more. However tenuous their well-being, however much they had suffered and would suffer again, they had found a way out of the wilderness.

My grandmother had a reverence for the sun, a holy regard that now is all but gone out of mankind. There was a wariness in her, and an ancient awe. She was a Christian in her later years, but she had come a long way about, and she never forgot her birthright. As a child she had been to the Sun Dances; she had taken part in those annual rites, and by them she had learned the restoration of her people in the presence of Tai-me. She was about seven when the last Kiowa Sun Dance was held in 1887 on the Washita River above Rainy Mountain Creek. The buffalo were gone. In order to consummate the ancient sacrifice—to impale the head of a buffalo bull upon the medicine tree—a delegation of old men journeyed into Texas, there to beg and barter for an animal from the Goodnight herd. She was ten when the Kiowas came together for the last time as a living Sun Dance culture. They could find no buffalo; they had to hang an old hide from the sacred tree. Before the dance could begin, a company of soldiers rode out from Fort Sill under orders to disperse the tribe. Forbidden without cause the essential act of their faith, having seen the wild herds slaughtered and left to rot upon the ground, the Kiowas backed away forever from the medicine tree. That was July 20, 1890, at the great bend of the Washita. My grandmother was there. Without bitterness, and for as long as she lived, she bore a vision of deicide.

Now that I can have her only in memory, I see my grandmother in the several postures that were peculiar to her: standing at the wood stove on a winter morning and turning meat in a great iron skillet; sitting at the south window, bent above her beadwork, and afterwards, when her vision had failed, looking down for a long time into the fold of her hands; going out upon a cane, very slowly as she did when the weight of age came upon her; praying. I remember her most often at prayer. She made long, rambling prayers out of suffering and hope, having seen many things. I was never sure that I had the right to hear, so exclusive were they of all mere custom and company. The last time I saw her she prayed standing by the side of her bed at night, naked to the waist, the light of a kerosene lamp moving upon her dark skin. Her long, black hair, always drawn and braided in the day, lay upon her shoulders and against her breasts like a shawl. I do not speak Kiowa, and I never understood her prayers, but there was something inherently sad in the sound, some merest hesitation upon the syllables of sorrow. She began in a high and descending pitch, exhausting her breath to silence; then again and again—and always the same intensity of effort, of something that is, and is not, like urgency in the human voice. Transported so in the dancing light among the shadows of her room, she seemed beyond the reach of time. But that was illusion; I think I knew then that I should not see her again.

Interpretations

1. According to tribal myth, the Kiowa "entered the world through a hollow log." From what sort of world did they consider themselves to have emerged? How might this tradition have shaped the Kiowas' attitude toward life and death?

2. Momaday says his grandmother regarded the last Kiowa Sun Dance (1887) as "a vision of deicide," or god-killing. Do you agree? Was it the death of a god or of a people?

3. What portrait of Momaday's grandmother emerges from the essay? How would you describe his relationship to her?

4. What is the significance of Momaday's equating family with tribe?

5. How does Momaday use description of the setting (the mountains and plains, the great spaces of the West) to control the mood or tone of his essay?

Correspondences

1. Memory plays an important role in the selections by Momaday and Baker. What do their memories suggest about the impact of the passage of time on family and tribe?

2. Momaday concludes his essay with a description of his grandmother praying, while Baker organizes his around his mother's funeral. How do these narrative techniques further contribute to the unity and purpose of the selections?

Applications

1. Momaday's vivid memories of his grandmother's house give rise to a sensuous re-creation of it. Describe a place you vividly recall because it played an important part in your life.

2. "My grandmother had a reverence for the sun, a holy regard that now is all but gone out of mankind. There was a wariness in her, and an ancient awe." What cultural conversation can you imagine having with Momaday's grandmother? Can you think of evidence to support his thesis that we have lost her sense of "ancient awe"?

Remarks at Amherst College upon Receiving an Honorary Degree

John F. Kennedy

John F. Kennedy (1917–1963), the thirty-fifth President of the United States, was the first Roman Catholic and one of the youngest Americans to be elected President. He received a B.S. from Harvard (1940), served in the Navy (1941–1945), and wrote the Pulitzer-Prize-winning book Profiles in Courage. *He served in Congress as both Representative and Senator from Massachusetts and in 1960 defeated Richard Nixon for President. Early in his administration a force of anti-Castro Cubans he sent to invade Cuba was defeated at the Bay of Pigs; the next year, however, he succeeded in forcing the Soviets to remove their missile bases from Cuba. Just as the nation remembers his assassination with horror, they remember the brief years of John and Jackie Kennedy in the White House as "Camelot," for it seemed to be a time of unusual respect for culture and wit, as illustrated by the following remarks and by the fact that Kennedy was the first President to invite an American poet—Robert Frost—to participate in his inauguration.*

. . . THE PROBLEMS WHICH this country now faces are staggering, both at home and abroad. We need the service, in the great sense, of every educated man or women to find 10 million jobs in the next 2½ years, to govern our relations—a country which lived in isolation for 150 years, and is now suddenly the leader of the free world—to govern our relations with over 100 countries, to govern those relations with success so that the balance of power remains strong on the side of freedom, to make it possible for Americans of all different races and creeds to live together in harmony, to make it possible for a world to exist in diversity and freedom. All this requires the best of all of us.

Therefore, I am proud to come to this college whose graduates have recognized this obligation and to say to those who are now here that the need is endless, and I am confident that you will respond.

Robert Frost said:

Two roads diverged in a wood, and I—
I took the one less traveled by,
And that has made all the difference.

I hope that road will not be the less traveled by, and I hope your commitment to the Great Republic's interest in the years to come will be worthy of your long inheritance since your beginning.

This day devoted to the memory of Robert Frost offers an opportunity for reflection which is prized by politicians as well as by others, and even by poets, for Robert Frost was one of the granite figures of our time in America. He was supremely two things: an artist and an American. A nation reveals itself not only by the men it produces but also by the men it honors, the men it remembers.

In America, our heroes have customarily run to men of large accomplishments. But today this college and country honors a man whose contribution was not to our size but to our spirit, not to our political beliefs but to our insight, not to our self-esteem, but to our self-comprehension. In honoring Robert Frost, we therefore can pay honor to the deepest sources of our national strength. That strength takes many forms, and the most obvious forms are not always the most significant. The men who create power make an indispensable contribution to the Nation's greatness, but the men who question power make a contribution just as indispensable, especially when that questioning is disinterested, for they determine whether we use power or power uses us.

Our national strength matters, but the spirit which informs and controls our strength matters just as much. This was the special significance of Robert Frost. He brought an unsparing instinct for reality to bear on the platitudes and pieties of society. His sense of the human tragedy fortified him against self-deception and easy consolation. "I have been," he wrote, "one acquainted with the night." And because he knew the midnight as well as the high noon, because he understood the ordeal as well as the triumph of the human spirit, he gave his age strength with which to overcome despair. At bottom, he held a deep faith in the spirit of man, and it is hardly an accident that Robert Frost coupled poetry and power, for he saw poetry as the means of saving power from itself. When power leads man towards arrogance, poetry reminds him of his limitations. When power narrows the area of man's concern, poetry reminds him of the richness and diversity of his existence. When power corrupts, poetry cleanses. For art establishes the basic human truth which must serve as the touchstone of our judgment.

The artist, however faithful to his personal vision of reality, becomes the last champion of the individual mind and sensibility against an intrusive society and an officious state. The great artist is thus a solitary figure. He has, as Frost said, a lover's quarrel with the world. In pursuing his perceptions of reality, he must often sail against the currents of his time. This is not a popular role. If Robert Frost was much honored during his lifetime, it was because a good many preferred to ignore his darker truths. Yet in retrospect, we see how the artist's fidelity has strengthened the fibre of our national life.

If sometimes our great artists have been the most critical of our society, it is because their sensitivity and their concern for justice, which must motivate any true artist, makes him aware that our Nation falls short of its highest potential. I see little of more importance to the future of our country and our civilization than full recognition of the place of the artist.

If art is to nourish the roots of our culture, society must set the artist free to follow his vision wherever it takes him. We must never forget that art is not a form of propaganda; it is a form of truth. And as Mr. MacLeish once remarked of poets, there is nothing worse for our trade than to be in style. In free society art is not a weapon and it does not belong to the sphere of polemics and ideology. Artists are not engineers of the soul. It may be different elsewhere. But democratic society—in it, the highest duty of the writer, the composer, the artist is to remain true to himself and to let the chips fall where they may. In serving his vision of the truth, the artist best serves his nation. And the nation which disdains the mission of art invites the fate of Robert Frost's hired man, the fate of having "nothing to look backward to with pride, and nothing to look forward to with hope."

I look forward to a great future for America, a future in which our country will match its military strength with our moral restraint, its wealth with our wisdom, its power with our purpose. I look forward to an America which will not be afraid of grace and beauty, which will protect the beauty of our natural environment, which will preserve the great old American houses and squares and parks of our national past, and which will build handsome and balanced cities for our future.

I look forward to an America which will reward achievement in the arts as we reward achievement in business or statecraft. I look forward to an America which will steadily raise the standards of artistic accomplishment and which will steadily enlarge cultural opportunities for all of our citizens. And I look forward to an America which commands respect throughout the world not only for its strength but for its civilization as well. And I look forward to a world which will be safe not only for democracy and diversity but also for personal distinction. . . .

Interpretations

1. Do you agree with Kennedy's implication that "every educated man or woman" can help "Americans of all different races and creeds to

live together in harmony"? and to "make it possible for a world to exist in diversity and freedom"? What can they do? What can *you* do?

2. Are colleges and universities the best places to find citizens who feel a responsibility to help with these tasks? What other places can you think of that could serve this purpose?

3. Kennedy says Frost's "contribution was not to our size but our spirit." Judging just by the poetic excerpt he has quoted, what has Frost contributed to our spirit? How does this excerpt relate to the idea that "the men who question power make a contribution"? What other poems can you cite by Frost that contribute to our "spirit"?

4. What rhetorical device do you find Kennedy using in these phrases: "our country will match its military strength with our moral restraint, its wealth with our wisdom, its power with our purpose"? Is his use of this device effective? Why or why not? What rhetorical device do you find Kennedy using in the last paragraph?

Correspondences

1. Apply Heraud's perspective (page 4) on poetry to Kennedy's concept of the poet expressed in his remarks at Amherst College. In what sense is the poet's role both public and private?

2. Momaday describes the storyteller in the Native American tradition as a "holyman; his function is sacred." Compare Kennedy's vision of the role of the poet to that of Momaday's storyteller. Do you agree that "when power narrows the area of man's concern, poetry reminds him of the richness and diversity of his existence"? What examples can you think of to support Kennedy's point of view?

Applications

1. Write a journal entry responding to Kennedy's statement that "if art is to nourish the roots of our culture, society must set the artist free to follow his vision wherever it takes him." Can you think of any circumstances in which artistic censorship should be imposed?

2. Is there a poet who has influenced you to the degree that Frost impressed Kennedy? Write an essay analyzing his or her influence.

from Life in the Villages

Jehan Sadat

Jehan Sadat (b. 1934) is the widow of Egyptian president Anwar el-Sadat, who was assassinated in 1981. As you will discover in Chapter 2, she grew up in Cairo as the daughter of an Egyptian civil servant and an English mother. In the selection here entitled "Life in the Villages," from her 1987 autobiography A Woman of Egypt, *Sadat is introduced to rural life by her husband. During her husband's eleven-year presidency, Jehan Sadat was active in social and humanitarian affairs, especially women's rights. Since his assassination in 1981, she has continued to fight for causes she believes in. At the same time, she has pursued an academic career as lecturer in Arabic literature at Cairo University and in the United States. Although she is a practicing Muslim, her efforts to increase Egyptian women's civil rights have met with frequent opposition from Muslim fundamentalists. For example, the decree her husband issued in 1979, popularly known as "Jehan's law" for her per-ceived influence, was abolished by the Egyptian supreme court in 1985. (This decree had allowed Egyptian women key civil rights: the right to sue for divorce and to retain custody of children if a husband was found to be polygamous. You will read of traditional Muslim child-custody practices in a Chapter 2 selection, Shusha Guppy's "Aunt Batool.")*

One of the oldest and culturally richest civilizations, at a crossroads between East and West, Egypt has been influenced by many invaders, among them the Persians, Greeks, Romans, and Arabs, the last of whom introduced the dominant religion (Islam) and language (Arabic) of Egypt. Egypt is a densely populated but largely barren country. Most of its population hugs the banks of the Nile. A British protectorate from 1914 to 1922, Egypt remained under British domination until 1952, when King Farouk was overthrown. Gamal Abdel Nasser be-came president in 1956. His protégé Anwar Sadat began his rise in the new government, becoming president in 1970. As the following selection shows, in spite of his revolutionary and re-forming sympathies, Sadat retained strong ties with village cul-ture and was able to inspire his city-bred wife with the same feelings.

"UM GAMAL, is your son well?"

"Um Gamal, I feel so sorry for you. You must have more children."

It did not matter to the women in Anwar's village of Mit Abul-Kum that I had three beautiful daughters as well as a son. No. I was known in the village only as Um Gamal, the Mother of Gamal. No matter how much I protested, in the village my daughters—or anyone's daughters—did not count. "You have only one child," the women would chide me even after my youngest daughter, Jehan, was born in 1961.

"I have four," I'd reply.

"But you have only one son. You must try to have another so he won't be all alone."

"He is not alone. He has three sisters and three half sisters as well," I would answer.

But the women would exchange side glances and shake their heads. "You should have more children," they would pronounce gravely. "Otherwise you might lose your husband."

I loved going to Anwar's village with him in the Nile Delta. The two-hour drive from Cairo was beautiful, the road lined with sycamore and eucalyptus trees and passing through miles and miles of cotton fields which were bright green in winter and filled with pale-yellow flowers in summer. As soon as we arrived in Mit Abul-Kum, my husband was transformed. Shedding his city business suit and putting on the long white galabiyya worn by all the men in the village, Anwar would go for long walks with me and the children, laughing while they rolled in the clover like puppies. Often Anwar would sing in his very loud voice the mournful songs of peasants toiling in the fields and I would wait for the neighbors to complain, but they never did. At home he taught the children to bake bread just the way he had loved to as a child, breaking an egg over the dough just before it went into the oven. They practiced and practiced to get it just right.

Anwar had been very nervous when he first brought me to his village. "You cannot go out during the day at all. You must stay inside until evening," he had told me. Not go out?

"Why?" I asked him.

"Because the people in my village will not understand you," he said.

"Anwar, what is it?" I pressed him.

He looked uneasy. "You are a woman used to the ways of the city," he explained. "The people in my village are very conservative. They will not respect you if they see you in your city clothes showing your arms and legs with your head uncovered. Such dress for women is not in our tradition."

Why, then, could I be seen in the evenings?

"That is the time set aside for visiting when the landowners and those with government jobs go out in the villages," Anwar explained. "The people are used to different ways then and accept it."

The next day I went to Tanta where I bought material for a long dress like those of the fellaheen, and a colorful scarf which I fixed to my head, as they did, with a band of flowers. And the next time we went to the village, I went out.

At first Mit Abul-Kum seemed as foreign to me as if we had gone not only to a different country but into a different century. The streets were unpaved, enveloping all who passed in their own little clouds of dust. The houses were made of baked mud and had very few windows; openings in the palm-thatched roofs let smoke out. On most roofs were piled stacks of fuel cakes made from animal dung and straw, drying in the sun. Deeply superstitious, many in the village painted their doors blue to ward off the jinns, the evil spirits described in the Quran.[1] For more insurance against the evil eye and the curses of the envious, villagers also dipped their hands into blue paint and placed their palmprints on the outside walls to evoke the protective symbol of Fatima, the Prophet's daughter. Horseshoes and ceramic hands bearing blue beads were also hung over the doors to the houses, fixed to the harnesses of their farm animals, even hung over the peasants' beds.

The lucky few in the village who had made their pilgrimage to Mecca had painted the story of their sacred journey on the outside walls of their houses as well. If they had crossed the Red Sea to Saudi Arabia by boat, there was a painting of a ship crossing the water. If they had flown, there was a painting of an airplane. Some had gone part of the way by bus or car. All this was depicted colorfully on the house walls, along with a rendition of the Kaaba, the black boxlike structure in the Great Mosque in Mecca which is the most sacred shrine in Islam.

The mud houses were very secure, as there was little rain, but they were very primitive. Before the power plant at the Aswan Dam was completed in 1968, there was no electricity in Mit Abul-Kum, no indoor plumbing or running water. The villagers rose by the sun and went to bed by the moon. Most of the houses were divided into two rooms, one used by the family to cook, sleep and pray in, the other to shelter their water buffaloes, donkeys, cows or even a camel, along with a few geese, ducks and chickens. In between the rooms there was usually an open area where the women hung their *basiras,* or bamboo mats. Salted yogurt was placed in them to drip until the yogurt turned into cheese.

In the center of the village there was a high tower for the pigeons to roost in, always noisy with the flapping of wings. The beautiful white birds were a food staple to the fellaheen[2] as well as a product to sell on market day. The only building taller than the pigeon tower was the village mosque, built shortly after the Revolution. Anwar had contributed some of its construction costs himself, donating his first paycheck from

[1]Or Koran, the sacred scriptures of Islam.
[2]Peasants, farmworkers.

el-Gumburiyya[3] so that the small mud mosque of Mit Abul-Kum could be replaced by one built with red bricks and a high minaret.

The sight of the village women depressed me at first. Older women over forty dressed always in black from head to toe and the women of all ages worked harder than the men. At dawn the women rose to the voice of the muezzin calling the faithful to the morning prayer, and then prepared the morning meal of white cheese and very sweet black tea for their families. Then there were the dirt floors of their houses to sweep out, the animals to feed, the dough to make for fresh bread, water which the women pumped by hand from the village well and carried back in jugs on their heads. Just in time they then hurried to carry lunch to their husbands in the fields, where, after the meal, they joined the men for the remainder of the day, weeding, hoeing and harvesting the crops of cotton, corn, clover and wheat.

The scene in Mit Abul-Kum was always the same, the dawn sky lighting the procession of the men in their galabiyyas toward the fields, followed by the children taking the water buffaloes and the cows out to graze and drink. Flocks of white egrets would fly behind them, settling in the early-morning fields to catch the worms which had come to the surface during the night. The egrets to me made the fields look like green carpets covered with white polka dots. By midmorning the egrets had moved, settling now on the animals, where they enthusiastically picked off the bugs from their backs.

At dusk the procession would be reversed, but it was now of a different shape. The flat horizon would silhouette not only the animals and the men in their robes, but the shapeless profiles of their long-robed wives walking behind, often carrying large loads of produce on their backs. The egrets would follow them home to roost in the trees, turning the branches totally white.

Though this view was always beautiful, I shivered when first I saw it. The women seemed like nothing but beasts of burden—or even less, because the men cared more for their cows than they did for their wives. The cow was the man's livelihood, bringing him milk and cheese and butter to eat and to sell. If his wife died he would be sad, of course. But if his cow died, he would be heartbroken, having lost his life savings and his economic future. It was cheaper, after all, for a man to add another wife than it was for him to buy a new cow.

The women were constantly kept in their place by the men. "Kill your cat on your wedding night," the men would say to each other after they married, stressing their need to be the dominant one in a marriage. The birth of a daughter was joyous, as all Egyptians love children, but it did not come close to the birth of a son. "*Illi taht el-tarha malhash farha*" was a common village expression: "What is under a veil brings no joy."

---

[3] *The Republic,* newspaper started by Anwar Sadat.

The men hardly referred to their wives by name, always calling out to them "Ya sitt," or "Hey, woman!" A woman could not interrupt her husband while he was talking with his friends, and had to walk behind him rather than beside him as they went to market. How miserable the women must be, I thought. I was wrong.

"Why are you looking so pleased, Amina?" one woman asked another at the waterwheel where all gathered to chat and gossip at noon before the women took the midday meal to their husbands in the fields.

"I sold three chickens and fourteen eggs yesterday at the market," Amina replied. "Now I can buy enough sugar and tea for the rest of the winter."

Another woman was also smiling. "Our cow is giving so much milk that I was able to sell ten kilos of cheese. My daughter's wedding will be the most splendid in the village."

Every day I joined the women at the waterwheel to listen to their conversation. And every day, while the yoked donkey or water buffalo drew the water by walking around and around the well, wearing a blindfold so that it wouldn't get dizzy and stop, my perception of these women changed. By modern standards they were disadvantaged, the great majority being illiterate. But compared to many middle-class women in Egypt in the fifties and even the sixties, the women of the village had far more freedom and independence.

What choices did middle-class women have except for those living in Cairo or Alexandria? In the smaller cities women had little education, certainly not enough to get a good job. Their husbands from the same class clung to the old traditions, expecting their wives to stay at home and care only for them and their children. These middle-class women lived in social isolation, sharing nothing of their husbands' lives and having no lives of their own outside the home.

In the rural areas the women worked side by side with the men, sharing in all aspects of their daily lives. Together they irrigated the fields, weeded and harvested the crops, sowed the new seeds. When the time came for a cow to bear a calf, the wife gladly assisted her husband in the delivery, for the birth of a calf was a blessing on any home. Not only would the family have milk to drink, but they would also prosper by having extra milk and cheese to sell. Individually, the women had their own businesses as well. They raised their own chickens and geese, collected the eggs, made their own cheese and sold what they could spare on market day. These were small freedoms, but it is many small things which make a whole. And in a way I envied them. They were certainly participating more in outside activities than I was when my children were small.

I loved the direct way the women talked. They were very bright and full of life, like my friend Hanem whose son was a nurse in the new village clinic. Hanem could neither read nor write, but because she, like many of the other women, listened to her portable radio all day, she was better informed than many of her contemporaries in the cities. Often I felt as though I were listening to a current-affairs professor when I visited with Hanem, she was so knowledgeable about events happening outside Egypt.

Though the men would certainly not admit it, it was the women in the village who made many of the decisions for the family, deciding when to build an extra room on their houses or to buy new animals to raise and sell. "The man is a river and the woman is a dike," went one popular expression in the villages. In Mit Abul-Kum the women had even organized a *gam'iyya*, a financial cooperative. Every month each woman would pay a small amount of money into a single fund, and each month a different woman would take the whole pot. In that way it was possible even for a very poor woman to get enough money to pay her son's bride-price or to buy a new sofa, straw rugs for her home, or a new dress which she would rush to show us all at the waterwheel.

The women helped each other in many ways. The oldest women in the village looked after the young children while their mothers worked in the fields. When one woman fell sick or had a baby, the other women served food to her family and cleaned her house. If a husband died—or a child—the women took turns bringing food to the poor widow, knowing she probably had little money and was not in the mood to cook anyway.

I had not been in the village long when Um Muhammad lost her son in a military accident. When I went to pay condolences, I had no difficulty locating her house. I simply followed sounds of grief. When I entered Um Muhammad's house, I found at least sixty women all dressed in black surrounding the poor mother, crying as if their own sons had died.

"I remember him as a little boy. I can see him now dressed in his military uniform coming to the village in a jeep just like a prince," one woman was crying out as I came through the door. Immediately all the women burst into wails, some beating their breasts and tearing at their clothes.

When the crying died down a little, another woman spoke. "I remember sitting at his wedding just five years ago," she cried out. "Never had he looked so beautiful dressed in his white galabiyya and a silk shawl. He looked like an angel." And again the women burst into shrieks of pain.

The atmosphere of loss was palpable. I began to cry myself, to feel the pain of the mother, and to share it. "We are never going to see Muhammad again," another woman sobbed, her arms around Um Muhammad. "Such a wonderful son. I remember when he brought you his first paycheck. 'Mother, this first salary is for you,' he said. 'You have suffered and sacrificed for me. You have been strict with me because you wanted to see me as an officer. Now it is my honor to thank you.'"

For three days the women came to lament with Um Muhammad, from the first rays of dawn until the evening, when they had to go tend to their own families. The village women did not leave their grieving sister for one minute. One third of them would bring lunch for everyone one day, another third the next, and so on. But they did not bring very good food, nor when they poured coffee and tea for those paying condolences did they offer sugar to sweeten it. This was not a time for pleasure. Only the food and drink offered to Um Muhammad, who would not eat, was sweetened.

"Try just this one bite of pigeon and take one swallow of this lemonade," the women urged Um Muhammad.

"Let me die," she cried out again and again. "Can there ever be happiness living without my son, never being able to see him again?" Immediately all the women would wail again.

The lamenting reached new peaks when Um Muhammad's grandchildren, who had been sent to another house during the day, returned at night. "See how small they are," the lament now ran. "It is too early for them to be orphans."

By the end of the three days, everyone, including Um Muhammad, was exhausted. By calling up every measure of grief at the young man's death, the women had helped to cleanse Um Muhammad's pain and to leave behind no hard grief. Nor did they desert her after the three days. Her close friends and neighbors stayed with her after that. And every Thursday afternoon until the fortieth-day ceremony, all the women returned to lament, though more quietly, with Um Muhammad while her grief began to fade. In Cairo we treated death much more privately and kept our sorrow to ourselves. But in the village everyone shared in everything.

Interpretations

1. What made the village of Mit Abul-Kum seem to Jehan Sadat like a visit to "a different century"?

2. "In the village everyone shared in everything." According to Sadat, what are the advantages of such a way of life? the disadvantages?

3. What did Sadat learn about the villagers and about herself as a result of her visit?

4. Most of the women Sadat writes about are illiterate and could never read this essay. How do you think they would react to it if they *could* read it? How would the male villagers react if they read it? For what audience do you think Sadat is writing, Egyptian or non-Egyptian, Muslim or non-Muslim? Support your answer.

5. What purpose does the dialogue in the introduction serve? How effective is it? (Does it present any problems for the general reader? If so, what are they and are they later solved?)

Correspondences

1. "Where there is pain, there are no words, all pain is the same." How is this Toni Morrison quotation borne in Sadat's description of village mourning rituals?

2. Sadat and Momaday are very aware of their surroundings. Compare Sadat's memories of village landscapes with those of Momaday's in the opening paragraph of "The Way to Rainy Mountain." How does each description contribute to the overall effectiveness of the whole selection?

Applications

1. "The man is a river and the woman is a dike." What examples does Sadat offer to support the village roles implied by this saying? How does this description apply to gender relationships in your culture?

2. Write a short cause-and-effect paragraph explaining why Jehan Sadat reformulates her original idea that the women in the villages were very unhappy.

Seven Days Of Mourning

Yael Yarimi

Yael Yarimi was born in Qiryat Eqron, Israel, a daughter of Jews of Yemenite descent. Like the majority of the sabras' (first generation who were born in the new land), Yael had a communication problem with the old generation, who tried to practice the culture they had brought with them. The gaps that were created among the generations were very common in the country in which they lacked identity. Naturally, Yael pursued the western lifestyle, the dominant one in Israel, and deserted the one of her ancestors, since the latter seemed to her obsolete. Yael rediscovered the richness of her roots only after she arrived in the United States in the late 1980s, when she reexamined her heritage.

In this essay, she expresses both appreciation and regret for the ignorance she had toward her heritage. She dedicates this essay to her parents Shalom and Yona ("peace" and "dove"), who endured many great ordeals when they came to the Holy Land. Going through a similar experience in America, Yael can now profoundly realize the high price her parents paid for their passage from the familiar to the strange. This is her way of thanking them for raising her with pride and confidence in spite of all the difficulties. She is now working on a second essay.

Tuesday

Dear Diary

It is eleven p.m. I hear unclear words coming from the next room. It is as if Mom and Dad entered an unfamiliar state and are speaking in a strange language . . . Among these odd words I can only understand one sentence Mom just said: "We must call everybody and inform them about the funeral time" . . . Now I hear my father crying. Oh my god! This is the first time in my life I have ever heard him crying just like us—the children.

I WAS TWELVE and too young to digest the significance of my grandfather's death. However, I was bothered with the notion that I would never see him again. I couldn't sleep. Constantly hiding my diary under the pillow,

I remember trying to strangle my weeping under the blanket. Threatening pictures emerged and floated in my mind.

I cannot forget the scene: our frontyard that was also our playground, turned overnight into a huge black tent made of strong, plastic canvas sheet and a great number of supporting rods. Strange people were unloading dozens of long tables and benches into the tent.

By the afternoon, all my relatives, neighbors and some other people had already arrived. Naturally, the men formed into a big rectangular pattern and began praying in loud voices, while the women were transferring large cooking pots from our house to the back of the tent. There, they installed a giant cooking stove which could be big enough for an army division. These volunteer ladies looked as if they were in a hurry. They worked so skillfully, that one might have thought that their lives depended on it.

We—the children—were running around between the legs and were scolded with blaming fingers. We were asked to be quiet. "This is not a time for joy" rebuked one of the ladies while holding my little brother by his ear. He was then sent away promising to keep quiet. Everything had happened very fast.

My father's eyes were an unforgettable sight. As the son of the deceased, my father was sitting on the ground, in one of the tent corners. Suddenly, he seemed so old, so infirm. My father, who was naturally a strong man, a towering figure, changed before my eyes into a helpless man with a saddened feeling of inner rage.

Not far from the men, in another corner, the mourning women were sitting on the ground as well. In the center of them, a woman I had never seen before was mourning in a heartbreaking wailing voice and caused all the other women to cry with her. I still remember her holding a square handkerchief with one hand on her forehead in a way that covered her entire face. Accompanying her sad songs, she then moved her upper body from side to side in a steady rhythm. Her mourning songs were interrupted by her outcries after every two stanzas that described my grandfather. I could see my grandmother's pleading facial expression as if she was trying to stop these words from being said.

I then was wondering how the mourning woman could cry and sob in such an honest way as if she knew my grandfather. I also could not understand why she had to add more agony to the already sad situation.

Dear Diary

I hate aunt Rina, I hate her so much. She had no right to push me and ask me to help the working ladies . . . I feel so sad today . . . I couldn't enter the cemetery this afternoon;

Mom says that women with periods are not clean; therefore I couldn't be present when my grandfather was buried. It is so corny . . . Grandpa, I know you hear me. I know you are watching me from heaven . . . This is a mad house. Mom says its going to be like that every day for the next seven days . . . My friend Sara, remember her?, the one you used to call "The Russian"?, she says they never cooked for funerals . . . She says our funeral is like camping. You would have been proud of me if you heard what a lecture I gave her about us, about our dream that came true; to be in the land of the Jews, about all the things you used to tell me.

I am still astonished each time I recall the dedication of the Yemenite Jewish Community during the Shiva—the seven days of mourning in Jewish tradition in which all the community has to console and help the family to get over the loss.

All men rose at dawn and were praying three times a day. After each prayer, meals were served, in a religious ceremony, first to the men, then to the mourning women and last to the congregation. Deep, stiff, plastic dishes were filled with soup and meat in the Yemenite style. Scattered pita breads were laid along the tables by the side of small round dishes that contained a spicy dip called *hilba*—made of herbs. Hilba is used to flavor the soup. People then were eating with their hands, and there were no conversations during the eating time.

Dear Diary

It has been a couple days that people are sleeping in my house. Everywhere I turn I encounter people, it's as if my house has turned into a hostel . . . Today it is an important day that's why I marked it in red ink. Today I have received my very first kiss.

Eddie, my cousin and I climbed the lemon tree in our back yard and kissed. . . . I love him so much . . . Dad must not know; he will kill me, like the time he beat me when I played with Eric.

I closed the diary, which had aged with the years. I held it to my bosom and allowed myself to cry. I can still feel the pain and the insult of the blows I received from my father. It was eighteen years ago, but I still remember him saying outrageously "Kiss is a half intercourse," then came a second round of blows.

Knocking on the door, my husband woke me up from the journey to my past. "Everybody is leaving," he shouted, "Hurry up." I wore a black dress with a black scarf as is customary at mourning in my family.

By the time we arrived at the cemetery, my grandmother had already been buried. Women were spread out on the grave, yelling and pulling their hair. Grandmother was eighty-nine years old when she died. I was so sorry that distance did not enable me to see her before.

Living in the Diaspora, I found myself torn apart between the home I am trying to establish with my American husband, and the great, rich and embracing tradition I have left in my land of birth. I miss the togetherness, the caring and the warmth among my people so much that I sometimes contemplate leaving everything I have accomplished here and just returning to my roots, to the familiar and run away from the ambiguous coldness I feel in America.

Entering the tent, my husband and I were sitting on the benches, in front of the same old tables, listening to the same heartbreaking weeping but this time from a different lady.

New generation of kids in our family were laughing and running around happy for the opportunity that brought them all together. Some of the traditional rituals will probably vanish among the new generation of Yemenite Jews in Israel, but in appearance only. I believe the essential tradition will remain forever.

Interpretations

1. How do you feel about the custom of a leader causing "all the other women to cry with her" even though the leader didn't know Yarimi's grandfather? What purpose does it serve?

2. Why do you think food has such an important place in these ceremonies? How common in other traditions is this attention to food?

3. Does moving away from one's home or native land strengthen or weaken the importance of tradition? What examples can you provide from your own experience?

4. What is added to this narrative by seeing most of it from the point of view of a twelve-year-old?

Correspondences

1. Review Schwartz's perspective on memory (page 4) and discuss its application to "Seven Days of Mourning." What do the journal entries reveal about the narrator's memories? What is her purpose in linking her grandfather's death to the present?

2. Sadat and Yarimi both focus on mourning rituals. Compare their responses. How do you account for differences in their emphases?

Applications

1. Write a journal entry responding to Yarimi's ambivalence about living in the Diaspora. Should she run away from the "ambiguous coldness of America"?

2. Discuss the last paragraph of the essay. To what extent do you agree that "the essential tradition will remain forever"? What values would be lost if that were not the case?

Taxidermist's Funeral

Andrew Rein

Andrew Rein (b. 1970) was born in New York City to a family whose religious beliefs are as diversified as a rich man's investments. He says,

> *I have Lutheran parents, Jewish grandparents, and Baptist aunts, uncles, and cousins. Although all of these religions are appealing in their own ways, I have chosen to be an Agnostic. My belief is that God exists, but is unknowable. Therefore, I follow no religious organization. Buddhaism, Judaism, and Christianity all have their beauty, mystery, and magic, but for me to follow any would be like a Christian breaking a commandment against my beliefs.*

TRADITIONS ARE NOT things that I've ever looked at in my family much less in myself. It's not that I considered them old fashioned or boring. They never seemed important enough to me to look at.

When I was ten years old, my Uncle Charlie died. He was the first person I had known who had died. I wasn't close to him, so when it happened I didn't feel a sense of loss, hurt or wanting to cry. The only memories I have of him are of going to his shop: Uncle Charlie was a taxidermist. When I would enter the shop, I would be overwhelmed by the pungent odor of formaldehyde; stuffed animals on wooden stands stared out at me with glass eyes. "Some man," my mom said about my uncle. He would pat me on the head with an old wrinkled hand and tell me through an old wrinkled mouth clinching a cigar, what a good boy I was.

One morning, my mom came into my room sobbing. "Uncle Charlie is dead." Two days later I was in a big, dark, creepy funeral home. My father came up to me with a yarmulka and put it on my head. "What is this for?" I questioned. "Tradition," he answered, "just wear it." I left it on my head and didn't think anything else of it.

The next memory I have of that day is standing in front of the open coffin, looking at my pale green, clammy looking, dead Uncle Charlie. "I thought they were supposed to make you look alive when you are dead," I thought to myself. He didn't look alive at all; not like the stuffed animals on wooden stands that stared with glass eyes. Uncle Charlie looked dead.

The ride to the cemetery was long and hot since the air conditioner was broken, and we couldn't open the windows more than a crack because the breeze would mess up my mother's hair. She was wearing a torn piece of cloth pinned to her lapel. "What's that for?" I asked pointing to the cloth. "When somebody close to you dies," she answered, "you tear a piece of your clothing as a sign of respect at the loss of a family member." "So why the cloth?" I asked. "Because this outfit was very expensive," she answered.

The rest of the day, the eulogy, the burial, is a blur. The only other memory I have of the event is getting a stuffed squirrel three weeks later.

Although traditions are not emphasized in my house, they're there and alive, just waiting for something to stir them from their sleep and come to us, unexpectedly.

Interpretations

1. How do you reconcile Rein's first-paragraph statement that traditions "never seemed important enough to me to look at" with his last paragraph? What is the essay's main point about tradition?

2. Why, or why not, would you agree with the last paragraph that traditions seem to have a life of their own independent of the individuals who practice them? What examples can you give?

3. How would you characterize Rein's mother's attitude toward tradition, especially as revealed in her answers on the way to the cemetery?

Correspondences

1. Rein and Yarimi recall their memories of a relative's funeral. How do you account for differences in their emotional responses to a similar event?

2. Analyze the tone of both essays. Is it appropriate to their subjects? How does tone affect purpose and meaning?

Applications

1. Write a journal entry on the significance of Rein's choice of title.

2. In Rein's essay objects such as the yarmulka and the torn piece of clothing are part of the mourning rituals of his cultural heritage. Discuss the importance of the symbolic in the preservation of family and cultural traditions.

from The Wedding

Shusha Guppy

*Shusha Guppy emigrated from Iran in the 1960s and is now a
folksinger and the London editor of* The Paris Review. *She is the
last child of Iran's leading philosopher, born during World War
II into a country that occupies a strategic place between the
Middle East and South Asia. In 1991 Shusha Guppy published*
Looking Back: A Panoramic View of a Literary Age by the Gran-
des Dames of European Letters.

*Once a powerful independent empire, Persia, Iran was later
conquered by the Turks and then the Mongols. In the nineteenth
century, Russia and the British vied for control of the oil-rich
country. In 1925 Reza Khan reestablished a native dynasty,
being succeeded by his son Reza Pahlavi in 1941. In an effort to
modernize Iran, the last shah made great changes in Iran's
economy and social and political systems. However, he was
intolerant of political opposition and had overlooked the power
of the Shiite branch of Islam (which claims over ninety percent
of the Iranian population, but a minority in the world of Islam)
and its conservative clergy, the mullahs. In January 1979, Pahlavi was driven into exile by revolution.*

*In the same month that the Pahlavi Dynasty was expelled, the
Ayatollah Ruhollah Khomeini returned from exile in France. In
the ensuing struggle, an Islamic republic was established that
gave supreme power to the Ayatollah. Iran quickly changed from
relative liberalism to strict conservatism. Guppy experienced
both swings of the political pendulum. She is therefore in a good
position to compare the Persia of her childhood and her parents' privileged lives—a Persia then already undergoing great
change—with postrevolutionary Iran. The following essay focuses on prerevolutionary times and is understandably nostalgic—in this case, for the traditional wedding customs of the
upper classes.*

HAJI SEYYED MOHAMMAD and Haji Ali-Baba: two more different men could
hardly be imagined, the one intelligent, shrewd, hedonistic, the other
imbued with the Northerner's simplicity of mind and heart—the cunning
and sophistication of the Bazaar versus the candour and nobility of the

land. Ali-Baba wore the white turban of the Sheikh, while Mohammad sported the black one of the Seyyed—the descendants of the Prophet.

Haji Ali-Baba's eldest daughter, Azra, was 17 when Kazem returned to Persia. She had unusual looks: blonde hair, grey-green eyes, high cheekbones and a very fair complexion, "just like a *Farangi* [European]." In reality she looked rather Russian, an impression enhanced by her intensely emotional and fiery temperament. She had had many suitors but her father had refused them all—they were "not good enough for her!"

As soon as the two men met, Ali-Baba fell completely under Kazem's spell; he was impressed by his erudition and captivated by his charm.

"I have found Azra's husband," he declared upon arriving home that evening. The snag was that Kazem had no wish to get married. On the contrary, he planned to lead the life of a celibate, ascetic philosopher and Sufi.

"I'm honoured by your generous interest," he rejoined, when his future father-in-law offered him his daughter's hand, "but I am in no position to marry, as I have no proper job and no money."

"Nonsense!" retorted the Sheikh. "I will give you both!" He was not a man to be contradicted, the offer was tempting and timely, and Kazem's resolve was broken.

"Oh, it was the grandest and loveliest wedding of the year!" recounted Aunt Ashraf. The story of my parents' nuptials was one of my favourites when I was a small child, and I often begged Aunt Ashraf to tell it.

"The preparations took months, at the end of which she had a fantastic trousseau—the finest rugs from Kerman and Kashan, gold-studded leather chests containing her clothes and linen—all finely embroidered—brocade spreads and wrappings, glass from Bohemia, china from France, and a large samovar from Tula (in Russia). She had enough for a whole house, although at first they were going to live at your grandfather, Haji Seyyed Mohammad's house."

"Then what happened?"

"Then came the wedding which lasted three days and three nights. The first day was devoted to the *Aqd* [the marriage ceremony and registration]. At dawn they brought the *Ghoncheh*. Now you probably don't know what that is, because it is going out of fashion among you modern people, but in those days it was part of the festivities. It consisted of two big trays, one containing coloured seeds arranged in decorative abstract patterns, the other a long flat bread, equally decorated with saffron and other vivid colours, and together they symbolised prosperity and fertility. The *Ghoncheh* was ordered from specialists in the Bazaar, and sent over with trays of cakes, biscuits, sweets and fruit arranged on silver dishes. Porters carried the enormous trays, precariously balanced on their heads, in a procession through the streets, followed by crowds of noisy urchins. It was displayed in the drawing room, around the bridal seat. When everything was ready and the guests arrived, they brought in the bride and sat her in the middle of the room on a *soozani* [an embroidered mat] in front of her wedding mirror, flanked by two candelabras and a glass lamp, to give light and happiness to the couple's life together.

"Then the groom's party arrived, headed by Haji Seyyed Mohammad, his secretary, and the mullah who was to perform the ceremony. Your mother sat there reading the Qoran while her younger sisters rubbed two pieces of block sugar above her head on a scarf. The sugar is supposed to make her life sweet ever after. Presently the mullah read the marriage contract from behind the door, and asked the bride if she agreed to it. When she said, 'Yes,' everyone cried, 'God be praised,' and the party began, for the women in the *andaroon* and for the men in the *birooni*. It wasn't like today when men and women are all mixed up together!"

"What happened the next day?"

"The next day was the public feast, when all the poor of the district were invited to a meal. They brought their containers, which were filled with delicious rice and stew, and went away to eat it with their families and pray for the couple's happiness and good health."

"And the third day?"

"Ah, that was the wedding proper! There was a sumptuous dinner for family and friends. Again outside caterers were hired—cooks, assistants, waiters. They arrived with cartloads of huge pots and pans and serving dishes. Smoke from the charcoal braziers drifted high above the roof of Haji Ali-Baba's house, streaked the turquoise-blue firmament, and filled the air with the aromas of barbecued lamb, spicy stews and saffron rice. The whole neighbourhood was abuzz with excitement and shared in the festivities. It was wonderful!"

On the wedding day, the *hammam* [public baths] had been rented exclusively; the women went in the morning and the men in the afternoon. My mother had been taken there, washed, rubbed with rosewater and made up with powder and rouge. She was dressed in white satin and lace, and wrapped in her black *chador*—it was several years before the veil was abolished. Her father had covered her in gold and jewellery, as an investment to be used in emergency or later to buy a house. Bangles jingled on her wrists and forearms; gold necklaces and chains, hung with sovereigns and half-sovereigns covered her chest, and her fingers flashed with rings. Her father ordered the most beautiful four-horse coach from the royal stables, complete with liveried footmen and grooms, and a fleet of lesser vehicles and droshkies for the guests to ride the short journey to the groom's house:

"I can see him standing outside his front door," went on Aunt Ashraf, "tears pouring down his cheeks, throwing fistfuls of *noql* [tiny pieces of almond coated with sugar] and silver coins to the crowds that lined the street. Urchins scrambled to pick up the coins while he showered more and more handfuls on them, until the bag was empty and the cortège had disappeared round the corner."

At its destination, the nuptial room had been prepared with the bride's trousseau. She sat on a brocade mat, ready to receive the groom. One by one the female guests kissed her goodbye:

"May God give you many sons," "May your household be blessed," "May God's shadow never leave your heads," were some of their valedictory blessings.

It was customary for an elderly relative—in this case, the old nanny—to remain outside the nuptial room. Sometime during the night, the door would be opened and the groom would give her a blood-stained handkerchief, proof of his bride's virginity. If, by any chance, the bride had turned out not to be a virgin, she would be sent back to her father's house, the marriage contract would be annulled, and her life thereafter blighted by opprobrium and dishonour. At other times, there would be cover-ups: stories were told of the knightly gallantry of husbands who had cut their own fingers to produce the necessary few drops of blood and save the honour of their wives. Other tales told of bloody battles that had resulted from a girl's dishonour and engulfed whole families for generations. Sometimes the bridegroom would be too nervous, chivvied by the presence of the old woman waiting outside and the rest of the family not far off, and would fail to "perform." His excruciating misery and humiliation the next morning can be imagined. But such customs were already considered barbaric by the educated people and the upper classes, and my father had sent the nanny to bed with a tip before entering the nuptial room, certain of his wife's virtue.

Left alone, Azra began to pray. Presently the door opened and the groom entered. My mother had never seen him, of course, except once, when she had caught a glimpse of him through a window as he was entering the *birooni* to visit her father. She had exclaimed: "Oh but he's so *old!*" Sharp glances had darted towards her like poisoned arrows and put an end to her comments. Nor had she ever been consulted about her wishes as to her future husband. At the wedding ceremony, the mullah had spoken the marriage formula, Will-you-take-this-man-as-your-husband, etc., and she had answered, "Yes," but then no bride in known memory had ever said, "No." There were instances of the bride being quite adamant—if the groom was a relative she had seen and disliked, or if she secretly desired another. But surrounded with threatening parents and relations, the prospect of dishonour and scandal, she had always ended up by saying, "Yes," only to regret it for the rest of her life. Why anyone bothered to ask the bride at all was only because Islam, in fairness to women, had insisted upon their consent, and so consent was duly extracted by hook or crook.

My mother told me the rest of the story herself . . .

"Father came in and greeted me with a *salam* [hello—peace be on you]. I was supposed to say it first, being his wife, but I could not open my mouth with nervousness. He then sat beside me on the mat, and took my hand, kissed it and said:

"Well, young lady, what brings you to our part of the world?"

That made me laugh and the ice was broken. I thought well what if he's a bit old? He is kind and charming, so perhaps I will like him . . .

In fact he was 23 years older than her, but she fell in love with him that night and loved him single-heartedly for the rest of her life. He died a few years before her, but she continued communicating with him through dreams and prayers: every night he came to her while she slept, as ever soothing, consoling, guiding her as he had done throughout their lives together.

My mother's old nanny stayed on with her for a few weeks to show her the ropes and give her moral support, then she returned home, leaving her to manage on her own and be absorbed into the *andaroon* life.

Eventually my mother sold her gold and jewellery, and with the proceeds my parents bought their first house. By then no one had separate *andaroon* and *birooni,* just one house divided into two spheres:

"We were so happy then," mother used to reminisce wistfully. "Your father helped me to cook as I learnt by trial and error, before we could afford a proper cook, and he shared the chores. Nowadays you modern people think it is natural for your husbands to help you, but in those days it was unheard of! Everybody was jealous of me, seeing how lovingly he treated me. He taught me everything I know about the world."

Of all the beautiful objects my mother had in her trousseau the finest was a filigree gold and tortoise-shell toilette set—Haji Ali-Baba's personal gift to his son-in-law. It consisted of a gold tray, with three gold bowls of varying sizes fitting into each other, a shaving brush of tortoise-shell decorated with gold, a mirror and a tortoise-shell comb framed with gold, all most delicately made. My mother did not display it, but kept it hidden in a box, and locked in a cupboard with other family documents, photograph albums, and a few objects of sentimental value. She kept the key to the cupboard always in her handbag. Twice she showed me the toilette set, and I remember marvelling, even as a small child, at the beauty of the design and the delicacy of its execution. Of all family heirlooms that disappeared in the events of 1979—stolen, looted or sold for a pittance—it was the loss of that gold and tortoise-shell set that I most regretted, for in my memory it symbolised my parents' union.

On my last visit to Persia in 1977, my mother gave me a few pieces from her trousseau: her French wedding lamp, painted with cherubs whirling among the clouds, a Bohemian glass water-pipe which I have converted into a lamp and which was made specially for the Qojar king, Nasserudin Shah, and her samovar from Tula. Everything else has gone. But it matters not, compared to the loss of innocent life other families have suffered from the revolution. I have often wondered where the filigree gold and tortoise-shell set now is. I was told that, soon after the revolution, Japanese antique dealers came to Persia and bought everything cheaply from those who had looted the houses. So I would like to think that today it is displayed in a Japanese home among other beautiful works of art.

Interpretations

1. What does the existence of separate parts of the house for women and men (*andaroon* and *birooni*) indicate about the relationship between the sexes? Do we have anything analogous to women's quarters and men's quarters (not counting restrooms)? Where can such relations between the sexes still be found today? How do you feel about such relations?

2. What does the "filigree gold and tortoise-shell toilette set" symbolize for the author's family?

3. Why would the "events of 1979" make the few family "heirlooms" that survived these events even more valuable to Guppy? Why do you suppose she elected to use "Persia" instead of the more current "Iran"?

4. Analyze use of narrative voice in this selection: What is gained by telling most of the story in the words of Aunt Ashraf? by switching at times to her mother's voice? by using "I" directly (that is, without quotation marks) only at the very end?

Correspondences

1. Social class is an important factor in both "The Wedding" and "Life in the Villages." How is social class revealed in the traditions of each culture? What examples attest to its influence on gender relationships? To what extent does it mirror (or not mirror) your own cultural traditions?

2. Attitudes toward personal space and territoriality differ among cultures. How do these affect traditions in the selections by Guppy and Sadat? To what extent have they been modified by the passing of time?

Applications

1. Would you ever consent to an arranged wedding? Why or why not? (In responding, consider the nature of the marriage that evolved in "The Wedding.")

2. Write a short essay explaining how funerals and weddings can serve tradition in Russell Baker's "Morrisonville" and Shusha Guppy's "The Wedding."

The Lottery

Shirley Jackson

Shirley Jackson (1919–1965) was born and raised in California. In 1933, she moved with her family to Rochester, New York, where she briefly attended the University of Rochester. Notable publications include the novel Hangsman *(1951), and the play* We Have Always Lived in the Castle *(1962). In "The Lottery" (1948), a frequently anthologized piece, Jackson scrutinizes scapegoating.*

THE MORNING OF June 27th was clear and sunny, with the fresh warmth of a full-summer day; the flowers were blossoming profusely and the grass was richly green. The people of the village began to gather in the square, between the post office and the bank, around ten o'clock; in some towns there were so many people that the lottery took two days and had to be started on June 26th, but in this village, where there were only about three hundred people, the whole lottery took less than two hours, so it could begin at ten o'clock in the morning and still be through in time to allow the villagers to get home for noon dinner.

The children assembled first, of course. School was recently over for the summer, and the feeling of liberty sat uneasily on most of them; they tended to gather together quietly for a while before they broke into boisterous play, and their talk was still of the classroom and the teacher, of books and reprimands. Bobby Martin had already stuffed his pockets full of stones, and the other boys soon followed his example, selecting the smoothest and roundest stones; Bobby and Harry Jones and Dickie Delacroix—the villagers pronounced this name "Dellacroy"—eventually made a great pile of stones in one corner of the square and guarded it against the raids of the other boys. The girls stood aside, talking among themselves, looking over their shoulders at the boys, and the very small children rolled in the dust or clung to the hands of their older brothers or sisters.

Soon the men began to gather, surveying their own children, speaking of planting and rain, tractors and taxes. They stood together, away from the pile of stones in the corner, and their jokes were quiet and they smiled rather than laughed. The women, wearing faded house dresses and sweaters, came shortly after their menfolk. They greeted one another and exchanged bits of gossip as they went to join their husbands. Soon the women, standing by their husbands, began to call to their children, and the children came reluctantly, having to be called four or five times. Bobby Martin ducked under his mother's grasping hand and ran, laughing, back to the pile of stones. His father spoke up sharply, and Bobby came quickly and took his place between his father and his oldest brother.

The lottery was conducted—as were the square dances, the teen-age club, the Halloween program—by Mr. Summers, who had time and energy to devote to civic activities. He was a round-faced, jovial man and he ran the coal business, and people were sorry for him, because he had no children and his wife was a scold. When he arrived in the square, carrying the black wooden box, there was a murmur of conversation among the villagers, and he waved and called, "Little late today, folks." The postmaster, Mr. Graves, followed him, carrying a three-legged stool, and the stool was put in the center of the square and Mr. Summers set the black box down on it. The villagers kept their distance, leaving a space between themselves and the stool, and when Mr. Summers said, "Some of you fellows want to give me a hand?" there was a hesitation before two men, Mr. Martin and his oldest son, Baxter, came forward to hold the box steady on the stool while Mr. Summers stirred up the papers inside it.

The original paraphernalia for the lottery had been lost long ago, and the black box now resting on the stool had been put into use even before Old Man Warner, the oldest man in town, was born. Mr. Summers spoke frequently to the villagers about making a new box, but no one liked to upset even as much tradition as was represented by the black box. There was a story that the present box had been made with some pieces of the box that had preceded it, the one that had been constructed when the first people settled down to make a village here. Every year, after the lottery, Mr. Summers began talking again about a new box, but every year the subject was allowed to fade off without anything's being done. The black box grew shabbier each year; by now it was no longer completely black but splintered badly along one side to show the original wood color, and in some places faded or stained.

Mr. Martin and his oldest son, Baxter, held the black box securely on the stool until Mr. Summers had stirred the papers thoroughly with his hand. Because so much of the ritual had been forgotten or discarded, Mr. Summers had been successful in having slips of paper substituted for the chips of wood that had been used for generations. Chips of wood, Mr. Summers had argued, had been all very well when the village was tiny, but now that the population was more than three hundred and likely to keep on growing, it was necessary to use something that would fit more easily into the black box. The night before the lottery, Mr. Summers and Mr. Graves made up the slips of paper and put them in the box, and it was then taken to the safe of Mr. Summers's coal company and locked up until Mr. Summers was ready to take it to the square next morning. The rest of the year, the box was put away, sometimes one place, sometimes another; it had spent one year in Mr. Graves's barn and another year underfoot in the post office, and sometimes it was set on a shelf in the Martin grocery and left there.

There was a great deal of fussing to be done before Mr. Summers declared the lottery open. There were the lists to make up—of heads of families, heads of households in each family, members of each household in each family. There was the proper swearing-in of Mr. Summers by the postmaster, as the official of the lottery; at one time, some people remembered, there had been a recital of some sort, performed by the official of the lottery, a perfunctory, tuneless chant that had been rattled off duly each year; some people believed that the official of the lottery used to stand just so when he said or sang it, others believed that he was supposed to walk among the people, but years and years ago this part of the ritual had been allowed to lapse. There had been, also, a ritual salute, which the official of the lottery had had to use in addressing each person who came up to draw from the box, but this also had changed with time, until now it was felt necessary only for the official to speak to each person approaching. Mr. Summers was very good at all this; in his clean white shirt and blue jeans, with one hand resting carelessly on the black box, he seemed very proper and important as he talked interminably to Mr. Graves and the Martins.

Just as Mr. Summers finally left off talking and turned to the assembled villagers, Mrs. Hutchinson came hurriedly along the path to the square, her sweater thrown over her shoulders, and slid into place in the back of the crowd. "Clean forgot what day it was," she said to Mrs. Delacroix, who stood next to her, and they both laughed softly. "Thought my old man was out back stacking wood," Mrs. Hutchinson went on, "and then I looked out the window and the kids was gone, and then I remembered it was the twenty-seventh and came a-running." She dried her hands on her apron, and Mrs. Delacroix said, "You're in time, though. They're still talking away up there."

Mrs. Hutchinson craned her neck to see through the crowd and found her husband and children standing near the front. She tapped Mrs. Delacroix on the arm as a farewell and began to make her way through the crowd. The people separated good-humoredly to let her through; two or three people said, in voices just loud enough to be heard across the crowd, "Here comes your Missus, Hutchinson," and "Bill, she made it after all." Mrs. Hutchinson reached her husband, and Mr. Summers, who had been waiting, said cheerfully, "Thought we were going to have to get on without you, Tessie." Mrs Hutchinson said, grinning, "Wouldn't have me leave m'dishes in the sink, now, would you, Joe?" and soft laughter ran through the crowd as the people stirred back into position after Mrs. Hutchinson's arrival.

"Well, now," Mr. Summers said soberly, "guess we better get started, get this over with, so's we can go back to work. Anybody ain't here?"

"Dunbar," several people said. "Dunbar, Dunbar."

Mr. Summers consulted his list. "Clyde Dunbar," he said. "That's right. He's broke his leg, hasn't he? Who's drawing for him?"

"Me, I guess," a woman said, and Mr. Summers turned to look at her. "Wife draws for her husband," Mr. Summers said. "Don't you have a grown boy to do it for you, Janey?" Although Mr. Summers and everyone else in the village knew the answer perfectly well, it was the business of the official of the lottery to ask such questions formally. Mr. Summers waited with an expression of polite interest while Mrs. Dunbar answered.

"Horace's not but sixteen yet," Mrs. Dunbar said regretfully. "Guess I gotta fill in for the old man this year."

"Right," Mr. Summers said. He made a note on the list he was holding. Then he asked, "Watson boy drawing this year?"

A tall boy in the crowd raised his hand. "Here," he said. "I'm drawing for m'mother and me." He blinked his eyes nervously and ducked his head as several voices in the crowd said things like "Good fellow, Jack," and "Glad to see your mother's got a man to do it."

"Well," Mr. Summers said, "guess that's everyone. Old Man Warner make it?"

"Here," a voice said, and Mr. Summers nodded.

A sudden hush fell on the crowd as Mr. Summers cleared his throat and looked at the list. "All ready?" he called. "Now, I'll read the names—heads of families first—and the men come up and take a paper out of the box. Keep the paper folded in your hand without looking at it until everyone has had a turn. Everything clear?"

The people had done it so many times that they only half listened to the directions; most of them were quiet, wetting their lips, not looking around. Then Mr. Summers raised one hand high and said, "Adams." A man disengaged himself from the crowd and came forward. "Hi, Steve," Mr. Summers said, and Mr. Adams said, "Hi, Joe." They grinned at one another humorlessly and nervously. Then Mr. Adams reached into the black box and took out a folded paper. He held it firmly by one corner as he turned and went hastily back to his place in the crowd, where he stood a little apart from his family, not looking down at his hand.

"Allen," Mr. Summers said, "Anderson. . . . Bentham."

"Seems like there's no time at all between lotteries any more," Mrs. Delacroix said to Mrs. Graves in the back row. "Seems like we got through with the last one only last week."

"Time sure goes fast," Mrs. Graves said.

"Clark. . . . Delacroix."

"There goes my old man," Mrs. Delacroix said. She held her breath while her husband went forward.

"Dunbar," Mr. Summers said, and Mrs. Dunbar went steadily to the box while one of the women said, "Go on, Janey," and another said, "There she goes."

"We're next," Mrs. Graves said. She watched while Mr. Graves came around from the side of the box, greeted Mr. Summers gravely, and selected a slip of paper from the box. By now, all through the crowd there were men holding the small folded papers in their large hands, turning them over and over nervously. Mrs. Dunbar and her two sons stood together, Mrs. Dunbar holding the slip of paper.

"Harburt. . . . Hutchinson."

"Get up there, Bill," Mrs. Hutchinson said, and the people near her laughed.

"Jones."

"They do say," Mr. Adams said to Old Man Warner, who stood next to him, "that over in the north village they're talking of giving up the lottery."

Old Man Warner snorted. "Pack of crazy fools," he said. "Listening to the young folks, nothing's good enough for *them*. Next thing you know, they'll be wanting to go back to living in caves, nobody work any more, live *that* way for a while. Used to be a saying about 'Lottery in June, corn be heavy soon.' First thing you know, we'd all be eating stewed chickweed and acorns. There's *always* been a lottery," he added petulantly. "Bad enough to see young Joe Summers up there joking with everybody."

"Some places have already quit lotteries," Mrs. Adams said.

"Nothing but trouble in *that*," Old Man Warner said stoutly. "Pack of young fools."

"Martin." And Bobby Martin watched his father go forward. "Overdyke. . . . Percy."

"I wish they'd hurry," Mrs. Dunbar said to her oldest son. "I wish they'd hurry."

"They're almost through," her son said.

"You get ready to run tell Dad," Mrs. Dunbar said.

Mr. Summers called his own name and then stepped forward precisely and selected a slip from the box. Then he called, "Warner."

"Seventy-seventh year I been in the lottery," Old Man Warner said as he went through the crowd. "Seventy-seventh time."

"Watson." The tall boy came awkwardly through the crowd. Someone said, "Don't be nervous, Jack," and Mr. Summers said, "Take your time, son."

"Zanini."

After that, there was a long pause, a breathless pause, until Mr. Summers, holding his slip of paper in the air, said, "All right, fellows." For a minute, no one moved, and then all the slips of paper were opened. Suddenly, all the women began to speak at once, saying, "Who is it?" "Who's got it?" "Is it the Dunbars?" "Is it the Watsons?" Then the voices began to say, "It's Hutchinson. It's Bill." "Bill Hutchinson's got it."

"Go tell your father," Mrs. Dunbar said to her older son.

People began to look around to see the Hutchinsons. Bill Hutchinson was standing quiet, staring down at the paper in his hand. Suddenly, Tessie Hutchinson shouted to Mr. Summers, "You didn't give him time enough to take any paper he wanted. I saw you. It wasn't fair!"

"Be a good sport, Tessie," Mrs. Delacroix called, and Mrs. Graves said, "All of us took the same chance."

"Shut up, Tessie," Bill Hutchinson said.

"Well, everyone," Mr. Summers said, "that was done pretty fast, and now we've got to be hurrying a little more to get done in time." He consulted his next list. "Bill," he said, "you draw for the Hutchinson family. You got any other households in the Hutchinsons?"

"There's Don and Eva," Mrs. Hutchinson yelled. "Make *them* take their chance! "

"Daughters drew with their husbands' families, Tessie," Mr. Summers said gently. "You know that as well as anyone else."

"It wasn't *fair,*" Tessie said.

"I guess not, Joe," Bill Hutchinson said regretfully. "My daughter draws with her husband's family, that's only fair, And I've got no other family except the kids."

"Then, as far as drawing for families is concerned, it's you," Mr. Summers said in explanation, "and as far as drawing for households is concerned, that's you, too. Right?"

"Right," Bill Hutchinson said.

"How many kids, Bill?" Mr. Summers asked formally.

"Three," Bill Hutchinson said. "There's Bill, Jr., and Nancy, and little Dave. And Tessie and me."

"All right, then," Mr. Summers said. "Harry, you got their tickets back?"

Mr. Graves nodded and held up the slips of paper. "Put them in the box, then," Mr. Summers directed. "Take Bill's and put it in."

"I think we ought to start over," Mrs. Hutchinson said, as quietly as she could. "I tell you it wasn't *fair.* You didn't give him time enough to choose. *Every*body saw that."

Mr. Graves had selected the five slips and put them in the box, and he dropped all the papers but those onto the ground, where the breeze caught them and lifted them off.

"Listen, everybody," Mrs. Hutchinson was saying to the people around her.

"Ready, Bill?" Mr. Summers asked, and Bill Hutchinson, with one quick glance around at his wife and children, nodded.

"Remember," Mr. Summers said, "take the slips and keep them folded until each person has taken one. Harry, you help little Dave." Mr. Graves took the hand of the little boy, who came willingly with him up to the box. "Take a paper out of the box, Davy," Mr. Summers said. Davy put his hand into the box and laughed. "Take just *one* paper," Mr. Summers said. "Harry, you hold it for him." Mr. Graves took the child's hand and removed the folded paper from the tight fist and held it while little Dave stood next to him and looked up at him wonderingly.

"Nancy next," Mr. Summers said. Nancy was twelve, and her school friends breathed heavily as she went forward, switching her skirt, and took a slip daintily from the box. "Bill, Jr.," Mr. Summers said, and Billy, his face red and his feet overlarge, nearly knocked the box over as he got a paper out. "Tessie," Mr. Summers said. She hesitated for a minute, looking around defiantly, and then set her lips and went up to the box. She snatched a paper out and held it behind her.

"Bill," Mr. Summers said, and Bill Hutchinson reached into the box and felt around, bringing his hand out at last with the slip of paper in it.

The crowd was quiet. A girl whispered, "I hope it's not Nancy," and the sound of the whisper reached the edges of the crowd.

"It's not the way it used to be," Old Man Warner said clearly. "People ain't the way they used to be."

"All right," Mr. Summers said. "Open the papers. Harry, you open little Dave's."

Mr. Graves opened the slip of paper and there was a general sigh through the crowd as he held it up and everyone could see that it was blank. Nancy and Bill, Jr., opened theirs at the same time, and both beamed and laughed, turning around to the crowd and holding their slips of paper above their heads.

"Tessie," Mr. Summers said. There was a pause, and then Mr. Summers looked at Bill Hutchinson, and Bill unfolded his paper and showed it. It was blank.

"It's Tessie," Mr. Summers said, and his voice was hushed. "Show us her paper, Bill."

Bill Hutchinson went over to his wife and forced the slip of paper out of her hand. It had a black spot on it, the black spot Mr. Summers had made the night before with the heavy pencil in the coal-company office. Bill Hutchinson held it up and there was a stir in the crowd.

"All right, folks," Mr. Summers said. "Let's finish quickly."

Although the villagers had forgotten the ritual and lost the original black box, they still remembered to use stones. The pile of stones the boys had made earlier was ready; there were stones on the ground with the blowing scraps of paper that had come out of the box. Mrs. Delacroix selected a stone so large she had to pick it up with both hands and turned to Mrs. Dunbar. "Come on," she said. "Hurry up."

Mrs. Dunbar had small stones in both hands, and she said, gasping for breath, "I can't run at all. You'll have to go ahead and I'll catch up with you."

The children had stones already, and someone gave little Davy Hutchinson a few pebbles.

Tessie Hutchinson was in the center of a cleared space by now, and she held her hands out desperately as the villagers moved in on her. "It isn't fair," she said. A stone hit her on the side of the head.

Old Man Warner was saying, "Come on, come on, everyone." Steve Adams was in the front of the crowd of villagers, with Mrs. Graves beside him

"It isn't fair, it isn't right," Mrs. Hutchinson screamed and then they were upon her.

Interpretations

1. What do the villagers mean by "fairness"? (What is implied by the fact that the only villager to complain about the lottery's consequences is Tessie Hutchinson?)

2. Why does Jackson use a flat, reportorial style to describe an event that would normally be headline news? (Consider the role of irony in this story.)

3. How important is it that the story is set in roughly contemporary New England? (How, for example, would its influence differ if the story were set in Aztec Mexico, a culture that routinely practiced human sacrifice?)

4. The tradition here depicted brings summary execution or reprieve. What traditions do we participate in that have life-or-death consequences, in either the short or the long run?

Correspondences

1. Review the Maugham quotation (page 3). What does it mean? How does it apply to "The Lottery"?

2. The selections by Jackson and Fairbank suggest that some traditions might benefit from a reevaluation. Do you agree? What criteria would you suggest?

Applications

1. When Shirley Jackson's story was first published in *The New Yorker* in 1948, she received hundreds of letters from people "who wanted to know where these lotteries were held, and whether they could go there and watch." What does this response suggest about human nature? (What was *your* response to the story?)

2. By showing how familiar the process of the lottery is to the villagers, what does Jackson imply about tradition, mass psychology, and social pressure?

The Water-Faucet Vision

Gish Jen

Gish Jen lives in Cambridge, Massachusetts. Support for her writing has come from the James Michener/Copernicus Society, the Bunting Institute, the Massachusetts Bay Transportation Authority, and The National Endowment for the Arts. Her fiction has appeared in The New Generation, *an anthology, and her most recent story, "What Means Switch" (1990), set in New York City, features an encounter between a polite Chinese girl and her Japanese boyfriend who knows Judo but not English. Jen was featured in the February 1990 issue of* Atlantic Monthly *as one of four prominent writers of the new generation. In 1991 Jen published the novel* Typical American.

TO PROTECT MY SISTER Mona and me from the pains—or, as they pronounced it, the "pins"—of life, my parents did their fighting in Shanghai dialect, which we didn't understand; and when my father one day pitched a brass vase through the kitchen window, my mother told us he had done it by accident.

"By accident?" said Mona.

My mother chopped the foot off a mushroom.

"By accident?" said Mona. "By *accident?*"

Later I tried to explain to her that she shouldn't have persisted like that, but it was hopeless.

"What's the matter with throwing things?" She shrugged. "He was *mad.*"

That was the difference between Mona and me: fighting was just fighting to her. If she worried about anything, it was only that she might turn out too short to become a ballerina, in which case she was going to be a piano player.

I, on the other hand, was going to be a martyr. I was in fifth grade then, and the hyperimaginative sort—the kind of girl who grows morbid in Catholic school, who longs to be chopped or frozen to death but then has nightmares about it from which she wakes up screaming and clutching a stuffed bear. It was not a bear that I clutched, though, but a string of three malachite beads that I had found in the marsh by the old aqueduct one day. Apparently once part of a necklace, they were each wonderfully striated and swirled, and slightly humped toward the center, like a jellyfish; so that if I squeezed one, it would slip smoothly away,

76

with a grace that altogether enthralled and—on those dream-harrowed nights—soothed me, soothed me as nothing had before or has since. Not that I've lacked occasion for soothing: though it's been four months since my mother died, there are still nights when sleep stands away from me, stiff as a well-paid sentry. But that is another story. Back then I had my malachite beads, and if I worried them long and patiently enough, I was sure to start feeling better, more awake, even a little special—imagining, as I liked to, that my nightmares were communications from the Almighty Himself, preparation for my painful destiny. Discussing them with Patty Creamer, who had also promised her life to God, I called them "almost visions"; and Patty, her mouth wadded with the three or four sticks of Doublemint she always seemed to have going at once, said, "I bet you'll be doin' miracleth by seventh grade."

Miracles. Today Patty laughs to think she ever spent good time stewing on such matters, her attention having long turned to rugs, and artwork, and antique Japanese bureaus—things she believes in.

"A good bureau's more than just a bureau," she explained last time we had lunch. "It's a hedge against life. I tell you: if there's one thing I believe, it's that cheap stuff's just money out the window. Nice stuff, on the other hand—now that you can always cash out, if life gets rough. *That* you can count on."

In fifth grade, though, she counted on different things.

"You'll be doing miracles too," I told her, but she shook her shaggy head and looked doleful.

"Na' me," she chomped. "Buzzit's okay. The kin' things I like, prayers work okay on."

"Like?"

"Like you 'member the dreth I liked?"

She meant the yellow one, with the crisscross straps.

"Well gueth what."

"Your mom got it for you."

She smiled. "And I only jutht prayed for it for a week," she said.

As for myself, though, I definitely wanted to be able to perform a wonder or two. Miracle-working! It was the carrot of carrots: it kept me doing my homework, taking the sacraments; it kept me mournfully on key in music hour, while my classmates hiccuped and squealed their carefree hearts away. Yet I couldn't have said what I wanted such powers *for,* exactly. That is, I thought of them the way one might think of, say, an ornamental sword—as a kind of collectible, which also happened to be a means of defense.

But then Patty's father walked out on her mother, and for the first time, there was a miracle I wanted to do. I wanted it so much I could see it: Mr. Creamer made into a spitball; Mr. Creamer shot through a straw into the sky; Mr. Creamer unrolled and replumped, plop back on Patty's doorstep. I would've cleaned out his mind and given him a shave en route. I would've given him a box of peanut fudge, tied up with a ribbon, to present to Patty with a kiss.

But instead all I could do was try to tell her he'd come back.

"He will not, he will not!" she sobbed. "He went on a boat to Rio Deniro. To Rio Deniro!"

I tried to offer her a stick of gum, but she wouldn't take it.

"He said he would rather look at water than at my mom's fat face. He said he would rather look at water than at me." Now she was really wailing, and holding her ribs so tightly that she almost seemed to be hurting herself—so tightly that just looking at her arms wound around her like snakes made my heart feel squeezed.

I patted her on the arm. A one-winged pigeon waddled by.

"He said I wasn't even his kid, he said I came from Uncle Johnny. He said I was garbage, just like my mom and Uncle Johnny. He said I wasn't even his kid, he said I wasn't his Patty, he said I came from Uncle Johnny!"

"From your Uncle Johnny?" I asked stupidly.

"From Uncle Johnny," she cried. "From Uncle Johnny!"

"He said that?" I said. Then, wanting to go on, to say *something*, I said, "Oh Patty, don't cry."

She kept crying.

I tried again. "Oh Patty, don't cry," I said. Then I said, "Your dad was a jerk anyway."

The pigeon produced a large runny dropping.

It was a good twenty minutes before Patty was calm enough for me just to run to the girls' room to get her some toilet paper; and by the time I came back she was sobbing again, saying "to Rio Deniro, to Rio Deniro" over and over again, as though the words had stuck in her and couldn't be gotten out. As we had missed the regular bus home and the late bus too, I had to leave her a second time to go call my mother, who was mad only until she heard what had happened. Then she came and picked us up, and bought us each a Fudgsicle.

Some days later, Patty and I started a program to work on getting her father home. It was a serious business. We said extra prayers, and lit votive candles; I tied my malachite beads to my uniform belt, fondling them as though they were a rosary, I a nun. We even took to walking about the school halls with our hands folded—a sight so ludicrous that our wheeze of a principal personally took us aside one day.

"I must tell you," she said, using her nose as a speaking tube, "that there is really no need for such peee-ity."

But we persisted, promising to marry God and praying to every saint we could think of. We gave up gum, then gum and Slim Jims both, then gum and Slim Jims and ice cream—and when even that didn't work, we started on more innovative things. The first was looking at flowers. We held our hands beside our eyes like blinders as we hurried by the violets by the flagpole, the window box full of tulips outside the nurse's office.

Next it was looking at boys: Patty gave up angel-eyed Jamie Halloran and I, gymnastic Anthony Rossi. It was hard, but in the end our efforts paid off. Mr. Creamer came back a month later, and though he brought with him nothing but dysentery, he was at least too sick to have all that much to say.

Then, in the course of a fight with my father, my mother somehow fell out of their bedroom window.

Recently—thinking a mountain vacation might cheer me—I sublet my apartment to a handsome but somber newlywed couple, who turned out to be every bit as responsible as I'd hoped. They cleaned out even the eggshell chips I'd sprinkled around the base of my plants as fertilizer, leaving behind only a shiny silverplate cake server and a list of their hopes and goals for the summer. The list, tacked precariously to the back of the kitchen door, began with a fervent appeal to God to help them get their wedding thank-yous written in three weeks or less. (You could see they had originally written "two weeks" but scratched it out—no miracles being demanded here.) It went on:

> Please help us, Almighty Father in Heaven Above, to get Ann a teaching job within a half-hour drive of here in a nice neighborhood.
> Please help us, Almighty Father in Heaven Above, to get John a job doing anything where he won't strain his back and that is within a half-hour drive of here.
> Please help us, Almighty Father in Heaven Above, to get us a car.
> Please help us, A.F. in H.A., to learn French.
> Please help us, A.F. in H.A., to find seven dinner recipes that cost less than 60 cents a serving and can be made in a half-hour. And that don't have tomatoes, since You in Your Heavenly Wisdom made John allergic.
> Please help us, A.F. in H.A., to avoid books in this apartment such as You in Your Heavenly Wisdom allowed John, for Your Heavenly Reasons, to find three nights ago (June 2nd).

Et cetera. In the left-hand margin they kept score of how they had fared with their requests, and it was heartening to see that nearly all of them were marked "Yes! Praise the Lord" (sometimes shortened to PTL), with the sole exception of learning French, which was mysteriously marked "No! PTL to the Highest."

That note touched me. Strange and familiar both, it seemed like it had been written by some cousin of mine—some cousin who had stayed home to grow up, say, while I went abroad and learned what I had to, though the learning was painful. This, of course, is just a manner of speaking; in fact I did my growing up at home, like anybody else.

But the learning *was* painful: I never knew exactly how it happened that my mother went hurtling through the air that night years ago, only that the wind had been chopping at the house, and that the argument had start about the state of the roof. Someone had been up to fix it the year before, but it wasn't a roofer, it was some man my father had insisted could do just as good a job for a quarter of the price. And maybe he could have, had he not somehow managed to step through a knot in the wood under the shingles and break his uninsured ankle. Now the shingles were coming loose again, and the attic insulation was mildewing besides, and my father was wanting to sell the house altogether, which he said my mother had wanted to buy so she could send pictures of it home to her family in China.

"The Americans have a saying," he said. "They saying, 'You have to keep up with Jones family,' I'm saying if Jones family in Shanghai, you can send any picture you want, *an-y* picture. Go take picture of those rich guys' house. You want to act like rich guys, right? Go take picture of those rich guys' house."

At that point my mother sent Mona and me to wash up, and started speaking Shanghaiese. They argued for some time in the kitchen while we listened from the top of the stairs, our faces wedged between the bumpy Spanish scrolls of the wrought-iron railing. First my mother ranted, then my father, then they both ranted at once until finally there was a thump, followed by a long quiet.

"Do you think they're kissing now?" said Mona. "I bet they're kissing, like this." She pursed her lips like a fish and was about to put them to the railing when we heard my mother locking the back door. We hightailed it into bed; my parents creaked up the stairs. Everything at that point seemed fine. Once in their bedroom, though, they started up again, first softly, then louder and louder, until my mother turned on a radio to try to disguise the noise. A door slammed; they began shouting at one another; another door slammed; a shoe or something banged the wall behind Mona's bed.

"How're we supposed to *sleep?*" said Mona, sitting up.

There was another thud, more yelling in Shanghaiese, and then my mother's voice pierced the wall, in English. "So what you want I should do? Go to work like Theresa Lee?"

My father rumbled something back.

"You think you're big shot because you have job, right? You're big shot, but you never get promotion, you never get raise. All I do is spend money, right? So what do you do, you tell me. So what do you do!"

Something hit the floor so hard that our room shook.

"So kill me," screamed my mother. "You know what you are? You are failure. Failure! You are failure!"

Then there was a sudden, terrific, bursting crash—and after it, as if on a bungled cue, the serene blare of an a cappella soprano, picking her way down a scale.

By the time Mona and I knew to look out the window, a neighbor's pet beagle was already on the scene, sniffing and barking at my mother's body, his tail crazy with excitement; then he was barking at my stunned and trembling father, at the shrieking ambulance, the police, at crying Mona in her bunnyfooted pajamas, and at me, barefoot in the cold grass, squeezing her shoulder with one hand and clutching my malachite beads with the other.

My mother wasn't dead, only unconscious, the paramedics figured that out right away, but there was blood everywhere, and though they were reassuring about her head wounds as they strapped her to the stretcher, commenting also on how small she was, how delicate, how light, my father kept saying, "I killed her, I killed her" as the ambulance screeched and screeched headlong, forever, to the hospital. I was afraid to touch her, and glad of the metal rail between us, even though its sturdiness made her seem even frailer than she was; I wished she was bigger, somehow, and noticed, with a pang, that the new red slippers we had given her for Mother's Day had been lost somewhere along the way. How much she seemed to be leaving behind as we careened along—still not there, still not there—Mona and Dad and the medic and I taking up the whole ambulance, all the room, so there was no room for anything else; no room even for my mother's real self, the one who should have been pinching the color back to my father's grey face, the one who should have been calming Mona's cowlick—the one who should have been bending over us, to help us to be strong, to help us get through, even as we bent over her.

Then suddenly we were there, the glowing square of the emergency room entrance opening like the gates of heaven; and immediately the talk of miracles began. Alive, a miracle. No bones broken, a miracle. A miracle that the hemlocks cushioned her fall, a miracle that they hadn't been trimmed in a year and a half. It was a miracle that all that blood, the blood that had seemed that night to be everywhere, was from one shard of glass, a single shard, can you imagine, and as for the gash in her head, the scar would be covered by hair. The next day my mother cheerfully described just how she would part it so that nothing would show at all.

"You're a lucky duck-duck," agreed Mona, helping herself, with a little *pirouette*, to the cherry atop my mother's chocolate pudding.

That wasn't enough for me, though. I was relieved, yes, but what I wanted by then was a real miracle, not for her simply to have survived, but for the whole thing never to have happened—for my mother's head never to have had to be shaved and bandaged like that, for her high, proud forehead never to have been swollen down over her eyes, for her face and neck and hands never to have been painted so many shades of blue-black, and violet, and chartreuse. I still want those things—for my parents not to have had to live with this affair like a prickle bush between them, for my father to have been able to look my mother in her swollen eyes and curse the madman, the monster that could have dared do this to the woman he loved. I wanted to be able to touch my mother without shuddering, to be able to console my father, to be able to get that crash out of my head, the sound of that soprano—so many things that I didn't know how to pray for them, that I wouldn't have known where to start even if I had the power to work miracles, right there, right then.

A week later, when my mother was home, and her head beginning to bristle with new hairs, I lost my malachite beads. I had been carrying them in a white cloth pouch that Patty had given me, and was swinging the pouch on my pinky on my way home from school, when I swung just a bit too hard, and it went sailing in a long arc through the air, whooshing like a perfectly thrown basketball through one of the holes of a nearby sewer. There was no chance of fishing it out: I looked and looked, crouching on the sticky pavement until the asphalt had crazed the skin of my hands and knees, but all I could discern was an evil-smelling musk, glassy and smug and impenetrable.

My loss didn't quite hit me until I was home, but then it produced an agony all out of proportion to my string of pretty beads. I hadn't cried at all during my mother's accident, and now I was crying all afternoon, all through dinner, and then after dinner too, crying past the point where I knew what I was crying for, wishing dimly that I had my beads to hold, wishing dimly that I could pray but refusing, refusing, I didn't know why, until I finally fell into an exhausted sleep on the couch, where my parents left me for the night—glad, no doubt, that one of the more tedious of my childhood crises seemed to be finally winding off the reel of life, onto the reel of memory. They covered me, and somehow grew a pillow under my head, and, with uncharacteristic disregard for the living room rug, left some milk and pecan sandies on the coffee table, in case I woke up hungry. Their thoughtfulness was prescient: I did wake up in the early part of the night; and it was then, amid the unfamiliar sounds and shadows of the living room, that I had what I was sure was a true vision.

Even now what I saw retains an odd clarity: the requisite strange light flooding the room, first orange, and then a bright yellow-green, then a crackling bright burst like a Roman candle going off near the piano. There was a distinct smell of coffee, and a long silence. The room seemed to be getting colder. Nothing. A creak; the light starting to wane, then waxing again, brilliant pink now. Still nothing. Then, as the pink started to go a little purple, a perfectly normal middle-aged man's voice, speaking something very like pig Latin, told me quietly not to despair, not to despair, my beads would be returned to me.

That was all. I sat a moment in the dark, then turned on the light, gobbled down the cookies—and in a happy flash understood I was so good, really, so near to being a saint that my malachite beads would come back through the town water system. All I had to do was turn on all the faucets in the house, which I did, one by one, stealing quietly into the bathroom and kitchen and basement. The old spigot by the washing machine was too gunked up to be coaxed very far open, but that didn't matter. The water didn't have to be full blast, I understood that. Then I gathered together my pillow and blanket and trundled up to my bed to sleep.

By the time I woke up in the morning I knew that my beads hadn't shown up, but when I knew it for certain, I was still disappointed; and as if that weren't enough, I had to face my parents and sister, who were all abuzz with the mystery of the faucets. Not knowing what else to do, I, like a puddlebrain, told them the truth. The results were predictably painful.

"Callie had a *vision*," Mona told everyone at the bus stop. "A vision with lights, and sinks in it!"

Sinks, visions. I got it all day, from my parents, from my classmates, even some sixth and seventh graders. Someone drew a cartoon of me with a halo over my head in one of the girls' room stalls; Anthony Rossi made gurgling noises as he walked on his hands at recess. Only Patty tried not to laugh, though even she was something less than unalloyed understanding.

"I don' think miracles are thupposed to happen in *thewers*," she said.

Such was the end of my saintly ambitions. It wasn't the end of all holiness; the ideas of purity and goodness still tippled my brain, and over the years I came slowly to grasp of what grit true faith was made. Last night, though, when my father called to say that he couldn't go on living in our old house, that he was going to move to a smaller place, another place, maybe a condo—he didn't know how, or where—I found myself still wistful for the time religion seemed all I wanted it to be. Back then the world was a place that could be set right: one had only to direct the hand of the Almighty and say, just here, Lord, we hurt here—and here, and here, and here.

Interpretations

1. What effect does attending a parochial school seem to have had on Callie's dreams and career plans? How are these religious matters connected with later events?

2. What does the list of hopes and goals left behind by the narrator's tenants reveal about them? Are they, in words from the last sentence of the story, attempting to "direct the hand of the Almighty"?

3. Would this list have been better placed at the *end* of the story, to keep the chronology unbroken? Why or why not?

4. When does the meaning of the title become clear?

5. What connection is there between the list the tenants left and Patty's belief that miracles aren't "thupposed to happen in *thewers*"? (Why do you think the author included this incident? What light does it shed on her plight?)

Correspondences

1. Review the Wilde quotation (page 3). How does it apply to "The Water-Faucet Vision"? What rituals and customs does the narrator "carry about with [her]"? What do they reveal about her? What do they contribute to the story?

2. Religious traditions are important in the selections by Gish Jen, Momaday, and Sadat. What role do they play in each narrative? How are the religious traditions of each author similar to or different from yours?

Applications

1. Write a journal entry on your first significant religious memory.

2. Parents and other adults are sometimes viewed by children as perfect people who will always protect them, a viewpoint encouraged by tradition. What do the children in Gish Jen's story discover about adults? If you have a similar recollection, develop it into an essay.

The Charles River's Song
Tells Me Back My Dreams
A Journey and a Memoir

Joan Ackermann

*Joan Ackermann is a freelance journalist who has been pub-
lished in* Time, Sports Illustrated, The Atlantic, Esquire, *and
many other publications. She is also a playwright whose plays
include* Zara Spook and Other Lures, Rescuing Greeland, *and*
Don't Ride the Clutch. *She lives in Berkshire County in western
Massachusetts with her rooster, rabbit, and dog.*

WHEN PEOPLE ASK me where I'm from and I tell them Cambridge, Massachusetts, they almost always say, "Yeah, but where are you *really* from?"
Cambridge is full of people who are from somewhere else.

"No, you see," I explain patiently, almost professorially, "I was born
there." My father, a professor at Boston University, is from Germany, and
my mother, who served a term as mayor, was born in Sweden. But I come
from Cambridge. Deep inside I always hope no one asks if I went to
Harvard, or MIT, because I didn't. I never applied to either place, because
(a) although I play the oboe and can flail a five-string banjo *and* ride a
unicycle, I would not have been accepted, and (b) to be rejected by one's
hometown seems to me an experience no one should have to take to her
grave.

Cambridge is a difficult enough hometown to please without having
to be issued a written certificate of denial from its admissions offices. A
native could go out into the world and cure cancer, solve the national
deficit, make the cover of *Time,* and head the first women's team up
Everest, and still not expect to get much of a homecoming for it. A person
from Cambridge can't go to Harvard Square after she's been away for a
while, throw up her arms, and announce, "I'm back!" and expect much
response.

A person from Cambridge is called a Cantabrigian, a word I never
learned to spell until just now. One of the advantages of growing up in a
town where gray matter is the most common geologic formation and the
person one thwacks with one's Frisbee is apt to be John Kenneth Galbraith is that one admits ignorance comfortably. Mainly because one is
used to it, but also because one is trained to think of ignorance as an

opportunity for learning, and learning in Cambridge is the local industry. It's an honest person's toil.

After I've explained to people that I'm really *from* Cambridge, I know they stand before me with some image resembling Harvard Square in their minds. In a way I am from Harvard Square, which is just seven blocks from my neighborhood. It was my local hangout, where I bought my ice cream, where I headed with a grubby handful of change I might have acquired dressed in a poncho and posing as a poor Mexican migrant with my friend Keil Choi, a young Korean, knocking on neighbors' doors, begging for work. "Job?" we asked, pathetically, as if it was the one English word we knew. Al Capp, the creator of L'il Abner, gave us some change, as did Dr. Cope, a world-famous surgeon.

I've left a lot of tracks in Harvard Square. Tracks to the Quaker Meeting House in Longfellow Park, to Brownie and Girl Scout meetings at the First Congregational Church where I got married and near where George Washington supposedly took command of the Continental Army, tracks on the way to grammar school, to high school, to Boston University, and to work as an editorial assistant at Little, Brown. Never did I feel more like a townie than when walking through Harvard Yard—past handsome ivy-covered walls and the grand stone staircase sweeping up to Widener Library—usually late on my way to high school. I went to Cambridge Rindge and Latin, an enormous public school, racially well mixed, with its share of fights, knives, pregnancies, adolescent trauma, and girl's gym.

Every day after school my friend Shelly and I would make our rounds in the Square, say hi to George at the Tasty and the parakeets in Woolworth's, cruise around through Bailey's ice cream shop, chat with the newsboy at Nini's, beat our way through the throng of tourists in the Harvard Coop buying glassware embossed with Harvard insignia. (My big brother Rick resented the tourists. "This is where I buy my *underwear,*" he used to say.) Shelly and I would go down to the ladies' room in the basement, sit on the floor, hang out, and check the Kotex machine for change.

I got my first job near Harvard Square, at Harkness Commons in the law school cafeteria, the day after I turned sixteen. I had to line up little patties of butter and break up rolls; I also, unfortunately, had to wear a hairnet and a heavily starched mid-calf-length uniform with a momentum of its own that had an adverse effect on the law students and that ultimately hastened my resignation. I also worked in the Square as a telephone operator at a Western Union office, which is no longer there on Boylston Street, which is now Kennedy Road, at the Wursthaus, and at Elsie's sandwich shop where my thick frappes were the talk of Adams House.

I took piano lessons in Harvard Square, consumed hundreds of pastries with my father, snuck into Robert Lowell's graduate poetry seminar, got teargassed often and chased by an angry squad of National Guardsmen. My brother and I used to enjoy driving around the Square in the mayor's car when our mother was mayor; there were four different sirens in the car and we played them all. Our mother preferred to get around on bicycle. A local hero in the peace movement, she worked hard to take care of people in the city, to provide decent housing and health care. I was enormously proud of her.

As a townie, I still find it hard to share Harvard Square with so many people. Truth (or "veritas," as it says on the sweatshirts) be known, I guess I feel somewhere that some bit of the Square is mine; a grand illusion, I know, but Cambridge is full of those. (The Brattle Theatre used to show Renoir's *La Grande Illusión* regularly. In a typically provincial hometown way, I assumed young Americans everywhere had to watch *Casablanca* once a year at their local theaters. I also assumed proper movie audience behavior was to sneer and hiss self-righteously and laugh at the wrong parts.)

What I would like to do in Harvard Square is lift my hand and stop the traffic; freeze all the movement, the frenzy, the noise, the cars, the hundreds of pedestrians, students, tourists, hippies; freeze the whole shebang so I could reach out and take hold of my past, wrench it from all the people tromping through it, hold it and peel off layer after layer of history, slip back through to older buried strata where I could watch myself at fourteen, mortified while buying my first bra at Corcoran's with my mother, or at eight, proudly going into Woolworth's and buying a Minnie Mouse Halloween costume with ninety-nine hard-saved pennies. But traffic in Cambridge, or in any other hometown, never stops. The only way to hold a place still is to close one's eyes and let the mind wander back.

I guess hometowns rarely wave hello, slap you on the back, and ask what you've got to show for yourself. What greets the returning native daughter is her own personal suspended text, stored in private landmarks. The Eliot Bridge, for instance, which spans the Charles River, is as aloof and ungiving as any other part of the city, but what welcomes me when I visit it is the echo of my ten-year-old voice down underneath the bridge screeching out, "Stroke! Stroke! Your mother's gonna croak!" to startled crews stroking by in their sculls. Or the memories of stalking big river rats along the sandy littered shore under the bridge, or of making out there with my high school boyfriend, Jed, on rainy afternoons.

My parents still live near the Eliot Bridge, in the same old neighborhood. I'm grateful for that, because every time I go home I'm going back to the very beginning. I walk up Shaler Lane to the Harvard graduate housing where we lived when my father was getting his PhD. I check out the old sandbox, turn the corner past the trash cans we used to pick through every Tuesday, and walk up Kenway Street under the maple trees whose falling leaves I caught and cooked in a pot on the stove and then buried in a ceremony designed to make Richie Cronin fall in love with me. (His brother Jed did; that was fine with me.) My parents' house up on the corner, where they moved when I was eleven, still has a lovely garden in the backyard with a fountain and bird feeders, my father's roses and my mother's vegetables. The neighborhood always feels the same, and for that I'm grateful too.

Just a block away, the Charles River croons an old Cambridge folk song, always more than willing to sit me down and tell me back my dreams. I was born in the Mount Auburn Hospital, which sits right smack on the river. Over the years, I have biked along the Charles, roller-skated, written poetry on the grassy banks, seen a drowned body hauled out of the river at night, picked forsythia, helped my mother fight to save the sycamore trees, gotten drunk, played guitar, had picnics, fished for catfish (Keil Choi and I caught eleven one Saturday afternoon with bamboo poles), strolled with my father, buried my baby teeth, buried friendship pacts smeared with blood, buried my canary, Cecil, who used to fly around my dorm room at B.U. (which was also on the Charles), danced barefoot at the Cambridge Boat Club at my wedding reception, reported a story for *Sports Illustrated* about sisters who rowed in the Olympics, and closed my eyes on balmy summer nights to savor the heady blossom-filled air.

For me, a hometown travels the psyche back through the senses and the heart, not through the brain. That's why I don't like to think of myself as a Cantabrigian. When I'm in Cambridge I prefer to think of myself as a hometown girl, someone who went to the public schools and played clarinet in the band, who spent hours and hours up in the branches of the giant squid tree on Lowell Street, got into occasional fights, and left chunks of cheese and Wonder Bread out for the river rats.

Interpretations

1. What kind of place do you know or imagine Cambridge to be even before you read this essay? What kind of place, according to Ackermann, is Cambridge?

2. Much of Ackermann's humor derives from the contrast between the kind of place Cambridge is (or is thought to be) and the ordinary human activities she describes, such as appealing for a job or a hand-out to world-famous neighbors like Al Capp. What other examples of such humorous contrast do you find?

3. One Cantabrigian tradition, Ackermann says, is admitting ignorance comfortably. Another is learning. What's the connection between

these two traditions? Do you think she has difficulty admitting ignorance? Why or why not?

4. Ackermann may not be able to "please" Cambridge," but Cambridge pleases her. Do people born in large cities have "home towns"? What do you consider yours? How do you feel about it?

Correspondences

1. Review the perspectives of Wilde and Schwartz (pages 3–4) and discuss their relevance to Ackermann's memoir. Cambridge has become part of Ackermann's "own personal suspended text" or memory. Is such a text or memory too private to be considered "tradition"? Are there both private and public traditions, or do the most public traditions have private aspects? Is tradition possible without memory?

2. A sense of place is central to the selections by Baker, Momaday, and Ackermann. What techniques do they use to establish the relationship between places and traditions?

Applications

1. Has any place affected you as intensely as Harvard Square did Ackermann? Describe this place, conveying your responses to it through your use of sensuous and visual imagery.

2. "For me, a hometown travels the psyche back through the senses and the heart, not through the brain." Discuss your emotional associations with your home town.

Kissing Customs

Michael T. Kaufman

Michael T. Kaufman (b. 1938) was born in Paris but raised and educated in the United States. He attended the City College of New York and Columbia University, He has worked for The New York Times *as a reporter and as bureau chief in Ottawa and Warsaw. His book about Poland,* Mad Dreams, Saving Graces, *was published in 1991. Here is a general description of that experience: "In the years I lived in Poland, the old order was crumbling, Solidarity had been temporarily driven underground and much of society was organized as a conspiracy. I loved it. Men and women validated themselves not by winning and losing, both of which were impossible, but by seeking honor and avoiding shame. I loved that too." The temporary outlawing of Solidarity that Kaufman refers to took place in 1981. A year earlier, the Polish government had made concessions to the demands of striking workers in the Lenin Shipyard in Gdansk. By 1981, nine million workers had joined Solidarity, the independent trade union. That same year, Lech Walesa and other Solidarity leaders were arrested. An irate United States retaliated with economic sanctions, which were lifted when martial law was suspended in 1982. Free elections, the first in more than forty years, were held on June 4, 1989, and Tadeusz Mazowiecki became the first non-Communist to head an Eastern bloc nation. Throughout this time of tremendous change, Poland's economy has continued to suffer. Housing and food are in chronic short supply, even though the "old order" that Kaufman knew is indeed gone.*

"Kissing Customs" was published in the "About Men" column of The New York Times *(1988).*

I RETURNED NOT long ago from a three-year assignment in Poland, where men kiss the hands of women as a matter of course when they meet. When I first arrived in Warsaw, I did not think this was such a great idea. At the time I thought of myself as a democratic kid from the streets of New York, and the notion of bending over and brushing my lips over the back of a woman's hand struck me as offensively feudal and hopelessly effete. Each time some perfectly fine woman offered me the back of her hand to kiss, I stammered my apology, saying something like, "Gosh, no offense intended, but where I come from we don't carry on like this, and while I respect you enormously, can't we make do with a simple handshake?"

I was at the time mindful of what my feminist friends back home might have said. I do not think they would have wanted me to kiss the hands of all women simply because they were women. They would have, rightly, seen this as a sexist custom, pointing out that not even in the grip of the most obsequious compulsions would anyone kiss the hand of a man.

But then I began to realize that the Polish custom had one particularly subtle and attractive aspect. After forty years of living under an unpopular Communist Government that sought to restrict society to the proletarian standard of some concocted Soviet model, the Poles were defending themselves with chivalrous customs. Instead of addressing each other with terms like "comrade citizen," as their Government had once urged them to do, Poles intuitively responded by assuming the manners of dukes and barons. In such circumstances it was pleasant and instructive to watch factory workers, mailmen, soldiers, peasants and high-school students kiss the hands held out them while the Communist Party people, often identifiable by their wide ties and out-of-date suits, maintained stiff though ideologically correct postures.

Under this kind of social pressure, I kissed. At first it was tricky. There was nothing in my Upper West Side of Manhattan public-school education that prepared me for the act. I had to experiment. I think my first attempts were perhaps too noisy. They may also have been too moist. I realized that generally what I was expected to communicate was respect and not ardor, but I didn't want to appear too distant. I had observed some aristocrats take the hands extended to them and swoosh down without making real contact. I was trying for slightly more commitment.

Eventually, I got it right. And, to my surprise, I liked it. Each new encounter became a challenge. I found I needed to make subtle little alterations in technique as the situations demanded. For instance, if the woman was younger, I would bring her hand to my lips. If she was older, I would bring my lips to her hand. When I could not tell if she was younger or older, I went on the premise that she was younger. Sometimes you could play out little dramas. It was nothing serious or marriage-threatening, but you could, by kissing with more than normal pressure, make yourself noticed—and you could notice yourself being noticed. Or you could imagine you were somebody else, which, at least in my case, can be pleasant.

The real advantage of hand-kissing, I came to realize, was that it provided a ritual that enriched the routine of everyday life. Whenever I returned to the West on holidays I was struck by how few such rituals existed in my own society. Hardly anyone shook hands, let alone kissed them. Instead, waiters would tell me their names before taking my order and wish me a good day as they took my money. But I never felt they really cared. I would be called by strangers who wanted to sell me something over the phone, and they would address me as Mike. I would try to squelch them with what I thought was chilling irony and say, "Make that Mr. Mike." No one got it, but some said, "That's cute: Mr. Mike."

In this cultural context, I doubt that the United States is ready for handkissing. We seem to lack the self-discipline, or perhaps the confidence, and then too, there is the real danger of insulting feminists and getting your nose broken. And, to our credit, we have limited tolerance for lah-di-dah.

Still, I think it would be good to have some gesture or ritual that signifies at least minimal mutual respect. The idea would be to affirm something less than intimacy but more than passing acquaintance. What I have in mind would be useful for both intersexual and intrasexual contacts. It would replace the exchange of monosyllables like "hi" and "yo."

My suggestion is that we shake hands every day with the people we hold in esteem. The practice, as common in Poland as hand-kissing, is, I realize, not unknown here. But in America it is sporadic and all too casual.

Since returning from Poland, I've renewed many acquaintances. Among them was a person whose actions had once offended my sense of ethics. We chatted civilly enough, talking of our families and our recent experiences, but I did not offer him my hand. I did this as a point of honor—and to send a message. Had I been talking to a Pole, he might have reddened, stammered or walked away. But my old acquaintance didn't even notice. In this country, the symbolism of such a small act is lost. Of course, I could have thrown a rock through one of his windows, or cursed his parentage, or even turned abruptly from him, but all that would have been overkill for the graveness of his offense.

As for kissing the hands of women, my reflex, unfortunately, is waning. Under the social pressures of democracy, the Polish impulses that would have me turn wrists and kiss are growing fainter and fainter. The kid from the streets of New York is reasserting himself on his home ground with authentic and atavistic boorishness. *Tant pis.*[1]

Interpretations

1. For what purpose, according to Kaufman, do Poles use hand-kissing? Do you expect the end of Soviet domination of Poland to affect this custom? Why or why not?

2. What does hand-kissing reveal about the relationship between the sexes in Poland? (Men kiss women's hands, but not vice versa, of course.)

---

[1]French idiom, "So much the worse [for us]"; "[That's] our loss."

3. Kaufman seems to associate hand-kissing with "dukes and barons." With whom else is hand-kissing associated, and why?

4. Kaufman despairs that North Americans will ever learn hand-kissing. However, he recommends that we restore handshaking—because we need "some gesture or ritual that signifies at least minimal mutual respect." Why is such ritual important? (Why is it important to show, and not just feel, respect? Are there larger implications of such rituals?)

Correspondences

1. "The real advantage of hand-kissing, I came to realize, was that it provided a ritual that enriched the routine of everyday life": What examples support this point? What role does social custom play in gender relationships in Sadat's essay? How do they support or contradict Kaufman's thesis?

2. To enhance their narratives, Gish Jen ("The Water-Faucet Vision") uses humor and Kaufman ("Kissing Customs") uses irony. What two examples of each do you find most effective?

Applications

1. Review Kaufman's comment about "the real danger of insulting feminists" in the United States. How "real" is the danger? Is the writer suggesting that Polish women are less liberated? (What is *your* response to the custom of hand-kissing?)

2. Expressions such as "Have a good day," "No problem," and "Take care" are common in conversation. What does their frequency suggest about how Americans relate to one another? Discuss the popularity and significance of these expressions. (Are such sayings to be taken more literally or symbolically? Can such sayings be considered rituals?)

ADDITIONAL WRITING TOPICS

1. Many writers in this chapter recall aspects of their family's traditions—weddings, funerals, and religious customs. Focus on a ritual that you would like to record, and do so from a cross-generational or a cross-cultural perspective. Interview members of your family and extended family on their memories and associations. Write an account of these recollections that illustrates and explains their importance.

2. Past experiences—their own or others—are important to Momaday, Sadat, and Guppy. Does the fact that each essay is about a particular culture and its traditions have any relevance to the writer's purpose? Have you had a similar experience that could be valuable to record? Before writing your essay, decide whether your purpose is to inform or persuade.

3. Review Bellah's statement in the chapter introduction: "In our forward-facing society, we are more apt to talk about the future than the past . . . yet even in the debate about our future, our cultural tradition, in its several strands, is still very much present." To what extent do the selections in this chapter support or refute Bellah? What is your own point of view?

4. According to Cesare Pavese, "We do not remember days, we remember moments." Freewrite about a moment of special significance for you. Then expand on the memory and its importance in a fully developed essay. (Why do you remember it so vividly? What do you remember? How might you best explain its effects on you?)

5. All cultures observe holidays of national or international importance. What functions do these observances serve? Write an essay about the holidays your family celebrates and the rituals you observe. How "traditional" are these observances—and your role in them?

6. Write a journal entry on what you know about your own roots. (What else would you like to discover about them? Which members of your immediate and extended family might you consult? What sources—letters, journals, family photographs—might be useful?) After compiling information from these various sources, write a narrative essay on what you discovered about your origins.

7. Some traditions, such as the observances on college campuses of African-American history month and women's history month, are fairly recent. What functions do such observances serve? (Are they important only to particular groups?)

8. Compare and contrast the role of *prayer* in Momaday and Gish Jen. Momaday's grandmother made "long, rambling prayers out of suffering and hope, having seen many things." Gish Jen dreamed of becoming a "miracle-worker." She speaks of her parents trying to spare their children the "pains of life," she is struck by the list of prayers of the newlyweds who sublet her apartment, she hears of the "miracle" of her mother's recovery, and finally she realizes that life is far too complicated to be set right by the childish wish for some miracle to make everything all right. Show how Momaday and Jen grow through their observations and experiences to the final somber and even fatalistic visions of human loss. Compare the Tai-me figure of the Kiowas with Jen's malachite beads as symbols. What did the loss of each mean to the characters?

9. In Sadat, the Folk Tales, and Fairbank, various traditions (or magic powers) are used to confine women, to control them in some way(s). In every case, women escape the controls or turn them, at least in part, to their advantage. Discuss for all these works the advantages and consolations that women in these cultures find even in their arduous and rigidly ordered lives. What qualities of human nature do they reveal, and are the qualities common to both men and women, or not?

CHAPTER 2

Relationships

Cross-cultural studies of relationships show incredible variations in social relationships, but one theme remains constant. We are social beings. Not many of us could or would want to live a life of isolation. The variations that exist in courtship, marriage, and family, friendship, and treatment of neighbors have been built on a changeless foundation of need.

The thousand-year-old parable of the Good Samaritan establishes a clear definition of "neighbor," a definition that transcends tribal and even family differences and calls on us to value service to others over our own comfort. Those who accept this definition as an ideal, however, admit that it is very difficult to practice.

Moving from the general "neighbor" to the specific "lover" or "daughter," we encounter few absolute guidelines. When personality, individualism, and sense of identity become all-important, who helps us reconcile self and society, independence and interdependence? The cross-cultural examples in this chapter may suggest some answers.

The most recurrent and controversial aspect of family relationships to be found in Chapter 2 selections is the debate between patriarchs and feminists. Are men rightly in charge of the family and tribe? Shouldn't women be accorded the same personal, political, and economic rights? Perhaps the impact of this debate is most evident in Mead's essay on the American family. Can it survive the challenge to traditionalism in changing personal and economic gender roles? Are women who return to the workplace surrendering their matriarchal role of nurturer of the family and tribe? The ancient idea of male supremacy has left its mark. In some selections it is taken for granted and in others it is vigorously rejected, and intrapersonal and intracultural harmony is shattered.

Some women steer a course between the two extremes: some do it well, but others are torn apart. Jehan Sadat's English mother holds on to her religious principles and her concepts of childraising without challenging or undermining the authority of her Muslim husband.

We generally think that romantic male-female relationships are a sign of modern times, but it would be hard to find a more romantic lover than Black Elk's lovesick swain High Horse. In our own not so traditional culture and in that relationship that we now call "a relationship," the battle between the romantics and the realists goes on. Bruce Weber says the realists are winning, and you may agree. Equality of the sexes is taken for granted in Penelope Lively's story about a modern couple troubled by the decision whether to continue living together or to marry.

Immigrant family relationships add different voices to the debate. The patriarchal family described in Julia Alvarez's "El Doctor" is transplanted from Santo Domingo to New York City, but the city hardly intrudes into this intimate portrait. The focus is not on language or generational conflicts, but rather on the continuity of the family across generational and national boundaries.

But immigration may put a heavy strain on family solidarity. Her family's immigration from China to California makes an angry feminist of Maxine Hong Kingston. Cultural differences in the way female children are treated are much greater between China and America than between the Dominican Republic and America. Kingston's Chinese family seems much more patriarchal than Alvarez's, in spite of *machismo*. Kingston must leave her family to find herself. The parent/child relationship is badly strained. The struggle turns Kingston into a "woman warrior."

Two student essays describe brother–sister relationships: Paul Cohen writes from a brother's point of view of a scheming, withdrawn sister; Danit Wehle tells what it's like to acquire a new brother at age fifteen.

The basic importance of family, whether it be patriarchal, matriarchal or some compromise between the two, is one of the lessons of a cross-cultural study of relationships. All of the Chapter 2 selections reinforce how much of our personal and cultural identity is deeply rooted in the need for community.

PERSPECTIVES

No people are ever as divided as those of the same blood.

Mavis Gallant

Your children are not your children. They are the sons and daughters of life's longing for itself. They come through you but not from you, and though they are with you, yet they belong not to you.

Kahlil Gibran

"Family" is not just a buzz word for reactionaries; for women, as for men, it is the symbol of the last area where one has any hope of control over one's destiny, of meeting one's most basic human needs, of nourishing that core of personhood, threatened now by vast impersonal institutions and uncontrollable corporate and government bureaucracies.

Betty Friedan

Love will redeem a man and change his entire character and existence; lack of love will literally drive a woman crazy.

Jean Anouilh

The word love *has by no means the same sense for both sexes, and this is one of the serious misunderstandings that divide them.*

Simone de Beauvoir

Friendship is by its very nature freer of deceit than any other relationship we can know because it is the bond least affected by striving for power, physical pleasure, or material profit, most liberated from any oath of duty or constancy.

Francine du Plessix Gray

Marriage is a lottery in which men stake their liberty and women their happiness.

Virginia des Rieux

Woman is woman's natural ally.

Euripides

Hold a true friend with both your hands.

Nigerian Proverb

Govern a family as you would cook a small fish—very gently.

Chinese Proverb

Every man's neighbor is his looking glass.

English Proverb

A good marriage is that in which each appoints the other the guardian of his solitude.

Rainer Maria Rilke

When Sleeping Beauty wakes up she is almost fifty years old.

Maxine Kumin

Why are women . . . so much more interesting to men than men are to women?

Virginia Woolf

People change and forget to tell each other.

Lillian Hellman

I have three chairs in my house; one for solitude, two for friendship, three for society.

Henry David Thoreau

Each friend represents a world in us, a world possibly not born until they arrive, and it is only by this meeting that a new world is born.

Anais Nin

The heart is a lonely hunter.

Carson McCullers

No people are uninteresting.

Yevgeny Yevtushenko

Applications

1. Freewrite on Gallant's perspective on families.

2. Discuss Woolf's perspective on men and women.

Women

Chinese Folk Tale

Milton Rugoff in his A Harvest of World Folk Tales *introduced this old Chinese story this way:*

> *Popular conceptions of China's isolation notwithstanding, Chinese folktales have been no more free of international influence than those of Europe or America. Coming mostly from India through the medium of Buddhism, but also from the Near East, many familiar themes, including those of "Cinderella," the Master Thief, and the trapping of a jinni (genie) in a bottle, appear in Chinese folklore. But the national temperament asserts itself in many ways. Ripened by centuries of a religious philosophy that makes for serenity, the Chinese have lent their stories many distinctive qualities: a gentle whimsicality, fantasy, pathos, the uncanny, a quiet resignation to fate.*

AFTER HE WAS MARRIED, Chang the Third no longer wanted to go to work. He sat at home the whole day and played with his wife. He gazed endlessly at her beautiful face, and the longer he looked the less he wanted to go out. Finally he gave up his job and remained night and day with his wife. He went on in this way for six months, and then for a year; but even the largest fortune is soon exhausted if one does nothing, and Chang had merely lived on his earnings. In two years all his wife's jewels, the chairs, the tables, the linen, the clothes, in fact everything they had, was pawned or sold, and they were left without a penny.

His wife was really unusually beautiful, but she thought to herself, "Since his marriage my husband has never left the house. Day and night he sits around doing nothing but eat. In a short while we shall no longer have the wherewithal to live." So she upbraided him, saying, "You really can't stay at home all day. All men must go to work." But Chang saw her beauty and he thought anxiously, "If I went out another man could come and make love to her." And instead of listening to her words he remained at home, preferring to eat the most miserable food.

But eventually their poverty became unbearable. They could no longer live if he did not work. Finally, one morning, he said good-by to his wife and decided to go to a village. On his way he met a fine-looking man of about fifty years, who said to him, "Which is the way to such and such a village?" Chang answered, "I am going there myself, so we can go together." During their walk Chang told the stranger his story. "I am so unhappy at leaving my wife," he said. "But I must look for work to enable us to live."

The stranger replied, "The simplest thing is to bottle up your wife. I will give you the bottle, and every day, when you leave, you will only need to look at your wife and blow into the bottle, and she will vanish inside at once. As you can always take it with you, you will never lose your wife. I must now take another road, so farewell." Then he handed Chang a large three-inch bottle from his bag and disappeared. Chang dropped the bottle into his bag, noting what the man had said, and set off gaily for the village. The next day he tried the gift. As his wife was combing her hair before the mirror he secretly blew into the bottle. The woman saw in the mirror the reflection of her husband blowing into a bottle, but then she lost consciousness and woke up to find herself inside the bottle. Chang put the bottle in his pocket and went off to his work in the village. He was quite contented, for now no other man could flirt with his wife. In the evening he tipped the bottle, and his beautiful wife stood before him as before.

One day, however, he was forced to leave his wife at home to do the washing. He begged her not to leave the house when the washing was finished, and then set off to the village, forgetting to take the bottle with him.

After her husband's departure the wife went down to the river to wash the clothes. While she was rinsing a shirt she suddenly felt a long, hard thing between her fingers. She took it out and looked at it carefully. "It's a bottle," she said to herself. "Every morning my husband blows into it and I vanish inside. Why has he forgotten it today?" While she was pondering over the matter, a handsome young man passed by on the other bank. She looked up at him, and without thinking what she was doing blew into the bottle, whereupon the young man disappeared. When she had finished the washing she replaced the bottle in her husband's clothes.

When the man arrived home he immediately asked for the bottle he had left behind, and his wife handed it to him without a word. The next day when he went out he blew into the bottle as usual, and his wife disappeared, and again he flattered himself that she was safe from the caresses of other men.

That evening on his return he tipped the bottle, but this time two people appeared, his wife and a handsome young man. He was very much surprised and said to himself, "How strange! I thought my wife was quite safe shut up in the bottle, but now she has got a man with her!

How odd it is! And how impossible it is to keep a beautiful wife to oneself."

Interpretations

1. Describe the relationship between Chang and his wife. How does it change in the course of the story?

2. What type of marriage does the bottle symbolize? What does the mirror symbolize?

3. What seems to be the point (moral) of this tale? (Consider that it was the husband himself who bottled up his wife with a potential lover.)

4. Do you think the title works? Why or why not? Would an equally good title be "Men"?

The Good Samaritan

Luke 10:29-37

*The parable of the Good Samaritan is one of a number of stories
told by Jesus to his followers. The original city of Samaria was
the center of a sect whose worship at a separate temple (on Mt.
Gerizim) and whose recognition of the authority of only the
Pentateuch (the first five books of the Bible) led to continual
tension with the Jews of Jerusalem and elsewhere.*

THEN ONE OF the experts in the Law stood up to test him and said,
"Master, what must I do to be sure of eternal life?"

"What does the Law say and what has your reading taught you?" said
Jesus.

"The Law says, 'Thou shalt love the Lord thy God with all thy heart
and with all thy soul and with all thy strength and with all thy mind—and
thy neighbor as thyself,'" he replied.

"Quite right," said Jesus. "Do that and you will live."

But the man, wanting to justify himself, continued, "But who is my
'neighbor'?"

And Jesus gave him the following reply:

"A man was once on his way down from Jerusalem to Jericho. He fell
into the hands of bandits who stripped off his clothes, beat him up, and
left him half dead. It so happened that a priest was going down that road,
and when he saw him he passed by on the other side. A Levite also came
on the scene, and when he saw him he too passed by on the other side.
But then a Samaritan traveler came along to the place where the man was
lying, and at the sight of him he was touched with pity. He went across
to him and bandaged his wounds, pouring on oil and wine. Then he put
him on his own mule, brought him to an inn and did what he could for
him. Next day he took out two silver coins and gave them to the inn-
keeper with the words: 'Look after him, will you? I will pay you back
whatever more you spend, when I come through here on my return.'
Which of these three seems to you to have been a neighbor to the bandits'
victim?"

"The man who gave him practical sympathy," he replied.

"Then you go and give the same," returned Jesus.

Interpretations

1. The lawyer wants to "test" Jesus and, after hearing Jesus' first answer, to "vindicate himself." How do you think he feels after hearing the parable and correctly answering Jesus' question? How do you explain the change?

2. Jesus connects salvation (inheriting "eternal life") with kind service to needy people. How important do *you* consider service to needy people? What's the best way to be of service? Can one do wrong in doing right? Do good works also require sensitivity and intelligence? health and wealth? Why or why not?

3. "Love thy neighbor" turns out to be, in this parable, something quite practical. What is *your* idea of love?

4. Jesus answers the lawyer's second question—"And who is my neighbour?"—with a story instead of a definition. What definition does the story imply? Do you agree with the definition? Why or why not? How does Jesus tailor his story to his audience? (Why does he choose a Samaritan as the hero of his story?)

Correspondences

1. "Every man's neighbor is his looking-glass." What point is this English proverb making about behavior? How might that point apply to the parable of the Good Samaritan?

2. Review the Rilke quotation (page 100). To what extent do you agree with his point about solitude in relationships? What might Chang the Third (of "Women") have learned from Rilke?

Applications

1. Consult a dictionary or thesaurus on the word *neighbor.* How has the concept of neighbor changed with time? (How have urbanization, industrialization, the rat race and a "looking out for Number One" mentality affected relationships among neighbors?) Answer these questions in an essay; use cause-and-effect organization.

2. Personal space and its effects on romantic relationships differ among cultures. Using "Women" as a point of departure, compare your ideas on personal space and romance with those of a classmate or friend from another culture.

Can the American Family Survive?

Margaret Mead

*Margaret Mead (1901–1978) was among the most widely recog-
nized of American anthropologists. She won early and immediate acclaim for her study of the transition from adolescence to
adulthood in* Coming of Age in Samoa *(1928). She also taught
for many years at Columbia University and wrote more than
twenty books, including* Culture and Commitment *(1970) and*
Blackberry Winter: A Memoir *(1972). In this essay, she examines
the troubled state of the contemporary American family and
suggests some stabilizing changes.*

ALL OVER THE United States, families are in trouble. It is true that there are
many contented homes where parents are living in harmony and raising
their children responsibly, and with enjoyment in which the children
share. Two out of three American households are homes in which a wife
and husband live together, and almost seven out of ten children are born
to parents living together in their first marriage.

However, though reassuring, these figures are deceptive. A great
many of the married couples have already lived through one divorce. And
a very large number of the children in families still intact will have to face
the disruption of their parents' marriage in the future. The numbers
increase every year.

It is also true that the hazards are much greater for some families
than for others. Very young couples, the poorly educated, those with
few skills and a low income, Blacks and members of other minority
groups—particularly if they live in big cities—all these are in danger of
becoming high-risk families for whose children a family breakdown is
disastrous.

But no group, whatever its status and resources, is exempt. This
in itself poses a threat to all families, especially those with young
children. For how can children feel secure when their friends in
other families so like their own are conspicuously lost and unhappy?
In one way or another we all are drawn into the orbit of families in
trouble.

Surely it is time for us to look squarely at the problems that beset
families and to ask what must be done to make family life more viable,

not only for ourselves now but also in prospect for all the children growing up who will have to take responsibility for the next generation.

The Grim Picture

There are those today—as at various times in the past—who doubt that the family can survive, and some who believe it should not survive. Indeed, the contemporary picture is grim enough.

- Many young marriages entered into with love and high hopes collapse before the first baby is weaned. The very young parents, on whom the whole burden of survival rests, cannot make it entirely on their own, and they give up.

- Families that include several children break up and the children are uprooted from the only security they have known. Some children of divorce, perhaps the majority, will grow up as stepchildren in homes that, however loving, they no longer dare to trust fully. Many—far too many—will grow up in single-parent homes. Still others will be moved, rootless as rolling stones, from foster family to foster family until at last they begin a rootless life on their own.

- In some states a family with a male breadwinner cannot obtain welfare, and some fathers, unable to provide adequately for their children, desert them so that the mothers can apply for public assistance. And growing numbers of mothers, fearful of being deserted, are leaving their young families while, as they hope and believe, they still have a chance to make a different life for themselves.

- As divorce figures have soared—today the proportion of those currently divorced is more than half again as high as in 1960, and it is predicted that one in three young women in this generation will be divorced—Americans have accepted as a truism the myth that from the mistakes made in their first marriage women and men learn how to do it better the second time around. Sometimes it does work. But a large proportion of those who have resorted to divorce once choose this as the easier solution again and again. Easily dashed hopes become more easily dashed.

- At the same time, many working parents, both of whom are trying hard to care for and keep together the family they have chosen to bring into being, find that there is no place at all where their children can be cared for safely and gently and responsibly during the long hours of their own necessary absence at their jobs. They have no relatives nearby and there is neither a day-care center nor afterschool care for their active youngsters. Whatever solution they find, their children are likely to suffer.

The Bitter Consequences

The consequences, direct and indirect, are clear. Thousands of young couples are living together in some arrangement and are wholly dependent on their private, personal commitment to each other for the survival of their relationship. In the years from 1970 to 1975 the number of single persons in the 25-to-34-year age group has increased by half. Some couples living together have repudiated marriage as a binding social relationship and have rejected the family as an institution. Others are delaying marriage because they are not sure of themselves or each other; still others are simply responding to what they have experienced of troubled family life and the effects of divorce.

At the end of the life span there are the ever-growing numbers of women and men, especially women, who have outlived their slender family relationships. They have nowhere to turn, no one to depend on but strangers in public institutions. Unwittingly we have provided the kind of assistance that, particularly in cities, almost guarantees such isolated and helpless old people will become the prey of social vultures.

And at all stages of their adult life, demands are made increasingly on women to earn their living in the working world. Although we prefer to interpret this as an expression of women's wish to fulfill themselves to have the rights that go with money earned and to be valued as persons, the majority of women who work outside their homes do so because they must. It is striking that ever since the 1950s a larger proportion of married women with children than of married but childless women have entered the labor force. According to recent estimates some 14 million women with children—four out of ten mothers of children under six years of age and more than half of all mothers of school-age children—are working, the great majority of them in full-time jobs.

A large proportion of these working women are the sole support of their families. Some 10 million children—more than one in six—are living with only one parent, generally with the mother. This number has doubled since 1960.

The majority of these women and their children live below the poverty level, the level at which the most minimal needs can be met. Too often the women, particularly the younger ones, having little education and few skills, are at the bottom of the paid work force. Though they and their children are in great need, they are among those least able to demand and obtain what they require merely to survive decently, in good health and with some hope for the future.

But the consequences of family trouble are most desperate as they affect children. Every year, all over the country, over 1 million adolescents, nowadays principally girls, run away from home because they have found life with their families insupportable. Some do not run very far and in the end a great many come home again, but by no means all of them. And we hear about only a handful whose terrifying experiences or whose death happens to come into public view.

In homes where there is no one to watch over them, elementary-school children are discovering the obliterating effects of alcohol; a growing number have become hard-case alcoholics in their early teens. Other young girls and boys, wanderers in the streets, have become the victims of corruption and sordid sex. The youngsters who vent their rage and desperation on others by means of violent crimes are no less social victims than are the girls and boys who are mindlessly corrupted by the adults who prey on them.

Perhaps the most alarming symptom of all is the vast increase in child abuse, which, although it goes virtually unreported in some groups, is not limited to any one group in our population. What seems to be happening is that frantic mothers and fathers, stepparents or the temporary mates of parents turn on the children they do not know how to care for, and beat them—often in a desperate, inarticulate hope that someone will hear their cries and somehow bring help. We know this, but although many organizations have been set up to help these children and their parents, many adults do not know what is needed or how to ask for assistance or whom they may expect a response from.

And finally there are the children who end their own lives in absolute despair. Suicide is now third among the causes of death for youngsters 15 to 19 years old.

What Has Gone Wrong?

In recent years, various explanations have been suggested for the breakdown of family life.

Blame has been placed on the vast movement of Americans from rural areas and small towns to the big cities and on the continual, restless surge of people from one part of the country to another, so that millions of families, living in the midst of strangers, lack any continuity in their life-style and any real support for their values and expectations.

Others have emphasized the effects of unemployment and underemployment among Blacks and other minority groups, which make their families peculiarly vulnerable in life crises that are exacerbated by economic uncertainty. This is particularly the case where the policies of welfare agencies penalize the family that is poor but intact in favor of the single-parent family.

There is also the generation gap, particularly acute today, when parents and their adolescent children experience the world in such very different ways. The world in which the parents grew up is vanishing, unknown to their children except by hearsay. The world into which adolescents are growing is in many ways unknown to both generations—and neither can help the other very much to understand it.

Then there is our obvious failure to provide for the children and young people whom we do not succeed in educating, who are in deep trouble and who may be totally abandoned. We have not come to grips with the problems of hard drugs. We allow the courts that deal with juveniles to become so overloaded that little of the social protection they were intended to provide is possible. We consistently underfund and understaff the institutions into which we cram children in need of re-education and physical and psychological rehabilitation, as if all that concerned us was to get them—and keep them—out of our sight.

Other kinds of explanations also have been offered.

There are many people who, knowing little about child development, have placed the principal blame on what they call "permissiveness"—on the relaxing of parental discipline to include the child as a small partner in the process of growing up. Those people say that children are "spoiled," that they lack "respect" for their parents or that they have not learned to obey the religious prohibitions that were taught to their parents, and that all the troubles plaguing family life have followed.

Women's Liberation, too, has come in for a share of the blame. It is said that in seeking self-fulfillment, women are neglecting their homes and children and are undermining men's authority and men's sense of responsibility. The collapse of the family is seen as the inevitable consequence.

Those who attribute the difficulties of troubled families to any single cause, whether or not it is related to reality, also tend to advocate panaceas, each of which—they say—should restore stability to the traditional family or, alternatively, supplant the family. Universal day care from birth, communal living, group marriage, contract marriage and open marriage all have their advocates.

Each such proposal fastens on some trouble point in the modern family—the lack of adequate facilities to care for the children of working mothers, for example, or marital infidelity, which, it is argued, would be eliminated by being institutionalized. Others, realizing the disastrous effects of poverty on family life, have advocated bringing the income of every family up to a level at which decent living is possible. Certainly this must be one of our immediate aims. But it is wholly unrealistic to suppose that all else that has gone wrong will automatically right itself if the one—but very complex—problem of poverty is eliminated.

A Look at Alternatives

Is there, in fact, any viable alternative to the family as a setting in which children can be successfully reared to become capable and responsible adults, relating to one another and a new generation of children as well as to the world around them? Or should we aim at some wholly new social invention?

Revolutionaries have occasionally attempted to abolish the family, or at least to limit its strength by such measures as arranging for marriages without binding force or for rearing children in different kinds of collectives. But as far as we know, in the long run such efforts have never worked out satisfactorily.

The Soviet Union, for instance, long ago turned away from the flexible, impermanent unions and collective child-care ideals of the early revolutionary days and now heavily emphasizes the values of a stable family life. In Israel the kibbutz, with its children's house and carefully planned, limited contact between parents and children, is losing out to social forms in which the family is both stronger and more closely knit. In Scandinavian countries, where the standards of child care are very high, serious efforts have been made to provide a viable situation for unmarried mothers and the children they have chosen to bring up alone; but there are disturbing indices of trouble, expressed, for example, in widespread alcoholism and a high rate of suicide.

Experience suggests that we would do better to look in other directions. Two approaches may be rewarding. First we can look at other kinds of societies—primitive societies, peasant societies and traditional complex but unindustrialized societies (prerevolutionary China, for example)—to discover whether there are ways in which families are organized that occur in all societies. This can give us some idea of needs that must be satisfied for families to survive and prosper.

Second we can ask whether the problems that are besetting American families are unique or are instead characteristic of families wherever modern industrialization, a sophisticated technology and urban living are drawing people into a new kind of civilization. Placing our own difficulties within a wider context can perhaps help us to assess what our priorities must be as we attempt to develop new forms of stability in keeping with contemporary expressions of human needs.

Looking at human behavior with all that we know—and can infer—about the life of our human species from earliest times, we have to realize that the family, as an association between a man and a woman and the children she bears, has been universal. As far as we know, both primitive "group" marriage and primitive matriarchy are daydreams—or nightmares, depending on one's point of view—without basis in historical reality. On the contrary, the evidence indicates that the couple, together with their children, biological or adopted, are everywhere at the core of human societies, even though this "little family" (as the Chinese called the nuclear family) may be embedded in joint families, extended families of great size, clans, manorial systems, courts, harems or other institutions that elaborate on kin and marital relations.

Almost up to the present, women on the whole have kept close to home and domestic tasks because of the demands of pregnancy and the nursing of infants, the rearing of children and the care of the disabled and the elderly. They have been concerned primarily with the conservation of intimate values and human relations from one generation to another over immense reaches of time. In contrast, men have performed tasks that require freer movement over greater distances, more intense physical effort and exposure to greater immediate danger; and everywhere men have developed the formal institutions of public life and the values on which these are based. However differently organized, the tasks of women and men have been complementary, mutually supportive. And where either the family or the wider social institutions have broken down, the society as a whole has been endangered.

In fact, almost everywhere in the world today societies *are* endangered. The difficulties that beset families in the United States are by no means unique. Families are in trouble everywhere in a world in which change—kinds of change that in many cases we ourselves proudly initiated—has been massive and rapid, and innovations have proliferated with only the most superficial concern for their effect on human lives and the earth itself. One difference between the United States and many other countries is that, caring so much about progress, Americans have moved faster. But we may also have arrived sooner at a turning point at which it becomes crucial to redefine what we most value and where we are headed.

Looking to the past does not mean that we should return to the past or that we can undo the experiences that have brought us where we are now. The past can provide us only with a base for what threatens sound family life and for considering whether our social planning is realistic and inclusive enough. Looking to the past is not a way of binding ourselves but of increasing our awareness, so that we are freer to find new solutions in keeping with our deepest human needs.

So the question is not whether women should be forced back into their homes or should have an equal say with men in the world's affairs. We urgently need to draw on the talents women have to offer. Nor is there any question whether men should be deprived of a more intimate family role. We have made a small beginning by giving men a larger share in parenting, and I believe that men and children have been enriched by it.

What we need to be sure of is that areas of caretaking associated in the past with families do not simply drop out of our awareness so that basic human needs go unmet. All the evidence indicates that this is where our greatest difficulties lie. The troubles that plague American families and families all over the industrialized world are symptomatic of the breakdown the responsible relationship between families and the larger communities of which they are part.

For a long time we have worked hard at isolating the individual family. This has increased the mobility of individuals; and by encouraging young families to break away from the older generation and the home community, we have been able to speed up the acceptance of change and the rapid spread of innovative behavior. But at the same time we have burdened every small family with tremendous responsibilities once shared within three generations and among a large number of people— the nurturing of small children, the emergence of adolescents into adulthood, the care of the sick and disabled and the protection of the aged. What we have failed to realize is that even as we have separated the single family from the larger society, we have expected each couple to take on a range of obligations that traditionally have been shared within a larger family and a wider community.

So all over the world there are millions of families left alone, as it were, each in its own box—parents faced with the specter of what may happen if either one gets sick, children fearful that their parents may end their quarrels with divorce, and empty-handed old people without any role in the life of the next generation.

Then, having pared down to almost nothing the relationship between families and the community, when families get into trouble because they cannot accomplish the impossible we turn their problems over to impersonal social agencies, which can act only in a fragmented way because they are limited to patchwork programs that often are too late to accomplish what is most needed.

Individuals and families do get some kind of help, but what they learn and what those who work hard within the framework of social agencies convey, even as they try to help, is that families should be able to care for themselves.

What Can We Do?

Can we restore family stability? Can we establish new bonds between families and communities? Perhaps most important of all, can we move to a firm belief that living in a family is worth a great effort? Can we move to a new expectation that by making the effort, families can endure? Obviously the process is circular. Both optimism and action are needed.

We shall have to distinguish between the things that must be done at once and the relations between families and communities that can be built up only over time. We shall have to accept willingly the cost of what must be done, realizing that whatever we do ultimately will be less costly than our present sorry attempts to cope with breakdown and disaster. And we shall have to care for the failures too.

In the immediate future we shall have to support every piece of Federal legislation through which adequate help can be provided for families, both single-parent families and intact poor families, so that they can live decently and safely and prepare their children for another kind of life.

We shall have to support Federal programs for day care and afterschool care for the children of working mothers and working parents, and for facilities where in a crisis parents can safely leave their small children for brief periods; for centers where the elderly can be cared for without being isolated from the rest of the world; for housing for young families and older people in communities where they can actually interact as friendly grandparents and grandchildren might; and for a national health program that is concerned not with fleecing the Government but with health care. And we must support the plea of Vice-President Walter F. Mondale, who, as chairman of the Senate Subcommittee on Children and Youth, called for "family impact" statements requiring Government agencies to account for what a proposed policy would do for families— make them worse off or better able to take care of their needs.

Government-funded programs need not be patchwork, as likely to destroy as to save. We need to realize that problems related to family and community life—problems besetting education, housing, nutrition, health care, child care, to name just a few—are interlocked. To solve them, we need awareness of detail combined with concern for the whole, and a wise use of tax dollars to accomplish our aims.

A great deal depends on how we see what is done—whether we value it because we are paying for it and because we realize that the protection given families in need is a protection for all families, including our own. Committing ourselves to programs of care—instead of dissociating ourselves from every effort—is one step in the direction of reestablishing family ties with the community. But this will happen only if we accept the idea that each of us, as part of a community, shares in the responsibility for everyone, and thereby benefits from what is done.

The changes that are needed cannot be accomplished by Federal legislation alone. Over a longer time we must support the design and building of communities in which there is housing for three generations, for the fortunate and the unfortunate, and for people of many backgrounds. Such communities can become central in the development of the necessary support system for families. But it will take time to build such communities, and we cannot afford just to wait and hope they will happen.

Meanwhile we must act to interrupt the runaway belief that marriages must fail, that parents and children can't help but be out of communication, that the family as an institution is altogether in disarray. There still are far more marriages that succeed than ones that fail; there are more parents and children who live in trust and learn from one another than ones who are out of touch; there are more people who care about the future than we acknowledge.

What we need, I think, is nationwide discussion—in magazines, in newspapers, on television panel shows and before Congressional committees—of how people who are happily married can help those who are not, how people who are fortunate can help those who are not and how people who have too little to do can help those who are not and how people who have too little to do can help those who are burdened by too much.

Out of such discussions can come a heightened awareness and perhaps some actual help, but above all, fresh thought about what must be done and the determination to begin to do it.

It is true that all over the United States, families are in trouble. Realizing this should not make us cynical about the family. It should start us working for a new version of the family that is appropriate to the contemporary world.

Interpretations

1. Does the section entitled "The Grim Picture" convince you that the American family is indeed in trouble? If so, how serious is the trouble? What evidence do you consider most convincing?

2. Do you agree that a cross-cultural study of the family might suggest ways to improve family life? Can you offer some insights into other family systems?

3. Mead believes that historical studies of the family will teach us how to provide the kind of caretaking that families used to provide. Do you agree with the author that such caretaking can be provided without asking women to leave the workplace and return to their "place" in the home? Cite reasons for your response.

4. Do you agree that the federal government must play a large part in saving the American family? Why or why not?

5. Which purpose does this essay's data, arguments, and tripartite organization (evidence, causes, solutions) serve better—to inform or to persuade? Cite examples to support your answer.

6. Does the author answer her title question? How? (What role do "optimism and action" play?)

Correspondences

1. Review the Friedan quotation (page 99). How does it apply to Mead's essay? To what extent do you share the anthropologist's views on the importance of family?

2. Mead focuses on the fragmentary nature of the American family. How do her portrayals of family life compare with those by Baker

and Sadat (Chapter 1)? What factors might account for any differences?

Applications

1. "Women's Liberation, too, has come in for a share of the blame. It is said that in seeking self-fulfillment, women are neglecting their homes and children and are undermining men's authority and men's sense of responsibility. The collapse of the family is seen as the inevitable consequence." To what extent has the feminist movement had adverse effects on the American family? Write an essay attacking or defending the charges in the quotation. Use specific examples to support your point of view.

2. In "Can the American Family Survive?" Margaret Mead presents a very grim picture of the American family in the 1970s. Write a short essay agreeing or disagreeing with Mead's view.

The Unromantic Generation

Bruce Weber

Bruce Weber (b. 1953) is an editor of The New York Times
Magazine. *He has written articles on such diverse topics as sports,
literary figures, and contemporary social life and has published
a collection of stories—*Look Who's Talking: An Anthology of
American Short Stories *(1986). In "The Unromantic Generation," published in the April 5, 1987, issue of* The New York
Times Magazine, *Weber discusses changing attitudes towards
gender relationships.*

HERE IS A contemporary love story.

Twenty-four-year-old Clark Wolfsberger, a native of St. Louis, and
Kim Wright, twenty-five, who is from Chicago, live in Dallas. They've
been going together since they met as students at Southern Methodist
University three years ago. They are an attractive pair, trim and athletic,
she dark and lissome, he broad-shouldered and square-jawed. They have
jobs they took immediately after graduating—Clark works at Talent
Sports International, a sports marketing and management company; Kim
is an assistant account executive at Tracy-Locke, a large advertising
agency—and they are in love.

"We're very compatible," she says.

"We don't need much time together to confirm our relationship," he
says.

When they speak about the future, they hit the two-career family
notes that are conventional now in the generations ahead of them. "At
thirty, I'll probably be married and planning a family," says Kim. "I'll stay
in advertising. I'll be a late parent."

"By thirty, I'll definitely be married; either that or water-skiing naked
in Monaco," Clark says, and laughs. "No. I'll be married. Well-established
in my line of work. Have the home, have the dog. Maybe not a kid yet,
but eventually. I'm definitely in favor of kids."

In the month I spent last winter visiting several cities around the
country, interviewing recent college graduates about marriage, relationships, modern romance, I heard a lot of this, life equations already
written, doubt banished. I undertook the trip because of the impression
so many of us have; that in one wavelike rush to business school and Wall

Street, young Americans have succumbed to a culture of immediate gratification and gone deep-down elitist on us. I set out to test the image with an informal survey meant to take the emotional temperature of a generation, not far behind my own, that *seems* so cynical, so full of such "material" girls and boys.

The sixty or so people I interviewed, between the ages of twenty-two and twenty-six, were a diverse group. They spoke in distinct voices, testifying to a range of political and social views. Graduate students, lawyers, teachers, entertainers, business people, they are pursuing a variety of interests. What they have in common is that they graduated from college, are living in or around an urban center, and are heterosexual, mirrors of myself when I graduated from college in 1975. And yet as I moved from place to place, beginning with acquaintances of my friends and then randomly pursuing an expanding network of names and phone numbers, another quality emerged to the degree that I'd call it characteristic: they are planners. It was the one thing that surprised me, this looking ahead with certainty. They have priorities. I'd ask about love; they'd give me a graph.

This isn't how I remember it. Twelve years ago, who knew? I was three years away from my first full-time paycheck, six from anything resembling the job I have now. It was all sort of desultory and hopeful, a time of dabbling and waiting around for some event that would sprout a future. Frankly, I had it in mind that meeting a woman would do it.

My cultural prototype was Benjamin Braddock, the character played by Dustin Hoffman in Mike Nichols's 1967 film *The Graduate,* who, returning home after his college triumphs, finds the prospect of life after campus daunting in the extreme, and so plunges into inertia. His refrain "I'm just a little worried about my future," served me nicely as a sort of wryly understated mantra.

What hauls Benjamin from his torpor is love. Wisely or not, he responds to a force beyond logic and turns the world upside down for Elaine Robinson. And though in the end their future together is undetermined, the message of the movie is that love is meant to triumph, that its passion and promise, however naïve, are its strength, and that if we are lucky it will seize us and transform our lives.

Today I'm still single and, chastened by that, I suppose, a little more rational about what to expect from love. Setting out on my trip, I felt as if I'd be plumbing a little of my past. But the people I spoke with reminded me more of the way I am now than the way I was then. I returned thinking that young people are older than they used to be, *The Graduate* is out of date, and for young people just out of college today, the belief that love is all you need no longer obtains.

"Kim's a great girl; I love her," Clark Wolfsberger says. "But she's very career-oriented. I am, too, and with our schedules the way they are, we haven't put any restrictions on each other. I think that's healthy."

"He might want to go back to St. Louis," Kim Wright says. "I want to go back to Chicago. If it works out, great. If not, that's fine, too. I can handle it either way."

They are not heartless, soulless, cold, or unimaginative. They *are* self-preoccupied, but that's a quality, it seems to me, for which youthful generations have always been known. What distinguishes this generation from mine, I think, is that they're aware of it. News-conscious, media-smart, they are sophisticated in a way I was not.

They have come of age, of course, at a time when American social traditions barely survive. Since 1975, there have been more than a million divorces annually, and it is well publicized that nearly half of all marriages now end in divorce. Yet the era of condoned casual promiscuity and sexual experimentation—itself once an undermining of the nation's social fabric—now seems to be drawing to a close with the ever-spreading plague of sexually transmitted disease.

The achievements of feminist activism—particularly the infusion of women into the work force—have altered the expectations that the sexes have for each other and themselves.

And finally, the new college graduates have been weaned on scarifying forecasts of economic gloom. They feel housing problems already; according to *American Demographics* magazine, the proportion of young people living at home with their parents was higher in 1985 than in the last three censuses. They're aware, too, of predictions that however affluent they are themselves, they're probably better off than their children will be.

With all this in mind, today's graduates seem keenly aware that the future is bereft of conventional expectations, that what's ahead is more chaotic than mysterious. I've come to think it ironic that in a youth-minded culture such as ours, one that ostensibly grants greater freedom of choice to young people than it ever has before, those I spoke with seem largely restrained. Concerned with, if not consumed by, narrowing the options down, getting on track, they are aiming already at a distant comfort and security. I spoke, on my travels, with several college counselors and administrators, and they concur that the immediate concerns of today's graduates are more practical than those of their predecessors. "I talk to them about sex," says Gail Short Hanson, dean of students at George Washington University, in Washington. "I talk about careers. And marriage, with women, because of the balancing act they have to perform these days. But love? I can't remember the last conversation I had about love."

Career-minded, fiercely self-reliant, they responded to me, a single man with a good job, with an odd combination of comradeliness and respect. When the interviews were over, I fielded a lot of questions about what it's like to work at *The New York Times*. How did I get my job? Occasionally, someone would ask about my love life. Considering the subject of our discussions, I was surprised it happened so rarely. When it did, I told them I'd come reasonably close to marriage once, but it didn't work out. Nobody asked me why. Nobody asked if I was lonely.

Micah Materre, twenty-five, recently completed an internship at CBS News in Chicago and is looking for a job in broadcast journalism. Like many of the young people I talked to, she is farsighted in her romantic outlook: "I went out with a guy last fall. He had a good job as a stockbroker. He was nice to me. But then he started telling me about his family. And there were problems. And I thought, 'What happens if I fall in love and we get married? What then?'"

It may be a memory lapse, but I don't recall thinking about marriage much at all until I fell in love. I was twenty-nine; late, that's agreed. But the point is that for me (and for my generation as a whole, I believe, though you hate to make a statement like that), marriage loomed only as an outgrowth of happenstance; you met a person. Today's graduates, however, seem uneasy with that kind of serendipity. All of the married couples I spoke with are delighted to be married, but they do say their friends questioned their judgment. "I heard a lot of reasons why I shouldn't do it," one recent bride told me "Finally, I just said to myself, 'I feel happier than I've ever felt. Why should I give this up just because I'm young?'"

Most of them too young to remember the assassination of *either* Kennedy, they are old enough to have romantic pasts, to have experienced the trauma of failure in love. What surprised me was how easily so many of them accepted it; it seems a little early to be resigned to the idea that things fall apart. In each interview, I asked about past involvements. Were you ever serious about anyone? Any marital close calls? And virtually everyone had a story. But I heard very little about heartbreak or lingering grief. Instead, with an almost uniform equanimity, they spoke of maturity gained, lessons learned. It isn't disillusionment exactly, and they *are* too young to be weary; rather, it sounds like determination.

Twenty-five-year-old Peter Mundy of San Francisco, for example, says that until six months ago he'd had a series of steady girlfriends. "I'm down on romance," he says. "There's too much pain, too much pressure. There are so many variables, and you can't tell until you're in the middle of it whether it'll be positive. It's only in retrospect that you can see how things went wrong. In the meantime, you end up neglecting other things."

The prevalent notion is that chemistry is untrustworthy; partners need to be up to snuff according to pretty rigorous standards. Ellen Lubin, twenty-six, of Los Angeles, for example, has just gotten engaged to the man been living with for two years. When she met him, she says: "I wasn't that attracted to him right away. But there were things about him that made me say, 'This is what I want in a man.' He's bright. He's a go-getter. He was making tons of money at the age of twenty-five. He's well-connected. He was like my mentor in coming to deal with life in the city."

At the end of *The Graduate,* Benjamin Braddock kidnaps his lady love at the altar, an instant after she has sealed her vows to someone else, and they manage to make their escape because Benjamin bolts the church door from the outside with a cross. That was the 1960s, vehement times. When I graduated, we were less obstreperous. Sacraments we could take or leave. And marriage wasn't much of an issue. If we put it off, it wasn't for the sake of symbolism so much as that it didn't seem necessary. In the last few years, I've been to a number of weddings among my contemporaries, people in their thirties, and that impression of us is still with me. What we did was drift toward marriage, arriving at it eventually, and with some surprise. Some of us are still drifting.

Today's graduates have forged a new attitude entirely. In spite of the high divorce rate, many of those I spoke with have marriage in mind. Overwhelmingly, they see it as not only desirable, but inevitable. Because of the odds, they approach it with wariness and pragmatism. More cautious than their parents (for American men in 1985, the median age at the time of their first marriage was 25.5, the highest since the turn of the century; it was 23.3 for women, a record), they are methodical in comparison with me.

Perhaps that explains why I find the way they speak about marriage so unromantic. Men and women tend to couch their views in different terms, but they seem to share the perception that marriage is necessarily restricting. Nonetheless they trust in its rewards, whatever they are. Overall, it doesn't represent the kind of commitment that seems viable without adequate preparation.

"I've been dating someone for a year and a half," says Tom Grossman, a twenty-four-year-old graduate of the University of Texas. "We don't talk about marriage, and frankly I don't think it'll occur." Currently area sales manager in San Antonio for the John H. Harland Company, a check-printing concern, Grossman says he has professional success in mind first. "I want to be really well-off financially, and I don't want that struggle to interfere with the marriage. There are too many other stress factors involved. I want to be able to enjoy myself right away. And I never want to look back and think that if I hadn't gotten married, I could have accomplished more."

Many young women say they responded with some alarm to last year's [1986] *Newsweek* report on the controversial demographic study conducted at Harvard, which concluded that once past thirty, a woman faces rapidly dwindling chances of marrying. At a time when women graduates often feel it incumbent on them to pursue careers, they worry that the possibility of "having it all" is, in fact, remote.

Janie Russell, twenty-five, graduated from the University of North Carolina in 1983, left a serious boyfriend behind, and moved to Los Angeles to pursue a career in the film industry. Working now as a director of production services at New Visions Inc., like many other young women she believes the independence fostered by a career is necessary, not only for her own self-esteem but as a foundation for a future partnership. "I look forward to marriage," she says. "But this is a very selfish time for me. I have to have my career. I have to say to myself, 'I did this on my own.' It makes me feel more interesting than I would otherwise. Of course, what may happen is that I'll look up one day and say, 'O.K., husband, where are you?' And he won't be there."

About halfway through my trip I stopped interviewing married couples because they tended to say similar things. They consider themselves the lucky ones. As twenty-four-year-old Adam Cooper put it, at dinner with his wife, Melanee, also twenty-four, in their Chicago apartment: "The grass is not greener on the other side."

I came away thinking it is as true as ever: all happy families are the same. But the couples I spoke with seemed to me part of a generation other than their own, older even than mine. Calling the Coopers to arrange an interview, I was invited for "a good, home-cooked meal."

The next day, I met Micah Materre, who expressed the prevailing contemporary stance as well as anyone. Outgoing and self-possessed, she gave me a long list of qualities she's looking for in a man: good looks, sense of humor, old-fashioned values, but also professional success, financial promise, and a solid family background. "Why not?" she said. "I deserve the best." But as I was folding up my notebook, she added a plaintive note: "I'll get married, won't I? It's the American way, right?"

Very early on in my sexual experience I was flattered by a woman who told me she ordinarily wouldn't go to bed with men who were under twenty-six. "Until then," she said, "all they're doing when they're with you is congratulating themselves." For whatever reason, she never returned my calls after that night. Not an untypical encounter, all in all. Congratulations to both of us.

We were a lusty, if callow, bunch, not least because we thought we could afford to be. Encouraged by the expansive social mores spawned by the sexual revolution, fortified by the advent of a widespread availability of birth control, and fundamentally unaware of germs, we interpreted sex, for our convenience, as pure pleasure shared by "consenting parties." If it feels good, do it. Remember that?

It is an attitude that the current generation inherited and put into practice at an early age. Asked about her circle of friends in Los Angeles, Lesley Bracker, twenty-three, puts it nonchalantly: "Oh, yeah, we were all sexually active as teenagers. When we were younger, it was considered O.K. to sleep around."

Now, however, they are reconsidering. In general, on this topic, I found them shy. They hesitate to speak openly about their sex lives, are prone to euphemism ("I'm not exactly out there, you know, mingling"), and say they worry about promiscuity only because they have friends who still practice it. According to Laura Kavesh and Cheryl Lavin, who write a column about single life, "Tales from the Front," for the *Chicago Tribune* that is syndicated in some sixty other papers around the country, a letter from a reader about the virtues of virginity generated more supportive mail than anything that has appeared in the column in its two years of existence. I'm not about to say there's a new celibacy among the young, but my impression is that even if they're having twice as much sex as they say they're having, it's not as much as you would think.

The AIDS scare, of course, is of primary relevance. "I talk about AIDS on first dates," says Jill Rotenberg, twenty-five, publishing manager of a rare-book company in San Francisco. "I talk about it all the time. I've spoken with the guy I'm dating about taking an AIDS test. Neither one of us is thrilled about condoms. But we use them. The first time we had sex, I was the one who had one in my wallet."

Not everyone is so vehement. But seriously or jokingly, in earnest tête-à-tête or idly at dinner parties, they all talk about it. To some, the new concern is merely a source of disappointment. Several of the young people I spoke with express the sense of having been robbed. It's tough to find sex when you want it, tougher than it used to be, is the lament of many, mostly men. As it was put to me at one point, "I wish I'd been born ten years earlier."

Jill Rotenberg says she feels betrayed: "I've had one long relationship in my life. He was my first lover, and for a long time my only one. So I feel I've had an untainted past. Now I feel I'm being punished anyway, even though I've been a good girl."

"I feel like I'm over the hurdle," says Douglas Ertman, twenty-two, of San Francisco, who got engaged last summer. "I'm really lucky to know that I'll have one sexual partner forever."

Most agree that the solution is monogamy, at least on a temporary basis. "It's a coupled-up society," says Alan Forman, twenty-six, a law student of George Washington University who, for the last several months, has been in a monogamous relationship. "Now more than ever. A lot of people I know are feeling the pressure to get hooked up with somebody."

I ask Forman and his girlfriend, twenty-four-year-old Debra Golden, about their future together. They say they don't know ("I'm too insecure to make a decision like that," she says), and I get the sense they never talk about it. Then she turns to him, genuinely curious. "Say you break up with me and go to New York next year," she says.

"I don't know," he says. "If I meet someone and I like her, what do I have to do, ask her to take a blood test?"

A decade ago, one of the privileges that my contemporaries and I inferred from our sexual freedom was more or less to deny that there might be, in the sexual act, an innately implied emotional exchange. It's no longer feasible, however, to explain away sex as frivolity, inconsequential gratification. And that has complicated things for all of us, of course, whatever age, single or not.

But for young people, it's an issue, like marriage, that has been raised early: what does sex mean, if it doesn't mean nothing?

It's clearly a struggle for them. In one of my first interviews, twenty-five-year-old Karl Wright of Chicago told me: "Maybe there's a silver lining in all this. Maybe AIDS will bring back romance." The more I think about that, the more chilling it gets.

Beverly Caro, a twenty-five-year-old associate in the Dallas law firm of Gardere & Wynne, graduated from Drake University, in Des Moines, in 1983, and attended law school there as well. Her office high above the street looks out on the city's jungle of futuristic skyscrapers. She had offers from firms in Denver and her hometown of Kansas City, Missouri, she says, but chose to come to Dallas because "I see upward mobility here; that's what I was looking for."

Ms. Caro has an attractive, thoughtful manner and a soft voice, but like many of her contemporaries, given the chance to discuss her personal goals, she speaks with a certitude that borders on defiance. Currently, she sees two men "somewhat regularly," she says. "I'd like to have a companion. A friend, I guess. But finding a man is not a top priority. I want to travel. I want to establish myself in the community. I don't see any drastic changes in my life by the time I turn thirty. Except that I'll be a property owner."

During my interviews, the theme of getting on track and staying there surfaced again and again. I came to think of it as the currency of self-definition. As a generation, they are not a particularly well-polled group, but certain figures bear out my impression.

According to annual surveys of 300,000 college freshmen conducted by the Higher Education Research Institute at the Graduate School of Education of the University of California at Los Angeles, young people today, by the time they *enter* college, are more inclined to express concrete life objectives than they've been for many years. Of those surveyed last fall, 73.2 percent cited being "very well off financially" as an essential or very important objective. That's up from 63.3 percent in 1980, 49.5 percent in 1975. Other objectives that the survey shows have risen in importance include "obtain recognition from colleagues for contributions to my special field"; "have administrative responsibility for the work of others"; "be successful in my own business"; and "raise a family." At the same time, the percentage of freshmen who consider it important to "develop a meaningful philosophy of life" has declined from 64.2 percent in 1975 to 40.6 percent last year.

Many of the people I spoke to feel the pressure of peer scrutiny. A status thing has evolved, to which many seem to have regretfully succumbed. Several expressed a weariness with meeting someone new and having to present themselves by their credentials. Yet, overwhelmingly, asked what they're looking for in a romantic partner, they responded first with phrases such as "an educated professional" and "someone with direction." They've conceded, more or less consciously, that unenlightened and exclusionary as it is, It's very uncool not to know what you want and not to be already chasing it.

"Seems like everyone in our generation has to be out there achieving," says Scott Birnbaum, twenty-five, who is the chief accountant for TIC United Corp., a holding company in Dallas.

Birnbaum graduated from the University of Texas in 1984, where, he says, "For me, the whole career-oriented thing kicked in." A native Texan with a broad drawl, he lives in the Greenville section of the city, an area populated largely by young singles. His apartment is comfortably roomy, not terribly well appointed. He shakes his head amiably as he points to the television set propped on a beer cooler. "What do I need furniture for?" he says. "Most of my time is taken up going to work."

Confident in himself professionally, Birnbaum was one of very few interviewees who spoke frankly about the personal cost of career success. Many speculated that they'll be worried if, in their thirties, they haven't begun to settle their love lives; this was more true of women than men. But Birnbaum confesses a desire to marry now. "It's kind of lonely being single," he says. "I'd hate to find myself successful at thirty without a family. Maybe once I'm married and have children, that might make being successful careerwise less important."

The problem, he goes on, is the collective outlook he's part and parcel of. "Here's how we think," he says. "Get to this point, move on. Get to that point, move on. Acquire, acquire. Career, career. We're all afraid to slow down for fear of missing out on something. That extends to your social life as well. You go out on a date and you're thinking, 'Hell, is there someone better for me?' I know how terrible that sounds but it seems to be my problem. Most of my peers are in the same position. Men and women. I tell you, its tough out there right now."

When I returned to New York, I called Alex de Gramont, whom I'd been saving to interview last. I've known Alex for a long time, since he was a gawky and curious high school student and I was his teacher. Handsome now, gentle-looking, he's a literary sort, prone to attractive gloom and a certain lack of perspective. He once told me that his paradigm of a romantic, his role model, was Heathcliff, the mad, doomed passion-monger from Emily Brontë's *Wuthering Heights*.

A year out of Wesleyan University in Middletown, Conn., Alex has reasons to be hopeful. His book-length senior thesis about Albert Camus has been accepted for publication, and on the strength of it, he has applied to four graduate programs in comparative literature. But he's unenthusiastic, and he has applied to law schools, too. In the meantime, he is living with his parents in New Jersey.

He tells me that last summer he went to West Germany in pursuit of a woman he'd met when he was in college. He expected to live there with her, but he was back in this country in a couple of weeks. "Camus has a line," Alex says, "'Love can burn or love can last. It can't do both.'" Like Benjamin Braddock, Alex is a little worried about his future.

Dustin Hoffman is forty-nine. I'm thirty-three. Both of us are doing pretty well. Alex, at twenty-three, confesses to considerable unease. "Every minute I'm not accomplishing something, I feel is wasted," he says, sort of miserably. "I feel a lot of pressure to decide what to do with my life. I'm a romantic, but these are very unromantic times."

Interpretations

1. The message of *The Graduate* is that love "is all you need." Weber believed that message when he was in college, and now he finds that his interviewees do not. Do you? Why or why not?

2. Can you formulate a definition of love as Weber and his interviewees are using it? Is it the same as sex? Can you define "romantic" as Weber uses it in his title and throughout the essay? Is "romantic" the opposite of "realistic"? Is it possible that there is an intellectual, nonromantic type of love that is not reducible to feelings? If so, frame your definition of love accordingly.

3. "Today's graduates . . . seem uneasy with . . . serendipity." How have divorce statistics, feminism, and "forecasts of economic gloom" converged to make today's graduates careful "planners"? Do you think being a planner and being open to pleasant surprises (serendipity) are mutually exclusive? Why or why not?

4. What is the main point of Weber's interview with Alex de Gramont? Why do you think he wanted to save that interview for last and to report on it last?

5. Is Weber's main purpose to inform or to persuade? Cite evidence to support your opinion.

Correspondences

1. Anouilh's quotation on human relationships (page 99) states that love is a powerful emotion. How is his concept similar to (or different

from) those expressed by Weber's interviewees? To what extent are their points of view attributable to what Weber terms "self-preoccupation"?

2. "The achievements of feminist activism—particularly the infusion of women into the work force—have altered the expectations that the sexes have for each other and themselves." How have expectations of relationships changed according to Weber? To what extent has women's liberation also affected the lifestyles of middle-class women in Egypt? (Sadat, Chapter 1).

Applications

1. Most recent graduates, say Weber, accept marriage as "inevitable." What effect might this attitude have on their marriages? Will other factors offset this fatalism? (What effect might the AIDS scare have?) Will AIDS "bring back romance"? How? Do you consider such a return a desirable development?

2. Most of the young people Weber interviewed felt a great pressure to accomplish much in a short time. To what extent does your generation share their ambition and sense of urgency? How do these factors affect your personal relationships? (For example, do you spend time with people who may not further your career?)

from Soviet Women Discuss Work, Marriage, and the Family

Francine du Plessix Gray

Francine du Plessix Gray (b. 1930), the daughter of a Russian mother, was born and lived in France until she was eleven, when she moved to the United States. She graduated from Barnard College, became a reporter, and joined the staff of The New Yorker *in 1968. She has taught at the City University of New York, Yale, and Columbia Universities. The following essay is an excerpt from her latest book* Soviet Women: Walking the Tightrope *(1990).*

Before December, 1991, the Russian women Gray portrays were citizens of the now-defunct Union of Soviet Socialist Republics. Russians, who were leaders of the 1917 revolution that led to the formation of the U.S.S.R., can trace their history to a state founded in the ninth century in Novgorod and Kiev. The Russian Empire was founded in 1721 by Peter the Great, who attempted with limited success to introduce Western European ideas and ideals into his huge domain. Political and technical modernization lagged behind the rest of Europe throughout the Czarist, and even the Communist, periods. The history of the twentieth century has been largely shaped by relations between the U.S.S.R. and the rest of the world: a brief period of friendship between Russia and the Allies during World War II was replaced by forty-five years of Cold War competition between Soviet totalitarian Communism and the traditional democratic/capitalistic West. Although the fifteen republics that made up the U.S.S.R. are only now embarked on a tumultuous and dangerous transition to a market economy and democracy, if the Russians can work out their problems and avoid civil war, the opportunities are tremendous for real improvement in relations with the rest of the world and living conditions for ordinary Russians. As you will see from what Gray writes about the place of women in Russian life, women will play a decisive role in this transition.

ON A CRYSTAL-COLD winter morning Professor Elvira Novikova—a historian and writer who has become a close friend—took me to visit a branch of her alma mater, the Moscow Lenin State Pedagogical Institute. Founded in 1890, it was the first center of higher learning in Moscow ever to open its doors to women. A highly competitive school, which accepts only one applicant out of thirty, the Vladimir Ilyich Lenin Branch of this institute now graduates many of the young women who will become the next generation of high school and university professors.

The walls of the institute's handsome neoclassical building, pale blue and green in color, filled with Doric colonnades, are still hung with posters of 1942 vintage reminding all onlookers of the Great Patriotic War: Mother and Child clutching each other before a bloodied Nazi bayonet, with the slogan "Warriors of the Red Army, Save Us!" The most famous war image of all, a powerful woman, her head wrapped in a peasant kerchief, her mouth open in a shout of alarm to call out the timeless slogan, "The Motherland calls you!"

For several hours, Elvira and I met with the university's rector, a genial woman of Elvira's stark old-fashioned style, with a messy bun of gray hair and flat, masculine shoes. She had asked eight students to talk to us over tea. These young women were enrolled in vastly different "faculties" of the five-thousand-member university, and were little acquainted with each other.

The first topic of conversation we shared seems to be obsessive to college-age women: The alarmingly growing rate of Soviet divorces, which they link to their mothers' tendency to pressure them too early into marriage.

"My mother and I are absolutely at odds on the issue," said Tatyana, a thoughtful twenty-year-old with long brown hair and an Alice in Wonderland face, whose parents are both factory workers. "All she can think of for me is marriage and kids, whereas my principal goal is to be wise and learned, so we argue a lot. The only support I get is from my grandmother, because of course in the 1930s women never questioned the central role of work and career."

"My grandmother, my parents, my brother, his wife, their child and I all live in the same two-room apartment," said Natasha, a young woman with attentive blue eyes, who is also the child of factory workers. "Seven people in two rooms . . . it's kind of wonderful to all dine together every night, we get a lot of discussion time together! I have the same problem as Tatyana, mother believes that women must start a family early on; my *babushka*'s the one who says it's essential to have both a career and a family."

"My *babushka*'s also the only one who understands why young people want to live together before marriage," Tatyana concurred, "mores were much freer in her time, in the twenties." All the young women nodded in agreement.

"Our mothers' postwar generation passed on this dangerous attitude, the terror that it's a stigma to stay unmarried, that if you wait too long you'll never get a man," said Olga, an aspiring zoologist. "It's a horrible side of our society; when a girl isn't married at nineteen or twenty-one she says, 'I'm an abandoned, useless woman, useless to all.'"

"I'm a very unusual case," said Ira, at twenty-three the oldest of the group. She was a trim blond linguist who had recently married a career army officer. "My mother is Estonian, so my parents are perhaps more geared to the Western tradition, they simply put me out of the house when I finished high school, and I had to get a room of my own . . ."

Ira's fellow students all turned around to stare at her. A room of her own! It was clear that they'd never laid eyes on a peer who'd become independent that early on.

". . . And I'll be grateful to them to the end of my days," Ira continued proudly. "I worked for two years before entering university, and it gave me time to prepare for marriage. My husband and I were twenty-three and twenty-eight when we married, and I think our union is . . . perfect."

"I was married at age eighteen and had my children in the following four years," said Masha, a smart-looking young matron with the round, pink face of a *matrioshka* doll. "But I couldn't have started university without my husband's help. He's twelve years older than I, a very serious man, and helps out with everything in the house, diapers, cooking. . . ."

This, too, seemed totally unusual. There were gasps of "Oh, you lucky thing!"

"Thirty percent of our divorces are caused by too many persons living in one crowded flat," said the very programmed Ira, a member of the linguistics faculty. "My husband and I were careful to wait two years; we only married when we were settled in a decent apartment, each earning a good salary." ("*Molodetz,* [Smart girl]," the rector acclaimed from her desk.)

"I, personally, wish to bring up a child by myself, without a man," said Tatyana. "A man! Who needs a *second* child?" The young women laughed and clapped in approval. The rector again rocked approvingly in her chair. I asked for a show of hands on the issue. Six out of nine young women asserted that if they hadn't found "an adequate husband" by the age of twenty-six or so, they'd have a child "by themselves."

"And I'm going to wait until I've finished my dissertation to have my first child," said provident Ira. "My field is the British contemporary novel. I'm writing my thesis on Graham Greene, and as soon as that's behind me I'll feel ready for pregnancy."

"*Tovarishch!*" my companion Elvira exclaimed. "Tell us how you go about planning a family that carefully!"

"Very simple," Ira answered forthrightly. "The spiral."

The young women shook their heads with envy. The group compared notes on the immense difficulty of obtaining spirals, or any effective contraceptive, outside of the country's main urban centers —Leningrad, Moscow. Even there, you had to find a particularly privileged doctor—only one out of ten gynecologists has access to them.

Throughout the discussion, at the back of the room there had sat a pretty, silent young woman wearing a gold-embroidered scarf and a large amount of eye makeup and gold jewelry. Her style differed strikingly from her peers' carefully groomed but simple style, and I asked for her point of view on the issues we'd been discussing.

"My father's a military man and my mother hasn't worked for twenty years," she said with a touch of self-consciousness. "She's brought us up and happily busied herself with her sewing and knitting, and I want to be just like her and have a husband and three children."

Heads turned toward this anomaly with looks of annoyance, dismissal. The painted young woman pouted and looked sorry to have spoken out at all. "Look at her, decked out like a strumpet, selling herself like a slave to the marriage market," my friend Elvira whispered to me. "To think that our government spends its precious money educating her, and all she wants to do is stay home with the kids and do needlework," the rector in turn grumbled to Elvira.

I then asked the young women to describe the most ideal life they could forecast for themselves fifteen years from now.

"My first priority is to love my work," Tatyana announced, "to become an outstanding specialist in the field of teaching English. Once that's established, I can support a child."

"I also want *liubimaya rabota,* a beloved work above all else," agreed Olga. "I wish to go to work everyday as if it were a festival."

"In fifteen years I want to have finished my *doctoral* dissertation in contemporary British fiction," energetic Ira announced. "I want to continue with my community work and Komsomol activities. I want my husband, who's now a major, to have become a colonel. I also want him to have finished his advanced degree in political science. And we have agreed that we want two children, so we'll need a slightly larger flat."

"I want a beloved work above all," said Natasha, the girl who lived with six members of her family in a two-room apartment. "I perhaps want a husband and children, but even more important—I want to remain very close to my parents, continue living with them."

"Bravo," the rector applauded again. "What if your husband doesn't like it that way?" I asked. "The marriage will end," Natasha flatly announced.

After the young women had left—we had talked for almost three hours—I stayed and chatted for another long while with Elvira and the rector.

The two educators continued to berate the societal pressures that forced women into early marriages. And then the rector—who has been married for thirty-five years to a man she describes as "a marvelous person, charmingly infantile," made a statement which might well sum up Soviet women's attitudes to life.

"I'll tell you," she said, "I only have a son. But if I had a daughter I'd suggest she go and have a child without a man. Because *the most important duty of a woman, along with her work, is to have children, far beyond the duty of being a wife.*"

"And the *next* most important thing," Elvira added, "is to keep a sense of duty toward your parents."

"Bravo!" the rector of the first Moscow university to allow women into its doors agreed.

Interpretations

1. The consensus of this group of women is that a woman's most important duty is to find satisfying work, and her next most important duty is to have children, with or without a husband. Perhaps the women would agree that the third most important duty is to honor one's parents. Would this list of women's duties be your list, and in this order? If not, how would you change the list, and why?

2. What do you take to be the significance of the "painted young woman's" gold-embroidered scarf, eye makeup, and gold jewelry? What clue does the essay provide as to why she seems to be more interested in a husband and children and even in "sewing and knitting"?

3. What connection do you see between the two posters Gray describes and the attitudes expressed by the women?

Correspondences

1. Weber in "The Unromantic Generation" discusses attitudes towards gender relationships in the United States. If the attitudes expressed by the Russian women interviewed by Gray are typical, how would you characterize gender relationships in Russia? How do they compare with those of Weber's interviewees? How do you account for the differences?

2. While rising divorce rates in the United States are attributable in part to the feminist movement according to Mead, the growing number of divorces in Russia is blamed on mothers pressuring daughters into early marriages. What other causes of divorce do they cite? Compare their attitudes toward divorce with yours.

Applications

1. Compare the responses toward single parenthood expressed by this group of Russian women with those in your English group. To what extent do you agree with them that being a wife is less important than being a mother?

2. Analyze the roles of family relationships in Russia based on this discussion among college-age women. Consider, for example, their attitudes toward parents and children.

High Horse's Courting

Black Elk

Black Elk (1863–1950) was a holy man of the Oglala Sioux of South Dakota. In 1930 he and the poet John G. Neihardt met and established a friendship that soon led to the publication of Black Elk Speaks *(1932). These memoirs paint a bleak picture of Indian life at the turn of the century, but "High Horse's Courting" provides a rare moment of comic relief. It also reveals something of Sioux courting customs "in the old days."*

The Oglala are a sub-branch of one of the seven tribes of Sioux (or Dakota), who in the mid-eighteenth century drove out the Cheyenne and Kiowas from the Black Hills of South Dakota and occupied the northern Great Plains. They sided with the British in the American Revolution and in the War of 1812, but later signed peace treaties with the United States. In 1867 the Sioux gave up a large section of territory and agreed to retire to a reservation in southwest Dakota, but the discovery of gold in the Black Hills and the resultant rush of prospectors brought on warfare led by such famous chiefs as Sitting Bull, Red Cloud, and Crazy Horse, who was Black Elk's second cousin. This was the outbreak that occasioned the famous last stand by General George A. Custer. Today the Sioux live on reservations in Minnesota, Nebraska, the Dakotas, and Montana. Those living on the nine reservations in South Dakota now number about 58,000.

YOU KNOW, in the old days, it was not very easy to get a girl when you wanted to be married. Sometimes it was hard work for a young man and he had to stand a great deal. Say I am a young man and I have seen a young girl who looks so beautiful to me that I feel all sick when I think about her. I cannot just go and tell her about it and then get married if she is willing. I have to be a very sneaky fellow to talk to her at all, and after I have managed to talk to her, that is only the beginning.

Probably for a long time I have been feeling sick about a certain girl because I love her so much, but she will not even look at me, and her parents keep a good watch over her. But I keep feeling worse and worse all the time; so maybe I sneak up to her tepee in the dark and wait until she comes out. Maybe I must wait there all night and don't get any sleep at all and she does not come out. Then I feel sicker than ever about her.

Maybe I hide in the brush by a spring where she sometimes goes to get water, and when she comes by, if nobody is looking, then I jump out and hold her and just make her listen to me. If she likes me too, I can tell that from the way she acts, for she is very bashful and maybe will not say a word or even look at me the first time. So I let her go, and then maybe I sneak around until I can see her father alone, and I tell him how many horses I can give him for his beautiful girl, and by now I am feeling so sick that maybe I would give him all the horses in the world if I had them.

Well, this young man I am telling about was called High Horse, and there was a girl in the village who looked so beautiful to him that he was just sick all over from thinking about her so much and he was getting sicker all the time. The girl was very shy, and her parents thought a great deal of her because they were not young any more and this was the only child they had. So they watched her all day long, and they fixed it so that she would be safe at night too when they were asleep. They thought so much of her that they had made a rawhide bed for her to sleep in, and after they knew that High Horse was sneaking around after her, they took rawhide thongs and tied the girl in bed at night so that nobody could steal her when they were asleep, for they were not sure but that their girl might really want to be stolen.

Well, after High Horse had been sneaking around a good while and hiding and waiting for the girl and getting sicker all the time, he finally caught her alone and made her talk to him. Then he found out that she liked him maybe a little. Of course this did not make him feel well. It made him sicker than ever, but now he felt as brave as a bison bull, so he went right to her father and said he loved the girl so much that he would give two good horses for her—one of them young and the other one not so very old.

But the old man just waved his hand, meaning for High Horse to go away and quit talking foolishness like that.

High Horse was feeling sicker than ever about it; but there was another young fellow who said he would loan High Horse two ponies and when he got some more horses, why, he could just give them back for the ones he had borrowed.

Then High Horse went back to the old man and said he would give four horses for the girl—two of them young and the other two not hardly old at all. But the old man just waved his hand and would not say anything.

So High Horse sneaked around until he could talk to the girl again, and he asked her to run away with him. He told her he thought he would just fall over and die if she did not. But she said she would not do that; she wanted to be bought like a fine woman. You see she thought a great deal of herself too.

That made High Horse feel so sick that he could not eat a bite, and he went around with his head hanging down as though he might just fall down and die any time.

Red Deer was another young fellow, and he and High Horse were great comrades, always doing things together. Red Deer saw how High Horse was acting, and he said: "Cousin, what is the matter? Are you sick in the belly? You look as though you were going to die."

Then High Horse told Red Deer how it was, and said he thought he could not stay alive much longer if he could not marry the girl pretty quick.

Red Deer thought awhile about it, and then he said: "Cousin, I have a plan, and if you are man enough to do as I tell you, then everything will be all right. She will not run away with you; her old man will not take four horses; and four horses are all you can get. You must steal her and run away with her. Then afterwhile you can come back and the old man cannot do anything because she will be your woman. Probably she wants you to steal her anyway."

So they planned what High Horse had to do, and he said he loved the girl so much that he was man enough to do anything Red Deer or anybody else could think up. So this is what they did.

That night late they sneaked up to the girl's tepee and waited until it sounded inside as though the old man and the old woman and the girl were sound asleep. Then High Horse crawled under the tepee with a knife. He had to cut the rawhide thongs first, and then Red Deer, who was pulling up the stakes around that side of the tepee, was going to help drag the girl outside and gag her. After that, High Horse could put her across his pony in front of him and hurry out of there and be happy all the rest of his life.

When High Horse had crawled inside, he felt so nervous that he could hear his heart drumming, and it seemed so loud he felt sure it would waken the old folks. But it did not, and afterwhile he began cutting the thongs. Every time he cut one it made a pop and nearly scared him to death. But he was getting along all right and all the thongs were cut down as far as the girl's thighs, when he became so nervous that his knife slipped and stuck the girl. She gave a big, loud yell. Then the old folks jumped up and yelled too. By this time High Horse was outside, and he and Red Deer were running away like antelope. The old man and some other people chased the young men but they got away in the dark and nobody knew who it was.

Well, if you ever wanted a beautiful girl you will know how sick High Horse was now. It was very bad the way he felt, and it looked as though he would starve even if he did not drop over dead sometime.

Red Deer kept thinking about this, and after a few days he went to High Horse and said: "Cousin, take courage! I have another plan, and I am sure, if you are man enough, we can steal her this time." And High

Horse said: "I am man enough to do anything anybody can think up, if I can only get that girl." So this is what they did.

They went away from the village alone, and Red Deer made High Horse strip naked. Then he painted High Horse solid white all over, and after that he painted black stripes all over the white and put black rings around High Horse's eyes. High Horse looked terrible. He looked so terrible that when Red Deer was through painting and took a good look at what he had done, he said it scared even him a little.

"Now," Red Deer said, "If you get caught again, everybody will be so scared they will think you are a bad spirit and will be afraid to chase you."

So when the night was getting old and everybody was sound asleep, they sneaked back to the girl's tepee. High Horse crawled in with his knife, as before, and Red Deer waited outside, ready to drag the girl out and gag her when High Horse had all the thongs cut.

High Horse crept up by the girl's bed and began cutting at the thongs. But he kept thinking, "If they see me they will shoot me because I look so terrible." The girl was restless and kept squirming around in bed, and when a thong was cut, it popped. So High Horse worked very slowly and carefully.

But he must have made some noise, for suddenly the old woman awoke and said to her old man: "Old Man, wake up! There is somebody in this tepee!" But the old man was sleepy and didn't want to be bothered. He said: "Of course there is somebody in this tepee. Go to sleep and don't bother me." Then he snored some more.

But High Horse was so scared by now that he lay very still and as flat to the ground as he could. Now, you see, he had not been sleeping very well for a long time because he was so sick about the girl. And while he was lying there waiting for the old woman to snore, he just forgot everything, even how beautiful the girl was. Red Deer who was lying outside ready to do his part, wondered and wondered what had happened in there, but he did not dare call out to High Horse.

Afterwhile the day began to break and Red Deer had to leave with the two ponies he had staked there for his comrade and girl, or somebody would see him.

So he left.

Now when it was getting light in the tepee, the girl awoke and the first thing she saw was a terrible animal, all white with black stripes on it, lying asleep beside her bed. So she screamed, and then the old woman screamed and the old man yelled. High Horse jumped up, scared almost to death, and he nearly knocked the tepee down getting out of there.

People were coming running from all over the village with guns and bows and axes, and everybody was yelling.

By now High Horse was running so fast that he hardly touched the ground at all, and he looked so terrible that the people fled from him and let him run. Some braves wanted to shoot at him, but the others said he might be some sacred being and it would bring bad trouble to kill him.

High Horse made for the river that was near, and in among the brush he found a hollow tree and dived into it. Afterwhile some braves came there and he could hear them saying that it was some bad spirit that had come out of the water and gone back in again.

That morning the people were ordered to break camp and move away from there. So they did, while High Horse was hiding in his hollow tree.

Now Red Deer had been watching all this from his own tepee and trying to look as though he were as much surprised and scared as all the others. So when the camp moved, he sneaked back to where he had seen his comrade disappear. When he was down there in the brush, he called, and High Horse answered, because he knew his friend's voice. They washed off the paint from High Horse and sat down on the river bank to talk about their troubles.

High Horse said he never would go back to the village as long as he lived and he did not care what happened to him now. He said he was going to go on the war-path all by himself. Red Deer said: "No, cousin, you are not going on the war-path alone, because I am going with you."

So Red Deer got everything ready, and at night they started out on the war-path all alone. After several days they came to a Crow camp just about sundown, and when it was dark they sneaked up to where the Crow horses were grazing, killed the horse guard, who was not thinking about enemies because he thought all the Lakotas were far away, and drove off about a hundred horses.

They got a big start because all the Crow horses stampeded and it was probably morning before the Crow warriors could catch any horses to ride. Red Deer and High Horse fled with their herd three days and nights before they reached the village of their people. Then they drove the whole herd right into the village and up in front of the girl's tepee. The old man was there, and High Horse called out to him and asked if he thought maybe that would be enough horses for his girl. The old man did not wave him away that time. It was not the horses that he wanted. What he wanted was a son who was a real man and good for something.

So High Horse got his girl after all, and I think he deserved her.

Interpretations

1. Black Elk sets his story "in the old days." How does this setting affect your response to the narrative?

2. What do you think is Black Elk's purpose in telling the story of High Horse's "sickness"?

3. What role does each participant perform in the courtship ritual? Is it significant that the girl is not named? Why or why not?

4. What is the tone of this narrative? Where does Black Elk use humor? What does the humor indicate about Black Elk's attitude toward the subject?

Correspondences

1. Wealth is important in the Black Elk and Weber selections: how does it affect gender relationships? Is economics important in such relationships, regardless of cultural background? Why or why not?

2. High Horse is romantic, while most of the young men Weber interviews are pragmatic. How does this difference influence their behavior, expectations, and relationships? Which term better describes you?

Applications

1. Write a speech for an unsympathetic audience on the following topic: "Traditional gender roles have contributed significantly to the stability and security of marriage." What tone should you adopt? What arguments will be most convincing? Include specific examples as supporting details.

2. How do generational differences affect concepts of romantic love and courtship customs? Interview some older people, asking them to define romantic love. Write a thesis statement based on their responses and plan an essay. (What other evidence will you need to develop your thesis into an essay?)

El Doctor

Julia Alvarez

*Julia Alvarez (b. 1950) was born in New York City but soon
moved to the Dominican Republic, returning to America ten
years later. A published essayist, poet, and writer of short fiction,
she has won several fellowships and prizes. She is currently on
the faculty at Middlebury College, Vermont, where she teaches a
course on Hispanic writers in the United States.*

*As you read "El Doctor," pay particular attention to the con-
versations between father and daughter. Notice that both are
interested in history, and that Dr. Alvarez is particularly interested in his ancestors' part in the history of the Dominican
Republic.*

*An island nation about the size of Vermont and New Hamp-
shire combined, the Dominican Republic shares with Haiti the
West Indian island of Hispaniola. It is also the site of Columbus's
landfall in 1492 and the capital Santo Domingo, the oldest
settlement by Europeans in the New World. From 1492 to 1863,
the republic remained intermittently under Spanish rule. A con-
stitutionally elected government was installed in 1924, but President Rafael Trujillo ruled as a dictator from 1930 until his
assassination in 1961, retaining power even when he was not
in office. U.S. Marines intervened to put down a revolt in 1965.
The country has enjoyed representative democracy since the
elections of 1966, but low prices for the main export commodity,
sugar, have caused widespread economic problems. These problems echo in the family tensions of "El Doctor." In 1991, Alvarez
published a collection of short stories,* How the Garcia Girls Lost
Their Accents.

"LIGHTS! At this hour?" my father asks, looking up from his empty dinner
plate at the glowing lamp my mother has just turned on above the table.
Are we in Plato's cave,[1] Mother?" He winks at me; as the two readers
in the family we show off by making allusions my mother and sisters
don't understand. He leans his chair back and picks up the hem of the
curtain. A dim gray light falls into the room. "See, Mother. It's still light
out there!"

---

[1]See Plato's "Allegory of the Cave," which compares our search for meaning in life to our
leaving the safe, dark but happy cave of illusions for the burning light of the sun of truth.

"*Ya, ya!*" she snaps, and flips the switch off.

"Your mother is a wonder," he announces, then he adds, "El Doctor is ready for bed." Dinner is over; every night my father brings the meal to a close with a third-person goodnight before he leaves the room.

Tonight he lingers, watching her. She says nothing, head bent, intent on her mashed plantains with oil and onions. "Yessir," he elaborates, "El Doctor—" The rest is garbled, for he's balled up his napkin and rubbed his lips violently as if he meant to erase them from his face. Perhaps he shouldn't have spoken up? She is jabbing at the few bites of beefsteak on her plate. Perhaps he should have just let the issue drop like water down his chest or whatever it is the Americans say. He scrapes his chair back.

Her scowl deepens. "Eduardo, please." And then, because he already knows better, she adds only, "The wax finish."

"*Por supuesto,*"[2] he says, his voice full of false concern as he examines her spotless kitchen floor for damages. Then, carefully, he lifts his chair up and tucks it back in its place. "This old man is ready for bed." He leans over and kisses the scowl off her face. "Mother, this country agrees with you. You look more beautiful every day. Doesn't she, girls?" And with a wink of encouragement to each of us, he leaves us in the dark.

I remember my mother mornings, slapping around in her comfortable slippers, polishing her windows into blinding panes of light. But I remember him mostly at night, moving down the dark halls, undressing as he climbed the dark stairs to bed.

I want to say there were as many buttons on his vest as stairs up to the bedroom: it seemed he unbuttoned a button on each step so that by the time he reached the landing, his vest was off. His armor, I thought, secretly pleased with all I believed I understood about him. But his vest couldn't have had more than six buttons, and the stairs were long and narrow. Of course, I couldn't see well in the dark he insisted on.

"I'm going to take this dollar," he showed me, holding a bill in one hand and a flickering lighter in the other, "and I'm going to set fire to it." He never actually did. He spoke in parables, he complained in metaphor because he had never learned to say things directly. I already knew what he meant, but I had my part to play.

"Why would you want to do something like that?" I asked.

"Exactly! Why burn up my money with all these lights in the house!" As we grew up, confirmed in our pyromania, he did not bother to teach us to economize, but went through the house, turning off lights in every room, not noticing many times that we were there, reading or writing a letter, and leaving us in the dark, hurt that he had overlooked us.

At the bedroom door he loosened his tie and, craning his neck, undid the top button of his shirt. Then he sat at the edge of the bed and turned on his bedside lamp. Not always; if a little reflected sun dappled the room with shadowy light, if it was late spring or early fall or summertime, he

[2]Of course.

waited until the last moment to turn on the lamp, sometimes reading in the dark until we came in and turned it on for him. "Papi, you're going to ruin your eyes," we scolded.

Once I worked it out for him with the pamphlet the electric company sent me. Were he to leave his bedside light, say, burning for the rest of his evenings—and I allowed him a generous four decades ("I won't need it for that long," he protested; I insisted)—the cost (side by side we multiplied, added, carried over to the next column) would be far less than if he lost his eyesight, was forced to give up his practice and had to spend the next four decades—

"Like your friend Milton," he said, pleased with the inspired possibilities of blindness.[3] Now that I was turning out to be the family poet, all the greats were my personal friends. "'When I consider how my light is spent,'" he began. He loved to recite, racing me through poems to see who would be the first one to finish.

"'How my light is spent,'" I echoed and took the lead. "'Ere half my days, in this dark world and wide . . .'"

Just as I was rounding the linebreak to the last line, he interjected it, "'They also serve who only stand and wait.'"

I scowled. How dare he clap the last line on after I had gone through all the trouble of reciting the poem! "Not every blind man is a Milton," I said, and I gave him the smirk I wore all through adolescence.

"Nutrition," he said mysteriously.

"What about nutrition?"

"Good nutrition, we're starting to see the effects: children grow taller; they have better teeth, better bones, better minds than their elders." And he reached for his book on the bedside table.

Actually, the reading came later. First there is the scene that labels him immigrant and shows why I could never call him, sweetly, playfully, *Daddy*. He took from his back pocket a wad of bills so big his hand could not close over it. And he began to count. If at this point we disturbed him, he waved us away. If we called from downstairs, he did not answer. All over the bed he shared with my mother were piles of bills: I do not know the system; no one ever did. Perhaps all the fives were together, all the tens? Perhaps each pile was a specific amount? But this was the one private moment he insisted on. Not even catching him undressing, which I never did, seems as intimate a glimpse of him.

After the counting came the binding and marking: each pile was held together with rubber bands he saved from the rolled-up *New York Times,* and the top bill was scribbled on. He marked them as a reminder of how much was in each pile, I'm sure, but I can't help thinking it was also his way of owning what he had earned, much as ranchers brand their cattle.

---

[3]Milton was an English poet (1608–1674) who, on becoming blind, wrote, "When I consider how my light is spent."

The Secretary of the Treasury had signed this twenty; there was Andrew Jackson's picture; he had to add his hand to it to make it his—to try to convince himself that it was his, for he never totally believed it was. Even after he was a successful doctor in New York with a house in the suburbs and lands at "home," his daughters in boarding schools and summer camps, a second car with enough gadgets to keep him busy in bad traffic, he was turning off lights, frequenting thrift shops for finds in ties, taking the 59th Street bridge even if it was out of his way to avoid paying a toll to cross the river.

He could not afford the good life, he could only pass it on. And he did. Beneath the surface pennypinching, his extravagance might have led him to bankruptcy several times had mother not been there to remind him that the weather was apt to change. "Save for a snowy day," she advised him.

"Julie! Isn't it rainy day?" he enlisted me. He was always happy to catch his wife at an error since she spoke English so much better than he did. "Save it for a rainy day?"

Eager to be an authority on anything, I considered Arbiter of Clichés a compliment to my literary talent. "Save it for a rainy day," I agreed.

"See, Mother."

She defended herself. "Snow is much worse than rain. For one thing, you need to own more clothes in the winter . . ."

Out from his pocket came a ten when we needed small change for the subway. Away at college I opened the envelope, empty but for the money order for fifty, a hundred; typed out in the blank beside *for* was his memo: "Get yourself a little something in my name." It was the sixties and parental money was under heavy suspicion; my friends needed me as a third world person to be a good example of poverty and oppression by the capitalist, military-industrial complex. I put my little somethings quietly in the bank. By the time I graduated from college, I had a small corrupt fortune.

But my rich father lived in the dark, saving string, going the long way. I've analyzed it with my economist friends. Perhaps since his fortune came from the same work which in his country had never earned him enough, he could never believe that his being well-to-do wasn't an I.R.S. oversight. My psychologist friends claim that it is significant that he was the youngest of twenty-five children. Coming after so many, he would always fear that the good things would run out. And indeed he had a taste for leftovers, which made his compliments come a day or two after a special meal. Whenever we had chicken, he insisted on the wings and the neck bone because those had been the portions left by the time the platter got to him, the baby. He liked the pale, bitter center of the lettuce. ("The leaves were gone when I got the salad bowl.") And when we had soup, he was surprised to find a piece of meat bobbing at the surface. "Someone missed this one."

Unlike mother, he saved for a sunny day. Extravaganza! On his birthday, on Christmas, on his saint's day which was never celebrated for anyone else, his presents multiplied before us. Beside the ones we had bought for him, there were always other glossy packages, ribboned boxes which dwarfed ours. The cards were forged: "To my dearest father from his loving daughter." "Which of you gave me this?" he asked with mock surprise and real delight. Cordelias[4] all, we shook our heads as he unwrapped a silk lounging jacket or a genuine leather passport case. I wish he had allowed someone to give him something.

Perhaps we did on those evenings after the money was counted and put away, and he was ready for company. With an instinct for his rituals, we knew when it was time to come into the bedroom. We heard the bathroom door click shut; he was undressing, putting on his pajamas. The hamper lid clapped on its felt lip. We heard steps. The bed creaked. We found him in the darkening room with a book. "Papi, you're ruining your eyes!" and we turned on the bedside lamp for him since he could not give himself the luxury of that light. "Oh my God, it's gotten dark already," he almost thanked us.

He wanted company, not conversation. He had us turn on the television so we could learn our English. This after years here, after his money had paid for the good private schools which unrolled our r's and softened our accents; after American boyfriends had whispered sweet colloquialisms in our ears. As the television's cowboys and beauty queens and ladies with disappointing stains in their wash droned on in their native English, he read the usual: a history book in Spanish. We sat at the edge of the king-size bed and wondered what he wanted from us. He wanted presences: Walter Cronkite, his children, his wife, the great gods of the past, Napoleon, Caesar, Maximilian.[5] If one of us, bored with his idea of company, got up to leave, he lowered his book. "Did you know that in the campaign of 1808, Napoleon left his General behind to cut off the enemy from the rear, and the two divisions totally missed each other?" That was the only way he knew to ask us to stay, appealing to history and defeat, to wintry campaigns, bloody frost-bitten feet, a field strewn with war dead.

I taste the mints that he gave us, one each. He kept a stash of them in a drawer next to his bed like a schoolboy and ate exactly one each night and gave away four. That was the other way he kept us there if we got up to go after Napoleon's troops had been annihilated. "Don't you want a mint?" He didn't mean right then and there. It was a promise we had to wait for, perhaps until the chapter ended or the Roman empire fell or he was sure we had given up on the evening and decided to stay,

[4]Cordelia is the daughter of King Lear (in Shakespeare's play) who remains devoted to her father.

[5]Maximilian was the Emperor of Mexico (1864–1867).

talking in code with each other about school, our friends, our wild (for that room) adventures.

We were not fooled into rash confessions there, for at the merest hint of misadventure, the book came down like a coffin lid on Caesar or Claudius.[6] Oh, we confessed, we were just exaggerating! Of course we didn't raid the dorm kitchen at midnight, our friends did. "Tell me who your friends are," he said in Spanish, "and I'll tell you who *you* are." No, we hadn't gotten help on our math. "The man who reaches the summit following another's trail will not find his way back to his own valley." If he caught us, hurrying, scurrying, here, there, he stopped us mid-flight to tell us what Napoleon had said to his valet, "Dress me slowly, I'm in a hurry."

But why look beyond one's own blood for good examples? "You come from good stock," he bragged when I came home from boarding school, my pride wounded. I'd been called ugly names by some great-great-granddaughters of the American Revolution. "You tell them your great-grandfather was the son of a count." He had paid a lot of money on a trip to Barcelona to find that out from a man who claimed he was licensed to do family trees. The elaborate chart, magnificently framed in curlicued wood, hung in the waiting room of his office in Spanish Brooklyn along with his medical degrees. His patients, I suppose, were meant to be reassured that their ailments would be treated, not only by the valedictorian of the faculty of medicine of La Universidad de Santo Domingo, but also by the descendant of a count. "We were in this hemisphere before they were. In fact, the first group of Puritans—"

"You don't understand, you don't understand," I wailed, hot tears welling in my eyes. And I closed the door of my room, forbidding anyone to enter.

"What's she doing in there, Mother?" I heard him ask her.

"I don't know. Writing poetry or something."

"Are you sure? You think she's all right?"

I had been reading Sylvia Plath and my talk was spiked with suicide.[7]

"These girls are going to drive us crazy!" My mother said. "That's what I'm sure of. One of them has to have straight hair. Straight hair, at this stage of the game! Another wants to spend the weekend at a boy's school. All the other girls get to! This one wants to die young and miserable!" Then she yelled at father. "I'm going to end up in Bellevue![8] And then you're all going to be very sorry!" I heard the rushed steps down the stairs, the bang of the screen door, finally the patter of the hose as she watered the obedient grass in the growing dark.

---

[6]Claudius was the Emperor of Rome (41–54 A. D.).

[7]Sylvia Plath was an American poet (1932–1963) who committed suicide.

[8]Psychiatric hospital in New York City.

He knocked first. "Hello?" he asked tentatively, the door ajar. "Hello, hello, Edgar Allan Poe," he teased, entering. He sat at the foot of my bed and told me the story of his life.

"The point is," he concluded, *"La vida es sueño y los sueños, sueños son."*[9] He stood by the window and watched my mother watering her fussy bushes as if she could flush roses out of them. "My father," he turned to me, "used to say that to my mother: Life is a dream, Mauran, and dreams are dreams."

He came across the shadowy room as if he did not want anyone to overhear. It was getting late. In the darkening garden she would be winding the hose into drooping coils. "Always, always," he said. "I always wanted to be a poet. *'La vida es sueño,'* 'They also serve who only stand and wait.' 'To be or not to be.' Can you imagine! To say such things! My God! Everyone gets a little something." He cupped his hands towards me. I nodded, too stunned at his flood of words to ask him what he meant. "And some make a building," he made a building with a wave of his hand. "Some," he rubbed his thumb and index finger together, "make money. Some make friends, connections, you know. But some, some make something that can change the thinking of mankind! Oh my God!" He smacked his forehead with his palm in disbelief. "Think of the Bible. Think of your friend Edgar Allan Poe. But then," he mused, "then you grow older, you discover . . ." He looked down at me. I don't know what he saw in my eyes, perhaps how young I still was, perhaps his eyes duplicated in my face. He stopped himself.

"You discover?" I said.

But he was already half way across the room. "Papi?" I tried to call him back.

"Your mother," he explained, letting himself out of the room and the revelation. "I think she is calling for me."

A few days later as I sat in his bedroom after supper, waiting for him to fall asleep, I tried to get him to finish his sentence. He couldn't remember what he was about to say, he said, but speaking of discoveries, "We're descended from the conquistadores, you know? Your grandfather traveled the whole north coast on horseback![10] Now there was a great man!" The supporting evidence was slim. "He looked like an Irishman. Ah, he was big and pink-tinted—what is that word, Julie? *Rowdy?*"

"You mean *ruddy?*" I said, knowing Don José de Jesus was probably ruddy with drink and rowdy with women. He had sired twenty-five children, widowed once, and kept four or five mistresses who raised the figure to thirty-five children. Of course, father never told us that; mother did when she explained how one of our uncles could be born within two

---

[9]Translated at the end of the paragraph, from *Life Is a Dream* by Spanish playwright Calderon (1600–1681).

[10]The north coast of the Caribbean island of Hispaniola.

months of father's birthday. She cautioned us never ever to mention to father what she had told us.

The youngest did, pretending ignorance, practicing addition. If Teolinda, the first wife, had ten children, and Mauran, the second one, had fifteen, and four of the kids had already died, then how come there were still thirty uncles and aunts left? "They were not hijos de padre y madre,"[11] he explained. "You know where that term came from? *Hijos de padre y madre?* When the Spaniards—"

"Where did the extra uncles and aunts come from?" She was not one to be diverted by a red herring twitching in the sun when a skeleton was rattling in the closet.

So, so he said. The time had come. The uncles and aunts were half brothers and sisters. The mothers *were* wives, yes, in the eyes of God, where it really mattered.

When we raised our eyebrows and pressed the smile out of our lips, he would have none of it. Customs changed. Our grandfather was a patriotic man. There had been a terrible epidemic, the island was underpopulated, the birthrate was low, the best men did what they had to do. "So," he looked pointedly at each of us. "There's a good *ejemplo*[12] for you. Always put in that extra little bit in whatever you do," he said, lifting up the history of Constantinople or Machu Picchu or Rome.

His mother? He sighed. Don't talk to him about his mother! A saint! Sweet, very religious, patience personified, always smiling. They didn't make them like that anymore, with a few exceptions, he winked at me.

But since Mauran knew about the half children, and being very religious, she must have believed her husband and she would spend eternity separated, I imagined her as a dour and dowdy woman alternately saying her rosary when her husband transgressed or having his children when he didn't.

"Does mother remind you of her?" I asked, thinking that leading questions might help him remember what he had been about to say in my room a few nights ago.

"Your mother is a wonder," he said. A good woman, so devoted, so thorough, a little nervous, so giving, a little forceful, a good companion, a little too used to her own way, so generous. "Every garland needs a few thorns," he added.

"I heard that," she said, coming into the room, "What was that about too used to my own way?"

"Did I say that, girls?" father turned to us. "No, Mami, you misheard."

"Then what did you say?"

"What did I say, girls?"

We shrugged, leaving him wide open.

[11]Children of father and mother.

[12]Example.

"I said, Mother," he said, unwrapping a rare second mint and putting it in his mouth to buy time. "I said: so used to giving to others. Mother, you're too generous!"

"Ay, put gravy on the chicken." She waved him off, terribly pleased as father winked at our knowing looks.

A few nights later, still on the track of his secret self, I asked him, "Papi, how do you see yourself?" Only I, who had achieved a mild reputation as a deep thinker, could get away with such questions.

"You ask deep questions," he mused, interrupting Napoleon's advance across the Russian steppes. "I like that."

He offered me my mint and unwrapped his. "I am the rock," he said, nodding.

"Ay, Papi, that's too impersonal. How do you perceive yourself. What kind of man are you?" I was young and thought such definitions could be given and trusted. I was young and ready to tear loose, but making it harder for myself by trying to understand those I was about to wound.

"I am a rock," he repeated, liking his analogy. "Mother, you girls, my sisters, everyone needs my support. I am the strong one!"

That admission put a mermaid on the rock, luring me back with a delicate song about loss and youth's folly and the loneliness of the father. "But, Papi," I whispered as I moved from the armchair to the foot of his bed, "you don't always have to be strong."

That was my mistake. The conversation was over. He hated touching scenes; they confused him. Perhaps as the last child of an older, disappointed woman, he was used to diffuse attention, not intimacy. To take hold of a hand, to graze a cheek and whisper an endearment were beyond him. Tenderness had to be mothered by necessity: he was a good doctor. Under the cover of Hippocrates' oath, with the stethoscope around his neck and the bright examination light flushing out the personal and making any interchange terribly professional, he was amazingly delicate: tapping a bone as if it were the fontanelle of a baby, easing a patient back on a pillow like a lover his sleeping beloved, stroking hair away from a feverish forehead. But now he turned away.

He fell asleep secretly in that room full of presences, my mother beside him. No one knew exactly when it happened. We looked to him during a commercial or when a slip had implicated us in some forbidden adventure, and the book had collapsed like a card house on his chest and his glasses rode the bridge of his nose like a schoolmarm's. Though if we got up to leave and one of us reached for his glasses he woke with a start. "I'm not asleep!" he lied. "Don't go yet, It's early."

He fell asleep in the middle of the Hundred Days while Napoleon marched towards Waterloo or, defeated, was shipped off to St. Helena. We stifled our giggles at his comic-book snores, the sheets pulled over his head, his nose poking out like a periscope. Very quietly, widening our eyes at each other as if that might stop any noise, we rose. One turned off the set and threw a kiss at mother, who put her finger to her lips from her far side of the bed. Another and another kiss traveled across the hushed room. A scolding wave from mother hurried my sisters out.

I liked to be the one who stayed, bending over the bedside table strewn with candy wrappers, slipping a hand under the tassled shade. I turned the switch over, once. The room burst into brighter light, the tassels swung madly, mother signaled to me, crossly, Out! Out at once! I shrugged apologies. Her scowl deepened. Father groaned. I bent closer. I turned again. The room went back into economical dark.

Interpretations

1. Why is it appropriate that Alvarez's father often describes his action in the third person?

2. What do you consider the doctor's outstanding personality trait? Cite two passages that reveal this trait.

3. In her portrayal of her father, Alvarez refers to several incidents that show that she and he shared a special empathy. Cite at least three examples and say how each contributes to your understanding this empathy.

4. "He wanted company, not conversation." Why would one want company without conversation? Is the doctor's desire unreasonable or uncommon? Is it hard to satisfy? Do you sympathize with it?

5. Alvarez tries many times to try to get her father to complete his statement: "But then, . . . then you grow older, you discover . . ." What do you think he might have intended to say?

6. What is the tone of this portrait? Where is it satirical? Where loving? Do you find that the doctor has an honest, healthy relationship with his daughters, especially the narrator, or does he patronize them? Where's the evidence?

Correspondences

1. Alvarez and Momaday (Chapter 1) talk about their ancestral pasts. In what aspects of that past do they take most pride? How has the past influenced their present? (Why is it important to understand one's past?)

2. Review the Gibran quotation on children (page 99). What does it mean? How might Julia's father respond to Gibran's thoughts on this subject? Cite evidence from the story to support your point of view.

Applications

1. Write an essay about your mother, father, or another adult to prove that you understand that person well. Include specific incidents, allusions, or metaphors that exemplify key personality traits.

2. Alvarez's father encouraged her to express her creativity. Write an essay about important encouragement you have received from an adult (parent, teacher, relative). How did this encouragement affect your relationship?

Quintana

John Gregory Dunne

John Gregory Dunne (b. 1932) was educated at Princeton University, served in the U.S. Army, and was a staff writer for Time *magazine for several years. He has written several screenplays with his wife, novelist and essayist Joan Didion, including* Play It as It Lays *(1972) and* True Confessions *(1982). His other publications include* The Studio *(1969) and* Quintana and Her Friends *(1978). In this essay about his daughter, Dunne shares his views on adoption.*

QUINTANA WILL BE eleven this week. She approaches adolescence with what I can only describe as panache, but then watching her journey from infancy has always been like watching Sandy Koufax pitch or Bill Russell play basketball. There is the same casual arrogance, the implicit sense that no one has ever done it any better. And yet it is difficult for a father to watch a daughter grow up. With each birthday she becomes more like us, an adult, and what we cling to is the memory of the child. I remember the first time I saw her in the nursery at Saint John's Hospital. It was after visiting hours and my wife and I stood staring through the soundproof glass partition at the infants in their cribs, wondering which was ours. Then a nurse in a surgical mask appeared from a back room carrying a fierce, black-haired baby with a bow in her hair. She was just seventeen hours old and her face was still wrinkled and red and the identification beads on her wrist had not our name but only the letters "NI." "NI" stood for "No Information," the hospital's code for an infant to be placed for adoption. Quintana is adopted.

It has never been an effort to say those three words, even when they occasion the well-meaning but insensitive compliment, "You couldn't love her more if she were your own." At moments like that, my wife and I say nothing and smile through gritted teeth. And yet we are not unaware that sometime in the not too distant future we face a moment that only those of us who are adoptive parents will ever have to face—our daughter's decision to search or not to search for her natural parents.

I remember that when I was growing up, a staple of radio drama was the show built around adoption. Usually the dilemma involved a child who had just learned by accident that it was adopted. This information could only come accidentally, because in those days it was considered a radical departure from the norm to inform your son or daughter that he or she was not your own flesh and blood. If such information had to be revealed, it was often followed by the specious addendum that the natural parents had died when the child was an infant. An automobile accident was viewed as the most expeditious and efficient way to get rid of both parents at once. One of my contemporaries, then a young actress, was not told she was adopted until she was twenty-two and the beneficiary of a small inheritance from her natural father's will. Her adoptive mother could not bring herself to tell her daughter the reason behind the bequest and entrusted the task to an agent from the William Morris office.

Today we are more enlightened, aware of the psychological evidence that such barbaric secrecy can only inflict hurt. When Quintana was born, she was offered to us privately by the gynecologist who delivered her. In California, such private adoptions are not only legal but in the mid-sixties, before legalized abortion and before the sexual revolution made it acceptable for an unwed mother to keep her child, were quite common. The night we went to see Quintana for the first time at Saint John's, there was a tacit agreement between us that "No Information" was only a bracelet. It was quite easy to congratulate ourselves for agreeing to be so open when the only information we had about her mother was her age, where she was from and a certified record of her good health. What we did not realize was that through one bureaucratic slipup she would learn her mother's name and that through another she would learn ours, and Quintana's.

From the day we brought Quintana home from the hospital, we tried never to equivocate. When she was little, we always had Spanish-speaking help and one of the first words she learned, long before she understood its import, was *adoptada*. As she grew older, she never tired of asking us how we happened to adopt her. We told her that we went to the hospital and were given our choice of any baby in the nursery. "No, not that baby," we had said, "not that baby, not that baby . . ." All this with full gestures of inspection, until finally: "That baby!" Her face would always light up and she would say: "Quintana." When she asked a question about her adoption, we answered, never volunteering more than she requested, convinced that as she grew her questions would become more searching and complicated. In terms I hoped she would understand, I tried to explain that adoption offered to a parent the possibility of escaping the prison of the genes, that no matter how perfect the natural child, the parent could not help acknowledging in black moments that some of his or her bad blood was bubbling around in the offspring; with an *adoptada*, we were innocent of any knowledge of bad blood.

In time Quintana began to intuit that our simple parable of free choice in the hospital nursery was somewhat more complex than we had indicated. She now knew that being adopted meant being born of another mother, and that person she began referring to as "my other mommy." How old, she asked, was my other mommy when I was born? Eighteen, we answered, and on her stubby little fingers she added on her own age, and with each birthday her other mommy became twenty-three, then twenty-five and twenty-eight. There was no obsessive interest, just occasional queries, some more difficult to answer, than others. Why had her other mother given her up? We said that we did not know—which was true—and could only assume that it was because she was little more than a child herself, alone and without the resources to bring up a baby. The answer seemed to satisfy, at least until we became close friends with a young woman, unmarried with a small child of her own. The contradiction was, of course, apparent to Quintana, and yet she seemed to understand, in the way that children do, that there had been a millenium's worth of social change in the years since her birth, that the pressures on a young unmarried mother were far more in 1966 than they were in 1973. (She did, after all, invariably refer to the man in the White House as President Nixon Vietnam Watergate, almost as if he had a three-tiered name like John Quincy Adams.) We were sure that she viewed her status with equanimity, but how much so we did not realize until her eighth birthday party. There were twenty little girls at the party, and as little girls do, they were discussing things gynecological, specifically the orifice in their mothers' bodies from which they had emerged at birth. "I didn't," Quintana said matter-of-factly. She was sitting in a large wicker fan chair and her pronouncement impelled the other children to silence. "I was adopted." We had often wondered how she would handle this moment with her peers, and we froze, but she pulled it off with such élan and aplomb that in moments the other children were bemoaning their own misfortune in not being adopted, one even claiming, "Well, I was almost adopted."

Because my wife and I both work at home, Quintana has never had any confusion about how we make our living. Our mindless staring at our respective typewriters means food on the table in a way the mysterious phrase "going to the office" never can. From the time she could walk, we have taken her to meetings whenever we were without help, and she has been a quick study on the nuances of our life. "She's remarkably well adjusted," my brother once said about her. "Considering that every time I see her she's in a different city." I think she could pick an agent out of a police lineup, and out of the blue one night at dinner she offered that all young movie directors were short and had frizzy hair and wore Ditto pants and wire glasses and shirts with three buttons opened. (As far as I know, she had never laid eyes on Bogdanovich, Spielberg or Scorsese.) Not long ago an actress received an award for a picture we had written for her. The actress's acceptance speech at the televised award ceremony drove Quintana into an absolute fury. "She never," Quintana reported, "thanked *us*." Since she not only identifies with our work but at times even considers herself an equal partner, I of course discussed this piece with her before I began working on it. I told her what it was about and said I would drop it if she would be embarrassed or if she thought the subject too private. She gave it some thought and finally said she wanted me to write it.

I must, however, try to explain and perhaps even try to justify my own motives. The week after *Roots* was televised, each child in Quintana's fifth-grade class was asked to trace a family tree. On my side Quintana went back to her great-grandfather Burns, who moved from Ireland shortly after the Civil War, a ten-year-old refugee from the potato famine, and on her mother's side to her great-great-great-great-grandmother Cornwall, who came west in a wagon train in 1846. As it happens, I have little interest in family beyond my immediate living relatives. (I can never remember the given names of my paternal grandparents and have never known my paternal grandmother's maiden name. This lack of interest mystifies my wife.) Yet I wanted Quintana to understand that if she wished, there were blood choices other than Dominick Burns and Nancy Hardin Cornwall. Over the past few years, there has been a growing body of literature about adoptees seeking their own roots. I am in general sympathetic to this quest, although not always to the dogged absolutism of the more militant seekers. But I would be remiss if I did not say that I am more than a little sensitive to the way the literature presents adoptive parents. We are usually shown as frozen in the postures of radio drama, untouched by the changes in attitudes of the last several generations. In point of fact we accept that our children might seek out their roots, even encourage it; we accept it as an adventure like life itself—perhaps painful, one hopes enriching. I know not one adoptive parent who does not feel this way. Yet in the literature there is the implicit assumption that we are threatened by the possibility of search, that we would consider it an act of disloyalty on the part of our children. The patronizing nature of this assumption is never noted in the literature. It is as if we were Hudson and Mrs. Bridges, below-stairs surrogates taking care of the wee one, and I don't like it one damn bit.

Often these days I find myself thinking of Quintana's natural mother. Both my wife and I admit more than a passing interest in the woman who produced this extraordinary child. (As far as we know, she never named the father, and even more interesting, Quintana has never asked about him.) When Quintana was small, and before the legalities of adoption were complete, we imagined her mother everywhere, a wraithlike presence staring through the chain-link fence at the blond infant sunbathing in the crib. Occasionally today we see a photograph of a young woman in a magazine—the mother as we imagine her to look—and we pass it to each other without comment. Once we even checked the name of a model in *Vogue* through her modeling agency; she turned out to be a Finn. I often wonder if she thinks of Quintana, or of us. (Remember, we know each other's names.) There is the possibility that having endured the twin traumas of birth and the giving up of a child, she blocked out the names the caseworker gave her, but I don't really believe it. I consider it more likely that she has followed the fairly well-documented passage of Quintana through childhood into adolescence. Writers are at least semipublic figures, and in the interest of commerce or selling a book or a movie, or even out of simple vanity, we allow interviews and photo layouts and look into television cameras; we even write about ourselves, and our children. I recall wondering how this sentient young woman of our imagination had reacted to four pages in *People*. It is possible, even likely, that she will read this piece. I know that it is an almost intolerable invasion of her privacy. I think it probable, however, that in the dark reaches of night she has considered the possibility of a further incursion, of opening a door one day and seeing a young woman who says, "Hello, Mother, I am your daughter."

Perhaps this is romantic fantasy. We know none of the circumstances of the woman's life, or even if she is still alive. We once suggested to our lawyer that we make a discreet inquiry and he quite firmly said that this was a quest that belonged only to Quintana, if she wished to make it, and not to us. What is not fantasy is that for the past year, Quintana has known the name of her natural mother. It was at dinner and she said that she would like to meet her one day, but that it would be hard, not knowing her name. There finally was the moment: we had never equivocated; did we begin now? We took a deep breath and told Quintana, then age ten, her mother's name. We also said that if she decided to search her out, we would help her in any way we could. (I must allow, however, that we would prefer she wait to make this decision until the Sturm and Drang of adolescence is past.) We then considered the possibility that her mother, for whatever good or circumstantial reasons of her own might prefer not to see her. I am personally troubled by the militant contention that the natural mother has no right of choice in this matter. "I did not ask to be born," an adoptee once was quoted in a news story I read. "She has to see me." If only life were so simple, if only pain did not hurt. Yet we would never try to influence Quintana on this point. How important it is to know her parentage is a question only she can answer; it is her decision to make.

All parents realize, or should realize, that children are not possessions, but are only lent to us, angel boarders, as it were. Adoptive parents realize this earlier and perhaps more poignantly than others. I do not know the end of this story. It is possible that Quintana will find more reality in family commitment and cousins across the continent and heirloom orange spoons and pictures in an album and faded letters from Dominick Burns and diary entries from Nancy Hardin Cornwall than in the uncertainties of blood. It is equally possible that she will venture into the unknown. I once asked her what she would do if she met her natural mother. "I'd put one arm around Mom," she said, "and one arm around my other mommy, and I'd say, 'Hello, Mommies.'"

If that's the way it turns out, that is what she will do.

Interpretations

1. How do you react to the parents' decision never to make a secret of Quintana's adoption? To the way they undertook to answer Quintana's questions about the way the adoption took place?

2. What "millenium's worth of social change" took place between 1966 and 1973?

3. What, according to Dunne, was his purpose in writing this piece? Why did he choose to write it in Quintana's twelfth year?

4. To what extent do you agree with the lawyer that only Quintana should make the decision to search for her natural mother? Should a natural mother have the right of choice not to see or recognize her adopted daughter? Why?

5. "It is possible, even likely, that [the natural mother] will read this piece." How do you think reading this piece would affect Quintana's natural mother?

Correspondences

1. "All parents realize, or should realize, that children are not possessions, but are only lent to us, angel boarders as it were." To what extent has being an adoptive parent shaped Dunne's philosophy about raising children? How is his perspective similar to or different from that of Gibran (page 99)?

2. The understanding of parent by child or child by parent occupies the families in "Quintana" and "El Doctor." Select an incident from each essay that results in an important mutual discovery. What did you learn about parent–child relationships?

Applications

1. Write an essay discussing your point of view on the subject of adoption that includes your thoughts about whether adopted children should be encouraged to seek their natural parents.

2. Analyze the role of cultural differences in Dunne's essay.

Noah

Danit Wehle

*Danit Wehle (b. 1973) was born in Israel and raised in Teaneck,
New Jersey. During her sophomore year of high school her
mother gave birth to her third child, Noah. Danit's essay "Noah"
depicts how the relationship with her new brother developed and
how it continues to grow while she is attending the University of
Massachusetts at Amherst.*

I ALWAYS HAD a very normal home life. You know, the typical two parents,
two kids. My mother and father used to take my brother and I on a family
outing every weekend and occasionally during the school week. I remember it was always so exciting when my father would come home
from work early because that meant we could all hang out together and
play cards or Monopoly. It was always the four of us. I mean as I got older
I did go out with my friends but when I came home my parents were
always there and even though I didn't spend as much time with them as
I had, when I did it was still the four of us and still just as much fun.

My life changed drastically when I was fifteen years old. My mother
announced to my brother and I that she was going to have a baby. My
first instinct was to cry and scream at her. How could she forget about us?
We were her kids. Didn't she love us? Weren't we what she wanted? Was
she getting sick of us? But then I thought about it some more and it
sounded great. How exciting! I loved babies and now I'd have my own
little brother or sister. I became very involved with her pregnancy. I read
up on all her books and kept track of the developing stages of the baby.
I remember the whole nine months all we talked about was the baby's
name. We each had our list and agreed that we didn't all have to love the
name, but we all have to at least be able to tolerate it. (My parents wanted
us to be involved so we wouldn't feel like they were leaving us and now
moving on to a new generation of kids.) It was good to be involved
because it brought us all together again.

The last month I rarely left the house and if I did, I called about every
five minutes to see if my mother was in labor. I drove her crazy but finally
it happened. The day my mother had the baby, I was at my piano lesson.
My teacher told me my mother was at the hospital and he would drive
me home. I don't remember exactly what I felt that day. I mean I know it
was intense excitement but I remember thinking then that when I look
back at this day in a few years, I'll forget how happy I was. So I don't

remember how it felt but I do know that I've never been so happy as the day when my little brother Noah was born.

The minute I saw him in the hospital, I fell in love with him. He was so tiny and soft. He came home the next day and I carried him into the house. From that day on, I was his little mother. I dressed him, fed him, bathed him, watched him grow and watched him develop. I was so proud.

It sounds like I adjusted perfectly but actually I didn't. Every once in a while I would blow up at my parents for ignoring me or for piling too much responsibility on me. Many times I wished that Noah was never born and our life was back to normal: how it used to be. It wasn't the four of us anymore. Our rhyming names didn't even work anymore. It was always Danit, Amit, Ronit, and John and now it was Danit, Amit, Ronit and John . . . and Noah. This all bothered me on and off for a while but really every time I saw Noah I forgot about my anger and just remembered how much I loved him.

Well, months went by and I spent a great deal of time with Noah. I watched him sit, crawl, stand, eat by himself, walk, talk. I was so proud of him. I was like typical mother; carrying pictures of him in my wallet. He was my baby.

Noah and I were very close. He really had fun with me. I taught him cute little sayings like, "Homey don't play dat" or "K-Mart sucks." I spoke to him as if he were my age so he began to talk like a little man. I couldn't get enough of him. He was a little man in an adorable body. I loved him.

A few days before college I took Noah to his first movie: 101 Dalmatians. It was our special day. I bought him popcorn, M&M's, and a lemonade. I'll never forget his face. He was sitting on the big theater seat holding a little bag of popcorn and a huge cup of lemonade, staring at the big, big TV screen in awe.

It was the hardest to say goodbye to Noah. I knew that my parents and I would be able to keep in touch over the phone or in letters. My brother the same thing. But Noah needed to see me, play with me. I remember I took him to the backyard and I told him that I'd be back in a little while, that he could send me pictures, talk to me on the phone, visit me. I told him never to forget that I love him and that he'll always be my little guy. Just as I was pulling out of the driveway, Noah shouted after me, "Danit, I love you!"

Interpretations

1. Compare Wehle's relationship with Noah and her relationship with the rest of her family. To what extent did the interfamily relationship before Noah's birth prepare Wehle for a new sibling?

2. Wehle says she was like a fifteen-year-old mother. How was her situation like that of a real mother? How different?

3. Wehle changed from initial resentment to eager acceptance of her mother's pregnancy. How adequate is Wehle's treatment of this change? How would the essay be affected if Wehle included her *brother's* reaction to the birth and growing up of Noah?

Correspondences

1. Contrast Wehle's description of her family relationships with those in Mead's essay. How do you account for differences in their points of view? How might Wehle's essay be considered an affirmative response to Mead's question regarding the survival of the American family?

2. "Quintana" is told from the point of view of a parent, while "Noah" is narrated from the perspective of a sibling. Analyze the differences in your responses to both selections. How does point of view also affect purpose and meaning as well as audience response?

Applications

1. How might the age at which one becomes a mother affect the way she feels and acts toward her child? Discuss the advantages and disadvantages of young parenthood.

2. Sometimes we can best illustrate the importance of a relationship by focusing on a particular event. Choose an event, action, or conversation to best explain a relationship that is important to you. Before writing, review Wehle's account of taking Noah to his first movie.

Alienation

Paul Cohen

Paul Cohen (b. 1966) was born in New York City, son of a civil-service worker (a policeman). He has recently returned to college after a break of fifteen years. These are his comments about himself:

I too entered the same field as my father which caused a social rift, since most Jewish families encourage learning and profess that you rise to success. I believe this as well, but have chosen the route of my father for a different reason. I wish to study the human condition first hand, and eventually I will attain a degree in psychology. I have been a cop for nine years and hope to write a novel (of which I already have a title and theme) studying a policeman's life from a psychological stand-point. I want to write what all civilians would like to read and what cops know and feel but do not admit.

THERE SHE WAS, as usual, playing dolls on the floor of her room. She would stay there for hours fantasizing about life; although, if you knew her, you would have sensed the pattern. It wasn't a fantasy; it was Phase One of a plan. She wasn't at play; she was practicing.

It was unusual that her door was open. Her brother peered into the room observing before announcing his presence. He had something important to say to her. He had to tell his sister to leave home. She was a junior in high school, seventeen years old and still playing Barbie dolls. She had spent most of her life in that room. It was filled with knick-knacks, mementos, stuffed animals and dolls all arranged like watchful eye of the curator. When he was younger, her brother would seek out some obscure detail in her room and change it. She would always know.

"Who's been in my room?" she screamed accusingly. She then would demand that her security be protected and her privacy not violated. Generally, she did not react well to criticism or any other unplanned emotion so it shocked her brother to pieces when she wholeheartedly accepted his plan that she attend college away from home. However, going away was part of the plan. After all, college was the best place to implement Phase Two of the plan—the "Mrs." degree.

In college, while preparing to become a school teacher, she majored in History. Her personal favorite was Jewish History. It seemed that she had found identity through Judaism; it is not unusual for a lonely person to find religion. At every family gathering she would soliloquize about being Jewish on an esoteric level. It was somewhat puzzling but not surprising that she met and married a Gentile man. He is a lawyer and works long hours which suits her just fine. That way, she could spend her day alone, meticulously "planning" every aspect of her life. They eventually bought a home in a predominantly Gentile neighborhood which was again puzzling because such a big deal was made about her being Jewish and raising her children Jewish, but her brother felt it was her attempt to once again isolate herself by contrasting her identity against the backdrop of another culture where it would be more noticeable than it would amongst its own. She knows that oil and water don't mix and she likes that distinction, maintaining control of her identity and not being absorbed by another person in marriage. Phase Two is complete.

Months before Phase Three was underway she began collecting baby things from friends and family. One day her brother came to visit and see the house for the first time. She was proud to show off her home and tell of her plans. The house was as meticulous as her room used to be. Everything was in place, museum style. Upon entering the nursery, her brother began to shiver and shake as if ants were crawling up his back. The room was eerie. It looked as if a baby was already living there—sheets, blankets and toys in the crib, clothes in the dressers, folded neatly. Everything was ready—except she wasn't pregnant yet.

After he stopped shaking, he realized: although she was missing a major piece of the interaction puzzle, she had achieved all she wanted out of life. From doll house to real house; baby dolls to babies, she is exactly where she wants to be—alone and in control.

Interpretations

1. Does this strike you as a fair, impartial, honest portrait? On what details do you base your answer? What do you consider the writer's emotional relationship to the character he is describing? When he speaks of "the plan," is he coolly describing her fantasies or projecting his own? What's the evidence?

2. The brother also has a "plan"—that, among other things, the sister go away to college. What is the writer's attitude toward the *brother's* plan?

3. How would this essay have to be rewritten if the girl became, in fact, pregnant? If she should have a baby, what would it indicate about the author's belief that she "wants to be—alone. . . ."?

Correspondences

1. Review Kumin's perspective (page 100). What does it imply about the costs of fantasy? Explain its connection to Cohen's "Alienation." Under what circumstances can you imagine his sister waking up?

2. Review McCullers's perspective on loneliness (page 100). To what extent might Cohen's sister be considered a hunter? For what is she searching? Would you characterize her as lonely? Why or why not?

Applications

1. Consult a *thesaurus* on the various meanings of *fantasy* and discuss the advantages and disadvantages of indulging in fantasies.

2. Analyze the functions of point of view in Cohen's essay. How does it affect his purpose and meaning? Is he merely describing a process or is he also making a judgment? How would you characterize his attitude toward his sister? Contrast his attitude with yours.

from Growing Up in Cairo

Jehan Sadat

Jehan Sadat (b. 1934) is the widow of Egyptian president Anwar el-Sadat, who was assassinated in 1981. You will discover in the following selection that she grew up in Cairo and was the daughter of an Egyptian civil servant and an English mother. For a fuller account of Ms. Sadat, see page 46.

I DID NOT KNOW until I was eleven that my name was Jehan, a Persian name picked out by my father which means "the world." My mother, who was English, had nicknamed me Jean, and that was what I was called by my father, an employee at the Ministry of Health, by my teachers at the Christian missionary school I attended, and by my friends. It was not at all strange for me or my classmates to have European names. I had friends named Mimi and Fifi, Helen and Betty. Egyptians had greatly admired European ways since our leader Muhammad Ali had opened Egypt to foreign influence one hundred years before, believing the Europeans to be much more advanced. But it was strange that I did not even know my proper name until I received my primary-school certificate before moving on to secondary school.

"Who is Jehan?" I asked the teacher, seeing it written on my certificate over my address.

"You," she told me.

I ran home to my mother. "What is my name?" I asked her.

"In school now you are Jehan," she told me. "In our family you are Jean." And to this day that is what my sister and brothers call me.

I was born on Roda Island, one of two islands in the Nile linked by bridges to Cairo in the east and Giza to the west. My island of Roda was a lovely area of gardens and gracious peach limestone villas populated by middle-class Egyptian families. The neighboring island of Zamalek was fancier, home to many British families and those of the Egyptian upper class. The Gezira Sporting Club on Zamalek, to which my family did not belong, boasted cricket pitches and polo fields, tennis courts and swimming pools and a bar at which liquor was served. The Gezira Club was in another world to me as a child, and to many other Egyptians as well. King Farouk was a member there, as were many of the foreign families, but there was a membership quota for Egyptians.

I was the third of four children in my family, and the first girl. A great space of age spread between my brothers and me. Magdi was ten years older, Ali seven. My mother, I was told, had yearned to have a girl, to comb a daughter's hair and embroider her dresses. The day of my birth was a cause of great celebration in our house, compounded by an *'allawa,* a raise in pay my father took that very same day from his government job. From the beginning, I was considered by my parents to be a good omen. Twenty-one months later, my sister Dalia was born and our family was complete.

We were all very light-skinned, a legacy not only from my English mother but on my father's side as well. My father's father was a Sa'idi, an Upper Egyptian from the tall, usually dark-skinned tribe descended from pure Pharaonic stock. Yet my grandfather too had been fair with blue eyes. His children—my father, my uncle and my two Egyptian aunts— were also fair, and, like all Egyptian families, we were all very close.

When I was a baby we lived with our relatives in one house, splitting up when I was five years old. But no one moved very far away. My bachelor Uncle Mustafa lived just one house away with his divorced sister, 'Aziza, it being his responsibility as a brother to look after her and her young daughter, 'Aida. I visited my Auntie 'Aziza, or Auntie Zouzou as she was nicknamed, every afternoon, and often she came to our home in the evenings. She was my favorite aunt and my Egyptian mother, showering me with affection and spoiling me.

After my Uncle Mustafa finally married at thirty-eight, Aunt Zouzou continued to live with him and his new wife, for it was improper then for a woman to live alone. I'm sure she was very lonely, but she continued to refuse many offers of marriage, fearing that her daughter might be mistreated by a stepfather.

My other aunt, Fatima, whom we fondly called Auntie Batta—Auntie "Duck"—lived just outside Cairo on the Pyramids Road. She was not as affectionate as Auntie Zouzou, but she was a very strong woman. After my grandmother died, Auntie Batta effectively took her place. It was to Auntie Batta's house that the whole family went to break the fast on the first day of Ramadan, and to her that they went to seek advice. Auntie Batta was married to Husni Abu Zaid, an official in the Wafd nationalist party who had served as governor of both Munufiyya province and Minia province. Uncle Husni had a government car, quite a symbol of prosperity at the time, and I loved to drive with him around Cairo. With its official license plate and the flag of Munufiyya fluttering on the fender, the car prompted all the soldiers who saw it to salute. As a little girl, I liked to imagine they were saluting me.

"The mother of the world," the historian Ibn el-Khaldun had called Cairo in the fourteenth century. As a child growing up in Roda, it was easy to see why. Everywhere were the signs of Cairo's rich past. Directly across the Nile to the east was Coptic Cairo, which for more than fifteen hundred years had been the center of Egyptian Christian art and religion. On my way to school I could see the spires of the fourth-century Abu Serga Church, built on the spot where it is believed the family of Jesus stayed during their flight into Egypt. Beyond Abu Serga, I could sometimes make out the thin Ottoman minarets of the Alabaster Mosque, built by Muhammad 'Ali in the nineteenth century. Still farther along was the Old City founded by the Fatimids in 973, and el-Azhar Mosque and University. El-Azhar is the oldest university in the world, and attracts more than 100,000 students from countries as far away as Mauritania and Indonesia. All who come are students of Islam, for though el-Azhar is old, our religion is still young and growing.

From the other side of Roda, I could look across the Nile to the west and see the river gardens of the rich merchants who lived in Giza, beyond to the campus of Cairo University, and to the Pyramids Road, which, if followed to the end, terminated at the Farafra Oasis in the Libyan Desert. On a clear day when no dust or sand blew, I could make out the tips of the Great Pyramids themselves. And always in the air, five times a day, I could hear the beautiful voices of the muezzins high up in the minarets of Cairo's thousands of mosques, calling the believers in Islam to prayer.

How lovely and quiet Roda Island was during my childhood. Everyone had green gardens, and between the villas on both sides of the island you could always see the Nile passing. In 1933, the population of Egypt was around 15 million, and the population of Cairo less than one million.

My mother must have been very brave to leave her native land of England to come live in Egypt. My father must have been brave also to have married a foreigner. Such a marriage was not against our religion of Islam, for the children of a Muslim man will always themselves be Muslim. It was forbidden only for a Muslim woman to marry into another religion, for her children would have to bear the religion of their father. No. My grandparents' objection to their marriage was not religious, but one of family tradition.

My father, Safwat Raouf, had met my mother, Gladys Charles Cotrell, in 1923 in Sheffield, England, where he was studying medicine at the University of Sheffield and she was a music teacher. Their love was very strong from the beginning. It had to be, for a marriage had already been arranged in Cairo between my father and his cousin. "No one in our family has ever married a foreigner," my grandfather wrote to my father in England. "I will not give you permission to marry this Englishwoman."

My grandparents were well used to the British, of course, for there were many, many British in Egypt at that time. Since the 1800s more than ten thousand British troops had been stationed in Egypt to "protect" our government. The British High Commissioner, Lord Cromer, was effectively ruling the country. Britain and France controlled Egypt's finances. Even Egypt's shares in the Suez Canal, completed in 1869, had had to be sold to the British by our then debt-ridden Khedive Isma'il. It was certainly not uncommon to see the British and many other foreigners in Cairo. But it was difficult for my conservative grandparents to adjust to new ways.

"If you do not allow this marriage, I will not eat until I am dead," my father wrote back to my grandfather. My grandfather was just as stubborn. "I will not give my permission," he replied. And back and forth the letters went until my grandmother grew worried that my father really might harm himself or, just as bad, not come back to Egypt at all. "You must give your permission," she told my grandfather. "Is it not better to welcome our son and his wife home to Egypt than to force him to live in a country foreign to our ways?"

Reluctantly my grandfather had agreed, and my grandmother had sent my mother the traditional Egyptian engagement present of jewelry, in this case a diamond ring and a diamond-and-sapphire necklace she had inherited from her grandfather, along with money for a honeymoon. My mother and father were married in a civil ceremony in England, and when my father returned home with my mother three years later it was with my brother, who had been born in Liverpool. As was the custom then, my parents moved into my grandparents' house on Roda Island. Quickly, my grandparents grew to love my mother, though it must not have been easy for any of them. Our society was more conservative then. And my mother's ways, indeed, were strange.

She never ate Egyptian food, but insisted on the Sudanese cook making a separate meal for her of boiled meat, boiled vegetables, boiled everything. The rest of the family ate the usual Egyptian fare: grilled pigeon; grilled fish; lamb kebab and *kufta,* spiced patties of minced lamb; *wara einab,* grape leaves stuffed with rice and minced meat; *molokhia,* a thick soup made of a minced green leaf and chicken stock; *bamia,* okra sautéed with butter, onion, garlic and tomato paste in broth, served almost always with rice, and different kinds of beans and salads. But my mother would eat boiled mutton and potatoes with mint sauce.

Breakfast was different for us also. In the morning, and indeed for all meals, Egyptians traditionally eat *ful medammes*—fava beans boiled into a thick paste with spices and topped with a fried egg. At our house we had cornflakes, boiled eggs, and thinly sliced toast instead of *'aish,* our flat, unleavened bread, along with jam my mother had made. Tea every afternoon at four was sacred, and she would serve us English tea instead of the sweet mint tea Egyptians drink, and wonderful British cakes, biscuits and sweets she'd made for us to eat. They were delicious, really, especially the lemon curd preserve which we didn't have in Egypt at all.

We shared our house with another family who lived in an apartment upstairs, and, to their wonder and the wonder of our other neighbors, my mother would bring a lovely pine tree into the house at Christmas and decorate it with shiny stars and balls, topping it off with a figure of Father Christmas. Nadia and Tahani, the children who lived upstairs, as well as other children in the neighborhood would rush to see our tree, because very few Egyptian families celebrated Christmas and none had ever seen a Christmas tree. Our friends envied us not only because of our tree and the delicious Christmas pudding my mother made, but because we received gifts as well.

It was difficult for my mother to live so far away from her country. During World War II all communication was cut off between England and Egypt. She heard no news from her family at all and was very worried. One day I found her crying in her room when I returned from school.

"What is wrong with Mummy?" I asked Betty, a friend of my mother's who had been visiting.

"She has just learned that her father passed away," Betty told me. "Her family has sent her some money and his watch." A few months later she lost her mother as well.

I felt so sorry for her. I would never have wanted to be away so long from my family. But she did not want to leave her children or her husband to go for a visit. For thirty years she did not return to England, and when she did she could not recognize the streets or even find her family house in Sheffield. To locate her family, my mother put a notice in the local newspaper, saying what hotel she was staying in. That afternoon her only living sister and other relatives rushed to see her. It was a very moving meeting after such a long separation, and the newspaper in Sheffield published a story about it.

My mother did not raise us to be British. Not at all. At home we all spoke Arabic, which she had learned to speak as well. She was not a proselytizer, so she did not influence us in any way from our Muslim traditions. But still it was a little bit confusing to me as a small child. My mother kept a crucifix of the prophet Jesus over her bed, and sometimes I would see her kneeling before it in prayer, her hands clasped together in the Christian manner though as small children we did not yet pray, I knew that the Muslims prayed differently, standing with the arms outstretched and prostrating themselves on the ground. I was confused by this difference between my mother and the rest of the family.

"Why are you Christian while we are all Muslim?" I asked her one afternoon after a classmate questioned me about it.

"Nobody chooses their religion," she explained to me in a very sweet way. "We are all what we are born to be. The important thing to remember is that all religions have just one God. It does not matter how we worship Him so long as we have faith."

But still it bothered me. My mother's Christian ways made me think more deeply about our Muslim traditions which others just took for granted. At the Coptic missionary school that all the children attended, the only primary school on Roda, the Christian teacher read stories to us several times a week from the Bible, stories about all the prophets and about Jesus Christ. Every morning before classes began there was a

Christian prayer service, which the teacher had told us we did not have to attend if we did not want to. So I didn't, staying at my desk in the classroom while all the other students went to the service, including my sister, who was too young to understand.

"Why don't you come with me?" my sister said.

"It is for the Christians and we are Muslim," I told her.

"But you will make the teacher angry," she said.

I didn't care. "I am not going to go listen to a priest just to please the teacher," I insisted.

But my sister was right. The teacher became cruel toward me, making me stand in the corner with my face to the wall every day during our recreational period.

"Your sister comes to prayers. So do the other students, both of whose parents are Muslim," the teacher said to me. "Why must you be different?"

"I am not a Christian," I would reply. And back I would go into the corner.

I was only eight at the time, and after three weeks of this I told my father how cruelly I felt the teacher was treating me. The next morning he came to see the British headmistress.

"I do not want either of my daughters to attend the Christian prayer service," he told her. "That is not their religion and the teacher is pressuring them."

The headmistress was evidently shocked when my father told her how severely I was being treated. She must have spoken to my teacher, because after my father's visit she treated me very kindly. From then on both Dalia and I stayed at our desks while the others went to chapel.

My mother never converted to Islam, though many of her British friends who were married to Egyptians did. Conversion was very simple, requiring registration as a Muslim at el-Azhar Mosque with two people as witnesses, and the recitation five times of the profession of faith: "I testify that there is no god but God, and Muhammad is His messenger." Her reluctance to convert perplexed my aunts and uncle. "Why doesn't Gladys change her religion?" my father's family and friends used to ask. But my father loved my mother very much and never wanted to pressure her. Instead, we would follow our tradition and holidays with my father's family. And my mother would share somewhat, even fasting a few days during Ramadan* to encourage us. We were a Muslim family with a Christian mother.

She was not a typical Egyptian mother, protectively hovering over her children. Not at all. When we fell playing games in the garden, our aunts would always rush to pick us up. "Let them get up by themselves," my

*The ninth month of the Muslim year spent in fasting from sunrise to sunset.

mother would say. Unlike many Egyptian mothers, who, after washing their children's hair, for example, made their children stay inside until their hair was dry, my mother would say, "Nonsense. Go outside and let the wind and sun dry it."

Many Egyptian mothers sat at night with their children until they fell asleep, then left a light burning for them so that they would not be frightened if they awoke. My mother disapproved of that, thinking it made the children dependent and soft. Instead she went in quite the other direction. Every night before we went to bed she made us go out into the black, black garden alone and find our way around it three times in the dark. That way, she said, we would learn not to be afraid of bring alone and not be afraid of the dark. And she was right.

Our home had a very warm, loving atmosphere. Every day my father returned from his office at two, the time all government offices closed for the day, with packets of chocolates, a new French cheese or a present of smoked tongue for us. Our main meal was at midday, after which all Cairenes including us, took naps until four or five. After his nap, my father never went out again the way many other Egyptian men did—going to the cafés to drink coffee, play backgammon or smoke the nargilehs or water pipes. Either we all went out together or he stayed home.

Sometimes on Friday, our Sabbath day, my father would take us to the Old City, marked by the Bab el-Metwalli, or Gate of the Holy Man, named after the Sufi sheikh who reportedly sat there centuries before, performing miracles for passersby. For all that Cairo was my hometown, I never ceased to marvel at the sights and the exotic history that made up my city. The streets of the Old City, far too narrow for automobiles, were choked instead with the traffic of horses, donkeys and even people laden down with loads of fresh vegetables, firesticks, vases of copper and brass to be sold in the bustling Khan el-Khalili bazaar. Cairo had been the greatest trading center in the world for centuries, and it was here in the caravanserai of the Khan el-Khalili that medieval traders from all over the Arab world had unloaded their camel trains. It was near here also that the Fatimid sultans had kept a zoo for the giraffes, ostriches and elephants sent to them as tribute from kingdoms in Africa.

The twelve thousand shops of the Khan el-Khalili were filled with remnants of the past being used in the present. My parents often took us through the dark, winding streets to the silver and gold market, located in the very heart of the bazaar so as to protect it from invaders. There my sister and I could buy silver bracelets for ten cents. While my mother stopped by the spice market to buy mint, thyme and sage for her British sauces, we children would strain to hear the clanking finger cymbals of the roving juice seller as children had for centuries, then pester our father to buy us glasses of the cold black syrupy sweet juice of the *tamarhindy*.

Interpretations

1. In what ways was Sadat's childhood Egyptian? European? What evidence is there that Sadat considers herself more Egyptian than European, or at least wants to establish that her Egyptian "half" is not secondary to her European "half"?

2. Which of Sadat's mother's traits do you think most influenced Sadat? Cite evidence. How did Sadat's Aunt Zouzou, her "Egyptian mother," influence her?

3. "Nobody chooses their religion," said Sadat's mother. How true is this? Do you think Sadat's mother should (or could) have changed to her husband's religion? Why or why not?

4. Compare the reactions of Sadat and her sister to the demands of their Christian school. On what principle did Sadat resist the Christian prayer service? (Which meant more to her, the freedom to be "different" or her Muslim religion?)

5. This essay discusses several kinds of cultural and national differences. What is its tone? (inflammatory? tolerant? arrogant? amused? serious? alarmed?)

Correspondences

1. Review the des Rieux quotation on marriage (page 99) and discuss its relevance to the relationship of Sadat's parents. (How did their different religious beliefs affect their marriage and their children's upbringing?)

2. Sadat and Alvarez vividly convey the inner workings of their families. How did their family life contribute to their personal sense of independence? How did their family customs enhance their sense of belonging?

Applications

1. Perhaps, like Sadat, you were raised by parents from different ethnic backgrounds, or, like Alvarez, by immigrant parents in a new culture. If so, write an essay describing and evaluating that experience.

2. Write an essay about someone in your family you once thought of as rather ordinary but whom you now appreciate and value highly. Focus on one event or experience that was most instrumental in your viewing this person in a new light.

from White Tigers

Maxine Hong Kingston

*Maxine Hong Kingston (b. 1940) grew up in the Chinese-Amer-
ican community of Stockton, California, and graduated from
the University of California. Her award-winning autobiographies* The Woman Warrior *(1976) from which "White Tigers" is
taken, and* China Man *(1980) focus on growing up female as a
first-generation Chinese-American. In 1988 she published a
novel,* Tripmaster Monkey. *As a writer, Kingston often blends
myth, history, and autobiography to illustrate the importance of
stories in the lives and culture of Chinese Americans.*

*For more information on China, see John King Fairbank,
"Footbinding," Chapter 1.*

MY AMERICAN LIFE has been such a disappointment.

"I got straight A's, Mama."

"Let me tell you a true story about a girl who saved her village."

I could not figure out what was my village. And it was important that
I do something big and fine, or else my parents would sell me when we
made our way back to China. In China there were solutions for what to
do with little girls who ate up food and threw tantrums. You can't eat
straight A's.

When one of my parents or the emigrant villagers said, "Feeding girls
is feeding cowbirds," I would thrash on the floor and scream so hard I
couldn't talk. I couldn't stop.

"What's the matter with her?"

"I don't know. Bad, I guess. You know how girls are. "There's no
profit in raising girls. Better to raise geese than girls.'"

"I would hit her if she were mine. But then there's no use wasting all
that discipline on a girl. 'When you raise girls, you're raising children for
strangers.'"

"Stop that crying!" my mother would yell. "I'm going to hit you if you
don't stop. Bad girl! Stop!" I'm going to remember never to hit or to scold
my children for crying, I thought, because then they will only cry more.

"I'm not a bad girl," I would scream. "I'm not a bad girl. I'm not a bad
girl." I might as well have said, "I'm not a girl."

"When you were little, all you had to say was 'I'm not a bad girl,' and
you could make yourself cry," my mother says, talking-story about my
childhood.

171

I minded that the emigrant villagers shook their heads at my sister and me. "One girl—and another girl," they said, and made our parents ashamed to take us out together. The good part about my brothers being born was that people stopped saying, "All girls," but I learned new grievances. "Did you roll an egg on *my* face like that when *I* was born?" "Did you have a full-month party for *me?*" "Did you turn on all the lights?" "Did you send *my* picture to Grandmother?" "Why not? Because I'm a girl? Is that why not?" "Why didn't you teach me English?" "You like having me beaten up at school, don't you?"

"She is very mean, isn't she?" the emigrant villagers would say.

"Come, children. Hurry. Hurry. Who wants to go out with Great-Uncle?" On Saturday mornings, my great-uncle, the ex-river pirate, did the shopping. "Get your coats, whoever's coming."

"I'm coming. I'm coming. Wait for me."

When he heard girls' voices, he turned on us and roared, "No girls!" and left my sisters and me hanging our coats back up, not looking at one another. The boys came back with candy and new toys. When they walked through Chinatown, the people must have said, "A boy—and another boy—and another boy!" At my great-uncle's funeral I secretly tested out feeling glad that he was dead—the six-foot bearish masculinity of him.

I went away to college—Berkeley in the sixties—and I studied, and I marched to change the world, but I did not turn into a boy. I would have liked to bring myself back as a boy for my parents to welcome with chickens and pigs. That was for my brother, who returned alive from Vietnam.

If I went to Vietnam, I would not come back; females desert families. It was said, "There is an outward tendency in females," which meant that I was getting straight A's for the good of my future husband's family, not my own. I did not plan ever to have a husband. I would show my mother and father and the nosey emigrant villagers that girls have no outward tendency. I stopped getting straight A's.

And all the time I was having to turn myself American-feminine, or no dates.

There is a Chinese word for the female *I*—which is "slave." Break the women with their own tongues!

I refused to cook. When I had to wash dishes, I would crack one or two. "Bad girl," my mother yelled, and sometimes that made me gloat rather than cry. Isn't a bad girl almost a boy?

"What do you want to be when you grow up, little girl?"

"A lumberjack in Oregon."

Even now, unless I'm happy, I burn the food when I cook. I do not feed people. I let the dirty dishes rot. I eat at other people's tables but won't invite them to mine, where the dishes are rotting.

If I could not-eat, perhaps I could make myself a warrior like the swords-woman who drives me. I will—I must—rise and plow the fields as soon as the baby comes out.

Once I get outside the house, what bird might call me; on what horse could I ride away? Marriage and childbirth strengthen the swordswoman, who is not a maid like Joan of Arc. Do the women's work; then do more work, which will become ours too. No husband of mine will say, "I could have been a drummer, but I had to think about the wife and kids. You know how it is." Nobody supports me at the expense of his own adventure. Then I get bitter: no one supports me; I am not loved enough to be supported. That I am not a burden has to compensate for the sad envy when I look at women loved enough to be supported. Even now China wraps double binds around my feet.

When urban renewal tore down my parents' laundry and paved over our slum for a parking lot, I only made up gun and knife fantasies and did nothing useful.

From the fairy tales, I've learned exactly who the enemy are. I easily recognize them—business-suited in their modern American executive guise, each boss two feet taller than I am and impossible to meet eye to eye.

I once worked at an art supply house that sold paints to artists. "Order more of that nigger yellow, willya?" the boss told me. "Bright, isn't it? Nigger yellow."

"I don't like that word," I had to say in my bad, small-person's voice that makes no impact. The boss never deigned to answer.

I also worked at a land developer's association. The building industry was planning a banquet for contractors, real estate dealers, and real estate editors. "Did you know the restaurant you chose for the banquet is being picketed by CORE and the NAACP?" I squeaked.

"Of course I know." The boss laughed. "That's why I chose it."

"I refuse to type these invitations," I whispered, voice unreliable.

He leaned back in his leather chair, his bossy stomach opulent. He picked up his calendar and slowly circled a date. "You will be paid up to here," he said. "We'll mail you the check."

If I took the sword, which my hate must surely have forged out of the air, and gutted him, I would put color and wrinkles into his shirt.

It's not just the stupid racists that I have to do something about, but the tyrants who for whatever reason can deny my family food and work. My job is my own only land.

To avenge my family, I'd have to storm across China to take back our farm from the Communists; I'd have to rage across the United States to take back the laundry in New York and the one in California. Nobody in history has conquered and united both North America and Asia. A descendant of eighty pole fighters, I ought to be able to set out confidently, march straight down our street, get going right now. There's work to do, ground to cover. Surely, the eighty pole fighters, though unseen would follow me and lead me and protect me, as is the wont of ancestors.

Or it may well be that they're resting happily in China, their spirits dispersed among the real Chinese, and not nudging me at all with their poles. I mustn't feel bad that I haven't done as well as the swordswoman did; after all, no bird called me, no wise old people tutored me. I have no magic beads, or water gourd sight, no rabbit that will jump in the fire when I'm hungry. I dislike armies.

I've looked for the bird. I've seen clouds make pointed angel wings that stream past the sunset, but they shred into clouds. Once at a beach after a long hike I saw a seagull, tiny as an insect. But when I jumped up to tell what miracle I saw, before I could get the words out I understood that the bird was insect-size because it was far away. My brain had momentarily lost its depth perception. I was that eager to find an unusual bird.

The news from China has been confusing. It also had something to do with birds. I was nine years old when the letters made my parents, who are rocks, cry. My father screamed in his sleep. My mother wept and crumpled up the letters. She set fire to them page by page in the ashtray, but new letters came almost every day. The only letters they opened without fear were the ones with red borders, the holiday letters that mustn't carry bad news. The other letters said that my uncles were made to kneel on broken glass during their trials and had confessed to being landowners. They were all executed, and the aunt whose thumbs were twisted off drowned herself. Other aunts, mothers-in-law, and cousins disappeared; some suddenly began writing to us again from communes or from Hong Kong. They kept asking for money. The ones in communes got four ounces of fat and one cup of oil a week, they said, and had to work from 4 A.M. to 9 P.M. They had to learn to do dances waving red kerchiefs; they had to sing nonsense syllables. The communists gave axes to the old ladies and said, "Go and kill yourself. You're useless." If we overseas Chinese would just send money to the Communist bank, our relatives said, they might get a percentage of it for themselves. The aunts in Hong Kong said to send money quickly; their children were begging on the sidewalks and mean people put dirt in their bowls.

When I dream that I am wire without flesh, there is a letter on blue airmail paper that floats above the night ocean between here and China. It must arrive safely or else my grandmother and I will lose each other.

My parents felt bad whether or not they sent money. Sometimes they got angry at their brothers and sisters for asking. And they would not simply ask but have to talk-story too. The revolutionaries had taken Fourth Aunt and Uncle's store, house, and lands. They attacked the house and killed the grandfather and oldest daughter. The grandmother escaped with the loose cash and did not return to help. Fourth Aunt picked up her sons, one under each arm, and hid in the pig house, where they slept that night in cotton clothes. The next day she found her husband, who had also miraculously escaped. The two of them collected twigs and yams to sell while their children begged. Each morning they tied the faggots on each other's back. Nobody bought from them. They ate the yams and some of the children's rice. Finally Fourth Aunt saw what was wrong. "We have to shout 'Fuel for sale' and 'Yams for sale,'" she said. "We can't just walk unobtrusively up and down the street." "You're right," said my uncle, but he was shy and walked in back of her. "Shout," my aunt ordered, but he could not. "They think we're carrying these sticks home for our own fire," she said. "Shout." They walked about miserably, silently, until sundown, neither of them able to advertise themselves. Fourth Aunt, an orphan since the age of ten, mean as my mother, threw her bundle down at his feet and scolded Fourth Uncle, "Starving to death, his wife and children starving to death, and he's too damned shy to raise his voice." She left him standing by himself and afraid to return empty-handed to her. He sat under a tree to think, when he spotted a pair of nesting doves. Dumping his bag of yams, he climbed up and caught the birds. That was when the Communists trapped him, in the tree. They criticized him for selfishly taking food for his own family and killed him, leaving his body in the tree as an example. They took the birds to a commune kitchen to be shared.

It is confusing that my family was not the poor to be championed. They were executed like the barons in the stories, when they were not barons. It is confusing that birds tricked us.

What fighting and killing I have seen have not been glorious but slum grubby. I fought the most during junior high school and always cried. Fights are confusing as to who has won. The corpses I've seen had been rolled and dumped, sad little dirty bodies covered with a police khaki blanket. My mother locked her children in the house so we couldn't look at dead slum people. But at news of a body, I would find a way to get out; I had to learn about dying if I wanted to become a swordswoman. Once there was an Asian man stabbed next door, words on cloth pinned to his corpse. When the police came around asking questions, my father said, "No read Japanese. Japanese words. Me Chinese."

I've also looked for old people who could be my gurus. A medium with red hair told me that a girl who died in a far country follows me wherever I go. This spirit can help me if I acknowledge her, she said. Between the head line and heart line in my right palm, she said, I have the mystic cross. I could become a medium myself. I don't want to be a medium. I don't want to be a crank taking "offerings" in a wicker plate from the frightened audience, who, one after another asked the spirits how to raise rent money, how to cure their coughs and skin diseases, how to find a job. And martial arts are for unsure little boys kicking away under fluorescent lights.

I live now where there are Chinese and Japanese, but no emigrants from my own village looking at me as if I had failed them. Living among one's own emigrant villagers can give a good Chinese far from China glory and a place. "That old busboy is really a swordsman," we whisper when he goes by, "He's a swordsman who's killed fifty. He has a tong ax in his closet." But I am useless, one more girl who couldn't be sold. When I visit the family now, I wrap my American successes around me like a private shawl; I *am* worthy of eating the food. From afar I can believe my family loves me fundamentally. They only say, "When fishing for treasures in the flood, be careful not to pull in girls," because that is what one says about daughters. But I watched such words come out of my own mother's and father's mouths; I looked at their ink drawing of poor people snagging their neighbor's flotage with long flood hooks and pushing the girl babies on down the river. And I had to get out of hating range. I read in an anthropology book that Chinese say, "Girls are necessary too"; I have never heard the Chinese I know make this concession. Perhaps it was a saying in another village. I refuse to shy my way anymore through our Chinatown, which tasks me with the old sayings and the stories.

The swordswoman and I are not so dissimilar. May my people understand the resemblance soon so that I can return to them. What we have in common are the words at our backs. The ideographs for *revenge* are "report a crime" and "report to five families." The reporting is the vengeance—not the beheading, not the gutting, but the words. And I have so many words—"chink" words and "gook" words too—that they do not fit on my skin.

Interpretations

1. Much of the "disappointment" Kingston has experienced is the result of an engrained favoritism of sons over daughters. How much of this attitude in these particular parents is traditional and how much is heartfelt? Cite details. Do you believe tradition is powerful enough to make parents truly hate a daughter?

2. How does Kingston react to her parents' treatment of her?

3. What obstacles lie in the way of Kingston making herself a "warrior" or "swordswoman"? What is her attitude toward these obstacles—self-pity, humor, philosophical acceptance? How can you tell?

4. What is the *tone* of the sentence, "Nobody in history has conquered and united both North America and Asia"? Where do you find other sentences in this same tone?

5. Speaking of marriage, the author says, "Even now China wraps double binds around my feet." What does she mean?

6. "From the fairy tales, I've learned exactly who the enemy are." What fairy-tale elements does the author weave into her narrative? What do these elements contribute to the narrative?

7. Kingston has described *The Woman Warrior* as complex and mosaic-like. For example, within a few paragraphs Kingston is a child being rejected by great-uncle, a college student at Berkeley, an indeterminate secondary-school student, and a "little girl." What is the effect of this multifaceted description?

Correspondences

1. "There's no profit in raising girls. Better to raise geese than girls," writes Kingston. "What is under a veil brings no joy," states Sadat (Chapter 1). According to these authors, how are female children traditionally regarded in China and in Egypt? What are the similarities and differences in their responses to this treatment?

2. According to Mead, the American family functions primarily as an individual unit. In Kingston's narrative the individual family functions with the clan. What examples of this interaction does Kingston cite? How might these different concepts of family affect competition among family members?

Applications

1. Prepare a presentation for a Parent Teachers Association meeting on the following topic: "Parental expectations of children often produce negative effects." (What *tone* should you adopt to best reach your audience?)

2. In one paragraph, discuss some of Kingston's ideas in the excerpt below:

   Nobody supports me at the expense of his own adventure. Then I get bitter: no one supports me; I am not loved enough to be supported.

Mother Tongue

Amy Tan

Amy Tan (b. 1952) is a second-generation Asian-American whose parents emigrated from China to Oakland, California, shortly before her birth. Her two novels include The Joy Luck Club *(1989) and* The Kitchen God's Wife *(1991). She lives in San Francisco and is currently working on essays about her recent trip to China and a new novel.*

For more information on China, see John King Fairbank's "Footbinding" in Chapter 1.

I AM NOT a scholar of English or literature. I cannot give you much more than personal opinions on the English language and its variations in this country or others.

I am a writer. And by that definition, I am someone who has always loved language. I am fascinated by language in daily life. I spend a great deal of my time thinking about the power of language—the way it can evoke an emotion, a visual image, a complex idea, or a simple truth. Language is the tool of my trade. And I use them all—all the Englishes I grew up with.

Recently, I was made keenly aware of the different Englishes I do use. I was giving a talk to a large group of people, the same talk I had already given to half a dozen other groups. The nature of the talk was about my writing, my life, and my book, *The Joy Luck Club*. The talk was going along well enough, until I remembered one major difference that made the whole talk sound wrong. My mother was in the room. And it was perhaps the first time she had heard me give a lengthy speech, using the kind of English I have never used with her. I was saying things like, "The intersection of memory upon imagination" and "There is an aspect of my fiction that relates to thus-and-thus"—a speech filled with carefully wrought grammatical phrases, burdened, it suddenly seemed to me, with nominalized forms, past perfect tenses, conditional phrases, all the forms of standard English that I had learned in school and through books, the forms of English I did not use at home with my mother.

Just last week, I was walking down the street with my mother, and I again found myself conscious of the English I was using, the English I do use with her. We were talking about the price of new and used furniture and I heard myself saying this: "Not waste money that way." My husband was with us as well, and he didn't notice any switch in my English. And then I realized why. It's because over the twenty years we've been together I've often used that same kind of English with him, and sometimes he even uses it with me. It has become our language of intimacy, a different sort of English that relates to family talk, the language I grew up with.

So you'll have some idea of what this family talk I heard sounds like, I'll quote what my mother said during a recent conversation which I videotaped and then transcribed. During this conversation, my mother was talking about a political gangster in Shanghai who had the same last name as her family's, Du, and how the gangster in his early years wanted to be adopted by her family, which was rich by comparison. Later, the gangster became more powerful, far richer than my mother's family, and one day showed up at my mother's wedding to pay his respects. Here's what she said in part:

"Du Yusong having business like fruit stand. Like off the street kind. He is Du like Du Zong—but not Tsung-ming Island people. The local people call putong, the river east side, he belong to that side local people. That man want to ask Du Zong father take him in like become own family. Du Zong father wasn't look down on him, but didn't take seriously, until that man big like become a mafia. Now important person, very hard to inviting him. Chinese way, came only to show respect, don't stay for dinner. Respect for making big celebration, he shows up. Mean gives lots of respect. Chinese custom. Chinese social life that way. If too important won't have to stay too long. He come to my wedding. I didn't see, I heard it. I gone to boy's side, they have YMCA dinner. Chinese age I was nineteen."

You should know that my mother's expressive command of English belies how much she actually understands. She reads the *Forbes* report, listens to *Wall Street Week,* converses daily with her stockbroker, reads all of Shirley MacLaine's books with ease—all kinds of things I can't begin to understand. Yet some of my friends tell me they understand 50 percent of what my mother says. Some say they understand 80 to 90 percent. Some say they understand none of it, as if she were speaking pure Chinese. But to me, my mother's English is perfectly clear, perfectly natural. It's my mother tongue. Her language, as I hear it, is vivid, direct, full of observation and imagery. That was the language that helped shape the way I saw things, expressed things, made sense of the world.

Lately, I've been giving more thought to the kind of English my mother speaks. Like others, I have described it to people as "broken" or "fractured" English. But I wince when I say that. It has always bothered me that I can think of no way to describe it other than "broken," as if it were damaged and needed to be fixed, as if it lacked a certain wholeness and soundness. I've heard other terms used, "limited English," for example. But they seem just as bad, as if everything is limited, including people's perceptions of the limited English speaker.

I know this for a fact, because when I was growing up, my mother's "limited" English limited *my* perception of her. I was ashamed of her English. I believed that her English reflected the quality of what she had to say. That is, because she expressed them imperfectly her thoughts were imperfect. And I had plenty of empirical evidence to support me: the fact that people in department stores, at banks, and at restaurants did not take her seriously, did not give her good service, pretended not to understand her, or even acted as if they did not hear her.

My mother has long realized the limitations of her English as well. When I was fifteen, she used to have me call people on the phone to pretend I was she. In this guise, I was forced to ask for information or even to complain and yell at people who had been rude to her. One time it was a call to her stockbroker in New York. She had cashed out her small portfolio and it just so happened we were going to go to New York the next week, our very first trip outside California. I had to get on the phone and say in an adolescent voice that was not very convincing, "This is Mrs. Tan."

And my mother was standing in the back whispering loudly, "Why he don't send me check, already two weeks late. So mad he lie to me, losing me money."

And then I said in perfect English, "Yes, I'm getting rather concerned. You had agreed to send the check two weeks ago, but it hasn't arrived."

Then she began to talk more loudly. "What he want, I come to New York tell him front of his boss, you cheating me?" And I was trying to calm her down, make her be quiet, while telling the stockbroker, "I can't tolerate any more excuses. If I don't receive the check immediately, I am going to have to speak to your manager when I'm in New York next week." And sure enough, the following week there we were in front of this astonished stockbroker, and I was sitting there red-faced and quiet, and my mother, the real Mrs. Tan, was shouting at his boss in her impeccable broken English.

We used a similar routine just five days ago, for a situation that was far less humorous. My mother had gone o the hospital for an appointment, to find out about a benign brain tumor a CAT scan had revealed a month ago. She said she had spoken very good English, her best English, no mistakes. Still, she said, the hospital did not apologize when they said they had lost the CAT scan and she had come for nothing. She said they did not seem to have any sympathy when she told them she was anxious to know the exact diagnosis, since her husband and son had both died of brain tumors. She said they would not give her any more information until the next time and she would have to make another appointment for that. So she said she would not leave until the doctor called her daughter. She wouldn't budge. And when the doctor finally called her daughter, me, who spoke in perfect English—lo and behold—we had assurances the CAT scan would be found, promise that a conference call on Monday would be held, and apologies for any suffering my mother had gone through for a most regrettable mistake.

I think my mother's English almost had an effect on limiting my possibilities in life as well. Sociologists and linguists probably will tell you that a person's developing language skills are more influenced by peers. But I do think that the language spoken in the family, especially in immigrant families which are more insular, plays a large role in shaping the language of the child. And I believe that it affected my results on achievement tests, IQ tests, and the SAT. While my English skills were never judged as poor, compared to math, English could not be considered my strong suit. In grade school I did moderately well, getting perhaps B's, sometimes B-pluses, in English and scoring perhaps in the sixtieth or seventieth percentile on achievement tests. But those scores were not good enough to override the opinion that my true abilities lay in math and science, because in those areas I achieved A's and scored in the ninetieth percentile or higher.

This was understandable. Math is precise; there is only one correct answer. Whereas, for me at least, the answers on English tests were always a judgment call, a matter of opinion and personal experience. Those tests were constructed around items like fill-in-the-blank sentence completion, such as, "Even though Tom was _____ , Mary thought he was _____ ." And the correct answer always seemed to be the most bland combinations of thoughts, for example, "Even though Tom was shy, Mary thought he was charming," with the grammatical structure "even though" limiting the correct answer to some sort of semantic opposites, so you wouldn't get answers like, "Even though Tom was foolish, Mary thought he was ridiculous." Well, according to my mother, there were very few limitations as to what Tom could have been and what Mary might have thought of him. So I never did well on tests like that.

The same was true with word analogies, pairs of words in which you were supposed to find some sort of logical, semantic relationship—for example, "*Sunset* is to *nightfall* as _____ is to _____ ." And here you would be presented with a list of four possible pairs, one of which showed the same kind of relationship: *red* is to *stoplight, bus* is to *arrival, chills* is to *fever, yawn* is to *boring*. Well, I could never think that way. I knew what the tests were asking, but I could not block out of my mind the images already created by the first pair, "*sunset* is to *nightfall*"—and I would see a burst of color against a darkening sky, the moon rising, the lowering of a curtain of stars. And all the other pairs of words—red, bus, stoplight, boring—just threw up a mass of confusing images, making it impossible for me to sort out something as logical as saying: "A sunset precedes nightfall" is the same as "a chill precedes a fever." The only way I would have gotten that answer right would have been to imagine an associative situation, for example, by being disobedient and staying out past sunset, catching a chill at night which turns into feverish pneumonia as punishment, which indeed did happen to me.

I have been thinking about all this lately, about my mother's English, about achievement tests. Because lately I've been asked, as a writer, why there are not more Asian Americans represented in American literature. Why are there few Asian Americans enrolled in creative writing programs? Why do so many Chinese students go into engineering? Well, these are broad sociological questions I can't begin to answer. But I have noticed in surveys—in fact, just last week—that Asian students, as a whole, always do significantly better on math achievement tests than in English. And this makes me think that there are other Asian-American students whose English spoken in the home might also be described as "broken" or "limited." And perhaps they also have teachers who are steering them away from writing and into math and science, which is what happened to me.

Fortunately, I happen to be rebellious in nature and enjoy the challenge of disproving assumptions made about me. I became an English major my first year in college, after being enrolled as pre-med. I started writing nonfiction as a freelancer the week after I was told by my former boss that writing was my worst skill and I should hone my talents toward account management.

But it wasn't until 1985 that I finally began to write fiction. And at first I wrote using what I thought to be wittily crafted sentences, sentences that would finally prove I had mastery over the English language. Here's an example from the first draft of a story that later made its way into *The Joy Luck Club,* but without this line: "That was my mental quandary in its nascent state." A terrible line, which I can hardly pronounce.

Fortunately, for reasons I won't get into today, I later decided I should envision a reader for the stories I would write. And the reader I decided upon was my mother, because these were stories about mothers. So with this reader in mind—and in fact she did read my early drafts—I began to write stories using all the Englishes I grew up with: the English I spoke to my mother, which for lack of a better term might be described as "simple"; the English she used with me, which for lack of a better term might be described as "broken"; my translation of her Chinese, which could certainly be described as "watered down"; and what I imagine to be her translation of her Chinese if she could speak in perfect English, her internal language, and for that I sought to preserve the essence, but neither an English nor a Chinese structure. I wanted to capture what language ability tests can never reveal: her intent, her passion, her imagery, the rhythms of her speech and the nature of her thoughts.

Apart from what any critic had to say about my writing, I knew I had succeeded where it counted when my mother finished reading my book and gave me her verdict: "So easy to read."

Interpretations

1. Tan's mother reads all kinds of books with ease. Why is it so much easier to "receive than to send"—to understand a new language than to speak it?

2. What several "Englishes" do you speak and why? What examples can you offer?

3. Students might take Tan's successful rebellion against her teachers' advice—her career as a novelist—as an example. Would you advise students in general to follow her lead? Why or why not?

4. Good writing, according to Tan, is easy reading. How good according to this criterion is this essay? What do you think contributes most to easy reading?

5. How can being bilingual make a writer better in both languages?

Correspondences

1. Kingston and Tan, Asian-American writers, describe their families' interactions with language. What role does English play in each selection? How do language barriers affect relationships among various family members?

2. Both writers also discuss the impact of language on their families' cultural interactions with the dominant culture. To what extent are their experiences similar? For what reasons do people ignore or make fun of those who speak "broken English"?

Applications

1. Tan writes that the "language spoken in the family, especially in immigrant families which are more insular, plays a large role in shaping the language of the child." Discuss how Kingston, Alvarez, and Tan have overcome that limitation.

2. Write a journal entry on the significance of Tan's title "Mother Tongue."

Grow Old Along with Me, The Best Is Yet to Be

Penelope Lively

Penelope Margaret Lively (b. 1933) was born in Cairo but lives in England. She graduated with an Honors Degree in Modern History from Oxford University and is a contributor to a variety of journals and magazines including Good Housekeeping *and* Vogue. *She has also authored numerous books, including* Judgement Day *(1980),* Next to Nature *(1982),* Corruption *(1984, from which the following story is taken) and* A House Inside Out *(1987).*

In "Grow Old Along with Me" you will encounter Sarah and Tony, a liberated British couple who are traveling in Gloucestershire, the county just to the west of Lively's home county of Oxfordshire. Around them are architectural reminders of England's long history, including the eighth-century church the couple reads about in "Pevsner." (Sir Nikolaus Pevsner, an architectural historian, wrote the Buildings of England *series.) By the eighth century, the British Isles had been invaded by the Angles, Saxons, and Jutes. The Danish would soon follow. In the eighth century the church in the story would, of course, have been Roman Catholic. By Sara and Tony's time—in fact in the sixteenth century under Henry VIII—the state church had become the Protestant Church of England. Sects such as the Separatists had begun to proliferate. These English Puritans were to found the Massachusetts Bay Colony in 1620.*

"OH, I DON'T KNOW . . ." said Sarah. "Decisions, decisions. I hate them. I mean, one of the things that bothers me is—would I stop being *me?* Would I change. If we did."

She wore dungarees in pale turquoise, and a white T-shirt. She drove the Fiat hunched forward over the steering-wheel. Her face was engulfed by large reflecting sun-glasses across which flew hedges, trees, a passing car. "It's rather gorgeous round here, isn't it? Half-asleep, as though nothing happens in a hundred years."

Tony said, "We both might. It's a significant step in a relationship—that's the point of it, I suppose."

"And the point of waiting. Thinking about it. Not rushing."

"Not that we have."

"Quite. Shall we stop and eat soon?"

"Yes—when there's a reasonable pub."

Gloucestershire unreeled at either side: dark green, straw-coloured, unpopulated. Trees drooped in the fields; a village was still and silent except for a lorry throbbing outside a shop. High summer gripped the landscape; birds twitched from hedge to hedge.

"Half the time," said Sarah, "it doesn't crop up. One sort of puts it out of one's mind—there are too many other things to think of. And then it begins to nag. We've got to either do it or not do it."

"We've been not doing it for three years, darling."

"I know, I know. But all the same, it looms."

"We are actually," he said, "better off, from a tax point of view, unmarried. Since your rise. We went into that in the winter—remember?"

"What about this—Free House, Bar Snacks. How much better off, exactly?"

"Oh, lord, I don't know. Hundreds, anyway."

She turned the car into the pub yard. "It's a point, then. Ma keeps saying, what happens if there's a baby? And I say well that would of course put a diffcrent complexion on things but *until* we are absolutely free to choose. The trouble is that dear ma thinks I'm on the shelf at twenty-six. I keep saying, there aren't shelves now."

The woman behind the bar watched them come in, a good-looking young couple, in the pink of health, not short of money, the kind of people who know their way around. She served them lagers and chicken salad, and noted Sarah's neat figure, not an ounce in the wrong place, which induced vague discontent. I'm dieting, she thought, as from Monday I am, I swear to God. She observed also Tony's tanned forearms, below the rolled sleeves of an indefinably modish shirt, like blokes in colour supp. ads. Thirtyish, nice voice. He didn't look at her, pocketing the change, turning away with the plates. She watched them settle in the corner by the window, sitting close, talking. In love, presumably, lucky so-and-so's.

"Tax is certainly a point," said Sarah. "Getting dependent on each other is another. Look at Tom and Alison. But one still feels that eventually we're going to have to make some kind of decision. You can have my pickled onion."

"Lots of people don't. Decide, I mean. Look at Blake and Susan."

"I don't want to look at Blake and Susan. Blake's forty-two, did you know that? And anyway he's *been* married. Oh, isn't it all difficult? We decided no baby, barring accidents, at least not yet, and that was one decision. Thank God for the pill, I suppose. I mean, imagine when they just *happened*."

"They still do sometimes. Look at Maggie."

"Oh, Maggie meant to, for goodness sake. That baby was no accident. It was psychological."

They ate, for a while, in silence. At the bar middle-aged men, locals, sporadically conversed, out of kilter like clocks ticking at different speeds. The woman wiped glasses. A commercial traveller came in and ordered a steak and kidney with chips. On the wall, hand-written posters advertised a Bring and Buy, a Darby and Joan Outing. Tony stacked their empty plates.

"Not exactly the hub of the universe, this."

"It's rather sweet. Laurie Lee country.[1] I used to adore that book—what's-it-called?—we did it for O-levels. Sex in the hedges and all that. O.K.—I'll find the loo and we'll get moving. Where are we, by the way, I've lost track?"

When she came back he had the map book open on his knee. "Let's have a look, there might be something to go and see. Oh, goodness, there is—we're not far from Deerhurst. Oh, we must see Deerhurst. You know—Saxon church, very special."

"Right you are. Do we have Pevsner?"

"On the back shelf of the car. What luck—I never realised Deerhurst was hereabouts."

"Aren't you a clever girl?" he said, patting her knee. "Knowing about Saxon churches."

The woman behind the bar, watching them, thought, yes, that's how it is when you're like that. Can't keep your hands off each other. Ah well. "How's the back, John?" she said. "That stuff I told you about do any good?" The young couple were getting up now, slinging sweaters about their shoulders, leaving without a backwards glance. People passing through, going off into other lives. Young intense lives. "What? Oh, thanks very much—I'll have a lager and lime. Cheers, John."

"Drive or navigate?" said Sarah, in the car park. "You're better with the map than I am, and it's all side roads to this church. I'll tell you one thing—if we do get married it's not going to be any flipping church business. That's what ma's got her eye on, you realise."

"There'd have to be some sort of do."

"We could have it at the flat. Cheaper. The do, I mean. And registry office. But it's all a bit academic, until we actually decide something. Do I go left or right?"

Signposts fingered toward slothful hinterlands. Cars glittered between the hedges, sparks of colour in a world of green and fawn. On the edge of the village, washing-lines held up stiff shapes of clothes, slumping pink and yellow sheets, a rank of nappies. A man scraped around young cabbages with a hoe.

"Corfu," said Tony, "was livelier."

"I thought we agreed never again a package holiday. Anyway, it's the new car this year instead."

"This is our fourth holiday together, Sarah."

[1] English poet and autobiographer born in 1914 in Gloucestershire.

"Cor . . . Hey—you're not directing me. That sign said Deerhurst."

"Sorry. My mind was on other things. Incidentally, what started us off on this marriage discussion? Today, I mean."

"I can't remember. Oh yes I can—it was you talking about this aunt of yours. Will you have to go to the wedding, by the way?"

"I hope not. I'd be the only person there under fifty, I should imagine. No—hearty good wishes over the phone and that kind of thing."

"It's nice for her," said Sarah charitably. "At that age. If a bit kind of fake, if you see what I mean."

"Yes. But for that generation there wouldn't be any alternative."

They nodded, sombrely.

"Here we are," said Sarah. "And this must be where you leave cars. Good—there's no one else there, I hate looking at churches when there's anyone else. Where's Pevsner? We're going to do this place properly—it's supposed to be important."

They advanced into the churchyard. The church, squatting amid yews, seemed almost derisive in its antiquity, tethered to something dark and incomprehensible, uncaring, too far away to be understood. Its stone was blurred, its shapes strange and unlovely. Gravestones drowned in grass. An aeroplane, unseen, rumbled across the milky sky.

"'. . . tall narrow nave of the C8,'" Tony read. "Seven hundred and something. "Jesus! That makes you think, doesn't it?"

"There's this famous sculpture thing over the door. An animal head. That's it, I suppose. Goodness, isn't it all sinister?"

They stood in silence. "Things that are so incredibly old," Sarah went on, "just leave you feeling respectful. I mean, that they're there at all."

They went into the church. Tony took a few steps down the nave. "Yes. I know what you mean. Even more so inside. All this stone standing for so long"—he gestured at piers, crossing arch, narrow uncompromising windows. "Read Pevsner," instructed Sarah. "I like to understand what I'm looking at." They toured the building, side by side, heads cocked from book to architectural feature, understanding.

The church door, which they had closed behind them, burst open. The sound made them both jump. Turning, they saw a man who stood framed in the gush of light from without: a tall man in tweed jacket and baggy-kneed trousers, an odd prophetic-looking figure with a mane of white hair, like a more robust version of the aged Bertrand Russell. A memorable person, who stood for a moment staring wildly round the church, at Sarah and Tony for one dismissive instant, and who then strode down the aisle searching, apparently, the pillars, and then back to the entrance and out, slamming the door.

"The vicar?" said Tony, after a moment.

"No. Frankly. That was no vicar. Funny to storm out like that, though. This place *vaut le détour,* as *Michelin*[2] says."

---

[2]Is worth a detour according to the *Michelin* travel guidebooks.

"P'raps he's seen it already."

"Presumably." Sarah turned back to Pevsner. "Apparently there's this other carving outside, round at the back, we'd better go and find it. We've done the rest, I think."

She led the way out of the church and round the side, through the long grass and the leaning grave-stones. And came, thus, upon them first.

In the angle of a buttress, up against the wall of the church. The man, the white-haired tall man, his back now turned. Turned because he was locked in an embrace, a succulent sexual embrace (the sound, just, of mouths—the impression of loins pushed together) with a woman little of whom could be seen as, eyes averted, Sarah scurried past, followed a few paces behind by Tony. Both of them at once seeing, and quickly looking away. Seeing of the man his tweed back and his mane of yellow-white hair and of the woman—well, little except an impression of blue denim skirt and plimsolls. And more white hair: crisp curly grey-white hair.

They achieved the back of the church and stood peering up at the wall.

"I can't see this sculpture," said Sarah (voice firm, ordinary, not lowered, rather loud indeed). "It's supposed to be a Virgin—ah, that must be it. Right up just under the window there."

When they came back past the buttress the couple were gone. The churchyard was quite empty. The whole place, which had briefly rocked, had sunk back into its lethargy. That crackling startling charge of passion had dissipated into the stagnant air of the summer afternoon. It was three o'clock, and felt as if it forever would be. Somewhere beyond the hedge a tractor ground across a field.

"Let's go," said Sarah brightly. "I think I've had Deerhurst."

The car was no longer alone. Two others, now, were parked alongside. Sarah whipped the key into the lock and opened the door. She plumped down into the driving-seat. "You know what? That was an assignation we stumbled into."

"So it would seem."

"Where are they now, do you imagine?"

Tony shrugged.

Sarah started the engine. She said with sudden violence, "You know, it was a bit revolting. They were seventy if they were a day."

Tony nodded. Embarrassment filled the car.

Interpretations

1. As the story opens, why don't Sarah and Tony call by name the subject they are discussing? Are they equally undecided, or is one trying to put pressure on the other?

2. How does Tony's aunt's marriage relate to the scene behind the church? What is Sarah's attitude towards his aunt's decision?

3. How does the white-haired couple's "succulent sexual embrace" affect Tony and Sarah? How does it relate to their own earlier discussion of marriage?

4. What do you think Sarah and Tony will decide about their own marriage? Cite reasons for your answer.

5. What is the tone of this story? Is it serious? objective? ironic?

6. For what audience is Lively writing? Do you think men and women respond differently to the story? (What is your response?)

Correspondences

1. Sarah and Tony consider themselves modern. Are they? How liberated are their attitudes? How tolerant? Is their outlook on relationships similar to or different from those of the American couples Weber interviewed?

2. Review the de Beauvoir quotation on love (page 99). To what extent does it apply to Tony and Sarah's relationship? Evaluate their relationship.

Applications

1. Assume you are about to enter a living-together arrangement. Write an essay to your parents explaining your decision. What tone should you adopt? What reasons might they find most convincing? Be sure to present your decision in a logical manner.

2. Write an essay analyzing the implications of the title of Lively's short story. How does it apply to the relationships she presents? What is her attitude towards Sarah and Tony?

ADDITIONAL WRITING TOPICS

1. "I'd like to have a companion. A friend, I guess. But finding a man is not a top priority. I want to travel. I want to establish myself in the community. I don't see any drastic changes in my life by the time I turn thirty. Except that I'll be a property owner." What factors might have contributed to the expectations of Weber's twenty-five-year-old interviewee? How does her attitude towards forming a primary relationship compare with yours? How might choosing pragmatically rather than romantically affect the longevity of the relationship?

2. Write an essay discussing whether it is realistic to expect marriage to last a lifetime today. (What expectations do most people have about marriage? What expectations should they have?)

3. Several selections focus on family members and their influence. Why are families so important? Write an essay answering this question. Use examples from this chapter and your own experience.

4. Does the observance of customs, rituals, or traditions promote unity and continuity within the family? What rituals has your family shared over the years? How have these contributed to family relationships? Write an essay explaining how the observance of rituals helps preserve the family.

5. Review Nin's perspective on friendship (page 100). What does it suggest about possibilities in relationships? Are old friends necessarily one's best friends? Write an essay comparing two friendships of varying durations. How has each contributed to your knowledge of yourself? How do the relationships differ?

6. Motherhood is an important theme in the selections by Mead, Sadat, Kingston, Gray, and Wehle. Analyze their views of motherhood in an essay that also includes your evaluation of the topic. Consider limiting your choice to any three selections.

7. A recurring and controversial aspect of family relationships is the debate between patriarchs and feminists evidenced in the selections by Kingston, Sadat, and Gray. Evaluate their conversations. To what extent do you find consensus? What might you add to the debate?

CHAPTER 3

Education

Human beings show a wonderful capacity to learn and un-learn—if it were not so you would not see such diversity in this and all the other chapters of this book. "The greatest happiness of man as a thinking being," said Goethe, "is to know what is knowable and quietly to revere what is unknowable." "What is knowable" is a vast area, as any college or library catalog can show, and just *how* vast is one more thing man—and woman—would like to know. Everything, then, about our varied fellow human beings, and not just their thinking, should interest us.

Perhaps the selections in this chapter that most clearly support Goethe's notion of the joy of learning are those by Marshall and Viloria. "Poets in the Kitchen" is an essay on the almost unconscious absorption of poetic language. Student Doris Viloria ("The Mistress of Make Believe") portrays a theatrical English teacher whose love of writing Viloria herself absorbed and displays.

There is a good deal of complaining about schools in the essays of this chapter. Is a school's curriculum to be regarded as a culture's propaganda machine, and the school's mission to conserve the culture's values in some pure form, pass them along to the next generation, and help immigrants to assimilate? How can goals be achieved? Marshall wishes that Barbadians had an institution like the Jewish *schul* so that assimilation into North American life and language did not strip Barbadians of their own culture. Is it desirable and possible for public schools to perform this mission without robbing students of their natal language and culture? Is it possible to achieve biculturalism, as well as bilingualism? Is it possible to tolerate, even respect, other religions, systems of law, forms of art and languages without losing respect for one's own? Is our idea of culture clear and distinct enough to speak of absolute boundaries between cultures? If we accept the concept of cultural differences, even cultural boundaries, is cultural exclusiveness the goal we want to pursue?

Armando Rendón regrets the way his schooling temporarily robbed him of his Hispanic heritage. The title character of Sophronia Liu's essay is a Chinese boy, a sacrifice, really, to his parents' aspirations-through-schooling. Norman Cousins says that he was miseducated: school taught him to look for differences rather than similarities between people.

Is a person educated who knows only his or her own culture as it is at that moment? Anyone who knows the *history* of his or her own culture expects change. But at what price? By what vehicle? Even to look at our own language or art or religion or social institutions a century or two ago is like a trip to another country.

PERSPECTIVES

During formal education, the child learns that life is for testing. This state lasts twelve years, a period during which the child learns that success comes from telling testers what they want to hear.

Russell Baker

Education is not a product: mark, diploma, job, money —in that order: it is a process, a never-ending one.

Bel Kaufman

The expression "a liberal education" originally meant one worthy of freemen. Such is education simply in a true and broad sense. But education ordinarily so called—the learning of trades and professions which is designed to enable men to earn their living, or to fit them for a particular station in life—is servile.

Henry David Thoreau

Education! Which of the various me's do you propose to educate, and which do you propose to suppress?

D. H. Lawrence

Knowledge without special capacity to teach is not the same as knowledge and capacity.

A Sufi Tale

A child cannot be taught by anyone who despises him, and a child cannot afford to be fooled.

James Baldwin

Education is hanging around until you've caught on.

Robert Frost

America's a hard school, I know, but hard schools make excellent graduates.

Oriana Fallaci

By doubting we are led to enquire: By enquiry we perceive the truth.

Abelard

If the word has the potency to revive and make us free, it has also the power to blind, imprison and destroy.

Ralph Ellison

I have always come to life after coming to books.

Jorge Luis Borges

Power is the ability to take one's place in whatever discourse is essential to action and the right to have one's part matter.

Carolyn Heilbrun

. . . That is what learning is. You suddenly understand something you've understood all your life, but in a new way.

Doris Lessing

Knowledge is power.

Francis Bacon

The mind is an enchanting thing.

Marianne Moore

Applications

1. Write a journal entry comparing these perspectives on education with yours.
2. In your group, discuss Baldwin's implied philosophy of education. Write a brief summary of the discussion.

The Creation of the Crow World

Crow Legend

The Crows, who were one of the most powerful tribes in Montana, are members of the second largest Indian language group north of Mexico (the Siouan; the largest is the Algonquian). They lived along the Yellowstone River and its tributaries and hunted across the plains and into the Rocky Mountains. Their reservation is in Montana near Billings. The name Crow *is thought to be a mistranslation of their name for themselves,* Apsaruke.

From the several versions of the Crow creation myth that have been recorded, this one has been selected because it is the most revealing of the material culture of the tribe and because it has less similarity with creation myths of other tribes. "The people of the old times referred to the Sun as the Old Man; he was the Supreme Being," wrote Lowie. Old Man was "identical with Old Man Coyote."

LONG BEFORE there was any land and before there was any living thing except four little ducks, the Creator, whom we call Old Man, came and said to the ducks, "Which one of you is brave?"

"I am the bravest," replied one duck.

"Dive into the water," Old Man said to the duck, "and get some dirt from the bottom. I will see what I can do with it."

The brave duck went down and was gone a long time. It came up again carrying on its beak some dirt that it gave to Old Man. He held it in his hand until it became dry. Then he blew the dirt in all directions and thus made the land and the mountains and the rivers.

Old Man, who was all-powerful, was asked by the ducks to make other living things. So he took more dirt in his hand and, after it had dried, he blew it off. And there stood a man and a woman, the first Crow Indians. Old Man explained to them how to increase their number. At first they were blind; when their eyes were opened and they saw their nakedness, they asked for something with which to clothe themselves.

So that they might have food and clothing, Old Man took the rest of the dirt brought up by Duck and made animals and plants. Then he killed one of the buffalo he had made, broke a rock, and with one of the pieces cut up the animal. Then he explained its parts and told the man and woman how to use them.

"To carry water," he said, "take the pouch from the inside of the buffalo and make a bucket. Make drinking cups from its horns and also from the horns of the mountain sheep. Use the best pieces of buffalo for food. When you have had enough to eat, make a robe from the hide."

Then he showed the woman how to dress the skin. He showed the man how to make arrowheads, axes, knives, and cooking vessels from hard stone. "To make a fire," said Old Man, "take two sticks and place a little sand on one of them and also some of the driest buffalo chips. Then take the other stick and roll it between your hands until fire comes."

Old Man told them to take a large stone and fasten to it a handle made from hide. "With it you can break animal bones to get the marrow for making soup," he said to the woman. He also showed her how to scrape skins with a bone from the foreleg of an animal, to remove the hair.

At first, Old Man gave the man and woman no horses; they had only dogs for carrying their things. Later he told them how to get horses. "When you go over that hill there, do not look back, no matter what you hear." For three days they walked without looking back, but on the third day they heard animals coming behind them. They turned around and saw horses, but the horses vanished.

Old Man told them how to build a sweat lodge and also explained its purpose. And he told the man how to get dreams and visions. "Go up in the mountains," he said, "cut a piece of flesh from yourself, and give it to me. Do not eat while you are there. Then you will have visions that will tell you what to do.

"This land is the best of the lands I have made," Old Man said to them. "Upon it you will find everything you need—pure water, vegetation, timber, game animals. I have put you in the center of it, and I have put people around you as your enemies. If I had made you in large numbers, you would be too powerful and would kill the other people I have created. You are few in number, but you are brave."

Interpretations

1. How important is Old Man's role as a teacher?

2. How apt are the Crows as students? What is the point of Old Man's lesson on how to get horses?

3. Old Man's last lesson is about the Crows' relations with other peoples—foreign affairs. How do you interpret this lesson? What does this lesson indicate about Old Man's nature, character, or qualities?

Correspondences

1. Compare "The Creation of the Crow World" with the creation stories in Chapter 1 and discuss the significance of differences in their emphases.

2. Review the Abelard perspective on education (page 194). What role does enquiry play in "The Creation of the Crow World"? In your educational experiences?

Applications

1. "The Creation of the Crow World" is part of the oral tradition of the Crow Indians. Consider the cultural functions of oral tradition. How might they shape the identity of the tribe as well as the individual? To what extent might they foster communal values? Freewrite about what you learned from a favorite childhood story.

2. Write your version of the creation story.

Kiss of Death

Armando Rendón

Armando Rendón (b. 1939) was raised in San Antonio, Texas, and is currently vice-president of ATM Systems, a Chicago counseling firm. He has written a film script, El Chicano in Washington, *and* Chicano Manifesto *(1971). He is a regular contributor to* Civil Rights Digest *and* The Washington Post. *In "Kiss of Death," Rendón presents his views on the importance of ethnic identity.*

For more information on Mexico, see Gary Soto, "Looking for Work," Chapter 4.

I NEARLY FELL VICTIM to the Anglo. My childhood was spent in the West Side barrio of San Antonio. I lived in my grandmother's house on Ruiz Street just below Zarzamora Creek. I did well in the elementary grades and learned English quickly.

Spanish was off-limits in school anyway, and teachers and relatives taught me early that my mother tongue would be of no help in making good grades and becoming a success. Yet Spanish was the language I used in playing and arguing with friends. Spanish was the language I spoke with my *abuelita,* my dear grandmother, as I ate *atole* on those cold mornings when I used to wake at dawn to her clattering dishes in the tiny kitchen; or when I would cringe in mock horror at old folk tales she would tell me late at night.

But the lesson took effect anyway. When, at the age of ten, I went with my mother to California, to the San Francisco Bay Area where she found work during the war years, I had my first real opportunity to strip myself completely of my heritage. In California the schools I attended were all Anglo except for this little mexicanito. At least, I never knew anyone who admitted he was Mexican and I certainly never thought to ask. When my name was accented incorrectly, Rendon instead of Rendón, that was all right; finally I must have gotten tired of correcting people or just didn't bother.

I remember a summertime visit home a few years after living on the West Coast. At an evening gathering of almost the whole family—uncles, aunts, nephews, nieces, my *abuelita*—we sat outdoors through the dusk until the dark had fully settled. Then the lights were turned on; someone brought out a Mexican card game, the Lotería El Diablito, similar to bingo. But instead of rows of numbers on a pasteboard, there were figures of persons, animals, and objects on cards corresponding to figures set in rows on a pasteboard. We used frijoles (pinto beans) to mark each figure on our card as the leader went through the deck one by one. The word for tree was called: *Arbol!* It completed a row; I had won. Then to check my card I had to name each figure again. When I said the word for tree, it didn't come at all as I wanted it to; AR-BOWL with the accent on the last syllable and sounding like an Anglo tourist. There was some all-around kidding of me and good-natured laughter over the incident, and it passed.

But if I had not been speaking much Spanish up until then, I spoke even less afterward. Even when my mother, who speaks both Spanish and English fluently, spoke to me in Spanish, I would respond in English. By the time I graduated from high school and prepared to enter college, the break was nearly complete. Seldom during college did I admit to being a Mexican-American. Only when Latin American students pressed me about my surname did I admit my Spanish descent, or when it proved an asset in meeting coeds from Latin American countries.

My ancestry had become a shadow, fainter and fainter about me. I felt no particular allegiance to it, drew no inspiration from it, and elected generally to let it fade away. I clicked with the Anglo mind-set in college, mastered it, you might say. I even became editor of the campus biweekly newspaper as a junior, and editor of the literary magazine as a senior—not bad, now that I look back, for a tortillas-and-beans Chicano upbringing to beat the Anglo at his own game.

The point of my "success," of course, was that I had been assimilated; I had bought the white man's world. After getting my diploma I was set to launch out into a career in newspaper reporting and writing. There was no thought in my mind of serving my people, telling their story, or making anything right for anybody but myself. Instead I had dreams of Pulitzer Prizes, syndicated columns, foreign correspondent assignments, front-page stories—that was for me. Then something happened.

A Catholic weekly newspaper in Sacramento offered me a position as a reporter and feature writer. I had a job on a Bay Area daily as a copyboy at the time, with the opportunity to become a reporter. But I'd just been married, and there were a number of other reasons to consider: there'd be a variety of assignments, Sacramento was the state capital, it was a good town in which to raise a family, and the other job lacked promise for upward mobility. I decided to take the offer.

My wife and I moved to Sacramento in the fall of 1961, and in a few weeks the radicalization of this Chicano began. It wasn't a book I read or a great leader awakening me, for we had no Chávezes or Tijerinas or Gonzálezes at the time; and it was no revelation from above. It was my own people who rescued me. There is a large Chicano population in Sacramento, today one of the most activist in northern California, but at the time factionalized and still dependent on the social and church organizations for identity. But together we found each other.

My job soon brought me into contact with many Chicanos as well as with the recently immigrated Mexicans, located in the barrios that Sacramento had allocated to the "Mexicans." I found my people striving to survive in an alien environment among foreign people. One of the stories I covered concerned a phenomenon called Cursillos de Cristiandad (Little Courses in Christianity), intense, three-day group-sensitivity sessions whose chief objective is the re-Christianization of Catholics. To cover the story properly I talked my editor into letting me make a Cursillo.

Not only was much revealed to me about the phony gilt lining of religion which I had grown up believing was the Church, but there was an added and highly significant side effect—cultural shock! I rediscovered my own people, or perhaps they redeemed me. Within the social dimension of the Cursillo, for the first time in many years I became reimmersed in a tough, *macho ambiente* (an entirely Mexican male environment). Only Spanish was spoken. The effect was shattering. It was as if my tongue, after being struck dumb as a child, had been loosened.

Because we were located in cramped quarters, with limited facilities, and the cooks, lecturers, priests, and participants were men only, the old sense of *machismo* and *camarada* was revived and given new perspective. I was cast in a spiritual setting which was a perfect background for reviving my Chicano soul. Reborn but imperfectly, I still had a lot to learn about myself and my people. But my understanding deepened and renewed itself as the years went by. I visited bracero camps with teams of Chicanos; sometimes with priests taking the sacraments; sometimes only Chicanos, offering advice or assistance with badly needed food and clothing, distributed through a bingo-game technique; and on occasion, music for group singing provided by a phonograph or a guitar. Then there were barrio organization work; migrant worker programs; a rural self-help community development project; and confrontation with anti-poverty agencies, with the churches, with government officials, and with cautious Chicanos, too.

In a little San Francisco magazine called *Way,* I wrote in a March 1966 article discussing "The Other Mexican-American":

> The Mexican-American must answer at the same time: Who am I? and Who are we? This is to pose then, not merely a dilemma of self-identity; but of self-in-group-identity. . . . Perhaps the answer to developing a total Mexican-American concept must be left in the hands of the artist, the painter, the writer, and the poet, who can abstract the essence of what it is to be Mexican in America. . . . When that understanding comes . . . the Mexican-

American will not only have acculturized himself, but he will have acculturized America to him.

If anyone knew what he was talking about when he spoke of the dilemma of who he was and where he belonged, it was this Chicano. I very nearly dropped out, as so many other Mexican-Americans have, under the dragging pressure to be someone else, what most of society wants you to be before it hands out its chrome-plated trophies.

And that mystique—I didn't quite have it at the time, or the right word for it. But no one did until just the last few years when so many of us stopped trying to be someone else and decided that what we want to be and to be called is Chicano.

I owe my life to my Chicano people. They rescued me from the Anglo kiss of death, the monolingual, monocultural, and colorless Gringo society. I no longer face a dilemma of identity or direction. That identity and direction have been charted for me by the Chicano—but to think I came that close to being sucked into the vacuum of the dominant society.

Interpretations

1. How does Rendón now regard his formal education? Do you think school would still have this effect today?

2. What did Rendón feel he still had to learn about his people? What evidence do you see in this essay that Rendón now has a clear understanding of Chicano culture?

3. What does the phrase "Anglo kiss of death" mean to Rendón? Do you think being Chicano means more to Rendón than ancestry, family, education, or culture? If so, what else does it mean?

4. "Monolingual, monocultural, and colorless" are three criticisms of Anglo society. How valid are these criticisms? Instead of becoming bicultural himself, Rendón says he rejected one culture and embraced another as if his life depended on it. Do you think he made the right choice? Why did he have to choose?

5. Do you think it desirable or even possible to value cultures other than your own as much as your own? Why or why not?

6. What is the tone of this essay? Is it constructively or destructively critical? objective or subjective? Has Rendón chosen the best tone to appeal to his (obviously English-speaking) audience? Why or why not?

Correspondences

1. Review the D. H. Lawrence quotation on education (page 193). To what extent does it apply to Rendón's experience as a Mexican-American student in the San Francisco school system?

2. Rendón rediscovers his ethnic identity when he "became reimmersed in a tough, *macho ambiente* (an entirely Mexican male environment)." What new perspectives does he gain? How does his experience with a patriarchal culture compare with that of Kingston (Chapter 2)?

Applications

1. Rendón states, "The Mexican-American must answer at the same time: Who am I? and Who are we? This is to pose, then, not merely a dilemma of self-identity, but of self-in-group identity." In an essay, explore this concept further. Focus on both self- and self-in-group identity in equal detail.

2. To what degree should a teacher of students from multicultural backgrounds assume responsibility for making them aware of their cultures? How might a teacher try to accomplish this? Read two or three sources on this subject and prepare a presentation for your English or speech class.

Confessions of a Miseducated Man

Norman Cousins

Norman Cousins was born (1912) in New York City. After his graduation from Teachers College of Columbia University he began his career in journalism. In 1940 he became editor of Saturday Review, *and for the next 29 years he wrote on a wide range of cultural and educational issues. In 1979 he published* Anatomy of an Illness, *an account of his struggle against a degenerative disease, followed by* Human Options: An Autobiographical Notebook *(1981), and* The Healing Heart: Antidotes to Panic and Helplessness *(1983). In* Confessions of a Miseducated Man, *which appeared as an editorial on May 10, 1952, Cousins evaluates his educational experiences.*

THESE NOTES ARE in the nature of a confession. It is the confession of a miseducated man.

I have become most aware of my lack of a proper education whenever I have had the chance to put it to the test. The test is a simple one: am I prepared to live in and comprehend a world in which there are 3 billion people? Not the world as it was in 1850 or 1900, for which my education might have been adequate, but the world today. And the best place to apply that test is outside the country—especially Asia or Africa.

Not that my education was a complete failure. It prepared me' superbly for a bird's-eye view of the world. It taught me how to recognize easily and instantly the things that differentiate one place or one people from another. Geography had instructed me in differences of terrain, resources, and productivity. Comparative culture had instructed me in the differences of background and group interests. Anthropology had instructed me in the differences of facial bone structure, skin pigmentation, and general physical aspect. In short, my education protected me against surprise. I was not surprised at the fact that some people lived in mud huts and others in bamboo cottages on stilts; or that some used peat for fuel and others dung; or that some enjoyed music with a five-note scale and others with twelve; or that some people were vegetarian by religion and others by preference.

In those respects my education had been more than adequate. But what my education failed to do was to teach me that the principal

significance of such differences was that they were largely without significance. The differences were all but obliterated by the similarities. My
education had bypassed the similarities. It had failed to grasp and define
the fact that beyond the differences are realities scarcely comprehended
because of their shattering simplicity. And the simplest reality of all was
that the human community was one—greater than any of its parts, greater
than the separateness imposed by the nations, greater than the divergent
faiths and allegiances or the depth and color of varying cultures. This
larger unity was the most important central fact of our time—something
on which people could build at a time when hope seemed misty, almost
unreal.

As I write this, I have the feeling that my words fall to give vitality to
the idea they seek to express. Indeed, the idea itself is a truism which all
peoples readily acknowledge even if they do not act on it. Let me put it
differently, then. In order to be at home anywhere in the world I had to
forget the things I had been taught to remember. It turned out that my
ability to get along with other peoples depended not so much upon my
comprehension of the uniqueness of their way of life as upon my comprehension of the things we had in common. It was important to respect
these differences, certainly, but to stop there was like clearing the ground
without any idea of what was to be built on it. When you got through
comparing notes, you discovered that you were both talking about the
same neighborhood, i.e., this planet, and the conditions that made it
congenial or hostile to human habitation.

Only a few years ago an education in differences fulfilled a specific
if limited need. That was at a time when we thought of other places and
peoples largely out of curiosity or in terms of exotic vacations. It was the
mark of a rounded man to be well traveled and to know about the
fabulous variations of human culture and behavior. But it wasn't the type
of knowledge you had to live by and build on.

Then overnight came the great compression. Far-flung areas which
had been secure in their remoteness suddenly became jammed together
in a single arena. And all at once a new type of education became
necessary, an education in liberation from tribalism. For tribalism had
persisted from earliest times, though it had taken refined forms. The new
education had to teach man the most difficult lesson of all: to look at
someone anywhere in the world and be able to recognize the image of
himself. It had to be an education in self-recognition. The old emphasis
upon superficial differences had to give way to education for mutuality
and for citizenship in the human community.

In such an education we begin with the fact that the universe itself
does not hold life cheaply. Life is a rare occurrence among the millions
of galaxies and solar systems that occupy space. And in this particular
solar system life occurs on only one planet. And on that one planet life
takes millions of forms. Of all these countless forms of life, only one, the

human species, possesses certain faculties in combination that give it supreme advantages over all the others. Among those faculties or gifts is a creative intelligence that enables man to reflect and anticipate, to encompass past experience, and also to visualize future needs. There are endless other wondrous faculties the mechanisms of which are not yet within the understanding of their beneficiaries—the faculties of hope, conscience, appreciation of beauty, kinship, love, faith.

Viewed in planetary perspective, what counts is not that the thoughts of men lead them in different directions but that all men possess the capacity to think; not that they pursue different faiths but that they are capable of spiritual belief; not that they write and read different books but that they are capable of creating print and communicating in it across time and space; not that they enjoy different art and music but that something in them enables them to respond deeply to forms and colors and ordered vibrations of sounds.

These basic lessons, then, would seek to provide a proper respect for man in the universe. Next in order would be instruction in the unity of man's needs. However friendly the universe may be to man, it has left the conditions of human existence precariously balanced. All men need oxygen, water, land, warmth, food. Remove any one of these and the unity of human needs is attacked and man with it. The next lesson would concern the human situation itself—how to use self-understanding in the cause of human welfare; how to control the engines created by man that threaten to alter the precarious balance on which life depends; how to create a peaceful society of the whole.

With such an education, it is possible that some nation or people may come forward not only with vital understanding but with the vital inspiration that men need no less than food. Leadership on this higher level does not require mountains of gold or thundering propaganda. It is concerned with human destiny; human destiny is the issue; people will respond.

Interpretations

1. Cousins never says that we should be *un*aware of (or disrespectful of) differences between cultures and/or peoples, but that awareness of differences is only a first step. Do you agree? What is "miseducation"? Do you think the process of education necessarily increases awareness of differences in people and things? Support your answer with examples.

2. Look at several of the examples of diversity in the third paragraph. Do you agree that "such differences [are] largely without significance"? Why or why not? (How important is the word "largely" here?)

3. What changed Cousins's mind about his education?

4. Some academic subjects or disciplines emphasize similarities between people while others emphasize differences. Which subjects fall into which group?

5. How effective a title is "Confessions of a Miseducated Man"?

Correspondences

1. Cousins states that his formal education highlighted differences among cultures, whereas Rendón feels that his education white-washed differences and emphasized similarities. What factors led to these opposite conclusions? (Should an education focus only on what people have in common and ignore their differences? Do you feel as they do that you have been "miseducated"? If so, how?)

2. While Cousins argues that the goal of education should be "to create a peaceful society of the whole," Rendón supports stressing ethnic identification. Is it possible to be assimilated yet preserve ethnic identification? Why or why not?

Applications

1. "The old emphasis upon superficial differences had to give way to education for mutuality and for citizenship in the human community." Write an essay agreeing with Cousins's point of view; assume an unsympathetic audience.

2. Cousins seems glad that his education at least "protected [him] against surprise." Do you agree that such protection is a valuable function of education? Is it a side function or a main goal? (What does Cousins mean by "surprise"? How is it a handicap?)

from Poets in the Kitchen

Paule Marshall

Paule Marshall was born (1929) in Brooklyn, New York, of West Indian (Barbadian) parents. She received her bachelor's degree from Brooklyn College and in 1959 she published her first novel Brown Girl, Brownstones. *In 1961 she published* Soul Clap Hands and Sing *and in 1969* The Chosen Place, the Timeless People, *a symbolic novel about the refusal of inhabitants of a small, underdeveloped Caribbean country to accept modernization. Her most recent novel is* Daughters *(1991). Marshall defines her work as an attempt "to trace history, because as a people we have not as yet really engaged our past." To what extent does she explore that past in "Poets in the Kitchen"?*

The history of Barbados, the most easterly of the West Indies, begins with the arrival of an English ship in 1605 and with British settlers at the uninhabited island in 1627. Slavery was abolished in 1834. The island, eighty percent of whose population of 256,000 is of African descent, declared its independence from Britain in 1966 but remains within the Commonwealth.

SOME YEARS AGO, when I was teaching a graduate seminar in fiction at Columbia University, a well-known male novelist visited my class to speak on his development as a writer. In discussing his formative years, he didn't realize it but he seriously endangered his life by remarking that women writers are luckier than those of his sex because they usually spend so much time as children around their mothers and their mothers' friends in the kitchen.

What did he say that for? The women students immediately forgot about being in awe of him and began readying their attack for the question and answer period later on. Even I bristled. There again was that awful image of women locked away from the world in the kitchen with only each other to talk to, and their daughters locked in with them.

But my guest wasn't really being sexist or trying to be provocative or even spoiling for a fight. What he meant—when he got around to examining himself more fully—was that, given the way children are (or were) raised in our society, with little girls kept closer to home and their mothers, the woman writer stands a better chance of being exposed, while growing up, to the kind of talk that goes on among women, more often than not in the kitchen; and that this experience gives her an edge over her male counterpart by instilling in her an appreciation for ordinary speech.

It was clear that my guest lecturer attached great importance to this, which is understandable. Common speech and the plain, workaday words that make it up are, after all, the stock in trade of some of the best fiction writers. They are the principal means by which a character in a novel or story reveals himself and gives voice sometimes to profound feelings and complex ideas about himself and the world. Perhaps the proper measure of a writer's talent is his skill in rendering everyday speech—when it is appropriate to his story—as well as his ability to tap, to exploit, the beauty, poetry and wisdom it often contains.

"If you say what's on your mind in the language that comes to you from your parents and your street and friends you'll probably say something beautiful." Grace Paley[1] tells this, she says, to her students at the beginning of every writing course.

It's all a matter of exposure and a training of the ear for the would-be writer in those early years of his or her apprenticeship. And, according to my guest lecturer, this training, the best of it, often takes place in as unglamorous a setting as the kitchen.

He didn't know it, but he was essentially describing my experience as a little girl. I grew up among poets. Now they didn't look like poets— whatever that breed is supposed to look like. Nothing about them suggested that poetry was their calling. They were just a group of ordinary housewives and mothers, my mother included, who dressed in a way (shapeless housedresses, dowdy felt hats and long, dark, solemn coats) that made it impossible for me to imagine they had ever been young.

Nor did they do what poets were supposed to do—spend their days in an attic room writing verses. They never put pen to paper except to write occasionally to their relatives in Barbados. "I take my pen in hand hoping these few lines will find you in health as they leave me fair for the time being," was the way their letters invariably began. Rather, their day was spent "scrubbing floor," as they described the work they did.

Several mornings a week these unknown bards would put an apron and a pair of old house shoes in a shopping bag and take the train or streetcar from our section of Brooklyn out to Flatbush. There, those who didn't have steady jobs would wait on certain designated corners for the white housewives in the neighborhood to come along and bargain with them over pay for a day's work cleaning their houses. This was the ritual even in the winter.

Later, armed with the few dollars they had earned, which in their vocabulary became "a few raw-mouth pennies," they made their way back to our neighborhood, where they would sometimes stop off to have

[1]Contemporary American fiction writer.

a cup of tea or cocoa together before going home to cook dinner for their husbands and children.

The basement kitchen of the brownstone house where my family lived was the usual gathering place. Once inside the warm safety of its walls the women threw off the drab coats and hats, seated themselves at the large center table, drank their cups of tea or cocoa, and talked. While my sister and I sat at a smaller table over in a corner doing our homework, they talked—endlessly, passionately, poetically, and with impressive range. No subject was beyond them. True, they would indulge in the usual gossip: whose husband was running with whom, whose daughter looked slightly "in the way" (pregnant) under her bridal gown as she walked down the aisle. That sort of thing. But they also tackled the great issues of the time. They were always, for example, discussing the state of the economy. It was the mid and late 30s then, and the aftershock of the Depression, with its soup lines and suicides on Wall Street, was still being felt.

Some people, they declared, didn't know how to deal with adversity. They didn't know that you had to "tie up your belly" (hold in the pain, that is) when things got rough and go on with life. They took their image from the bellyband that is tied around the stomach of a newborn baby to keep the navel pressed in.

They talked politics. Roosevelt was their hero. He had come along and rescued the country with relief and jobs, and in gratitude they christened their sons Franklin and Delano and hoped they would live up to the names.

If F. D. R. was their hero, Marcus Garvey was their God. The name of the fiery, Jamaican-born black nationalist of the 20s was constantly invoked around the table. For he had been their leader when they first came to the United States from the West Indies shortly after World War I. They had contributed to his organization, the United Negro Improvement Association (UNIA), out of their meager salaries, bought shares in his ill-fated Black Star Shipping Line, and at the height of the movement they had marched as members of his "nurses' brigade" in their white uniforms on Seventh Avenue in Harlem during the great Garvey Day parades. Garvey: He lived on through the power of their memories.

And their talk was of war and rumors of wars. They raged against World War II when it broke out in Europe, blaming it on the politicians. "It's these politicians. They're the ones always starting up all this lot of war. But what they care? It's the poor people got to suffer and mothers with their sons." If it was *their* sons, they swore they would keep them out of the Army by giving them soap to eat each day to make their hearts sound defective. Hitler? He was for them "the devil incarnate."

Then there was home. They reminisced often and at length about home. The old country, Barbados—or Bimshire, as they affectionately called it. The little Caribbean island in the sun they loved but had to leave. "Poor—poor but sweet" was the way they remembered it.

And naturally they discussed their adopted home. America came in for both good and bad marks. They lashed out at it for the racism they encountered. They took to task some of the people they worked for, especially those who gave them only a hard-boiled egg and a few spoonfuls of cottage cheese for lunch. "As if anybody can scrub floor on an egg and some cheese that don't have no taste to it!"

Yet although they caught H in "this man country," as they called America, it was nonetheless a place where "you could at least see your way to make a dollar." That much they acknowledged. They might even one day accumulate enough dollars, with both them and their husbands working, to buy the brownstone houses which, like my family, they were only leasing at that period. This was their consuming ambition: to "buy house" and to see the children through.

There was no way for me to understand it at the time, but the talk that filled the kitchen those afternoons was highly functional. It served as therapy, the cheapest kind available to my mother and her friends. Not only did it help them recover from the long wait on the corner that morning and the bargaining over their labor, it restored them to a sense of themselves and reaffirmed their self-worth. Through language they were able to overcome the humiliations of the work-day.

But more than therapy, that freewheeling, wide-ranging, exuberant talk functioned as an outlet for the tremendous creative energy they possessed. They were women in whom the need for self-expression was strong, and since language was the only vehicle readily available to them they made of it an art form that—in keeping with the African tradition in which art and life are one—was an integral part of their lives.

And their talk was a refuge. They never really ceased being baffled and overwhelmed by America—its vastness, complexity and power. Its strange customs and laws. At a level beyond words they remained fearful and in awe. Their uneasiness and fear were even reflected in their attitude toward the children they had given birth to in this country. They referred to those like myself, the little Brooklyn-born Bajans (Barbadians), as "these New York children" and complained that they couldn't discipline us properly because of the laws here. "You can't beat these children as you would like, you know, because the authorities in this place will dash you in jail for them. After all, these is New York children." Not only were we different, American, we had, as they saw it, escaped their ultimate authority.

Confronted therefore by a world they could not encompass, which even limited their rights as parents, and at the same time finding themselves permanently separated from the world they had known, they took refuge in language. "Language is the only homeland," Czeslaw Milosz, the emigré Polish writer and Nobel Laureate, has said. This is what it became for the women at the kitchen table.

It served another purpose also, I suspect. My mother and her friends were after all the female counterpart of Ralph Ellison's invisible man.[2] Indeed, you might say they suffered a triple invisibility, being black, female and foreigners. They really didn't count in American society except as a source of cheap labor. But given the kind of women they were, they couldn't tolerate the fact of their invisibility, their powerlessness. And they fought back, using the only weapon at their command: the spoken word.

Those late afternoon conversations on a wide range of topics were a way for them to feel they exercised some measure of control over their lives and the events that shaped them. "Soully-gal, talk yuh talk!" they were always exhorting each other. "In this man world you got to take yuh mouth and make a gun!" They were in control, if only verbally and if only for the two hours or so that they remained in our house.

For me, sitting over in the corner, being seen but not heard, which was the rule for children in those days, it wasn't only what the women talked about—the content—but the way they put things—their style. The insight, irony, wit, and humor they brought to their stories and discussions and their poet's inventiveness and daring with language—which of course I could only sense but not define back then.

They had taken the standard English taught them in the primary schools of Barbados and transformed it into an idiom, an instrument that more adequately described them—changing around the syntax and imposing their own rhythm and accent so that the sentences were more pleasing to their ears. They added the few African sounds and words that had survived, such as the derisive suck-teeth sound and the word "yam," meaning to eat. And to make it more vivid, more in keeping with their expressive quality, they brought to bear a raft of metaphors, parables, Biblical quotations, sayings and the like:

"The sea ain' got no back door," they would say, meaning that it wasn't like a house where if there was a fire you could run out the back. Meaning that it was not to be trifled with. And meaning perhaps in a larger sense that man should treat all of nature with caution and respect.

"I has read hell by heart and called every generation blessed!" They sometimes went in for hyperbole.

A woman expecting a baby was never said to be pregnant. They never used that word. Rather, she was "in the way" or, better yet, "tumbling big." "Guess who I butt up on in the market the other day tumbling big again!"

And a woman with a reputation of being too free with her sexual favors was known in their book as a "thoroughfare"—the sense of men like a steady stream of cars moving up and down the road of her life. Or

[2]Title of novel published in 1947 which has become the seminal metaphor for African-Americans.

she might be dubbed "a free-bee," which was my favorite of the two. I liked the image it conjured up of a woman scandalous perhaps but independent, who flitted from one flower to another in a garden of male beauties, sampling their nectar, taking her pleasure at will, the roles reversed.

And nothing, no matter how beautiful, was ever described as simply beautiful. It was always "beautiful-ugly": the beautiful-ugly dress, the beautiful-ugly house, the beautiful-ugly car. Why the word "ugly," I used to wonder, when the thing they were referring to was beautiful, and they knew it. Why the antonym, the contradiction, the linking of opposites? It used to puzzle me greatly as a child.

There is the theory in linguistics which states that the idiom of a people, the way they use language, reflects not only the most fundamental views they hold of themselves and the world but their very conception of reality. Perhaps in using the term "beautiful-ugly" to describe nearly everything, my mother and her friends were expressing what they believed to be a fundamental dualism in life: the idea that a thing is at the same time its opposite, and that these opposites, these contradictions make up the whole. But theirs was not a Manichaean brand of dualism[3] that sees matter, flesh, the body, as inherently evil, because they constantly addressed each other as "soully-gal"— soul: spirit; gal: the body, flesh, the visible self. And it was clear from their tone that they gave one as much weight and importance as the other. They had never heard of the mind/body split.

As for God, they summed up His essential attitude in a phrase, "God," they would say, "don' love ugly and He ain' stuck on pretty."

Using everyday speech, the simple commonplace words—but always with imagination and skill—they gave voice to the most complex ideas. Flannery O'Connor[4] would have approved of how they made ordinary language work, as she put it, "double-time," stretching, shading, deepening its meaning. Like Joseph Conrad[5] they were always trying to infuse new life in the "old old words worn thin . . . by . . . careless usage." And the goals of their oral art were the same as his: "to make you hear, to make you feel . . . to make you *see*." This was their guiding esthetic.

By the time I was 8 or 9, I graduated from the corner of the kitchen to the neighborhood library, and thus from the spoken to the written word. The Macon Street Branch of the Brooklyn Public Library was an imposing half block long edifice of heavy gray masonry, with glass-paneled doors at the front and two tall metal torches symbolizing the light that comes of learning flanking the wide steps outside.

---

[3]Religious sect founded in 276 A.D. in Persia, which teaches the release of the spirit from matter through asceticism.

[4]Flannery O'Connor (1925–1964) American writer.

[5]Joseph Conrad (1857–1924) British fiction writer.

The inside was just as impressive. More steps—of pale marble with gleaming brass railings at the center and sides—led up to the circulation desk, and a great pendulum clock gazed down from the balcony stacks that faced the entrance. Usually stationed at the top of the steps like the guards outside Buckingham Palace was the custodian, a stern-faced West Indian type who for years, until I was old enough to obtain an adult card, would immediately shoo me with one hand into the Children's Room and with the other threaten me into silence, a finger to his lips. You would have thought he was the chief librarian and not just someone whose job it was to keep the brass polished and the clock wound. I put him in a story called "Barbados" years later and had terrible things happen to him at the end.

I was sheltered from the storm of adolescence in the Macon Street library, reading voraciously, indiscriminately, everything from Jane Austen to Zane Grey, but with a special passion for the long, full-blown, richly detailed 18th- and 19th-century picaresque tales: *Tom Jones, Great Expectations, Vanity Fair.*

But although I loved nearly everything I read and would enter fully into the lives of the characters—indeed, would cease being myself and become them—I sensed a lack after a time. Something I couldn't quite define was missing. And then one day, browsing in the poetry section, I came across a book by someone called Paul Laurence Dunbar, and opening it I found the photograph of a wistful, sad-eyed poet who to my surprise was black. I turned to a poem at random. "Little brown-baby wif spa'klin'/eyes/Come to yo' pappy an set on his knee." Although I had a little difficulty at first with the words in dialect, the poem spoke to me as nothing I had read before of the closeness, the special relationship I had had with my father, who by then had become an ardent believer in Father Divine and gone to live in Father's "kingdom" in Harlem. Reading it helped to ease somewhat the tight knot of sorrow and longing I carried around in my chest that refused to go away. I read another poem, "Lias! Lias! Bless de Lawd!/Don' you know de day's/erbroad?/Ef you don' get up, you scamp/Dey'll be trouble in dis camp." I laughed. It reminded me of the way my mother sometimes yelled at my sister and me to get out of bed in the mornings.

And another: "Seen my lady home las' night/Jump back, honey, jump back./Hel'/huh han'/an'/sque'z it tight . . ." About love between a black man and a black woman. I had never seen that written about before and it roused in me all kinds of delicious feelings and hopes.

And I began to search then for books and stories and poems about "The Race" (as it was put back then), about my people. While not abandoning Thackeray, Fielding, Dickens and the others, I started asking the reference librarian, who was white, for books by Negro writers, although I must admit I did so at first with a feeling of shame—the shame I and many others used to experience in those days whenever the word "Negro" or "colored" came up.

No grade school literature teacher of mine had ever mentioned Dunbar or James Weldon Johnson or Langston Hughes.[6] I didn't know that Zora Neale Hurston[7] existed and was busy writing and being published during those years. Nor was I made aware of people like Frederick Douglass and Harriet Tubman[8]—their spirit and example—or the great 19th-century abolitionist and feminist Sojourner Truth. There wasn't even Negro History Week when I attended P.S. 35 on Decatur Street!

What I needed, what all the kids—West Indian and native black American alike—with whom I grew up needed, was an equivalent of the Jewish shul, someplace where we could go after school—the schools that were shortchanging us—and read works by those like ourselves and learn about our history.

It was around that time also that I began harboring the dangerous thought of someday trying to write myself. Perhaps a poem about an apple tree, although I had never seen one. Or the story of a girl who could magically transplant herself to wherever she wanted to be in the world—such as Father Divine's kingdom in Harlem. Dunbar—his dark, eloquent face, his large volume of poems—permitted me to dream that I might someday write, and with something of the power with words my mother and her friends possessed.

When people at readings and writers' conferences ask me who my major influences were, they are sometimes a little disappointed when I don't immediately name the usual literary giants. True, I am indebted to those writers, white and black, whom I read during my formative years and still read for instruction and pleasure. But they were preceded in my life by another set of giants whom I always acknowledge before all others: the group of women around the table long ago. They taught me my first lesson in the narrative art. They trained my ear. They set a standard of excellence. This is why the best of my work must be attributed to them; it stands as testimony to the rich legacy of language and culture they so freely passed on to me in the wordshop of the kitchen.

Interpretations

1. What does their choice of such subjects as politics reveal about these women's interests and needs? Why were their conversations so crucial to their survival?

---

[6]Paul Laurence Dunbar (1870–1906), James Weldon Johnson (1871–1938), Langston Hughes (1902–1967)—African-American poets of the Harlem Renaissance.

[7]Zora Neale Hurston (1901–1961)—African-American novelist.

[8]"Frederick Douglass (1817–1895), Harriet Tubman (1820–1913)—African-American abolitionists.

2. Were these "poets of the kitchen" as interesting on paper as in their conversation? Why? What does Marshall think their use of English shows about them? What do you think is the best example of this quality?

3. Marshall—and the "well-known male novelist" who visited her classroom, as well as Grace Paley, another well-known fiction writer—say that the most important language for a novelist is "everyday speech," the language of "your parents and your street and friends." Do you agree? Do you think beginning writers are inclined to resist this lesson? Are they contemptuous of using everyday speech in their stories and novels? Why?

Correspondences

1. To what extent do Paule Marshall and Armando Rendón both discover that "language is the only homeland"?

2. Marshall writes, "what I needed, what all kids—West Indian and native black American alike—with whom I grew up needed, was an equivalent of the Jewish shul, someplace where we could go after school—the schools that were shortchanging us—and read works by those like ourselves and learn about our history." How might this also apply to Rendón? Should their educational systems have taught them about their own heritage? Why or why not? What has your education taught you about your cultural heritage?

Applications

1. "In this man world you got to take yuh mouth and make a gun" and "The sea ain' got no back door" are sayings the author heard as a child. Are there proverbs which you heard frequently as you were growing up? Write an essay about two or three proverbs or folk expressions. Demonstrate clearly, as does Marshall, the effects of such sayings on your educational development.

2. Marshall's "unknown bards" used language to combat their sense of powerlessness in a culture in which they experienced the "triple invisibility of being black, female and foreigners." Which expressions best reflect this? Are there other situations in which language might be a source of empowerment? Cite examples.

Discovering Books

Richard Wright

Richard Wright (1906–1960) was born on a plantation near Natchez, Mississippi. He had little formal education and dropped out of school at fifteen. He then moved to Chicago and worked in the post office. In the 1930s he began writing fiction. His first collection of short stories, Uncle Tom's Children *(1938), won the annual award of* Story *magazine. His* Native Son *(1940) was the first novel by an African-American writer to enter the mainstream of American literature. The following selection is from* Black Boy, *an autobiographical account of Wright's Southern childhood.*

ONE MORNING I arrived early at work and went into the bank lobby where the Negro porter was mopping. I stood at a counter and picked up the Memphis *Commercial Appeal* and began my free reading of the press. I came finally to the editorial page and saw an article dealing with one H. L. Mencken. I knew by hearsay that he was the editor of the *American Mercury,* but aside from that I knew nothing about him. The article was a furious denunciation of Mencken, concluding with one, hot, short sentence: Mencken is a fool.

I wondered what on earth this Mencken had done to call down upon him the scorn of the South. The only people I had ever heard denounced in the South were Negroes, and this man was not a Negro. Then what ideas did Mencken hold that made a newspaper like the *Commercial Appeal* castigate him publicly? Undoubtedly he must be advocating ideas that the South did not like. Were there, then, people other than Negroes who criticized the South? I knew that during the Civil War the South had hated northern whites, but I had not encountered such hate during my life. Knowing no more of Mencken than I did at that moment, I felt a vague sympathy for him. Had not the South, which had assigned me the role of a nonman, cast at him its hardest words?

Now, how could I find out about this Mencken? There was a huge library near the riverfront, but I knew that Negroes were not allowed to patronize its shelves any more than they were the parks and playgrounds of the city. I had gone into the library several times to get books for the white men on the job. Which of them would now help me to get books? And how could I read them without causing concern to the white men with whom I worked? I had so far been successful in hiding my thoughts and feelings from them, but I knew that I would create hostility if I went about this business of reading in a clumsy way.

I weighed the personalities of the men on the job. There was Don, a Jew; but I distrusted him. His position was not much better than mine and I knew that he was uneasy and insecure; he had always treated me in an offhand, bantering way that barely concealed his contempt. I was afraid to ask him to help me to get books; his frantic desire to demonstrate a racial solidarity with the whites against Negroes might make him betray me.

Then how about the boss? No, he was a Baptist and I had the suspicion that he would not be quite able to comprehend why a black boy would want to read Mencken. There were other white men on the job whose attitudes showed clearly that they were Kluxers or sympathizers, and they were out of the question.

There remained only one man whose attitude did not fit into an anti-Negro category, for I had heard the white men refer to him as a "Pope lover." He was an Irish Catholic and was hated by the white Southerners. I knew that he read books, because I had got him volumes from the library several times. Since he, too, was an object of hatred, I felt that he might refuse me but would hardly betray me. I hesitated, weighing and balancing the imponderable realities.

One morning I paused before the Catholic fellow's desk.

"I want to ask you a favor," I whispered to him.

"What is it?"

"I want to read. I can't get books from the library. I wonder if you'd let me use your card?"

He looked at me suspiciously.

"My card is full most of the time," he said.

"I see," I said and waited, posing my question silently.

"You're not trying to get me into trouble, are you, boy?" he asked, staring at me.

"Oh, no, sir."

"What book do you want?"

"A book by H. L. Mencken."

"Which one?"

"I don't know. Has he written more than one?"

"He has written several."

"I didn't know that."

"What makes you want to read Mencken?"

"Oh, I just saw his name in the newspaper," I said.

"It's good of you to want to read," he said. "But you ought to read the right things."

I said nothing. Would he want to supervise my reading?

"Let me think," he said. "I'll figure out something."

I turned from him and he called me back. He stared at me quizzically.

"Richard, don't mention this to the other white men," he said.

"I understand," I said. "I won't say a word."

A few days later he called me to him.

"I've got a card in my wife's name," he said. "Here's mine."

"Thank you, sir."

"Do you think you can manage it?"

"I'll manage fine," I said.

"If they suspect you, you'll get in trouble," he said.

"I'll write the same kind of notes to the library that you wrote when you sent me for books," I told him. "I'll sign your name."

He laughed.

"Go ahead. Let me see what you get," he said.

That afternoon I addressed myself to forging a note. Now, what were the names of books written by H. L. Mencken? I did not know any of them. I finally wrote what I thought would be a foolproof note: *Dear Madam: Will you please let this nigger boy*—I used the word "nigger" to make the librarian feel that I could not possibly be the author of the note—*have some books by H. L. Mencken?* I forged the white man's name.

I entered the library as I had always done when on errands for whites, but I felt that I would somehow slip up and betray myself. I doffed my hat, stood a respectful distance from the desk, looked as unbookish as possible, and waited for the white patrons to be taken care of. When the desk was clear of people, I still waited. The white librarian looked at me.

"What do you want, boy?"

As though I did not possess the power of speech, I stepped forward and simply handed her the forged note, not parting my lips.

"What books by Mencken does he want?" she asked.

"I don't know, ma'am," I said, avoiding her eyes.

"Who gave you this card?"

"Mr. Falk," I said.

"Where is he?"

"He's at work, at the M—— Optical Company," I said. "I've been in here for him before."

"I remember," the woman said. "But he never wrote notes like this."

Oh, God, she's suspicious. Perhaps she would not let me have the books? If she had turned her back at that moment, I would have ducked out the door and never gone back. Then I thought of a bold idea.

"You can call him up, ma'am," I said, my heart pounding.

"You're not using these books, are you?" she asked pointedly.

"Oh, no, ma'am. I can't read."

"I don't know what he wants by Mencken," she said under her breath.

I knew now that I had won; she was thinking of other things and the race question had gone out of her mind. She went to the shelves. Once or twice she looked over her shoulder at me, as though she was still doubtful. Finally she came forward with two books in her hand.

"I'm sending him two books," she said. "But tell Mr. Falk to come in next time, or send me the names of the books he wants. I don't know what he wants to read."

I said nothing. She stamped the card and handed me the books. Not daring to glance at them, I went out of the library, fearing that the woman would call me back for further questioning. A block away from the library I opened one of the books and read a title: *A Book of Prefaces*. I was nearing my nineteenth birthday and I did not know how to pronounce the word *preface*. I thumbed the pages and saw strange words and strange names. I shook my head, disappointed. I looked at the other book; it was called *Prejudices*. I knew what that word meant; I had heard it all my life. And right off I was on guard against Mencken's books. Why would a man want to call a book *Prejudices?* The word was so stained with all my memories of racial hate that I could not conceive of anybody using it for a title. Perhaps I had made a mistake about Mencken? A man who had prejudices must be wrong.

When I showed the books to Mr. Falk, he looked at me and frowned.

"That librarian might telephone you," I warned him.

"That's all right," he said. "But when you're through reading those books, I want you to tell me what you get out of them."

That night in my rented room, while letting the hot water run over my can of pork and beans in the sink, I opened *A Book of Prefaces* and began to read. I was jarred and shocked by the style, the clear, clean, sweeping sentences. Why did he write like that? And how did one write like that? I pictured the man as a raging demon, slashing with his pen, consumed with hate, denouncing everything American, extolling everything European or German, laughing at the weaknesses of people, mocking God, authority. What was this? I stood up, trying to realize what reality lay behind the meaning of the words. . . . Yes, this man was fighting, fighting with words. He was using words as a weapon, using them as one would use a club. Could words be weapons? Well, yes, for here they were. Then, maybe, perhaps, I could use them as a weapon? No. It frightened me. I read on and what amazed me was not what he said, but how on earth anybody had the courage to say it.

Occasionally I glanced up to reassure myself that I was alone in the room. Who were these men about whom Mencken was talking so passionately? Who was Anatole France? Joseph Conrad? Sinclair Lewis, Sherwood Anderson, Dostoevski, George Moore, Gustave Flaubert, Maupassant, Tolstoy, Frank Harris, Mark Twain, Thomas Hardy, Arnold Bennett, Stephen Crane, Zola, Norris, Gorky, Bergson, Ibsen, Balzac, Bernard Shaw, Dumas, Poe, Thomas Mann, O. Henry, Dreiser, H. G. Wells, Gogol, T. S. Eliot, Gide, Baudelaire, Edgar Lee Masters, Stendhal, Turgenev, Huneker, Nietzsche, and scores of others? Were these men real? Did they exist or had they existed? And how did one pronounce their names?

I ran across many words whose meanings I did not know, and I either looked them up in a dictionary or, before I had a chance to do that, encountered the word in a context that made its meaning clear. But what strange world was this? I concluded the book with the conviction that I had somehow overlooked something terribly important in life. I had once tried to write, had once reveled in feeling, had let my crude imagination roam, but the impulse to dream had been slowly beaten out of me by experience. Now it surged up again and I hungered for books, new ways of looking and seeing. It was not a matter of believing or disbelieving what I read, but of feeling something new, of being affected by something that made the look of the world different.

As dawn broke I ate my pork and beans, feeling dopey, sleepy. I went to work, but the mood of the book would not die; it lingered, coloring everything I saw, heard, did. I now felt that I knew what the white men were feeling. Merely because I had read a book that had spoken of how they lived and thought, I identified myself with that book. I felt vaguely guilty. Would I, filled with bookish notions, act in a manner that would make the whites dislike me?

I forged more notes and my trips to the library became more frequent. Reading grew into a passion. My first serious novel was Sinclair Lewis's *Main Street*. It made me see my boss, Mr. Gerald, and identify him as an American type. I would smile when I saw him lugging his golf bags into the office. I had always felt a vast distance separating me from the boss, and now I felt closer to him, though still distant. I felt now that I knew him, that I could feel the very limits of his narrow life. And this had happened because I had read a novel about a mythical man called George F. Babbitt.

The plots and stories in the novels did not interest me so much as the point of view revealed. I gave myself over to each novel without reserve, without trying to criticize it; it was enough for me to see and feel something different. And for me, everything was something different. Reading was like a drug, a dope. The novels created moods in which I lived for days. But I could not conquer my sense of guilt, my feeling that the white men around me knew that I was changing, that I had begun to regard them differently.

Whenever I brought a book to the job, I wrapped it in newspaper—a habit that was to persist for years in other cities and under other circumstances. But some of the white men pried into my packages when I was absent and they questioned me.

"Boy, what are you reading those books for?"

"Oh, I don't know, sir,"

"That's deep stuff you're reading, boy."

"I'm just killing time, sir."

"You'll addle your brains if you don't watch out."

I read Dreiser's *Jennie Gerhardt* and *Sister Carrie* and they revived in me a vivid sense of my mother's suffering; I was overwhelmed, I grew silent, wondering about the life around me. It would have been impossible for me to have told anyone what I derived from these novels, for it was nothing less than a sense of life itself. All my life had shaped me for the realism, the naturalism of the modern novel, and I could not read enough of them.

Steeped in new moods and ideas, I bought a ream of paper and tried to write; but nothing would come, or what did come was flat beyond telling. I discovered that more than desire and feeling were necessary to write and I dropped the idea. Yet I still wondered how it was possible to know people sufficiently to write about them? Could I ever learn about life and people? To me, with my vast ignorance, my Jim Crow* station in life, it seemed a task impossible of achievement. I now knew what being a Negro meant. I could endure the hunger. I had learned to live with hate. But to feel that there were feelings denied me, that the very breath of life itself was beyond my reach, that more than anything else hurt, wounded me. I had a new hunger.

In buoying me up, reading also cast me down, made me see what was possible, what I had missed. My tension returned, new, terrible, bitter, surging, almost too great to be contained. I no longer felt that the world about me was hostile, killing; I *knew* it. A million times I asked myself what I could do to save myself, and there were no answers. I seemed forever condemned, ringed by walls.

I did not discuss my reading with Mr. Falk, who had lent me his library card; it would have meant talking about myself and that would have been too painful. I smiled each day, fighting desperately to maintain my old behavior, to keep my disposition seemingly sunny. But some of the white men discerned that I had begun to brood.

"Wake up there, boy!" Mr. Olin said one day.

"Sir!" I answered for the lack of a better word.

"You act like you've stolen something," he said.

I laughed in the way I knew he expected me to laugh, but I resolved to be more conscious of myself, to watch my every act, to guard and hide the new knowledge that was dawning within me.

If I went north, would it be possible for me to build a new life then? But how could a man build a life upon vague, unformed yearnings? I wanted to write and I did not even know the English language. I bought English grammars and found them dull. I felt that I was getting a better sense of the language from novels than grammars. I read hard, discarding a writer as soon as I felt that I had grasped his

*Segregation and suppression of African-Americans in public places such as buses, restaurants, and educational institutions.

point of view. At night the printed page stood before my eyes in sleep.

Mrs. Moss, my landlady, asked me one Sunday morning:

"Son, what is this you keep on reading?"

"Oh, nothing. just novels."

"What you get out of 'em?"

"I'm just killing time," I said.

"I hope you know your own mind," she said in a tone which implied that she doubted if I had a mind.

I knew of no Negroes who read the books I liked and I wondered if any Negroes ever thought of them. I knew that there were Negro doctors, lawyers, newspapermen, but I never saw any of them. When I read a Negro newspaper I never caught the faintest echo of my preoccupation in its pages. I felt trapped and occasionally, for a few days, I would stop reading. But a vague hunger would come over me for books, books that opened up new avenues of feeling and seeing, and again I would forge another note to the white librarian. Again I would read and wonder as only the naive and unlettered can read and wonder, feeling that I carried a secret, criminal burden about with me each day.

That winter my mother and brother came and we set up house-keeping, buying furniture on the installment plan, being cheated and yet knowing no way to avoid it. I began to eat warm food and to my surprise found the regular meals enabled me to read faster. I may have lived through many illnesses and survived them, never suspecting that I was ill. My brother obtained a job and we began to save toward the trip north, plotting our time, setting tentative dates for departure. I told none of the white men on the job that I was planning to go north; I knew that the moment they felt I was thinking of the North they would change toward me. It would have made them feel that I did not like the life I was living, and because my life was completely conditioned by what they said or did, it would have been tantamount to challenging them.

I could calculate my chances for life in the South as a Negro fairly clearly now.

I could fight the southern whites by organizing with other Negroes, as my grandfather had done. But I knew that I could never win that way; there were many whites and there were but few blacks. They were strong and we were weak. Outright black rebellion could never win. If I fought openly I would die and I did not want to die. News of lynchings were frequent.

I could submit and live the life of a genial slave, but that was impossible. All of my life had shaped me to live by my own feelings and thoughts. I could make up to Bess and marry her and inherit the house. But that, too, would be the life of a slave; if I did that, I would crush to death something within me, and I would hate myself as much as I knew the whites already hated those who had submitted. Neither could I ever willingly present myself to be kicked, as Shorty had done. I would rather have died than do that.

I could drain off my restlessness by fighting with Shorty and Harrison. I had seen many Negroes solve the problem of being black by transferring their hatred of themselves to others with a black skin and fighting them. I would have to be cold to do that, and I was not cold and I could never be.

I could, of course, forget what I had read, thrust the whites out of my mind, forget them; and find release from anxiety and longing in sex and alcohol. But the memory of how my father had conducted himself made that course repugnant. If I did not want others to violate my life, how could I voluntarily violate it myself?

I had no hope whatever of being a professional man. Not only had I been so conditioned that I did not desire it, but the fulfillment of such an ambition was beyond my capabilities. Well-to-do Negroes lived in a world that was almost as alien to me as the world inhabited by whites.

What, then, was there? I held my life in my mind, in my consciousness each day, feeling at times that I would stumble and drop it, spill it forever. My reading had created a vast sense of distance between me and the world in which I lived and tried to make a living, and that sense of distance was increasing each day. My days and nights were one long, quiet, continuously contained dream of terror, tension, and anxiety. I wondered how long I could bear it.

Interpretations

1. What details most vividly bring home Wright's poverty?

2. How did Wright's forged note show an understanding of white racism? What lessons for surviving in a racist society does the young Wright learn?

3. What effect does exposure to Mencken have on Wright?

4. Do you think books and libraries are as important as Wright thinks? Would you, if you had to, go to the same lengths he does to borrow books? Why or why not? Is it possible to be too respectful of the written word? If so, what are the signs of this excessive respect—in young Wright? in others?

5. Wright is best known as a writer of fiction, especially of novels. What techniques usually associated with fiction does Wright use here? How do these techniques contribute to the excerpt's effectiveness?

Correspondences

1. Compare and contrast the role of the library in the education of Wright and Marshall.

2. Review the Ellison perspective (page 194). To what extent did Wright's experience with "word . . . potency" influence him to become a writer?

Applications

1. Richard Wright's educational experiences were shaped primarily by his awareness of himself as an outsider. Have you ever felt like an outsider to the education establishment? Freewrite about the experience and expand on it for an essay.

2. Wright implies that books and reading are *the* most important means of education. Do you agree? Why or why not? (How have TV and radio affected the role of books in education?)

The Lesson

Toni Cade Bambara

Toni Cade Bambara (b. 1939) grew up in New York City deeply conscious of the inequities of race and class. She graduated from Queens College in 1959 and received her M.A. from City College of New York. Her publications include Gorilla, My Love *(1972),* The Sea Birds Are Still Alive *(1977), and* The Salt Eaters *(1980). This is how she perceives her role as a writer:*

> *Stories are important. They keep us alive. In the ships, in the camps, in the quarters, fields, prisons, on the road, on the run, underground, under siege, in the throes, on the verge—the storyteller snatches us back from the edge to hear the next chapter in which we are the subjects. We, the hero of the tales. Our lives preserved. How it was, how it be. Passing it along in the relay. That is what I work to do, to produce stories that save our lives.*

As you read "The Lesson," set in New York City, pay particular attention to Bambara's use of dialogue.

BACK IN THE DAYS when everyone was old and stupid or young and foolish and me and Sugar were the only ones just right, this lady moved on our block with nappy hair and proper speech and no makeup. And quite naturally we laughed at her, laughed the way we did at the junk man who went about his business like he was some big-time president and his sorry-ass horse his secretary. And we kinda hated her too, hated the way we did the winos who cluttered up our parks and pissed on our handball walls and stank up our hallways and stairs so you couldn't halfway play hide-and-seek without a goddamn gas mask. Miss Moore was her name. The only woman on the block with no first name. And she was black as hell, cept for her feet, which were fish-white and spooky. And she was always planning these boring-ass things for us to do, us being my cousin, mostly, who lived on the block cause we all moved North the same time and to the same apartment then spread out gradual to breathe. And our parents would yank our heads into some kinda shape and crisp up our clothes so we'd be presentable for travel with Miss Moore, who always looked like she was going to church, though she never did. Which is just one of things the grownups talked about when they talked behind her back like a dog. But when she came calling with some sachet she'd sewed up or some gingerbread she'd made or some book, why then they'd all be too embarrassed to turn her down and we'd get handed over all spruced up. She'd been to college and said it was only right that she should take responsibility for the young ones' education, and she not even related by marriage or blood. So they'd go for it. Specially Aunt Gretchen. She was the main gofer in the family. You got some old dumb shit foolishness you want somebody to go for, you send for Aunt Gretchen. She been screwed into the go-along for so long, it's a blood-deep natural thing with her. Which is how she got saddled with me and Sugar and Junior in the first place while our mothers were in a la-de-da apartment up the block having a good ole time.

So this one day Miss Moore rounds us all up at the mailbox and it's puredee hot and she's knockin herself out about arithmetic. And school suppose to let up in the summer I heard, but she don't never let up. And the starch in my pinafore scratching the shit outta me and I'm really hating this nappy-head bitch and her goddamn college degree. I'd much rather go to the pool or to the show where it's cool. So me and Sugar leaning on the mailbox being surly, which is a Miss Moore word. And Flyboy checking out what everybody brought for lunch. And Fat Butt already wasting his peanutbutter-and-jelly sandwich like the pig he is. And Junebug punchin on Q.T.'s arm for potato chips. And Rosie Giraffe shifting from one hip to the other waiting for somebody to step on her foot or ask if she from Georgia so she can kick ass, preferably Mercedes'. And Miss Moore asking us do we know what money is, like we a bunch of retards. I mean real money, she say, like it's only poker chips or monopoly papers we lay on the grocer. So right away I'm tired of this and say so. And would much rather snatch Sugar and go to the Sunset and terrorize the West Indian kids and take their hair ribbons and their money too. And Miss Moore files that remark away for next week's lesson on brotherhood, I can tell. And finally I say we oughta get to the subway cause it's cooler and besides we might meet some cute boys. Sugar done swiped her mama's lipstick, so we ready.

So we heading down the street and she's boring us silly about what things cost and what our parents make and how much goes for rent and how money ain't divided up right in this country. And then she get to the part about we all poor and live in the slums, which I don't feature. And I'm ready to speak on that, but she steps out in the street and hails two cabs just like that. Then she hustles half the crew in with her and hands me a five-dollar bill and tells me to calculate 10 percent tip for the driver. And we're off. Me and Sugar and Junebug and Flyboy hanging out the window and hollering to everybody, putting lipstick on each other cause Flyboy a faggot anyway, and making farts with our sweaty armpits. But I'm mostly trying to figure how to spend this money. But they all fascinated with the meter ticking and Junebug starts laying bets as to how much it'll read when Flyboy can't hold his breath no more. Then Sugar lay bets as to how much it'll be when we get there. So I'm stuck. Don't nobody want to go for my plan, which is to jump out at the next light and run off to the first bar-b-que we can find. Then the driver tells us to get the hell out cause we there already. And the meter reads eight-five cents. And I'm stalling to figure out the tip and Sugar say give him a dime. And I decided he don't need it bad as I do, so later for him. But then he tries to take off with Junebug foot still in the door so we talk about his mama something ferocious. Then we check out that we on Fifth Avenue and everybody dressed up in stockings. One lady in a fur coat, hot as it is. White folks crazy.

"This is the place," Miss Moore say, presenting it to us in the voice she uses at the museum. "Let's look in the windows before we go in."

"Can we steal?" Sugar asks very serious like she's getting the ground rules squared away before she plays. "I beg your pardon," say Miss Moore, and we fall out. So she leads us around the windows of the toy store and me and Sugar screamin, "This is mine, that's mine, I gotta have that, that was made for me, I was born for that," till Big Butt drowns us out.

"Hey, I'm goin to buy that there."

"That there? You don't even know what it is, stupid."

"I do so," he say punchin on Rosie Giraffe. "It's a microscope."

"Whatcha gonna do with a microscope, fool?"

"Look at things."

"Like what, Ronald?" ask Miss Moore. And Big Butt ain't got the first notion. So here go Miss Moore gabbing about the thousands of bacteria in a drop of water and the somethinorother in a speck of blood and the million and one living things in the air around us is invisible to the naked eye. And what she say that for? Junebug go to town on that "naked" and we rolling. Then Miss Moore ask what it cost. So we all jam into the window smudgin it up and the price tag say $300. So then she ask how long'd take for Big Butt and Junebug to save up their allowances. "Too long," I say. "Yeh," adds Sugar, "outgrown it by that time." And Miss Moore say no, you never outgrow learning instruments. "Why, even medical students and interns and," blah, blah, blah. And we ready to choke Big Butt for bringing it up in the first damn place.

"This here costs four hundred eighty dollars," say Rosie Giraffe. So we pile up all over her to see what she pointin out. My eyes tell me it's a chunk of glass cracked with something heavy, and different-color inks dripped into the splits, then the whole thing put into a oven or something. But for $480 it don't make sense.

"That's a paperweight made of semi-precious stones fused together under tremendous pressure," she explains slowly, with her hands doing the mining and all the factory work.

"So what's a paperweight?" asks Rosie Giraffe.

"To weigh paper with, dumbbell," say Flyboy, the wise man from the East.

"Not exactly," say Miss Moore, which is what she say when you warm or way off too. "It's to weigh paper down so it won't scatter and make your desk untidy." So right away me and Sugar curtsy to each other and then to Mercedes who is more the tidy type.

"We don't keep paper on top of the desk in my class," say Junebug, figuring Miss Moore crazy or lyin one.

"At home, then," she say. "Don't you have a calendar and a pencil case and a blotter and a letter-opener on your desk at home where you do your homework?" And she know damn well what our homes look like cause she nosys around in them every chance she gets.

"I don't even have a desk," say Junebug. "Do we?"

"No. And I don't get no homework neither," says Big Butt.

"And I don't even have a home," say Flyboy like he do at school to keep the white folks off his back and sorry for him. Send this poor kid to camp posters, is his specialty.

"I do," says Mercedes. "I have a box of stationery on my desk and a picture of my cat. My godmother bought the stationery and the desk. There's a big rose on each sheet and the envelopes smell like roses."

"Who wants to know about your smelly-ass stationery," say Rosie Giraffe fore I can get my two cents in.

"It's important to have a work area all your own so that . . ."

"Will you look at this sailboat, please," say Flyboy, cuttin her off and pointin to the thing like it was his. So once again we tumble all over each other to gaze at this magnificent thing in the toy store which is just big enough to maybe sail two kittens across the pond if you strap them to the posts tight. We all start reciting the price tag like we in assembly. "Hand-crafted sailboat of fiberglass at one thousand one hundred ninety-five dollars."

"Unbelievable," I hear myself say and am really stunned. I read it again for myself just in case the group recitation put me in a trance. Same thing. For some reason this pisses me off. We look at Miss Moore and she lookin at us, waiting for I dunno what.

"Who'd pay all that when you can buy a sailboat set for a quarter at Pop's, a tube of glue for a dime, and a ball of string for eight cents? It must have a motor and a whole lot else besides," I say. "My sailboat cost me about fifty cents."

"But will it take water?" say Mercedes with her smart ass.

"Took mine to Alley Pond Park once," say Flyboy. "String broke. Lost it. Pity."

"Sailed mine in Central Park and it keeled over and sank. Had to ask my father for another dollar."

"And you got the strap," laugh Big Butt. "The jerk didn't even have a string on it. My old man wailed on his behind."

Little Q.T. was staring hard at the sailboat and you could see he wanted it bad. But he too little and somebody'd just take it from him. So what the hell. "This boat for kids, Miss Moore?"

"Parents silly to buy something like that just to get all broke up," say Rosie Giraffe.

"That much money it should last forever," I figure.

"My father'd buy it for me if I wanted it."

"Your father, my ass," say Rosie Giraffe getting a chance to finally push Mercedes.

"Must be rich people shop here," say Q.T.

"You are a very bright boy," say Flyboy. "What was your first clue?" And he rap him on the head with the back of his knuckles, since Q.T. the only one he could get away with. Though Q.T. liable to come up behind you years later and get his licks in when you half expect it.

"What I want to know is," I says to Miss Moore though I never talk to her, I wouldn't give the bitch that satisfaction, "is how much a real boat costs? I figure a thousand'd get you a yacht any day?"

"Why don't you check that out," she says, "and report back to the group?" Which really pains my ass. If you gonna mess up a perfectly good swim day least you could do is have some answers. "Let's go in," she say like she got something up her sleeve. Only she don't lead the way. So me and Sugar turn the corner to where the entrance is, but when we get there I kinda hang back. Not that I'm scared, what's there to be afraid of, just a toy store. But I feel funny, shame. But what I got to be shamed about? Got as much right to go in as anybody. But somehow I can't seem to get hold of the door, so I step away for Sugar to lead. But she hangs back too. And I look at her and she looks at me and this is ridiculous. I mean, damn, I have never ever been shy about doing nothing or going nowhere. But then Mercedes steps up and then Rosie Giraffe and Big Butt crowd in behind and shove, and next thing we all stuffed into the doorway with only Mercedes squeezing past us, smoothing out her jumper and walking right down the aisle. Then the rest of us tumble in like a glued-together jigsaw done all wrong. And people lookin at us. And it's like the time me and Sugar crashed into the Catholic church on a dare. But once we got in there and everything so hushed and holy and the candles and the bowin and the handkerchiefs on all the drooping heads, I just couldn't go through with the plan. Which was for me to run up to the altar and do a tap dance while Sugar played the nose flute and messed around in the holy waters. And Sugar kept givin me the elbow. Then later teased me so bad I tied her up in the shower and turned it on and locked her in. And she'd be there till this day if Aunt Gretchen hadn't finally figured I was lyin about the boarder takin a shower.

Same thing in the store. We all walkin on tiptoe and hardly touchin the games and puzzles and things. And I watched Miss Moore who is steady watchin us like she waiting for a sign. Like Mama Drewery watches the sky and sniffs the air and takes note of just how much slant is in the bird formation. Then me and Sugar bump smack into each other, so busy gazing at the toys, 'specially the sailboat. But we don't laugh and go into our fat-lady bump-stomach routine. We just stare at that price tag. Then Sugar run a finger over the whole boat. And I'm jealous and want to hit her. Maybe not her, but I sure want to punch somebody in the mouth.

"Watcha bring us here for, Miss Moore?"

"You sound angry, Sylvia. Are you mad about something?" Givin me one of them grins like she tellin a grown-up joke that never turns out to be funny. And she's lookin very closely at me like maybe she plannin to do my portrait from memory. I'm mad, but I won't give her that satisfaction. So I slouch around the store bein very bored and say, "Let's go."

Me and Sugar at the back of the train watchin the tracks whizzin by large then small then gettin gobbled up in the dark. I'm thinkin about this tricky toy I saw in the store. A clown that somersaults on a bar then does chin-ups just cause you yank lightly at his leg. Cost $35. I could see me askin my mother for a $35 birthday clown. "You wanna who that costs what?" she'd say, cocking her head to the side to get a better view of the hole in my head. Thirty-five dollars and the whole household could go visit Grandaddy Nelson in the country. Thirty-five dollars would pay for the rent and the piano bill too. Who are these people that spend that much for performing clowns and $1000 for toy sailboats? What kinda work they do and how they live and how come we ain't in on it? Where we are is who we are, Miss Moore always pointin out. But it don't necessarily have to be that way, she always adds then waits for somebody to say that poor people have to wake up and demand their share of the pie and don't none of us know what kind of pie she talkin about in the first damn place. But she ain't so smart cause I still got her four dollars from the taxi and she sure ain't gettin it. Messin up my day with this shit. Sugar nudges me in my pocket and winks.

Miss Moore lines us up in front of the mailbox where we started from, seem like years ago, and I got a headache for thinkin so hard. And we lean all over each other so we can hold up under the draggy-ass lecture she always finishes us off with at the end before we thank her for borin us to tears. But she just looks at us like she readin tea leaves. Finally she say, "Well, what did you think of F.A.O. Schwartz?"

Rosie Giraffe mumbles, "White folks crazy."

"I'd like to go there again when I get my birthday money," says Mercedes, and we shove her out the pack so she has to lean on the mailbox by herself.

"I'd like a shower. Tiring day," say Flyboy.

Then Sugar surprises me by saying, "You know, Miss Moore, I don't think all of us here put together eat in a year what that sailboat costs." And Miss Moore lights up like somebody goosed her. "And?" she say, urging Sugar on. Only I'm standin on her foot so she don't continue.

"Imagine for a minute what kind of society it is in which some people can spend on a toy what it would cost to feed a family of six or seven. What do you think?"

"I think," say Sugar pushing me off her feet like she never done before, cause I whip her ass in a minute, "that this is not much of a democracy if you ask me. Equal chance to pursue happiness means an equal crack at the dough, don't it?" Miss Moore is besides herself and I am disgusted with Sugar's treachery. So I stand on her foot one more time to see if she'll shove me. She shuts up, and Miss Moore looks at me, sorrowfully I'm thinkin. And somethin weird is goin on. I can feel it in my chest.

"Anybody else learn anything today?" lookin dead at me. I walk away and Sugar has to run to catch up and don't even seem to notice when I shrug her arm off my shoulder.

"Well, we got four dollars anyway," she says.

"Uh hunh."

"We could go to Hascombs and get half a chocolate layer and then to the Sunset and still have plenty of money for potato chips and ice cream sodas."

"Uh hunh."

"Race you to Hascombs," she say.

We start down the block and she gets ahead which is O.K. by me cause I'm goin to the West End and then over the Drive to think this day through. She can run if she want to and even run faster. But ain't nobody gonna beat me at nuthin.

Interpretations

1. What does Miss Moore hope to accomplish during the class outing? What lesson does she want to teach? Do you agree that the lesson needs teaching? Why? Has Miss Moore chosen an effective method of teaching?

2. What evidence is there that this outing is only the latest in a series of attempts to teach a lesson and that the children already know what they are expected to "learn"? How does that repetition affect your reaction to Sylvia's irritation at Sugar's "treachery" in saying what Sugar believes to be the lesson: "Equal chance to pursue happiness means an equal crack at the dough, don't it?" Has Sylvia failed to understand the lesson or is she irritated at the repetition?

3. Although Sylvia says "I'm mad," she will not admit her anger to Miss Moore. Why not? Does Sylvia know what has made her angry? Do we know?

4. Is Sylvia a reliable informant? (How does she feel about Miss Moore? Is she cooperative?)

5. Why do you think Miss Moore never demands change due her from the narrator?

6. How would this story be different if Miss Moore were the narrator? Would that be an improvement? Why or why not?

7. What do you consider the more important element of this story, the lesson itself or the personalities and/or attitudes of the three or four main characters? Why?

Correspondences

1. Sylvia in "The Lesson" has mixed emotions towards Miss Moore, the mentor of the neighborhood children. What role does she play in the children's lives? What is her purpose in exposing them to new experiences? To what extent did she contribute positively or negatively to their education? Review the last paragraph of Wright's "Discovering Books." Does Mr. Falk serve as a mentor? Why or why not?

2. "White folks crazy" appears twice in "The Lesson." What situations give rise to this conclusion? What emotions are the children expressing through these words? (What is the significance of Sylvia's resolve that "ain't nobody gonna beat me at nothin"?) How is Sylvia's attitude towards white people similar to or different from that of Rendón?

Applications

1. Write an essay about an adult who has had a positive or negative influence on your education. Include in your portrayal an experience which clearly illustrates that influence.

2. According to fiction writer Grace Paley, "If you say what's on your mind in the language that comes to you from your parents and your street and friends you'll probably say something beautiful." Write an essay showing the extent to which "The Lesson" supports Paley's point of view.

The Stolen Party

Liliana Heker

Liliana Heker was editor of the Argentinian literary magazine
El Ornitorrinco *(The Platypus) during the years of military dictatorship between 1976 and 1983. She published her first book
of short stories,* Those Who Beheld the Burning Bush, *while she
was a teenager. Her second novel,* Zona de Clivage, *was published in 1988.*

*The second largest country in South America, Argentina re-
mained a Spanish colony from 1515 until 1916. By the end of
the nineteenth century nearly all the native Indians had been
killed and replaced by Italian, German, and Spanish immigrants. For a few decades Argentina was the most industrialized
and prosperous of the major Latin American nations, but Juan
Perón, first elected president in 1946, ran the country into debt
and suppressed freedom of speech and press. After Perón's death,
his wife Isabel became the first woman elected to head a Western
nation; she was ousted in 1976 by a military junta which for
seven years jailed, tortured, and killed 5,000 people and
plunged the society into a continuous state of siege, an especially
dangerous period for a journalist like Heker. Since the failed
attempt in 1982 to oust the British from the Islas Malvinas
(Falkland Islands), democratic regimes have tried to curb runaway inflation and restore civil rights to the population.*

AS SOON AS SHE arrived she went straight to the kitchen to see if the
monkey was there. It was: what a relief! She wouldn't have liked to admit
that her mother had been right. *Monkeys at a birthday?* her mother had
sneered. *Get away with you, believing any nonsense you're told!* She was
cross, but not because of the monkey, the girl thought; it's just because
of the party.

"I don't like you going," she told her. "It's a rich people's party."

"Rich people go to Heaven too," said the girl, who studied religion at
school.

"Get away with Heaven," said the mother. "The problem with you,
young lady, is that you like to fart higher than your ass."

The girl didn't approve of the way her mother spoke. She was barely
nine, and one of the best in her class.

"I'm going because I've been invited," she said. "And I've been
invited because Luciana is my friend. So there."

233

"Ah yes, your friend," her mother grumbled. She paused. "Listen, Rosaura," she said at last. "That one's not your friend. You know what you are to them? The maid's daughter, that's what."

Rosaura blinked hard: she wasn't going to cry. Then she yelled: "Shut up! You know nothing about being friends!"

Every afternoon she used to go to Luciana's house and they would both finish their homework while Rosaura's mother did the cleaning. They had their tea in the kitchen and they told each other secrets. Rosaura loved everything in the big house, and she also loved the people who lived there.

"I'm going because it will be the most lovely party in the whole world, Luciana told me it would. There will be a magician, and he will bring a monkey and everything."

The mother swung around to take a good look at her child, and pompously put her hands on her hips.

"Monkeys at a birthday?" she said. "Get away with you, believing any nonsense you're told!"

Rosaura was deeply offended. She thought it unfair of her mother to accuse other people of being liars simply because they were rich. Rosaura too wanted to be rich, of course. If one day she managed to live in a beautiful palace, would her mother stop loving her? She felt very sad. She wanted to go to that party more than anything else in the world.

"I'll die if I don't go," she whispered almost without moving her lips.

And she wasn't sure whether she had been heard, but on the morning of the party, she discovered that her mother had starched her Christmas dress. And in the afternoon, after washing her hair, her mother rinsed it in apple vinegar so that it would be all nice and shiny. Before going out, Rosaura admired herself in the mirror, with her white dress and glossy hair, and thought she looked terribly pretty.

Señora Ines also seemed to notice. As soon as she saw her, she said: "How lovely you look today, Rosaura."

Rosaura gave her starched skirt a slight toss with her hands and walked into the party with a firm step. She said hello to Luciana and asked about the monkey. Luciana put on a secretive look and whispered into Rosaura's ear: "He's in the kitchen. But don't tell anyone, because it's a surprise."

Rosaura wanted to make sure. Carefully she entered the kitchen and there she saw it: deep in thought, inside its cage. It looked so funny that the girl stood there for a while, watching it, and later, every so often, she would slip out of the party unseen and go and admire it. Rosaura was the only one allowed into the kitchen. Señora Ines had said: "You yes, but not the others, they're much too boisterous, they might break something." Rosaura had never broken anything. She even managed the jug of orange juice, carrying it from the kitchen into the dining room. She held it carefully and didn't spill a single drop. And Señora Ines had said: "Are you sure you can manage a jug as big as that?" Of course she could manage. She wasn't a butterfingers, like the others. Like that blonde girl with the bow in her hair. As soon as she saw Rosaura, the girl with the bow had said:

"And you? Who are you?"

"I'm a friend of Luciana," said Rosaura.

"No," said the girl with the bow, "you are not a friend of Luciana because I'm her cousin and I know all her friends. And I don't know you."

"So what," said Rosaura. "I come here every afternoon with my mother and we do our homework together."

"You and your mother do your homework together?" asked the girl, laughing.

"I and Luciana do our homework together," said Rosaura, very seriously.

The girl with the bow shrugged her shoulders.

"That's not being friends," she said. "Do you go to school together?"

"No."

"So where do you know her from?" said the girl, getting impatient.

Rosaura remembered her mother's words perfectly. She took a deep breath.

"I'm the daughter of the employee," she said.

Her mother had said very clearly: "If someone asks, you say you're the daughter of the employee; that's all." She also told her to add: "And proud of it." But Rosaura thought that never in her life would she dare say something of the sort.

"What employee?" said the girl with the bow. "Employee in a shop?"

"No," said Rosaura angrily. "My mother doesn't sell anything in any shop, so there."

"So how come she's an employee?" said the girl with the bow.

Just then Señora Ines arrived saying *shh shh,* and asked Rosaura if she wouldn't mind helping serve out the hotdogs, as she knew the house so much better than the others.

"See?" said Rosaura to the girl with the bow, and when no one was looking she kicked her in the shin.

Apart from the girl with the bow, all the others were delightful. The one she liked best was Luciana, with her golden birthday crown; and then the boys. Rosaura won the sack race, and nobody managed to catch her when they played tag. When they split into two teams to play charades, all the boys wanted her for their side. Rosaura felt she had never been so happy in all her life.

But the best was still to come. The best came after Luciana blew out the candles. First the cake. Señora Ines had asked her to help pass the cake around, and Rosaura had enjoyed the task immensely, because everyone called out to her, shouting "Me, me!" Rosaura remembered a story in which there was a queen who had the power of life or death over her subjects. She had always loved that, having the power of life or death. To Luciana and the boys she gave the largest pieces, and to the girl with the bow she gave a slice so thin one could see through it.

After the cake came the magician, tall and bony, with a fine red cape. A true magician: he could untie handkerchiefs by blowing on them and make a chain with links that had no openings. He could guess what cards were pulled out from a pack, and the monkey was his assistant. He called the monkey "partner." "Let's see here, partner," he would say, "turn over a card." And, "Don't run away, partner: time to work now."

The final trick was wonderful. One of the children had to hold the monkey in his arms and the magician said he would make him disappear.

"What, the boy?" they all shouted.

"No, the monkey!" shouted back the magician.

Rosaura thought that this was truly the most amusing party in the whole world.

The magician asked a small fat boy to come and help, but the small fat boy got frightened almost at once and dropped the monkey on the floor. The magician picked him up carefully, whispered something in his ear, and the monkey nodded almost as if he understood.

"You mustn't be so unmanly, my friend," the magician said to the fat boy.

"What's unmanly?" said the fat boy.

The magician turned around as if to look for spies.

"A sissy," said the magician. "Go sit down."

Then he stared at all the faces, one by one. Rosaura felt her heart tremble.

"You, with the Spanish eyes," said the magician. And everyone saw that he was pointing at her.

She wasn't afraid. Neither holding the monkey, nor when the magician made him vanish; not even when, at the end, the magician flung his red cape over Rosaura's head and uttered a few magic words . . . and the monkey reappeared, chattering happily, in her arms. The children clapped furiously. And before Rosaura returned to her seat, the magician said:

"Thank you very much, my little countess."

She was so pleased with the compliment that a while later, when her mother came to fetch her, that was the first thing she told her.

"I helped the magician and he said to me, 'Thank you very much, my little countess.' "

It was strange because up to then Rosaura had thought that she was angry with her mother. All along Rosaura had imagined that she would say to her: "See that the monkey wasn't a lie?" But instead she was so thrilled that she told her mother all about the wonderful magician.

Her mother tapped her on the head and said: "So now we're a countess!"

But one could see that she was beaming.

And now they both stood in the entrance, because a moment ago Señora Ines, smiling, had said: "Please wait here a second."

Her mother suddenly seemed worried.

"What is it?" she asked Rosaura.

"What is what?" said Rosaura. "It's nothing; she just wants to get the presents for those who are leaving, see?"

She pointed at the fat boy and at a girl with pigtails who were also waiting there, next to their mothers. And she explained about the presents. She knew, because she had been watching those who left before her. When one of the girls was about to leave, Señora Ines would give her a bracelet. When a boy left, Señora Ines gave him a yo-yo. Rosaura preferred the yo-yo because it sparkled, but she didn't mention that to her mother. Her mother might have said: "So why don't you ask for one, you blockhead?" That's what her mother was like. Rosaura didn't feel like explaining that she'd be horribly ashamed to be the odd one out. Instead she said:

"I was the best-behaved at the party."

And she said no more because Señora Ines came out into the hall with two bags, one pink and one blue.

First she went up to the fat boy, gave him a yo-yo out of the blue bag, and the fat boy left with mother. Then she went up to the girl and gave her a bracelet out of the pink bag, and the girl with the pigtails left as well.

Finally she came up to Rosaura and her mother. She had a big smile on her face and Rosaura liked that. Señora Ines looked down at her, then looked up at her mother, and then said something that made Rosaura proud:

"What a marvelous daughter you have, Herminia."

For an instant, Rosaura thought that she'd give her two presents: the bracelet and the yo-yo. Señora Ines bent down as if about to look for something. Rosaura also leaned forward, stretching out her arm. But she never completed the movement.

Señora Ines didn't look in the pink bag. Nor did she look in the blue bag. Instead she rummaged in her purse. In her hand appeared two bills.

"You really and truly earned this," she said handing them over. "Thank you for all your help, my pet."

Rosaura felt her arms stiffen, stick close to her body, and then she noticed her mother's hand on her shoulder. Instinctively she pressed herself against her mother's body. That was all. Except her eyes. Rosaura's eyes had a cold, clear look that fixed itself on Señora Ines's face.

Señora Ines, motionless, stood there with her hand outstretched. As if she didn't dare draw it back. As if the slightest change might shatter an infinitely delicate balance.

Interpretations

1. What is the significance of Señora Ines offering Rosaura money? Why are Rosaura's eyes "cold" and "clear"?

2. What did Rosaura learn at this party? To what extent was the monkey part of this lesson?

3. Explain the implications of the story's last paragraph. If the story were told from Señora Ines's point of view, would we see that the problem was not just Rosaura's but also Ines's?

Correspondences

1. Review Heilbrun's perspective (page 194) and discuss its application to "The Stolen Party." To what extent will Rosaura feel more or less powerful in the future as a result of her final encounter with Señora Ines?

2. Part of the education of Sylvia in "The Lesson" and Rosaura in "The Stolen Party" concerns their becoming aware of the implications of differences in social class. What do they learn? How are their responses similar? different?

Applications

1. Write an analysis of the mother–daughter relationship in "The Stolen Party." How does it change during the course of the story? What "lesson" does each learn during the course of the story?

2. Discuss the significance of the story's title.

Looking for a Lost Dog

Gretel Ehrlich

Gretel Ehrlich (b. 1946) was born in California and educated at Bennington College. She now lives on a ranch in Wyoming and has published two collections of essays: The Solace of Open Spaces *(1985) and* Islands, Universe, and Home *(1988). She frequently uses nature as a catalyst for her writing.*

The most valuable thoughts which I entertain are anything but what I thought. Nature abhors a vacuum, and if I can only walk with sufficient carelessness I am sure to be filled.
Henry David Thoreau

I STARTED OFF this morning looking for my lost dog. He's a red heeler, blotched brown and white, and I tell people he looks like a big saddle shoe. Born at Christmas on a thirty-below-zero night, he's tough, though his right front leg is crooked where it froze to the ground.

It's the old needle-in-the-haystack routine: small dog, huge landscape, and rugged terrain. While moving cows once, he fell in a hole and disappeared. We heard him whining but couldn't see him. When we put our ears to the ground, we could hear the hole that had swallowed him.

It's no wonder human beings are so narcissistic. The way our ears are constructed, we can only hear what's right next to us or else the internal monologue inside. I've taken to cupping my hands behind my ears—mule-like—and pricking them all the way forward or back to hear what's happened or what's ahead.

"Life is polyphonic," a Hungarian friend in her eighties said. She was a child prodigy from Budapest who had soloed on the violin in Paris and Berlin by the time she was twelve. "Childishly, I once thought hearing had mostly to do with music," she said. "Now that I'm too old to play the fiddle, I know it has to do with the great suspiration of life everywhere."

But back to the dog. I'm walking and looking and listening for him, though there is no trail, no clue, no direction to the search. Whimsically, I head north toward the falls. They're set in a deep gorge where Precambrian rock piles up to ten thousand feet on either side. A raven creaks overhead, flies into the cleft, glides toward a panel of white water splashing over a ledge, and comes out cawing.

To find out what is lost is an art in some cultures. The Navajos employ "hand tremblers," usually women, who go into a trance and "see" where the lost article or person is located. When I asked one such diviner what it was like when she was in trance, she said, "Lots of noise, but noise that's hard to hear."

Near the falls the ground flattens into a high-altitude valley before the mountains rise vertically. The falls roar, but they're overgrown with spruce, pine, willow, and wild rose, and the closer I get, the harder it is to see the water. Perhaps that is how it will be in my search for the dog.

We're worried about Frenchy because last summer he was bitten three times by rattlesnakes. After the first bite he walked toward me, reeled dramatically, and collapsed. I could see the two holes in his nose where the fangs went in, and I felt sure he was dying. I drove him twenty miles to the vet; by the time we arrived, Frenchy resembled a monster. His nose and neck had swollen as though a football had been sewn under the skin.

I walk and walk. Past the falls, through a pass, toward a larger, rowdier creek. The sky goes black. In the distance snow on the Owl Creek Mountains glares. A blue ocean seems to stretch between, and the black sky hangs over like a frown. A string of cottonwoods whose new, tender leaves are the color of limes pulls me downstream. I come into the meadow with the abandoned apple orchard. The trees have leaves but have lost most of their blossoms. I feel as if I had caught strangers undressed.

The sun comes back, and the wind. It brings no dog, but ducks slide overhead. An Eskimo from Barrow, Alaska, told me the reason spring has such fierce winds is so birds coming north will have something to fly on.

To find what's lost; to lose what's found. Several times I've thought I might be "losing my mind." Of course, minds aren't literally misplaced— on the contrary, we live too much under them. As with viewing the falls, we can lose sight of what is too close. It is between the distant and close-up views that the struggle between impulse and reason, logic and passion takes place.

The feet move; the mind wanders. In his journals Thoreau wrote: "The saunterer, in the good sense, is not more vagrant than the meandering river, which is all the while sedulously seeking the shortest course to the sea."

Today I'm filled with longings—for what I'm not, for what is impossible, for people I love who can't be in my life. Passions of all sorts struggle soundlessly, or else, like the falls, they are all noise but can't be seen. My hybrid anguish spends itself as recklessly and purposefully as water.

Now I'm following a game trail up a sidehill. It's a mosaic of tracks—elk, deer, rabbit, and bird. If city dwellers could leave imprints in cement, it would look this way: tracks would overlap, go backward and forward like the peregrine saunterings of the mind.

I see a dog's track, or is it a coyote's? I get down on my hands and knees to sniff out a scent. What am I doing? I entertain expectations of myself as preposterous as when I landed in Tokyo—I felt so at home there that I though I would break into fluent Japanese. Now I sniff the ground and smell only dirt. If I spent ten years sniffing, would I learn scents?

The tracks veer off the trail and disappear. Descending into a dry wash whose elegant, tortured junipers and tumbled boulders resemble a Japanese garden, I trip on a sagebrush root. I look. Deep in the center of the plant there is a bird's nest, but instead of eggs, a locust stares up at me.

Some days I think this one place isn't enough. That's when nothing is enough, when I want to live multiple lives and be allowed to love without limits. Those days, like today, I walk with a purpose but no destination. Only then do I see, at least momentarily, that everything is here. To my left a towering cottonwood is lunatic with birdsong. Under it I'm a listening post while its great gray trunk—like a baton or the source of something—heaves its green symphony into the air.

I walk and walk: from the falls, over Grouse Hill, to the dry wash. Today it is enough to make a shadow.

Interpretations

1. How does the Thoreau quotation (page 239) apply to the essay? Try, for a start, to relate the quotation to "Life is polyphonic" and "we live too much under 'our minds' " and "I want to live multiple lives." What place is there in the process of learning or education for a certain "carelessness"?

2. The dog keeps getting lost in—or at least disappearing from—this essay. What seems more important to Ehrlich here than telling a story? At one point Ehrlich herself seems to turn into a dog: "Now I sniff the ground. . . ." How important is it to Ehrlich's purpose that the dog really exist?

3. Characterize the prevailing mood of the essay. What is the essay's main point?

4. What do you think would make one feel that one must not love beyond certain limit? ("I want to . . . love without limits.") What does "love" mean in this case? What would be the object of such love?

Correspondences

1. Review Lessing's perspective on learning (page 194) and discuss its applications to "Looking for a Lost Dog." What does Ehrlich "learn" from her experiences?

2. "To find what is lost is an art in some cultures." How might stories like "The Creation of the Crow World" help us rediscover what has been lost? What conversations can you imagine having with "hand tremblers and diviners"? Explain what Erlich thinks we can learn from folk culture.

Applications

1. Compare Erhlich's point about the relation between listening and learning with Marshall's in "Poets in the Kitchen." To whom and to what should we listen?

2. Interpret "today it is enough to make a shadow."

The Mistress of Make Believe

Doris Viloria

Doris Viloria (b. 1972) was brought up and educated in Queens,
N.Y., and is currently in her first year of college.

SHE WAS HUGE, but in a majestic awe-inspiring way like a mountain that
only added to her enigma. The word fat never came to mind.

"Good morning class," she'd briskly salute each day, as she marched
in on stiletto heels. Her hair would be piled high on her head, in a fountain
of honey blond and gray tendrils that was most undoubtedly dyed. The
heady scent of lilacs drenched the room as she entered; a tornado of
fragrances, heavy make-up, and shopping bags, her gaudy jewelry sending out smart metallic clinks. She always squeezed herself into tight "form
fitting" cashmere turtlenecks, which emphasized her rather copious stomach and voluptuous bosom and created the illusion of a kind of fanciful,
woman–caterpillar hybrid. Then shifting her bulk considerably, she
would sit atop her tall, rickety wooden swivel chair, crossing her legs
jauntily, and bringing one polished long red fingernail to her lips. As her
meaty arms settled on her lectern, one perfectly tweezed eyebrow lan-
guidly drifted up like a cobra, contemplating the class.

"Aaah," she'd purr in her thick coppery, baritone New England accent, as she towered over us, her mouth curling up in a sly grin. "How
many of you are ready to let your imagination take you off to distant
mystical lands"?

Together we explored the unbridled savagery of William Golding's
The Lord of the Flies, the silent yearnings and personal betrayals of John
Knowles' *A Separate Peace,* and the coming of age in the heart of injustice
of a young girl in Harper Lee's *To Kill a Mockingbird.* Golding's desolate,
desperate island sprang to life as she needled us with questions.

"Is man simply a beast temporarily tamed by years of affecting proper
etiquette, whose mask might drop if taken out of his 'civilized' environment?" she'd fire at us. "How would any of you react if placed in a jungle
where your actions were accountable to no one? Would you aspire to rule
as a belligerent dictator, or would you struggle to maintain your moralistic
humanity and preserve democracy?"

Having thus spat out these challenges she would take a long draught
of steaming black coffee from her styrofoam cup, leaving a sharp stain of
fuschia lipstick on the rim. Then in a smokey, hypnotic tone she would
read a passage from the book. The mood became trancelike as we

followed her into the story. Afterwards, those characters would linger about the room like inspirational phantoms as I slaved over my writing assignment.

Creating solely on pure instinct and guided by the illuminations of those benevolent daimons, I wrote a short story based on a gripping terrifying nightmare I'd had. It was as though I had exorcised all the horrors of my dream from myself, and they had metamorphosized into a story that had a life of its own. With a feeling of deep-seated pride and accomplishment, I turned it in.

Walking out of class one day, I heard that unmistakable voice ask for a moment of my time. I was brimming with curiosity as I approached her desk. Those penetrating blue eyes gazed at me with a mixture of respect and mischief. Tapping my story gently on her desk, she inclined that lion's mane of a head to the side and whispered in a close and confidential way, "Where did it come from"?

My eyes darted about the room as I searched for some response. Finally, I turned to her levelly and said honestly, "It just sort of wove itself."

Nodding her head in understanding after what seemed like an hour, she handed me the paper. "It really is very special," she said with a sigh. "You have a way with words that is a talent, a gift. I expect you to be a woman of great individual distinction."

Those words have bolstered me like iron saviors through countless fits of self doubt and introspection over the past few years. I walked out of the room that day with charmed visions of exquisitely soaring dragonflies before me. The spell has never waned.

Interpretations

1. What scene and what group of people do you assume the author to be describing? How effective is that description? What purpose does the description seem intended to serve?

2. How do you interpret the question "Where did it [the story] come from"? How important to the meaning of the essay is this question?

3. How would this essay be affected if the story itself were included or appended here?

4. How do you react to the words "You have a way with words that is a talent, a gift"?

5. The last paragraph is perhaps the most important in terms of the meaning of the essay. Comment on the effectiveness of saving this information until the end.

Correspondences

1. Review Moore's perspective (page 194). How does it apply to Viloria's educational experience? How many "enchanting" minds are there in her essay?

2. Review Borges's perspective on books (page 194). To what extent does it apply to Viloria's essay? To your own experiences with reading?

Applications

1. Viloria is excited by using language effectively. You may be creative in another medium such as photography, music, art, or dance. Write an essay describing your creative process and the emotions it evokes.

2. Write a journal entry responding to the questions posed by Viloria's teacher in paragraph 5. What do they reveal about her teaching techniques? About what she expects from her students?

from I Just Wanna Be Average

Mike Rose

Mike Rose (b. 1944) grew up in Los Angeles, the son of immigrants from southern Italy. He attended Loyola University, the University of Southern California, and the University of California at Los Angeles, where he is now Associate Director of Writing Programs. He has received awards from the National Academy of Education, the McDonnell Foundation, and the National Council of Teachers of English for his books and articles on language and literacy. "I Just Wanna Be Average" is a chapter from Lives on the Boundary *(1989).*

IT'S POPULAR these days to claim you grew up on the streets. Men tell violent tales and romanticize the lessons violence brings. But, though it was occasionally violent, it wasn't the violence in South L.A. that marked me, for sometimes you can shake that ugliness off. What finally affected me was subtler, but more pervasive: I cannot recall a young person who was crazy in love or lost in work or one old person who was passionate about a cause or an idea. I'm not talking about an absence of energy—the street toughs and, for that fact, old Cheech had energy. And I'm not talking about an absence of decency, for my father was a thoughtful man. The people I grew up with were retired from jobs that rub away the heart or were working hard at jobs to keep their lives from caving in or were anchorless and in between jobs and spouses or were diving headlong into a barren tomorrow: junkies, alcoholics, and mean kids walking along Vermont looking to throw a punch. I developed a picture of human existence that rendered it short and brutish or sad and aimless or long and quiet with rewards like afternoon naps, the evening newspaper, walks around the block, occasional letters from children in other states. When, years later, I was introduced to humanistic psychologists like Abraham Maslow and Carl Rogers, with the visions of self-actualization, or even Freud with his sober dictum about love and work, it all sounded like a glorious fairy tale, a magical account of a world full of possibility, full of hope and empowerment. Sindbad and Cinderella couldn't have been more fanciful.

Some people who manage to write their way out of the working class describe the classroom as an oasis of possibility. It became their intellectual playground, their competitive arena. Given the richness of my memories of this time, it's funny how scant are my recollections of school. I remember the red brick building of St. Regina's itself, and the topography of the playground: the swings and basketball courts and peeling benches. There are images of a few students: Erwin Petschaur, a muscular German boy with a strong accent; Dave Sanchez, who was good in math; and Sheila Wilkes, everyone's curly-haired heartthrob. And there are two nuns: Sister Monica, the third-grade teacher with beautiful hands for whom I carried a candle and who, to my dismay, had wedded herself to Christ; and Sister Beatrice, a woman truly crazed, who would sweep into class, eyes wide, to tell us about the Apocalypse.

All the hours in class tend to blend into one long, vague stretch of time. What I remember best, strangely enough, are the two things I couldn't understand and over the years grew to hate: grammar lessons and mathematics. I would sit there watching a teacher draw her long horizontal line and her short, oblique lines and break up sentences and put adjectives here and adverbs there and just not get it, couldn't see the reason for it, turned off to it. Students will float to the mark you set. I and the others in the vocational classes were bobbing in pretty shallow water. Vocational education was aimed at increasing the economic opportunities of students who do not do well in our schools. Some serious programs succeed in doing that, and through exceptional teachers—like Mr. Gross in *Horace's Compromise*—students learn to develop hypotheses and troubleshoot, reason through a problem, and communicate effectively—the true job skills. The vocational track, however, is most often a place for those who are just not making it, a dumping ground for the disaffected. There were a few teachers who worked hard at education; young Brother Slattery, for example, combined a stern voice with weekly quizzes to try to pass along to us a skeletal outline of world history. But mostly the teachers had no idea of how to engage the imaginations of us kids who were scuttling along at the bottom of the pond.

And the teachers would have needed some inventiveness, for none of us was groomed for the classroom. It wasn't just that I didn't know things—didn't know how to simplify algebraic fractions, couldn't identify different kinds of clauses, bungled Spanish translations—but that I had developed various faulty and inadequate ways of doing algebra and making sense of Spanish. Worse yet, the years of defensive tuning out in elementary school had given me a way to escape quickly while seeming at least half alert. During my time in Voc. Ed., I developed further into a mediocre student and a somnambulant problem solver, and that affected the subjects I did have the wherewithal to handle: I detested Shakespeare; I got bored with history. My attention flitted here and there. I fooled around in class and read my books indifferently—the intellectual equivalent of playing with your food. I did what I had to do to get by, and I did it with half a mind.

But I did learn things about people and eventually came into my own socially. I liked the guys in Voc. Ed. Growing up where I did, I understood and admired physical prowess, and there was an abundance of muscle here. There was Dave Snyder, a sprinter and halfback of true quality. Dave's ability and his quick wit gave him a natural appeal, and he was welcome in any clique, though he always kept a little independent. He enjoyed acting the fool and could care less about studies, but he possessed a certain maturity and never caused the faculty much trouble. It was a testament to his independence that he included me among his friends—I eventually went out for track, but I was no jock. Owing to the Latin alphabet and a dearth of *R*s and *S*s, Snyder sat behind Rose, and we started exchanging one-liners and became friends.

There was Ted Richard, a much-touted Little League pitcher. He was chunky and had a baby face and came to Our Lady of Mercy as a seasoned street fighter. Ted was quick to laugh and he had a loud, jolly laugh, but when he got angry he'd smile a little smile, the kind that simply raises the corner of the mouth a quarter of an inch. For those who knew, it was an eerie signal. Those who didn't found themselves in big trouble, for Ted was very quick. He loved to carry on what we would come to call philosophical discussions: What is courage? Does God exist? He also loved words, enjoyed picking up big ones like *salubrious* and *equivocal* and using them in our conversations—laughing at himself as the word hit a chuckhole rolling off his tongue. Ted didn't do all that well in school— baseball and parties and testing the courage he'd speculated about took up his time. His textbooks were *Argosy* and *Field and Stream,* whatever newspapers he'd find on the bus stop—from the *Daily Worker* to pornography—conversations with uncles or hobos or businessmen he'd meet in a coffee shop, *The Old Man and the Sea.* With hindsight, I can see that Ted was developing into one of those rough-hewn intellectuals whose sources are a mix of the learned and the apocryphal, whose discussions are both assured and sad.

And then there was Ken Harvey. Ken was good-looking in a puffy way and had a full and oily ducktail and was a car enthusiast . . . a hodad. One day in religion class, he said the sentence that turned out to be one of the most memorable of the hundreds of thousands I heard in those Voc. Ed. years. We were talking about the parable of the talents, about achievement, working hard, doing the best you can do, blah-blah-blah, when the teacher called on the restive Ken Harvey for an opinion. Ken thought about it, but just for a second, and said (with studied, minimal affect), "I just wanna be average." That woke me up. Average?! Who wants to be average? Then the athletes chimed in with the clichés that make you want to laryngectomize them, and the exchange became a platitudinous melee. At the time, I thought Ken's assertion was stupid, and I wrote him off. But his sentence has stayed with me all these years, and I think I am finally coming to understand it.

Ken Harvey was gasping for air. School can be a tremendously disorienting place. No matter how bad the school, you're going to encounter notions that don't fit with the assumptions and beliefs that you grew up with—maybe you'll hear these dissonant notions from teachers, maybe from the other students, and maybe you'll read them. You'll also be thrown in with all kinds of kids from all kinds of backgrounds, and that can be unsettling—this is especially true in places of rich ethnic and linguistic mix, like the L.A. basin. You'll see a handful of students far excel you in courses that sound exotic and that are only in the curriculum of the elite: French, physics, trigonometry. And all this is happening while you're trying to shape an identity, your body is changing, and your emotions are running wild. If you're a working-class kid in the vocational track, the options you'll have to deal with this will be constrained in certain ways: You're defined by your school as "slow"; you're placed in a curriculum that isn't designed to liberate you but to occupy you, or, if you're lucky, train you, though the training is for work the society does not esteem; other students are picking up the cues from your school and your curriculum and interacting with you in particular ways. If you're a kid like Ted Richard, you turn your back on all this and let your mind roam where it may. But youngsters like Ted are rare. What Ken and so many others do is protect themselves from such suffocating madness by taking on with a vengeance the identity implied in the vocational track. Reject the confusion and frustration by openly defining yourself as the Common Joe. Champion the average. Rely on your own good sense. Fuck this bullshit. Bullshit, of course, is everything you—and the others—fear is beyond you: books, essays, tests, academic scrambling, complexity, scientific reasoning, philosophical inquiry.

The tragedy is that you have to twist the knife in your own gray matter to make this defense work. You'll have to shut down, have to reject intellectual stimuli or diffuse them with sarcasm, have to cultivate stupidity, have to convert boredom from a malady into a way of confronting the world. Keep your vocabulary simple, act stoned when you're not or act more stoned than you are, flaunt ignorance, materialize your dreams. It is a powerful and effective defense—it neutralizes the insult and the frustration of being a vocational kid and, when perfected, it drives teachers up the wall, a delightful secondary effect. But like all strong magic, it exacts a price.

Interpretations

1. How common is it in neighborhoods such as Rose describes for young people not to be "crazy in love or lost in work" or for old persons not to be "passionate about a cause or an idea"? What would you call the missing quality in the lives of such people?

2. What does Rose's statement that "The vocational track . . . is most often a place for those who are just not making it, a dumping ground for the disaffected" imply about our educational system?

3. Rose says that "students will float to the mark you set" but also that "none of us were groomed for the classroom." To what extent is it possible for teachers to resolve this paradox?

4. Rose says working-class vocational ed. students "champion the average" as a defense against confusion and frustration. What evidence can you cite, from your own experience, that this defense is "powerful and effective"?

Correspondences

1. Contrast Rose's classroom experiences with those of Viloria and speculate on their psychological effects.

2. Review Bacon's perspective on knowledge and power (page 194) and discuss its relevance to Rose and his classmates. Explain the connection between education and empowerment. What factors contributed to their powerlessness?

Applications

1. Evaluate Rose's evidence in support of the thesis that "school can be a tremendously disorienting place."

2. Imagine yourself as a vocational teacher. What strategies would you use to engage your students? What possibilities would you offer them? How might you contribute to their sense of empowerment?

So Tsi-fai

Sophronia Liu

Sophronia Liu (b. 1953) was born in Hong Kong and came to America at age 10. She received her Master's Degree in English from the University of South Dakota and is currently working on her doctorate at the University of Minnesota. These are her reasons for writing "So Tsi-fai": "I wrote 'So Tsi-fai' as a response to an assignment in a feminist creative writing course. The assignment was to describe a person who had given me my first inkling about social class. I guess for me, my awareness of social class and of the meaning of colonial oppression happened simultaneously in my sixth-grade classroom."

The events of this narrative occurred in Hong Kong, an island ninety miles south of Canton, China. Hong Kong has been a British colony since 1841 and is scheduled to revert to the People's Republic of China in 1997. Only 20,000 of its 5.7 million inhabitants are British. Hong Kong and its mainland adjunct the New Territories have been the destination of more than a million refugees from China, but since the Chinese crackdown on political dissidents in Tiananmen Square in June 1989, many Hong Kong citizens, fearful that the Chinese Communist government in Beijing will not honor the agreement allowing Hong Kong to retain its capitalist system, are themselves contemplating emigration.

For more information on China, see John King Fairbank, "Footbinding," Chapter 1.

VOICES, IMAGES, SCENES from the past—twenty-three years ago, when I was in sixth grade:

"Let us bow our heads in silent prayer for the soul of So Tsi-fai. Let us pray for God's forgiveness for this boy's rash taking of his own life . . ." Sister Marie (Mung Gu-liang). My sixth-grade English teacher. Missionary nun from Paris. Principal of The Little Flower's School. Disciplinarian, perfectionist, authority figure: awesome and awful in my ten-year-old eyes.

"I don't need any supper. I have drunk enough insecticide." So Tsi-fai. My fourteen-year-old classmate. Daredevil; good-for-nothing lazy-bones (according to Mung Gu-liang). Bright black eyes, disheveled hair, defiant sneer, creased and greasy uniform, dirty hands, careless walk,

251

shuffling feet. Standing in the corner for being late, for forgetting his homework, for talking in class, for using foul language. ("Shame on you! Go wash your mouth with soap!" Mung Gu-liang's sharp command. He did, and came back with a grin.) So Tsi-fai: Sticking his tongue out behind Mung Gu-liang's back, passing secret notes to his friends, kept behind after school, sent to the Principal's office for repeated offense. So Tsi-fai: incorrigible, hopeless, and without hope.

It was a Monday in late November when we heard of his death, returning to school after the weekend with our parents' signatures on our midterm reports. So Tsi-fai also showed his report to his father, we were told later. He flunked three out of the fourteen subjects: English Grammar, Arithmetic, and Chinese Dictation. He missed each one by one to three marks. That wasn't so bad. But he was a hopeless case. Overaged, stubborn, and uncooperative; a repeated offender of school rules, scourge of all teachers; who was going to give him a lenient passing grade? Besides, being a few months over the maximum age—fourteen— for sixth graders, he wasn't even allowed to sit for the Secondary School Entrance Exam.

All sixth graders in Hong Kong had to pass the SSE before they could obtain a seat in secondary school. In 1964 when I took the exam, there were more than twenty thousand candidates. About seven thousand of us passed: four thousand were sent to government and subsidized schools, the other three thousand to private and grant-in-aid schools. I came in around no. 2000; I was lucky. Without the public exam, there would be no secondary school for So Tsi-fai. His future was sealed.

Looking at the report card with three red marks on it, his father was furious. So Tsi-fai was the oldest son. There were three younger children. His father was a vegetable farmer with a few plots of land in Wong Jukhang, by the sea. His mother worked in a local factory. So Tsi-fai helped in the fields, cooked for the family, and washed his own clothes. ("Filthy, dirty boy!" gasped Mung Gu-liang. "Grime behind the ears, black rims on the fingernails, dirty collar, crumpled shirt. Why doesn't your mother iron your shirt?") Both his parents were illiterate. So Tsi-fai was their biggest hope: He made it to the sixth grade.

Who woke him up for school every morning and had breakfast waiting for him? Nobody. ("Time for school! Get up! Eat your rice!" Ma nagged and screamed. The aroma of steamed rice and Chinese sausages spread all over the house. "Drink your tea! Eat your oranges! Wash your face! And remember to wash behind your ears!") And who helped So Tsi-fai do his homework? Nobody. Did he have older brothers like mine who knew all about the arithmetic of rowing a boat against the currents or with the currents, how to count the feet of chickens and rabbits in the same cage, the present perfect continuous tense of "to live" and the future perfect tense of "to succeed"? None. Nil. So Tsi-fai was a lost cause.

I came first in both terms that year, the star pupil. So Tsi-fai was one of the last in the class: He was lazy; he didn't care. Or did he?

When his father scolded him, So Tsi-fai left the house. When he showed up again, late for supper, he announced, "I don't need any supper. I have drunk enough insecticide." Just like another one of his practical jokes. The insecticide was stored in the field for his father's vegetables. He was rushed to the hospital; dead upon arrival.

"He gulped for a last breath and was gone," an uncle told us at the funeral. "But his eyes wouldn't shut. So I said in his ear, 'You go now and rest in peace.' And I smoothed my hand over his eyelids. His face was all purple."

His face was still purple when we saw him in his coffin. Eyes shut tight, nostrils dilated and white as if fire and anger might shoot out, any minute.

In class that Monday morning, Sister Marie led us in prayer. "Let us pray that God will forgive him for his sins." We said the Lord's Prayer and the Hail Mary. We bowed our heads. I sat in my chair, frozen and dazed, thinking of the deadly chill in the morgue, the smell of disinfectant, ether, and dead flesh.

"Bang!" went a gust of wind, forcing open a leaf of the double door leading to the back balcony. "Flap, flap, flap." The door swung in the wind. We could see the treetops by the hillside rustling to and fro against a pale blue sky. An imperceptible presence had drifted in with the wind. The same careless walk and shuffling feet, the same daredevil air—except that the eyes were lusterless, dripping blood; the tongue hanging out, gasping for air. As usual, he was late. But he had come back to claim his place.

"I died a tragic death," his voice said. "I have as much right as you to be here. This is my seat." We heard him; we knew he was back.

. . . So Tsi-fai: Standing in the corner for being late, for forgetting his homework, for talking in class, for using foul language. So Tsi-fai: Palm outstretched, chest sticking out, holding his breath: "Tat. Tat. Tat." Down came the teacher's wooden ruler, twenty times on each hand. Never batting an eyelash: then back to facing the wall in the corner by the door. So Tsi-fai: grimy shirt, disheveled hair, defiant sneer. So Tsi-fai. Incorrigible, hopeless, and without hope.

The girls in front gasped and shrank back in their chairs. Mung Gu-liang went to the door, held the doorknob in one hand, poked her head out, and peered into the empty balcony. Then, with a determined jerk, she pulled the door shut. Quickly crossing herself, she returned to the teacher's desk. Her black cross swung upon the front of her gray habit as she hurried across the room. "Don't be silly!" she scolded the frightened girls in the front row.

What really happened? After all these years, my mind is still haunted by this scene. What happened to So Tsi-fai? What happened to me? What happened to all of us that year in sixth grade, when we were green and young and ready to fling our arms out for the world? All of a sudden, death claimed one of us and he was gone.

Who arbitrates between life and death? Who decides which life is worth preserving and prospering, and which to nip in its bud? How did it happen that I, at ten, turned out to be the star pupil, the lucky one, while my friend, a peasant's son, was shoveled under the heap and lost forever? How could it happen that this world would close off a young boy's life at fourteen just because he was poor, undisciplined, and lacked the training and support to pass his exams? What really happened?

Today, twenty-three years later, So Tsi-fai's ghost still haunts me. "I died a tragic death. I have as much right as you to be here. This is my seat." The voice I heard twenty-three years ago in my sixth-grade classroom follows me in my dreams. Is there anything I can do to lay it to rest?

Interpretations

1. To what extent does So Tsi-fai's family help him realize his aspirations? What relation do you see between these aspirations and So Tsi-fai's suicide?

2. What does the statement, "I don't need any supper. I have drunk enough insecticide" show about So Tsi-fai's personality?

3. In two paragraphs of questions, the author tries to convey her feelings about So Tsi-fai's "ghost." Describe these feelings. (Can you answer any of the story questions?)

4. Specifically, which phrases, sentences, or passages control the tone of the essay and most aptly convey the author's feelings about the events surrounding So Tsi-fai's death?

5. Sometimes poor and uneducated but ambitious parents are surprised to find their educated children alienated. How do you think such alienation can be avoided so that the whole family benefits from the newly educated generation?

Correspondences

1. Review the Baker perspective on American education (page 193). How does it apply to the educational experience of students in Hong Kong? Should educational systems focus less on testing? Why or why not?

2. Parents play an important role in the education of their children. How did So Tsi-fai's parents affect his? How was their attitude towards education different from that of Kingston's parents (Chapter 2)?

Applications

1. "Voices, images, scenes from the past—twenty-three years ago, when I was in sixth grade." Write an essay about a classmate who, like So Tsi-fai, made a deep impression. Describe the person's effect on your education.

2. Do the children of poor, uneducated parents indeed have a right to a good education? If so, whose responsibility is it to provide that education? Is this a particularly Chinese problem, or do we face it also in the United States?

ADDITIONAL WRITING TOPICS

1. Is community part of the educational experiences of Rendón, Kontor, Liu, or Cousins? How does its presence or absence affect their experiences? To what extent was your educational experience shaped by the presence or absence of a sense of community? Should educational institutions be responsible for fostering a sense of community?

2. Review the Kaufman quotation (page 193). What are the ramifications of viewing education as a process rather than a product? To what extent do the selections in this chapter support or refute Kaufman? Write an essay responding to these questions concluding with your views on this issue.

3. According to the Ellison quotation (page 194), language can create or destroy, liberate or imprison. How do the selections by Rendón, Wright, and Marshall attest to Ellison's point of view? To what extent do you agree or disagree with Ellison? What educational experience led to your conclusions about the power of language? Frame your reply in a chronological narrative. Include insights gained from the experience.

4. Should a teacher serve as a role model for students? How important is it that he or she be a member of the students' ethnic group? Do teachers have too much or too little influence on their students? Write an essay that answers these questions.

5. Review the Bambara headnote (p. 225). Why does she think stories are important? How have stories that you were told and that you have read contributed to your knowledge of your cultural heritage and to your education? Write a speech for your local school board in which you argue for the inclusion of a storytelling component in each of the elementary grades.

6. Some educational theorists argue that because students have grown up with television they prefer the visual to the linear—the image to the word. For such learners, "a picture is worth a thousand words." To what extent do you agree? How has the visual affected information processing? Should more visual techniques of communication be incorporated into the classroom? Write an essay responding to these questions.

7. Review Ehrlich's essay and write an essay interpreting the motifs of "looking" and "finding." What role does curiosity play in the learning process? Discuss the connection between "finding" and "learning."

8. According to Rose, students tend to respond to the expectations of their teachers. Apply this thesis to the selections by Liu, Rose, and/or Viloria. What might you conclude about the effects of lack of expectation on student performance?

CHAPTER 4

Work

We spend a great deal of our lives choosing, preparing for, and doing our work. "What do you do?" is perhaps the first question we want to ask about a new acquaintance. "Talking shop" is supposed to be taboo everywhere except at the office, factory, or construction site, yet no taboo is more frequently, and more gladly, broken. For many people, the workplace is life. Talk about it ranges from the personal and particular to the abstract, whatever one's culture.

As you will discover, attitudes towards work and its value differ among cultures and exist in a matrix of customs, traditions, education, and class. In the Genesis account, work is viewed as a punishment for human disobedience, while in the Nez Percé selection work is portrayed as interfering with dreams.

In the traditional, pre-industrial economy of Guinea, in western Africa, goldsmithing is highly ritualistic work akin to religious "mysteries." From it the craftsman gains an identity and a social status as well as an income. The identity is particularly satisfying and the status exalted.

The most abstract treatment of work in this chapter is Lance Morrow's consideration of recent developments in the nature and psychological impact of work, mostly on Americans, and the American attitude toward work. Ouchi's "The Competitive Edge" is a sociological treatise on cultural and national traits revealed in work habits. He finds the Japanese more suited by temperament than Americans to industrial work because of the Japanese emphasis on cooperation.

Most of the other selections of the chapter focus on individual workers, mostly blue collar, who experience problems: immigrant conditions and the effects of national, racial, or sexual prejudice. Steve Olson, a construction worker, sees his co-workers, the BCGs (blue-collar guys) as a "much maligned group" who "have been portrayed as beer-drinking, big-bellied, bigoted rednecks who dress badly. . . . While white-collar types are debating the value of reading over watching TV, BCGs are doing stuff." (*Newsweek,* November 6, 1989).

In immigrant families work provides, above all, for education. It serves that end however it can. And workers suffer for it. Mario Puzo's family "did stuff," in addition to raising a son who would become a best-selling novelist. The Puzos exchanged a small farm in Italy for working on the railroad in one of the roughest neighborhoods of New York, Hell's Kitchen. The main character of Ann Petry's story is a black factory worker whose white female boss calls him a "nigger." You will see how Johnson handles the problem in "Like a Winding Sheet." Rachel Jones, a black reporter for a Florida newspaper, and one of the few white-collar workers in this chapter, finds work made almost impossible by racial prejudice when she tries to cover a Ku Klux Klan rally. The title character in Bharati Mukherjee's "Jasmine" will put up with almost any indignity and do almost any work in America to escape her home in Trinidad. Gary Soto, our youngest worker, accepts any job on the block in "Looking for Work," but the consequences are much less serious. Unlike blacks and first-generation immigrants, he is not exploited or foiled.

"Procrastination," by a student (Sharon Friedner) who seems to know the subject first-hand, puts a light-hearted spin on a problem that plagues all workers, and students too. And another student, Michael Gnolfo, treats a topic much in the news these days in "A View of Affirmative Action in the Workplace."

PERSPECTIVES

Work spares us from three great evils: boredom, vice and need.

Voltaire

How will you know when you have found work you love? One symptom is that you will lose track of time, You'll look at your watch and wonder where the hours have gone, at your calendar and wonder what happened to the week. And that loss of time sense is a symbol as well as a symptom. We are time-bound creatures, but meaningful work can make us forget our mortal limitation—because it helps us transcend it.

Lynne V. Cheney

If people are highly successful in their professions they lose their senses. Sound goes. They have no time to listen to music. Speech goes. They have no time for conversation. They lose their sense of proportion—the relations between one thing and another. Humanity goes.

Virginia Woolf

Work is a necessity for man. Man invented the alarm clock.

Pablo Picasso

Life is a continual distraction which does not allow us to reflect on that from which we are distracted.

Franz Kafka

Women feel just as men feel . . . and it is narrowminded in their more privileged fellow creatures to say that they ought to confine themselves to making pudding and knitting stockings.

Charlotte Brontë

This book, being about work, is, by its very nature, about violence—to the spirit as well as the body.

Studs Terkel

In fact, there is perhaps only one human being in a thousand who is passionately interested in his job for the job's sake.

Dorothy Sayers

More and more, we take for granted that work must be destitute of pleasure. More and more, we assume that if we want to be pleased we must wait until evening, or the weekend, or vacation, or retirement. More and more, our farms and forests resemble our factories and offices, which in turn more and more resemble prisons—why else should we be so eager to escape them? We recognize defeated landscapes by the absence of pleasure from them. We are defeated at work because our work gives us no pleasure.

Wendell Berry

Increased means and increased leisure are the two civilizers of man.

Disraeli

We are not far from the time when a man after a hard weekend of leisure will thankfully go back to work.

Russell Baker

Applications

1. Write a journal entry comparing the Perspectives on work to your own ideas about work.
2. Discuss Picasso's viewpoint with your group and write an analysis of their responses.

The Fall

Genesis 3:1-9

The Genesis account of the Fall explains among other things, the origin of work, painful childbirth, and death. This seminal story following immediately after the Genesis account of Creation continues to exert an influence on Western culture out of proportion to its modest length.

THE SERPENT WAS more crafty than any wild creature that the LORD God had made. He said to the woman, "Is it true that God has forbidden you to eat from any tree in the garden?" The woman answered the serpent, "We may eat the fruit of any tree in the garden, except for the tree in the middle of the garden; God has forbidden us either to eat or to touch the fruit of that; if we do, we shall die." The serpent said, "Of course you will not die. God knows that as soon as you eat it, your eyes will be opened and you will be like gods knowing both good and evil." When the woman saw that the fruit of the tree was good to eat, and that it was pleasing to the eye and tempting to contemplate, she took some and ate it. She also gave her husband some and he ate it. Then the eyes of both of them were opened and they discovered that they were naked; so they stitched fig-leaves together and made themselves loincloths.

The man and his wife heard the sound of the LORD God walking in the garden at the time of the evening breeze and hid from the LORD God among the trees of the garden. But the LORD God called to the man and said to him, "Where are you?" He replied, "I heard the sound as you were walking in the garden, and I was afraid because I was naked, and I hid myself." God answered, "Who told you that you were naked? Have you eaten from the tree which I forbade you?" The man said, "The woman you gave me for a companion, she gave me fruit from the tree and I ate it." Then the LORD God said to the woman, "What is this that you have done?" The woman said, "The serpent tricked me, and I ate." Then the LORD God said to the serpent:

> Because you have done this you are accursed
> more than all cattle and all wild creatures.
> On your belly you shall crawl, and dust you shall eat
> all the days of your life.
> I will put enmity between you and the woman,
> between your brood and hers.

> They shall strike at your head,
> and you shall strike at their heel.

To the woman he said:

> I will increase your labour and your groaning,
> and in labour you shall bear children.
> You shall be eager for your husband,
> and he shall be your master.

And to the man he said:

> Because you have listened to your wife
> and have eaten from the tree which I forbade you,
> accursed shall be the ground on your account.
> With labour you shall win your food from it
> all the days of your life.
> It will grow thorns and thistles for you,
> none but wild plants for you to eat.
> You shall gain your bread by the sweat of your brow
> until you return to the ground;
> for from it you were taken.
> Dust you are, to dust you shall return.

Interpretations

1. What attitude toward work does the passage reveal?

2. What attitude toward woman does the story reveal? Does the story explain why the serpent chose to speak to the woman, not the man? Of what significance is this choice?

3. What attributes of God does this story reveal? Does God's ban on the knowledge of good and evil (morality?) play into the serpent's evil designs, making the man and woman unnecessarily vulnerable? Is obedience God's main objective, and is this simply a test case to see if the new man and woman can obey orders, no matter what the orders?

4. Whom does the story hold ultimately responsible for the existence of evil?

5. Do you think the punishments in this case fit the crime? Why or why not?

My Young Men Shall Never Work

Chief Smohalla as told by Herbert J. Spinden

The Nez Percé are a tribe of American Indians formerly occupy-ing much of the Pacific Northwest whose reservation is in Idaho.

Because Native Americans resisted giving up their homes and nomadic way of life to become farmers, white people have often called them lazy, stubborn, and impractical. But to Indians, whose homes, land, and hunting were sacred, anything that threatened any one of these, threatened their whole system of beliefs and values, in short, their very life.

MY YOUNG MEN shall never work. Men who work cannot dream and wisdom comes in dreams.

You ask me to plow the ground. Shall I take a knife and tear my mother's breast? Then when I die she will not take me to her bosom to rest.

You ask me to dig for stone. Shall I dig under her skin for bones? Then when I die I cannot enter her body to be born again.

You ask me to cut grass and make hay and sell it and be rich like white men. But how dare I cut off my mother's hair?

It is a bad law and my people cannot obey it. I want my people to stay with me here. All the dead men will come to life again. We must wait here in the house of our fathers and be ready to meet them in the body of our mother.

Interpretations

1. Are the Nez Percé objecting to all work? Would you define work to include hunting?

2. What is the Nez Percé's reason for rejecting what they call "work"? What do they value more than work? How common is it for a culture to place the highest value on something other than work? Is work the highest value of American culture? What's the evidence?

3. To what extent is the misunderstanding between the Nez Percé and the whites a matter of language (definition)? of tradition? What is the Nez Percé attitude towards earth? (What metaphor extends through and is elaborated within the whole passage?)

Correspondences

1. Review the Voltaire quotation (page 259). How does it apply to the Genesis account of the origins of work? Which attitude towards work best reflects your own?

2. Review the Kafka quotation (page 259). What does it mean? To what extent does it reflect the sentiments about work expressed by Smohalla of the Nez Percé?

Applications

1. Write a journal entry on work as punishment.

2. Compare and contrast the attitudes toward the earth as a place of human habitation as revealed in Genesis and the words of Chief Smohalla and examine the concept of human responsibility in each reading. Be specific, using examples and brief quotations to enforce your points.

What Is the Point of Working?

Lance Morrow

Lance Morrow is a poet and playwright. He worked as a reporter on the Washington Star *before becoming a contributing editor to* Time *magazine. In 1981 he won the National Magazine Award for his essays regularly featured in* Time, *and in 1985 he published a book on fatherhood,* The Chief: A Memoir of Fathers and Sons. *In "What Is the Point of Working?" Morrow explores American attitudes toward the workplace.*

WHEN GOD FORECLOSED on Eden, he condemned Adam and Eve to go to work. Work has never recovered from that humiliation. From the beginning, the Lord's word said that work was something bad: a punishment, the great stone of mortality and toil laid upon a human spirit that might otherwise soar in the infinite, weightless playfulness of grace.

A perfectly understandable prejudice against work has prevailed ever since. Most work in the life of the world has been hard, but since it was grindingly inevitable, it hardly seemed worth complaining about very much. Work was simply the business of life, as matter-of-fact as sex and breathing. In recent years, however, the ancient discontent has grown elaborately articulate. The worker's usual old bitching has gone to college. Grim tribes of sociologists have reported back from office and factory that most workers find their labor mechanical, boring, imprisoning, stultifying, repetitive, dreary, heartbreaking. In his 1972 book *Working,* Studs Terkel began: "This book, being about work, is, by its very nature, about violence—to the spirit as well as to the body." The historical horrors of industrialization (child labor, Dickensian squalor, the dark satanic mills) translate into the 20th century's robotic busywork on the line, tightening the same damned screw on the Camaro's fire-wall assembly, going nuts to the banging, jangling Chaplinesque whirr of modern materialism in labor, bringing forth issue, disgorging itself upon the market.

The lamentations about how awful work is prompt an answering wail from the management side of the chasm: nobody wants to work any more. As American productivity, once the exuberant engine of national wealth, has dipped to an embarrassingly uncompetitive low, Americans have shaken their heads: the country's old work ethic is dead. About the only good words for it now emanate from Ronald Reagan and certain beer commercials. Those ads are splendidly mythic playlets, romantic idealizations of men in groups who blast through mountains or pour plumingly molten steel in factories, the work all grit and grin. Then they retire to flip around iced cans of sacramental beer and debrief one another in a warm sundown glow of accomplishment. As for Reagan, in his presidential campaign he enshrined work in his rhetorical "community of values," along with family, neighborhood, peace and freedom. He won by a landslide.

Has the American work ethic really expired? Is some old native eagerness to level wilderness and dig and build and invent now collapsing toward a decadence of dope, narcissism, income transfers and aerobic self-actualization?

The idea of work—work as an ethic, an abstraction—arrived rather late in the history of toil. Whatever edifying and pietistic things may have been said about work over the centuries (Kahlil Gibran called work "love made visible," and the Benedictines say, "To work is to pray"), humankind has always tried to avoid it whenever possible. The philosophical swells of ancient Greece thought work was degrading; they kept an underclass to see to the laundry and other details of basic social maintenance. That prejudice against work persisted down the centuries in other aristocracies. It is supposed, however, to be inherently un-American. Edward Kennedy likes to tell the story of how, during his first campaign for the Senate, his opponent said scornfully in a debate: "This man has never worked a day in his life!" Kennedy says that the next morning as he was shaking hands at a factory gate, one worker leaned toward him and confided, "You ain't missed a goddamned thing."

The Protestant work ethic, which sanctified work and turned it into vocation, arrived only a few centuries ago in the formulations of Martin Luther and John Calvin. In that scheme, the worker collaborates with God to do the work of the universe, the great design. One scholar, Leland Ryken of Illinois' Wheaton College, has pointed out that American politicians and corporate leaders who preach about the work ethic do not understand the Puritans' original, crucial linkage between human labor and God's will.

During the 19th century industrialization of America, the idea of work's inherent virtue may have seemed temporarily implausible to generations who labored in the mines and mills and sweatshops. The century's huge machinery of production punished and stunned those who ran it.

And yet for generations of immigrants, work *was* ultimately availing; the numb toil of an illiterate grandfather got the father a foothold and a high school education, and the son wound up in college or even law school. A woman who died in the Triangle Shirtwaist Co. fire [1911] in lower Manhattan had a niece who made it to the halcyon Bronx, and another generation on, the family went to Westchester County. So for millions of Americans, as they labored through the complexities of generations, work worked, and the immigrant work ethic came at last to merge with the Protestant work ethic.

The motive of work was all. To work for mere survival is desperate. To work for a better life for one's children and grandchildren lends the labor a fierce dignity. That dignity, an unconquerably hopeful energy and aspiration—driving, persisting like a life force—is the American quality that many find missing now.

The work ethic is not dead, but it is weaker now. The psychology of work is much changed in America. The acute, painful memory of the Great Depression used to enforce a disciplined and occasionally docile approach to work—in much the way that older citizens in the Soviet Union do not complain about scarce food and overpopulated apartments, because they remember how much more horrible everything was during the war. But the generation of the Depression is retiring and dying off, and today's younger workers, though sometimes laid off and kicked around by recessions and inflation, still do not keep in dark storage that residual apocalyptic memory of Hoovervilles and the Dust Bowl and banks capsizing.

Today elaborate financial cushions—unemployment insurance, union benefits, welfare payments, food stamps and so on—have made it less catastrophic to be out of a job for a while. Work is still a profoundly respectable thing in America. Most Americans suffer a sense of loss, of diminution, even of worthlessness, if they are thrown out on the street. But the blow seldom carries the life-and-death implications it once had, the sense of personal ruin. Besides, the wild and notorious behavior of the economy takes a certain amount of personal shame out of joblessness; if Ford closes down a plant in New Jersey and throws 3,700 workers into the unemployment lines, the guilts falls less on individuals than on Japanese imports or American car design or an extortionate OPEC.

Because today's workers are better educated than those in the past, their expectations are higher. Many younger Americans have rearranged their ideas about what they want to get out of life. While their fathers and grandfathers and great-grandfathers concentrated hard upon plow and drill press and pressure gauge and tort, some younger workers now ask previously unimaginable questions about the point of knocking themselves out. For the first time in the history of the world, masses of people in industrially advanced countries no longer have to focus their minds upon work as the central concern of their existence.

In the formulation of Psychologist Abraham Maslow, work functions in a hierarchy of needs: first, work provides food and shelter, basic human maintenance. After that, it can address the need for security and then for friendship and "belongingness." Next, the demands of the ego arise, the need for respect. Finally, men and women assert a larger desire for "self-actualization." That seems a harmless and even worthy enterprise but sometimes degenerates into self-infatuation, a vaporously selfish discontent that dead-ends in isolation, the empty face that gazes back from the mirror.

Of course in patchwork, pluralistic America, different classes and ethnic groups are perched at different stages in the work hierarchy. The immigrants—legal and illegal—who still flock densely to America are fighting for the foothold that the jogging tribes of self-actualizers achieved three generations ago. The zealously ambitious Koreans who run New York City's best vegetable markets, or boat people trying to open a restaurant, or chicanos who struggle to start a small business in the *barrio* are still years away from est and the Sierra Club. Working women, to the extent that they are new at it, now form a powerful source of ambition and energy. Feminism—and financial need—have made them, in effect, a sophisticated-immigrant wave upon the economy.

Having to work to stay alive, to build a future, gives one's exertions a tough moral simplicity. The point of work in that case is so obvious that it need not be discussed. But apart from the sheer necessity of sustaining life, is there some inherent worth in work? Carlyle believed that "all work, even cotton spinning, is noble; work is alone noble." Was he right?

It is seigneurial cant to romanticize work that is truly detestable and destructive to workers. But misery and drudgery are always comparative. Despite the sometimes nostalgic haze around their images, the pre-industrial peasant and the 19th century American farmer did brutish work far harder than the assembly line. The untouchable who sweeps excrement in the streets of Bombay would react with blank incomprehension to the malaise of some $17-an-hour workers on a Chrysler assembly line. The Indian, after all, has passed from "alienation" into a degradation that is almost mystical. In Nicaragua, the average 19-year-old peasant has worked longer and harder than most Americans of middle age. Americans prone to restlessness about the spiritual disappointments of work should consult unemployed young men and women in their own ghettos: they know with painful clarity the importance of the personal dignity that a job brings.

Americans often fall into fallacies of misplaced sympathy. Psychologist Maslow, for example, once wrote that he found it difficult "to conceive of feeling proud of myself, self-loving and self-respecting, if I were working, for example, in some chewing-gum factory . . ." Well, two weeks ago, Warner-Lambert announced that it would close down its gum-manufacturing American Chicle factory in Long Island City, N.Y.; the workers who had spent years there making Dentyne and Chiclets were distraught. "It's a beautiful place to work," one feeder-catcher-packer of chewing gum said sadly. "It's just like home." There is a peculiar elitist arrogance in those who discourse on the brutalizations of work simply because they cannot imagine themselves performing the job. Certainly workers often feel abstracted out, reduced sometimes to dreary robotic functions. But almost everyone commands endlessly subtle systems of adaptation; people can make the work their own and even cherish it against all academic expectations. Such adaptations are often more important than the famous but theoretical alienation from the process and product of labor.

Work is still the complicated and crucial core of most lives, the occupation melded inseparably to the identity; Freud said that the successful psyche is one capable of love and of work. Work is the most thorough and profound organizing principle in American life. If mobility has weakened old blood ties, our co-workers often form our new family, our tribe, our social world; we become almost citizens of our companies, living under the protection of salaries, pensions and health insurance. Sociologist Robert Schrank believes that people like jobs mainly because they need other people; they need to gossip with them, hang out with them, to schmooze. Says Schrank: "The workplace performs the function of community."

Unless it is dishonest or destructive—the labor of a pimp or a hit man, say—all work is intrinsically honorable in ways that are rarely understood as they once were. Only the fortunate toil in ways that express them directly. There is a Renaissance splendor in Leonardo's effusion: "The works that the eye orders the hands to make are infinite." But most of us labor closer to the ground. Even there, all work expresses the laborer in a deeper sense: all life must be worked at, protected, planted, replanted, fashioned, cooked for, coaxed, diapered, formed, sustained. Work is the way that we tend the world, the way that people connect. It is the most vigorous, vivid sign of life—in individuals and in civilizations.

Interpretations

1. What do you consider the most interesting or valuable point Morrow makes about work? Why?

2. Have you ever considered not working at all, just avoiding any kind of work for your whole life? Probably not, but *why* not? Aside from food and shelter, what do you expect to get out of work? What portion of your identity do you expect to derive from your work? If your work is not the "central concern of [your] existence," what else could occupy that position? Are your educational choices (or your choice of friends or of entertainment) shaped wholly by your work plans? If not, by what?

3. "Because today's workers are better educated than those in the past, their expectations are higher." Do you agree that education raises expectations? Expectations of what? If you agree, can you explain

how this relationship works? What are the advantages and disadvantages of being governed by "higher" expectations?

4. Is it possible to be a failure in your chosen profession and still be a success in life? Explain.

5. How has Morrow limited his subject and where in the essay does he indicate which aspect of work he intends to cover?

Correspondences

1. Review the Cheney quotation (page 259). To what extent is it applicable to Morrow's essay? Do you agree with Morrow that the work ethic is weaker now in America than it was in the past. Why or why not?

2. Morrow suggests that the hardest workers in the United States are immigrants. How does Weber's essay (Chapter 2) or Marshall's story (Chapter 3) contradict or support this? (What attitudes toward work are expressed by those Weber interviewed? How do they compare with those of Marshall's "poets"?)

Applications

1. Discuss in your group Schrank's thesis that "the workplace performs the function of community." Have you found that to be true of your working experience? Might Schrank's thesis also apply to the homeless? What is the relationship of homelessness to work?

2. Morrow's essay traces a changing concept of work from "grindingly inevitable . . . simply the business of life" to the activity that brings "personal dignity" and "identity," and provides "the organizing principle in American life . . . the way that we tend the world, . . . the way that people connect." How much does Morrow think (and do you think) automation and better education have changed our concept(s) of work?

Choosing a Dream: Italians in Hell's Kitchen

Mario Puzo

Mario Puzo (b. 1920) is from New York City. The son of a railroad trackman, he was educated at the New School for Social Research and Columbia University. He has received numerous awards and honors from the American Academy of Motion Picture Arts and Sciences, the Writers Guild of America, West, Inc., for The Godfather *(1972) and* The Godfather, Part II *(1974). In "Italians in Hell's Kitchen," Puzo explains why his youthful contempt for his Italian parents and relatives changed to awe and admiration.*

A major world power under the Romans, the birthplace of the Renaissance and the site of the mother church of Roman Catholicism, Italy was prevented until 1860 by German, French, Spanish, and Austrian intervention from transforming its city states into a unified modern nation (under King Victor Emmanuel II). Even after unification, economic progress, especially in the south, was slow, sending millions of Italians abroad in search of a better life. In the century and a half before 1988, almost ten percent of immigrants to the United States were Italian, among them Puzo's parents.

AS A CHILD and in my adolescence, living in the heart of New York's Neapolitan ghetto, I never heard an Italian singing. None of the grown-ups I knew were charming or loving or understanding. Rather they seemed coarse, vulgar, and insulting. And so later in my life when I was exposed to all the clichés of lovable Italians, singing Italians, happy-go-lucky Italians, I wondered where the hell the moviemakers and story-writers got all their ideas from.

At a very early age I decided to escape these uncongenial folk by becoming an artist, a writer. It seemed then an impossible dream. My father and mother were illiterate, as were their parents before them. But practicing my art I tried to view the adults with a more charitable eye and so came to the conclusion that their only fault lay in their being foreigners; I was an American. This didn't really help because I was only half right. I was the foreigner. They were already more "American" than I could ever become.

But it did seem then that the Italian immigrants, all the fathers and mothers that I knew, were a grim lot; always shouting, always angry, quicker to quarrel then embrace. I did not understand that their lives were a long labor to earn their daily bread and that physical fatigue does not sweeten human natures.

And so even as a very small child I dreaded growing up to be like the adults around me. I heard them saying too many cruel things about their dearest friends, saw too many of their false embraces with those they had just maligned, observed with horror their paranoiac anger at some small slight or a fancied injury to their pride. They were, always, too unforgiving. In short, they did not have the careless magnanimity of children.

In my youth I was contemptuous of my elders, including a few under thirty. I thought my contempt special to their circumstances. Later when I wrote about these illiterate men and women, when I thought I understood them, I felt a condescending pity. After all, they had suffered, they had labored all the days of their lives. They had never tasted luxury, knew little more economic security than those ancient Roman slaves who might have been their ancestors. And alas, I thought, with new-found artistic insight, they were cut off from their children because of the strange American tongue, alien to them, native to their sons and daughters.

Already an artist but not yet a husband or father, I pondered omnisciently on their tragedy, again thinking it special circumstance rather than a constant in the human condition. I did not yet understand why these men and women were willing to settle for less than they deserved in life and think that "less" quite a bargain. I did not understand that they simply could not afford to dream; I myself had a hundred dreams from which to choose. For I was already sure that I would make my escape, that I was one of the chosen. I would be rich, famous, happy. I would master my destiny. . . .

My family and I grew up together on Tenth Avenue, between Thirtieth and Thirty-first streets, part of the area called Hell's Kitchen. This particular neighborhood could have been a movie set for one of the Dead End Kid flicks or for the social drama of the East Side in which John Garfield played the hero. Our tenements were the western wall of the city. Beneath our windows were the vast black iron gardens of the New York Central Railroad, absolutely blooming with stinking boxcars freshly unloaded of cattle and pigs for the city slaughterhouse. Steers sometimes escaped and loped through the heart of the neighborhood followed by astonished young boys who had never seen a live cow.

The railroad yards stretched down to the Hudson River, beyond whose garbagey waters rose the rocky Palisades of New Jersey. There were railroad tracks running downtown on Tenth Avenue itself to another freight station called St. Johns Park. Because of this, because these trains cut off one side of the street from the other, there was a wooden bridge over Tenth Avenue, a romantic-looking bridge despite the fact that no sparkling water, no silver flying fish darted beneath it; only heavy dray carts drawn by tired horses, some flat-boarded trucks, tin lizzie automobiles and, of course, long strings of freight cars drawn by black, ugly engines. . . .

My father supported his wife and seven children by working as a trackman laborer for the New York Central Railroad. My oldest brother worked for the railroad as a brakeman, another brother was a railroad shipping clerk in the freight office. Eventually I spent some of the worst months of my life as the railroad's worst messenger boy.

My oldest sister was just as unhappy as a dressmaker in the garment industry. She wanted to be a school teacher. At one time or another my other two brothers also worked for the railroad—it got all six males in the family. The two girls and my mother escaped, though my mother felt it her duty to send all our bosses a gallon of homemade wine on Christmas. But everybody hated their jobs except my oldest brother who had a night shift and spent most of his working hours sleeping in freight cars. My father finally got fired because the foreman told him to get a bucket of water for the crew and not to take all day. My father took the bucket and disappeared forever.

Nearly all the Italian men living on Tenth Avenue supported their large families by working on the railroad. Their children also earned pocket money by stealing ice from the refrigerator cars in summer and coal from the open stoking cars in the winter. Sometimes an older lad would break the seal of a freight car and take a look inside. But this usually brought down the "Bulls," the special railroad police. And usually the freight was "heavy" stuff, too much work to cart away and sell, something like fresh produce or boxes of cheap candy that nobody would buy.

The older boys, the ones just approaching voting age, made their easy money by hijacking silk trucks that loaded up at the garment factory on Thirty-first Street. They would then sell the expensive dresses door to door, at bargain prices no discount house could match. From this some graduated into organized crime, whose talent scouts alertly tapped young boys versed in strongarm. Yet despite all this, most of the kids grew up honest, content with fifty bucks a week as truck drivers, deliverymen, and white-collar clerks in the civil service.

I had every desire to go wrong but I never had a chance. The Italian family structure was too formidable.

I never came home to an empty house; there was always the smell of supper cooking. My mother was always there to greet me, sometimes with a policeman's club in her hand (nobody ever knew how she acquired it). But she was always there, or her authorized deputy, my older sister, who preferred throwing empty milk bottles at the heads of her little brothers when they got bad marks on their report cards. During the great Depression of the 1930s, though we were the poorest of the poor, I never remember not dining well. Many years later as a guest of a millionaire's club, I realized that our poor family on home relief ate better than some of the richest people in America.

My mother would never dream of using anything but the finest imported olive oil, the best Italian cheeses. My father had access to the fruits coming off ships, the produce from railroad cars, all before it went through the stale process of middlemen; and my mother, like most Italian women, was a fine cook in the peasant style. . . .

I had to help support my family by working on the railroad. After school hours of course. This was the same railroad that had supplied free coal and free ice to the whole Tenth Avenue when I was young enough to steal with impunity. After school finished at 3 P.M. I went to work in the freight office as a messenger. I also worked Saturdays and Sundays when there was work available.

I hated it. One of my first short stories was about how I hated that job. But of course what I really hated was entering the adult world. To me the adult world was a dark enchantment, unnatural. As unnatural to the human dream as death. And as inevitable. . . .

Then why do I dream of those immigrant Italian peasants as having been happy? I remember how they spoke of their forebears, who spent all their lives farming the arid mountain slopes of Southern Italy. "He died in that house in which he was born," they say enviously. "He was never more than an hour from his village, not in all his life," they sigh. And what would they make of a phrase like "retrospective falsification"?

No, really, we are all happier now. It is a better life. And after all, as my mother always said, "Never mind about being happy. Be glad you're alive."

When I came to my "autobiographical novel," the one every writer does about himself, I planned to make myself the sensitive, misunderstood hero, much put upon by his mother and family. To my astonishment my mother took over the book and instead of my revenge I got another comeuppance. But it is, I think, my best book. And all those old-style grim conservative Italians whom I hated, then pitied so patronizingly, they also turned out to be heroes. Through no desire of mine. I was surprised. The thing that amazed me most was their courage. Where were their Congressional Medals of Honor? Their Distinguished Service Crosses? How did they ever have the balls to get married, have kids, go out to earn a living in a strange land, with no skills, not even knowing the language? They made it without tranquillizers, without sleeping pills, without psychiatrists, without even a dream. Heroes. Heroes all around me. I never saw them.

But how could I? They wore lumpy work clothes and handlebar moustaches, they blew their noses on their fingers and they were so short that their high-school children towered over them. They spoke a laughable broken English and the furthest limit of their horizon was their daily bread. Brave men, brave women, they fought to live their lives without dreams. Bent on survival, they narrowed their minds to the thinnest line of existence.

It is no wonder that in my youth I found them contemptible. And yet they had left Italy and sailed the ocean to come to a new land and leave their sweated bones in America. Illiterate Colombos, they dared to seek the promised land. And so they, too, dreamed a dream.

Interpretations

1. Puzo says of the Italians he knew in his childhood, "[T]heir lives were a long labor to earn their daily bread." To what extent were their lives and personalities shaped by their work? Do you think their work played an unusually large part in their lives? Cite evidence. Are most people so shaped by their jobs?

2. How does Puzo use description to support his thesis on these Italian immigrants? Which images back up his point best?

3. Why does Puzo credit his family with saving him and his brothers from a life of crime?

4. What did Puzo consider these Italians' "tragedy"? What effect did it have on Puzo? What is his final explanation for the "tragedy"?

5. Why doesn't Puzo feel guilty for having misjudged his fellow Italians?

6. How does Puzo use his introduction and his conclusion as organizing devices?

Correspondences

1. Review the comments on work by Smohalla of the Nez Percé. How does it apply to the Italian immigrants in Puzo's essay? How does Puzo's last paragraph contradict the Nez Percé sentiments?

2. Review Morrow's comments about ethnic attitudes towards work. How does "Italians in Hell's Kitchen" support or contradict his point of view? How do Morrow's comments apply to the work habits of your ethnic group?

Applications

1. Puzo says of his early attitudes towards his family: "I did not understand that they simply could not afford to dream; I myself had a

hundred dreams from which to choose." Show how Puzo eventually came to discover that this family did dream, in spite of being "bent on survival." What did he discover was the nature of their dreams, and how did writing his autobiographical novel help him to rediscover and reevaluate his family, his roots?

2. Study dictionary and thesaurus definitions of *work, trade, drudgery,* and *vocation.* How do they differ in meaning and applicability? Which best describe what Puzo's family members did to earn a living?

The Competitive Edge: Japanese and Americans

William Ouchi

William Ouchi (b. 1943) was born in Honolulu. He is now a professor of management at UCLA and the author of Theory Z: How American Business Can Meet the Japanese Challenge *(1981) and* The M-Form Society: How American Teamwork Can Recapture the Competitive Edge *(1984). In the following essay you will see his interests in business management, competition, the United States and Japan come together.*

A centralized feudal government ruled Japan from 1192 to 1867, with very little contact with Westerners until the American Commodore Matthew Perry opened Japan to U.S. trade with a treaty in 1854. The modernizing Emperor Meiji set Japan on a new course in 1868, and in the century and a half since then, Japan has become increasingly involved in the history of other nations (in wars with Russia, China, Korea, and the United States). Since her defeat in 1945, Japan has become one of the most powerful economies in the world and a leader in technology. Japan's growth rate, the highest in the industrial world, has led writers like Ouchi to examine the causes of her success and to ask which factors might be exportable (record on unemployment? high savings rate?). Analysts usually turn sooner or later to the unusual homogeneity of Japan's population. Less than one percent of the Japanese belong to non-Japanese ethnic groups, and a large majority share religions (Buddhism and Shintoism). The "strong orientation to collective values" Ouchi describes is one of the effects of this homogeneity.

PERHAPS THE MOST difficult aspect of the Japanese for Westerners to comprehend is the strong orientation to collective values, particularly a collective sense of responsibility. Let me illustrate with an anecdote about a visit to a new factory in Japan owned and operated by an American electronics company. The American company, a particularly creative firm, frequently attracts attention within the business community for its novel approaches to planning, organizational design, and management systems. As a consequence of this corporate style, the parent company determined to make a thorough study of Japanese workers and to design a plant that would combine the best of East and West. In their study they discovered that Japanese firms almost never make use of individual work incentives, such as piecework or even individual performance appraisal tied to salary increases. They concluded that rewarding individual achievement and individual ability is always a good thing.

In the final assembly area of their new plant, long lines of young Japanese women wired together electronic products on a piece-rate system: the more you wired, the more you got paid. About two months after opening, the head foreladies approached the plant manager. "Honorable plant manager," they said humbly as they bowed, "we are embarrassed to be so forward, but we must speak to you because all of the girls have threatened to quit work this Friday." (To have this happen, of course, would be a great disaster for all concerned.) "Why," they wanted to know, "can't our plant have the same compensation system as other Japanese companies? When you hire a new girl, her starting wage should be fixed by her age. An eighteen-year-old should be paid more than a sixteen-year-old. Every year on her birthday, she should receive an automatic increase in pay. The idea that any of us can be more productive than another must be wrong, because none of us in final assembly could make a thing unless all of the other people in the plant had done their jobs right first. To single one person out as being more productive is wrong and is also personally humiliating to us." The company changed its compensation system to the Japanese model.

Another American company in Japan had installed a suggestion system much as we have in the United States. Individual workers were encouraged to place suggestions to improve productivity into special boxes. For an accepted idea the individual received a bonus amounting to some fraction of the productivity savings realized from his or her suggestion. After a period of six months, not a single suggestion had been submitted. The American managers were puzzled. They had heard many stories of the inventiveness, the commitment, and the loyalty of Japanese workers, yet not one suggestion to improve productivity had appeared.

The managers approached some of the workers and asked why the suggestion system had not been used. The answer: "No one can come up with a work improvement idea alone. We work together, and any ideas that one of us may have are actually developed by watching others and talking to others. If one of us was singled out for being responsible for such an idea, it would embarrass all of us." The company changed to a group suggestion system, in which workers collectively submitted suggestions. Bonuses were paid to groups which would save bonus money until the end of the year for a party at a restaurant or, if there was enough money, for family vacations together. The suggestions and productivity improvements rained down on the plant.

One can interpret these examples in two quite different ways. Perhaps the Japanese commitment to collective values is an anachronism that does not fit with modern industrialism but brings economic success despite that collectivism. Collectivism seems to be inimical to the kind of maverick creativity exemplified in Benjamin Franklin, Thomas Edison, and John D. Rockefeller. Collectivism does not seem to provide the individual incentive to excel which has made a great success of American enterprise. Entirely apart from its economic effects, collectivism implies a loss of individuality, a loss of the freedom to be different, to hold fundamentally different values from others.

The second interpretation of the examples is that the Japanese collectivism is economically efficient. It causes people to work well together and to encourage one another to better efforts. Industrial life requires interdependence of one person on another. But a less obvious but far-reaching implication of the Japanese collectivism for economic performance has to do with accountability.

In the Japanese mind, collectivism is neither a corporate or individual goal to strive for nor a slogan to pursue. Rather, the nature of things operates so that nothing of consequence occurs as a result of individual effort. Everything important in life happens as a result of teamwork or collective effort. Therefore, to attempt to assign individual credit or blame to results is unfounded. A Japanese professor of accounting, a brilliant scholar trained at Carnegie-Mellon University who teaches now in Tokyo, remarked that the status of accounting systems in Japanese industry is primitive compared to those in the United States. Profit centers, transfer prices, and computerized information systems are barely known even in the largest Japanese companies, whereas they are a commonplace in even small United States organizations. Though not at all surprised at the difference in accounting systems, I was not at all sure that the Japanese were primitive. In fact, I thought their system a good deal more efficient than ours.

Most American companies have basically two accounting systems. One system summarizes the overall financial state to inform stockholders, bankers, and other outsiders. That system is not of interest here. The other system, called the managerial or cost accounting system, exists for an entirely different reason. It measures in detail all of the particulars of transactions between departments, divisions, and key individuals in the organization, for the purpose of untangling the interdependencies between people. When, for example, two departments share one truck for deliveries, the cost accounting system charges each department for part of the cost of maintaining the truck and driver, so that at the end of the year, the performance of each department can be individually assessed, and the better department's manager can receive a larger raise. Of course, all of this information processing costs money, and furthermore may lead to arguments between the departments over whether the costs charged to each are fair.

In a Japanese company a short-run assessment of individual performance is not wanted, so the company can save the considerable expense of collecting and processing all of that information. Companies still keep track of which department uses a truck how often and for what purposes, but like-minded people can interpret some simple numbers for themselves and adjust their behavior accordingly. Those insisting upon clear and precise measurement for the purpose of advancing individual interests must have an elaborate information system. Industrial life, however, is essentially integrated and interdependent. No one builds an automobile alone, no one carries through a banking transaction alone. In a sense the Japanese value of collectivism fits naturally into an industrial setting, whereas the Western individualism provides constant conflicts. The image that comes to mind is of Chaplin's silent film "Modern Times" in which the apparently insignificant hero played by Chaplin successfully fights against the unfeeling machinery of industry. Modern industrial life can be aggravating, even hostile, or natural: all depends on the fit between our culture and our technology.

The *shinkansen* or "bullet train" speeds across the rural areas of Japan giving a quick view of cluster after cluster of farmhouses surrounded by rice paddies. This particular pattern did not develop purely by chance, but as a consequence of the technology peculiar to the growing of rice, the staple of the Japanese diet. The growing of rice requires the construction and maintenance of an irrigation system, something that takes many hands to build. More importantly, the planting and the harvesting of rice can only be done efficiently with the cooperation of twenty or more people. The "bottom line" is that a single family working alone cannot produce enough rice to survive, but a dozen families working together can produce a surplus. Thus the Japanese have had to develop the capacity to work together in harmony, no matter what the forces of disagreement or social disintegration, in order to survive.

Japan is a nation built entirely on the tips of giant, suboceanic volcanoes. Little of the land is flat and suitable for agriculture. Terraced hillsides make use of every available square foot of arable land. Small homes built very close together further conserve the land. Japan also suffers from natural disasters such as earthquakes and hurricanes. Traditionally homes are made of light construction materials, so a house falling down during a disaster will not crush its occupants and also can be quickly and inexpensively rebuilt. During the feudal period until the Meiji restoration of 1868, each feudal lord sought to restrain his subjects from moving from one village to the next for fear that a neighboring lord might amass enough peasants with which to produce a large agricultural surplus, hire an army and pose a threat. Apparently bridges were not commonly built across rivers and streams until the late nineteenth century, since bridges increased mobility between villages.

Taken all together, this characteristic style of living paints the picture of a nation of people who are homogeneous with respect to race, history, language, religion, and culture. For centuries and generations these people have lived in the same village next door to the same neighbors. Living in close proximity and in dwellings which gave very little privacy, the Japanese survived through their capacity to work together in harmony. In this situation, it was inevitable that the one most central social value which emerged, the one value without which the society could not continue, was that an individual does not matter.

To the Western soul this is a chilling picture of society. Subordinating individual tastes to the harmony of the group and knowing that individual needs can never take precedence over the interests of all is repellent to the Western citizen. But a frequent theme of Western philosophers and sociologists is that individual freedom exists only when people willingly subordinate their self-interests to the social interest. A society composed entirely of self-interested individuals is a society in which each person is at war with the other, a society which has no freedom. This issue, constantly at the heart of understanding society, comes up in every century, and in every society, whether the writer be Plato, Hobbes, or B. F. Skinner.

In order to complete the comparison of Japanese and American living situations, consider flight over the United States. Looking out of the window high over the state of Kansas, we see a pattern of a single farmhouse surrounded by fields, followed by another single homestead surrounded by fields. In the early 1800s in the state of Kansas there were no automobiles. Your nearest neighbor was perhaps two miles distant; the winters were long, and the snow was deep. Inevitably, the central social values were self-reliance and independence. Those were the realities of that place and age that children had to learn to value.

The key to the industrial revolution was discovering that non-human forms of energy substituted for human forms could increase the wealth of a nation beyond anyone's wildest dreams. But there was a catch. To realize this great wealth, non-human energy needed huge complexes called factories with hundreds, even thousands of workers collected into one factory. Moreover, several factories in one central place made the generation of energy more efficient. Almost overnight, the Western world was transformed from a rural and agricultural country to an urban and industrial state. Our technological advance seems to no longer fit our social structure: in a sense, the Japanese can better cope with modern industrialism. While Americans still busily protect our rather extreme form of individualism, the Japanese hold their individualism in check and emphasize cooperation.

Interpretations

1. What is Ouchi's thesis or main idea? Where does he first state it? How does he attempt to support or develop it?

2. What factors does Ouchi think have caused the Japanese preference for cooperation?

3. According to Ouchi, what is the basic difference between Japanese and Western workers? Do you think Westerners could benefit by becoming more like the Japanese?

4. "Industrial life requires interdependence. . . ." Do other areas besides industry require interdependence? Is it possible that we Westerners have taken independence too far? Does collectivism necessarily imply a loss of freedom? (What difference do you see between the Japanese ideal of cooperation and what Westerners call unselfishness?)

5. If, as Ouchi thinks, modern industrialism is better suited to Japan than to the West, why do you think industrialism began in the West?

Correspondences

1. What are the economic and cultural implications of the collective sense of responsibility of the Japanese towards work as opposed to the individual's responsibility advocated in the United States? Compare Ouchi and Morrow.

2. "Collective solidarity" is an important aspect of Japanese ethics. Just what does it mean? How does it apply to the experiences of Sadat, Momaday (Chapter 1), and Kingston (Chapter 2)? To what extent is it part of the American work ethic?

Applications

1. Test Ouchi's thesis on American individualism in the workplace by conducting an informal survey of workers varying in age, occupation, and ethnic background on their views on cooperation in the workplace. What conclusions did you reach? Write an essay supporting or refuting Ouchi's thesis.

2. Using your group experience as a basis, write an analysis of how working collaboratively has affected your ability to learn. How has it changed your attitudes toward learning? Be specific.

Like a Winding Sheet

Ann Petry

Ann Petry (b. 1912) was born and raised in Old Saybrook, Connecticut, but has lived most of her adult life in Harlem. She worked as a journalist with the Amsterdam News *and as an editor of the* People's Voice. *For her first novel,* The Street *(1946), she was awarded a Houghton Mifflin Literary Fellowship. Other publications include* Country Place *(1947),* The Narrows *(1953) and* Miss Muriel and Other Stories *(1971). Her fiction reflects her interest in the naturalist school and many of her stories are set in large cities. In "Like a Winding Sheet," Petry explores some causes and effects of boredom in the workplace.*

HE HAD PLANNED to get up before Mae did and surprise her by fixing breakfast. Instead he went back to sleep and she got out of bed so quietly he didn't know she wasn't there beside him until he woke up and heard the queer soft gurgle of water running out of the sink in the bathroom.

He knew he ought to get up but instead he put his arms across his forehead to shut the afternoon sunlight out of his eyes, pulled his legs up close to his body, testing them to see if the ache was still in them.

Mae had finished in the bathroom. He could tell because she never closed the door when she was in there and now the sweet smell of talcum powder was drifting down the hall and into the bedroom. Then he heard her coming down the hall.

"Hi, babe," she said affectionately.

"Hum," he grunted, and moved his arms away from his head, opened one eye.

"It's a nice morning."

"Yeah." He rolled over and the sheet twisted around him, outlining his thighs, his chest. "You mean afternoon, don't ya?"

Mae looked at the twisted sheet and giggled. "Looks like a winding sheet," she said. "A shroud—" Laughter tangled with her words and she had to pause for a moment before she could continue. "You look like a huckleberry—in a winding sheet—"

"That's no way to talk. Early in the day like this," he protested.

He looked at his arms silhouetted against the white of the sheets. They were inky black by contrast and he had to smile in spite of himself and he lay there smiling and savoring the sweet sound of Mae's giggling.

"Early?" She pointed a finger at the alarm clock on the table near the bed and giggled again. "It's almost four o'clock. And if you don't spring up out of there, you're going to be late again."

"What do you mean 'again'?"

"Twice last week. Three times the week before. And once the week before and—"

"I can't get used to sleeping in the daytime," he said fretfully. He pushed his legs out from under the covers experimentally. Some of the ache had gone out of them but they weren't really rested yet. "It's too light for good sleeping. And all that standing beats the hell out of my legs."

"After two years you oughta be used to it," Mae said.

He watched her as she fixed her hair, powdered her face, slipped into a pair of blue denim overalls. She moved quickly and yet she didn't seem to hurry.

"You look like you'd had plenty of sleep," he said lazily. He had to get up but he kept putting the moment off, not wanting to move, yet he didn't dare let his legs go completely limp because if he did he'd go back to sleep. It was getting later and later but the thought of putting his weight on his legs kept him lying there.

When he finally got up he had to hurry, and he gulped his breakfast so fast that he wondered if his stomach could possibly use food thrown at it at such a rate of speed. He was still wondering about it as he and Mae were putting their coats on in the hall.

Mae paused to look at the calendar. "It's the thirteenth," she said. Then a faint excitement in her voice, "Why, it's Friday the thirteenth." She had one arm in her coat sleeve and she held it there while she stared at the calendar. "I oughta stay home," she said. "I shouldn't go outa the house."

"Aw, don't be a fool," he said. "Today's payday. And payday is a good luck day everywhere, any way you look at it." And as she stood hesitating he said, "Aw, come on."

And he was late for work again because they spent fifteen minutes arguing before he could convince her she ought to go to work just the same. He had to talk persuasively, urging her gently, and it took time. But he couldn't bring himself to talk to her roughly or threaten to strike her like a lot of men might have done. He wasn't made that way.

So when he reached the plant he was late and he had to wait to punch the time clock because the day-shift workers were streaming out in long lines, in groups and bunches that impeded his progress.

Even now just starting his workday, his legs ached. He had to force himself to struggle past the outgoing workers, punch the time clock, and get the little cart he pushed around all night, because he kept toying with the idea of going home and getting back in bed.

He pushed the cart out on the concrete floor, thinking that if this was his plant he'd make a lot of changes in it. There were too many standing-up jobs for one thing. He'd figure out some way most of 'em could be done sitting down and he'd put a lot more benches around. And this job he had—this job that forced him to walk ten hours a night, pushing this little cart, well, he'd turn it into a sitting-down job. One of those little trucks they used around railroad stations would be good for a job like this. Guys sat on a seat and the thing moved easily, taking up little room and turning in hardly any space at all, like on a dime.

He pushed the cart near the foreman. He never could remember to refer to her as the forelady even in his mind. It was funny to have a white woman for a boss in a plant like this one.

She was sore about something. He could tell by the way her face was red and her eyes were half-shut until they were slits. Probably been out late and didn't get enough sleep. He avoided looking at her and hurried a little, head down, as he passed her though he couldn't resist stealing a glance at her out of the corner of his eyes. He saw the edge of the light-colored slacks she wore and the tip end of a big tan shoe.

"Hey, Johnson!" the woman said.

The machines had started full blast. The whirr and the grinding made the building shake, made it impossible to hear conversations. The men and women at the machines talked to each other but looking at them from just a little distance away, they appeared to be simply moving their lips because you couldn't hear what they were saying. Yet the woman's voice cut across the machine sounds—harsh, angry.

He turned his head slowly. "Good evenin,' Mrs. Scott," he said, and waited.

"You're late again."

"That's right. My legs were bothering me."

The woman's face grew redder, angrier looking. "Half this shift comes in late," she said. "And you're the worst one of all. You're always late. Whatsa matter with ya?"

"It's my legs," he said. "Somehow they don't ever get rested. I don't seem to get used to sleeping days. And I just can't get started."

"Excuses. You guys always got excuses," her anger grew and spread. "Every guy comes in here late always has an excuse. His wife's sick or her grandmother died or somebody in the family had to go to the hospital," she paused, drew a deep breath. "And the niggers is the worse. I don't care what's wrong with your legs. You get in here on time. I'm sick of you niggers—"

"You got the right to get mad," he interrupted softly. "You got the right to cuss me four ways to Sunday but I ain't letting nobody call me a nigger."

He stepped closer to her. His fists were doubled. His lips were drawn back in a thin narrow line. A vein in his forehead stood out swollen, thick.

And the woman backed away from him, not hurriedly but slowly—two, three steps back.

"Aw, forget it," she said. "I didn't mean nothing by it. It slipped out. It was an accident." The red of her face deepened until the small blood vessels in her cheeks were purple. "Go on and get to work," she urged. And she took three more slow backward steps.

He stood motionless for a moment and then turned away from the sight of the red lipstick on her mouth that made him remember that the foreman was a woman. And he couldn't bring himself to hit a woman. He felt a curious tingling in his fingers and he looked down at his hands. They were clenched tight, hard, ready to smash some of those small purple veins in her face.

He pushed the cart ahead of him, walking slowly. When he turned his head, she was staring in his direction, mopping her forehead with a dark blue handkerchief. Their eyes met and then they both looked away.

He didn't glance in her direction again but moved past the long work benches, carefully collecting the finished parts, going slowly and steadily up and down, back and forth the length of the building, and as he walked he forced himself to swallow his anger, get rid of it.

And he succeeded so that he was able to think about what had happened without getting upset about it. An hour went by but the tension stayed in his hands. They were clenched and knotted on the handles of the cart as though ready to aim a blow.

And he thought he should have hit her anyway, smacked her hard in the face, felt the soft flesh of her face give under the hardness of his hands. He tried to make his hands relax by offering them a description of what it would have been like to strike her because he had the queer feeling that his hands were not exactly a part of him anymore—they had developed a separate life of their own over which he had no control. So he dwelt on the pleasure his hands would have felt—both of them cracking at her, first one and then the other. If he had done that his hands would have felt good now—relaxed, rested.

And he decided that even if he'd lost his job for it, he should have let her have it and it would have been a long time, maybe the rest of her life, before she called anybody else a nigger.

The only trouble was he couldn't hit a woman. A woman couldn't hit back the same way a man did. But it would have been a deeply satisfying thing to have cracked her narrow lips wide open with just one blow, beautifully timed and with all his weight in back of it. That way he would have gotten rid of all the energy and tension his anger had created in him. He kept remembering how his heart had started pumping blood so fast he had felt it tingle even in the tips of his fingers.

With the approach of night, fatigue nibbled at him. The corners of his mouth drooped, the frown between his eyes deepened, his shoulders sagged; but his hands stayed tight and tense. As the hours dragged by he noticed that the women workers had started to snap and snarl at each other. He couldn't hear what they said because of the sound of machines but he could see the quick lip movements that sent words tumbling from the sides of their mouths. They gestured irritably with their hands and scowled as their mouths moved.

Their violent jerky motions told him that it was getting close on to quitting time but somehow he felt that the night still stretched ahead of him, composed of endless hours of steady walking on his aching legs. When the whistle finally blew he went on pushing the cart, unable to believe that it had sounded. The whirring of the machines died away to a murmur and he knew then that he'd really heard the whistle. He stood still for a moment, filled with a relief that made him sigh.

Then he moved briskly, putting the cart in the storeroom, hurrying to take his place in the line forming before the paymaster. That was another thing he'd change, he thought. He'd have the pay envelopes handed to the people right at their benches so there wouldn't be ten or fifteen minutes lost waiting for the pay. He always got home about fifteen minutes late on payday. They did it better in the plant where Mae worked, brought the money right to them at their benches.

He stuck his pay envelope in his pants' pocket and followed the line of workers heading for the subway in a slow-moving stream. He glanced up at the sky. It was a nice night, the sky looked packed full to running over with stars. And he thought if he and Mae would go right to bed when they got home from work they'd catch a few hours of darkness for sleeping. But they never did. They fooled around—cooking and eating and listening to the radio and he always stayed in a big chair in the living room and went almost but not quite to sleep and when they finally got to bed it was five or six in the morning and daylight was already seeping around the edges of the sky.

He walked slowly, putting off the moment when he would have to plunge into the crowd hurrying toward the subway. It was a long ride to Harlem and tonight the thought of it appalled him. He paused outside an all-night restaurant to kill time, so that some of the first rush of workers would be gone when he reached the subway.

The lights in the restaurant were brilliant, enticing. There was life and motion inside. And as he looked through the window he thought that everything within range of his eyes gleamed—the long imitation marble counter, the tall stools, the white porcelain-topped tables and especially the big metal coffee urn right near the window. Steam issued from its top and a gas flame flickered under it—a lively, dancing, blue flame.

A lot of the workers from his shift—men and women—were lining up near the coffee urn. He watched them walk to the porcelain-topped tables carrying steaming cups of coffee and he saw that just the smell of the coffee lessened the fatigue lines in their faces. After the first sip their faces softened, they smiled, they began to talk and laugh.

On a sudden impulse he shoved the door open and joined the line in front of the coffee urn. The line moved slowly. And as he stood there the smell of the coffee, the sound of the laughter and of the voices, helped dull the sharp ache in his legs.

He didn't pay any attention to the white girl who was serving the coffee at the urn. He kept looking at the cups in the hands of the men who had been ahead of him. Each time a man stepped out of the line with one of the thick white cups the fragrant steam got in his nostrils. He saw that they walked carefully so as not to spill a single drop. There was a froth of bubbles at the top of each cup and he thought about how he would let the bubbles break against his lips before he actually took a big deep swallow.

Then it was his turn. "A cup of coffee," he said, just as he had heard the others say.

The white girl looked past him, put her hands up to her head and gently lifted her hair away from the back of her neck, tossing her head back a little. "No more coffee for a while," she said.

He wasn't certain he'd heard her correctly and he said, "What?" blankly.

"No more coffee for a while," she repeated.

There was silence behind him and then uneasy movement. He thought someone would say something, ask why or protest, but there was only silence and then a faint shuffling sound as though the men standing behind him had simultaneously shifted their weight from one foot to the other.

He looked at the girl without saying anything. He felt his hands begin to tingle and the tingling went all the way down to his finger tips so that he glanced down at them. They were clenched tight, hard, into fists. Then he looked at the girl again. What he wanted to do was hit her so hard that the scarlet lipstick on her mouth would smear and spread over her nose, her chin, out toward her cheeks, so hard that she would never toss her head again and refuse a man a cup of coffee because he was black.

He estimated the distance across the counter and reached forward, balancing his weight on the balls of his feet, ready to let the blow go. And then his hands fell back down to his sides because he forced himself to lower them, to unclench them and make them dangle loose. The effort took his breath away because his hands fought against him. But he couldn't hit her. He couldn't even now bring himself to hit a woman, not even this one, who had refused him a cup of coffee with a toss of her head. He kept seeing the gesture with which she had lifted the length of her blond hair from the back of her neck as expressive of her contempt for him.

When he went out the door he didn't look back. If he had he would have seen the flickering blue flame under the shiny coffee urn being extinguished. The line of men who had stood behind him lingered a moment to watch the people drinking coffee at the tables and then they left as he had without having had the coffee they wanted so badly. The girl behind the counter poured water in the urn and swabbed it out and as she waited for the water to run out, she lifted her hair gently from the back of her neck and tossed her head before she began making a fresh lot of coffee.

But he had walked away without a backward look, his head down, his hands in his pockets, raging at himself and whatever it was inside of him that had forced him to stand quiet and still when he wanted to strike out.

The subway was crowded and he had to stand. He tried grasping an overhead strap and his hands were too tense to grip it. So he moved near the train door and stood there swaying back and forth with the rocking of the train. The roar of the train beat inside his head, making it ache and throb, and the pain in his legs clawed up into his groin so that he seemed to be bursting with pain and he told himself that it was due to all that anger-born energy that had piled up in him and not been used and so it had spread through him like a poison—from his feet and legs all the way up to his head.

Mae was in the house before he was. He knew she was home before he put the key in the door of the apartment. The radio was going. She had it tuned up loud and she was singing along with it.

"Hello, babe," she called out, as soon as he opened the door.

He tried to say "hello" and it came out half grunt and half sigh.

"You sure sound cheerful," she said.

She was in the bedroom and he went and leaned against the door-jamb. The denim overalls she wore to work were carefully draped over the back of a chair by the bed. She was standing in front of the dresser, tying the sash of a yellow housecoat around her waist and chewing gum vigorously as she admired her reflection in the mirror over the dresser.

"Whatsa matter?" she said. "You get bawled out by the boss or somep'n?"

"Just tired," he said slowly. "For God's sake, do you have to crack that gum like that?"

"You don't have to lissen to me," she said complacently. She patted a curl in place near the side of her head and then lifted her hair away from the back of her neck, ducking her head forward and then back.

He winced away from the gesture. "What you got to be always fooling with your hair for?" he protested.

"Say, what's the matter with you anyway?" She turned away from the mirror to face him, put her hands on her hips. "You ain't been in the house two minutes and you're picking on me."

He didn't answer her because her eyes were angry and he didn't want to quarrel with her. They'd been married too long and got along too well and so he walked all the way into the room and sat down in the chair by the bed and stretched his legs out in front of him, putting his weight on the heels of his shoes, leaning way back in the chair, not saying anything.

"Lissen," she said sharply. "I've got to wear those overalls again tomorrow. You're going to get them all wrinkled up leaning against them like that."

He didn't move. He was too tired and his legs were throbbing now that he had sat down. Besides the overalls were already wrinkled and dirty, he thought. They couldn't help but be for she'd worn them all week. He leaned farther back in the chair.

"Come on, get up," she ordered.

"Oh, what the hell," he said wearily, and got up from the chair. "I'd just as soon live in a subway. There'd be just as much place to sit down."

He saw that her sense of humor was struggling with her anger. But her sense of humor won because she giggled.

"Aw, come on and eat," she said. There was a coaxing note in her voice. "You're nothing but an old hungry nigger trying to act tough and—" she paused to giggle and then continued, "You—"

He had always found her giggling pleasant and deliberately said things that might amuse her and then waited, listening for the delicate sound to emerge from her throat. This time he didn't even hear the giggle. He didn't let her finish what she was saying. She was standing close to him and that funny tingling started in his finger tips, went fast up his arms and sent his fist shooting straight for her face.

There was the smacking sound of soft flesh being struck by a hard object and it wasn't until she screamed that he realized he had hit her in the mouth—so hard that the dark red lipstick had blurred and spread over her full lips, reaching up toward the tip of her nose, down toward her chin, out toward her cheeks.

The knowledge that he had struck her seeped through him slowly and he was appalled but he couldn't drag his hands away from her face. He kept striking her and he thought with horror that something inside him was holding him, binding him to this act, wrapping and twisting about him so that he had to continue it. He had lost all control over his hands. And he groped for a phrase, a word, something to describe what this thing was like that was happening to him and he thought it was like being enmeshed in a winding sheet—that was it—like a winding sheet. And even as the thought formed in his mind, his hands reached for her face again and yet again.

Interpretations

1. Explain the meaning of Mae's statement in the beginning of the story, "You look like a huckleberry in a winding sheet." What further significance does the title acquire at the end? Do you think a person like Mae would use this language or the closely related "shroud"? Why or why not? Do you find the dialogue in general to be natural? Support your answer with examples. How important is dialogue to the success or failure of the story? Do you find the story to be a success? Why?

2. What part does their work play in Mae's and Johnson's lives? Would different jobs make them different people? What's the evidence? Do you think sedentary jobs are necessarily better jobs? Why?

3. Johnson's forewoman values punctuality, an attitude which provides much of the momentum for the story. In the world of real work, do you find punctuality to be a highly valued quality in an employee? What experiences led you to that conclusion? Do you think it *should* be highly valued? If so, why?

4. What role does race play in the relationships between Johnson and Mrs. Scott? Johnson and the girl at the coffee shop? Johnson and Mae?

5. Discuss how traditional restrictions on men's behavior affect Johnson. Why does he finally "hit a lady"?

6. Which is the primary cause of Johnson's behavior—that you can't hit *any* woman but you can hit your wife or that you can't hit a white person but you can hit another black?

7. The story organization is generally chronological. How does Petry keep it moving forward without having the time structure become obtrusive?

Correspondences

1. Review the Terkel quotation (page 260). What does it mean? How does it apply to Petry's story? Cite examples of physical and spiritual violence. Which were worse in your opinion?

2. Ouchi talks about the spirit of cooperation and participation in the Japanese workplace. To what extent were these part of Johnson's experience in the American workplace? How was Johnson interested in participating?

Applications

1. Show how a person, if degraded and belittled enough, may come to absorb and even accept a negative image of himself. Trace Johnson's progression from a nonviolent to a violent person by examining these encounters: Mrs. Scott (oppressor); coffee shop waitress (oppressor); Mae (wife/mirror). Also examine the role played by Johnson's legs (aching, static) and his hands (tingling, tense, active).

2. Assume the role of Mae, Mrs. Scott, or the girl at the lunch counter and freewrite exploring the relationships of wife–husband, supervisor–subordinate, customer–waitress.

Year of the
Blue-Collar Guy

Steve Olson

Steve Olson is a construction worker living in Madison, Wisconsin. In the following selection, he focuses on the contributions and the values of blue-collar workers.

WHILE THE LEARNED are attaching appropriate labels to the 1980s and speculating on what the 1990s will bring, I would like to steal 1989 for my own much maligned group and declare it "the year of the blue-collar guy (BCG)." BCGs have been portrayed as beer-drinking, big-bellied, bigoted rednecks who dress badly. Wearing a suit to a cement-finishing job wouldn't be too bright. Watching my tie go around a motor shaft followed by my neck is not the last thing I want to see in this world. But, more to the point, our necks are too big and our arms and shoulders are too awesome to fit suits well without expensive tailoring. Suits are made for white-collar guys.

But we need big bellies as ballast to stay on the bar stool while we're drinking beer. And our necks are red from the sun and we are somewhat bigoted. But aren't we all? At least our bigotry is open and honest and worn out front like a tattoo. White-collar people are bigoted, too. But it's disguised as the pat on the back that holds you back: "You're not good enough so you need affirmative action." BCGs aren't smart enough to be that cynical. I never met a BCG who didn't respect an honest day's work and a job well done—no matter who did it.

True enough, BCGs aren't perfect. But, I believe this: we are America's last true romantic heroes. When some 21st-century Louis L'Amour writes about this era he won't eulogize the greedy Wall Street insider. He won't commend the narrow-shouldered, wide-hipped lawyers with six-digit unearned incomes doing the same work women can do. His wide-shouldered heroes will be plucked from the ranks of the blue-collar guy. They are the last vestige of the manly world where strength, skill and hard work are still valued.

To some extent our negative ratings are our own fault. While we were building the world we live in, white-collar types were sitting on their ever-widening butts redefining the values we live by. One symbol of America's opulent wealth is the number of people who can sit and ponder and comment and write without producing a usable product or

292

skill. Hey, get a real job—make something—then talk. These talkers are the guys we drove from the playgrounds into the libraries when we were young and now for 20 years or more we have endured the revenge of the nerds.

BCGs fidgeted our way out of the classroom and into jobs where, it seemed, the only limit to our income was the limit of our physical strength and energy. A co-worker described a BCG as "a guy who is always doing things that end in the letter 'n'—you know—huntin', fishin', workin' . . ." My wise friend is talking energy! I have seen men on the job hand-nail 20 square of shingles (that's 6,480 nails) or more a day, day after day, for weeks. At the same time, they were remodeling their houses, raising children, and coaching Little League. I've seen crews frame entire houses in a day—day after day. I've seen guys finish concrete until 11 P.M., go out on a date, then get up at 6 A.M. and do it all over again the next day.

These are amazing feats of strength. There should be stadiums full of screaming fans for these guys. I saw a 40-year-old man neatly fold a 350-pound piece of rubber roofing, put it on his shoulder and, alone, carry it up a ladder and deposit it on a roof. Nobody acknowledged it because the event was too common. One day at noon this same fellow wrestled a 22-year-old college summer worker. In the prime of his life, the college kid was a 6-foot-3, 190-pound body-builder and he was out of his league. He was on his back to stay in 90 seconds flat.

Great Skilled Work Force

Mondays are tough on any job. But in our world this pain is eased by stories of weekend adventure. While white-collar types are debating the value of reading over watching TV, BCGs are doing stuff. I have honest to God heard these things on Monday mornings about BCG weekends: "I tore out a wall and added a room," "I built a garage," "I went walleye fishing Saturday and pheasant hunting Sunday," "I played touch football both days" (in January), "I went skydiving," "I went to the sports show and wrestled the bear." Pack a good novel into these weekends.

My purpose is not so much to put down white-collar people as to stress the importance of blue-collar people to this country. Lawyers, politicians and bureaucrats are necessary parts of the process, but this great skilled work force is so taken for granted it is rarely seen as the luxury it truly is. Our plumbing works, our phones work and repairs are made as quickly as humanly possible. I don't think this is true in all parts of the world. But this blue-collar resource is becoming endangered. Being a tradesman is viewed with such disdain these days that most young people I know treat the trades like a temporary summer job. I've seen young guys take minimum-wage jobs just so they can wear suits. It is as if any job without a dress code is a dead-end job. This is partly our own fault. We even tell our own sons, "Don't be like me, get a job people respect." Blue-collar guys ought to brag more, even swagger a little. We should drive our families past the latest job site and say "That house was a piece of junk, and now it's the best one on the block. I did that." Nobody will respect us if we don't respect ourselves.

Our work is hard, hot, wet, cold, and always dirty. It is also often very satisfying. Entailing the use of both brain and body there is a product—a physical result of which to be proud. We have fallen from your roofs, died under heavy equipment and been entombed in your dams. We have done honest, dangerous work. Our skills and energy and strength have transformed lines on paper into physical reality. We are this century's Renaissance men. America could do worse than to honor us. We still do things the old-fashioned way, and we have earned the honor.

Interpretations

1. Do you agree with Olson that blue-collar workers deserve more respect? Do you agree with his analysis of how and why they were short-changed on respect and with his prescription for regaining it? Why or why not?

2. Which aspect of his subject does Olson emphasize in the essay, the negative (the low morale of BCGs and its causes) or the positive (BCGs' pleasure in their work, their heroic strength, and their contribution to the country)? Do you think he has chosen an appropriate tone?

3. "Nobody will respect us if we don't respect ourselves." Do you consider Olson's primary audience for this essay to be his fellow BCGs or another group? If another, what group? Cite evidence.

4. Olson says his purpose is "not so much to put down white-collar people as to stress the importance of blue-collar people to this country." To what extent does he fulfill his stated purpose? Cite phrases that white-collar workers might find offensive.

Correspondences

1. "While we were building the world we live in, white-collar types were sitting on their ever-widening butts redefining the values we live by": To what extent does this comment apply to Morrow's essay?

2. "Being a tradesman is viewed with such disdain these days that most young people I know treat the trades like a temporary summer job":

What factors have contributed to such disdain? To what extent do you agree with Olson's assertion? How does Puzo regard tradesmen?

Applications

1. Conduct an informal survey on attitudes of college administrators, faculty, and counselors towards blue-collar work. Write an analysis of their responses.

2. Show how Olson, in defending the group he identifies with, "the blue-collar guys (BCGs)," at the same time stereotypes a group he dislikes, the white-collar guys he calls "nerds." Show the reasons he dislikes the second group and to what extent he presents an unbiased picture of them.

The Mysteries of My Father's Workshop

Camara Laye

Camara Laye (1928–1980) was born in Guinea into a family that combined tribal culture with the religion of Islam. He is the author of three highly acclaimed novels, The Radiance of the King *(1956),* A Dream of Africa *(1966), and* The Guardian of the Word *(1984). His autobiography* The Dark Child *(1954), written in French, from which the following selection is excerpted, traces his life to the time when he left Guinea to study engineering in France. There he found the differences between African and European culture overwhelming. His books, however, succeed in combining these discordant elements into unified wholes. In "The Mysteries of My Father's Workshop" Laye portrays his father's pride in his work.*

Guinea is located on the Atlantic coast of West Africa. About the size of Oregon, it was under French control from the middle of the nineteenth century until 1958, when President Sékou Touré demanded immediate French withdrawal. Within days, the French withdrew all aid, administrators, and technicians. (Laye was living in Guinea in 1956–1966, working part of this time for the state.) By the 1970s Touré turned Guinea into a Soviet-aligned, one-party state; his dictatorship lasted 26 years. Laye spent his last years as a teacher in neighboring Sénégal, one of only five sub-Saharan countries that now govern themselves under systems of majority rule. Guinea, on the other hand, has been ruled by a military government since the death of Touré in 1984. The country has the world's largest bauxite deposits, as well as other natural resources, although most of the resources remain undeveloped. French is still the official language. About one quarter of the population is Malinké, the tribe to which Laye belonged, with the remainder divided among seventeen other tribes. A large majority of Guineans are Muslim.

OF ALL THE DIFFERENT kinds of work my father performed, none fascinated me so much as his skill with gold. No other occupation was so noble, no other needed such a delicate touch; and, moreover, this sort of work was always a kind of festival: it was a real festival that broke the monotony of ordinary working days.

So if a woman, accompanied by a go-between, crossed the threshold of the workshop, I would follow her in at once. I knew what she wanted: she had brought some gold and wanted to ask my father to transform it into a trinket. The woman would have collected the gold in the placers of Siguiri, where, for months on end, she would have crouched over the river, washing the mud and patiently extracting from it the grains of gold. These women never came alone: they were well aware that my father had other things to do than to make trinkets for all and sundry; and even if the making of jewellery had been his main occupation, they would have realized that they were not his first or his only customers, and that their wants could not be immediately attended to.

Generally these women required the trinket for a certain date, either for the festival of Ramadan or for the Tabaski; or for some other family festivity, or for a dance ceremony.

Thereupon, to better their chance of being quickly served, and the more easily to persuade my father to interrupt the work he had in hand, they would request the services of an official praise-singer, a go-between, and would arrange with him in advance what fee they would pay for his good offices.

The praise-singer would install himself in the workshop, tune up his cora, which is our harp, and would begin to sing my father's praises. This was always a great event for me. I would hear recalled the lofty deeds of my father's ancestors, and the names of these ancestors from the earliest times; as the couplets were reeled off, it was like watching the growth of a great genealogical tree that spread its branches far and wide and flourished its boughs and twigs before my mind's eye. The harp played an accompaniment to this vast utterance of names, expanding it and punctuating it with notes that were now soft, now shrill. Where did the praise-singer get his information from? He must certainly have developed a very retentive memory stored with facts handed down to him by his predecessors, for this is the basis of all our oral traditions. Did he embellish the truth? It is very likely: flattery is the praise-singer's stock in trade! · Nevertheless, he was not allowed to take too many liberties with tradition, for it is part of the praise-singer's task to preserve it. But in those days such considerations did not enter my head, which I would hold high and proud; for I used to feel quite drunk with so much praise, which seemed to reflect some of its effulgence upon my own small person.

I could tell that my father's vanity was being inflamed, and I already knew that after having sipped this milk-and-honey he would lend a favourable ear to the woman's request. But I was not alone in my knowledge; the woman also had seen my father's eyes gleaming with contented pride; and she would hold out her grains of gold as if the whole thing were settled: my father, taking up his scales, would weigh the gold.

"What sort of trinket do you desire?" he would ask.

"I want . . ."

And often it would happen that the woman did not know really what she wanted, because she would be so torn by desire, because she would have liked to have many, many trinkets, all out of the same small quantity of gold: but she would have had to have much more than she had brought with her to satisfy such a desire, and eventually she would have to content herself with some more modest wish.

"When do you want it for?" my father would ask.

And she would always want it at once.

"Why are you in such a hurry? How do you expect me to find the time?"

"It's very urgent, I can assure you," the woman would reply.

"That's what all women say, when they want an ornament. Well, I'll see what I can do. Now are you happy?"

Then he would take the clay pot that was kept specially for the smelting of gold and pour in the grains; thereupon he would cover the gold with powdered charcoal, a charcoal which he obtained by the use of plant juices of exceptional purity; finally he would place a large lump of the same kind of charcoal over the whole thing.

Then, having seen the work duly undertaken, the woman, by now quite satisfied, would go back to her household tasks, leaving her go-between to carry on with the praise-singing which had already proved so advantageous to her.

On a sign from my father, the apprentices would start working the two pairs of sheep-skin bellows which were placed on the ground at each side of the forge and linked to it by earthen pipes. These apprentices remained seated all the time, with crossed legs, in front of the bellows; at least the younger did, for the elder would sometimes be allowed to take part in the craftsmen's work and the younger—in those days it was Sidafa—only had to work the bellows and watch the proceedings while awaiting his turn to be elevated to less rudimentary tasks. For a whole hour they would both be working the levers of the bellows till the fire in the forge leapt into flame, becoming a living thing, a lively and merciless spirit.

Then my father, using long pincers, would lift the clay pot and place it on the flames.

Immediately all work would more or less stop in the workshop: actually while the gold is being melted and while it is cooling all work with copper or aluminum is supposed to stop, for fear that some fraction of these less noble metals might fall among the gold. It is only steel that can still be worked at such times. But workmen who had some piece of steel work in hand would either hasten to finish it or would openly stop work to join the other apprentices gathered round the forge. In fact, there were often so many of them at these times pressing round my father that I, the smallest, would have to get up and push my way in among them, so as not to miss any of the operation.

It might happen that, feeling he had too little room to work in, my father would make his apprentices stand well away from him. He would merely raise his hand in a simple gesture: at that particular moment he would never utter a word, and no one else would, no one was allowed to utter a word, even the go-between's voice would no longer be raised in song; the silence would be broken only by the panting of the bellows and by the faint hissing of the gold. But if my father never used to utter actual words at this time, I know that he was uttering them in his mind; I could see it by his lips that kept working while he bent over the pot and kept stirring the gold and the charcoal with a bit of wood that would keep bursting into flame, and so had to be constantly replaced by a fresh bit.

What were the words my father's lips were forming? I do not know; I do not know for certain: I was never told what they were. But what else could they have been, if not magical incantations? Were they not the spirits of fire and gold, of fire and air, air breathed through the earthen pipes, of fire born of air, of gold married with fire—were not these the spirits he was invoking? Was it not their help and their friendship he was calling upon in this marriage of elemental things? Yes, it was almost certainly those spirits he was calling upon, for they are the most elemental of all spirits, and their presence is essential at the melting of gold.

The operation that was going on before my eyes was simply the smelting of gold; but it was something more than that: a magical operation that the guiding spirits could look upon with favour or disfavour; and that is why there would be all round my father that absolute silence and that anxious expectancy. I could understand, though I was just a child, that there was no craft greater than the goldsmith's. I expected a ceremony, I had come to be present at a ceremony, and it really was one, though very protracted. I was still too young to be able to understand why it was so protracted; nevertheless, I had an inkling, beholding the most religious concentration of all those present as they watched the mixing process.

When finally the gold began to melt, I used to feel like shouting, and perhaps we would all have shouted if we had not been forbidden to make a sound: I would be trembling, and certainly everyone else would be trembling as we sat watching my father stirring the mixture, still a heavy paste in which the charcoal was gradually being consumed. The next stage followed swiftly; the gold now had the fluidity of water. The guiding spirits had smiled on the operation!

"Bring me the brick!" my father would say, thus lifting the ban that until then had kept us all silent.

The brick, which an apprentice would place beside the fire, was hollowed out, generously greased with Galam butter. My father would take the pot off the fire, tilt it carefully, and I would watch the gold flowing into the brick, flowing like liquid fire. True, it was only a very sparse trickle of fire, but oh, how vivid, how brilliant! As the gold flowed into the brick, the grease would splutter and flame and give off a thick smoke that caught in the throat and stung the eyes, leaving us all weeping and coughing.

It occurred to me later on that my father could easily have relinquished all the work of smelting the gold to one or other of his assistants: they were not without experience in these matters; they had taken part hundreds of times in the same preparations and they would certainly have brought the work to a successful conclusion. But as I have told you, my father kept moving his lips! We could not hear those words, those secret words, those incantations which he addressed to powers that we should not, that we could not hear or see: this was essential. Only my father was versed in the science of conjuring the spirits of fire, air and gold, and conjuring evil spirits, and that is why he alone conducted the whole operation.

By now the gold would have cooled in the hollow of the brick, and my father would begin to hammer and stretch it. This was the moment when his work as a goldsmith really began. I noticed that before embarking on it he never failed to stroke stealthily the little snake coiled up under the sheepskin; one can only assume that this was his way of gathering strength for what remained to be done, and which was the most difficult.

But was it not extraordinary, was it not miraculous that on these occasions the little black serpent always coiled up under the sheepskin? He was not always there, he did not visit my father every day, but he was always present whenever there was gold to be worked.

Moreover, it is our custom to keep apart from the working of gold all influences outside those of the jeweller himself. And indeed it is precisely because the jeweller alone possesses the secret of his incantations; but also because the working of gold, besides being a task of the greatest skill, is a matter of confidence, of conscience, a task which is not undertaken excepting after due reflection and experiment. Finally, I do not think that any jeweller would renounce the opportunity of performing such a task—I ought to say, such a spectacle!—in which he can display his abilities with a virtuosity that his work as a blacksmith or a mechanic or even as a sculptor is never invested with; even though in these more humble tasks his skill is no less wonderful, even though the statues which he carves in wood with his adze are not insignificant works!

The snake's presence came as no surprise to me; ever since that evening when my father had talked to me about the guiding spirit of our race, it had ceased to surprise me; it was quite natural that the snake should be there: he had knowledge of the future. Did he impart any of that knowledge to my father? It seemed to me quite obvious that he did: did he not always warn him of what was going to happen? But I had another reason for believing implicitly in the powers of the little snake.

The craftsman who works in gold must first of all purify himself, that is, he must wash himself all over and, of course, abstain from all sexual relationships during the whole time. Great respecter of ceremony as he was, it would have been impossible for my father to ignore these rules. Now I never saw him make these preparations. I would see him address himself to his work without any apparent preliminaries. But from that moment it was obvious that, forewarned by his black guiding spirit in a dream of the task that would await him in the morning, my father must have prepared for it as soon as he arose, and had entered his workshop in a state of purity, his body smeared with the magical substances hidden in his numerous pots full of secret potions. So I believe my father never entered his workshop except in a state of ritual purity; and that is not because I want to make him out as being better than he is—he is a man like any other, and has a man's weaknesses—but always when it was a matter of ritual he was uncompromisingly strict.

The woman for whom the trinket was being made, and who would often have looked in to see how the work was getting on, would come for the final time, not wanting to miss anything of the marvelous sight as the gold wire, which my father had succeeded in spinning, was transformed into a trinket. She was here now, devouring with her eyes the fragile golden wire, following its tranquil and inevitable spirals round the little metal cone which gave the trinket its shape. My father would be watching her out of the corner of his eye, and sometimes I would see the corners of his mouth twitch into a smile: the woman's avid attentiveness amused him.

"Are you trembling?" he would say to her.

"*Am* I trembling?" she would ask.

And we would all burst out laughing at her. For she *was* trembling! She was trembling with covetousness for the spiral pyramid in which my father was inserting, among the convolutions, tiny grains of gold. When finally he terminated the work by placing at the summit the largest grain of gold, the woman would jump excitedly to her feet.

Then, while my father was slowly turning the trinket round in his fingers, smoothing it into perfect shape, no one could have displayed such utter happiness as the native woman, not even the praise-singer, whose trade it was to do so, and who, during the whole process of transformation, had kept on singing his praises, accelerating his rhythm, increasing his flatteries as the trinket took shape, and praising my father's talents to the skies.

Indeed, the praise-singer participated in a curious—I was going to say direct, effective—way in the work. He, too, was intoxicated with the joy of creation; he declaimed his rapture, and plucked his harp like a man inspired; he warmed to the task as if he had been the craftsman himself, as if the trinket had been made by his own hands. He was no longer a paid thurifer; he was no longer just the man whose services each and anyone could hire: he had become a man who creates his song under the influence of some very personal, interior necessity.

When my father, after having soldered the large grain of gold that crowned the summit, held out his work to be admired, the go-between would no longer be able to contain himself, and would intone the douga—the great chant which is only sung for celebrated men, and which is danced to only for them.

But the douga is a tremendous chant, a provocative chant, a chant that the go-between would not venture to sing, and that the man for whom it is sung would not venture to dance to, without certain precautions.

My father, forewarned in a dream, had been able to take these precautions as soon as he got up; the praise-singer had taken them as a matter of course when he had made his bargain with the woman. Just as my father had done, he had smeared his body with magic lotions and so had rendered himself invulnerable to the bad spirits which the douga would undoubtedly stir into activity, invulnerable also even to his fellow praise-singers who, jealous perhaps, were only waiting to hear the chant, the note of exaltation and the loss of control which that exaltation entails, to cast their evil spells upon him.

At the first notes of the douga, my father would rise and utter a cry in which happiness and triumph were equally mingled; and brandishing in his right hand the hammer that was the symbol of his profession, and in his left a ram's horn filled with magic substances, he would dance the glorious dance.

No sooner had he finished than workmen and apprentices, friends and customers in their turn, not forgetting the woman for whom the trinket had been created, would flock round him, congratulating him, showering praises on him, and complimenting at the same time the go-between, who found himself laden with gifts, gifts that are almost the only resources he has in his wandering life, that he leads after the fashion of the troubadours of old. Beaming, aglow with dancing and the praises he had received, my father would offer kola nuts, that small change of Guinean civility.

All that now remained to be done was to redden the trinket in a little water mixed with chlorine and seasalt. I could go now: the ceremony was over! But often, as I was leaving the workshop, my mother, who might be in the yard pounding millet or rice, would call me.

"Where have you been?" she would ask, although she knew very well where I had been.

"In the workshop."

"Oh, yes, your father was making something out of gold. Gold! It's always gold!"

And she would pound furiously the helpless bowl of rice or millet. "Your father's ruining his health! You see what he's doing."

"He's been dancing the douga," I would reply.

"The douga! The douga won't stop him ruining his eyesight! And you would be better off playing here in the yard instead of going and breathing the dust and smoke in the workshop!"

My mother did not like my father to work with gold. She knew how harmful the soldering of gold can be: a jeweller can wear his lungs out, puffing at his blowpipe, and his eyes suffer by being so close to the intense heat of the forge; and even more perhaps from the microscopic delicacy of the work. But even if there had been no danger in it, my mother still would have disliked this work: she held it in suspicion, for you cannot solder gold without the help of other metals, and my mother used to think that it was not strictly honest to keep the gold which was saved by its alloys, although this was the accepted thing; and she, too, was quite prepared, whenever she took cotton to be woven, to receive in return a piece of cloth of only half the original weight.

Interpretations

1. How did Laye's father feel about his work? What were his working conditions? (What were the economic pressures and rewards? the non-economic rewards?) Where are such conditions and rewards still possible in an industrialized country like ours?

2. The praise-singer sang the praises—sometimes exaggerating them—of the ancestors of the person whose favors were sought. Does our culture have the equivalent of a praise-singer (in a perhaps disguised form)? If so, where? Do we still identify with our ancestors to the point of "vanity . . . inflamed" when we hear them praised? If so, give an example.

3. What was the meaning and purpose of the gold-smelting ceremony? How did the snake contribute to the aura? What did the dream contribute? Do you think smelting gold deserves this special attention or aura? Why or why not? What economic and cultural factors in the American workplace make such a mixing of religion and work unlikely? Is any work in our culture such a mixture? What? Why?

4. What is Laye's attitude toward the customs and the people he describes? (Approving, critical, apologetic, impressed, detached, amused?) Cite details to support your answer.

5. At times Laye seems to fear he might be misunderstood. What aspect of Laye's story do you think a general audience would have the most trouble understanding? Where do you find Laye attempting to bridge the gap in understanding between his reading audience and the events he describes?

Correspondences

1. Review the Berry perspective on work (page 260) and discuss its application to Laye's essay.

2. Discuss how cultural traditions affect attitudes toward work in the selections by Ouchi and Laye.

Applications

1. Laye's father was part of an agrarian as opposed to an industrial economy. How are they different? How might these differences affect attitudes towards quality as opposed to quantity of work as well as towards creativity and productivity?

2. What is the evidence that Laye sees a connection between a praise-singer and an author—for example, a poet or dramatist or novelist—or, for that matter an autobiographer like himself? Write a journal entry explaining this connection.

The Price of Hate: Thoughts on Covering a Ku Klux Klan Rally

Rachel L. Jones

Rachel Jones (b. 1961) was born in Cairo, Illinois. She attended Northwestern University and Southern Illinois University and held internships at The New York Times *and the* Washington Post *before working as a general assignment reporter with* The Miami Herald.

We think you will be interested in Jones's reasons for choosing journalism as a profession:

> I decided at a relatively early age that I would use words to make a living. I was fascinated by them and the images they could evoke, how they could make you feel, hear, smell and taste power there, and decided that I would attempt some profession that used words.
>
> My approach to reporting was based in practicality; the love of words and writing had to be channeled into a realistic endeavor. I had followed newspapers like The Chicago Tribune and The St. Louis Post-Dispatch all my life and was curious about the process of putting out a whole paper every day.
>
> Ironically, the first newspaper I ever worked at was The New York Times, and it was an awe-inspiring way to learn about journalism. But it taught me a respect for the field that remains to this day. I learned that what a reporter does is to translate events—everyday and extraordinary—into digestible bites for the reader at home. We are like walking lightning rods, collecting the information, putting ourselves into someone else's shoes and then writing about it so that even more people can understand. Or, as one editor once told me, we're the guys who have to make John Q. Public believe that the sewage treatment plant really IS important. We have to write the stories that even if they aren't read, will make people aware that their world is growing and changing

and they ought to keep up—and that they CAN, if they'll read a newspaper.

In "The Price of Hate," Jones's dedication to covering an assignment is put to an unusual test.

I WAS SITTING at my computer terminal when I overheard someone in the office mention his concern because he thought a black couple was moving into a house on his street.

He was standing only four feet away from me, yet lacked a mechanism that would prevent him from making racist statements in front of a black person. I stopped typing and stared at his back. He froze momentarily, and the woman he was talking to glanced at me.

I didn't confront him. I had to transmit copy to St. Petersburg and then leave to cover a graduation. Besides, my stomach was churning. Just seven days earlier, at a Ku Klux Klan rally in Clearwater, I had stood only four feet away from a Tarpon Springs man who told me he was tired of "the n——s getting everything."

I'd be lying if I said that the possibility of covering a Ku Klux Klan rally didn't cause me a few moments' concern about my physical well-being. But when another reporter came over to tell me about the May 28th Klan rally in front of Clearwater City Hall, I reasoned, "It's just another assignment. I am a reporter, and I know my life isn't all budget meetings."

I must also admit to a curiosity about the Klan, and it seemed a good opportunity to take a look at that sideshow of human nature. Now, I *could* have asked to be excused from that particular assignment. As a police reporter, my Saturdays are sometimes very busy. Had I approached my editor to delicately decline, we could have both made ourselves believe it was only natural to send a burly young man into the fray. Anything could have happened that day—traffic accidents, drownings, first-degree murders at the jail.

I couldn't be two places at once, could I?

But two days before the event, I turned to my editor and asked, "I AM covering the rally on Saturday, aren't I?"

She didn't miss a beat. Yes, of course. Just a short story, unless the streets were running with blood or something.

I jokingly told her about the only slightly feigned horror of my older sister, who shrieked into the phone, "They're letting a black reporter cover the KLAN?"

At the Klan rally, the man from Tarpon Springs saw my press badge and figured I was a part of something he called the "Black Associated Press," which he swore was denying white journalism graduates jobs. Mr.

Tarpon told me that n——s weren't qualified to get the jobs they were getting through affirmative action, and that America is for white people.

I paused momentarily and asked what he thought should be done about black people. He didn't know or care.

"Send 'em all to hell," he said, while I took notes.

It's funny—it was all so clinical. My voice held an even tone, and while he talked I searched his contorted face for some glimmer of recognition on his part that *I* was a human being, and the words that he spat just might hurt me.

Just as I later waited for Mr. Welcome Wagon to turn around and apologize for his blunder, I waited for the Tarpon Springs man to show some spark of humanity, but he finished his conversation and walked away.

My stomach was still churning hours later as I relived that rally. The whole experience was like being scalded, like having something sharp raked over my flesh until it was raw.

After it was over I went home and drank a shot from the bottle of brandy I'd bought last Christmas. In Harlequin romances, handsome princes always proffered hard liquor to soothe the jangled nerves of a distraught heroine.

But I was alone, and I was no heroine. That night, every noise from the apartment upstairs made me jump, and the pattern of trees against the curtains frightened me as I tossed and turned. I called three of my siblings, but other than offering sympathy, they felt helpless to ease my trauma.

I had been so naive about the whole assignment. The thing is, I never thought it would change me. I figured it would be difficult, but I didn't want it to *change* me.

What you must understand about the Klan is that its members and supporters have been stripped of their humanity. I gained that insight and feel stronger for it. It was easy enough on one level to say, "These people are stupid, so I shouldn't be bothered by what they say."

But that was cold comfort as I walked across the City Hall parking lot, feeling a numbness creep through my arms and legs. I thought I must have been walking like the Scarecrow in *The Wizard of Oz,* but figured if I could just make it to the church across the street, I'd be fine.

At the church, I asked to use the phone and was sent down a hall and to the left. My fingers felt like sausages as I tried to use the rotary dial, muttering curses as I fouled up several times. Finally managing to reach an editor, I was coherent enough to give her information for a brief summary of the rally.

But when the next editor picked up the phone, I dissolved in tears after three words. He was puzzled, and I think unaware of what was wrong at first. I whimpered that I was sorry and didn't know what was wrong, either. I gasped and caught a few breaths before describing in a wavering voice what had happened.

He tried calming me down to discuss the facts. How many people attended? Had there been any clashes? What did police have to say? I planned to write a full story.

The editor said maybe we should just ignore the event. He asked if any of the Klan members had been abusive to me. I mumbled, "Uh hum," and the tears flowed fresh. He told me to get as much police information as I could and to call him back later.

I placed the phone on the hook and buried my face in my hands, letting the sobs come freely. The man who had let me use the church phone brought me a box of tissues and a Coke.

After I splashed my face with cold water and controlled the sobs, I headed back to the rally, just as the Klansmen were loading up to leave. Shouts of "white supremacy" rang through the air as they rolled out, and my photographer walked over to give me the Klansmen's names. I turned away, telling her that I probably wouldn't use them anyway.

"I didn't think it would affect me," I whispered.

"Don't cry. They aren't worth it, Rachel," she said.

But even then, it had started to change me . . .

When you have stared into the twisted face of hate, you *must* change. I remember watching the documentary *Eyes on the Prize,* in particular the segment on the desegregation of Little Rock High School in 1957, and being disturbed by the outpouring of rage against those nine students.

The whites who snarled into the camera back then had no explanation for their vitriol and violence other than that the students were black, and they didn't care who knew it. They weren't going to let those n———s into the school, no matter what.

I've struggled all my life against a visceral reaction to that kind of racism. I have been mistreated because of my color, but nothing ever came near to what those students went through on a daily basis.

That and countless other examples let me know what I'd been spared, and I decided to choose the path of understanding, realizing that some people are always going to fear or even hate me because of my color alone.

It's a burden blacks must carry no matter how high a level of achievement they reach, and I sought to incorporate that into my own striving. Watching films of what hate turned those people into made me choose to reject it, to deal with people individually and not tarnish all whites with the same obscene images. *I would not hate.*

But as one Klan supporter muttered, "N—— b——," at me as I weaved my way through the crowd, that resolve crumbled. It stung as much as if he *had* slapped me or thrown something.

The leader shouted taunts and epithets at a black woman who was infuriated by the proceedings, and who had even lunged at several people in the small group of supporters.

As the black woman walked away, the leader shouted, "Why don't you go back to Nee-gor Africa where you came from!" I laughed because he sounded foolish, but he saw me and sent a fresh stream of obscenity my way.

A Jewish woman who came to protest was heaped with stinging abuse, and the rabble was ingenious in its varied use of sexual and racial obscenities directed toward her.

Other reporters and photographers eyed me warily throughout the rally, watching for my reactions to the abuse. When the leader started passing out leaflets and avoided my outstretched hand, a photographer asked for two and brought me one.

I said thank you. He said quietly, "You're very, very welcome," and was embarrassed when I caught his eye.

When it was all over, several police officials called me brave. But I felt cold, sick and empty. I felt like such a naive fool. I felt bitter. So this is what it feels like, I thought. Why *shouldn't* I just hate them right back, why couldn't I diffuse this punch in the gut?

What is noble about not flinching in the face of hate? Slavery, lynchings, rape, inequality, was that not enough? If they want to send me to hell, shouldn't I want to take them along for the ride?

But I still couldn't hate. I was glad I had cried, though. It defied their demented logic. It meant I was human.

Interpretations

1. Jones felt that her work did not absolutely require her to jeopardize her "physical well-being" by covering a Klan rally. What would she have lost if she had "delicately" asked her editor "to send a burly young man" to cover the story? Do you think she was right to undertake the assignment? (She admits to extreme naiveté.) If so, why? Do you think she will do it again? Do you think she could have better prepared herself emotionally for the experience? If so, how?

2. What is the tone of the essay? Why do you think she failed to quote the "fresh stream of obscenity" at several points? Do you find any humor?

3. One thing Jones learned from the assignment was how emotionally vulnerable she was. What else did she learn? She mistakenly thought that by remembering how "stupid" Klansmen are, she would be protected. Do you think remembering how stupid one's enemy is can

sometimes protect one from that enemy? Why? Under what circumstances?

4. "I planned to write a full story of the rally," says the author. Did she? Would you like to read it? Why?

5. What is Jones's purpose in comparing her experience with that of the students at Little Rock High School in 1957?

6. What *is* the price of hate? Jones says that even after this experience she "still couldn't hate." Is it really possible to "turn the other cheek"? How do you know?

7. What instances of kindness in this hateful scene does Jones report? Why do you think she included them?

Correspondences

1. Review the Ellison quotation (page 194). How does it apply to the people Jones encountered on her assignment? To what extent do you agree with Jones's conclusion that "[they] have been stripped of their humanity"?

2. Jones, a black journalist, covers an assignment in Florida in 1988. How does her experience in the workplace compare with that of Johnson, an unskilled worker in Petry's story in New York in 1945?

Applications

1. Review Jones's biography (page 305). Why did she want to become a journalist? Characterize *your* goals with respect to future work. What criteria will you use? Write an essay defining your career goals.

2. Discuss the Woolf quotation on work (page 259) with your group and write an analysis of their responses.

Free and Equal

Lalita Gandbhir

Lalita Gandbhir (b. 1938) works as a physician in the Boston area, where she has lived since coming to the United States in 1963. She has published stories in the Toronto South Asian Review, *the* Massachusetts Review, Spotlight, *and other journals, as well as two collections of short stories in India. Before reading her short story, freewrite about your association with its title.*

RAMESH CAREFULLY STUDIED his reflection in the mirror hung in the hallway. His hair, shirt, tie, suit, nothing escaped his scrutiny. His tie seemed a little crooked, so he undid it and fixed it with slow deliberate movements. Then he reexamined the tie. A conservative shade of maroon, not too wide, not too narrow, just right for the occasion, for the image he wanted to project.

All of a sudden he was aware of two eyes staring at him. He turned to Jay, his little son. Jay sat on the steps leading to the second floor, his eyes focused on his father.

"Why are you staring at me?" Ramesh inquired.

"Going to work now?" Jay intimated the reason for the surprised stare.

Ramesh understood the reason behind Jay's confusion. He used to go to work dressed like this in the mornings. Jay had not seen him dressed in a suit in the evening.

For a moment Ramesh was proud of his son. "What a keen observer Jay is!" Ramesh thought to himself. "For six months I have not worked, yet he noticed a change in my old routine."

However, the implications behind the question bothered Ramesh.

"I am going to a job fair," he answered irritably and again attempted to focus on his tie.

"Can I come?" Jay promptly hurled a question in Ramesh's direction. To him a fair was a fun event. He had been to fairs with his mother before and did not wish to miss this one.

"Jay, this is not the kind of fair you are thinking of. This is a job fair."

"Do they sell jobs at job fairs?"

"Yes." Jay's question struck a sensitive spot. "No, they don't sell jobs. They are buyers. They shop for skills. It's me who is selling my skills. Unfortunately, it's a buyer's market."

The question stimulated Ramesh's chain of thought. "Is my skill for sale?" Ramesh wondered. "If that is true, then why did I dress so carefully? Why did I rehearse answers to imaginary questions from interviewers?"

"No, this job hunting is no longer a simple straightforward business transaction like it used to be when engineers were in demand. I am desperate. I am selling my soul. The job market is no longer a two-way street. I have no negotiating power. I just have to accept what I can get."

Ramesh pulled on his socks mechanically and longingly thought of the good old days like a sick old man thinking of his healthful youth.

Just ten years ago he had hopped from job to job at will. Money, interesting work, more responsibility, benefits, a whim for any reason that appealed to him, and he had switched jobs. Responding to advertisements was his hobby. Head hunters called him offering better and better situations. He went to job fairs casually dressed and never gave a second thought to his attire.

He had job offers, not one or two, but six or seven. The industry needed him then. It was so nice to be coveted!

Ramesh wiped his polished, spotless shoes with a soft cloth.

How carefree he used to be! He dressed like this every morning in five minutes and, yes, Jay remembers.

He never polished his shoes then. His hand moving the cloth on his shoes stood still for a minute. Yes, Rani, his wife, did it for him. Nowadays she seemed to do less and less for him. Why? He asked himself.

Rani had found a part-time job on her own when companies in the area had started to lay off engineers. She had not bothered to discuss the matter with him, just informed him of her decision. In a year she accepted a full-time slot. "How did she manage to receive promotions so soon?" Ramesh wondered.

Rani still ran the home and cared for their young children. Ramesh had seen her busy at all kinds of tasks from early morning until late at night.

Over the last three months she did less and less for Ramesh. She no longer did his laundry or ironing. She had stopped polishing his shoes and did not wait up for him when he returned late from job fairs.

"She is often tired," Ramesh tried to understand, but he felt that she had let him down, wronged him just when his spirit was sinking and he needed her most.

"She should have made an effort for the sake of appearance. It was her duty toward a jobless, incomeless husband.

He pushed all thoughts out of his mind.

He tied his polished shoes, dragged his heavy winter coat out of the closet, and picked up his keys.

"Tell your Ma that I have left," he ordered Jay, and closed the door without saying good-bye to Rani.

In the car, thoughts flooded his mind again.

Perhaps he made a mistake in coming to study abroad for his Masters in engineering. No! That was not the error. He should not have stayed on after he received his Masters. He should have returned home as he originally planned.

He intended to return, but unfortunately he attended a job fair after graduation just for fun and ended up accepting a job offer. A high salary in dollars converted into a small fortune in rupees, proved impossible to resist. He always converted dollars into rupees then, before buying or selling. He offered himself an excuse of short-term American experience and stayed on. The company that hired him sponsored him for a green card.

He still wanted to return home, but he postponed it, went for a visit instead and picked Rani from several prospective brides, married her and returned to the United States.

The trip left bitter memories, especially for Rani. He could not talk his mother out of accepting a dowry.

"Mother, Rani will earn the entire sum of a dowry in a month in the United States. A dowry is a hardship for her middle-class family. Let us not insist on it. Just accept what her family offers."

But Mother, with Father's tacit support, insisted. "You are my only son. I have waited for this occasion all my life. I want a proper wedding, the kind of wedding our friends and relatives will remember forever."

Ramesh gave in to her wishes and had a wedding with pomp and special traditional honors for his family. His mother was only partially gratified because she felt that their family did not get what was due them with her foreign returned son! The dowry, however, succeeded in upsetting Rani, who looked miserable throughout the ceremony.

"We will refund all the money once you come to the United States," Ramesh promised her. "It's a minor sum when dollars are converted to rupees."

Instead of talking in his conciliatory tone, Rani demanded, too harshly for a bride, "If it's a minor sum, why did you let your family insist on a dowry? You know my parents' savings are wiped out."

Over a few years they refunded the money, but Rani's wounds never healed and during fights she referred to the dowry spitefully.

Her caustic remarks did not bother Ramesh before, but now with her income supporting the family, they were beginning to hurt. "Write your mother that your wife works and makes up for part of the dowry her father failed to provide!" she had remarked once.

"Don't women ever forgive?" he had wondered.

"I am extra sensitive." He brushed off the pain that Rani's words caused.

The job fair was at a big hotel. He followed the directions and turned into a full parking lot. As he pulled into the tight space close to the exit, he glanced at the hotel lobby. Through the glass exterior wall, underneath a brightly lit chandelier, he could see a huge crowd milling in the lobby.

Panic struck him. He was late. So many people had made it there ahead of him. All applicants with his experience and background might be turned away.

Another car approached and pulled into the last parking space in the lot. The engine noise died and a man roughly his height and build stepped out, just as Ramesh shut his car door. Out on the walkway Ramesh heard a greeting.

"Hello, how are you?"

Ramesh looked up.

In the fluorescent lights his eyes met friendly blue eyes. He noticed a slightly wrinkled forehead and receding hairline, like his own.

"Hello," Ramesh responded.

The stranger smiled. "Sometimes I wonder why I come to these fairs. In the last six months I must have been to at least ten."

"Really? So have I!" He must have been laid off at the same time, Ramesh thought.

"We must have attended the same ones. I don't remember seeing you," the newcomer said.

"Too many engineers looking for a job—you know," Ramesh offered as explanation.

The pair had approached the revolving lobby doors. Ramesh had a strong urge to turn back and return home.

"Come on, we must try." The newcomer apparently had sensed the urge. "My name is Bruce. Would you like to meet me at the door in an hour? We will have a drink before we go home. It will—kind of lift my spirits."

"All right," Ramesh agreed without thinking and added, "I am Ramesh."

Bruce waited for Ramesh to step into the revolving door.

Ramesh mechanically pushed into the lobby. His heart sagged even further. "With persons like Bruce looking for a job, who will hire a foreigner like me?" he wondered. He looked around. Bruce had vanished into the crowd.

Ramesh looked at a row of booths set up by the side wall. He approached one looking for engineers with his qualifications. A few Americans had already lined up to talk to the woman screening the applicants.

She looked at him and repeated the same questions she had asked applicants before him. "Your name, sir?"

He had to spell it. She made a mistake in noting it down. He had to correct her.

"Please fill out this application." He sensed a slight irritation in her voice.

"Thank you," he said. His accent seemed to have intensified. He took the application and retreated to a long table.

He visited six or seven booths of companies who might need—directly, indirectly, or remotely—someone of his experience and education; challenge, benefit package, location, salary, nothing mattered to him any more. He had to find a job.

An hour and a half later, as he approached the revolving door, he noticed Bruce waiting for him.

During the discussion over drinks, he discovered that Bruce had the same qualifications as himself. However, Bruce had spent several years wandering around the world, so he had only four years of experience. Ramesh had guessed right. Bruce had been laid off the same time as himself.

"It's been very hard," Bruce said. "What little savings we had are wiped out and my wife is fed up with me. She thinks I don't try hard. This role reversal is not good for a man's ego."

"Yes," Ramesh agreed.

"I may have to move but my wife doesn't want to. Her family is here."

"I understand."

"I figure you don't have that problem."

"No. You must have guessed I'm from India."

After a couple of drinks they walked out into an empty lobby and empty parking lot.

Two days later Bruce called. "Want to go to a job fair? It's in Woodland, two hundred miles from here. I hate to drive out alone." Ramesh agreed.

"Who will hire me when Americans are available?" he complained to Rani afterward.

"You must not think like that. You are as good as any of them," Rani snapped. "Remember what Alexander said."

Ramesh remembered. Alexander was a crazy history student with whom he had shared an apartment. Rani always referred to Alexander's message.

Ramesh had responded to an advertisement on his university's bulletin board and Alexander had answered the phone.

"You have to be crazy to share an apartment with me. My last roommate left because he could not live with me."

"What did you do? I mean, why did he leave?" Ramesh asked.

"I like to talk. You see, I wake up people and tell them about my ideas at night. They call me crazy Alexander . . ."

"I will get back to you." Ramesh put the receiver down and talked to the student who had moved out.

"You see, Alexander's a nut. He sleeps during the day and studies at night. He's a history buff. He studies revolutions. He wakes up people just to talk to them, about theories, others and his own! He will offer to discount the rent if you put up with him."

Short of funds, Ramesh moved in with Alexander.

Much of Alexander's oratory bounced off Ramesh's half-asleep brain, but off and on a few sentences made an impression and stuck in his memory.

"You must first view yourself as free and equal," Alexander had said.

"Equal to whom?"

"To those around you who consider you less than equal . . ."

"Me? Less than equal?"

"No! Not you, stupid. The oppressed person. Oppression could be social, religious, foreign, traditional."

"Who oppressed me?"

"No! No! Not you! An imaginary oppressed person who must first see himself as the equal of his oppressors. The idea of equality will ultimately sow seeds of freedom and revolution in his mind. That idea is the first step. You see . . . stop snoring . . . That's the first step toward liberation."

Soon Ramesh walked like a zombie.

In another month, he too moved out.

After his marriage he told Rani some of his conversations with Alexander.

"Makes sense," she said, looking very earnest.

"Really! You mean you understand?" Rani's reaction amazed Ramesh.

"Yes, I do. I am an oppressed person, socially and traditionally. That's why my parents had to come up with a dowry."

A month went by and Ramesh was called for an interview.

Bruce telephoned the same night. He and some other engineers he knew had also been called. Had Ramesh received a call, too?

Ramesh swallowed hard. "No, I didn't." He felt guilty and ashamed. He had lied to Bruce, who was so open, friendly, and supportive, despite his own difficulties.

Ramesh's ego had already suffered a major trauma. He was convinced that he would not get a job if Americans were available and he did not wish to admit to Bruce later on, "I had an interview, but they didn't hire me." It was easier to lie now.

The interview over, Ramesh decided to put the job out of his mind. His confidence at a low ebb, he dared not hope.

Three weeks went by and he received a phone call from the company that interviewed him. He had the job.

"They must have hired several engineers," Ramesh thought, elated.

Bruce called again. "I didn't get the job. The other guys I know have also received negative replies."

The news stunned Ramesh. He could not believe that he had the job and the others did not. As he pondered this, he realized he owed an embarrassing explanation to Bruce. How was he going to tell him that he had the job?

As Bruce jabbered about something, Ramesh collected his courage.

"I have an offer from them," he stated in a flat tone and strained his ear for a response.

After a few unbearable seconds of silence, Bruce exclaimed, "Congratulations! At least one of us made it. Now we can all hope. I know you have better qualifications."

Ramesh knew that the voice was sincere, without a touch of the envy he had anticipated.

They agreed to meet Saturday for a drink, a small celebration, Bruce suggested.

"Rani, I got the job. The others didn't." Ramesh hung up the receiver and bounded up to Rani.

"I told you are as good as any of them," Rani responded nonchalantly and continued to fold laundry.

"Maybe . . . possibly . . . they needed a minority candidate," Ramesh muttered.

Rani stopped folding. "Ramesh," she said as her eyes scanned Ramesh's face, "You may have the job and the knowledge and the qualifications, but you are not free and equal."

"What do you mean?" Ramesh asked.

Interpretations

1. Alexander, for all his eccentricities, is portrayed as the voice of wisdom. How does his "message" of free and equal relate to the problems of job seeking? to the problems of competition between foreign and native-born job seekers? to the problem of dowries?

2. How realistic is Bruce's lack of resentment that Ramesh got a job? How well does the story make us believe in Ramesh's "better qualifications"?

3. From you own experience, what is the usual relationship between two candidates competing in a limited job market? Do they confide in each other or share tips? Does the first one to get a job feel guilty?

4. What do you think was Gandbhir's purpose in writing this story—to show human nature in action, to entertain, to make a point, or for some other reason? If you think the story was written primarily to make a point, what is it?

Correspondences

1. Jones and Gandbhir raise the issue of affirmative action in the workplace and its implications for "minority candidates." How do their perspectives differ? Consider how competition for jobs affects attitudes toward affirmative action.

2. Olson and Gandbhir discuss how one's job affects self-respect. Which examples did you find most convincing? How might material success in the workplace also affect self-image?

Applications

1. "You may have the job and the knowledge and the qualifications, but you are not free and equal." Discuss Rani's assessment of her husband. Is it possible for Ramesh to be "free and equal" in the United States? Why or why not?

2. Freewrite on your associations with success. Is it possible for everyone to be successful? How might our individual strivings for success affect our social and communal values?

A View of Affirmative Action in the Workplace

Michael Gnolfo

Michael Gnolfo was born in Brooklyn, N.Y., in 1951. He grew up in Queens, and lives in Nassau County on Long Island with his wife and son. He works for a major utility company as a customer-service supervisor. He returned to college after a sixteen-year absence and is now a graduate of Queensborough Community College.

AFFIRMATIVE ACTION is by definition any plan or program that promotes the employment of women and of members of minority groups. This has come about to right all the wrongs suffered by these groups in the past. It is intended to be a positive force for civil rights.

Directly or indirectly, because of Affirmative Action women and minorities have increasingly found more opportunity where none existed for them. Traditional role separation is disappearing. Society is realizing an untapped wealth of talent and business is reaping a whirlwind of benefits from this new diversity.

Jobs that were traditionally male dominated have had major inroads by women. Bus drivers, construction workers, telephone technicians and pilots now count women among their numbers as do the management staffs of many corporations. The reverse is also true. Men have increasingly entered such fields as nursing, secretarial sciences and flight attendants which have been traditionally female occupations. It seems that no barriers exist to an individual with the skills to perform a job.

While all of this is good and the proper course to pursue, there are problems. We can all agree that the protection and promotion of one group in society is wrong. So, when does a program designed to promote fairness become discriminatory? When capable people are neglected at the expense of less capable or similarly capable politically correct/connected candidates. A glaring example of this is the New York City Police exam and requirements. A comparison of physical requirements from today versus thirty years ago reveals a less demanding test of strength and physique. The requirements were relaxed to allow lesser physical candidates to pass. Minority candidates with lower written test marks are also taken over other candidates if a certain percentage of those minorities are not represented on the force. We are legislating mediocrity at best. What is more desirable, a competent organization or a gender/racially correct structure?

Private business is doing just the same. It is especially true in any large company that is contractually obligated to the government or is regulated by it. Those not included in Affirmative Action become less likely to be successful despite qualification. They are fast becoming a new oppressed minority. Companies are zealous in their adherence to Affirmative Action not out of altruism but of fear of loss of contract or stiffer regulation. Remember that while there has been much progress by minorities in business there is a dearth of minority CEOs in the major corporations and that says so much about the reality of Affirmative Action.

The time is right for another step in the evolution of American society. We all realize the positive contributions of the groups protected by Affirmative Action. They have been valuable additions to our society. But abuses have now surfaced. Let's not make the same mistakes we made before. We need a Positive Fairness principle to replace Affirmative Action. Qualification and achievement should be the deciding factors in society and business. Quotas are abhorrent. Discrimination is bad, be it directed toward a race, gender, religion or anyone for any reason. Affirmative Action is becoming a racist, sexist instrument that is quickly turning into a tool of those who would replace one form of dominance with another. Contrary to the belief of feminists, the best man for the job is not a WOMAN but the most qualified individual.

Interpretations

1. Gnolfo says that the purpose of Affirmative Action has been "to right all the wrongs suffered by these groups in the past." If this was once a worthwhile goal, has the goal been met? Are there perhaps other reasons for Affirmative Action (such as diversification) that make it still worthwhile?

2. What is the relationship between economic hard times and Affirmative Action in the workplace?

3. What is the legal status of Affirmative Action? Gnolfo says that companies don't practice Affirmative Action out of "altruism." What difference would it make if it were voluntary? Would it still accomplish its goal without the "abuses" Gnolfo attributes to it?

4. Gnolfo assumes that his readers will understand "politically correct-connected candidates." Has he correctly judged his audience? Political correctness—or PC—has become a frequently encountered short-hand or code designation for what set of ideas or beliefs? How

does political correctness relate to Affirmative Action? to freedom of speech and other Bill-of-Rights issues?

5. Comment on the relationship between Gnolfo's first three paragraphs and the rest of the essay. How effective is this two-part organization?

Correspondences

1. Gnolfo examines the effects of Affirmative Action in the workplace. What conversation can you imagine him having with Ramesh in "Free and Easy"?

2. "Affirmative Action is becoming a racist, sexist instrument that is quickly turning into a tool of those who would replace one form of dominance with another." To what extent do you agree or disagree? Compare Gnolfo's assessment of Affirmative Action with that expressed by Olson in paragraph 2 of "Year of the Blue-Collar Guy."

Applications

1. Affirmative Action is a controversial issue. If you are a member of a minority group who could benefit from Affirmative Action, write an essay citing reasons why your choice to do so is ethical. If you are in a position to be hurt by Affirmative Action, write an essay citing reasons why Affirmative Action programs offer unfair opportunities to minorities. Be as specific as you can.

2. Discuss Gnolfo's thesis that "contrary to the belief of feminists, the best man for the job is not a WOMAN but the most qualified individual."

Procrastination

Sharon Y. Friedner

Sharon Friedner (b. 1974) was born in New York, but was raised and educated through high school in Massachusetts. She will further her education at Oberlin College (Ohio) where she plans to major in English. About her essay, she says:

> *"Procrastination" was originally a college application essay. I chose the topic because I feel that procrastination is a trait many people see as a flaw. I wanted to show how this "flaw" can, indeed, be a virtue. There is nothing that can spur the imagination more than trying to write an essay at midnight.*

It is two o'clock in the morning and the wires that connect my brain to my mind are smoldering as they hover precariously near their melting point. Once again I am imprisoned by the shackles of procrastination. Once again I try in vain to capture time—the elusive monster. But, as always, my efforts are for naught, and I am left with nothing but a blank piece of notebook paper that must be magically transformed into a literary masterpiece before sunrise.

The force of gravity inevitably becomes too much for my weary eyelids, and they finally give in—momentarily shutting out the clock that progresses unceasingly toward my deadline. A familiar scene begins to creep into my mind. . . .

It is morning and the sun comes up but no one—absolutely no one—awakens. In a sense, the progression of time is ignored—completely denied by the happy slumberers. The following morning everything proceeds as usual, and not a soul is aware of the day that has been skipped. Oh, how easy it seems to outsmart this thing we call time. I smile inwardly as I recall the fact that if everyone in the world could agree that today is Friday, it would be. But no one has agreed to this; and in the morning everyone will wake up as usual; and the clock in its perpetual rush has not stopped to wait for me to think; and the paper in front of me is still as blank as it was the day the factory spit it out.

I count to three and heave my eyelids open. I glance at the clock and grin, knowing that I have been tempting time to catch up with me. Half an hour—shot! It used to be at this point that panic would begin to set in. For I have reached the point of no return. From now until dawn I must use every ounce of my academic prowess to create not only a mechanically perfect essay, but an essay on *paper* that does justice to the essay in my *mind*. I am tired and unsure, yet hopeful that my skill will come through for me this time. Fortunately I have long ago learned to overcome my "after midnight panic." Indeed, I am calm. I have been in this exact situation an uncountable number of times and, admittedly I have come to enjoy it. For me procrastination is a challenge, a skill, an art—maybe even an addiction. It is the thrill of mental stamina and survival. It is the feeling of being alone, utterly alone in a race against time—and against myself; a race that I have initiated and a contest that I *must* win. Procrastination is the ability to look time in the eye and laugh. An ability that I have only begun to master.

I stand up, stretch, and walk over to the window. One at a time I lift the shade, the glass, the screen, and the storm window. Nature rushes in. I breathe the sweet, frigid morning air and look out at the obscure and soundless world that is my inspiration. The cold wind revives my body and I find that my mind is still surprisingly lucid. I sit down in my favorite spot by the bed where the carpet is worn from all the nights I've spent like this one. Confidently I grasp my pen, and take one final glance at the clock. I am surprised that an hour has passed in what seemed like only a moment. Time hits me with all the harsh exactness of its reality. It is now that the true race begins.

Interpretations

1. Figurative language like metaphor, hyperbole, and personification enliven Friedner's essay. What examples of such language can you find?

2. How effective is Friedner's redefinition of procrastination as an "ability"?

3. Why is the light tone of this essay appropriate—or inappropriate—for this subject?

Correspondences

1. Review Picasso's perspective (page 259) and discuss its relevance to "procrastination." To what extent do you agree with Friedner that the clock is an enemy?

2. Compare and contrast attitudes toward time expressed by Laye and Friedner. To what extent is it true that we are in a race against time?

Applications

1. In what areas of life besides work is procrastination a challenge? What is your way of dealing with it?

2. Friedner wrote "procrastination" as part of college application. Imagine yourselves as members of a college admissions committee. How might "procrastination" affect your judgment on her college acceptance?

Looking for Work

Gary Soto

Gary Soto (b. 1952) is a second-generation Mexican-American from Fresno, California. He earned degrees from California State University and from the University of California at Berkeley, where he teaches English and Chicano studies, He has received numerous awards, including the Academy of American Poets prize (1975), a Guggenheim Fellowship (1979–1980), Levinson Award (1984), and American Book Award (1985) for Living Up the Street: Narrative Recollections. *"Looking for Work" shows more of Soto's consciousness of his Mexican-American identity than does his essay in Chapter 3, "Summer School."*

Mexicans can boast of a series of advanced civilization. The Olmec, Toltec, Mayan, and Aztec cultures flourished variously between 100 and 900. Hernando Cortez, a Spanish conquistador, defeated the Aztecs in 1519–1521, establishing the Spanish rule that would last until independence was declared in 1821.

The California in which Soto grew up, along with much of the present American Southwest, was part of Mexico until the Mexican-American War (1848) stripped Mexico of all its territory north of the Rio Grande. Only 13 percent of Mexico's land is arable. The per capita annual income in 1984 was about $2,000. Some land redistribution and the discovery of oil in the 1970s brightened Mexico's economic prospects somewhat. However, large numbers of Mexicans continue to flow into the United States in search of employment. In the 1970s, fourteen percent of immigrants to the United States, or six million people, came from Mexico. In 1988 alone, almost a million Mexicans came north over the Rio Grande.

ONE JULY, while killing ants on the kitchen sink with a rolled newspaper, I had a nine-year-old's vision of wealth that would save us from ourselves. For weeks I had drunk Kool-Aid and watched morning reruns of *Father Knows Best*, whose family was so uncomplicated in its routine that I very much wanted to imitate it. The first step was to get my brother and sister to wear shoes at dinner.

"Come on, Rick—come on, Deb," I whined. But Rick mimicked me and the same day that I asked him to wear shoes he came to the dinner table in only his swim trunks. My mother didn't notice, nor did my sister, as we sat to eat our beans and tortillas in the stifling heat of our kitchen. We all gleamed like cellophane, wiping the sweat from our brows with the backs of our hands as we talked about the day: Frankie our neighbor was beat up by Faustino; the swimming pool at the playground would be closed for a day because the pump was broken.

Such was our life. So that morning, while doing-in the train of ants which arrived each day, I decided to become wealthy, and right away! After downing a bowl of cereal, I took a rake from the garage and started up the block to look for work.

We lived on an ordinary block of mostly working class people: ware-housemen, egg candlers, welders, mechanics, and, a union plumber. And there were many retired people who kept their lawns green and the gutters uncluttered of the chewing gum wrappers we dropped as we rode by on our bikes. They bent down to gather our litter, muttering at our evilness.

At the corner house I rapped the screen door and a very large woman in a muu-muu answered. She sized me up and then asked what I could do.

"Rake leaves," I answered, smiling.

"It's summer, and there ain't no leaves," she countered. Her face was pinched with lines; fat jiggled under her chin. She pointed to the lawn, then the flower bed, and said: "You see any leaves there—or there?" I followed her pointing arm, stupidly. But she had a job for me and that was to get her a Coke at the liquor store. She gave me twenty cents, and after ditching my rake in a bush, off I ran. I returned with an unbagged Pepsi, for which she thanked me and gave me a nickel from her apron.

I skipped off her porch, fetched my rake, and crossed the street to the next block where Mrs. Moore, mother of Earl the retarded man, let me weed a flower bed. She handed me a trowel and for a good part of the morning my fingers dipped into the moist dirt, ripping up runners of Bermuda grass. Worms surfaced in my search for deep roots, and I cut them in halves, tossing them to Mrs. Moore's cat who pawed them playfully as they dried in the sun. I made out Earl whose face was pressed to the back window of the house, and although he was calling to me I couldn't understand what he was trying to say. Embarrassed, I worked without looking up, but I imagined his contorted mouth and the ring of keys attached to his belt—keys that jingled with each palsied step. He scared me and I worked quickly to finish the flower bed. When I did finish Mrs. Moore gave me a quarter and two peaches from her tree, which I washed there but ate in the alley behind my house.

I was sucking on the second one, a bit of juice staining the front of my T-shirt, when Little John, my best friend, came walking down the alley with a baseball bat over his shoulder, knocking over trash cans as he made his way toward me.

Little John and I went to St. John's Catholic School, where we sat among the "stupids." Miss Marino, our teacher, alternated the rows of good students with the bad, hoping that by sitting side-by-side with the bright students the stupids might become more intelligent, as though intelligence were contagious. But we didn't progress as she had hoped. She grew frustrated when one day, while dismissing class for recess, Little John couldn't get up because his arms were stuck in the slats of the chair's backrest. She scolded us with a shaking finger when we knocked over the globe, denting the already troubled Africa. She muttered curses when Leroy White, a real stupid but a great softball player with the gift to hit to all fields, openly chewed his host when he made his First Communion; his hands swung at his sides as he returned to the pew looking around with a big smile.

Little John asked what I was doing, and I told him that I was taking a break from work, as I sat comfortably among high weeds. He wanted to join me, but I reminded him that the last time he'd gone door-to-door asking for work his mother had whipped him. I was with him when his mother, a New Jersey Italian who could rise up in anger one moment and love the next, told me in a polite but matter-of-fact voice that I had to leave because she was going to beat her son. She gave me a homemade popsicle, ushered me to the door, and said that I could see Little John the next day. But it was sooner than that. I went around to his bedroom window to suck my popsicle and watch Little John dodge his mother's blows, a few hitting their mark but many whirring air.

It was midday when Little John and I converged in the alley, the sun blazing in the high nineties, and he suggested that we go to Roosevelt High School to swim. He needed five cents to make fifteen, the cost of admission, and I lent him a nickel. We ran home for my bike and when my sister found out that we were going swimming, she started to cry because she didn't have the fifteen cents but only an empty Coke bottle. I waved for her to come and three of us mounted the bike—Debra on the cross bar, Little John on the handle bars and holding the Coke bottle which we would cash for a nickel and make up the difference that would allow all of us to get in, and me pumping up the crooked streets, dodging cars and pot holes. We spent the day swimming under the afternoon sun, so that when we got home our mom asked us what was darker, the floor or us? She feigned a stern posture, her hands on her hips and her mouth puckered. We played along. Looking down, Debbie and I said in unison, "Us."

That evening at dinner we all sat down in our bathing suits to eat our beans, laughing and chewing loudly. Our mom was in a good mood, so I took a risk and asked her if sometime we could have turtle soup. A few days before I had watched a television program in which a Polynesian tribe killed a large turtle, gutted it, and then stewed it over an open fire. The turtle, basted in a sugary sauce, looked delicious as I ate an afternoon bowl of cereal, but my sister, who was watching the program with a glass of Kool-Aid between her knees, said, "Caca."

My mother looked at me in bewilderment. "Boy, are you a crazy Mexican. Where did you get the idea that people eat turtles?"

"On television," I said, explaining the program. Then I took it a step further. "Mom, do you think we could get dressed up for dinner one of these days? David King does."

"*Ay, Dios,*" my mother laughed. She started collecting the dinner plates, but my brother wouldn't let go of his. He was still drawing a picture in the bean sauce. Giggling, he said it was me, but I didn't want to listen because I wanted an answer from Mom. This was the summer when I spent the mornings in front of the television that showed the comfortable lives of white kids. There were no beatings, no rifts in the family. They wore bright clothes; toys tumbled from their closets. They hopped into bed with kisses and woke to glasses of fresh orange juice, and to a father sitting before his morning coffee while the mother buttered his toast. They hurried through the day making friends and gobs of money, returning home to a warmly lit living room, and then dinner. *Leave It To Beaver* was the program I replayed in my mind:

"May I have the mashed potatoes?" asks Beaver with a smile.

"Sure, Beav," replies Wally as he taps the corners of his mouth with a starched napkin.

The father looks on in his suit. The mother, decked out in earrings and a pearl necklace, cuts into her steak and blushes. Their conversation is politely clipped.

"Swell," says Beaver, his cheeks puffed with food.

Our own talk at dinner was loud with belly laughs and marked by our pointing forks at one another. The subjects were commonplace.

"Gary, let's go to the ditch tomorrow," my brother suggests. He explains that he has made a life preserver out of four empty detergent bottles strung together with twine and that he will make me one if I can find more bottles. "No way are we going to drown."

"Yeah, then we could have a dirt clod fight," I reply, so happy to be alive.

Whereas the Beaver's family enjoyed dessert in dishes at the table, our mom sent us outside, and more often than not I went into the alley to peek over the neighbor's fences and spy out fruit, apricots or peaches.

I had asked my mom and again she laughed that I was a crazy *chavalo* as she stood in front of the sink, her arms rising and falling with suds, face glistening from the heat. She sent me outside where my brother and sister were sitting in the shade that the fence threw out like a blanket. They were talking about me when I plopped down next to them. They looked at one another and then Debbie, my eight-year-old sister, started in.

"What's this crap about getting dressed up?"

She had entered her profanity stage. A year later she would give up such words and slip into her Catholic uniform, and into squealing on my brother and me when we "cussed this" and "cussed that."

I tried to convince them that if we improved the way we looked we might get along better in life. White people would like us more. They might invite us to places, like their homes or front yards. They might not hate us so much.

My sister called me a "craphead," and got up to leave with a stalk of grass dangling from her mouth. "They'll never like us."

My brother's mood lightened as he talked about the ditch—the white water, the broken pieces of glass, and the rusted car fenders that awaited our knees. There would be toads, and rocks to smash them.

David King, the only person we knew who resembled the middle class, called from over the fence. David was Catholic, of Armenian and French descent, and his closet was filled with toys. A bear-shaped cookie jar, like the ones on television, sat on the kitchen counter. His mother was remarkably kind while she put up with the racket we made on the street. Evenings, she often watered the front yard and it must have upset her to see us—my brother and I and others—jump from trees laughing, the unkillable kids of the very poor, who got up unshaken, brushed off, and climbed into another one to try again.

David called again. Rick got up and slapped grass from his pants. When I asked if I could come along he said no. David said no. They were two years older so their affairs were different from mine. They greeted one another with foul names and took off down the alley to look for trouble.

I went inside the house, turned on the television, and was about to sit down with a glass of Kool-Aid when Mom shooed me outside.

"It's still light," she said. "Later you'll bug me to let you stay out longer. So go on."

I downed my Kool-Aid and went outside to the front yard. No one was around. The day had cooled and a breeze rustled the trees. Mr. Jackson, the plumber, was watering his lawn and when he saw me he turned away to wash off his front steps. There was more than an hour of light left, so I took advantage of it and decided to look for work. I felt suddenly alive as I skipped down the block in search of an overgrown flower bed and the dime that would end the day right.

Interpretations

1. How does Soto keep the idea of work from getting lost in a welter of detail and digressions? Does he value work more for itself or for what it can bring him? Cite evidence for your response.

2. What are the major character traits of the nine-year-old Soto?

3. It is of course not true that the "kids" of "the very poor" are "unkillable." But why do they sometimes seem so to middle-class people? What is the truth about the health and life expectancy of poor kids vs. that of middle-class or wealthy kids? (Do you think Soto's aspirations for his family and himself are unkillable? Why or why not?)

4. How seriously do you take the nine-year-old Soto's claims that he, alone of his family, had aspirations to rise above the "commonplace" subjects discussed at table and longings for the "wealth that would save [them] from [themselves]"? What would it mean for the Soto family to be "saved from" itself?

5. What do you think is Soto's thesis or main point in this essay? Contrast Soto's interests with those of his brother. What is the effect of this discrepancy on the tone of the essay and on the thesis or main point?

6. How, in general, does the Soto family get along with the other families on the block? Do you think the Sotos feel discriminated against or disliked? What's the evidence? What was the range of income and ethnic groups among the families on the block?

7. How does the chronology provide unity?

Correspondences

1. "Little John and I went to St. John's Catholic School, where we sat among the 'stupids.' Miss Marino, our teacher, alternated the rows of good students with the bad, hoping that by sitting side-by-side with the bright students, the stupids might become more intelligent, as though intelligence were contagious." In "So Tsi-Fai" (Chapter 3) Liu's teacher viewed So Tsi-fai as "incorrigible, hopeless and without hope." Do people get tracked for the future as early as grammar school? In a parochial school in Fresno as well as in Hong Kong? How does such stereotyping affect future work choices?

2. Soto and Bambara (Chapter 3) use a child as narrator. How does that affect their use of dialogue, their portrayals of relationships, and your response as reader? Cite examples from both selections.

Applications

1. In "Looking for Work" Soto compares his working-class way of life with that of middle-class white families exemplified by "Father Knows Best" and "Leave It to Beaver." How are their work habits similar and different?

2. "One July, while killing ants on the kitchen sink with a rolled newspaper, I had a nine-year-old's vision of wealth that would save us from ourselves." Write a journal entry on your motivation for looking for your first "job."

Jasmine

Bharati Mukherjee

Bharati Mukherjee (b. 1940) was raised in Calcutta, India, and came to the United States in 1961. She lived in Canada from 1968 to 1972 before returning to the United States, where she is now a permanent resident. She received her Ph.D. from the University of Iowa and has taught at several academic institutions, including Skidmore College and Columbia University. Her novels include The Tiger's Daughter *(1972),* The Wire *(1975), and* Jasmine *(1989), an expansion of the story "Jasmine." With her husband, she also co-authored* Days and Nights in Calcutta *(1977), a journal of their impression of a return visit to India. In "Jasmine," taken from* The Middleman and Other Stories *(1988), the title character is a young immigrant from Trinidad who becomes infatuated with Ann Arbor, Michigan.*

Trinidad and Tobago is an island republic off the eastern coast of Venezuela about the size of Delaware. Its population of 1,262,000 is forty-three percent African and forty percent East Indian. Trinidad and Tobago, a parliamentary democracy, won independence from Britain in 1962 and became a republic in 1976. One of the most prosperous countries in the Caribbean, much of its prosperity is based on oil drilling and refining.

JASMINE CAME TO Detroit from Port-of-Spain, Trinidad, by way of Canada. She crossed the border at Windsor in the back of a gray van loaded with mattresses and box springs. The plan was for her to hide in an empty mattress box if she heard the driver say, "All bad weather seems to come down from Canada, doesn't it?" to the customs man. But she didn't have to crawl into a box and hold her breath. The customs man didn't ask to look in.

The driver let her off at a scary intersection on Woodward Avenue and gave her instructions on how to get to the Plantations Motel in Southfield. The trick was to keep changing vehicles, he said. That threw off the immigration guys real quick.

Jasmine took money for cab fare out of the pocket of the great big raincoat that the van driver had given her. The raincoat looked like something that nuns in Port-of-Spain sold in church bazaars. Jasmine was glad to have a coat with wool lining, though; and anyway, who would know in Detroit that she was Dr. Vassanji's daughter?

All the bills in her hand looked the same. She would have to be careful when she paid the cabdriver. Money in Detroit wasn't pretty the way it was back home, or even in Canada, but she liked this money better. Why should money be pretty, like a picture? Pretty money is only good for putting on your walls maybe. The dollar bills felt businesslike, serious. Back home at work, she used to count out thousands of Trinidad dollars every day and not even think of them as real. Real money was worn and green, American dollars. Holding the bills in her fist on a street corner meant she had made it in okay. She'd outsmarted the guys at the border. Now it was up to her to use her wits to do something with her life. As her Daddy kept saying, "Girl, is opportunity come only once." The girls she'd worked with at the bank in Port-of-Spain had gone green as bananas when she'd walked in with her ticket on Air Canada. Trinidad was too tiny. That was the trouble. Trinidad was an island stuck in the middle of nowhere. What kind of place was that for a girl with ambition?

The Plantations Motel was run by a family of Trinidad Indians who had come from the tuppenny-ha'penny country town, Chaguanas. The Daboos were nobodies back home. They were lucky, that's all. They'd gotten here before the rush and bought up a motel and an ice cream parlor. Jasmine felt very superior when she saw Mr. Daboo in the motel's reception area. He was a pumpkin-shaped man with very black skin and Elvis Presley sideburns turning white. They looked like earmuffs. Mrs. Daboo was a bumpkin, too; short, fat, flapping around in house slippers. The Daboo daughters seemed very American, though. They didn't seem to know that they were nobodies, and kept looking at her and giggling.

She knew she would be short of cash for a great long while. Besides, she wasn't sure she wanted to wear bright leather boots and leotards like Viola and Loretta. The smartest move she could make would be to put a down payment on a husband. Her Daddy had told her to talk to the Daboos first chance. The Daboos ran a service fixing up illegals with islanders who had made it in legally. Daddy had paid three thousand back in Trinidad, with the Daboos and the mattress man getting part of it. They should throw in a good-earning husband for that kind of money.

The Daboos asked her to keep books for them and to clean the rooms in the new wing, and she could stay in 16B as long as she liked. They showed her 16B. They said she could cook her own roti; Mr. Daboo would bring in a stove, two gas rings that you could fold up in a metal box. The room was quite grand, Jasmine thought. It had a double bed, a TV, a pink sink and matching bathtub. Mrs. Daboo said Jasmine wasn't the big-city Port-of-Spain type she'd expected. Mr. Daboo said that he wanted her to stay because it was nice to have a neat, cheerful person around. It wasn't a bad deal, better than stories she'd heard about Trinidad girls in the States.

All day every day except Sundays Jasmine worked. There wasn't just the bookkeeping and the cleaning up. Mr. Daboo had her working on the match-up marriage service. Jasmine's job was to check up on social security cards, call clients' bosses for references, and make sure credit information wasn't false. Dermatologists and engineers living in Bloomfield Hills, store owners on Canfield and Woodward: she treated them all as potential liars. One of the first things she learned was that Ann Arbor was a magic word. A boy goes to Ann Arbor and gets an education, and all the barriers come crashing down. So Ann Arbor was the place to be.

She didn't mind the work. She was learning about Detroit, every side of it. Sunday mornings she helped unload packing crates of Caribbean spices in a shop on the next block. For the first time in her life, she was working for a black man, an African. So what if the boss was black? This was a new life, and she wanted to learn everything. Her Sunday boss, Mr. Anthony, was a courtly, Christian, church-going man, and paid her the only wages she had in her pocket. Viola and Loretta, for all their fancy American ways, wouldn't go out with blacks.

One Friday afternoon she was writing up the credit info on a Guyanese Muslim who worked in an assembly plant when Loretta said that enough was enough and there was no need for Jasmine to be her father's drudge.

"Is time to have fun," Viola said, "We're going to Ann Arbor."

Jasmine filed the sheet on the Guyanese man who probably now would never get a wife and got her raincoat. Loretta's boyfriend had a Cadillac parked out front. It was the longest car Jasmine had ever been in and louder than a country bus. Viola's boyfriend got out of the front seat. "Oh, oh, sweet things," he said to Jasmine. "Get in front." He was a talker. She'd learned that much from working on the matrimonial match-ups. She didn't believe him for a second when he said that there were dudes out there dying to ask her out.

Loretta's boyfriend said, "You have eyes I could leap into, girl."

Jasmine knew he was just talking. They sounded like Port-of-Spain boys of three years ago. It didn't surprise her that these Trinidad country boys in Detroit were still behind the times, even of Port-of-Spain. She sat very stiff between the two men, hands on her purse. The Daboo girls laughed in the back seat.

On the highway the girls told her about the reggae night in Ann Arbor. Kevin and the Krazee Islanders. Malcolm's Lovers. All the big reggae groups in the Midwest were converging for the West Indian Students Association fall bash. The ticket didn't come cheap but Jasmine wouldn't let the fellows pay. She wasn't that kind of girl.

The reggae and steel drums brought out the old Jasmine. The rum punch, the dancing, the dreadlocks, the whole combination. She hadn't heard real music since she got to Detroit, where music was supposed to be so famous. The Daboo girls kept turning on rock stuff in the motel lobby whenever their father left the area. She hadn't danced, really *danced,* since she'd left home. It felt so good to dance. She felt hot and sweaty and sexy. The boys at the dance were more than sweet talkers; they moved with assurance and spoke of their futures in America. The bartender gave her two free drinks and said, "Is ready when you are, girl." She ignored him but she felt all hot and good deep inside. She knew Ann Arbor was a special place.

When it was time to pile back into Loretta's boyfriend's Cadillac, she just couldn't face going back to the Plantations Motel and to the Daboos with their accounting books and messy files.

"I don't know what happen, girl," she said to Loretta. "I feel all crazy inside. Maybe is time for me to pursue higher studies in this town."

"This Ann Arbor, girl, they don't just take you off the street. It *cost* like hell.

She spent the night on a bashed-up sofa in the Student Union. She was a well-dressed, respectable girl, and she didn't expect anyone to question her right to sleep on the furniture. Many others were doing the same thing. In the morning, a boy in an army parka showed her the way to the Placement Office. He was a big, blond, clumsy boy, not bad-looking except for the blond eyelashes. He didn't scare her, as did most Americans. She let him buy her a Coke and a hotdog. That evening she had a job with the Moffitts.

Bill Moffitt taught molecular biology and Lara Hatch-Moffitt, his wife, was a performance artist. A performance artist, said Lara, was very different from being an actress, though Jasmine still didn't understand what the difference might be. The Moffitts had a little girl, Muffin, whom Jasmine was to look after, though for the first few months she might have to help out with the housework and the cooking because Lara said she was deep into performance rehearsals. That was all right with her, Jasmine said, maybe a little too quickly. She explained she came from a big family and was used to heavy-duty cooking and cleaning. This wasn't the time to say anything about Ram, the family servant. Americans like the Moffitts wouldn't understand about keeping servants. Ram and she weren't in similar situations. Here mother's helpers, which is what Lara had called her—Americans were good with words to cover their shame—seemed to be as good as anyone.

Ann Arbor was a huge small town. She couldn't imagine any kind of school the size of the University of Michigan. She meant to sign up for courses in the spring. Bill brought home a catalogue bigger than the phonebook for all of Trinidad. The university had courses in everything. It would be hard to choose; she'd have to get help from Bill. He wasn't like a professor, not the ones back home where even high school teachers called themselves professors and acted like little potentates. He wore blue jeans and thick sweaters with holes in the elbows and used phrases like "in vitro" as he watched her curry up fish. Dr. Parveen back home— he called himself "doctor" when everybody knew he didn't have even a Master's degree—was never seen without his cotton jacket which had gotten really ratty at the cuffs and lapel edges. She hadn't learned any-thing in the two years she'd put into college. She'd learned more from working in the bank for two months than she had at college. It was the assistant manager, Personal Loans Department, Mr. Singh, who had turned her on to the Daboos and to smooth, bargain-priced emigration.

Jasmine liked Lara. Lara was easygoing. She didn't spend the time she had between rehearsals telling Jasmine how to cook and clean American-style. Mrs. Daboo did that in 16B. Mrs. Daboo would barge in with a plate of stale samosas and snoop around giving free advice on how mainstream Americans did things. As if she were dumb or something! As if she couldn't keep her own eyes open and make her mind up for herself. Sunday mornings she had to share the butcher-block workspace in the kitchen with Bill. He made the Sunday brunch from new recipes in *Gourmet* and *Cuisine*. Jasmine hadn't seen a man cook who didn't have to or wasn't getting paid to do it. Things were topsy-turvy in the Moffitt house. Lara went on two- and three-day road trips and Bill stayed home. But even her Daddy, who'd never poured himself a cup of tea, wouldn't put Bill down as a woman. The mornings Bill tried out something com-plicated, a Cajun shrimp, sausage, and beans dish, for instance, Jasmine skipped church services. The Moffitts didn't go to church, though they seemed to be good Christians. They just didn't talk church talk, which suited her fine.

Lara showed her the room she would have all to herself in the finished basement. There was a big, old TV, not in color like the motel's and a portable typewriter on a desk which Lara said she would find handy when it came time to turn in her term papers. Jasmine didn't say anything about not being a student. She was a student of life, wasn't she? There was a scary moment after they'd discussed what she could expect as salary, which was three times more than anything Mr. Daboo was supposed to pay her but hadn't. She thought Bill Moffitt was going to ask her about her visa or her green card* number and social security. But all Bill did was smile and smile at her—he had a wide, pink, baby face—and play with a button on his corduroy jacket. The button would need sewing back on, firmly.

Lara said, "I think I'm going to like you, Jasmine. You have a some-thing about you. A something real special. I'll just bet you've acted, haven't you?" The idea amused her, but she merely smiled and accepted Lara's hug. The interview was over.

Then Bill opened a bottle of Soave and told stories about camping in northern Michigan. He'd been raised there. Jasmine didn't see the point in sleeping in tents; the woods sounded cold and wild and creepy. But she said, "Is exactly what I want to try out come summer, man. Campin and huntin."

---

*Work permit issued only to immigrants who have permanent resident status in the U.S.

Lara asked about Port-of-Spain. There was nothing to tell about her hometown that wouldn't shame her in front of nice white American folk like the Moffitts. The place was shabby, the people were grasping and cheating and lying and life was full of despair and drink and wanting. But by the time she finished, the island sounded romantic. Lara said, "It wouldn't surprise me one bit if you were a writer, Jasmine."

Two months passed. Jasmine knew she was lucky to have found a small, clean, friendly family like the Moffitts to build her new life around. "Man!" she'd exclaim as she vacuumed the wide-plank wood floors or ironed (Lara wore pure silk or pure cotton). "In this country Jesus givin out good luck only!" By this time they knew she wasn't a student, but they didn't care and said they wouldn't report her. They never asked if she was illegal on top of it.

To savor her new sense of being a happy, lucky person, she would put herself through a series of "what ifs": what if Mr. Singh in Port-of-Spain hadn't turned her on to the Daboos and loaned her two thousand! What if she'd been ugly like the Mintoo girl and the manager hadn't even offered! What if the customs man had unlocked the door of the van! Her Daddy liked to say, "You is a helluva girl, Jasmine."

"Thank you, Jesus," Jasmine said, as she carried on.

Christmas Day the Moffitts treated her just like family. They gave her a red cashmere sweater with a V neck so deep it made her blush. If Lara had worn it, her bosom wouldn't hang out like melons. For the holiday weekend Bill drove her to the Daboos in Detroit. "You work too hard," Bill said to her. "Learn to be more selfish. Come on, throw your weight around." She'd rather not have spent time with the Daboos, but that first afternoon of the interview she'd told Bill and Lara that Mr. Daboo was her mother's first cousin. She had thought it shameful in those days to have no papers, no family, no roots. Now Loretta and Viola in tight, bright pants seemed trashy like girls at Two-Johnny Bissoondath's Bar back home. She was stuck with the story of the Daboos being family. Village bumpkins, ha! She would break out. Soon.

Jasmine had Bill drop her off at the RenCen. The Plantations Motel, in fact, the whole Riverfront area, was too seamy. She'd managed to cut herself off mentally from anything too islandy. She loved her Daddy and Mummy, but she didn't think of them that often anymore. Mummy had expected her to be homesick and come flying right back home. "Is blowin sweat-of-brow money is what you doin, Pa," Mummy had scolded. She loved them, but she'd become her own person. That was something that Lara said: "I am my own person."

The Daboos acted thrilled to see her back. "What you drinkin, Jasmine girl?" Mr. Daboo kept asking. "You drinkin sherry or what?" Pouring her little glasses of sherry instead of rum was a sure sign he thought she had become whitefolk-fancy. The Daboo sisters were very friendly, but Jasmine considered them too wild. Both Loretta and Viola had changed boyfriends. Both were seeing black men they'd danced with in Ann Arbor. Each night at bedtime, Mr. Daboo cried. "In Trinidad we stayin we side, they stayin they side. Here, everything mixed up. Is helluva confusion, no?"

On New Year's Eve the Daboo girls and their black friends went to a dance. Mr. and Mrs. Daboo and Jasmine watched TV for a while. Then Mr. Daboo got out a brooch from his pocket and pinned it on Jasmine's red sweater. It was a Christmasy brooch, a miniature sleigh loaded down with snowed-on mistletoe. Before she could pull away, he kissed her on the lips. "Good luck for the New Year!" he said. She lifted her head and saw tears. "Is year for dreams comin true."

Jasmine started to cry, too. There was nothing wrong, but Mr. Daboo, Mrs. Daboo, she, everybody was crying.

What for? This is where she wanted to be. She'd spent some damned uncomfortable times with the assistant manager to get approval for her loan. She thought of Daddy. He would be playing poker and fanning himself with a magazine. Her married sisters would be rolling out the dough for stacks and stacks of roti, and Mummy would be steamed purple from stirring the big pot of goat curry on the stove. She missed them. But. It felt strange to think of anyone celebrating New Year's Eve in summery clothes.

In March Lara and her performing group went on the road. Jasmine knew that the group didn't work from scripts. The group didn't use a stage, either; instead, it took over supermarkets, senior citizens' centers, and school halls, without notice. Jasmine didn't understand the performance world. But she was glad that Lara said, "I'm not going to lay a guilt trip on myself. Muffie's in super hands," before she left.

Muffie didn't need much looking after. She played Trivial Pursuit all day, usually pretending to be two persons, sometimes Jasmine, whose accent she could imitate. Since Jasmine didn't know any of the answers, she couldn't help. Muffie was a quiet, precocious child with see-through blue eyes like her dad's, and red braids. In the early evenings Jasmine cooked supper, something special she hadn't forgotten from her island days. After supper she and Muffie watched some TV, and Bill read. When Muffie went to bed, Bill and she sat together for a bit with their glasses of Soave. Bill, Muffie, and she were a family, almost.

Down in her basement room that late, dark winter, she had trouble sleeping. She wanted to stay awake and think of Bill. Even when she fell asleep it didn't feel like sleep because Bill came barging into her dreams in his funny, loose-jointed, clumsy way. It was mad to think of him all the time, and stupid and sinful; but she couldn't help it. Whenever she put back a book he'd taken off the shelf to read or whenever she put his clothes through the washer and dryer, she felt sick in a giddy, wonderful way. When Lara came back things would get back to normal. Meantime she wanted the performance group miles away.

Lara called in at least twice a week. She said things like, "We've finally obliterated the margin between realspace and performancespace." Jasmine filled her in on Muffie's doings and the mall. Bill always closed with, "I love you. We miss you, hon."

One night after Lara had called—she was in Lincoln, Nebraska—Bill said to Jasmine, "Let's dance."

She hadn't danced since the reggae night she'd had too many rum punches. Her toes began to throb and clench. She untied her apron and the fraying, knotted-up laces of her running shoes.

Bill went around the downstairs rooms turning down lights. "We need atmosphere," he said. He got a small, tidy fire going in the living room grate and pulled the Turkish scatter rug closer to it. Lara didn't like anybody walking on the Turkish rug, but Bill meant to have his way. The hissing logs, the plants in the dimmed light, the thick patterned rug: everything was changed. This wasn't the room she cleaned every day.

He stood close to her. She smoothed her skirt down with both hands.

"I want you to choose the record," he said.

"I don't know your music."

She brought her hand high to his face. His skin was baby smooth.

"I want *you* to pick," he said. "You are your own person now."

"You got island music?"

He laughed, "What do you think?" The stereo was in a cabinet with albums packed tight alphabetically into the bottom three shelves. "Calypso has not been a force in my life."

She couldn't help laughing. "Calypso? Oh, man." She pulled dust jackets out at random. Lara's records. The Flying Lizards. The Violent Femmes. There was so much still to pick up on!

"This one," she said, finally.

He took the record out of her hand. "God!" he laughed. "Lara must have found this in a garage sale!" He laid the old record on the turntable. It was "Music for Lovers," something the nuns had taught her to foxtrot to way back in Port-of-Spain.

They danced so close that she could feel his heart heaving and crashing against her head. She liked it, she liked it very much. She didn't care what happened.

"Come on," Bill whispered. "If it feels right, do it." He began to take her clothes off.

"Don't Bill," she pleaded.

"Come on, baby," he whispered again. "You're a blossom, a flower."

He took off his fisherman's knit pullover, the corduroy pants, the blue shorts. She kept pace. She'd never had such an effect on a man:

He nearly flung his socks and Adidas into the fire. "You feel so good," he said. "You smell so good. You're really something, flower of Trinidad."

"Flower of Ann Arbor," she said, "not Trinidad."

She felt so good she was dizzy. She'd never felt this good on the island where men did this all the time, and girls went along with it always for favors. You couldn't feel really good in a nothing place. She was thinking this as they made love on the Turkish carpet in front of the fire: she was a bright, pretty girl with no visa, no papers, and no birth certificate. No nothing other than what she wanted to invent and tell. She was a girl rushing wildly into the future.

His hand moved up her throat and forced her lips apart and it felt so good, so right, that she forgot all the dreariness of her new life and gave herself up to it.

Interpretations

1. Jasmine is "a girl with ambition." Ambition for what? Does she accomplish her ambition? How? What are Jasmine's other outstanding character traits? Where do they appear in the story?

2. What is Jasmine's relation with the Moffitts? How does it change? Why? What makes theirs, at least, a confusing relationship?

3. Jasmine glamourizes her hometown when describing it to Lara because she is ashamed of it. What does this indicate about Jasmine and her motivation for emigrating to Canada and then the United States? Do you feel that you understand Jasmine better than she understands herself. Why?

4. Jasmine thinks what she learned about "bargain-priced emigration" from the assistant bank manager in Trinidad more important than anything she had learned in two years of college. What does this tell us about Jasmine? What is the tone of the phrase "bargain-priced emigration"? How do you interpret the sentence, "She'd spent some damned uncomfortable times with the assistant manager to get approval for her loan"?

5. Stories develop mainly from conflict: between two or more characters, within a character as the result of some psychological force (guilt, jealousy), or between a character and some impersonal force like poverty or disease. What is the main conflict in this story? Between what or whom? Is the struggle resolved?

6. What do you think is the point or thesis of the story?

Correspondences

1. "In this country Jesus givin out good luck only!" Why did Jasmine feel "Ann Arbor was the place to be"? To what extent was she, like Puzo's immigrants, captured by the American dream? Was she lucky to work for the Moffitts? Why or why not?

2. Review the Voltaire quotation (page 259). How does it apply to Jasmine's work experiences in the United States? Had Jasmine entered the country legally, might she have chosen differently? Explain your answer.

Applications

1. "Trinidad was an island stuck in the middle of nowhere. What kind of place was that for a girl with ambition?" What evidence is there of Jasmine's ambition? Compare her experiences in Trinidad with those in Michigan.

2. What does the future hold for Jasmine? Write a journal entry on what you can imagine her doing five years from now.

The Cotton Picker

Nicholas Lemann

*Nicholas Lemann was born in 1952 and raised in New Orleans.
He has worked for* The Washington Monthly, Texas Monthly, *and
the* Washington Post, *and has been a national correspondent for*
The Atlantic *since 1983. He also writes regularly for* The New
York Review of Books *and other publications. He lives in New
York City. "Cotton Picker" is excerpted from the* The Promised
Land: The Great Black Migration and How It Changed America
(1991).

THREE OR FOUR miles south of the town of Clarksdale, Mississippi, there is
a shambling little hog farm on the side of the highway. It sits right up next
to the road, on cheap land, unkempt. A rutted dirt path leads back to a
shack made of unpainted wood; over to the side is a makeshift wire fence
enclosing the pen where the hogs live. Behind the fence, by the bank of
a creek, under a droopy cottonwood tree, is an old rusted-out machine
that appears to have found its final resting place. The vines have taken
most of it over. It looks like a tractor from the 1930s with a very large
metal basket mounted on top. Abandoned machinery is so common a
sight in front of poor folks' houses in the South that it is completely
inconspicuous.

The old machine, now part of a hoary Southern set-piece, is actually
important. It is the last tangible remnant of a great event in Clarksdale:
the day of the first public demonstration of a working, production-ready
model of the mechanical cotton picker, October 2, 1944. A crowd of
people came out on that day to the Hopson plantation, just outside of
town on Highway 49, to see eight machines pick a field of cotton.

Like the automobile, the cotton picker was not invented by one
person in a blinding flash of inspiration. The real breakthrough in its
development was building a machine that could be reliably mass-pro-
duced, not merely one that could pick cotton. For years, since 1927,
International Harvester had been field-testing cotton-picking equipment
at the Hopson place; the Hopsons were an old and prosperous planter
family in Clarksdale, with a lot of acreage and a special interest in the
technical side of farming. There were other experiments with mechanical
cotton pickers going on all over the South. The best-known of the exper-
imenters were two brothers named John and Mack Rust, who grew up
poor and populist in Texas and spent the better part of four decades

trying to develop a picker that they dreamed would be used to bring decent pay and working conditions to the cotton fields. The Rusts demonstrated one picker in 1931 and another, at an agricultural experiment station in Mississippi, in 1933; during the late 1930s and early 1940s they were field-testing their picker at a plantation outside Clarksdale, not far from the Hopson place. Their machines could pick cotton, but they couldn't be built on a factory assembly line. In 1942 the charter of the Rust Cotton Picker Company was revoked for nonpayment of taxes, and Mack Rust decamped for Arizona; the leadership in the development of the picker inexorably passed from a pair of idealistic self-employed tinkerers to a partnership between a big Northern corporation and a big Southern plantation, as the International Harvester team kept working on a machine that would be more sturdy and reliable than the Rusts'. With the advent of World War II, the experiments at the Hopson plantation began to attract the intense interest of people in the cotton business. There were rumors that the machine was close to being perfected, finally. The price of cotton was high, because of the war, but hands to harvest it were short, also because of the war. Some planters had to leave their cotton to rot in the fields because there was nobody to pick it.

Howell Hopson, the head of the plantation, noted somewhat testily in a memorandum he wrote years later, "Over a period of many months on end it was a rare day that visitors did not present themselves, more often than otherwise without prior announcement and unprepared for. They came individually, in small groups, in large groups, sometimes as organized delegations. Frequently they were found wandering around in the fields, on more than one occasion completely lost in outlying wooded areas." The county agricultural agent suggested to Hopson that he satisfy everyone's curiosity in an orderly way by field-testing the picker before an audience. Hopson agreed, although, as his description of the event makes clear, not with enthusiasm: "An estimated 2,500 to 3,000 people swarmed over the plantation on that one day. 800 to 1,000 automobiles leaving their tracks and scars throughout the property. It was always a matter of conjecture as to how the plantation managed to survive the onslaught. It is needless to say this was the last such 'voluntary' occasion."

In group photographs of the men developing the cotton picker, Howell Hopson resembles Walt Whitman's self-portrait in the frontispiece of *Leaves of Grass:* a casually dressed man in a floppy hat, standing jauntily with a hip cocked and a twig in his hand. In truth he was more interested in rationalizing nature than in celebrating it. Perhaps as a result of an injury in early childhood that kept his physical activity limited, Hopson became a devoted agricultural tinkerer. His entrancement with efficiency was such that after he took over the family plantation, he numbered the fields so that he could keep track of them better. The demonstration was held in C-3, a field of forty-two acres.

The pickers, painted bright red, drove down the white rows of cotton. Each one had mounted in front a row of spindles, looking like a wide mouth, full of metal teeth, that had been turned vertically. The spindles, about the size of human fingers, rotated in a way that stripped the cotton from the plants; then a vacuum pulled it up a tube and into the big wire basket that was mounted on top of the picker. In an hour, a good field hand could pick twenty pounds of cotton; each mechanical picker, in an hour, picked as much as a thousand pounds—two bales. In one day, Hopson's eight machines could pick all the cotton in C-3, which on October 2, 1944, was sixty-two bales. The unusually precise cost-accounting system that Hopson had developed showed that picking a bale of cotton by machine cost him $5.26, and picking it by hand cost him $39.41. Each machine did the work of fifty people.

Nobody bothers to save old farm equipment. Over the years the Hopsons' original cotton pickers disappeared from the place. Nearly forty years later, a family son-in-law discovered the one rusty old picker that sits in the pigpen south of town; where the other ones are today, nobody knows. Howell Hopson had some idea of the importance of his demonstration in C-3, though. In his memorandum, he wrote that "the introduction of the cotton harvester may have been comparable to the unveiling of Eli Whitney's first hand operated cotton gin. . . ." He was thinking mostly of the effect on cotton farming, but of course the cotton gin's impact on American society was much broader than that. It set off some of the essential convulsions of the nineteenth century in this country. The cotton gin made it possible to grow medium- and short-staple cotton commercially, which led to the spread of the cotton plantation from a small coastal area to most of the South. As cotton planting expanded, so did slavery, and slavery's becoming the central institution of the Southern economy was the central precondition of the Civil War.

What the mechanical cotton picker did was make obsolete the share-cropper system, which arose in the years after the Civil War as the means by which cotton planters' need for a great deal of cheap labor was satisfied. The issue of the labor supply in cotton planting may not sound like one of the grand themes in American history, but it is, because it is really the issue of race. African slaves were brought to this country mainly to pick cotton. For hundreds of years, the plurality of African-Americans were connected directly or indirectly to the agriculture of cotton; at the time of the demonstration on the Hopson plantation, this was still true. Now, suddenly, cotton planters no longer needed large numbers of black people to pick their cotton, and inevitably the nature of black society and of race relations was going to have to change.

Slavery was a political institution that enabled an economic system, the antebellum cotton kingdom. Sharecropping began in the immediate aftermath of the end of slavery, and was the dominant economic institution of the agrarian South for eighty years. The political institution that paralleled sharecropping was segregation; blacks in the South were denied social equality from Emancipation onward, and, beginning in the 1890s, they were denied the ordinary legal rights of American citizens as well. Segregation strengthened the grip of the sharecropper system by ensuring that most blacks would have no arena of opportunity in life except for the cotton fields. The advent of the cotton picker made the maintenance of segregation no longer a matter of necessity for the economic establishment of the South, and thus it helped set the stage for the great drama of segregation's end.

In 1940, 77 per cent of black Americans still lived in the South—49 per cent in the rural South. The invention of the cotton picker was crucial to the great migration by blacks from the Southern countryside to the cities of the South, the West, and the North. Between 1910 and 1970, six and a half million black Americans moved from the South to the North; five million of them moved after 1940, during the time of the mechanization of cotton farming. In 1970, when the migration ended, black America was only half Southern, and less than a quarter rural; "urban" had become a euphemism for "black." The black migration was one of the largest and most rapid mass internal movements of people in history—perhaps *the* greatest not caused by the immediate threat of execution or starvation. In sheer numbers it outranks the migration of any other ethnic group—Italians or Irish or Jews or Poles—to this country. For blacks, the migration meant leaving what had always been their economic and social base in America and finding a new one.

During the first half of the twentieth century, it was at least possible to think of race as a Southern issue. The South, and only the South, had to contend with the contradiction between the national creed of democracy and the local reality of a caste system; consequently the South lacked the optimism and confidence that characterized the country as a whole. The great black migration made race a national issue in the second half of the century—an integral part of the politics, the social thought, and the organization of ordinary life in the United States. Not coincidentally, by the time the migration was over, the country had acquired a good measure of the tragic sense that had previously been confined to the South. Race relations stood out nearly everywhere as the one thing most plainly wrong in America, the flawed portion of the great tableau, the chief generator of doubt about how essentially noble the whole national enterprise really was.

The story of American race relations after the mechanical cotton picker is much shorter than the story of American race relations during the period when it revolved around the cultivation and harvesting of cotton by hand: less than half a century, versus three centuries. It is still unfolding. Already several areas of the national life have changed completely because of the decoupling of race from cotton: popular culture, presidential politics, urban geography, education, justice, social welfare.

To recount what has happened so far is by no means to imply that the story has ended. In a way it has just begun, and the racial situation as it stands today is not permanent—is not, should not be, will not be.

Interpretations

1. When sharecropping ended and five million African-Americans moved north, where did they move to? What are the main effects of this migration?

2. Why wasn't emancipation—the end of slavery—the end of racial problems in the United States?

3. How do Lemann's descriptive opening paragraphs about an old rusted-out machine and the Hopson plantation help awaken the reader's interest in the rather abstract subjects of work and race?

4. "The great black migration made race a national issue. . . ." How important an issue in American society do you find race to be? What is the general American attitude toward race and racial issues? Do Americans generally agree that race is a national, as opposed to a sectional, issue?

Correspondences

1. Review Terkel's perspective on work (page 260) and discuss its application to Lehmann's essay.

2. "For Blacks, the migration meant leaving what had always been their economic and social base in America and finding a new one." To what extent do the work situations of immigrants to the United States discussed by Puzo, Morrow, and/or Mukherjee parallel those of the black migrant?

Applications

1. Analyze the relationship between race and the U.S. economy—work, employment, taxes, and governmental involvement.

2. "In 1970, when the migration ended, Black America was only half southern, and less than a quarter rural; 'urban' had become a euphemism for 'Black'." How might "urban" be defined in the 1990s? Discuss the ramifications for the workplace.

ADDITIONAL WRITING TOPICS

1. Review Sayers's perspective on work (p. 260) and test its validity by interviewing people you know in various occupations on their attitudes towards working and the workplace. What conclusions did you reach? Write an analysis based on their responses.

2. Baker (Chapter 1) writes that "one defect of my mother's code was the value it placed on money and position. The children never cared a lot for that. To care, I suppose, you had to have been there with her during the depression." Compare Baker's mother's ideas of ambition and attitude towards work with those of a parent, teacher, counselor or employer. How do they differ? What cultural and generational factors have influenced them?

3. "Our work is hard, hot, wet, cold and always dirty. It is also very satisfying." Test Olson's thesis by interviewing several BCGs; ask them to what extent they are satisfied with their work. Use their responses to support or refute Olson.

4. Olson, Jones, Gnolfo, and Gandbhir note attitudes toward Affirmative Action in the workplace. Review their comments. Then conduct an informal survey by interviewing several people affected by Affirmative Action programs. Summarize your findings.

5. According to Morrow, "Work is the way we tend the world, the way that people connect. It is the most vigorous vivid sign of life—in individuals and in civilizations." Test his thesis by asking several people of varying gender, ages and occupations to write a paragraph responding to Morrow's statement. Analyze their responses in a fully developed essay that clearly refutes or supports Morrow's point of view.

6. Despite the fact that teachers have longer vacations and more autonomy than do people in many other professions, statistics indicate a decline in college graduates choosing teaching as a profession. Conduct an informal survey among classmates on their attitudes towards teaching and teachers to try to determine the causes for this decline. Summarize your findings.

7. Sociologists argue that—despite stress, boredom, and burnout in the workplace—many Americans are unable to enjoy their leisure time in simple pursuits. Do you agree? Why is it difficult for people to relax off the job? (Have leisure activities become more sophisticated, expensive, and complex?) To what extent has leisure become another burden?

8. Ouchi shows how a nation's history and geography, its ethnic diversity or homogeneity, and its cultural values shape its orientation toward work: Americans emphasize individual effort; Japanese collective effort. Using Ouchi's overview and your own knowledge and experience, show why it would be difficult for Americans to change their emphasis, even if collective effort would be more efficient and profitable.

CHAPTER 5

Interactions

Peaceful interactions among cultures take many forms: treaties, trade, tourism, art exhibits, drama, movies, dance, student exchanges, exchange of scientific information, world fairs, conferring of awards and honors like the Nobel Prizes, sports events, musical events, conferences, emergency and other aid, cooperation in law enforcement, the United Nations. In general, these interactions please, intrigue, or interest us. Variety enhances—in food, dress, language, religion, art, celebrations, government. However, as the Senegalese folktale that begins this chapter implies, there is another side to human nature, and it is bleak. People may be so fond of their vested arrangements, so afraid that change will be for the worse, that they prefer falsehood to truth. Exposure to other cultures, the sifting of truth, the juxtaposition of another's knowledge and our ignorance, for example, are sometimes more than we can stand: "Better the devil we know than the devil we don't" expresses an enduring attitude that quickly surfaces when cultures compete rather than complement. Such clashes exact a price and take various forms.

Lack of awareness of cultural differences or the assumption of one cultural group that another is inferior results in interactions that are painful power struggles. These struggles run the gamut from personal suffering to temporary feuds to civil war or full-scale war. For example, had we known more about Vietnamese culture, we might not have blundered into the Vietnam War. On a more personal scale, Michael Novak thinks that the American majority makes too little effort to understand and include

349

immigrants from Italy, Greece, Poland, and other Eastern European countries. Distress can become internalized. Jim Fusilli struggles to understand and reconcile his Italian and Irish halves. The "Englishwoman" in Jhabvala's story of that name could have spared herself a good deal of unhappiness had she known more about upperclass Indian family life and sexual mores.

Student Juliet Wright was thrown into a sink-or-swim year in Brazil as an exchange student and forced to interact with a culture very different from her native Jamaica. Another student, Brian Delaney, interacting with his girlfriend, found that the different styles of childraising in their Irish and Indian homes had given them different but perhaps complementary values.

The shock of cross-cultural interactions may also occur between members of the same culture, as when an emigrant returns home after a long absence. Time and distance can make an alien of a native. Alastair Reid is such an immigrant; a cosmopolitan world traveler and resident of New York City, he returns to his homeland of Scotland to find a place that has "changed less" than any other he can think of. It has "the air of a museum." Peripatetic Reid is amazed at the kind of rootedness that can develop when a Scotsman makes his "peace with place," with Scottish landscapes and people. Likewise, the culture shock in Matshoba's story occurs, not in the interaction between blacks and whites in apartheid-ridden South Africa, but between blacks united against apartheid and reservists (certain black policemen in the story) who cooperate with the whites to keep blacks in their "place."

In the interactions of this chapter sometimes falsehood prevails and the result is disruptive and destructive. But other interactions are based on a respect for truth and on acceptance of the world's cultural variety.

PERSPECTIVES

Culture is that which binds men together.

Ruth Benedict

We are creatures of outside *influences. We originate*
nothing *within. Whenever we take a new line of thought*
and drift into a new line of belief and action, the
impulse is always suggested from the outside.

Mark Twain

The planet has become an intricate convergence—of
acid rains and ruin forests burning, of ideas and
Reeboks and stock markets that ripple through time
zones, of satellite signals and worldwide television, of
advance-purchase airfares, fax machines, the mini-
aturization of the universe by computer, of T-shirts and
mutual destinies.

Lance Morrow

As social equality spreads there are more and more
people who, though neither rich nor powerful enough to
have much hold over others, have gained or kept enough
wealth and enough understanding to look after their
own needs. Such folk owe no man anything and hardly
expect anything from anybody. They form the habit of
thinking of themselves in isolation and imagine that
their whole destiny is in their own hands.

Thus, not only does democracy make men forget their
ancestors, but it also clouds their view of their descen-
dants and isolates them from their contemporaries.
Each man is forever thrown back on himself alone, and
there is danger that he may be shut in the solitude of
his own heart.

Alexis de Tocqueville

The only way to make sure people you agree with can speak is to support the rights of people you don't agree with.

Eleanor Holmes Norton

Man is an animal suspended in webs of significance which he himself has created. I take culture to be those webs.

Clifford Geertz

No man is an iland, intire of it selfe; every man is a peece of the Continent, a part of the maine; if a Clod bee washed away by the Sea, Europe is the lesse, as well as if a Promontorie were, as well as if a Mannor of thy friends or of thine owne were; any man's death diminishes me, because I am involved in Mankinde; And therefore never send to know for whom the bell tolls; It tolls for thee.

John Donne

Culture regulates our lives at every turn. From the moment we are born until we die there is, whether we are conscious of it or not, constant pressure upon us to follow certain types of behavior that other men have created for us.

Clyde Kluckhohn

It is a terrible, an inexorable, law that one cannot deny the humanity of another without diminishing one's own; in the face of one's victim one sees oneself.

James Baldwin

Where justice is denied, where poverty is enforced, where ignorance prevails and where any one class is made to feel that society is in an organized conspiracy to oppress, rob and degrade them, neither persons nor property will be safe.

Frederick Douglass

Our great mistake is to try to exact from each person virtues which he does not possess, and to neglect the cultivation of those which he has.

Marguerite Yourcenar

"E Pluribus Unum" has never had more meaning than it has today . . . because we are a diverse community, we must exercise more tolerance than ever before. Tolerance for each other's differences is the only way we can survive.

Whoopi Goldberg

Applications

1. Select a perspective on interactions with which you agree or disagree. In your journal, record and analyze the reasons for your point of view.

2. Select two perspectives for discussion in your group. What insights did you gain? Record them in your journal.

The Falsehood of Truth

Senegalese Myth

*Senegal is a republic in western Africa, which gained indepen-
dence from France in 1960.*

FENE-FALSEHOOD and Deug-Truth started out on a journey one day.

Fene-Falsehood said, "Everyone says that the Lord loves truth
better than falsehood, so I think that you had better do all the talking
for us."

Deug-Truth agreed, and when they came to a village, Deug-Truth
greeted the first woman they met and asked if they could have a drink.
She gave them a filthy bowl full of lukewarm water and then sat down in
the doorway of her hut and began to eat a big meal of rice. While the two
travelers were still there, the woman's husband came home and asked for
his supper.

"It's not ready," replied the woman insolently.

The husband then turned to the two strangers who were watching
and asked, "What would you say about a woman like that?"

"I would say that she is the worst wife I have seen in a long time. It's
bad enough for her not to be hospitable to strangers, but it is really
disgraceful when she doesn't feed her own husband," replied Deug-
Truth. Fene-Falsehood didn't say a word.

The woman became furious and began to yell and scream louder
than either of the two travelers had ever heard anyone scream before.
"Are you going to stand by and let these strangers insult me!" she
screamed to her husband. "If so, I will go home to my father and you will
have to raise a bride-price for a new wife."

Then the husband, too, became angry and chased the two strangers
out of town.

So Deug and Fene continued their travels and next came to a village
where they found several children dividing up a bull that had just been
slaughtered. They thought that this was rather strange, for it was the
custom that meat was always divided by the head-man. While they were
still watching, they saw the chief come up and take a very poor share of
meat which the children handed him. The chief saw the two strangers and
asked, "Who do you think is the leader in this village?"

Fene said nothing but Deug immediately answered, "It seems to me
that these children must be the leaders of this village, for they are dividing
the meat."

The chief immediately became angry and chased them out of that village.

As they continued to walk along, Fene said to Deug, "It is said that the Lord loves you the best, but I am beginning to wonder if man is not rather different from God. It seems to me that men do not like you very well. I think I will try my luck at the next village."

At the next village, they found that all the people were weeping because the favorite wife of the king had just died. Fene thought for a minute and then said, "Go tell the king that a man is here who can raise people from the dead."

Soon Fene was brought before the king and said, "I will raise your wife from the dead if you will give me half of your fortune."

The king immediately agreed and Fene had a hut built above the family grave. The king and all of the people waited outside and listened to the strange noises. First they heard huffing and panting and strange chants, but then they began to hear Fene talking loudly as if he were arguing. Finally he burst out of the door and slammed it shut—holding it tightly.

"Oh, dear," he said, "you did not tell me that your whole family was buried in there. When I woke your wife up, your father and your grandfather both came out too. I thought I had better check before I let them all out."

The king and his advisers began to look frightened, for the king's father had been a very cruel king and the new king and his friends had given his death a little assistance.

I think you had better leave them all," said the king. "We would have a lot of trouble here with three kings."

"Well, it's not that easy," said Fene slyly. "Your father has offered me half of this property to let him out. I am certainly not going to send him back for nothing."

"I will still give you half of my property," said the desperate king. "Just get rid of them all."

So Fene received half of the king's fortune and concluded that while truth might have the favor of God, falsehood was the best way to get ahead with men.

Interpretations

1. Before you read this story, cover up the last sentence, beginning with "concluded that. . . ." When you reach this point in the story, write your own conclusion. Compare your conclusion and the storyteller's. Do you generally like the point of a story stated outright, or would you rather deduce it for yourself. Why? Do you agree with the stated conclusion? Why or why not? If the conclusion is true, why should

the reader, of all people, want to learn this "truth"? Isn't it also a falsehood?

2. Are the incidents along the journey well chosen illustrations of the moral? Are people indeed more apt to prefer falsehood in the areas of marriage and tribal leadership (politics?)? Why or why not? Do you think the husband and the chief make real choices or merely bow to necessity? What makes you think so?

3. Allegorical stories, whose characters are abstractions (like Falsehood and Truth), are rare in American contemporary literature. Why? (What expectations do characters like this set up?)

4. Is it wise to alert the readers or hearers that the story is didactic— meant to teach a lesson? Why or why not? Would we derive the same point from the story if the names Fene and Deug had not been translated for us? Would the story's mood or tone (and thus its effect) be the same? If not, how would it be different?

5. What cultural interaction do you find in the story?

The Wise Rogue

Jewish Folk Tale as told by Moses Gaster

The editor of A Harvest of World Folk Tales *describes the origins of "The Wise Rogue" as follows:*

> *The keynotes of Jewish folk story are wisdom, humor, and piety, and its favorite form is the parable. It is plainly the product of a society that was in its early days priestly and in its later days persecuted, Rare are the mighty, muscular heroes (Samson was one, of course, but David against Goliath and Judith against Holofernes seem much more characteristic); nor are there any authentic fire-breathing dragons or broom-riding witches. The heroes of the Jews are wise kings, learned rabbis, or rogues who live by their wits; their dragons are the Devil and the Temptations; their witches are those who have historically oppressed them. Even their humor is of a worldly-wise or satiric sort; and their sillies, the Wise Men of Helm, are not so much numskulls as absent-minded philosophers, men whose heads are filled with more than is commonly useful.*

A MAN WHO was once caught stealing was ordered by the king to be hanged. On the way to the gallows he said to the governor that he knew a wonderful secret, and it would be a pity to allow it to die with him, and he would like to disclose it to the king. He would put a seed of a pomegranate in the ground, and through the secret taught to him by his father he would make it grow and bear fruit overnight. The thief was brought before the king, and on the morrow the king, accompanied by the high officers of state, came to the place where the thief was waiting for them. There the thief dug a hole and said, "This seed must be put in the ground only by a man who has never stolen or taken anything which did not belong to him. I being a thief cannot do it." So he turned to the vizier who, frightened, said that in his younger days he had retained something which did not belong to him. The treasurer said that in dealing with large sums he might have entered too much or too little, and even the king owned that he had kept a necklace of his father's. The thief then said, "You are all mighty and powerful and want nothing, and yet you cannot plant the seed, whilst I who have stolen a little because I was starving am to be hanged." The king, pleased with the ruse of the thief, pardoned him.

Interpretations

1. Did the king do the right thing? Why or why not?

2. "The king, pleased with the ruse of the thief, pardoned him." Usually people do not enjoy being tricked; what was different about this case? How would you have felt if the trick had been played on you?

3. What does this story imply about the relationship between justice and mercy?

4. The laws broken seem insignificant. Are they the tip of the iceberg? If officials commit petty crimes, will they also commit serious ones? How can a society prevent lawless people from administering the law?

5. What is the tone of this story? How does it affect the meaning?

Correspondences

1. Review the Donne quotation (page 352). How does it apply to "The Falsehood of Truth?" (What episodes in the folktale contradict it? Do you agree with Fene's conclusion about human interactions? Why or why not?)

2. Review the Geertz quotation (page 352). What does it mean? How does it relate to "The Wise Rogue"? What does the story imply about human interactions?

Applications

1. "Honesty is the best policy." Do you believe so? Should honesty be the basis of all human interactions? Write an essay explaining why it is possible or impossible to be totally honest with your best friend.

2. What do both stories suggest about success? Are rogues likely to achieve success? What examples can you think of? Discuss these questions in your group and record your conclusions.

Does America Still Exist?

Richard Rodriguez

Richard Rodriguez (b. 1944) is a Mexican-American who grew up in California. He has studied at Stanford University, Columbia University, and the University of California at Berkeley—where he teaches. In addition to writing essays, he has published the autobiographical Hunger of Memory: The Education of Richard Rodriguez *(1981). The following essay first appeared in* Harper's *(March 1984) as part of a group of essays written in response to the question "Does America Still Exist?"*

FOR THE CHILDREN of immigrant parents the knowledge comes easier. America exists everywhere in the city—on billboards, frankly in the smell of French fries and popcorn. It exists in the pace: traffic lights, the assertions of neon, the mysterious bong- bong-bong through the atriums of department stores. American exists as the voice of the crowd, a menacing sound—the high nasal accent of American English.

When I was a boy in Sacramento (California, the fifties), people would ask me, "Where you from?" I was born in this country, but I knew the question meant to decipher my darkness, my looks.

My mother once instructed me to say, "I am an American of Mexican descent." By the time I was nine or ten, I wanted to say, but dared not reply, "I am an American."

Immigrants come to America and, against hostility or mere loneliness, they recreate a homeland in the parlor, tacking up postcards or calendars of some impossible blue—lake or sea or sky. Children of immigrant parents are supposed to perch on a hyphen between two countries. Relatives assume the achievement as much as anyone. Relatives are, in any case, surprised when the child begins losing old ways. One day at the family picnic the boy wanders away from their spiced food and faceless stories to watch other boys play baseball in the distance.

There is sorrow in the American memory, guilty sorrow for having left something behind—Portugal, China, Norway. The American story is the story of immigrant children and of their children—children no longer able to speak to grandparents. The memory of exile becomes inarticulate as it passes from generation to generation, along with wedding rings and pocket watches—like some mute stone in a wad of old lace. Europe. Asia. Eden.

But, it needs to be said, if this is a country where one stops being Vietnamese or Italian, this is a country where one begins to be an American. America exists as a culture and a grin, a faith and a shrug. It is clasped in a handshake, called by a first name.

As much as the country is joined in a common culture, however, Americans are reluctant to celebrate the process of assimilation. We pledge allegiance to diversity. America was born Protestant and bred Puritan, and the notion of community we share is derived from a seventeenth-century faith. Presidents and the pages of ninth-grade civics readers yet proclaim the orthodoxy: We are gathered together—but as individuals, with separate pasts, distinct destinies. Our society is as paradoxical as a Puritan congregation: We stand together, alone.

Americans have traditionally defined themselves by what they refused to include. As often, however, Americans have struggled, turned in good conscience at last to assert the great Protestant virtue of tolerance. Despite outbreaks of nativist frenzy, America has remained an immigrant country, open and true to itself.

Against pious emblems of rural America—soda fountain, Elks hall, Protestant church, and now shopping mall—stands the cold-hearted city, crowded with races and ambitions, curious laughter, much that is odd. Nevertheless, it is the city that has most truly represented America. In the city, however, the millions of singular lives have had no richer notion of wholeness to describe them than the idea of pluralism.

"Where you from?" the American asks the immigrant child. "Mexico," the boy learns to say.

Mexico, the country of my blood ancestors, offers formal contrast to the American achievement. If the United States was formed by Protestant individualism, Mexico was shaped by a medieval Catholic dream of one world. The Spanish journeyed to Mexico to plunder, and they may have gone, in God's name, with an arrogance peculiar to those who intend to convert. But through the conversion, the Indian converted the Spaniard. A new race was born, the *mestizo,* wedding European to Indian. José Vasconcelos, the Mexican philosopher, has celebrated this New World creation, proclaiming it the "cosmic race."

Centuries later, in a San Francisco restaurant, a Mexican-American lawyer of my acquaintance says, in English, over *salade niçoise,* that he does not intend to assimilate into gringo society. His claim is echoed by a chorus of others (Italian-Americans, Greeks, Asians) in this era of ethnic pride. The melting pot has been retired, clanking, into the museum of quaint disgrace, alongside Aunt Jemima and the Katzenjammer Kids.* But resistance to assimilation is characteristically American. It only makes clear how inevitable the process of assimilation actually is.

*Aunt Jemima—stereotypical black mammy; Katzenjammer Kids— stereotypical cartoon characters.

For generations, this has been the pattern. Immigrant parents have sent their children to school (simply, they thought) to acquire the "skills" to survive in the city. The child returned home with a voice his parents barely recognized or understood, couldn't trust, and didn't like.

In Eastern cities—Philadelphia, New York, Boston, Baltimore— class after class gathered immigrant children to women (usually women) who stood in front of rooms full of children, changing children. So also for me in the 1950s. Irish-Catholic nuns. California. The old story. The hyphen tipped to the right, away from Mexico and toward a confusing but true American identity.

I speak now in the chromium American accent of my grammar school classmates—Billy Reckers, Mike Bradley, Carol Schmidt, Kathy O'Grady. . . . I believe I became like my classmates, became German, Polish, and (like my teachers) Irish. And because assimilation is always reciprocal, my classmates got something of me. (I mean sad eyes; belief in the Indian Virgin; a taste for sugar skulls on the Feast of the Dead.) In the blending, we became what our parents could never have been, and we carried America one revolution further.

"Does America still exist?" Americans have been asking the question for so long that to ask it again only proves our continuous link. But perhaps the question deserves to be asked with urgency now. Since the black civil rights movement of the 1960s, our tenuous notion of a shared public life has deteriorated notably.

The struggle of black men and women did not eradicate racism, but it became the great moment in the life of America's conscience. Water hoses, bulldogs, blood—the images, rendered black, white, rectangular, passed into living rooms.

It is hard to look at a photograph of a crowd taken, say, in 1890 or in 1930 and not notice the absence of blacks. (It becomes an impertinence to wonder if America *still* exists.)

In the sixties, other groups of Americans learned to champion their rights by analogy to the black civil rights movement. But the heroic vision faded. Dr. Martin Luther King, Jr. had spoken with Pauline eloquence of a nation that would unite Christian and Jew, old and young, rich and poor. Within a decade, the struggles of the 1960s were reduced to a bureaucratic competition for little more than pieces of a representational pie. The quest for a portion of power became an end in itself. The metaphor for the American city of the 1970s was a committee: one black, one woman, one person under thirty . . .

If the small town had sinned against America by too neatly defining who could be an American, the city's sin was a romantic secession. One noticed the romanticism in the antiwar movement—certain demonstrators who demonstrated a lack of tact or desire to persuade and seemed content to play secular protestants. One noticed the romanticism in the competition among members of "minority groups" to claim the status of

Primary Victim. To Americans unconfident of their common identity, minority standing became a way of asserting individuality. Middle-class Americans—men and women clearly not the primary victims of social oppression—brandished their suffering with exuberance.

The dream of a single society probably died with *The Ed Sullivan Show*. The reality of America persists. Teenagers pass through big-city high schools banded in racial groups, their collars turned up to a uniform shrug. But then they graduate to jobs at the phone company or in banks, where they end up working alongside people unlike themselves. Typists and tellers walk out together at lunchtime.

It is easier for us as Americans to believe the obvious fact of our separateness—easier to imagine the black and white Americas prophesied by the Kerner report (broken glass, street fires)—than to recognize the reality of a city street at lunchtime. Americans are wedded by proximity to a common culture. The panhandler at one corner is related to the pamphleteer at the next who is related to the banker who is kin to the Chinese old man wearing an MIT sweatshirt. In any true national history, Thomas Jefferson begets Martin Luther King, Jr., who begets the Gray Panthers. It is because we lack a vision of ourselves entire—the city street is crowded and we are each preoccupied with finding our own way home—that we lack an appropriate hymn.

Under my window now passes a little white girl softly rehearsing to herself a Motown obbligato.

Interpretations

1. In the seventh through ninth paragraphs, Rodriguez comes rather close to defining "American" as diversity, tolerance, and pluralism. Do you agree that Americans "pledge allegiance" to these principles? Why do you think Rodriguez did not explicitly define "American" and organize his essay around such a definition?

2. Why was the question "Where you from?" so unsettling, so important to answer "correctly"? What has the boy learned when he learns to answer "Mexico"?

3. Rodriguez frequently uses specifics to stand for something more general, as in "spiced food" and "baseball." What do these two details stand for? Can you find other examples of this kind of symbolic detail?

4. How, according to Rodriguez, do some people misuse their "minority standing"? What has been the result of such misuse?

5. How do you interpret the last sentence? Which do you consider to be the most important words in this sentence?

Correspondences

1. Review the de Tocqueville quotation on social equality (page 351). What points does he make about democracy? How does Rodriguez's essay support or contradict de Tocqueville's views? With whom do you agree more?

2. "Americans have traditionally defined themselves by what they refused to include." What does Rodriguez mean? Cite examples from Rendón or Bambara (Chapter 3) to support or refute his point of view.

Applications

1. To Rodriguez, "The American story is the story of immigrant children and of their children—children no longer able to speak to their grandparents." Write an analysis of the personal and cultural ramifications of this thesis.

2. Bilingual education is a complex and controversial issue. Some theorists believe that immersion in the English language results in alienation from family and culture. Others advocate that all students become part of the educational mainstream. Present these differing viewpoints to several students for whom English is a second language. What are their views? With whom do they agree? for what reasons? Write an essay summarizing your findings. To what extent do their responses alter your views on this issue?

Silent Dancing

Judith Ortiz Cofer

Judith Ortiz Cofer (b. 1952) is the author of a novel, The Line of
the Sun *(1989), two poetry collections, and* Peregrina, *a chap-
book that won the 1985 Riverstone Press International Poetry
Competition. Her writings have appeared in numerous magazines and she has received several fellowships, from, for example, the National Endowment for the Arts. "Silent Dancing" is the
title essay of a collection published in 1990.*

*Puerto Rico is a self-governing Commonwealth of about three
million people, 99.9 percent of whom are Hispanic. Puerto
Ricans are citizens of the U.S., although they do not pay federal
income tax, vote in national elections, or send senators or rep-
resentatives to Congress. About two million Puerto Ricans like
Cofer's father have emigrated to the mainland, although since
1974 there has been a reverse migration. The easternmost island
of the West Indies group called the Greater Antilles, Puerto Rico
was discovered by Columbus in 1493 and conquered for Spain
by Ponce de León. Slaves were imported to grow the main crop,
sugar cane. The island was ceded to the U.S. after the Spanish-
American War in 1898. The population voted to accept Commonwealth status in 1952. Although the per capita income
($4,301 in 1985) is low in comparison to that of the U.S., it is
the highest of any area in Latin America, thanks primarily to
programs developed since the late 1940s to encourage manufacturing and tourism.*

*We have a home movie of this party. Several times my mother and I have
watched it together, and I have asked questions about the silent revelers
coming in and out focus. It is grainy and of short duration, but it's a
great visual aid to my memory of life at that time. And it is in color—the
only complete scene in color I can recall from those years.*

WE LIVED IN Puerto Rico until my brother was born in 1954. Soon after,
because of economic pressures on our growing family, my father joined
the United States Navy. He was assigned to duty on a ship in Brooklyn
Yard—a place of cement and steel that was to be his home base in the
States until his retirement more than twenty years later. He left the Island
first, alone, going to New York City and tracking down his uncle who

lived with his family across the Hudson River in Paterson, New Jersey. There my father found a tiny apartment in a huge tenement that had once housed Jewish families but was just being taken over and transformed by Puerto Ricans, overflowing from New York City. In 1955 he sent for us. My mother was only twenty years old, I was not quite three, and my brother was a toddler when we arrived at El Building, as the place had been christened by its newest residents.

My memories of life in Paterson during those first few years are all in shades of gray. Maybe I was too young to absorb vivid colors and details, or to discriminate between the slate blue of the winter sky and the darker hues of the snow-bearing clouds, but that single color washes over the whole period. The building we lived in was gray, as were the streets, filled with slush the first few months of my life there. The coat my father had bought for me was similar in color and too big; it sat heavily on my thin frame.

I do remember the way the heater pipes banged and rattled, startling all of us out of sleep until we got so used to the sound that we automatically shut it out or raised our voices above the racket. The hiss from the valve punctuated my sleep (which has always been fitful) like a nonhuman presence in the room—a dragon sleeping at the entrance of my childhood. But the pipes were also a connection to all the other lives being lived around us. Having come from a house designed for a single family back in Puerto Rico—my mother's extended-family home—it was curious to know that strangers lived under our floor and above our heads, and that the heater pipe went through everyone's apartment. (My first spanking in Paterson came as a result of playing tunes on the pipes in my room to see if there would be an answer.) My mother was as new to this concept of beehive life as I was, but she had been given strict orders by my father to keep the doors locked, the noise down, ourselves to ourselves.

It seems that Father had learned some painful lessons about prejudice while searching for an apartment in Paterson. Not until years later did I hear how much resistance he had encountered with landlords who were panicking at the influx of Latinos into a neighborhood that had been Jewish for a couple of generations. It made no difference that it was the American phenomenon of ethnic turnover which was changing the urban core of Paterson, and that the human flood could not be held back with an accusing finger.

"You Cuban?" one man had asked my father, pointing at his name tag on the navy uniform—even though my father had the fair skin and light brown hair of his northern Spanish background, and the name Ortiz is as common in Puerto Rico as Johnson is in the United States.

"No," my father had answered, looking past the finger into his adversary's angry eyes. "I'm Puerto Rican."

"Same shit." And the door closed.

My father could have passed as European, but we couldn't. My brother and I both have our mother's black hair and olive skin, and so we lived in El Building and visited our great-uncle and his fair children on the next block. It was their private joke that they were the German branch of the family. Not many years later that area too would be mainly Puerto Rican. It was as if the heart of the city map were being gradually colored brown—*café con leche* brown. Our color.

The movie opens with a sweep of the living room. It is a "typical' immigrant Puerto Rican decor for the time: the sofa and chairs are square and hard-looking, upholstered in bright colors (blue and yellow in this instance) and covered with the transparent plastic that furniture salesmen then were so adept at convincing women to buy. The linoleum on the floor is light blue; where it had been subjected to spike heels, as it was in most places, there were dime-size indentations all over it that cannot be seen in this movie. The room is full of people dressed up: dark suits for the men, red dresses for the women. When I have asked my mother why most of the women are in red that night, she has shrugged and said, "I don't remember. Just a coincidence." She doesn't have my obsession for assigning symbolism to everything.

The three women in red sitting on the couch are my mother, my eighteen-year-old cousin, and her brother's girlfriend. The novia *is just up from the Island, which is apparent in her body language. She sits up formally, her dress pulled over her knees. She is a pretty girl, but her posture makes her look insecure, lost in her full-skirted dress, which she has carefully tucked around her to make room for my gorgeous cousin, her future sister-in-law. My cousin has grown up in Paterson and is in her last year of high school. She doesn't have a trace of what Puerto Ricans call* la mancha *(literally, the stain: the mark of the new immigrant—something about the posture, the voice, or the humble demeanor that makes it obvious to everyone the person has just arrived on the mainland). My cousin is wearing a tight, sequined, cocktail dress. Her brown hair has been lightened with peroxide around the bangs, and she is holding a cigarette expertly between her fingers, bringing it up to her mouth in a sensuous arc of her arm as she talks animatedly. My mother, who has come up to sit between the two women, both only a few years younger than herself, is somewhere between the poles they represent in our culture.*

It became my father's obsession to get out of the barrio, and thus we were never permitted to form bonds with the place or with the people who lived there. Yet El Building was a comfort to my mother, who never got over yearning for *la isla*. She felt surrounded by her language: the walls were thin, and voices speaking and arguing in Spanish could be heard all day. *Salsas* blasted out of radios, turned on early in the morning and left on for company. Women seemed to cook rice and beans perpetually—the strong aroma of boiling red kidney beans permeated the hallways.

Though Father preferred that we do our grocery shopping at the supermarket when he came home on weekend leaves, my mother insisted that she could cook only with products whose labels she could read. Consequently, during the week I accompanied her and my little brother to La Bodega—a hole-in-the-wall grocery store across the street from El Building. There we squeezed down three narrow aisles jammed with various products. Goya and Libby's—those were the trademarks that were trusted by her *mamá*, so my mother bought many cans of Goya beans, soups, and condiments, as well as little cans of Libby's fruit juices for us. And she also bought Colgate toothpaste and Palmolive soap. (The final *e* is pronounced in both these products in Spanish, so for many years I believed that they were manufactured on the Island. I remember my surprise at first hearing a commercial on television in which "Colgate" rhymed with "ate.") We always lingered at La Bodega, for it was there that Mother breathed best, taking in the familiar aromas of the foods she knew from Mamá's kitchen. It was also there that she got to speak to the other women of El Building without violating outright Father's dictates against fraternizing with our neighbors.

Yet Father did his best to make our "assimilation" painless. I can still see him carrying a real Christmas tree up several flights of stairs to our apartment, leaving a trail of aromatic pine. He carried it formally, as if it were a flag in a parade. We were the only ones in El Building that I knew of who got presents on both Christmas and *día de Reyes,* the day when the Three Kings brought gifts to Christ and Hispanic children.

Our supreme luxury in El Building was having our own television set. It must have been a result of Father's guilt feelings over the isolation he had imposed on us, but we were among the first in the barrio to have one. My brother quickly became an avid watcher of Captain Kangaroo and Jungle Jim, while I loved all the series showing families. By the time I started first grade, I could have drawn a map of Middle America as exemplified by the lives of characters in *Father Knows Best, The Donna Reed Show, Leave It to Beaver, My Three Sons,* and (my favorite) *Bachelor Father,* where John Forsythe treated his adopted teenage daughter like a princess because he was rich and had a Chinese houseboy to do everything for him. In truth, compared to our neighbors in El Building *we* were rich. My father's navy check provided us with financial security and a standard of living that the factory workers envied. The only thing his money could not buy us was a place to live away from the barrio—his greatest wish, Mother's greatest fear.

In the home movie the men are shown next, sitting around a card table set up in one corner of the living room, playing dominoes. The clack of the ivory pieces was a familiar sound. I heard it in many houses on the

Island and in many apartments in Paterson. In Leave it to Beaver, *the Cleavers played bridge in every other episode; in my childhood, the men started every social occasion with a hotly debated round of dominoes. The women would sit around and watch, but they never participated in the games.*

Here and there you can see a small child. Children were always brought to parties and, whenever they got sleepy, were put to bed in the host's bedroom. Babysitting was a concept unrecognized by the Puerto Rican women I knew: a responsible mother did not leave her children with any stranger. And in a culture where children are not considered intrusive, there was no need to leave the children at home. We went where our mother went.

Of my preschool years I have only impressions: the sharp bite of the wind in December as we walked with our parents toward the brightly lit stores downtown; how I felt like a stuffed doll in my heavy coat, boots, and mittens; how good it was to walk into the five-and-dime and to sit at the counter drinking hot chocolate. On Saturdays our whole family would walk downtown to shop at the big department stores on Broadway. Mother bought all our clothes at Penney's and Sears, and she liked to buy her dresses at the women's specialty shops like Lerner's and Diana's. At some point we'd go into Woolworth's and sit at the soda fountain to eat.

We never ran into other Latinos at these stores or when eating out, and it became clear to me only years later that the women from El Building shopped mainly in other places—stores owned by other Puerto Ricans or by Jewish merchants who had philosophically accepted our presence in the city and decided to make us their good customers, if not real neighbors and friends. These establishments were located not downtown but in the blocks around our street, and they were referred to generically as La Tienda, El Bazar, La Bodega, La Botánica. Everyone knew what was meant. These were the stores where your face did not turn a clerk to stone, where your money was as green as anyone else's.

One New Year's Eve we were dressed up like child models in the Sears catalogue: my brother in a miniature man's suit and bow tie, and I in black patent-leather shoes and a frilly dress with several layers of crinoline underneath. My mother wore a bright red dress that night, I remember, and spike heels; her long black hair hung to her waist. Father, who usually, wore his navy uniform during his short visits home, had put on a dark civilian suit for the occasion: we had been invited to his uncle's house for a big celebration. Everyone was excited because my mother's brother Hernan—a bachelor who could indulge himself with luxuries—had bought a home movie camera, which he would be trying out that night.

Even the home movie cannot fill in the sensory details such a gathering left imprinted in a child's brain. The thick sweetness of women's perfumes mixing with the ever-present smells of food cooking in the kitchen: meat and plantain *pasteles,* as well as the ubiquitous rice dish made special with pigeon peas— *gandules*—and seasoned with precious *sofrito* sent up from the Island by somebody's mother or smuggled in by a recent traveler. *Sofrito* was one of the items that women hoarded, since it was hardly ever in stock at La Bodega. It was the flavor of Puerto Rico.

The men drank Palo Viejo rum, and some of the younger ones got weepy. The first time I saw a grown man cry was at a New Year's Eve party: he had been reminded of his mother by the smells in the kitchen. But what I remember most were the boiled *pasteles,* plantain or yucca rectangles stuffed with corned beef or other meats, olives, and many other savory ingredients, all wrapped in banana leaves. Everybody had to fish one out with a fork. There was always a "trick" *pastel*—one without stuffing—and whoever got that one was the "New Year's Fool."

There was also the music. Long-playing albums were treated like precious china in these homes. Mexican recordings were popular, but the songs that brought tears to my mother's eyes were sung by the melancholy Daniel Santos, whose life as a drug addict was the stuff of legend. Felipe Rodríguez was a particular favorite of couples, since he sang about faithless women and brokenhearted men. There is a snatch of one lyric that has stuck in my mind like a needle on a worn groove: *De piedra ba de ser mi cama, de piedra la cabezera . . . la mujer que a mi me quiera . . . ba de quererme de veras. Ay, Ay, Ay, corazón, porque no amas . . .* I must have heard it a thousand times since the idea of a bed made of stone, and its connection to love, first troubled me with its disturbing images.

The five-minute home movie ends with people dancing in a circle— the creative filmmaker must have set it up, so that all of them could file past him. It is both comical and sad to watch silent dancing. Since there is no justification for the absurd movements that music provides for some of us, people appear frantic, their faces embarrassingly intense. It's as if you were watching sex. Yet for years, I've had dreams in the form of this home movie. In a recurring scene, familiar faces push themselves forward into my mind's eye, plastering their features into distorted close-ups. And I'm asking them: "Who is *she?* Who is the old woman I don't recognize? Is she an aunt? Somebody's wife? Tell me who she is."

> "See the beauty mark on her cheek as big as a hill on the lunar landscape of her face—well, that runs in the family. The women on your father's side of the family wrinkle early; it's the price they pay for that fair skin. The young girl with the green stain on her wedding dress is *la novia*—just up from the Island. See, she

lowers her eyes when she approaches the camera, as she's supposed to. Decent girls never look at you directly in the face. *Humilde,* humble, a girl should express humility in all her actions. She will make a good wife for your cousin. He should consider himself lucky to have met her only weeks after she arrived here. If he marries her quickly, she will make him a good Puerto Rican–style wife; but if he waits too long, she will be corrupted by the city, just like your cousin there."

"She means me, I do what I want. This is not some primitive island I live on. Do they expect me to wear a black mantilla on my head and go to mass every day? Not me. I'm an American woman, and I will do as I please. I can type faster than anyone in my senior class at Central High, and I'm going to be a secretary to a lawyer when I graduate. I can pass for an American girl anywhere—I've tried it. At least for Italian, anyway—I never speak Spanish in public. I hate these parties, but I wanted the dress. I look better than any of these *humildes* here. *My* life is going to be different. I have an American boyfriend. He is older and has a car. My parents don't know it, but I sneak out of the house late at night sometimes to be with him. If I marry him, even my name will be American. I hate rice and beans—that's what makes these women fat."

"Your *prima* is pregnant by that man she's been sneaking around with. Would I lie to you? I'm your *tía política,* your great-uncle's common-law wife—the one he abandoned on the Island to go marry your cousin's mother. *I* was not invited to this party, of course, but I came anyway. I came to tell you that story about your cousin that you've always wanted to hear. Do you remember the comment your mother made to a neighbor that has always haunted you? The only thing you heard was your cousin's name, and then you saw your mother pick up your doll from the couch and say: 'It was as big as this doll when they flushed it down the toilet.' This image has bothered you for years, hasn't it? You had nightmares about babies being flushed down the toilet, and you wondered why anyone would do such a horrible thing. You didn't dare ask your mother about it. She would only tell you that you had not heard her right, and yell at you for listening to adult conversations. But later, when you were old enough to know about abortions, you suspected.

"I am here to tell you that you were right. Your cousin was growing an *americanito* in her belly when this movie was made. Soon after, she put something long and pointy into her pretty self, thinking maybe she could get rid of the problem before breakfast and still make it to her first class at the high school.

Well, *niña,* her screams could be heard downtown. Your aunt, her *mamá,* who had been a midwife on the Island, managed to pull the little thing out. Yes, they probably flushed it down the toilet. What else could they do with it—give it a Christian burial in a little white casket with blue bows and ribbons? Nobody wanted that baby—least of all the father, a teacher at her school with a house in West Paterson that he was filling with real children, and a wife who was a natural blonde.

"Girl, the scandal sent your uncle back to the bottle. And guess where your cousin ended up? Irony of ironies. She was sent to a village in Puerto Rico to live with a relative on her mother's side: a place so far away from civilization that you have to ride a mule to reach it. A real change in scenery. She found a man there—women like that cannot live without male company—but believe me, the men in Puerto Rico know how to put a saddle on a woman like her. *La gringa,* they call her. Ha, ha, ha. *La gringa* is what she always wanted to be . . ."

The old woman's mouth becomes a cavernous black hole I fall into. And as I fall, I can feel the reverberations of her laughter. I hear the echoes of her last mocking words: *la gringa, la gringa!* And the conga line keeps moving silently past me. There is no music in my dream for the dancers.

When Odysseus visits Hades to see the spirit of his mother, he makes an offering of sacrificial blood, but since all the souls crave an audience with the living, he has to listen to many of them before he can ask questions. I, too, have to hear the dead and the forgotten speak in my dream. Those who are still part of my life remain silent, going around and around in their dance. The others keep pressing their faces forward to say things about the past.

My father's uncle is last in line. He is dying of alcoholism, shrunken and shriveled like a monkey, his face a mass of wrinkles and broken arteries. As he comes closer I realize that in his features I can see my whole family. If you were to stretch that rubbery flesh, you could find my father's face, and deep within *that* face—my own. I don't want to look into those eyes ringed in purple. In a few years he will retreat into silence, and take a long, long time to die. *Move back, Tío,* I tell him. *I don't want to hear what you have to say. Give the dancers room to move. Soon it will be midnight. Who is the New Year's Fool this time?*

Interpretations

1. How did Cofer's father's policy of isolating his family affect the family and Cofer specifically? Was assimilation the goal of this policy of isolation? If so, how would you have expected Cofer's father to

regard the cousin—as, for example, a model for his family? Can you find evidence to show Cofer's own attitude toward this policy?

2. How do you interpret the statement that "La Gringa is what she always wanted to be . . ."? What point about assimilation does the cousin's life make? What point about assimilation does the essay finally imply?

3. Why do you think Cofer sees her whole family in her alcoholic uncle's face?

4. What would you say are Cofer's feelings about these "dead and forgotten" relations that make her think of Odysseus in Hades? If she identifies or sympathizes with them, why does she say, "I don't want to hear what you have to say"?

Correspondences

1. Although her father was determined to take his family out of the Barrio, Cofer states that "the only thing his money could not buy us was a place to live away from the Barrio—his greatest wish, mother's greatest fear." Contrast her father's experiences with assimilation with those of Rodriguez. How do you account for differences in their points of view? Would Cofer's father be able to leave the Barrio today? Why or why not?

2. Evaluate the influence of television in Cofer's early childhood. How did it shape her concepts of family relationships and customs? Compare her media experiences with those of Soto (Chapter 4). Speculate as to its effect on their assimilation processes.

Applications

1. Cofer describes the family home movie as a powerful visual aid to her childhood memories. How do her visual recollections affect the text's meaning? Where in her descriptions do you also find Cofer appealing to the sense of taste and smell? With what effects?

2. Analyze the implications of Cofer's title. Explain why "there is no music in my dream for the dancers."

The Drama of an Exchange Student

Juliet Wright

Juliet Wright was born in 1969 in Savanna-la-mar, Jamaica, West Indies. She attended the Hampton High School boarding institution for girls in Malvern, Jamaica, and emigrated to New York in 1987 to further her education. She currently attends Queensborough Community College; her ultimate goal is to study International Relations and Portuguese and become an ambassador from Jamaica to Brazil.

IT WAS A hot humid day in August. There was yelling and screaming in the grandstands of the Jamaica National Stadium. The Jamaica All Stars were playing against the Brazilian team of São Paulo. I recognized a few of the players on the Brazilian team from the World Cup of 1986. I remember how they lost to France, and all of Brazil cried with them, including me, but that was not the only time I cried.

I remember how I cried when I first heard that I had gained a scholarship through the American Field Service to go on an intercultural exchange to Brazil. The first two weeks of my trip to Brazil are now so distinct in my mind.

I arrived in Pôrto Alegre, a shy and timid fifteen-year-old girl, embarking on a one-year adventure. I walked through the airport with pictures of my host family in my hand. The little I knew about them was deciphered from the few abstract lines they had written on the back of the photos in the worst form of English. Already I knew they did not speak English, and I most definitely did not speak Portuguese.

I spotted a fat friendly looking Italian woman with a sign that said, "Julie," never mind that was not my real name, but I was sure the sign was meant for me. It was the only name that looked familiar. I greeted her and the rest of the family with hugs and smiles. Soon we were off to my new home. Everyone else laughed and talked for the duration of the journey. They spoke at such an incredible speed. They tried to speak to me, but I could not understand; when I tried to tell them I was tired, they only smiled. So we stuck to the exchange of smiles and funny gestures.

We arrived in the little town of Montenegro which had a population of no more than three hundred people. For a city girl, I knew this was going to be very different. The town was in a valley surrounded by hills, as far as the eyes could see. The earth on the bare hillsides was fire red, and the streets were made of cobblestone. The cars were like none I had ever seen. The only familiar sight was a Volkswagen Bug. There were many cyclists on the road and even a few horses and carts.

We arrived at my new home. It was a very huge white house with a brick red roof. It looked warm and friendly. The design was very different and interesting. The kitchen and the dining room were detached from the rest of the house. The driveway was long and winding and had a healthy grapevine running overhead. Where the lawn should have been was a huge vegetable garden. It was very unattractive growing there in front of such a beautiful house.

I learned my sisters' names, Rosanne, Rosa, Regina. They pronounced their names with a silent 'R', which gave the effect Hosanne, Hausa, Hegina. I could not even begin to learn my father's name. My mother's name was nice and easy. Her name was Ines, and something told me I would get along with her just fine.

The relatives came over to see the new addition to the family. I don't know if these four or five people were related. But they were all very interesting. A very cute and friendly little girl came and sat beside me. I smiled at her. I supposed she must have asked me a question. She looked at me puzzled and could not understand why I did not respond. I heard her mother calling her name and she rattled off a few lines of something to her. Andresa, the little innocent girl looked at me strangely. I knew she was baffled that I did not speak her language and I guess she had never encountered this before. "Hello Andresa, how are you?" I said that although I knew she would not understand, just to clear in her mind that it was not a matter that I could not speak, but that I spoke something she could not understand. She was intrigued by the idea and stared at me for the rest of the evening. I could not imagine that a little four year old could make me feel so uncomfortable at this stage of life.

During the next few days, the people I had seen seemed to be very light skinned. Somehow that was strange to me. I had the impression that Brazil was a large melting pot of different ethnic groups. Coming directly from a Caribbean island which was eighty percent Black and the difference a combination of other ethnic groups, it was difficult to relate to these people with whom I had no previous contact. Nothing was familiar to me. All I heard of Brazil was the Carnival, Rio, football and the Amazons. "I wish I had read more about this place."

I went to see what their clothing might have to offer. I could not decide whether their styles were way ahead or way behind. I knew something for sure—they were different.

It was time to begin school. My host family had already registered me in school. I learnt one word on my first day of school: 'la estrangeira'. I can now tell you that means foreign girl. All day the students were constantly pointing out the foreigner to each other. They must have welcomed something new to break the monotony of their small town. At eleven-thirty the nearby church bell began tolling. Suddenly, classes adjourned and everyone was rushing somewhere, some students on bicycles, some on foot. They all seemed to have something important to do. I did not. In a matter of fifteen minutes there was no one in sight. I was leaning against the wall by the school gate watching a postal worker close the office across the street. I had to assume that the whole town went home for lunch. As I walked home I felt like an outcast. I felt no one cared enough to let me know what happened next. "Maybe they thought the whole world went home for lunch." When classes resumed we had Physics. I could never understand Physics in English let alone in Portuguese. So I took out my writing pad and wrote home. Every Monday and Wednesday at one o'clock I wrote home.

Home at this point seemed so out of reach, almost as if it were in a completely different galaxy, separate and apart. I could never imagine that two places in this world could be so different.

Gradually I became withdrawn from everyone. Basically, I read books, listened to English music from my audio tapes, and slept. This was my own world. The TV, the radio, playing games with the family, all these activities I was automatically excluded from. I was handicapped, I could not communicate. I was confused and angry at myself. Why couldn't I fit in? Was this all part of the culture shock they spoke about in our orientations?

Before students went to a foreign country on an exchange, the American Field Service gave orientations. This was the only thing that made me feel now that my situation was normal. The volunteers of the Service had counseled us in depth on what to expect. But the excitement at that time had flustered my mind and I never stopped to think of what the situation would really be like. Would I like the people, their dress, their food?

I understood when it was dinner time because they would ring the dinner bell, not that this interested me because I hated the food. They cooked in olive oil which I disliked, and they loved to mix all their different foods together. After dinner, everyone sat together and shared a traditional drink of ground herbs with hot water. Chimarrau, as they called it, was served in a hollow wood- like cone with a thick silver straw. Everyone took turns drinking, refilled the cone with hot water and passed it along. Oh how I despised this Southern tradition. I would sit there aloof as everyone nonchalantly socialized. I wondered if anyone understood what I was going through. Did they have any idea what turmoil my mind was in? I was in a new system, a new way of life, and a whole new culture. I wanted to be back on the plane home to my own country, my own culture, something I understood. But it was too late, I was there to stay.

For the next two months this miserable existence was all I knew. I think the one thing that saved me was my encounter with a lady by the name of Maria who had been an exchange student herself from Brazil to New York five years ago. She now taught English conversation at the language center in a town called Yazigi. She helped me immensely with my Portuguese. I attended her English classes sometimes and conversed with her students on different topics. In this exchange, Maria and I became good friends.

At the beginning of my third month, I received a bulletin from the American Field Service informing me of an orientation which was to be held in the big city of Pôrto Alegre. Oh how I looked forward to this event. Finally, the weekend of the orientation was here. I boarded the bus to Pôrto Alegre with much anxiety. It was a pleasant change to see tall buildings and the hustle and bustle of the city. At the bus station in Pôrto Alegre a handsome young male was holding a yellow and red sign that said A.F.S. I went over and he greeted me in the traditional Southern way. Three kisses on the cheek, from left to right then left again. He had been an A.F.S. student from Brazil to California years ago, and now he was an A.F.S. volunteer. He took me back to the orientation site, where I met students from all over the world who were staying in three adjoining Southern states. We played getting-to-know-you games, and everyone felt very relaxed with each other. There were some fifteen students and about five volunteers. We had different rap sessions in which each student shared their experience with the group. To my amazement I was not in such a bad position after all. There were students who could not get along with their families. There was a Japanese girl who spoke neither English nor Portuguese and for her the language barrier was far greater than it was for me. Eventually she had to return home sooner than planned.

That weekend I considered myself fortunate. There were some students who were requesting a change of families, but I did not. Thanks to Maria, the counselors said my Portuguese was picking up well. We did many things together on the weekend. We went out on the town to a movie, discos and all the historical sights. I made a few friends that weekend, and the good thing was that some of them were no further than an hour from Montenegro. We already planned to meet on the upcoming weekend. I shared my room with a girl named Cathy from Blumenau. She was going to New York for one year as an exchange student. We had a lot in common and became good friends.

I returned to Montenegro on Sunday evening with renewed spirits. I borrowed my sister's bicycle and rode over to Maria to tell her all about my weekend. She was so excited for me. When I got home, my sister told me we were going to get together at her friend's house. She took up my Walkman and took out the cassette saying I should bring it along and teach them to dance my kind of music. This was truly an exchange of cultures I thought to myself. We all enjoyed ourselves thoroughly, and they loved my Reggae music.

As time went by, I began feeling more comfortable in my new environment. I had made a conscious decision from the time of my orientation to put my all into this experience and make the best of it. I continued my Portuguese classes with Maria and I studied my verbs and conjugations constantly.

My mother suggested to me that instead of going straight home after school, I should go to her store in the town and stay with her until closing. She owned a hardware store on the main street of the town. I accepted the suggestion and was glad I did. I got to know her much better. On slow evenings she taught me to knit and to type. She really made me feel like one of her daughters. I became more acquainted with the people in the community who enjoyed interviewing me as they stopped in for a tin of paint.

My mother discovered through our chit-chats every evening that I played the piano and hence signed me up for classes at the local community center on Mondays and Wednesdays. I met new faces of all ages, some of them more patient than others. The younger children loved practicing their English on me and sometimes brought me their English homework.

For the next few months my Portuguese continued to improve. I was even doing Math and Chemistry tests, never Physics. There was a mandatory class in the curriculum called Organization of Social and Political Brazil, which I was actually beginning to understand.

I went to the school soccer games and cheered for my class. When the volley ball season started, Montenegro was high in spirits and had their very own team playing on the national level. I attended every home game and had the opportunity of meeting a few of the players since my sister played on a team herself. Not all the players were from Montenegro, and there were three handsome Black players from the North, one of whom taught me a lot about relating to my friends and family of different color.

My youngest sister Rosanne was very athletic and pursuing a degree in Physical Education. Since Montenegro had no physical fitness center, she rented a large room and began having exercise classes. Her friend was also teaching Samba classes in the same room after Rosanne's classes. Therefore, every Tuesday and Thursday I went with them and worked out and learnt a few Samba moves. I now had a full schedule. I was becoming very involved.

My next orientation was held in Blumenau, where the Oktoberfest was being held. As you may imagine, there were many people of German descent living there. I exchanged families for one week, and I stayed with Cathy's family. This was the girl I had roomed with at my first orientation. Cathy was now away in New York on an exchange herself. Her family was very interested to hear about all the dislikes, challenges and successes of my experience so far. It gave them a good idea of what their daughter's trip was like so far.

I now had many friends in Montenegro. We would always visit each other and drink Chimarrau which I by now had acquired a taste for, and eat Churrasco, which is grilled chicken, steak, fish, or whatever you pleased. By this time, I had gained so much weight, it was obvious that I had become fond of the food. My favorite past-time, however, was to go to the river and sit on my special boulder at the bank side and record my deepest thoughts and feelings. My little friend Andresa had stopped speaking to me because she complained that I never rode her around on the back of my bicycle anymore. I had to patch things up with her, because she was really my very first friend, and I dared not forget those rough days. So I made sure whenever I went to the river, Andresa was on the back of my bike.

Towards the end of my experience when I would call home, I found myself speaking in Portuguese to my parents. It gave them such a thrill to hear me. We were making arrangements for me to return home to Jamaica. Yes I had not seen my natural family in one year, and without doubt, I missed them, but I could never picture giving up my new way of life, my friends, my new tongue and all my newly acquired traditions of the past year.

Interpretations

1. What was Wright's final evaluation of her exchange experience? How would *you* rate her experience? How does Wright's relationship with little Andresa symbolize the year's experience?

2. What qualifications should a student have in order to benefit from an exchange program? Compare the two experiences of living abroad (a) as a tourist and (b) as a student. What foreign countries would most interest you as a place to study?

3. What are the strengths of Wright's essay? How effective is the opening paragraph in introducing the main idea(s) of the essay? What would you say is her purpose in writing this essay?

Correspondences

1. Compare the causes of cultural alienation in the essays by Cofer and Wright. Consider the role of language in both essays.

2. Review Morrow's perspective on global interactions (page 351) and discuss its relevance to Wright's essay. Trace her process in reaching a realization of "mutual destinies."

Applications

1. Discuss the importance of the orientation phase of a student exchange program like Wright's. How effective was it? What changes would you suggest? How can you imagine yourself participating in a similar interaction?

2. Since we all respond in part to other people's definitions of ourselves, freewrite on your reaction to being described as "the foreign one." How might this experience affect the self-concepts of new immigrants to the United States?

In Ethnic America

Michael Novak

Michael Novak (b. 1933), from Johnstown, Pennsylvania, is an American of Slovak descent. A distinguished scholar, he has earned several degrees, including an M.A. (1966) from Harvard University. His teaching career has spanned a number of prestigious universities, and he is currently a Professor of American Studies at the University of Notre Dame. Mr. Novak has authored numerous books, including Naked I Leave *(1970),* The Rise of the Unmeltable Ethnics *(1972),* Confession of a Catholic *(1983), and* Human Rights and the New Realism *(1986). In this selection from* The Rise of the Unmeltable Ethnics, *Novak examines the difficulties many southern and eastern European immigrants encountered as they attempted cultural assimilation in the United States.*

For information on Poland, see Michael T. Kaufman's "Kissing Customs," Chapter 1; on Italy, see Mario Puzo's "Italians in Hell's Kitchen," Chapter 4; and on Czechoslovakia, see Hana Wehle's "The Impossible Became No Longer Unthinkable," Chapter 6.

GROWING UP IN America has been an assault upon my sense of worthiness. It has also been a kind of liberation and delight.

There must be countless women in America who have known for years that something is peculiarly unfair, yet who only recently have found it possible, because of Women's Liberation, to give tongue to their pain. In recent months I have experienced a similar inner thaw, a gradual relaxation, a willingness to think about feelings heretofore shepherded out of sight.

I am born of PIGS—those Poles, Italians, Greeks, and Slavs, those non-English-speaking immigrants numbered so heavily among the workingmen of this nation. Not particularly liberal or radical; born into a history not white Anglo-Saxon and not Jewish; born outside what, in America, is considered the intellectual mainstream—and thus privy to neither power nor status nor intellectual voice.

Those Poles of Buffalo and Milwaukee—so notoriously taciturn, sullen, nearly speechless. Who has ever understood them? It is not that Poles do not feel emotion—what is their history if not dark passion, romanticism, betrayal, courage, blood? But where in America is there anywhere a language for voicing what a Christian Pole in this nation feels? He has no Polish culture left him, no Polish tongue. Yet Polish feelings do not go easily into the idiom of happy America, the America of the Anglo-Saxons and yes, in the arts, the Jews. (The Jews have long been a culture of the word, accustomed to exile, skilled in scholarship and in reflection. The Christian Poles are largely of peasant origin, free men for hardly more than a hundred years.) Of what shall the young man of Lackawanna think on his way to work in the mills, departing his relatively dreary home and street? What roots does he have? What language of the heart is available to him?

The PIGS are not silent willingly. The silence burns like hidden coals in the chest.

All four of my grandparents, unknown to one another, arrived in America from the same county in Slovakia. My grandfather had a small farm in Pennsylvania; his wife died in a wagon accident. Meanwhile, Johanna, fifteen, arrived on Ellis Island, dizzy from witnessing births and deaths and illnesses aboard the crowded ship. She had a sign around her neck lettered PASSAIC. There an aunt told her of a man who had lost his wife in Pennsylvania. She went. They were married. She inherited his three children.

Each year for five years Grandma had a child of her own. She was among the lucky; only one died. When she was twenty-two and the mother of seven (my father was the last), her husband died. "Grandma Novak," as I came to know her many years later, resumed the work she had begun in Slovakia at the town home of a man known to my father only as "the Professor"; she housecleaned and she laundered.

I heard this story only weeks ago. Strange that I had not asked insistently before. Odd that I should have such shallow knowledge of my roots. Amazing to me that I do not know what my family suffered, endured, learned, and hoped these last six or seven generations. It is as if there were no project in which we all have been involved, as if history in some way began with my father and with me.

The estrangement I have come to feel derives not only from lack of family history. Early in life, I was made to feel a slight uneasiness when I said my name. When I was very young, the "American" kids still made something out of names unlike their own, and their earnest, ambitious mothers thought long thoughts when I introduced myself.

Under challenge in grammar school concerning my nationality, I had been instructed by my father to announce proudly: "American." When my family moved from the Slovak ghetto of Johnstown to the WASP suburb on the hill, my mother impressed upon us how well we must be dressed, and show good manners, and behave—people think of us as "different" and we mustn't give them any cause. "Whatever you do, marry a Slovak girl," was other advice to a similar end: "They cook. They clean. They take good care of you. For your own good." I was taught to be proud of being Slovak, but to recognize that others wouldn't know what it meant, or care.

Nowhere in my schooling do I recall any attempt to put me in touch with my own history. The strategy was clearly to make an American of me. English literature, American literature, and even the history books, as I recall them, were peopled mainly by Anglo-Saxons from Boston (where most historians seemed to live). Not even my native Pennsylvania, let alone my Slovak forebears, counted for very many paragraphs. (We did have something called "Pennsylvania History" somewhere; I seem to remember its puffs for industry. It could have been written by a Mellon. I don't remember feeling envy or regret: a feeling, perhaps, of unimportance, of remoteness, of not having heft enough to count.

The fact that I was born a Catholic also complicated life. What is a Catholic but what everybody else is in reaction against? Protestants reformed "the whore of Babylon." Others were "enlightened" from it, and Jews had reason to help Catholicism and the social structure it was rooted in fall apart. The history books and the whole of education hummed in upon that point (for during crucial years I attended a public school): to be modern is decidedly not to be medieval; to be reasonable is not to be dogmatic; to be free is clearly not to live under ecclesiastical authority; to be scientific is not to attend ancient rituals, cherish irrational symbols, indulge in mythic practices. It is hard to grow up Catholic in America without becoming defensive, perhaps a little paranoid, feeling forced to divide the world between "us" and "them."

We had a special language all our own, our own pronunciation for words we shared in common with others (Augústine, contémplative), sights and sounds and smells in which few others participated (incense at Benediction of the Most Blessed Sacrament, Forty Hours, wakes, and altar bells at the silent consecration of the Host); and we had our own politics and slant on world affairs. Since earliest childhood, I have known about a "power elite" that runs America: the boys from the Ivy League in the State Department as opposed to the Catholic boys in Hoover's FBI who (as Daniel Moynihan once put it), keep watch on them. And on a whole host of issues, my people have been, though largely Democratic, conservative: on censorship, on communism, on abortion, on religious schools, etc. "Harvard" and "Yale" long meant "them" to us.

We did not feel this country belonged to us. We felt fierce pride in it, more loyalty than anyone could know. But we felt blocked at every turn. There were not many intellectuals among us, not even very many professional men. Laborers mostly. Small businessmen, agents for corporations perhaps. Content with a little, yes, modest in expectation, and content. But somehow feeling cheated. For a thousand years the Slovaks survived Hungarian hegemony and our strategy here remained the same: endurance and steady work. Slowly, one day, we would overcome.

A special word is required about a complicated symbol: sex. To this day my mother finds it hard to spell the word intact, preferring to write "s–." Not that much was made of sex in our environment. And that's the point: silence. Demonstrative affection, emotive dances, an exuberance Anglo-Saxons seldom seem to share; but on the realities of sex, discretion. Reverence, perhaps; seriousness, surely. On intimacies, it was as though our tongues had been stolen, as though in peasant life for a thousand years—as in the novels of Tolstoi, Sholokhov, and even Kosinski—the context had been otherwise. Passion, certainly; romance, yes; family and children, certainly; but sex rather a minor if explosive part of life.

Imagine, then, the conflict in the generation of my brothers, sister, and myself. Suddenly, what for a thousand years was minor becomes an all-absorbing investigation. Some view it as a drama of "liberation" when the ruling classes (subscribers to the *New Yorker,* I suppose) move progressively, generation by generation since Sigmund Freud, toward concentration upon genital stimulation, and latterly toward consciousness-raising sessions in Clit. Lib. But it is rather a different drama when we stumble suddenly upon mores staggering any expectation our grandparents ever cherished.

Yet more significant in the ethnic experience in America is the intellectual world one meets: the definition of values, ideas, and purposes emanating from universities, books, magazines, radio, and television. One hears one's own voice echoed back neither by spokesmen of "middle America" (so complacent, smug, nativist, and Protestant), nor by the "intellectuals." Almost unavoidably, perhaps, education in America leads the student who entrusts his soul to it in a direction which, lacking a better word, we might call liberal: respect for individual conscience, a sense of social responsibility, trust in the free exchange of ideas and procedures of dissent, a certain confidence in the ability of men to "reason together" and adjudicate their differences, a frank recognition of the vitality of the unconscious, a willingness to protect workers and the poor against the vast economic power of industrial corporations, and the like.

On the other hand, the liberal imagination has appeared to be astonishingly universalist and relentlessly missionary. Perhaps the metaphor "enlightenment" offers a key. One is *initiated into light.* Liberal education tends to separate children from their parents, from their roots, from their history, in the cause of a universal and superior religion.

In particular, I have regretted and keenly felt the absence of that sympathy for PIGS which simple human feeling might have prodded intelligence to muster, that same sympathy which the educated find so easy to conjure up for black culture, Chicano culture, Indian culture, and other cultures of the poor. In such cases one finds the universalist pretensions of liberal culture suspended; some groups, at least, are entitled to be both different and respected. Why do the educated classes find it so difficult to want to understand the man who drives a beer truck, or the fellow with a helmet working on a site across the street with plumbers and electricians, while their sensitivities race easily to Mississippi or even Bedford-Stuyvesant?

There are deep secrets here, no doubt, unvoiced fantasies and scarcely admitted historical resentments. Few persons in describing "middle Americans," "the silent majority," or Scammon and Wattenberg's "typical American voter" distinguish clearly enough between the nativist American and the ethnic American. The first is likely to be Protestant, the second Catholic. Both may be, in various ways, conservative, loyalist, and unenlightened. Each has his own agonies, fears, betrayed expectations. Neither is ready, quite, to become an ally of the other. Neither has the same history behind him here. Neither has the same hopes. Neither lives out the same psychic voyage, shares the same symbols, has the same sense of reality. The rhetoric and metaphors proper to each differ from those of the other.

There is overlap, of course. But country music is not a polka; a successful politician in a Chicago ward needs a very different "common touch" from the one needed by the county clerk in Normal. The urban experience of immigration lacks that mellifluous, optimistic, biblical vision of the good America which springs naturally to the lips of politicians from the Bible Belt. The nativist tends to believe with Richard Nixon that he "knows America, and the American heart is good." The ethnic tends to believe that every American who preceded him has an angle, and that he, by God, will some day find one, too. (Often, ethnics complain that by working hard, obeying the law, trusting their political leaders, and relying upon the American dream, they now have only their own naiveté to blame for rising no higher than they have.)

Unfortunately, it seems, the ethnics erred in attempting to Americanize themselves before clearing the project with the educated classes. They learned to wave the flag and to send their sons to war. They learned to support their President—an easy task, after all, for those accustomed to obeying authority. And where would they have been if Franklin Roosevelt had not sided with them against established interests? They knew a little about communism—the radicals among them in one way, and by far the larger number of conservatives in another. To this day not a few exchange letters with cousins and uncles who did not leave for America when they might have, whose lot is demonstrably harder than their own and less than free.

Finally, the ethnics do not like, or trust, or even understand the intellectuals. It is not easy to feel uncomplicated affection for those who call you "pig" "fascist," "racist." One had not yet grown accustomed to not hearing "hunkie," "Polack," "spic," "mick," "dago," and the rest.

At no little sacrifice, one had apologized for foods that smelled too strong for Anglo-Saxon noses; moderated the wide swings of Slavic and Italian emotion; learned decorum; given oneself to education, American style; tried to learn tolerance and assimilation. Each generation criticized the earlier for its authoritarian and European and old-fashioned ways. "Up-to-date" was a moral lever. And now when the process nears completion, when a generation appears that speaks without accent and goes to college, still you are considered "pigs" "fascists," and "racists." Racists? Our ancestors owned no slaves. Most of us ceased being serfs only in the last two hundred years—the Russians in 1861. . . .

Whereas the Anglo-Saxon model appears to be a system of atomic individuals and high mobility, our model has tended to stress communities of our own, attachment to family and relatives, stability, and roots. Ethnics tend to have a fierce sense of attachment to their homes, having been homeowners for less than three generations: a home is almost fulfillment enough for one man's life. Some groups save arduously in a passion to *own;* others rent. We have most ambivalent feelings about suburban assimilation and mobility. The melting pot is a kind of homogenized soup, and its mores only partly appeal to ethnics: to some, yes, and to others, no.

It must be said that ethnics think they are better people than the blacks. Smarter, tougher, harder working, stronger in their families. But maybe many are not sure. Maybe many are uneasy. Emotions here are delicate; one can understand the immensely more difficult circumstances under which the blacks have suffered; and one is not unaware of peculiar forms of fear, envy, and suspicion across color lines. How much of this we learned in America by being made conscious of our olive skin, brawny backs, accents, names, and cultural quirks is not plain to us. Racism is not our invention; we did not bring it with us; we had prejudices enough and would gladly have been spared new ones. Especially regarding people who suffer more than we.

Interpretations

1. The first two sentences of this essay serve as a striking introduction; they grab the reader's interest. Do they also state the main point (thesis) of the essay? Is each sentence equally important to the thesis?

2. Novak says that his "estrangement" resulted from lack of knowledge of his family's history and from his sense—symbolized in his name—of being different and not understood. Is not knowing one's family history a common condition among immigrants? What else contributed to Novak's sense of alienation?

3. Those who lived through the 1988 Presidential campaign have become very conscious of the word *liberal*. Examine Novak's extended definition of this word and evaluate it. How does it compare to yours?

4. What reasons does Novak give to support his thesis that the educated classes are more likely to sympathize with blacks than with Slovaks, Poles, Italians, or Greeks? If you agree, why do you? Cite supporting evidence.

5. Why do you think Novak wrote this essay? What was his purpose?

Correspondences

1. "Nowhere in my schooling do I recall any attempt to put me in touch with my own history. The strategy was clearly to make an American out of me." Should such a "strategy" be the purpose of American education? How does Novak's educational experience compare to that of Marshall and Rendón (Chapter 3)? What might each of the three writers have gained emotionally and intellectually from a curriculum that clearly reflected the contribution of their cultures?

2. Looking for work is an integral part of the immigrant experience. Compare the work experiences of Novak's grandmother (paragraphs six and seven) with those of Jasmine in the story of the same name (Chapter 4). Who has the more fortunate interaction? Why do you say so?

Applications

1. "We did not feel this country belonged to us" reflects not only Novak's point of view but that of many other immigrants. To whom, then, does America belong? How might cultural interactions contribute to better communication and a wider sense of belonging?

2. "[T]he ethnics do not like, or trust, or even understand the intellectuals." Why not? What characteristics do the ethnics associate with intellectuals? What is your definition of an intellectual? How does it compare to Novak's? What interactions can you imagine taking place between ethnics and intellectuals that would contribute to better personal and cultural understanding?

Black Men and
Public Spaces

Brent Staples

Brent Staples (b. 1951) is from Chester, Pennsylvania. He has a Ph.D. in psychology from the University of Chicago and is currently on the editorial board of The New York Times, *where he writes on culture and politics. We asked him why he selected* Ms. *for his essay "Black Men and Public Spaces" and he responded:*

> Ms. *is a women's magazine. Women are more vulnerable to street violence, and judgments about who is safe and who is dangerous is an urgent priority for them.*

My FIRST VICTIM was a woman—white, well dressed, probably in her early twenties. I came upon her late one evening on a deserted street in Hyde Park, a relatively affluent neighborhood in an otherwise mean, impoverished section of Chicago. As I swung onto the avenue behind her, there seemed to be a discreet, uninflammatory distance between us. No so. She cast back a worried glance. To her, the youngish black man—a broad six feet two inches with a beard and billowing hair, both hands shoved into the pockets of a bulky military jacket—seemed menacingly close. After a few more quick glimpses, she picked up her pace and was soon running in earnest. Within seconds she disappeared into a cross street.

That was more than a decade ago. I was 22 years old, a graduate student newly arrived at the University of Chicago. It was in the echo of that terrified woman's footfalls that I first began to know the unwieldy inheritance I'd come into—the ability to alter public space in ugly ways. It was clear that she thought herself the quarry of a mugger, a rapist or worse. Suffering a bout of insomnia, however, I was stalking sleep, not defenseless wayfarers. As a softy who is scarcely able to take a knife to a raw chicken—let alone hold it to a person's throat—I was surprised, embarrassed, and dismayed all at once. Her flight made me feel like an accomplice in tyranny. It also made it clear that I was indistinguishable from the muggers who occasionally seeped into the area from the surrounding ghetto. That first encounter, and those that followed, signified that a vast, unnerving gulf lay between nighttime pedestrians—particularly women—and me. And I soon gathered that being perceived as dangerous is a hazard in itself. I only needed to turn a corner into a dicey situation, or crowd some frightened, armed person in a foyer somewhere, or make an errant move after being pulled over by a policeman. Where fear and weapons meet—and they often do in urban America—there is always the possibility of death.

In that first year, my first away from my hometown, I was to become thoroughly familiar with the language of fear. At dark, shadowy intersections in Chicago, I could cross in front of a car stopped at a traffic light and elicit the *thunk, thunk, thunk, thunk* of the driver—black, white, male, or female—hammering down the door locks. On less traveled streets after dark, I grew accustomed to but never comfortable with people who crossed to the other side of the street rather than pass me. Then there were the standard unpleasantries with police, doormen, bouncers, cab drivers, and others whose business it is to screen out troublesome individuals *before* there is any nastiness.

I moved to New York nearly two years ago and I have remained an avid night walker. In central Manhattan, the near-constant crowd cover minimizes tense one-on-one street encounters. Elsewhere—visiting friends in SoHo, where sidewalks are narrow and tightly spaced buildings shut out the sky—things can get very taut indeed.

Black men have a firm place in New York mugging literature. Norman Podhoretz in his famed (or infamous) 1963 essay, "My Negro Problem—And Ours," recalls growing up in terror of black males; they "were tougher than we were, more ruthless," he writes—and as an adult on the Upper West Side of Manhattan, he continues, he cannot constrain his nervousness when he meets black men on certain streets. Similarly, a decade later, the essayist and novelist Edward Hoagland extols a New York where once "Negro bitterness bore down mainly on other Negroes." Where some see mere panhandlers, Hoagland sees "a mugger who is clearly screwing up his nerve to do more than just *ask* for money." But Hoagland has "the New Yorker's quick-hunch posture for broken-field maneuvering," and the bad guy swerves away.

I often witness that "hunch posture," from women after dark on the warrenlike streets of Brooklyn where I live. They seem to set their faces on neutral and, with their purse straps strung across their chests bandolier style, they forge ahead as though bracing themselves against being tackled. I understand, of course, that the danger they perceive is not a hallucination. Women are particularly vulnerable to street violence, and young black males are drastically overrepresented among the perpetrators of that violence. Yet these truths are no solace against the kind of alienation that comes of being ever the suspect, against being set apart, a fearsome entity with whom pedestrians avoid making eye contact.

It is not altogether clear to me how I reached the ripe old age of 22 without being conscious of the lethality nighttime pedestrians attributed to me. Perhaps it was because in Chester, Pennsylvania, the small, angry industrial town where I came of age in the 1960s, I was scarcely noticeable against a backdrop of gang warfare, street knifings, and murders. I grew up one of the good boys, had perhaps a half-dozen fist fights. In retrospect, my shyness of combat has clear sources.

Many things go into the making of a young thug. One of those things is the consummation of the male romance with the power to intimidate. An infant discovers that random flailings send the baby bottle flying out of the crib and crashing to the floor. Delighted, the joyful babe repeats those motions again and again, seeking to duplicate the feat. Just so, I recall the points at which some of my boyhood friends were finally seduced by the perception of themselves as tough guys. When a mark cowered and surrendered his money without resistance, myth and reality merged—and paid off. It is, after all, only manly to embrace the power to frighten and intimidate. We, as men, are not supposed to give an inch of our lane on the highway; we are to seize the fighter's edge in work and in play and even in love; we are to be valiant in the face of hostile forces.

Unfortunately, poor and powerless young men seem to take all this nonsense literally. As a boy, I saw countless tough guys locked away; I have since buried several, too. They were babies, really—a teenage cousin, a brother of 22, a childhood friend in his mid-twenties—all gone down in episodes of bravado played out in the streets. I came to doubt the virtues of intimidation early on. I chose, perhaps even unconsciously, to remain a shadow—timid, but a survivor.

The fearsomeness mistakenly attributed to me in public places often has a perilous flavor. The most frightening of these confusions occurred in the late 1970s and early 1980s when I worked as a journalist in Chicago. One day, rushing into the office of a magazine I was writing for with a deadline story in hand, I was mistaken for a burglar. The office manager called security and, with an ad hoc posse, pursued me through the labyrinthine halls, nearly to my editor's door. I had no way of proving who I was. I could only move briskly toward the company of someone who knew me.

Another time I was on assignment for a local paper and killing time before an interview. I entered a jewelry store on the city's affluent near north side. The proprietor excused herself and returned with an enormous red Doberman pinscher straining at the end of a leash. She stood, the dog extended toward me, silent to my questions, her eyes bulging nearly out of her head. I took a cursory look around, nodded, and bade her good night. Relatively speaking, however, I never fared as badly as another black male journalist. He went to nearby Waukegan, Illinois, a couple of summers ago to work on a story about a murderer who was born there. Mistaking the reporter for the killer, police hauled him from his car at gunpoint and but for his press credentials would probably have tried to book him. Such episodes are not uncommon. Black men trade tales like this all the time.

In "My Negro Problem—And Ours," Podhoretz writes that the hatred he feels for blacks makes itself known to him through a variety of avenues—one being his discomfort with that "special brand of paranoid touchiness" to which he says blacks are prone. No doubt he is speaking here of black men. In time, I learned to smother the rage I felt at so often being taken for a criminal. Not to do so would surely have led to madness—via that special "paranoid touchiness" that so annoyed Podhoretz at the time he wrote the essay.

I am uneasy with the word "paranoid" in this context because the term refers to a delusionary state, something wholly imagined. But what do we say of a man who is driven to distraction by very real irritations, by a culture that consistently views him as sinister, for example? Since it isn't possible to unpack the entire issue here, we must let "paranoid" stand for the time being, even though it falls far short of describing the state of mind in question.

I take precautions to make myself less threatening. I move about with care, particularly in the late evening. I give a wide berth to nervous people on subway platforms during the wee hours, particularly when I have exchanged business clothes for jeans. If I happen to be entering a building behind some people who appear skittish, I may walk by, letting them clear the lobby before I return, so as not to seem to be following them. I have been calm and extremely congenial on those rare occasions when I've been pulled over by the police.

And on late-evening constitutionals along streets less traveled by, I employ what has proved to be an excellent tension-reducing measure: I whistle melodies from Beethoven and Vivaldi and the more popular classical composers. Even steely New Yorkers hunching toward nighttime destinations seem to relax, and occasionally they even join in the tune. Virtually everybody seems to sense that a mugger wouldn't be warbling bright, sunny selections from Vivaldi's *Four Seasons*. It is my equivalent of the cowbell that hikers wear when they know they are in bear country.

Interpretations

1. What evidence does Staples provide to make a convincing case that "being perceived as dangerous is a hazard in itself"?

2. ". . . some of my boyhood friends were finally seduced by the perception of themselves as tough guys." Do you think being perceived as tough has a natural attraction to boys and/or men of any race? What's the difference between virility (or manliness) and toughness?

3. To what extent does Staples think there is any justification for New York women's precautions against young black males?

4. Has our society had any success so far in reducing "touchiness" of blacks and the fears of whites? What more can be done? Does an essay like this one contribute to the solution or to the problem? Explain.

Correspondences

1. Review the Douglass perspective (page 352) and discuss its relevance to the selection by Staples.

2. Analyze the roles of ethnicity and class in the selections by Novak and Staples. What insights did you gain from reading about their experiences?

Applications

1. Discuss the precautions Staples takes to make himself less threatening. How do you respond to his reaction to the problem of "so often being taken for a criminal"? Does he exaggerate the problem? Is there a better solution—or precaution—than his?

2. Staples writes that "when fear and weapons meet . . . there is always the possibility of death." Which—fear or weapons—lies more within the control of society or the individual? Assuming we must start controlling one or the other, with which one do we have the best chance of beginning?

Opting for the Light

Jim Fusilli

Jim Fusilli (b. 1954) is a graduate of St. Peter's College in Jersey City. He has published essays in the Wall Street Journal *and the* New York Times Magazine *as well as in other periodicals. Here are his reasons for writing "Opting for the Light," a personal essay about his family's ethnic backgrounds: "I wrote 'Opting for the Light' for several reasons. I wanted to go beyond my customary critical essays. I hoped the experience would be cathartic (it was not), and I wanted to have something by way of explanation to show my Irish relatives and friends so they'd know there were reasons for the way I feel."*

IT IS A TRUTH long held among my family and friends that I hate being half Irish rather than fully Italian. It is not an unspoken truth. "You hate being Irish," a distant Irish relative recently snapped, because I said her granddaughter looked more like the girl's Italian father than her mother. And: "He is?" said the incredulous Italian wife of an Irish friend. "Yeah," replied the friend, "and he hates it."

There is but a morsel of truth in what they say. "Hate" would imply outright disdain for all things Irish, and I count among my favorite things Joyce's *Dubliners* and the evocative work of Van Morrison. I marvel at Shaw, admire the nationalist fervor of the Irish Renaissance, and relish Yeats's transcendental eloquence and his revision of the English romanticists, who, to me, somehow seem to have found their reverence of nature in the impossible beauty of the green Sheeffry Hills of County Mayo.

Nor can it be said that I don't love my mother or enjoy several other members of the Irish side of my family. My Irish grandmother was perhaps my favorite relative, witty and caustic, a lovable curmudgeon. I can hear her gravel voice now, and see the sheen of her silver hair, the pink frame of her eyeglasses. She was my mother's best friend and a friend of mine, ever present, seemingly as much a part of my life as my parents. (I never lived more than short walk from her until after college; we never took a vacation without her.) So deeply embedded was she in my life that on the way to the funeral home for her wake I paused to help her across the slippery pavement. For the first time, she was not there.

Further, several of my closest friends are Irish-Americans; their importance to me is immeasurable. And as a child, my hero was a family friend named Molloy, who seemed to me larger than life. He had a big black car with leather seats, and took me to see baseball games in Philadelphia. We cheered Jim Maloney and Jim O'Toole when the Reds came to town.

That said, I can't now deny that if there isn't genuine hate there is at least a deep resentment. For years, I refused to acknowledge it; no one likes a bigot, and I had worked hard to reject the bigotry that surrounded me as a child. (I never understood the sense of pride displayed by my aunt when she related how my Irish great-grandfather, a bartender, would shatter a glass after it was used by a black man.) To admit the resentment would have meant, at some point, to fall to a compulsion to further examine it. That, I knew, would be painful; "An intellectual hatred is the worst," Yeats thought. Briefly, I considered my "hate" the product of what I'd begun to see as a characteristic Irish-American self-loathing. It was plausible: Never did I not *know* that I was Irish; what was Irish in me was what in me was *wrong*.

But, no, despite knowing well what Joyce meant when he wrote, "All the indignities of his life enraged him," instead, I clung to a skittish belief that I simply preferred to be Italian, and was claiming a birthright. I want to be solely Italian, I had told myself, because Italians are wonderful: warm, gregarious, loving. I opted for the light.

Like scores of other seaport cities dotting the Northeast, my hometown was a hub for poor immigrants; the flood of Irish preceded the influx of Italians by several decades. By the time my grandfather arrived in 1903 as a little boy from Foggia, a town in Apulia in southern Italy, the city was largely populated by the Irish; the Irish lived uptown in brownstone houses with lace curtains, the Italians in the downtown tenements recently vacated by the Irish. Having suffered the indignities of prejudice—according to Lawrence J. McCaffrey's *The Irish Diaspora in America,* the Catholic Irish were considered by Anglo-Americans "belligerent, animal-like people with strong backs (and) weak minds" best suited for sports—the Irish seemed intent on heaping similar suffering on the new Italians. They ran City Hall and the police; they could do it, despite the teachings of the church to which they claimed allegiance.

Thus, in the late '40s, my mother was chided by her own for dating and then marrying an Italian, despite my father's reputation as a crooner in the Sinatra mold. (And my immigrant grandfather had a piece of his own small business: a barbershop at Twenty-Third and Seventh in the heart of Manhattan's fur district. He was, as he might have said, "no greenhorn.") As a youngster, I felt at odds straddling the two groups, and saw the tension as caused by the Irish. I remember my Italian grandparents as people who adored my mother—perhaps they saw the marriage of their oldest son as a sign of assimilation—and were baffled by her reserve. ("Cold Irish," I'm told, is the expression.) She almost never attended the splendid Sunday afternoon meals made by my grandmother—dubbed by me Nana Popone; I was her little *popone,* her little melon. My Irish uncles thought these meals were somehow comic—"Did you go to Nana Popone's for 'bisgetti'?" they'd mock. Those meals were magnificent. I can still smell the aroma of my grandmother's cooking as my father and I came up the stairs toward her small kitchen; the garlic simmering in olive oil, the fresh, pungent cheese, her remarkable tomato sauce. I can feel her sloppy kisses, and the huge hugs my grandfather— Papa Popone, of course—gave me. They had a one-eyed black bulldog who could eat an olive and leave behind the pit. My grandmother served me Hoffman's Cream Soda; *my* glass was purple, with a silver base. (How my grandmother wanted to please me; she always asked after my mother.) I loved it there; I resent having been made to feel that it was foolish.

I recall my father accepting the jibes of his Irish in-laws with grace; somehow, whether it was lighthearted or sharp-tongued, it *always* came up. The only time I can remember him exploding over a slight was when my red-headed cousin taunted *me.* (I didn't tell my father that while he was out of earshot my aunt also called me "guinea.") As for me, though we lived in an apartment complex uptown, I can recall only one boy who loved to taunt with ethnic slurs, but even as a child he was viewed as troubled. As for the sour mother of a neighbor who spit ethnic invectives at my friend Leonard Minervini at the 1964 New York World's Fair, I then attributed her misbehavior to a miserable disposition rather than a particular prejudice.

Much of the bias I felt was unspoken, and inferred. The prevailing attitude was that uptown was the preferred place to be and that the Irish had made it so; clearly, my Italian grandparents could not have lived comfortably there. Though I didn't mind my neighborhood—there was a black-topped alley behind the complex where my friends and I could play without worrying about cars and such— there was something appealing about the other. Downtown had a lovely aesthetic: the best food, boisterous shopkeepers, the friendliest people; it was loud, *alive.* (For me, a walk down New York's Carmine Street or in Boston's North End is a taste of the past.) Its two Catholic churches throughout the year sponsored a variety of "feasts"; there were oom-pah bands, zeppole, fireworks, green-white-and-red flags, and men in baggy suits carrying statues of saints. I sat on the curb and, surrounded by the crack and sizzle of sausage rings on open grills, ate fresh watermelon down to the rind. Priests in brown, flowing robes tied with rope played with little boys in short pants and scuffed black shoes.

Uptown turned up its nose at such behavior—at best, it was viewed with superior bemusement—there is nothing quite like Irish condescension—but I loved it. It was such a marked contrast. My parish priest, Father Meehan, was an austere man; the lapels of his black suit jacket were military crisp. Revelry was permitted in the alley, thankfully, but I recall a walk around the block required propriety, unless a fire hydrant had been opened, or Mr. Softee had arrived. I assume there was nightlife in my neighborhood—there must have been; there were four taverns at each intersection—but my memory is of looking out the window and seeing silence. A sense of forced dignity permeated us; today, nothing reminds me so much of uptown as a freshly made hotel room. Downtown, I knew, they were wrapped in joy.

As I grew older and expanded my world, I became less concerned with what the Irish thought of me. Most of my Irish family moved away, taking their jibes with them. With the advent of a maturing second generation, Italians became the political force in my town, thus making them less fashionable to openly mock. I went to a Catholic high school in a neighboring city; my peers were mostly Italians and Hispanics. My first steady girlfriend was Italian; her mother's kitchen reminded me of my grandmother's. My stance became one of Italian pride, and I believed I had struck it without rancor toward the Irish. By then, I almost never heard bitter ethnic insults, and no one knew I was half Irish. (Although, to my amazement, at a party with my mother's family, a cousin called *me* "cold Irish.") I didn't think it would ever be an issue again; at least if it was, I was no longer cluttered with confused feelings: Avoiding the mirror, I knew who I was.

After college, long after my steady girl and I had parted, for a brief time I dated a woman who was fiercely Irish; her father belonged to a Hibernia Club, a bar that did not reflect Irish pride so much as an affinity toward bias and intolerance. In their small home, there were musty pictures of saints and needlepoint samplers of Irish prayers on the wall; her father often drank until he fell. He would sleep in the bedroom that separated the tiny living room and kitchen; no one could speak above a whisper for he might awaken abruptly in a foul mood. No one would turn on the TV.

There was always tension between the two of us. I thought it was because I was five years older than his daughter, a college freshman. ("Oh, so you're a *man,*" he sneered when we first met.) But he worked weeknights, and I rarely saw him.

One rainy Saturday evening, there was a party at the Hibernia Club: hot dogs, sauerkraut, cabbage, cold salads. The jukebox played buoyant Irish jigs and baleful ballads. Since women were not allowed beyond the club's backroom, my girlfriend asked me to slip inside and fetch her mother and sister a few hot dogs, which sat in a steaming vat across the crowded bar. As I filled a plate, I heard the girl's father shout above the din, "Hey, look at the guinea going at the free food! No extra food for guineas!" There was great laughter; I died. I was seven years old again, and covered in shadows. I was ashamed of my grandmother and grandfather, the oom- pah bands and the gilded statues of saints; I live *uptown,* I wanted to shout.

That night, at that moment, the knot in my chest that had been gone for years returned.

Fifteen years later, it will not go away.

There is a picture of my grandmother and grandfather on my desk. They are holding me.

Interpretations

1. According to Fusilli, *Irish*-Americans, who themselves were once victims of discrimination by Anglo-Americans, tend to discriminate against blacks and later immigrant groups and use labels like "guinea." How common is this behavior among immigrant groups? How does it qualify the popular concept of America as a melting pot?

2. As he grew up, most of his Irish family moved away, and Fusilli thought he had solved his "Irish problem." How did he react to its resurfacing? (Explain the last line of the essay.)

3. Fusilli's first sentence sounds like a thesis statement. Does it in fact turn out to express his main point? If not, what is his thesis? At what point in the essay are you sure of it? What event confirms the thesis?

Correspondences

1. Fusilli focuses on bigotry within his own family. How does that affect his personal interactions? To what extent is his experience with ethnic bigotry similar to or different from Novak's?

2. Fusilli and Sadat (Chapter 2) were each raised by parents from different ethnic backgrounds. How did the cultural interactions of their parents affect their sense of ethnic identity and their concept of family?

Applications

1. Review the Fusilli biography (page 392) and his reasons for writing "Opting for the Light." Write an analysis of the personal and cultural implications of his interactions.

2. Consult dictionary and thesaurus definitions of *bigotry, prejudice, racism,* and *bias.* How do their connotations differ? To what extent is each the result of cultural conditioning?

An Indian/Irish
Interaction

Brian Delaney

Brian Delaney (b. 1963) was born in New York City to parents of Irish descent. In July 1991, he married a woman from Madras, India, first in a traditional Indian ceremony and two weeks later in a Catholic Mass. His wife is a school psychologist for the Board of Education in New York, and Brian is in the nursing program of the Catholic Medical Center.

AS A RESULT of having many discussions with my girlfriend, who is Indian, I have discovered that our upbringings differ a great deal. In traditional American families, there seems to be more freedom of choice than within the traditional Indian families.

The information that I obtained from my girlfriend and my personal observation of the Indian culture has given me insight into some of the traditions of her culture. Indians emphasize a good education, respect for their elders, and other figures of authority. My girlfriend, who grew up in the city of Madras in the southern part of India, has had the traditions of her culture forced upon her. As she was growing up, her father, like his father, set rules that molded every aspect of her life. Since there was not any real wealth in her family, the emphasis was on becoming the best person one can become. Her father was educated primarily in India and considered himself fortunate to have been given the chance to go to school, since the opportunity of going to school is a luxury, and not everyone in India can afford it.

In Indian culture children are not given much of a chance to develop social skills. My girlfriend was always told by her father that she was to come home from school and study. I am sure it was the same way for her brother and sister. Even in high school she was not allowed to visit a friend's house after school. Instead, she was allowed to have friends over to her house. But she was so ashamed of the strict manner in which her father treated her that she would never invite anyone. These traditions were instilled in her brother and sister as well. Their strict upbringing was maybe one of the reasons why her family as a unit has grown apart. Now that they are old enough to make their own decisions, they resent their father for depriving them of the right to make their own choices. This seems to be the outcome of having Indian traditions ingrained into a person who is being raised in an American society.

I do believe that the Indian father only wants what is best for his children. My girlfriend's father has raised two medical doctors and a psychologist. I think this is what he set out to do, and probably feels as though he has done a successful job of raising his children. The traditional Indian culture believes that once success is achieved, then happiness will follow. These same traditions that tend to drive the Indian families living in America apart are those I wish I had had more of in my Irish-American upbringing. In my childhood there were rules but they were lenient. My mother and father showed their love for me in a different manner. They wanted me to be happy and, therefore, allowed me greater freedom. In an American-Irish tradition, a lot of trust is placed in their children. In my family, the traditions were modeled for us to emulate rather than be enforced. This is where I was given the freedom to choose the traditional way (my parents' way) or my own. Either way, unless the outcome of my actions was hurtful or truly opposed their beliefs, I preferred to make my own decisions. In the Irish-American tradition, rather than the emphasis being placed on becoming a professional and a high achiever, the emphasis was on good judgment and on good moral character. In this respect, I feel that the traditions that were instilled in me were very important.

These traditions affect all aspects of our lives. I think that the traditional Irish-American family believes that if a child is given the sense of good judgment and trust a child will have all he or she needs to become a successful person.

I think traditions are a very important part of life and a balance between the Indian traditions and the Irish-American traditions would be a good way to raise children these days. The Indian traditions involving respect for elders, emphasis of education, and protectiveness along with the American traditions which allow greater freedom of choice and emphasis on trust would be a good way to raise strong independent individuals.

Interpretations

1. To what extend to you agree that Irish-Americans are less ambitious for their children than Indian-Americans? Which evidence from the essay best supports this idea?

2. Delaney's final paragraph calls for a balance between the Irish and the Indian ways of raising children. Do you think such a balance is possible? Why or why not? How, for example, would a family com-

bining Irish-Indian methods handle vocational plans for their children? What attitude might they take toward developing "social skills"?

3. What other areas of childraising would need to be "balanced" in an Indian-Irish household? What accommodations would be necessary and what success would you predict?

Correspondences

1. Jackson and Fairbank (Chapter 1) advocate reassessing traditions. To what extent does Delaney agree? What added dimension does he introduce as a result of his cultural interaction?

2. Contrast Fusilli's evaluation of Irish-American family life with that of Delaney. What factors might explain differences in their points of view?

Applications

1. Have you, like Delaney, had the opportunity to compare another culture's traditions and values? What attitudes did you modify as a result of this cultural interaction? Write an evaluation of your experience.

2. Discuss Delaney's thesis that "the traditional Indian culture believes that once success is achieved, happiness will follow." To what extent do you agree or disagree?

from A Life in Contrasts

Russell Howe

Russell Howe (b. 1925) was born in London, attended Cambridge University and the Sorbonne, and now lives in Washington, D.C. He has been foreign correspondent for Reuters and various newspapers, a professor at Dakar University in Senegal, and a media consultant. His writings include novels, diplomatic history, and travel accounts, of which The Koreans *(1988)— from which the following excerpt is taken—is an example.*

The Korea of which Howe writes is located in northeast Asia between China and Japan. It has played a prominent part in twentieth-century history and economics, and is now celebrated for its surge toward modernization, industrialization, and economic success. It traces its history at least to the first century B.C. and was a united kingdom by the seventh century. At times a vassal state to the Chinese Empire, it was forcibly annexed by Japan in 1910 and remained a Japanese colony until the end of World War II, when it was divided into North Korea and South Korea by the occupying troops of the Soviet Union and the United States. The Korean War (1950–1953) involved United States, UN, and South Korean troops against invading Chinese and North Koreans, with 157,000 U.S. casualties. College students have played significant roles in recent Korean politics, spearheading the resignation of the first President of the newly formed (1948) Republic of Korea Syngman Rhee in 1960. Korea was a police state under the next two presidents, but in 1987 students and middle-class office workers, shopkeepers, and business executives, following weeks of violence, forced a popular election in which Roh Tae Woo was elected president.

WHEN I FIRST CAME to Korea two decades ago, my host, the Food and Agriculture Organization of the United Nations, took me around the country to see projects connected with the peasant society which Korea was then still expected to remain. This afforded me a view of Korea which is disappearing and which, for the casual visitor, has disappeared already. Agricultural and fishing projects tend to be in remote places far from towns, places where there were then no modern hotels, in most places no traditional inn—*yŏgwan*—and sometimes not even a real *yŏ-in-suk,* or mom-and-pop guest house. My FAO escort and I would sleep on a thin *yo* of artificial sponge or on mats on the wood-heated floor, our heads on tiny *pe-gae* pillows filled with dried beans or barley husks. We would breakfast on a dozen or so minuscule traditional dishes, which nearly always included grasshoppers in a black-bean, sesame, garlic, and chili-pepper sauce. At the projects, the local official on whom we called would receive the visiting reporter with the self-abnegating grace of a West African chief; but instead of tumblers of schnapps he would offer barley tea, a beverage even more bland than American office coffee. Almost everyone wore traditional dress of white cotton.

Sometimes, I would be left to travel on my own, and once when I doubted my driver's ability to hurl a Toyota wagon through a mountain stream two feet deep, he promised to resign if he stalled in mid-current. He did it all in reverse—out of consideration for me, so that getting out of the torrent, if he failed, would be easier than getting in. On the other side, he checked the chassis and found no damage, bowed, and apologized for the discomfort. I bowed and apologized for doubting his skill and obvious experience. Today, the perfume of that sunset afternoon comes back; one surveys Seoul's cityscape conscious that this is a population made for the graces and also for the risks and relaxations of country life, yet inhabiting a megalopolis— not exactly unwillingly, but with reservations.

Other apparent contradictions abound: a high-fashion secretary with a poodle cut and Lancôme makeup waits at a yellow taxi shelter along with some elderly peasant from the countryside in his loose, off-white *chŏ-g'i* waistcoat, white raffia hat and pantaloons, or perhaps a long gray *paji* tied with a bow. Each understands the other more than each cares to admit. Close by, an expensive French restaurant run by Koreans with *cordon bleu* diplomas is neighbor to a noodle stall. A business administration graduate of Seoul National leaves his skyscraper office to prepare for his promotion interview with the boss by going to a *han-yak,* or traditional apothecary's shop, for a concoction that will make him, he hopes, alert or even brilliant. Both he and the high-fashion secretary, as well as the rice farmer in his country clothes, may have postponed everything from the day before—a fourth or thirteenth or twenty-second of the lunar month, therefore an unpropitious day for action. The young executive's boss may even have stayed away from the office the entire day, to avoid being led by his *in-yon,* or karma, into dire misfortune.

To prepare for his meeting, the young man has read W. Edwards Deming, Dale Carnegie, Galbraith and Schumacher (in pirated Korean editions, of course) and has prayed to Buddha and Jesus and conferred with his late father in meditation; and in order to go to a *han-yak,* he has had to resort to a thin subterfuge. Although it is the lunch hour, his immediate supervisor has stayed at his desk, meaning that none of his staff can decently leave their desks either. It is, however, acceptable to do so briefly if you stay behind in spirit, so the young executive has left his

gabardine raincoat and umbrella on the office hatstand, even though it
has started to rain.

In the *han-yak*, the apothecary takes down a few bottles with labels
handwritten in Chinese ideographs, the Latin of traditional Korean medicine. He mixes chrysanthemum seeds with some tree bark and the grated
brainbox of a frog. He pestles all this together and pours it into tamarind
juice. The drenched young man pays and swills the potion down on the
spot. Despite the expense, he also decides to ask for some deer horn
gratings. He and his girlfriend are going dancing in a psychedelic disco
that night; he has high hopes of what will follow, and wants to be at the
peak of his sexual powers. He hurries through the rain shower, back to
his office building, and is soon seated once more in front of his Samsung
computer, working on the new import contract proposals from Philadelphia and Bombay.

His supervisor finally leaves at eight P.M., and the staff make a dignified rush for the door two minutes, or one elevator run, later. The young
executive walks down a narrow street, pausing to watch a traditional
cloisonné artist at work in his shabby shop, which bears the official sign
that confirms that he is a government-recognized craftsman. The young
man's attention has been attracted by the fact that the artisan is using a
computer not much different from his own to compose a version of a
traditional graphic design for a vase.

Continuing on his way, the young man comes to a street stall where
he takes a seat along with other well-dressed businessmen, a housewife
with a child, and a couple of van drivers, and orders a bowl of *mae-un-
t'ang*, seafood and vegetables in a steaming broth. He drinks a pint of
so-ju with his dinner, then chews a breath deodorant. Now, it is dark
everywhere, but a department store is still open and he goes in to buy a
gift for his girl. The store resembles its counterparts in Paris or San
Francisco or Tokyo except that, as he steps onto the escalator, a sixteen-
year-old maiden in traditional Lyi dynasty *hanbok* dress bows to him, and
again to the woman customer behind him, thus completing her 5,137th
bow of the day.

You could spend an hour at a Tokyo bus stop in a freak electric storm, and
your sole neighbor in the shelter might never say a word to you. Only the
British are as covetous of their privacy. There is, however, a logical reason
preventing the Japanese from addressing a stranger: he cannot know *how*,
because the person *is* a stranger. Koreans share the same necessity to know
if you are superior, equal, or inferior; like the Japanese, they would prefer
to know what you do and what rank you occupy in your company or
profession. And in this, you cannot be too precise. There are, for instance,
different words in both languages for *writer*, according to whether you
write fiction or nonfiction. There is no word for *broadcaster*; one has to
be more specific—radio? television? scriptwriter? anchorperson?

But the Koreans have a solution which few Japanese would attempt. They ask questions. They are curious. They *stare*. Other Asian peoples may appear inscrutable to us, and us to them, but the Koreans are not inscrutable. They dare not be, because they *scrute*. Those of us who had mothers who wisely boxed our ears if we focussed our gaze on a passerby with only one arm, or an oriental face, or who had just fallen facedown in a puddle, are startled by the unabashed inquisitiveness everywhere in Korea, in spite of the general insistence on *mŏt*— manners, taste. Even shy sales assistants will ask about your work, your family situation, your age—the latter being an important determinant in societal rank. All Koreans go up one rank in prestige every year; they even start with a bonus—time in the womb counts as the first year of life, so that you are born at the age of one. Moreover, all birthdays occur on the lunar new year: if you are born in December, you are two almost before you can even gurgle.

Modern Japanese comedy films like *Tampōpo* or *The Family Game* are as daring in their environment as the first erotic photo-essay magazines in America a generation or so ago; but in Korea, humor is endemic. Although the slapstick of television kitchen-sink comedies and soap operas borrows routines from Tinseltown, the genre was always there. However, like most people who love clowning, Koreans are sad and stoical at heart; the vague-à-l'âme courses through every artery of Korean life. If your taxi driver switches on his radio, and you are not forced to listen to outdated Western rhythms, you will hear Korean pop music as sad as Portuguese fado. Understanding the words isn't necessary. The themes are those of American country music: lovers and mistresses are ever unfaithful, absent, or gone forever; and as the voice of the singer breaks with spurious emotion, you usually hear the word *nun-mul* (eye-water). What other language has an onomatopoeic for sobbing? For that matter, in what other tongue do birds or bells weep instead of singing or pealing?

This is, at base, a Confucian society. The most important relationship was always between father and son, followed by ruler and subject, then husband and wife, then elders and youth, then loyalty between friends. The first four are different forms of the same. The second relationship, that of ruler and subject, which successive militaro-republican regimes have sought to exploit in recent times, is increasingly challenged in an era when the taxpayer has ascended the throne and begun to assert that generals are nothing more than armed usurpers.

The quality of loyalty, as important to Koreans as to Turks or Scots, is commanded by more than blood and friendship. As in Africa, there is an automatic kithship involving loyalties between classmates—people of the same age who have gone through high school, military service, university and so on together. In 1987, a great debate emerged as to how President Chon Du-hwan, before he retired, would ensure that all his fellow-members of the eleventh graduating class of the Military Academy would have suitable civil posts to take care of their military retirement years.

However, social rank, including rank by age, is primordial. Superiors—or elders—go first. For instance, a husband enters a taxi, bus, or theater ahead of his wife. There are five different ways of saying he and she, according to whether the person is an elder or an employer or, at the other end of the scale, a child or a servant. As in French, the way an officer speaks to a soldier, or a farmer to his laborers, or a policeman to a pimp, is also the way you address a colleague when you finally recognize him as a close friend, or a member of the opposite sex when you want to convey a trembling heart.

For twelve and a half centuries, from 667 to 1905, when Korea became a Japanese protectorate, much of the battle for rank revolved around the annual civil service examinations, prepared for by rote learning, Chinese fashion. These examinations assigned literate Koreans to their rung on the social ladder. This Confucian concept of the *yang-ban* (member of the gentry) has given way to the global ethos of our meritocratic era; but militarism has often replaced Confucianism, and the university or military college entrance examinations are now the master keys of the career gate. Two-thirds of all who take them fail; there is usually only one second chance a year later, and that's it! And even passing successfully doesn't guarantee a place. The old Confucian exams could be taken over and over again, into old age, and people who never passed still pridefully noted their improved scores every year.

Chinese influence also remains in the ideograph, still used alongside the Korean *han-gŭl* alphabet in publications, because ideographs distinguish between different meanings for the same word and also make for briefer headlines and titles. As in Japan, a high school student must learn eighteen hundred Chinese characters to graduate.

These days, of course, he or she must also study English, from middle school on, with its vastly more illogical alphabet than *han-gŭl,* its often confusingly dissimilar "big" and "small" letters, its seven different ways of pronouncing *-ough,* its differences between Standard English and Indian English and American English, its galaxy of geographical accents, and so on. There are also lessons on how to use a knife and fork: Koreans must be the only East Asians who sometimes prefer to eat rice with a spoon instead of *jŏtgarak,* chopsticks.

Interpretations

1. Russell says "apparent contradictions abound" in Korea. Contradictions between what? Would you call them contradictions, cultural crossings, or perhaps just interactions? In the hypothetical day in the life of the young business executive, what are the most obvious "contradictions"?

2. Compare Korean, Japanese, and American interactions with strangers. Why do you think Howe makes the comparison?

3. Why has cultural crossing apparently always been a feature of Korean life? What has been the effect of this crossing on Korea and on her neighbors?

4. What's the evidence that Howe aims to entertain as well as inform? Do you see a plan or organization to his arrangement of detail, or is it random? Do you think he gives enough detail to satisfy his purpose in writing? If not, where would you like to see more detail?

5. What is the tone of this essay? What do you think is Howe's purpose in writing? What is the tone of the concocted word *scrute?* Although he uses both words, which word better suits Howe's purpose in describing Korean life, *contradictions* or *contrasts?* What is the connotation of each? Is his use of both words confusing? Why or why not?

6. In explaining that Korea is "a Confucian society," Howe describes various relationships and paths to advancement. How different are these relationships and paths from the ones Americans are familiar with? How are they similar?

Correspondences

1. Howe and Jhabvala discuss marriage. What evidence is there of patriarchy in both selections? How does the marriage of the Englishwoman compare to that of Guppy's parents (Chapter 1) in another patriarchal culture?

2. Review Goldberg's perspective (page 353) and discuss its application to Howe's essay.

Applications

1. According to Howe, Korea is currently involved in an interaction between the traditions of the past and the intrusions of the present. What evidence does he offer to support his point of view? Which cultural interactions might prove most difficult to reconcile?

2. Write a journal entry about an interaction in which you were involved that affirmed or contradicted Benedict's perspective that "culture is that which binds men together."

The Englishwoman

Ruth Prawer Jhabvala

Ruth Prawer Jhabvala (b. 1927) was born in Cologne, Germany, emigrated to England in 1939, and became a British citizen in 1948. She married C.S.H. Jhabvala, an architect, in 1951, and currently lives in New York. They have three children. She has published many novels—among them Amrita *(1956),* The Nature of Passion *(1956),* The Householder *(1960), and* Three Continents *(1988)—and many collections of stories. Her screenplays include* A Passage to India *and* Room with a View, *for which she won an Academy Award in 1987. In "The Englishwoman" she returns to a prevalent theme in her writings, being an outsider in an Indian family.*

The India to which Jhabvala moved from England in 1951 had just (in 1947) declared its independence from the British, who had controlled most of India for about 300 years. Colonial India had at the same time been partitioned into Pakistan and India, creating in the same year about 12 million Hindu and Muslim refugees, of whom about 200,000 were killed. Mohandas K. Gandhi (known as the Mahatma), the leader of Indian independence who had advocated nonviolent civil disobedience and abolition of the Untouchable caste, was assassinated the year after independence. The Congress Party dominated Indian politics for forty years (from Independence until late 1989) under Prime Ministers Jawaharlal Nehru, his daughter Indira Gandhi (no relation to Mohandas), and her son Rajiv Gandhi. Indian history, one of the oldest in the world, can be traced to at least 5,000 B.C. The founder of Buddhism lived in 5th-century India. In the 3rd century B.C. Buddhism became the established religion; the native Hinduism revived, however, and eventually prevailed, and now claims well over three-quarters of the Indian population of 800 million.

THE ENGLISHWOMAN—her name is Sadie—was fifty-two years old when she decided to leave India. She could hardly believe it. She felt young and free. At fifty-two! Her bag is packed and she is running away. She is eloping, leaving everything behind her—husband, children, grandchildren, thirty years of married life. Her heart is light and so is her luggage. It is surprising how few things she has to take with her. Most of her

406

clothes are not worth taking. These last years she has been mostly wearing dowdy cotton frocks sewn by a little turbaned tailor. She still has a few saris but she is not taking them with her. She doesn't ever intend to wear those again.

The person who is crying the most at her impending departure is Annapurna, her husband's mistress. Annapurna has a very emotional nature. She looks into the packed bag; like Sadie, she is surprised by its meager contents. "Is that all you are taking with you?" she asks. Sadie answers, "It's all I've got." Annapurna breaks into a new storm of tears.

"But that's good," Sadie urges. "Not to accumulate things, to travel light—what could be better?"

"Oh, you're so spiritual," Annapurna tells her, wiping her eyes on the other's sleeve. "Really you are far more Indian than I am."

"Nonsense," Sadie says, and she means it. What nonsense.

But it is true that if Indian means "spiritual"—as so many people like to believe—then Annapurna is an exception. She is a very, very physical sort of person. She is stout, with a tight glowing skin, and shining eyes and teeth, and hair glossy with black dye. She loves clothes and jewelry and rich food. Although she is about the same age as the Englishwoman, she is far more vigorous, and when she moves, her sari rustles and her bracelets jingle.

"But are you really going?"

Annapurna keeps asking this question. And Sadie keeps asking it of herself too. But they ask it in two very different ways. Annapurna is shocked and grieved (yes, grieved—she loves the Englishwoman). But Sadie is incredulous with happiness. Can it really be true? she keeps asking herself. I'm going? I'm leaving India? Her heart skips with joy and she has difficulty in repressing her smiles. She doesn't want anyone to suspect her feelings. She is ashamed of her own callousness—and yet she goes on smiling, more and more, and happiness wells up in her like a spring.

Last week she went to say goodbye to the children. They are both settled in Bombay now with their families. Dev, her son, has been married for two years and has a baby girl; Monica, the daughter, has three boys. Dev has a fine job with an advertising company; and Monica is working too, for she has too much to drive to be content with just staying at home. She calls herself a go-go girl and that is what she is, charging around town interviewing people for the articles she writes for a women's magazine, talking in the latest slang current in Bombay, throwing parties of which she herself is the life and soul. Monica looks quite Indian—her eyes are black, her skin glows; she is really more like Annapurna than like the Englishwoman, who is gaunt and pale.

Although so gay, Monica also likes to have serious discussions. She attempted to have such a discussion with her mother. She said, "But, Mummy, *why* are you going?" and she looked at her with the special serious face she has for serious moments.

Sadie didn't know what to answer. What could she say? But she had to say something, or Monica would be hurt. So she too became solemn, and she explained to her daughter that when people get older they begin to get very homesick for the place in which they were born and grew up and that this homesickness becomes worse and worse till in the end life becomes almost unbearable. Monica understood what she said and sympathised with it. She made plans how they would all come and visit her in England. She promised that when the boys became bigger, she would send them to her for long holidays. She was now in full agreement with her mother's departure, so Sadie was glad she told her what she did. She was prepared to tell Dev the same thing if he asked her, but he didn't ask. He and his wife were rather worried in those days because there was an outbreak of chicken pox in their apartment building and they were afraid Baby might catch it. But they too promised frequent visits to her in England.

Only Annapurna is still crying. She looks at Sadie's little suitcase and cries, and then she looks at Sadie and cries. She keeps asking, "But why, *why?*" Sadie tries to tell her what she told Monica, but Annapurna waves her aside; for her it is not a good enough reason and she is right, Sadie herself knows it isn't. She asks wouldn't Sadie miss all of them and their love for her, and wouldn't she miss the life she has lived and the place in which she has lived it, her whole past, everything she has been and done for thirty years? Thirty years! she cries, again and again, appalled—and Sadie too is appalled, it is such a long time. Annapurna says that an Indian wife also yearns for her father's house, and at the beginning of her marriage she is always waiting to go off there to visit; but as the years progress and she becomes deeper and deeper embedded in her husband's home, these early memories fade till they are nothing more than a sweet sensation enshrined in the heart. Sadie knows that what Annapurna is saying is true, but also that it does not in the least apply in her own case because her feelings are not ones of gentle nostalgia.

The Englishwoman doesn't like to remember the early years when she first came to live here. It is as if she wished to disown her happiness then. How she loved everything! She never gave a backward glance to home or England. Her husband's family enjoyed and abetted her attempts to become Indian. A whole lot of them—mother-in-law, sister-in-law, aunts, cousins and friends—would cram into the family car (with blue silk curtains discreetly drawn to shield them from view) and drive to the bazaar to buy saris for Sadie. She was never much consulted about their choice, and when they got home, she was tugged this way and that while they argued with each other about the best way to drape it round her. When they had finished, they stood back to admire, only instead of admiring they often could not help sailing at her appearance. She didn't care. Yes, she knew she was too tall for the sari, and too thin, and too English, but she loved wearing it and to feel herself Indian. She also made attempts to learn Hindi, and this too amused everyone and they never tired of making her repeat certain words, going into peals of laughter at her pronunciation. Everyone, all the ladies of the household, had a lot of fun. They were healthy, rich and gay. They were by no means a tradition-bound family, and although their life in the house did have something of the enclosed, languorous quality of purdah living, the minds flowering within it were full of energy and curiosity. The mother-in-law herself, at that time well over sixty, spent a lot of her time reading vernacular novels, and she also attempted to write some biographical sketches of her own, describing life in a high-caste household in the 1880s. She took to smoking cigarettes quite late in life and liked them so much that she ended up as a chain-smoker. When Sadie thinks of her, she sees her reclining on an embroidered mat spread on the floor, one elbow supported on a bolster, some cushions at her back, reading a brown tattered little volume through her glasses and enveloping herself in clouds of scented cigarette smoke.

Annapurna often speaks about those days. Annapurna was a relative, some sort of cousin. She had run away from her husband (who drank and, it was whispered, went in for unnatural practices) and had come to live with them in the house. When Annapurna speaks about those distant times, she does so as if everyone were still alive and all of them as young and gay as they were then. Often she says, "If only Srilata [or Radhika—or Raksha—or Chandralekha] were here now, how she would laugh!" But Srilata died of typhoid twenty yens ago; Raksha married a Nepalese general and has gone to live in Kathmandu; Chandralekha poisoned herself over an unhappy love affair. To Annapurna, however, it is as if everyone is still there and she recalls and brings to life every detail of a distant event so that to Sadie too it begins to appear that she can hear the voices of those days. Till Annapurna returns to the present and with an outstretched hand, her plump palm turned up to heaven, she acknowledges that they are all gone and many of them are dead; and she turns and looks at the Englishwoman and says, "And now you are going too," and her eyes are full of reproach.

It may seem strange that the mistress should reproach the wife, but Annapurna is within her rights to do so. For so many years now it is she who has taken over from the Englishwoman all the duties of a wife. There has never been any bitterness or jealousy between them. On the contrary, Sadie has always been grateful to her. She knows that before her husband became intimate with Annapurna, he used to go to other women. He *had* to go; he was such a healthy man and needed women as strong and healthy as he was. These were often young prostitutes. But for a long time now he has been content with Annapurna. He has put on an enormous amount of weight in these last years. It is Annapurna's fault; she feeds him too well and panders to his passion for good food. His meals are frequent and so heavy that in between them, he is not capable of moving. He lies on a couch arranged for him on a verandah and breathes heavily. Sometimes he puffs at a hookah which stands within easy reach. He lies there for hours while Annapurna sits on the other end of the couch and entertains him with lively gossip. He enjoys that, but doesn't mind at all if she has no time for him. When he feels like talking, he summons one of the servants to come and squat on the carpet near his couch.

When Sadie first knew him, as a student at Oxford, he was a slim boy with burning eyes and a lock of hair on his forehead. He was always smiling and always on the go. He loved being a student, and though he never managed to graduate, got a lot out of it. He gave breakfast parties and had his own wine merchant and a red car in which he drove up to London several times a week; he was always discovering new pleasures, like hampers from Fortnum and Mason's and champagne parties on the river. Sadie had grown up in rather an austere atmosphere. Her family were comfortably off but had high principles of self-restraint and preferred lofty thought to lavish living. Sadie herself—a serious girl, a spare, stringent, high-bred English beauty—thought she had the same principles, but the young Indian made her see another side to her nature. When he went back to India, it was impossible to stay behind. She followed him, married him, and loved him even more than she had in England. He belonged here so completely. Sometimes Sadie didn't see him for days on end—when he went on shooting parties and other expeditions with his friends—but she didn't mind. She stayed at home with the other women and enjoyed life as much as he did. There were summer nights when they all sat out in the garden by the fountain, and Chandralekha, who had a very sweet voice, sang sad songs from the hills while Radhika accompanied her on a lutelike instrument; and the moon shone, and Annapurna cut up mangoes for all of them, and the smell of these mangoes mingled with that exuding from the flowering bushes in a mixture so pungent, so heady, that when the Englishwoman recalls those nights now, it is always by their scent that they become physical and present to her.

Annapurna and Sadie's husband play cards every evening. They play for money and Annapurna usually loses and then she gets cross; she always refuses to pay up, and the next evening they conveniently forget her debt and start again from scratch. But if he loses, then she insists on immediate payment: she laughs in triumph, and holding out her hand, opens and shuts it greedily and shouts, "Come on, pay up!" She also calls to Sadie and the servants to witness his discomfiture; those evenings are always merry. But sooner or later, and often in the middle of a game, she falls asleep. Once Annapurna is asleep, everything is very quiet. The servants turn off the lights and go to their quarters; the husband sits on his couch and looks out into the garden and takes a few puffs at his hookah; Sadie is upstairs in her bedroom. Nothing stirs, there isn't a sound, until the husband gives a loud sigh as he heaves himself up. He wakes Annapurna and they support each other up the stairs to their bedroom, where they sink onto their large, soft bed and are asleep immediately and totally until it is morning. It is a long time before Sadie can get to sleep. She walks up and down the room. She argues with herself to and fro, and her mind heaves in turmoil like a sea in storm. The fact that everything else is calm and sleeping exacerbates her restlessness. She longs for some response, for something or someone other than herself to be affected by what is going on within her. But there is only silence and sleep. She steps out of her room and onto the verandah. The garden is in imperfect darkness, dimly and fitfully lit by the moon. Occasionally—very, very occasionally—a bird wakes up and rustles in a tree.

It was during these hours of solitude that she came to her decision to leave. To others—and at the actual moment of making it, even to herself—it seemed like a sudden decision, but in fact, looking back, she realizes that she has been preparing for it for twenty years. She can even mark the exact day, twenty years ago, when first she knew that she did not want to go on living here. It was when her son was sick with one of those sudden mysterious illnesses that so often attack children in India. He lay burning in the middle of a great bed, with his eyes full of fever; he was very quiet except for an occasional groan. All the women in the house had gathered round his bedside and all were giving advice and different remedies. Some sat on chairs, some on the floor; the mother-in-law squatted crosslegged on the end of his bed; her spectacles on her nose, smoking cigarettes and turning the pages of a novel; from time to time she made soothing noises at Dev and squeezed his ankles. Annapurna sat by his side and rubbed ice on his head. Every time Dev groaned they all said, "Oh, poor Baba, poor Baba." The servants moved in and out; they too said, "Oh, poor Baba," and looked at him pityingly. The Englishwoman remembered the sickbeds of her own childhood, how she lay for hours comfortable and bored with nothing to do except watch the tree outside the window and the fat wet raindrops squashing against and sliding down the window-pane. The only person who ever came in was her mother, when it was time for her medicine. But Dev wouldn't have liked that. He wanted everyone with him, and if one of the aunts was out of the room for too long a time, he would ask for her in a weak voice and someone would have to go and fetch her.

Sadie went out onto the verandah. But it was no better there. The day was one of these murky yellow ones when the sun is stifled in vapours of dust. She felt full of fears, for Dev and for herself, as if they were both being sucked down by—what was it? the heat? the loving women inside? the air thick as a swamp in which fevers breed? She longed to be alone with her sick child in some cool place. But she knew this was not possible and that they belonged here in this house crammed full with relatives and choking under a yellow sky. She could never forget the despair of that moment, though in the succeeding years there were many like it. But that was the first.

As she stood there on the verandah, she saw her husband arrive home. He was a very bright spot in that murky day. He was dressed in a starched white kurta with little jewels for buttons, and his face was raised towards her as she stood up on the verandah, and he was smiling. He was no longer the slim boy she had first known but neither was he as fat as he is today: no, he was in the prime of life then, and what a prime! He came bounding up the outside staircase toward toward her and said, "How is he?"

"How can he be," she answered, "with all of them in there?"

Surprised at her tone, he stopped smiling and looked at her anxiously. Her anger mounted, and there were other things mixed in with it now: not only the heat and the overcrowded room but also that he was so sleek and smiling and young while she—oh, she felt worn out, wrung out, and knew she looked it. She thought of the prostitutes he went to. It seemed to her that she could see and smell their plump, brown, wriggling young bodies greasy with scented oil.

In a shaking voice she said, "They're stifling that poor boy—they won't let him breathe. No one seems to have the least idea of hygiene."

He knew it was more than she was saying and continued to look at her anxiously. "Are you ill?" he asked and put out his hand to feel her forehead. When she drew back, he asked, "What is it?" full of sympathy.

They had been speaking in low voices, but all the same from inside the crowded room Annapurna had sensed that something was wrong. She left the bedside and came out to join them. She looked enquiringly at Sadie's husband. They were not yet lovers at the time, but there was that instinctive understanding between them there was between all the members of that household.

"She is not well," he said.

"I *am* well! I'm perfectly well!" Sadie burst into tears. She had no control over this. Furiously she wiped the foolish tears from her cheeks.

Both of them melted with tenderness. Annapurna folded her in an embrace; the husband stroked her back. When she struggled to get free, they thought it was a new outbreak of anguish and redoubled their attentions. At last she cried, "It's so *hot!*" and indeed she could hardly breathe and perspiration ran down her in runnels from her being squashed against fat Annapurna. Then Annapurna let her go. They both stood and looked at her, full of anxiety for her; and these two round healthy shining faces looking at her with love, *pitying* her, were so unbearable to her that, to prevent herself from bursting into the tears that she despised but that they, she knew, not only awaited but even expected, she turned and, hurrying along the verandah that ran like a gallery all round the house, she hid herself in her bedroom and locked the door. They followed and knocked urgently and begged to be allowed to enter. She refused to open. She could hear them discussing her outside the door: they were full of understanding; they realized that people did get upset like this and that then it was the duty of others to soothe and help them.

She was always being soothed and helped. She is still being soothed and helped. Annapurna has taken everything out of her suitcase and is repacking it in what she considers is a better way. She has had special shoe bags sewn. As a matter of fact, she would like to have a completely new outfit of clothes made for her. She says how will it look if Sadie arrives with nothing better than those few shabby rags in that little suitcase? Sadie thinks silently to herself: Look to whom? She knows almost no one there. A few distant relatives, one old school friend; she hasn't been there for thirty years, she has no contacts, no correspondence—and yet she is going home! Home! And again happiness rushes over her in waves, and she takes a deep breath to be able to bear it.

"And not a single piece of jewelry," Annapurna grumbles.

Sadie laughs. She has given it all away long ago to Monica and to Dev's wife: and very glad she was to get rid of all those heavy costly gold ornaments. They were her share of the family jewels, but she never knew what to do with them. Certainly she couldn't wear them—she was always too thin and pale to be able to carry off those pieces fit for a barbarian queen; so she had left them lying around for years in a cupboard till Annapurna had taken them away from her to lock up in a safe.

"At least *one* piece you could have let me keep for you," Annapurna now says. "Then you would have had something to show them. What will they think of us?"

"What will *who* think?" Sadie asks, and the idea of the distant relatives and her poor school friend (Clare, still unmarried and still teaching) having any thoughts on the subject of what properties she has brought back with her from India makes her laugh again. And there is a lightheartedness in her laughter that hasn't been there for a long time, and Annapurna hears it and is hurt by it.

They are both hurt by her attitude. It has been years since Sadie saw her husband so upset; but then it has been years since anything really upset him. He has led a very calm life lately. Not that his life was not always calm and comfortable, but there were times in his younger days when he, like everyone else in the house, had his outbursts. She particularly remembers one he had with his sister Chandralekha. Actually, at that time, the whole house was in upheaval. Chandralekha had formed an unfortunate attachment to a man nobody approved of. They were not a rigid family that way—there had been several love matches—but it seemed Chandralekha's choice was entirely unsuitable. Sadie had met the man, who struck her as intelligent and of a strong character. In fact, she thought Chandralekha had shown excellent taste. But when she told her husband so, he waved her aside and said she didn't understand. And it was true, she didn't; everything that went on in the house during those days was a mystery to her. Oh, she understood vaguely what it was all about—the man was of *low birth,* and all his virtues of character and self-made position could not wipe that stain away—but the passions that were aroused, the issues that were thought to be at stake, were beyond her comprehension. Yet she could see that all of them were suffering deeply, and Chandralekha was in a torment of inner conflict (indeed, she later committed suicide).

One day Chandralekha came in carrying a dish of sweet rice which she had made herself. She said, "Just wait till you taste this," and she lovingly ladled a spoonfull onto her brother's plate. He began to eat with relish, but quite suddenly he pushed the plate away and began to cry out loud. Everyone at once knew why, of course. The only person who was surprised was Sadie— both at the suddenness of the outburst and at the lengths to which he went. He banged his head against the wall, flung himself on the ground at Chandralekha's feet, and at one point he snatched up a knife and held it at his own throat and had to have it wrested away from him by all the women there surrounding him. "The children, the children!" he kept crying, and at first Sadie thought he meant their own children, Monica and Dev, and she couldn't understand what was threatening them; but everyone else knew he meant Chandralekha's children who were yet unborn but who would be born, and if she married this man, born with polluted blood. Sadie didn't know how that scene ended; she went away and locked herself up in her bedroom. She covered her ears with her hands to shut out the noise and cries that echoed through the house.

When he learned of her decision to leave, Sadie's husband begged and pleaded with her in the same way he had done with Chandralekha all those years ago. The Englishwoman felt embarrassed and ashamed for him. He looked so ridiculous, being so heavy and fat, with his great bulk heaving, and emitting cries like those of a hysterical woman. No one else found him ridiculous—on the contrary, the servants and Annapurna were deeply affected by his strong emotions and tried to comfort him. But he wouldn't be comforted till in the end his passion spent itself. Then he became resigned and even quite practical and sent for his lawyer to make a settlement. He was very generous toward his wife, and indeed keeps pressing her to accept more and is distressed because she doesn't need it. So now she feels ashamed not of him but of herself and her own lack of feeling.

It is her last night in India. As usual, her husband and Annapurna are playing cards together. When she joins them, they look at her affectionately and treat her like a guest. Annapurna offers tea, sherbet, lime water, and is distressed when she declines all these suggestions. She is always distressed by the fact that Sadie needs less food than she does. She says, "How can you live like that?" After a moment's thought, she adds, "How

will you live *there?* Who will look after you and see that you don't starve
yourself to death?" When Sadie looks at her it is as she feared: tears are
again flowing down Annapurna's cheeks. A sob also breaks from out of
her bosom. It is echoed by another sob: Sadie looks up and sees that tears
are also trickling down her husband's face. Neither of them speaks, and
in fact they go on playing cards. The Englishwoman lowers her eyes away
from them; she sits there, silent, prim, showing no emotion. She hopes
they think she *has* no emotion; she does her best to hide it—the happiness that will not be suppressed, even at the sight of their tears.

Annapurna has had enough of playing. She flings down the cards
(she has been losing). She wipes her tears away with her forearm like a
child, yawns, sighs, says, "Well, time to go to bed," in resignation. He
says, "Yes, it's time," with the same sigh and the same resignation. They
have accepted the Englishwoman's departure; it grieves them, but they
submit to it, as human beings have to submit to everything, such as old
age and disease and loss of every kind. They walk upstairs slowly,
leaning on each other.

When Sadie goes up to her own room, she is almost running in her
excitement. She looks in the mirror and is surprised at the drained face
that looks back at her. She doesn't feel like that at all—no, she feels the
way she used to do, so that now she expects her bright eyes back again
and her pink cheeks. She turns away from the mirror, laughing at her own
foolishness; and she can hear her own laughter and it is just the way it
used to be. She knows she won't sleep tonight. She doesn't want to sleep.
She loves this feeling of excitement and youth and to pace the room with
her heart beating and wild thoughts storming in her head. The servants
have turned out the lights downstairs and gone to bed. The lights are out
in her husband and Annapurna's room too; they must be fast asleep, side
by side on their bed.

The Englishwoman can't see the moon, but the garden is lit up by
some sort of faint silver light. She can make out the fountain with the
stone statue, and the lime trees, and the great flowering bush of Queen
of the Night; there is the bench where they used to sit in the evenings
when Chandralekha sang in her sweet voice. But as she goes on looking,
the moonlit scene brightens until it is no longer that silver garden but
English downs spreading as far as the eye can see, yellow on one side,
green on another. The green side is being rained upon by mild soft rain
coming down like a curtain, and the yellow side is being shone upon by
a sun as mild and soft as that rain. On a raised knoll in the foreground
there is an oak tree with leaves and acorns, and she is standing by this
tree; and as she stands there, on that eminence overlooking the downs,
strong winds blow right through her. They are as cold and fresh as the
waters of a mountain torrent. They threaten to sweep her off her feet so
that she has to plant herself down very firmly and put out her hand to
support herself against the trunk of the tree (she can feel the rough

texture of its bark). She raises her face, and her hair—not *her* hair but the shining hair of her youth—flies wild and free in that strong wind.

Interpretations

1. Sadie's decision to leave India is connected in her mind with what happened to her son when he was sick twenty years ago. Why does she feel such despair? What aspects of Indian culture does she find most difficult to accept?

2. To what extent does her husband's relationship with Annapurna contribute to the decision?

3. Why does Jhabvala use the generic "The Englishwoman" as a title instead of "Sadie"? What is the difference in implication?

4. Why is Sadie's husband never given a name or allowed to speak, except in one scene?

5. What is Jhabvala's purpose in writing this story?

Correspondences

1. Jhabvala's Englishwoman is ambivalent about India, her adopted country. How does her ambivalence affect her personality, family and choices? Contrast her reaction to India with that of Sadat's mother (Chapter 2), also English, to Egypt, her adopted country. What factors might account for the differences in their reactions?

2. Rank and social class are important in Korean culture (Howe), while the caste system is an integral part of Indian society (Jhabvala). What role does social rank play in the social interactions in each selection?

Applications

1. The Englishwoman felt alienated in India. Have you also ever felt like a stranger in a different environment? How did cultural differences contribute to your alienation? Describe the place, then analyze the experience and its effects.

2. According to the Englishwoman, she and Annapurna had never been jealous of each other. Do you find this plausible? To what extent does the account of their social interactions refute or support her assertion?

A Few Pointers

James Fallows

James Fallows was born in Philadelphia in 1949 and graduated from Harvard University in 1970. He worked as an editor of the Washington Monthly *and the* Texas Monthly *and for two years was speech writer for President Jimmy Carter. His latest book,* More Like Us: Making America Great Again *(1989), which takes the reader on a tour of Japan and other Asian countries, grew out of three years' residence with his wife and two sons in Malaysia and Japan. A regular broadcaster on National Public Radio, Fallows is Washington editor of* The Atlantic Monthly.

LIVING IN A FOREIGN culture is, most of the time, exhilarating and liberating. You don't have to feel responsible for the foibles of your temporary home; you can forget about the foibles of your real home for a while. Your life seems longer, because each day is dense with new and surprising experiences. I can remember distinctly almost every week of the past three and a half years. The preceding half dozen years more or less run together in a blur.

But there is also distress in foreign living, particularly in living in Asia at this time in its history. It comes not from daily exasperations, which after all build character, but from the unsettling thoughts that living in Asia introduces. As I head for home, let me mention the thought that disturbs me most.

It concerns the nature of freedom: whether free societies are fit to compete, in a Darwinian sense. Until the repression in China last summer [1989], many Westerners assumed that the world had entered an era of overall progress. True, environmental problems were getting worse rather than better, and many African and Latin American societies were still in bad shape. But in Asia it seemed possible to believe that people had learned how to make their societies both richer and freer year by year. As countries in Asia became more advanced and prosperous, they loosened their political controls—and as the controls came off, economic progress speeded up. This was the moral of the Korean and Taiwanese success stories, as those countries evolved toward the ideal set by stable, prosperous Japan. Even China, before the summer [of 1989], seemed to be loosening up, both economically and politically. China's crackdown made the spread of democracy and capitalism seem less certain than it had seemed before, but even this step backward confirmed the idea that political freedoms and economic progress were naturally connected. Everyone assumes that as China makes its political system more repressive, its economy will stagnate.

I draw a darker conclusion from the rise of the Asian economies. The economic success stories of Asia do not prove that political freedom and material progress go hand in hand. On the contrary: the Asian societies are, in different ways, fundamentally more repressive than America is, and their repression is a key to their economic success. Japan, Korea, Taiwan, and Singapore allow their citizens much less latitude than America does, and in so doing they make the whole society, including the business sector, function more efficiently than ours does. The lesson of the Soviet economic collapse would seem to be that a completely controlled economy cannot survive. The lesson of the rising Asian system is that economics with some degree of control can not only survive but prevail.

The crucial concepts here are "excessive" choice and "destructive" competition. Classical free-market economic theory says that these are impossibilities; a person can never have too much choice, and there can never be too much competition in a market. Asian societies approach this issue from a fundamentally different perspective. They were built on neither an Enlightenment concept of individual rights nor a capitalist concept of free and open markets, and they demonstrate in countless ways that less choice for individuals can mean more freedom and success for the social whole.

The examples of economic efficiency are the most familiar. Japanese businessmen have almost no freedom to move to another company, even if they're dissatisfied with conditions where they're working. (Of course, they're technically free to quit, but very few reputable big companies will hire someone who has left another big firm.) This may be frustrating for the businessmen, but so far it has been efficient for the companies. For instance, they can invest in employee training programs without fear that newly skilled workers will use their skills somewhere else. Singaporeans have been forced to put much of their income into a national retirement fund; Koreans have been discouraged from squandering their money overseas on tourism (until this year, only people planning business trips and those in a few other narrow categories were granted passports); Japanese consumers are forced to pay inflated prices for everything they buy. All these measures have been bad for individuals but efficient for the collective. In different ways they have transferred money from people to large institutions, which then invest it for future productivity. To illustrate the point the opposite way: Korea has in the past two years become a more successful democracy and a less successful export economy. Precisely because workers have been going on strike and consumers demanding a higher standard of living, Korean companies have temporarily lost their edge against competitors in Taiwan and Japan.

Yu-Shan Wu, of The Brookings Institution, has suggested a useful way to think about this combination of economic freedom and political control. In communist economies, he says, property is owned by the state, and investment decisions are made by the state. The result is a disaster. The style of capitalism practiced in the United States takes the opposite approach: Private owners control most property, and private groups make most investment decisions. The result over the past century has been a big success, but now some inefficiencies are showing up. Japan, Wu says, has pioneered a new approach: private ownership of property, plus public guidance of investment decisions. The big industrial combines of Japan are as private and profit-oriented as those of the United States, and therefore at least as efficiency-minded (unlike state enterprises in Russia or China). But in Japan's brand of capitalism some of the largest decisions are made by the state, not the "invisible hand." This private-public approach, Wu concludes, reduces the freedom of people and single companies, but it has certain long-term advantages over the private-private system.

Last year two U.S. companies made supercomputers, the Cray corporation and a subsidiary of Control Data. This year only one does. Control Data abandoned the business, finding it unprofitable. The same circumstances have applied to Japan—difficult but important technology, lean or nonexistent profits for the foreseeable future—but the results have been different, because the state occasionally overrules the invisible hand. It is inconceivable that the Japanese government would have let one of only two participants abandon an area of obvious future technical importance. If Japan left decisions to the invisible hand, there would be no aircraft engineers at work in the country, because Mitsubishi and Kawasaki cannot hope to earn a profit competing against Boeing. But the big Japanese companies keep their aerospace-engineering departments active, in part because of government-directed incentives to do so. (These range from explicit subsidies, like the FSX fighter-plane contracts, to a system of industrial organization that makes it possible for companies to subsidize unprofitable divisions for years.) Eventually, Japanese planners believe, the aerospace expertise will pay off.

Americans should not be surprised by what the private-public system can accomplish. It's essentially the way our economy worked during the Second World War. People were forced to save, through Liberty Bonds, and forced not to consume, through rationing. Big companies were privately owned and run, but overall goals were set by the state. Under this system the output of the U.S. economy rose faster than ever before or since. (Part of the reason for the rapid rise, of course, was that wartime production finally brought America out of the Great Depression.) For the

United States this managed economy was a wartime exception. For the Japanese-style economic systems of Asia it has been the postwar rule. This is not to say that we need a wartime mentality again but, rather, to show that the connection between individual freedom and collective prosperity is more complicated than we usually think. We may not like the way the Japanese-style economic system operates, but we'd be foolish not to recognize that it does work, and in many ways works better than ours.

Here's an even harder truth to face: The most successful Asian economies employ a division of labor between men and women that we may find retrograde but that has big practical advantages for them. Despite some signs of change—for instance, the rising influence of Takako Doi at the head of the Socialist Party in Japan—the difference between a man's role and a woman's is much more cut and dried in Asia than in the United States. It is tempting to conclude that a time lag is all that separates Asian practices from American, and that Japanese and Korean women will soon be demanding the rights that American women have won during the past generation. But from everything I've seen, such an assumption is as naive as imagining that Japan is about to be swept by an American-style consumer-rights movement.

There is a lot to dislike in this strict assignment of sex roles. It's unfair in an obvious way to women, because 99 percent of them can never really compete for business, political, academic, or other opportunities and success. I think it's ultimately just as bad for men, because most of them are cut off from the very idea of dealing with women as equals, and have what we would consider emotionally barren family lives. The average Japanese salaryman takes more emotional satisfaction in his workplace life than the average American does, but less in his relations with wife and children. Nonetheless, this system has one tremendous practical advantage. By making it difficult for women to do anything except care for their families, the traditional Asian system concentrates a larger share of social energy on the preparation of the young.

The best-educated American children are a match for the best in Asia, but the average student in Japan, Korea, Singapore, or Taiwan does better in school than the average American. The fundamental reason, I think, is that average students in these countries come from families with two parents, one of whom concentrates most of her time and effort on helping her children through school. Limits on individual satisfaction undergird this educational achievement in two ways: The mother is discouraged from pursuing a career outside the house, and she and the father are discouraged from even thinking about divorce. The typical Asian marriage is not very romantic. In most countries arranged marriages are still common, and while extramarital affairs are at least as frequent as they are in the United States, they seem to cause less guilt. But because most husbands and wives expect less emotional fulfillment from marriage, very few marriages end in divorce. Individual satisfaction from marriage may be lower, but the society enjoys the advantages of having families that are intact.

The Asian approach to the division of labor is not one that Americans want to emulate, or can. Except in emergencies we have believed in satisfying individual desires rather than suppressing them. But, to come back to the central point, we shouldn't fool ourselves about the sheer effectiveness of the system that the Asian societies have devised. Their approach to child-rearing, as to economic development, is worse for many individuals but better for the collective welfare than ours seems to be. The Asian model is not going to collapse of its own weight, unlike the Soviet communist system. So the puzzle for us is to find ways to evoke similar behavior—moderation of individual greed, adequate attention to society's long-term interests, commitment to raising children—within our own values of individualism and free choice.

I hope somebody has figured out the answer to this while I've been away.

Interpretations

1. What is the thesis of Fallows' article? Where is it first expressed? What evidence of its truth, according to Fallows, does Japan provide?

2. Recent history in Korea, says Fallows, seems to indicate a conflict between democracy and capitalism. Can you provide other examples of such conflict?

3. Fallows refers three times to "the invisible hand" without defining it. What does it mean?

4. What, according to Fallows, is the relation between the sexes in Asia? What advantages of this relationship does he mention? what disadvantages?

5. What's the evidence that Fallows believes that the Asian system is more efficient in the short than in the long run? How realistic do you find the solution he proposes?

Correspondences

1. ". . . the Asian societies are, in different ways, fundamentally more repressive than America is, and their repression is a key to their economic success." To what extent is Fallows' point of view confirmed or contradicted by Howe?

2. According to Fallows, "we may not like the way the Japanese-style economic system operates, but we'd be foolish not to recognize that it does work, and in many ways works better than ours." Review Ouchi's comments (Chapter 4) on Japan's economy. How is his assessment similar to or different from Fallows'?

Applications

1. Do citizens of the United States enjoy any freedoms that you feel should be curtailed or abolished for the common good? What are they and how do they harm the commonwealth?

2. "Living in a foreign culture is, most of the time, exhilarating and liberating." Write an essay contrasting Fallows' responses to this experience with those of Jhabvala's Englishwoman.

Digging Up Scotland

Alastair Reid

Alastair Reid (b. 1926) was born in Scotland and lives in New York and the Dominican Republic. He is a poet, translator, essayist, and author of books for children. He has published some volumes of poetry, including Weathering: New and Selected Poems *(1978), and contributes frequently to the* Atlantic Monthly, Encounter, *and* The New Yorker. *He comments on being a writer in exile: "I like the state of being a foreigner. It sharpens the ear and eye, and the kind of alienation it implies is not a bad wavelength for a writer to work on, as long as his nerve and curiosity are up to it, and as long as the mails still go through." In the following excerpt from* Whereabouts: Notes on Being a Foreigner, *Reid recalls his impressions of a visit to his Scottish roots.*

Scotland, now joined with England and Wales in the United Kingdom of Great Britain and Northern Ireland, occupies the northern third of the main island. About 75 percent of the population of five million and most of the industry are found in a 60-mile-wide belt of land from the Firth of Clyde on the west to the Firth of Forth on the east. In this belt are the capital Edinburgh and the industrial center Glasgow; St. Andrews, one of eight Scottish universities, is a few miles north of the Firth of Forth. The kingdoms of Scotland, founded in 1018, and England have shared a common monarch since 1603 and a common parliament since 1707. Monuments to Scotland's Robert Burns, Sir Walter Scott, the Calvinist reformer John Knox and Mary, Queen of Scots draw many tourists, as do the "unfailingly beautiful" land- and seascapes that also draw Reid back from time to time.

I HAVE A FRIEND in Scotland, a painter, who still lives in the fishing town he was born in, grew up in, went to school in, was married in, raised his children in, works in, and clearly intends to die in. I look on him with uncomprehending awe, for although I had much the same origins that he had, born and sprouting in rural Scotland, close to the sea, living more by the agrarian round than by outside time, I had in my head from an early age the firm notion of leaving, long before I knew why or how. Even less did I realize then that I would come to restless rest in a whole slew of places, countries, and languages—the shifting opposite of my rooted friend. Walking with him through his parish, I am aware that the buildings and trees are as familiar to him as his own fingernails; that the people he throws a passing word to he has known, in all their changings, over a span of some fifty years; that he has surrounding him his own history and the history of the place, in memory and image, in language and stone; that his past is ever present to him, whereas my own is lost, shed. He has made his peace with place in a way that to me is, if not unimaginable, at least by now beyond me.

I spent a part of the summer of 1980 digging up Scotland and to some extent coming to terms with it, for although I have gone back to it at odd intervals since I first left, I have always looked on it more as past than as present. My childhood is enclosed, encapsulated in it somewhere, but the threads that connect me to it have long been ravelled. When I return, however, I realize that the place exists spinally in my life, as a kind of yardstick against which I measure myself through time—a setting against which I can assess more clearly the changes that have taken place in me, and in it. When I go back, I am always trying on the country to see if it still fits, or fits better than it did. In one sense, the place is as comfortable to me as old clothes; in another, it is a suit that did not fit me easily from the beginning.

Still, the landscapes of childhood are irreplaceable, since they have been the backdrops for so many epiphanies, so many realizations. I am acutely aware, in Scotland, of how certain moods of the day will put me suddenly on a sharp edge of attention. They have occurred before, and I experience a time warp, past and present in one, with an intense physicality. That double vision is enough to draw anyone back anywhere, for it is what gives us, acutely, the experience of living *through* time, rather than simply living in time. People's faces change when they begin to say, "I once went back to . . ." Something is happening to them, some rich realization, the thrill of retrieval that pervades Nabokov's writing, past and present in one. Places provide these realizations more readily than people do: places have longer lives, for one thing, and they weather in less unpredictable ways. Places are the incarnations of a modus vivendi and the repositories of memory, and so always remain accessible to their own children; but they make very different demands on their inhabitants. In Scotland, the sense of place is strong; when I had left that attachment behind me, I had a loose curiosity about new places, and I still spark up at the notion of going somewhere I have never been to before.

Nevertheless (a favorite Scottish qualification), places embody a consensus of attitudes; and while I lived in a cheerful harmony with the places I grew up in, as places, I did not feel one with them. The natural world and the human world separated early for me. I felt them to be somehow in contradiction, and still do. The Scottish landscape—misty, muted, in constant flux and shift—intrudes its presence in the form of endlessly changing weather; the Scottish character, eroded by a bitter history and a stony morality, and perhaps in reaction to the changing turbulence of weather, subscribes to illusions of permanence, of durability, asking for a kind of submission, an obedience. I felt, from the beginning, exhilarated by the first, fettered by the second. Tramps used to stop at our house, men of the road, begging a cup of tea or an old shirt, and in my mind I was always ready to leave with them, because between Scotland and myself I saw trouble ahead.

When I go back to Scotland, I gravitate mostly to the East Neuk of Fife, that richly farmed promontory jutting into the North Sea to the northeast of Edinburgh, specifically to the town of St. Andrews, a well-worn place that has persisted in my memory from the time I first went there, a very young student at a very ancient university. I have come and gone at intervals over some thirty years, and St. Andrews has changed less in that time than any other place I can think of. It is a singular place, with an aura all its own. For a start, it has a setting unfailingly beautiful to behold in any weather—the curve of St. Andrews Bay sweeping in from the estuary of the River Eden across the washed expanse of the West Sands, backed by the windy green of the golf courses, to the town itself, spired, castled, and cathedraled, punctuated by irregular bells, cloistered and grave, with gray stone roofed in slate or red tile, kempt ruins and a tidy harbor, the town backed by green and gold fields with their stands of ancient trees. If it has the air of a museum, that is no wonder, for it sits placidly on top of a horrendous past. From the twelfth century on, it was in effect the ecclesiastical capital of Scotland, but the Reformation spelled its downfall: its vast cathedral was sacked, and by the seventeen-hundreds the place had gone into a sad decline. Its history looms rather grimly, not just in the carefully tended ruins of castle and cathedral but in the well-walked streets; inset in the cobblestones at the entrance to St. Salvator's College quadrangle are the initials "P.H.," for Patrick Hamilton, who was burned as a martyr on that spot in 1528; students acquire the superstition of never treading on the initials. With such a weighty past so tangibly present, the townspeople assume the air and manner of custodians, making themselves as comfortable and inconspicuous as they can among the ruins, and turning up their noses at the transients—the students, the golfers, the summer visitors. Yet, as in all such situations, it is the transients who sustain the place, who flock into it, year in, year out, to the present-day shrines of the university and the golf courses.

The date of the founding of the University of St. Andrews is given, variously, as 1411 or 1412: the ambiguity arises from the fact that in fifteenth-century Scotland the year began on March 25, and the group of scholars who founded the institution received their charter in February of that dubious year. Such matters are the stuff of serious controversy in St. Andrews. As students, we felt admitted to a venerable presence, even if the curriculum appeared to have undergone only minimal alteration since

1411. A kind of wise mist enveloped the place, and it seemed that we could not help absorbing it, unwittingly. The professors lectured into space, in an academic trance; we took notes, or borrowed them; the year's work culminated in a series of written examinations on set texts, which a couple of weeks of intense immersion, combined with native cunning and a swift pen, could take care of. What that serious, gravid atmosphere did was to make the present shine, in contradistinction to the past. Tacitly and instinctively, we relished the place more than the dead did or could, and we felt something like an obligation to fly in the face of the doleful past. The green woods and the sea surrounded us, the library, and an ocean of time. When I left St. Andrews to go into the Navy in the Second World War, the place, over my shoulder, took on a never-never aura—not simply the never-neverness of college years but as contrast to the troubled state of the times. It appeared to me, in that regard, somewhat unreal.

In its human dimension, St. Andrews embodied the Scotland I chose to leave behind me. The spirit of Calvin, far from dead, stalked the countryside, ever present in a pinched wariness, a wringing of the hands. We were taught to expect the worst—miserable sinners, we could not expect more. A rueful doom ruffles the Scottish spirit. It takes various spoken forms. That summer, a man in Edinburgh said to me, "See you tomorrow, if we're spared," bringing me to a horrified standstill. "Could be worse" is a regular verbal accolade; and that impassioned cry from the Scottish spirit "It's no' right!" declares drastically that *nothing* is right, nothing will ever be right—a cry of doom. Once at an international rugby match between Scotland and England in which the Scots, expected to win comfortably, doggedly snatched defeat from the jaws of victory, a friend of mine noticed two fans unroll a carefully prepared, hand-stitched banner bearing the legend "WE WUZ ROBBED." The wariness is deep-rooted. I prize the encounter I once had with a local woman on the edge of St. Andrews, on a heady spring day. I exclaimed my pleasure in the day, at which she darkened and muttered, "We'll pay for it, we'll pay for it"—a poem in itself.

> It was a day peculiar to this piece of the planet,
> when larks rose on long thin strings of singing
> and the air shifted with the shimmer of actual angels.
> Greenness entered the body. The grasses
> shivered with presences, and sunlight
> stayed like a halo on hair and heather and hills.
> Walking into town, I saw, in a radiant raincoat,
> the woman from the fish-shop. "What a day it is!"
> cried I, like a sunstruck madman.
> And what did she have to say for it?
> Her brow grew bleak, her ancestors raged in their graves

as she spoke with their ancient misery:
"We'll pay for it, we'll pay for it, we'll pay for it!"

And my father, who gleefully collected nuggets of utterance, often told of
an old parishioner of his who, in the course of a meeting, rose to his feet
and declared, "Oh, no, Mr. Reid. We've *tried* change, and we know it
doesn't work." I noticed on a bus I caught in St. Andrews on my last visit,
a sign that read "PLEASE LOWER YOUR HEAD"—a piece of practical advice that
had, for me, immediate Calvinist overtones.

Some of that girn and grumble lingers on in the Scots. The choice is
to succumb to it or to struggle energetically against it. Or, of course, to
leave it behind—the woe and the drear weather—and begin again in
kinder climates. What Calvin ingrained in the Scottish spirit was an
enduring dualism. *The Strange Case of Dr. Jekyll and Mr. Hyde* is the
quintessential Scottish novel. The mysterious elixir of transformation is
simply whisky, which quite often turns soft-spoken Scots into ranting
madmen. Mr. Hyde lurks in these silent depths. Virtue had to be achieved
at the expense of the flesh and the physical world, in which we were
always being judged and found wanting—the world, it seemed, had a
vast, invisible scoreboard that gave no marks for virtue but buzzed mer-
cilessly at miscreants. It buzzed for me. It buzzed for me and for Kathleen,
one of my sisters, so regularly that we became renegades, outwitting the
system when we could. In St. Andrews, that dreich outlook regularly took
the form of an audible sniff of disapproval.

Interpretations

1. Reid distinguishes between living "*through* time" and "living *in* time."
   What does he mean?

2. What elements, according to Reid, created the Scottish character? To
   what extent does he find this character appealing?

3. What do the teaching methods at St. Andrews University suggest
   about education philosophy in Scotland? How do they compare with
   methods at your own college?

4. What cultural clashes or interactions are depicted in this essay?

Correspondences

1. Memory plays an important role in the Reid and Jhabvala narratives.
   How are their attitudes toward their pasts and presents similar and

different? What do they suggest about their responses to the choices they have made?

2. According to Reid, the curriculum at St. Andrews University has changed little since 1411, yet "students felt admitted to a venerable presence." How do you explain their attitude? Might it be due partly to Scotland's homogeneity? Contrast the Scottish students' attitude with that of Novak. Might his dissatisfaction with education be accounted for by America's heterogeneity? What other reasons can you offer?

Applications

1. Reid says of Scotland: "In one sense, the place is as comfortable to me as old clothes; in another, it is a suit that did not fit me easily from the beginning." Write an essay about a place to which you have a similar paradoxical reaction. Include both what is appealing and unappealing about the place.

2. "A rueful doom muffles the Scottish spirit. It takes various spoken forms." What examples does Reid offer to support this thesis? Which did you find most effective? How do they help explain why Reid became a renegade from his native land?

Call Me Not a Man

Mtutuzeli Matshoba

Mtutuzeli Matshoba (b. 1950) is from Soweto, South Africa, and was educated at the University of Fort Hare. In 1978, reception of his first literary contribution, by the newspaper The Voice, *encouraged him to continue writing. He is the author of* Seeds of War *(1981) a novel, and* Call Me Not a Man *(stories, 1979), which was inspired by his dealings with police reservists, who openly practiced robbery and thievery.*

Apartheid ("apartness") became law in South Africa in 1948. Under the law of segregation, blacks, who comprise over two-thirds of the population, live separately from whites and have been forced into overcrowded and poverty-striken townships. Blacks are severely restricted to certain occupations, and are paid far lower wages than whites for similar work. Only whites may vote or run for public office. Blacks must carry permits or passbooks. In 1948 alone, more than 238, 000 blacks were jailed for entering a white area without a passbook.

South African antagonisms are exacerbated by the presence of both black reservests and black policemen. Although black policemen in South Africa are "shunned as quislings [traitors] by some other blacks," more than half of the country's 65,000 policemen and policewomen are nonwhite and their numbers are increasing. "The pay is good by black standards and job security attractive. Many volunteers come from rural areas where unemployment is rampant and political protest minimal." (New York Times, *January 1, 1990)*

Black protests against apartheid have increased in recent years. In retaliation, the government has since 1986 declared a nationwide state of emergency, which gives almost unlimited power to the police. In 1988 two million black workers staged a massive strike to protest new labor laws and the prohibition on political activity by anti-apartheid groups, led, among others, by Nobel Peace Prize-winner Archbishop Desmond Tutu. Nelson Mandela's release from prison in February 1990, is expected to signal the end of apartheid.

For neither am I a man in the eyes of the law,
Nor am I a man in the eyes of my fellow man.

By dodging, lying, resisting where it is possible, bolting when I'm already cornered, parting with invaluable money, sometimes calling my sisters into the game to get amorous with my captors, allowing myself to be slapped on the mouth in front of my womenfolk and getting sworn at with my mother's private parts, that component of me which is man has died countless times in one lifetime. Only a shell of me remains to tell you of the other man's plight, which is in fact my own. For what is suffered by another man in view of my eyes is suffered also by me. The grief he knows is a grief I know. Out of the same bitter cup do we drink. To the same chain-gang do we belong.

Friday has always been their chosen day to go plundering, although they come only occasionally, maybe once a month. Perhaps they have found better pastures elsewhere, where their prey is more predictable than at Mzimhlope, the place which has seen the tragic demise of three of their accomplices who had taken the game a bit too far by entering the hostel on the northern side of our location and fleecing the people right in the midst of their disgusting labour camps. Immediately after this there was a notable abatement in the frequency of their visits to both the location and the adjacent hostel. However the lull was short-lived, lasting only until the storm had died down, because the memory tarnishes quickly in the locations, especially the memory of death. We were beginning to emit sighs of relief and to mutter "good riddance" when they suddenly reappeared and made their presence in our lives felt once again. June 'seventy-six had put them out of the picture for the next year, during which they were scarcely seen. Like a recurring pestilence they refuse to vanish absolutely from the scene.

A person who has spent some time in Soweto will doubtless have guessed by now that the characters I am referring to are none other than some of the so-called police reservists who roam our dirty streets at weekends, robbing every timid, unsuspecting person, while masquerading as peace officers to maintain law and order in the community. There are no greater thieves than these men of the law, men of justice, peace officers and volunteer public protectors in the whole of the slum complex because, unlike others in the same trade of living off the sweat of their victims, they steal out in the open, in front of everybody's eyes. Of course nothing can be done about it because they go out on their pillaging exploits under the banners of the law, and to rise in protest against them is analogous to defiance of the powers that be.

So, on this Friday too we were standing on top of the station bridge at Mzimhlope. It was about five in the afternoon and the sun hung over the western horizon of spectacularly identical coalsmoke-puffing roof-tops like a gigantic, glowing red ball which dyed the foamy clouds with the crimson sheen of its rays. The commuter trains in from the city paused below us every two or three minutes to regurgitate their infinite human cargo, the greater part of whom were hostel-dwellers who hurried up Mohale Street to cook their meagre suppers on primus stoves. The last train we had seen would now be leaving Phefeni, the third station from Mzimhlope. The next train had just emerged from the bridge this side of New Canada, junction to East and West Soweto. The last group of the hostel people from the train now leaving Phefeni had just turned the bend at Mohale Street where it intersects with Elliot. The two-hundred-metre stretch to Elliot was therefore relatively empty, and people coming towards the station could be clearly made out.

As the wheels of the train from New Canada squealed on the iron tracks and it came to a jerking stop, four men, two in overalls and the others in dustcoats, materialized around the Mohale Street bend. There was no doubt who they were, from the way they filled the whole width of the street and walked as if they owned everything and everybody in their sight. When they came to the grannies selling vegetables, fruit and fried mealies along the ragged, unpaved ides of the street, they grabbed what they fancied and munched gluttonously the rest of the way towards us. Again nothing could be done about it, because the poverty-stricken vendors were not licensed to scrape together some crumbs to ease the gnawing stomachs of their fatherless grandchildren at home, which left them wide open for plunder by the indifferent "reserves." "*Awu!* The Hellions," remarked Mandla next to me, "Let's get away from here, my friend."

He was right. They reminded one of the old western film; but I was not moving from where I was simply because the reservists were coming down the street like a bunch of villains. One other thing I knew was that the railway constable who was on guard duty that Friday at the station did not allow the persecution of the people on his premises. I wanted to have my laugh when they were chased off the station.

"Don't worry about them. Just wait and see how they're going to be chased away by this copper. He won't allow them on the station," I answered.

They split into twos when they arrived below us. Two of them, a tall chap with a face corroded by skin-lightening cream and wearing a yellow golf cap on his shaven head, and another stubby, shabbily dressed, middle-aged man with a bald frontal lobe and a drunk face, chewing at a cooked sheep's foot that he had taken from one of the grannies, climbed the stairs on our right-hand side. The younger man took the flight in fours. The other two chose to waylay their unsuspecting victims on the street corner at the base of the left-hand staircase. The first wave of the people who had alighted from the train was in the middle of the bridge when the second man reached the top of the stars.

Maybe they knew the two reservists by sight, maybe they just smelt cop in the smoggy air, or it being a Friday, they were alert for such possibilities. Three to four of the approaching human wall turned suddenly in their tracks and ran for their dear freedom into the mass behind them. The others were caught unawares by this unexpected movement and they staggered in all directions trying to regain balance. In a split second there was commotion on the station, as if a wild cat had found its way into a fowl-run. Two of those who had not been quick enough were grabbed by their sleeves, and their passes demanded. While they were producing their books the wolves went over their pockets, supposedly feeling for dangerous weapons, *dagga*[1] and other illegal possessions that might be concealed in the clothes, but really to ascertain whether they had caught the right people for their iniquitous purposes. They were paging through the booklets when the Railway policeman appeared.

"Wha . . . ? Don't you fools know that you're not supposed to do that shit here? Get off! Get off and do that away from Railway property. Fuck off!" He screamed at the two reservists so furiously that the veins threatened to burst in his neck.

"Arrest the dogs, *baba!* Give them a chance also to taste jail!" Mandla shouted.

"*Ja,*" I said to Mandla, "you bet, they've never been where they are so prepared to send others."

The other people joined in and we jeered the cowards off the station. They descended the stairs with their tails tucked between their legs and joined their companions below the station. Some of the commuters who had been alerted by the uproar returned to the platform to wait there until the reservists had gone before they would dare venture out of the station.

We remained where we had been and watched the persecution from above. I doubted if they even read the passes (if they could), or whether the victims knew if their books were right or out of order. Most likely the poor hunted men believed what they were told by the licensed thieves. The latter demanded the books, after first judging their prey to be weak propositions, flicked through the pages, put the passes into their own pockets, without which the owners could not continue on their way, and told the dumbfounded hostel men to stand aside while they accosted other victims. Within a very short while there was a group of confused men to one side of the street, screaming at their hostel mates to go to room so-and-so and tell so-and-so that they had been arrested at the station, and to bring money quickly to release them. Few of those who were being sent heard the messages since they were only too eager to leave the danger zone. Those who had money shook hands with their captors, received their books back and ran up Mohale Street. If they were unlucky they came upon another "roadblock" three hundred metres up

[1] Marijuana.

the street where the process was repeated. Woe unto them who had paid their last money to the first extortionists, for this did not matter. The police station was their next stopover before the Bantu Commissioners, and thence their final destination, Modderbee Prison, where they provided the farmers with ready cheap labour until they had served their terms for breaking the law. The terms vary from a few days to two years for *loaferskap*,[2] which is in fact mere unemployment, for which the unfortunate men are not to blame. The whole arrangement stinks of forced labour.

The large *kwela-kwela*[3] swayed down Mohale Street at breakneck speed. The multitudes scattered out of its way and hung on to the sagging fences until it had passed. To be out of sight of the people on the station bridge, it skidded and swerved into the second side street from the station. More reservists poured out of it and went immediately to their dirty job with great zeal. The chain-gang which had been lined up along the fence of the house nearest the station was kicked and shoved to the *kwela-kwela* into which the victims were bundled under a rain of fists and boots, all of them scrambling to go in at the same time through the small door. The driver of the *kwela-kwela,* the only uniformed constable among the group, clanged the door shut and secured it with the locking lever. He went to stand authoritatively near one of the vendors, took a small avocado pear, peeled it and put it whole into a gargantuan mouth, spitting out the large stone later. He did not have to take the trouble of accosting anyone himself. His gangsters would all give him a lion's share of whatever they made, and moreover buy him some beers and brandy. He kept adjusting his polished belt over his potbelly as the .38 police special in its leather holster kept tugging it down. He probably preferred to wear his gun unconventionally, cowboy style.

A boy of about seventeen was caught with a knife in his pocket, a dangerous weapon. They slapped him a few times and let him stand handcuffed against the concrete wall of the station. Ten minutes later his well-rounded sister alighted from the train to find her younger brother among the prisoners. As she was inquiring from him why he had been arrested, and reprimanding him for carrying a knife, one of the younger reservists came to stand next to her and started pawing her. She let him carry on, and three minutes later her brother was free. The reservist was beaming all over his face, glad to have won himself a beautiful woman in the course of his duties and little knowing that he had been given the wrong address. Some of our Black sisters are at times compelled to go all the way to save their menfolk, and, as always, nothing can be done about it.

[2]Vagrancy.

[3]Police van.

There was a man coming down Mohale Street, conspicuous amidst the crowd because of the bag and baggage that was loaded on his overall-clad frame. On his right shoulder was a large suitcase with a grey blanket strapped to it with flaxen strings. From his left hand hung a bulging cardboard box, only a few inches from the ground, and tilting him to that side. He walked with the bounce of someone used to walking in gumboots or on uneven ground. There was the urgency of someone who had a long way to travel in his gait. It was doubtless a *goduka* on his way home to his family after many months of work in the city. It might even have been years since he had visited the countryside.

He did not see the hidden *kwela-kwela*, which might have fore-warned him of the danger that was lurking at the station. Only when he had stumbled into two reservists, who stepped into his way and ordered him to put down his baggage, did he perhaps remember that it was Friday and raid-day. A baffled expression sprang into his face as he realized what he had walked into. He frantically went through the pockets of his overalls. The worried countenance deepened on his dark face. He tried again to make sure, but he did not find what he was looking for. The men who had stopped him pulled him to one side, each holding him tightly by the sleeve of his overall. He obeyed meekly like a tame animal. They let him lift his arms while they searched him all over the body. Finding nothing hidden on him, they demanded the inevitable book, although they had seen that he did not have it. He gesticulated with his hands as he explained what had caused him not to be carrying his pass with him. A few feet above them, I could hear what was said.

"Strue, *madoda*,"[4] he said imploringly, "I made a mistake. I luggaged the pass with my trunk. It was a jacket that I forgot to search before I packed it into the trunk."

"How do we know that you're not lying?" asked one of the reservists in a querulous voice.

"I'm not lying, *mfowethu*.[5] I swear by my mother, that's what happened," explained the frightened man.

The second reservist had a more evil and uncompromising attitude. "That was your own stupidity, mister. Because of it you're going to jail now; no more to your wife."

"Oh, my brother. Put yourself in my shoes. I've not been home to my people for two years now. It's the first chance I have to go and see my twin daughters who were born while I've been here. Feel for another poor Black man, please, my good brother. Forgive me only for this once."

"What? Forgive you? And don't give us that slush about your children. We've also got our own families, for whom we are at work right now, at this very moment," the obstinate one replied roughly.

"But, *mfo*. Wouldn't you make a mistake too?"

[4,5]Terms of respect.

That was a question the cornered man should not have asked. The reply this time was a resounding slap on the face. "You think I'm stupid like you, huh? Bind this man, Mazibuko, put the bloody irons on the dog."

"No, man. Let us talk to the poor bloke. Perhaps he can do something for us in exchange for the favour of letting him proceed on his way home," the less volatile man suggested, and pulled the hostel man away from the rest of the arrested people.

"*Ja.* Speak to him yourself, Mazibuko. I can't bear talking to rural fools like him. I'll kill him with my bare hands if he thinks that I've come to play here in Johannesburg!" The anger in the man's voice was faked, the fury of a coward trying to instill fear in a person who happened to be at his mercy. I doubted if he could face up to a mouse. He accosted two boys and ran his hands over their sides, but he did not ask for their passes.

"You see, my friend, you're really in trouble. I'm the only one who can help you. This man who arrested you is not in his best mood today. How much have you got on you? Maybe if you give something he'll let you go. You know what wonders money can do for you. I'll plead for you; but only if I show him something can he understand." The reservist explained the only way out of the predicament for the trapped man, in a smooth voice that sounded rotten through and through with corruption, the sole purpose for which he had joined the "force."

"I haven't got a cent in my pocket. I bought provisions, presents for the people at home and the ticket with all the money they gave me at work. Look, *nkosi,*[6] I have only the ticket and the papers with which I'm going to draw my money when I arrive at home." He took out his papers, pulled the overall off his shoulders and lowered it to his thighs so that the brown trousers he wore underneath were out in the open. He turned the dirty pockets inside out. "There's nothing else in my pockets except these, mister, honestly."

"Man!"

"Yessir?"

"You want to go home to your wife and children?"

"Yes, *please,* good man of my people. Give me a break."

"Then why do you show me these damn papers? They will feed your own children, but not mine. When you get to your home you're going to draw money and your kids will be scratching their tummies and dozing after a hectic meal, while I lose my job for letting you go and my own children join the dogs to scavenge the trashbins. You're mad, *mos.*" He turned to his mate. "Hey, Baloyi. Your man says he hasn't got anything, but he's going to his family which he hasn't seen for two years."

"I told you to put the irons on him. He's probably carrying a little fortune in his underpants. Maybe he's shy to take it out in front of the

---

[6]Term of respect.

people. It'll come out at the police station, either at the charge office or in the cells when the small boys shake him down."

"Come on, you. Your hands maan!"

The other man pulled his arms away from the manacles. His voice rose desperately, "*Awu* my people. You mean you're really arresting me? Forgive me! I pray do."

A struggle ensued between the two men.

"You're resisting arrest? You—" and a stream of foul vitriolic words concerning the anatomy of the hostel man's mother gushed out of the reservist's mouth.

"I'm not, I'm not! But please listen!" The hostel man heaved and broke loose from the reservist's grip. The latter was only a lump of fat with nothing underneath. He staggered three steps back and flopped on his rump. When he bounced back to his feet, unexpectedly fast for his bulk, his eyes were blazing murder. His companions came running from their own posts and swarmed upon the defenceless man like a pack of hyenas upon a carcass. The other people who had been marooned on the bridge saw a chance to go past while the wolves were still preoccupied. They ran down the stairs and up Mohale like racehorses. Two other young men who were handcuffed together took advantage of the diversion and bolted down the first street in tandem, taking their bracelets with them. They ran awkwardly with their arms bound together, but both were young and fit and they did their best in the circumstances.

We could not stand the sickening beating that the other man was receiving any more.

"Hey! Hey. *Sies,* maan. Stop beating the man like that. Arrest him if you want to arrest him. You're killing him, dogs!" we protested loudly from the station. An angry crowd was gathering.

"Stop it or we'll stop you from doing anything else forever!" someone shouted.

The psychopaths broke their rugger scrum and allowed us to see their gruesome handiwork. The man was groaning at the base of the fence, across the street where the dirt had gathered. He twisted painfully to a sitting position. His face was covered with dirt and blood from where the manacles that were slipped over the knuckles had found their marks, and his features were grotesquely distorted. In spite of that, the fat man was not satisfied. He bent and gathered the whimpering man's wrists with the intention of fastening them to the fence with the handcuffs.

"Hey, hey, hey, Satan! Let him go. Can't you see that you've hurt that man enough?"

The tension was building up to explosion point and the uniformed policeman sensed it.

"Let him go, boys. Forgive him. Let him go," he said, shooting nervous glances in all directions.

Then the beaten-up man did the most unexpected and heart-rending thing. He knelt before the one ordering his release and held his dust-covered hands with the palms together in the prayer position, and still kneeling he said, "Thank you very much, my lord. God bless you. Now I can go and see my twins and my people at home."

He would have done it. Only it never occurred in his mind at that moment of thanksgiving to kiss the red gleaming boots of the policeman.

The miserable man beat the dust off his clothes as best he could, gathered his two parcels and clambered up the stairs, trying to grin his thanks to the crowd that had raised its voice of protest on his behalf. The policeman decided to call it a day. The other unfortunates were shepherded to the waiting *kwela-kwela*.

I tried to imagine how the man would explain his lumps to his wife. In the eye of my mind I saw him throwing his twins into the air and gathering them again and again as he played with them.

"There's still a long way to cover, my friend," I head Mandla saying into my ear.

Interpretations

1. What is the evidence that both the police reservists and their victims are black? How does their blackness affect your response to their behavior? Do you think this point should be made clear earlier in the story? Why?

2. To what extent does the scene with the *avocado* serve as a symbol of the relationship between the reservists and the black citizens of Soweto?

3. The story is told in the first person by an unnamed narrator. What do we know about this narrator? What are his dominant traits? What is his relation to the events he narrates? Would the story be improved if told by the hostel man or by the author in the third person? Why or why not?

4. Does the attitude in the hostel man upon his release strip him of his manhood, as the title suggests? Why or why not?

5. What is the tone of this story? What is implied by the use of three different terms to suggest respect? Is the style appropriate to the subject? Describe the style and give examples to support your description.

Correspondences

1. Review the first paragraph of Matshoba's story. Why does he use the word "man" so often? What is he implying about his own manhood and that of the other members of the symbolic chain gang? Review Jones's essay (Chapter 4) on covering the Klan rally in Florida in 1988. How do whites refer to her? How does this interaction affect her concept of herself.

2. Review the Baldwin quotation (page 352). What does it mean? To what extent do you agree with it? How does it apply to social interactions in "Call Me Not a Man"? *Who* saw himself in the eyes of the victim?

Applications

1. Review the Kluckhohn quotation (page 352). How does it apply to the beaten man's interaction with the policeman who sprayed him? to the last line of the story? How pertinent is it to Wright's interactions with whites (Chapter 3)? What might you conclude about the cost of survival?

2. What more did you learn about the political system depicted in Matshoba's story? What can an individual living under apartheid do to end this system? Does he or she have any choice but to support and accept it? What can people living outside the system do?

ADDITIONAL WRITING TOPICS

1. "Growing up in America has been an assault upon my sense of worthiness. It has also been a kind of liberation and delight." What aspects of Novak's interactions reflect this paradox? To what extent does the paradox also apply to the experiences of Fusilli and Cofer?

2. Review the Norton quotation (page 352). Is it easier to support theoretically than practically? To what extent do the interactions presented in the selections in this textbook reflect the kinds of tolerance of individual differences Norton advocates?

3. Review the Morrow quotation (page 351). What does it suggest about interactions? How do the selections by Howe, Fallows, Wright, and Jhabvala support or refute Morrow's thesis?

4. Write about a group you participated in recently. Analyze how the group members interact with one another. By what means do they communicate with one another? How do they handle disagreement or friction? Write an essay on what you learned about group relations.

5. Lack of awareness of cultural differences or the assumption by one cultural group that another is inferior results in interactions that are painful power struggles. Apply this thesis to any three selections in this chapter.

6. Although "the melting pot" is the traditional metaphor associated with the immigrant experience in the United States, many sociologists now believe that "the fusion chamber" is a more accurate description of current cultural interacting. Contrast the implications of both terms and, using any three essays in this chapter, justify your choice of metaphor.

7. Review Goldberg's perspective on cultural interactions (page 353) and evaluate its relevance to any three cultural interactions in this chapter.

8. Rodriguez concludes his essay on American identity by claiming that "Americans are wedded by proximity to a common culture." That is, in spite of our enormous ethnic diversity and the "hyphenated identity" of the children of immigrant parents, we are on the whole shaped by a common culture. Agree or disagree with Rodriguez by examining the impact of *some* of the following American innovations and customs. *Your own experience is important here:* you may write from the point of view of a native-born American, a member of an immigrant family (recent or established), a member of America's youth, a student-visa resident, an older adult. What do you believe is

the impact on you and your identity group of these common culture realities:

easily available credit ("plastic money")

access to affordable (if expensive) higher education

fast-food services

multiple-earners households

latch-key children

multiple-car households

rapidly changing hair and clothing styles

TV, both programming and advertisements

cheap, abundant print resources (newspapers, magazines, FAX, etc.)

shopping malls

huge supermarkets and chain stores

early access to sex education and sexual activity

very mobile lifestyles (the average American homeowner moves every seven years)

shortening of the generation gap from twenty-five to about ten years

dominance of superstar, celebrity, culture hero images

CHAPTER 6

Choices

Culture, according to anthropologist Bronislaw Malinowski, is the "artificial, secondary environment" that human beings superimpose on nature. We human beings, then, are "in" both nature and culture, and both influence our choices. A diversity of cultures, which the following selections illustrate, makes for great choice and sometimes great difficulty of choice. Cultures are "dramatic conversations about things that matter," says Robert Bellah, (see the introduction to Chapter 1) and those conversations are about choices.

While nature is passively selecting the fittest organisms for survival, we humans are actively, sometimes painfully, choosing, making a variety of choices—ethical, political, economic—for a variety of reasons both rational and emotional. If we make the same choice time after time, such as training ourselves to set the alarm clock and getting up when it rings, it becomes "second" nature, and we are on time for work or school without having to think much about it. Where life runs its traditional course, unconscious habit often replaces conscious choice, but when crises arise, social or personal, habit is useless and all kinds of choices must be made, including painful ones. This is the complex situation in the essays of this chapter.

Is culture, like nature, a limitation on freedom of choice, or does it allow more free play of individual wisdom and imagination? Do we increase our own choices to the degree we free ourselves from culture? The first selection in the chapter poses such a possibility. The young man in the Swahili tale chooses a wife and finds that the choice is involved with such cultural requirements as a bride price. The wife's culture denies her the choice of husband, but her wisdom, which is even greater than her beauty, shows to her subsequent choices which allow her to triumph.

In a crisis, habit cannot necessarily ease the pain of choice. When she decided one December day in 1955 not to sit in the back of the bus in Montgomery, Alabama, Rosa Parks made a painful choice whose effects are still being felt all over the world. She rejected her enslaved grandfather's fierce hatred of whites, but still reads her American history with an eye for hypocrisy. Leonardo, facing a crisis in "A Train Ride," is forced into a painful "dramatic conversation" with himself that leads to a surprising and momentous choice.

It would be hard to imagine more painful choices than those made by Anna in the impossible political situation of Hana Wehle's "The Impossible Became No Longer Unthinkable." Uprooted from her home in Prague and transported with her husband and his parents to the Theresienstadt ghetto (where they were later joined by Anna's mother), the twenty-five-year-old Anna tried to keep together the "little cluster of three broken women" after the two men died.

A change of place may also alter the significance of moral, economic and social choices. Several of the selections in this chapter show immigrants to the United States faced with changing choices. Manuela's early life ("A Tale of Two Moralities") seems to have offered few choices, but once she began to extricate herself from the traditional village, the choices (and problems) increased. Richard Rodriguez in "To the Border" sympathetically, poetically, recreates the emotions and wrenching choices of a boy (Rodriguez's father?) who is one of the lonely "Mexicans without Mexico."

Phan Huu Thanh fled South Vietnam when it fell into Communist hands and resumed his education many miles later at the University of Massachusetts. Another student, Lev Tagayev, tells in "No Sacrifice Too Great" how he interrupted his schooling with a "star-crossed" choice that took him on almost the same journey, but in the opposite direction, and that turned him from a promising student into a soldier in the country Thanh had fled.

Marshall Glickman reaches across cultural lines to choose Zen Buddhism. In so doing, he changes his definitions of success and failure and, along with them, his behavior, his health, and his goals. In "Banderillero" we see a bullfighter in Spain struggle with success and failure and make a difficult career choice. And the Afrikaner farmer Marais Van der Vyver in Nadine Gordimer's story makes a series of life-and-death choices. In the following selections nature, culture, and choice—three sometimes incompatible but essential elements—combine in uneasy and interesting ways.

PERSPECTIVES

January 1
Look to this day,
For it is life, the very life of life.
In its brief course lie all the varieties and realities of
*   your existence,*
The bliss of growth, the glory of action, the splendor of
*   beauty;*
For yesterday is but a dream; and tomorrow is only a
*   vision,*
But today well lived makes
Every yesterday a dream of happiness
And every tomorrow a vision of hope.

Bhagavad-Gita

People are trapped in history and history is trapped in
them.

James Baldwin

Look out how you use proud words.
When you let proud words go, it is
*   not easy to call them back.*
They wear long boots, hard boots; they
*   walk off proud; they can't hear you calling—*
Look out how you use proud words.

Carl Sandburg

Troubles overcome are good to tell.

Yiddish Proverb

If man's condition is unjust, he has only one alternative,
which is to be just himself.

Albert Camus

One doesn't throw the stick after the snake has gone.

Liberian Proverb

Once to every man and nation comes the moment to decide
In the strife of truth with falsehood, for the good or evil side.

James Russell Lowell

Two roads diverged in a wood, and I—I took the one less traveled by, and that has made all the difference.

Robert Frost

Every time a man has contributed to the victory of the dignity of the spirit, every time a man has said no to an attempt to subjugate his fellows, I have felt solidarity with his act.

Frantz Fanon

No day comes back again; an inch of time is worth a foot of jade.

Zen Proverb

There is, I think, an essential difference of character in mankind, between those who wish to do, *and those who wish to* have *certain things.*

William Hazlitt

All life is an experiment. The more experiments you make the better.

Ralph Waldo Emerson

If I had to choose between betraying my country and betraying my friend, I hope I should have the guts to betray my country.

E. M. Forster

Applications

1. Write a journal entry on one of the perspectives on choices. To what extent do you consider yourself free to make choices?
2. Discuss the perspective of the Zen proverb. What does it imply about time and choice? To what extent do you agree that time is more important than wealth?

The Wise Daughter

Swahili Folk Tale

Swahili is spoken widely in East Africa and is an official language of Kenya and Tanzania.

THERE WAS ONCE a young man whose parents died and left him a hundred cattle. He was lonely after the death of his parents, so he decided to get married. He went to his neighbors and asked them to help him find a wife.

Soon one of the neighbors came to tell him that he had found the most beautiful girl in the country for him to marry. "The girl is very good and wise and beautiful, and her father is very wealthy," he said. "Her father owns six thousand cattle."

The young man became very excited when he heard about this girl. But then he asked, "How much is the bride price?"

"The father wants a hundred cattle," was the reply.

"A hundred cattle! That is all I have. How will we be able to live?" replied the young man.

"Well, make up your mind. I have to take an answer to the father soon," said the neighbor.

The young man thought, "I cannot live without this girl." So he said, "Go and tell the father that I want to marry his daughter."

So the two were married. But after they returned home, they quickly ran out of food, and the young man had to herd cattle for a neighbor to get anything to eat. What he got was not very much for a young lady who was used to eating well and living in style.

One day as the young wife was sitting outside the house, a strange man came by and was struck by her beauty. He decided to try to seduce her and sent a message to her. The young wife told him that she could not make up her mind and he would have to come back later.

Several months later, the girl's father came to visit. She was very upset because she did not have anything to feed him. But on that same day, the seducer came back. So the young wife told the seducer that she would give in to his requests if he would bring her some meat to cook for her father.

Soon the seducer returned with the meat and the girl went inside to cook it. Her husband returned, and he and her father sat down to eat and have a good time. The seducer was standing outside listening. Soon he became angry and went inside to see what was happening. The young husband, who was hospitable, invited him in.

The young wife then brought in the meat and said, "Eat, you three fools."

445

"Why do you call us fools?" the three men said all together.

"Well, Father," the girl replied. "You are a fool because you sold something precious for something worthless. You had only one daughter and traded her for a hundred cattle when you already had six thousand."

"You are right," said her father. "I was a fool."

"As for you, husband," she went on. "You inherited only a hundred cattle and you went and spent them all on me, leaving us nothing to eat. You could have married another woman for ten or twenty cows. That is why you were a fool."

"And why am I a fool?" asked the seducer.

"You are the biggest fool of all. You thought you could get for one piece of meat what had been bought for a hundred cattle."

At that, the seducer ran away as fast as he could. Then the father said, "You are a wise daughter. When I get home, I will send your husband three hundred cattle so that you shall live in comfort."

Interpretations

1. Is this tale about how *not* to make choices? Explain your answer.

2. In many cultures the bride must provide a dowry, whereas in the East African culture of this story the groom must pay a bride price; how do you feel about these customs? How do you think they affect relations between the sexes? Why?

Correspondences

1. Review the Liberian proverb on page 443. How does it apply to the Swahili tale? What does the latter suggest about making choices based on emotions? Do you agree? Why?

2. In the Swahili tale, the women are described as wise, the men foolish. Compare the woman in this selection with Effua in "Anticipation" (Chapter 2). How are they similar? Are women, as the selections suggest, more logical than men in affairs of the heart? Cite evidence.

Applications

1. Write a journal entry about a choice that you regret having made. What did you learn from the experience?

2. Study a dictionary or thesaurus entry for *wisdom*. Which connotations best express your associations with wisdom? Can wisdom be taught? Do we value wise people? How might wisdom affect choices?

The Zen Master, My Father, and Me

Marshall Glickman

Marshall Glickman (b. 1961) majored in philosophy at North-western University and after graduation worked for three years for Shearson Lehman Brothers. Since then he has been traveling, reading, meditating, writing, and spending time with family and friends. This is how he describes his purpose in writing "The Zen Master, My Father, and Me."

> *After I was beaten with the stick, I spent the night think-ing about what had happened and why. I consoled myself that at the very least the experience would make an interesting story. In my mind I saw a catchy opening line for an essay: "A Zen master beat me so hard my back swelled a purple lump the size of a baseball." Then I realized that I was composing an essay as an escape, using it to make a scary event safe. So I dropped the idea.*
>
> *Years later, I told my girlfriend (now wife) Margaret about my experiences at camp. After I told her, I made a nonverbal connection to my experience at a sesshin. Writing the essay allowed me to figure out what that connection was.*

THE ZEN MASTER pulled my shoulder forward with one hand and grabbed his stick with the other. "Shout!" he commanded. As I bent over, his wooden stick cracked across my back. "Louder!" he roared. I yelled again. Another sharp slap stung my back. I screamed as loud as I could. He hit me again— and again— until I lost count of the blows and my hoarse screams.

When he rang his bell, indicating the end of our meeting, I was dazed and shaken. I bowed and left the room, resuming my vow of silence.

I was at a *sesshin,* a week-long meditation retreat. Seven days without phones, TV, radio, or showers. Seven days spent meditating eleven hours a day.

I am nine; my brother Joe eleven. We're at a sleepaway sports camp. My father's red and contorted face is inches from mine. His glasses are crooked; his neck strained from yelling.

447

He's in a rage because we've called home every day for a week, crying, begging mom to bring us home. We hate camp. We hate waking at 6:30 to a recording of reveille and laps around the obstacle course. We hate the drills and swimming lessons. The bathrooms stink; the food is worse. The kids are mean. My first nights were spent wet and cold from midnight water raids.

"THE WORLD IS A TOUGH PLACE!" he screams. "YOU'VE GOT TO BE STRONG. OTHERWISE YOU'LL END UP STARVING IN A CONCEN-TRATION CAMP. IF SOMEONE PICKS ON YOU, PUNCH THEM IN THE FACE."

I am dazed and shaken—too shocked to speak or cry. Normally, my dad isn't scary. He never hit me. He rarely raised his voice to Mom. He usually only yelled at football games or on the tennis court. Joe and I don't wave as we watch my parents' car disappear past the camp gates.

The next day I got into a fight. I can't remember with who, or why, but I know I didn't cry.

Camp was a distant memory until I saw my bruised back in a bathroom mirror in the monastery. A bright purple lump the size of a baseball swelled from a sea of lavender and blue. I was shocked. Why had I let myself be beaten? I spent a sleepless night wondering if I should leave the *sesshin*.

Zen Buddhism had been my anchor since college. From day one freshman year, I practically lived at the library. My major was philosophy, but my real interest was Harvard Law School. I obsessed over A's and worked hard to stay motivated—even tacking a sign over my bed that read: "WAKE UP ASSHOLE." By my junior year, a persistent tension rash covered my legs.

During a study break in the library, I came across a book about Zen. Its philosophy was much different from the metaphysics I studied in class. Zen wasn't concerned with logic. Its wisdom came from direct experience. And better yet, Zen offered a way to be—a take-life-as-it-comes fluidity that I lacked.

The book said to meditate and concentrate on the present. It also said something that sounded surprising, but somehow felt true: the ego is an illusion. The self does not exist as a separate unchanging entity and we cause ourself needless pain by clinging to the idea of self. What we really want is simply a full deep experience of life—not achievements.

It made sense to me. If I lived in the moment, waking up late wouldn't ruin my day. If I wasn't dominated by my ego, I wouldn't worry about my grades. I read more books about Zen, savoring descriptions of *satori* (enlightenment) like a prisoner dreams of freedom.

I started meditating. For half an hour a day, I tried to sit still in the half-lotus position, letting thoughts pass like clouds in the sky. My mind would calm down for about fifteen minutes, until the only thing I could think about were my aching back and burning thighs and ankles. Yet rather than move my legs, I would scream into a pillow or throw my alarm clock across the room. I was determined to relax. Within a few months, I was meditating two hours a day.

The more I meditated, the more I wanted to be released from my desire to succeed. Happiness shouldn't depend on getting into Harvard or landing a good job. It was more important to learn how to live. Unfortunately, there was a problem: I needed an income.

After graduating, I got a job as a stockbroker. I wanted to save enough money to be freed from a regular job. I disciplined myself even more than I had in college. I woke up at 5:30 in the morning, meditated before work and made calls until nine or ten at night. My savings goal and the words "DO IT" were taped to my phone. I became both the demanding boss and the down-trodden worker. A new rash covered my dialing hand.

Two years later, the lump on my back told me I was doing the same thing with Zen. I had turned *satori* into an accomplishment that demanded sacrifice. I embraced the Zen tradition of yelling and blows to the back because they gave increased energy for concentration. Like volunteering for extra credit, I always asked to be hit when monks prowled the meditation hall with sticks.

But I hadn't asked the Zen master (*roshi*) to hit me during our meeting—and even if I had, he'd gone beyond "extra credit" or a little shot of energy.

The *roshi* seemed to be the consummate wise sage. He spoke carefully and intelligently with an endearing Japanese accent. His movements were measured and graceful; his advice penetrating and funny. I didn't know him intimately, but I idolized him in the way I had my dad as a kid. I wanted his approval; wanted to know what he knew. And I assumed he knew better than I did.

Maybe the *roshi's* austere training as a monk in Japan made him believe that a serious student had to be beaten for insight. Maybe he wanted his students to have *satori* so much that he turned it into a goal too. In college, as I developed what I thought were my own values, I had learned that my father could make mistakes. Now I saw that the *roshi* could too.

The point isn't to blame the *roshi* or my dad; what mattered was the problem in me. For the first time, I clearly saw how I was living for results. I had thought that the West in me pushed for success, while the East tried to let go. But the truth was, I was always pushing, always putting the goal first. Camp had made me tougher. It taught me some discipline. But the real lesson I learned wasn't "stand up for myself"; it was DON'T FAIL.

After realizing this at the *sesshin,* my first reaction was: get rid of goals and discipline because they cause anxiety—I'm going home. But that wasn't the answer; discipline can be a good tool. It had enabled me to save enough money to quit my job. And the discipline of meditating is basically healthy. What I needed to remember is failing isn't a disgrace. Because when failing isn't an option, discipline turns into dictatorship.

I decided to finish the *sesshin* and not push anymore. I didn't ask for the stick. I didn't attend meetings. I just sat still. As hours slipped into days, I found a deeper level of awareness than ever before. I experienced a glimpse of pure boundless energy—life without the ego. Maybe the *roshi* thought that would happen. It's hard to tell.

I haven't attended another *sesshin,* but I still meditate every day—although I don't call it Zen. I just try to sit still, relax, and be aware. My rash has gotten smaller, but it hasn't disappeared. It's a reminder that it may take a lifetime to truly learn that while goals aren't that important, trusting myself and listening are.

Interpretations

1. What is Glickman's purpose in juxtaposing the Zen master and his father in the first two sections of the story? What elements do the scenes share? How are they different?

2. Without having suffered a "persistent tension rash," would Glickman have started studying Zen? Why does he say the lump on his back was "doing the same thing with Zen"?

3. Judging from Glickman's summary of Zen Buddhism, what does it teach about human aspiration? about the "desire to succeed"? Are aspiring and succeeding the same? Why or why not?

4. Right from the beginning of the essay, discipline is an important idea. What are the stages in the development of Glickman's final conception of discipline? To what extent do you agree with his conception? Why is it valuable? Can discipline be developed? If so, how? Is discipline of value only as a "tool," or does it have intrinsic value?

5. How does Glickman change in the course of the story? How does he account for the change? Is it an improvement? Is it a common change? What is Glickman's final attitude toward meditation? Do you share his attitude? Why or why not? What is his final attitude toward Zen?

6. What does Glickman mean by learning to "trust [oneself]"? Why might learning to do so take a lifetime? How does trusting oneself relate to relaxing, meditating, and/or deemphasizing goals?

Correspondences

1. "What I needed to remember is failing isn't a disgrace. Because when failing isn't an option, discipline turns into dictatorship." To what extent do you agree with Glickman? Can one learn from failure? How might adherence to this same philosophy have altered the destiny of So Tsi-fai (Chapter 3)?

2. "It's a reminder that it may take a lifetime to truly learn that while goals aren't that important, trusting myself and listening are." What brings Glickman to this conclusion? How does it affect his choices? How might Baker's mother (Chapter 1) respond to such a philosophy?

Applications

1. Glickman feels that his preoccupation with success in the future has diminished his enjoyment of the present. To what extent do you agree? Does this insight change your own outlook?

2. Glickman says that he was first attracted to Zen Buddhism because it "wasn't concerned with logic." Might Zen also have appealed to Glickman simply because it came from another culture?

from A Long Way to Go

Rosa Parks

Rosa Parks (b. 1913) from Pine Level, Alabama, became the center of civil rights controversy in 1955 when she was arrested for refusing to give up her seat on a bus to a white man in Montgomery, Alabama. In protest, the blacks of the city, led by 26-year-old Dr. Martin Luther King, Jr., boycotted the segregated buses. One year later the buses were desegregated. The Statue of Liberty is the fitting focal point of "A Long Way to Go," for it reflects Ms. Parks's assessment of complex race relations in the United States, past and present. Rosa Parks just published (with Jim Haskins) My Story *(Dial Books, 1992).*

WHEN I WAS COMING UP, I went to a one-room country school in Pine Level, Alabama, where all the pupils and the teachers were black. In the sixth grade, my mother sent me to Montgomery, where I went to the Montgomery Industrial School, which was run by Miss Alice White. She was a very proper older woman who ran the school with a group of Northern white ladies who were sympathetic to the plight of Negroes. That's what they called us back then.

In school, we learned all of the civics lessons that children were supposed to learn. We had to memorize Abraham Lincoln's Gettysburg Address and portions of the Constitution. We recited the Pledge of Allegiance. We studied all of the Presidents—Washington, Jefferson, Lincoln—and we knew about all the wars.

I guess for most of us children, the Statue of Liberty was just something we read about in a civics book. We learned that poem about the statue, but it was just another lesson we had to recite, just like the Civil War poem about the Blue and the Gray, or the Gettysburg Address.

The Africans who came over on the slave ships never saw the statue. Of course, they didn't mention that in the history books. The studies we did in our books were based on freedom and equality and the pursuit of happiness and all. But in reality we had to face the fact that we were not as free as the books said. What they taught us in school didn't apply to us as a race. We were being told to be as submissive and as useful as possible to white people, to do their work and see to their comforts and be segregated from them when they saw fit for us not to be around.

Even Miss Alice White, who had all the best intentions in the world, was part of the system. In her lectures, she would tell us how horrible slavery was, but then she would say that at least it brought the Negro out of savagery in Africa. Of course, none of those slave traders ever asked the Africans whether they wanted to come to America. I imagine that if the Africans had come around after the statue was built, they would have had some terrible ideas about what it meant to them. I don't think they would have written any poems.

My family knew the brutality and disillusionment of not being treated like human beings. My grandfather was a slave. He was the son of the plantation owner, so he was very white in appearance. My grandfather used to say that the overseer took an instant dislike to him because he looked so white. He would always tell me how he had to dodge and hide to keep out of trouble with the overseer. Until the day he died, my grandfather had a fierce hatred of white people.

My mother had a mind of her own. She always held to the belief that none of us should be mistreated because of our race. She was pretty outspoken, and of course that didn't endear her to too many whites. It didn't endear her to too many blacks, either, because in those days the general attitude among our people was to go along in silence. If you differed with that, you had to stand pretty much alone.

I remember that one of the first books I read, back when I was 8 years old, was called *Is the Negro a Beast?* That was the kind of attitude that white people had in Alabama in those days. It was so different from what we were reading about in our American history and civics lessons, with all the positive messages about life in this country, and I could see that what we were being taught wasn't so, at least as far as black people were concerned.

It didn't change much when I was working. I encountered all kinds of discrimination. If you were black in the South, it was just something you lived with all the time. I would just meet it in silence, bite my lip, go on. I saw it a lot with the bus drivers. If they thought you were about to make trouble, they would just shut the door on you and drive on off. In fact, the same red-headed driver who arrested me in 1955 [starting the Montgomery bus boycott led by Martin Luther King] had evicted me from a bus in 1943. He didn't want me to walk through the white section of the bus to get to the section for blacks, and I told him I wasn't going to get off the bus while I was already on. He took me by the sleeve of my winter coat and led me off. When I got on his bus again 12 years later, I remembered him very well, but I didn't expect him to disturb me a second time.

I didn't actually get to see the Statue of Liberty until about a year after the boycott. By that time, my attitude was a little different. I thought that saying—"Give me your tired, your poor . . ."—was impressive, that we should help people who come to the United States. This was a better place than where they had been.

I was invited to come to New York by Dr. Ralph Bunche and met him at the United Nations. I stayed with a Quaker couple, Mr. and Mrs. Stuart Meacham, who lived on Franklin D. Roosevelt Drive in Manhattan, right on the East River. Mr. Meacham asked me what was the first thing I wanted to do in New York. I told him, to see the Statue of Liberty. I had always been fascinated by tall buildings and monuments.

We went across the water by ferry about noon. It was just the way I thought it would be, that big arm waving the torch high above everything. We walked up all those stairs to the very top, right in the crown. We looked out from the windows in the crown, and we could see for miles. When we went back down, Mr. Meacham took my picture at the foot of the statue.

I guess the statue should be a symbol of freedom. I would not want our young people to be so disillusioned that they couldn't feel a sense of awe about it. But I can't find myself getting overwhelmed. We are supposed to be loyal and dedicated and committed to what America stands for. But we are still being denied complete equality. We have to struggle to gain a little bit, and as soon as it seems we make some gains for all our sacrifices, there are new obstacles, and people trying to take away what little we have.

Certainly there is a degree of freedom in America that we can celebrate, but as long as a difference in your complexion or your background can be used against you, we still have a long way to go.

Interpretations

1. How was Parks influenced by her family (for example, by choices her mother made and by her grandfather's reaction to slavery)?

2. How do the writer's childhood and adult responses to the Statue of Liberty differ? What accounts for the difference?

3. Do you agree with the writer's assessment of the current "degree of freedom in America" (last two paragraphs)?

4. Explain the significance of the title.

Correspondences

1. Review the Baldwin perspective on choices (page 443). How does it apply to "A Long Way to Go"? Does Parks accept "being trapped in history"? Cite evidence for your answer.

2. As a student in sixth grade, Parks concludes that "what they taught us in school didn't apply to us as a race." How might her educational

experience, that of Marshall and Rendón (Chapter 3), and that of Rodriguez and Novak (Chapter 5) be used to convince educators of the need for a multicultural curriculum in American elementary schools? (Also cite evidence from your own experience.)

Applications

1. Which is the more courageous response to the violence of others, violence or nonviolence? Narrate an incident that illustrates your position. Use the third person.

2. Rosa Parks was arrested for civil disobedience. Is there a cause for which you too would be willing to break the law? Under what circumstances can you imagine making such a choice?

Not Too Young to Understand Communism

Phan Huu Thanh

Phan Huu Thanh, born in the countryside of South Vietnam, moved with his family to Saigon in 1961. Thanh left Vietnam in 1980, leaving his family behind. He graduated from the University of Massachusetts in 1988 with a major in electrical engineering.

Since 1975, when American troops withdrew from Vietnam, approximately one million Vietnamese, Cambodians, and Laotians have fled their countries and settled in the United States. About the size of New Mexico, Vietnam enters history as a vassal state of China from 111 B.C. until 939 A.D., and from time to time thereafter. France conquered the area in 1858. After the Japanese occupation during World War II, guerilla leader Ho Chi Minh established a communist government in the North, and the French were defeated at Dienbienphu in 1954. The country was divided that same year into North Vietnam with Ho in firm control in his capital of Hanoi, and South Vietnam, with its capital at Saigon, which was soon racked with military coups and Buddhist opposition to the authoritarian government. Also in that same year the communists in the North began their attempts to conquer the South. U.S. airstrikes against the North began in 1964 and continued until U.S. troop strength reached a peak of 543,000 in 1969. U.S. troops began withdrawing in 1969, and ceasefires were signed in the hopes that South Vietnam could defend itself. Instead, the Saigon regime surrendered to the North Vietnamese in 1976, and the country was reunited as a communist state. The toll of the war was horrible: over a million civilian casualties, more than 58,000 U.S. combat deaths, and over 200,000 South Vietnamese combat deaths. Over six and a half million South Vietnamese war refugees like Thanh's family were displaced.

I WAS BORN in a poor family, in a far countryside. My parents were hard-working, ingenuous farmers. When I was two years old, my parents wanted to look for a better life so they decided to move to Saigon. With hard work, my parents succeeded in their business in the first years. At

456

the beginning of our stay in Saigon, with pockets almost empty, my parents bought a small house. This happened when I was six and started my schooling.

Like other children, beside studying and playing, I did not pay attention to the outside society or to the ups and downs of my family's life. When I entered high school, my parents opened a fabric and sewing store. Because the financial situation of my family became better, my everyday life improved. Time went by until I was seventeen years old. It was 1975, when the "Civil War" between the north and south of Vietnam reached a climax. It was the time when the Communists from the north were about to take over the south. I was called to join the army of South Vietnam in February and was ordered to report in July. Tragically, South Vietnam fell into the Communist hands in April 1975.

As a young boy, I was indifferent to political events, even to the biggest events which resulted in the disappearance of a country from the world's map. I was not shocked when the Communists took over my homeland. At that time, I was mistaken in thinking that the differences between the two regimes would not harm me. Living under communism, I realized that everybody's life was controlled completely by the Communists and that people were expected to become communists. I remember when I was a college freshman in 1978. I had to talk and act like a Communist. Otherwise, I would be considered bad and would be kicked out of school. I was told to join the Communist Youth party many times. I always thought of my future as a feeble one. I would never have a chance to follow my ideals. Hating the regime, hating the situation, I quit school and went to work.

At that time my parents' fabric and sewing goods store was closed because there were not as many customers as before. Perhaps people no longer cared about their appearance. People just hoped to have enough food for everyday survival. My parents had to change their business and they worked harder. After I quit school, I worked for a soy sauce factory that formerly belonged to my cousin but that was now controlled by the government. Not too long after I went to work, I was forced to join the Communist army. My parents were very upset about this, especially when they thought of my cousin who had been in the same situation as I was now and who was forced to join the Communist army. He fought and then died in Cambodia as a soldier.

My parents decided to prevent me from joining. They tried to convince me to leave Vietnam, and in the meantime, tried to find a way for me to escape. I disagreed because I knew that I would be far away from my family forever. I moved far away from my home to live with a cousin in the countryside because I would be arrested if I stayed home.

In 1980 I changed my mind and decided to leave Vietnam. My parents found an organization designed to help people leave the country. This group was organized by some officials of the former government in the south. They received very bad treatment after 1975. The Communists forced them into concentration camps for the purpose of brainwashing. After many years of being held, they were released and forced to live in the "New Economic Zones," which were in the wild and primitive jungles far away from civilization. Upon being put into such a situation, these people wanted to resist, but they could do nothing, so the idea of escaping communism and finding freedom in another country appealed to them. This was the only thing they could do, and they began to carry out the idea.

However, at first they had a lot of problems. One was financial. The amount of money they had altogether was not enough, so they had to look for companions. I was one of three people who responded. As my contribution I gave then two pieces of gold. The financial problem was finally solved. We now had money in hand. The next step was to buy a boat. Someone had to go to the fishing areas to seek information about this business. This work was not easy since in some areas like fishing and manufacturing, private business was no longer permitted. The Communist government tightly controlled everything. We tried and failed many times; however, at last we obtained a small boat from some fishermen who also wanted to leave the country due to Communist persecution. The boat was small, about 15 meters long and 2.5 meters wide, and was not in good condition for a long trip. We quickly rebuilt it. Some parts were replaced, and the boat was ready at last.

As a part of the preparation for the trip, we had ten days to buy food and gasoline. We bought rice and various canned foods. We did not forget to prepare a large amount of water. Also, we bought a compass, which would help us go in the right direction. Of great concern was a place to moor the boat and how to get people into it. The boat would never depart if we did not offer twenty pieces of gold to a high official in the local area. However, before departure the boat was searched and kept two days at a police post.

The boat sailed to the sea at dawn on October 25, 1980. With the help of a map and the compass, we were on our way to Singapore. Thinking about the promised land, we all were happy. We wished to see a ship from West Germany or England or the United States, because it would help make our trip shorter. Some people started to be seasick. They vomited. Some girls did the cooking and food was distributed sparingly. Night came, but nobody could sleep. The ocean looked dangerous in the dark.

A day went by and the second day began. At 10 A.M. we saw a ship. We did not know which country it was from because it was far away. To make a signal, we burned some clothing, hoping it would attract help. People yelled at the ship, but nothing worked. The ship kept its direction and disappeared on the horizon. The people became silent once again. In the evening, our captain was the first one to see a boat approaching.

People were perky and started talking. The coming boat was from Singapore, where we wanted to go. It was big, about forty meters in length, five meters in width. We saw just six people on the boat. It came within twenty meters of us. Two people used a small canoe to come to talk. They spoke Chinese. Luckily, there were some Chinese-Vietnamese people on our boat. When we asked them to take us to land, they said that they could not do that since the situation was politically related; however, they would pull our boat toward a beach provided we paid them fifteen pieces of gold. We did not have that much gold because most of it had gone in the preparation. Before leaving, they gave us some water, noodles, and two cartons of cigarettes. Also, they told us the direction to get to the island nearest our position. Someone got sick as another day went by.

I felt terrible when I remembered a story about boat people who were three weeks on the sea without food and water. Their boat was without gasoline. It went in no direction while people were dying. As for us, the boat was on its third day. People were very tired, except for the fishermen and people who were in the navy before. The captain always encouraged people. He said that without storms, pirates, or something wrong with the engine, we would get to Singapore within three more days. He paid attention to sick people and gave them medicine. Also, he did not forget to remind people to stay calm in any situation.

People in our situation fear the natural environment. In the evening, the sky was cloudy. It was the beginning of a storm. People were even more afraid, but we still hoped that the storm would be light. Once again we did not get our wish. It was a big storm, lasting more than twelve hours. It began at 9 P.M. and ended at 9:30 A.M. the next morning. The small boat had to fight with huge waves. It went up and down and seemed like it would capsize at any moment. The captain and fishermen were calm. Not only were they keeping us composed, but they also had to work at keeping the boat balanced. Aside from the sound of water beating on the sides of the boat, I heard prayers from many people. We stood at the threshold of death. Some water started to get in the boat through gaps made as waves beat over it breaking down the caulking that held the wood together. A fisherman went down to check and reported that the gaps were not dangerous. The skills of the captain and fishermen were wonderful. They did not let the boat "fall" in the face of the huge waves. The boat kept going slowly in the storm.

The sky returned to its beauty as the black clouds departed. Thank God, we were still alive. As if coming back from death, we were happy and started talking. Some men volunteered to do the cooking while some others made fun of girls who had been so scared during the storm the night before. It was the first time on the trip that I saw people laugh. I tried to sleep to pass another day.

We started the fifth day with an engine problem. Smoke came out of the smokestack in circular shapes. Someone said that the engine was about to stop. To relax the people, the captain said it would be all right if we turned off the engine for a while. (We thought that without a working engine the boat would be capsized if it met another storm. This was a terrible thought.) About 10 A.M., someone woke up the others when he first saw a helicopter coming. One can imagine how happy we were. With newly found energy, everybody waved and yelled at the helicopter. A woman was crying. Perhaps she was so happy because she knew that the coming helicopter was from the United States. The captain reminded people to stay calm again. He then tried to communicate with the pilots, but the helicopter just flew around and around and finally flew away. Some people felt bad, but the captain said "The Americans would never go away when they know we are in a situation like this. They will come back." He was right. Another helicopter and a warship came toward us. The captain told us that the ship and the helicopters belonged to the Seventh Fleet of the U.S. Navy, which was on mission in the Pacific Ocean. The warship came closer and closer. We could see soldiers in uniforms. They waved at us as they saw us waving at them. Many other soldiers came out. No action was taken for twenty minutes. (I knew later that the ship was waiting for an order from its headquarters, telling them what to do with us.) At last, the ship started rescuing us. Some soldiers were ordered to do the job. One of them, with one hand on the cable, used the other hand to pull each of us up to the ship while other soldiers got ready to help if someone fell into the sea. Person after person, finally all of us, got on the ship safely. We were so happy that we seemed to forget tiredness. We talked about the storm, the boat from Singapore, and everything that had happened. We all agreed that this was the luckiest thing that happened in our lives. Someone noticed an interesting thing when we were rescued: around the ship, in the distance, there were four other U.S. warships. They went away as we left our boat behind. The warship's captain ordered it to fire at our boat. We felt a loss as we saw the sinking boat.

A doctor came to take care of us. He passed out different kinds of medicines for the skin, and directed us on their use. He especially paid attention to sick people. After taking a shower, everybody felt better. We looked funny in oversized T-shirts, jeans, and navy uniforms. Later we took turns in going to the cafeteria for food while some soldiers prepared a place for us to sleep at night. We were on the way to Subic Bay, a U.S. Navy base in the Philippines. We arrived at Subic Bay two days later and stayed there for three days. We were then transferred to Manila by bus. After a week, we were once again transferred by plane to Palawan, a big island in the Philippines where there was a refugee camp.

In the camp, I did not have to do anything but study English. I often felt lonely and homesick. I missed my mother whose whole life was lived for her children. She never seemed tired of working hard. She often said to the children "I'm working for you, for your future. To make me happy, just try to study hard, just try to be useful." Before I left the country, she repeated it, but in another way, another emotion. She said "Be a good person in your new country, and study as much as you can. You've had no chances here, so don't miss your chances there. We'll be happy with your success. Write home often." I promised her, and she cried. I had never seen her cry before. I also missed my father, my brothers and sisters. However, I felt more independent, more self-confident, and stronger than ever.

After nine months of living in the camp, I left for the United States under the sponsorship of the International Rescue Committee. In July 1981, I was resettled in Boston, Massachusetts. The first months were a time of struggle. I faced so many problems, especially the language problem. I cannot forget the day I was beaten by some American teenagers. The scars are still on my hands, in front of my eyes. Every time I look at them, I see a group of young men standing at a corner. My sixth sense told me that something bad was about to happen. I passed the street and started to go faster, hoping nothing would happen, but the young men passed the street and chased after me. I ran and fell. One guy hit my back with a baseball bat as I stood up. Some others punched me. They left when a car stopped at the scene. I felt very bad and was sick for two days. Also, I lost my new watch.

I applied for admission to a high school. Although I was a college freshman in my country, I applied for the eleventh grade. I knew that the language problem would hinder me a lot. My new life began with disappointments; however, when I thought of my parents, of their sacrifice, I felt stronger. I tried to study harder and harder and hoped that my success in school would make my family happy. I got on many honor rolls in my two years in high school. Then I received the Boston Teachers' Union scholarship and the Franklin Medal on my graduation day. I was accepted by three universities: Northeastern University, Wentworth Institute of Technology, and the University of Massachusetts. Because of financial problems, I decided to go to UMass, a state university. I also decided to live in a dormitory because I thought that my studies would not be affected by my surroundings as much.

Until now, I have done nothing but study in my second country. I hope that I will get a good job in the future and become useful to society. One thing which is encouraging is that my family is very happy with what I am doing so far here in the United States.

I promised myself to do the best I can.

Interpretation

1. Of the choices Thanh makes here, how many were made or influenced by his family? How important to him is his family?

2. Most of Thanh's story—especially the first part—is summarized. Which part of this story does he tell in the greatest detail? Do you think it a wise decision to elaborate on this part? Why? Where would you recommend still more detail?

3. What is his greatest problem as a refugee in the United States? What do you think would be your greatest problem if you were in Thanh's shoes?

4. Why do you suppose Thanh makes no mention of the United States' part in the Vietnam War?

Correspondences

1. Thanh choose, for political reasons, to leave his native country. Compare his experience as an immigrant and student. To what extent does the United States fulfill Thanh's expectations as "the promised land"?

2. Review Frost's perspective on choices (page 444) and discuss its application to Thanh's essay. What "differences" has he confronted as a result of his choices? Under what circumstances can you imagine making a similar choice?

Applications

1. "I cannot forget the day I was beaten by some American teenagers." How does this experience compare with Thanh's treatment by Vietnamese Communists and as a "boat person"? Characterize his present attitude toward this beating.

2. Imagine being forced to leave your country. Freewrite on your possible responses to this situation.

To the Border

Richard Rodriguez

Richard Rodriguez (b. 1944) is from San Francisco and the child of Spanish-speaking Mexican immigrants. He entered school with little knowledge of English but graduated with a Ph.D. in literature from the University of California at Berkeley. Rodriguez has received critical acclaim for his autobiography Hunger of Memory: The Education of Richard Rodriguez *(1982). In "To the Border," he focuses on the plight and perils of Mexicans who have illegally crossed the Mexican-American border or have been contracted to work as farm workers in the United States.*

For more information on Mexico and Mexican immigration to the United States see Gary Soto, "Looking for Work," Chapter 4.

YOU STAND AROUND. You smoke. You spit. You are wearing your two shirts, two pants, two underpants. Jesús says if they chase you, throw that bag down. Your plastic bag is your mama, all you have left: the yellow cheese she wrapped has formed a translucent rind; the laminated scapular of the Sacred Heart nestles flame in its cleft. Put it in your pocket. Inside. Put it in your underneath pants' pocket. The last hour of Mexico is twilight, the shuffling of feet. Jesús says they are able to see in the dark. They have X rays and helicopters and searchlights. Jesús says wait, just wait, till he says. Though most of the men have started to move. You feel the hand of Jesús clamp your shoulder, fingers cold as ice. *Venga, corre.*[1] You run. All the rest happens without words. Your feet are tearing dry grass, your heart is lashed like a mare. You trip, you fall. You are now in the United States of America. You are a boy from a Mexican village. You have come into the country on your knees with your head down. You are a man.

Papa, what was it like?

I am his second son, his favorite child, his confidant. After we have polished the De Soto, we sit in the car and talk. I am sixteen years old. I fiddle with the knobs of the radio. He is fifty.

He will never say. He was an orphan there. He had no mother, he remembered none. He lived in a village by the ocean. He wanted books and he had none.

You are lucky, boy.

[1]Go, run.

In the Fifties, Mexican men were contracted to work in America as *braceros,* farm workers. I saw them downtown in Sacramento. I saw men my age drunk in Plaza Park on Sundays, on their backs on the grass. I was a boy at sixteen, but I was an American. At sixteen, I wrote a gossip column, "The Watchful Eye," for my school paper.

Or they would come into town on Monday nights for the wrestling matches or on Tuesdays for boxing. They worked over in Yolo County. They were men without women. They were Mexicans without Mexico.

On Saturdays, they came into town to the Western Union office where they sent money—money turned into humming wire and then turned back into money—all the way down into Mexico. They were husbands, fathers, sons. They kept themselves poor for Mexico.

Much that I would come to think, the best I would think about male Mexico, came as much from those chaste, lonely men as from my own father who made false teeth and who—after thirty years in America—owned a yellow stucco house on the east side of town.

The male is responsible. The male is serious. A man remembers.

Fidel, the janitor at church, lived over the garage at the rectory. Fidel spoke Spanish and was Mexican. He had a wife down there, people said; some said he had grown children. But too many years had passed and he didn't go back. Fidel had to do for himself. Fidel had a clean piece of linoleum on the floor, he had an iron bed, he had a table and a chair. He had a coffeepot and a frying pan and a knife and a fork and a spoon, I guess. And everything else Fidel sent back to Mexico. Sometimes, on summer nights, I would see his head through the bars of the little window over the garage at the rectory.

The migration of Mexico is not only international, south to north. The epic migration of Mexico, and throughout Latin America, is from the village to the city. And throughout Latin America, the city has ripened, swollen with the century. Lima, Caracas, Mexico City. So the journey to Los Angeles is much more than a journey from Spanish to English. It is the journey from *tú*—the familiar, the erotic, the intimate pronoun—to the repellent *usted* of strangers' eyes.

It is 1986 and I am a journalist. I am asking questions of a Mexican womon in her East L.A. house. She is watchful and pretty, in her thirties, she wears an apron. Her two boys—Roy and Danny—are playing next door. Her husband is a tailor. He is sewing in a bright bedroom at the back of the house. His feet work the humming treadle of an old Singer machine as he croons Mexican love songs by an open window.

I will send for you or I will come home rich.

Mexico is poor. But my mama says there are no love songs like the love songs of Mexico. She hums a song she can't remember. The ice cream there is creamier than here. Someday we will see. The people are kinder—poor, but kinder to each other.

My mother's favorite record is *"Mariachis de Mexico y Pepe Villa con Orquesta."*

Men sing in Mexico. Men are strong and silent. But in song the Mexican male is granted license he is otherwise denied. The male can admit longing, pain, desire.

HAIII—EEEE—a cry like a comet rises over the song. A cry like mock weeping tickles the refrain of Mexican love songs. The cry is meant to encourage the balladeer—it is the raw edge of his sentiment. HAIII-EEEE. It is the man's sound. A ticklish arching of semen, a node wrung up a guitar string, until it bursts in a descending cascade of mockery. HAI. HAI. HAI. The cry of a jackal under the moon, the whistle of the phallus, the maniacal song of the skull.

Mexico is on the phone—long-distance.

A crow alights upon a humming wire, bobs up and down, needles the lice within his vest, surveys with clicking eyes the field, the cloud of mites, then dips into the air and flies away.

Juanito killed! My mother shrieks, drops the phone in the dark. She cries for my father. For light.

The earth quakes. The peso flies like chaff in the wind. The police chief purchases his mistress a mansion on the hill.

The door bell rings. I split the blinds to see three nuns standing on our front porch.

Mama. Mama.

Monsignor Lyons has sent three Mexican nuns over to meet my parents. The nuns have come to Sacramento to beg for Mexico at the eleven o'clock Mass. We are the one family in the parish that speaks Spanish. As they file into our living room, the nuns smell pure, not sweet, pure like candles or like laundry.

The nun with a black mustache sighs at the end of each story the other two tell. Orphan. Leper. Crutch. Dry land. One eye. Casket.

¡Que lástima![2]
Tell me, Papa.
What?
About Mexico.

---

[2]What a pity!

I lived with the family of my uncle. I was the orphan in the village. I used to ring the church bells in the morning, many steps up in the dark. When I'd get up to the tower I could see the ocean.

The village, Papa, the houses too . . .

The ocean. He studies the polished hood of our beautiful blue De Soto.

Relatives invited relatives. Entire Mexican villages got re-created in three stories of a single house. In the fall, after the harvest in the Valley, families of Mexican adults and their American children would load up their cars and head back to Mexico in caravans, for weeks, for months. The schoolteacher said to my mother what a shame it was the Mexicans did that—took their children out of school.

Like Wandering Jews. They carried their home with them, back and forth; they had no true home but the tabernacle of memory.

Each year the American kitchen takes on a new appliance.

The children are fed and grow tall. They go off to school with children from Vietnam, from Kansas, from Hong Kong. They get into fights. They come home and they say dirty words.

The city will win. The city will give the children all the village could not—VCRs, hairstyles, drumbeat. The city sings mean songs, dirty songs. But the city will sing the children a great Protestant hymn.

You can be anything you want to be.

Your coming of age. It is early. From your bed you watch your mama moving back and forth under the light. The bells of the church ring in the dark. Mama crosses herself. From your bed you watch her back as she wraps the things you will take.

You are sixteen. Your father has sent for you. That's what it means. He has sent an address in Nevada. He is there with your uncle. You remember your uncle remembering snow with his beer.

You dress in the shadows. You move toward the table, the circle of light. You sit down. You force yourself to eat. Mama stands over you to make the sign of the cross on your forehead with her thumb. You are a man. You smile. She puts the bag of food in your hands. She says she has told *La Virgen*.

Then you are gone. It is gray. You hear a little breeze. It is the rustle of your old black Dueña, the dog, taking her shortcuts through the weeds, crazy Dueña, her pads on the dust. She is following you.

You pass the houses of the village, each window is a proper name. You pass the store. The bar. The lighted window of the clinic where the pale medical student from Monterrey lives alone and reads his book full of sores late into the night.

You want to be a man. You have the directions in your pocket: an address in Tijuana and a map with a yellow line that leads from the highway to an X on a street in Reno. You are afraid, but you have never seen snow.

You are just beyond the cemetery. The breeze has died. You turn and throw a rock back at La Dueña, where you know she is—where you will always know where she is. She will not go past the cemetery. She will turn in circles like a *loca*[3] and bite herself.

The dust takes on gravel, the path becomes a rutted road which leads to the highway. You walk north. The sky has turned white overhead. Insects click in the fields. In time, there will be a bus.

I will send for you or I will come home rich.

Interpretations

1. Who is the "you" in the first (and subsequent) sentence? What choice has been made?

2. What attitude did the sixteen-year-old Rodriguez have toward the Mexican farm workers he saw downtown in Sacramento? How far removed from their situation was his? (How does this account for his attitude?)

3. What attitude toward the United States is revealed by the last line of the essay?

4. The last vignette of this essay describes the beginning of a voyage from the known to the unknown: ". . . each window is a proper name." What are some of the "knowns" the Mexican boy is leaving? Why do you think Rodriguez chose to include each of them? What is their combined impact?

5. Rodriguez avoids a bald statement of his main point or thesis, apparently preferring to create a mood and force his reader to intuit meaning. What is the mood and the point?

Correspondences

1. "So the journey to Los Angeles is much more than a journey from Spanish to English. It is the journey from *tú*—the familiar, the erotic, the intimate pronoun—to the repellant *usted* of strangers' eyes." What is Rodriguez implying about the personal costs involved in "choosing" to cross the border? To what extent did Thanh's decision to leave Vietnam involve similar costs?

[3]Crazy woman.

2. "The male is responsible. The male is serious. A man remembers." What did Rodriguez learn from his male role models? How does his experience compare to that of Rendón (Chapter 3)? How did their mentors affect their choices?

Applications

1. Rodriguez writes that the Mexican migrant workers are "[l]ike Wandering Jews. They carried their home with them, back and forth; they had no true home but the tabernacle of memory." What is the meaning here of "tabernacle"? In what sense does memory serve as a refuge? At what price does one "choose" to become a migrant worker?

2. *"You can be anything you want to be."* Is this belief a realistic basis on which to choose to emigrate to the United States? Does the United States offer this possibility to all of its citizens? Write an essay stating specific reasons for your point of view.

The Moment Before the Gun Went Off

Nadine Gordimer

Nadine Gordimer (b. 1923) was born in Johannesburg, South Africa, and educated at the University of Witwatersrand. She is the renowned author of nine novels and eight volumes of short stories, the recipient of numerous international awards, and an outspoken critic of South African apartheid policies. Her most recent novel is My Son's Story *(1990). Nadine Gordimer was awarded the Nobel Prize for Literature in 1991.*

Apartheid (apartness) became law in South Africa in 1948; under it blacks and those of mixed race (coloreds) live separately from whites and have been forced into overcrowded and poverty-stricken townships.

For more information on South Africa see Mtutuzeli Matshoba, "Call Me Not a Man," In Chapter 5.

MARAIS VAN DER VYVER shot one of his farm laborers, dead. An accident, there are accidents with guns every day of the week—children playing a fatal game with a father's revolver in the cities where guns are domestic objects, nowadays, hunting mishaps like this one, in the country—but these won't be reported all over the world. Van der Vyver knows his will be. He knows that the story of the Afrikaner farmer—regional leader of the National Party and commandant of the local security commando— shooting a black man who worked for him will fit exactly *their* version of South Africa, it's made for them. They'll be able to use it in their boycott and divestment campaigns, it'll be another piece of evidence in their truth about the country. The papers at home will quote the story as it has appeared in the overseas press, and in the back and forth he and the black man will become those crudely drawn figures on anti-apartheid banners, units in statistics of white brutality against blacks quoted at the United Nations—he, whom they will gleefully be able to call "a leading member" of the ruling Party.

People in the farming community understand how he must feel. Bad enough to have killed a man, without helping the Party's, the government's, the country's enemies as well. They see the truth of that. They know, reading the Sunday papers, that when Van der Vyver is quoted saying he is "terribly shocked," he will "look after the wife and children," none of those Americans and English, and none of those people at home who want to destroy the white man's power will believe him. And how they will sneer when he even says of the farm boy (according to one paper, if you can trust any of those reporters), "He was my friend, I always took him hunting with me." Those city and overseas people don't know it's true: farmers usually have one particular black boy they like to take along with them in the lands; you could call it a kind of friend, yes, friends are not only your own white people, like yourself, whom you take into your house, pray with in church, and work with on the Party committee. But how can those others know that? They don't want to know it. They think all blacks are like the bigmouth agitators in town. And Van der Vyver's face in the photographs, strangely opened by distress—everyone in the district remembers Marais Van der Vyver as a little boy who would go away and hide himself if he caught you smiling at him, and everyone knows him now as a man who hides any change of expression round his mouth behind a thick, soft mustache, and in his eyes by always looking at some object in hand, a leaf or a crop fingered, pen or stone picked up, while concentrating on what he is saying, or while listening to you. It just goes to show what shock can do; when you look at the newspaper photographs you feel like apologizing, as if you had stared in on some room where you should not be.

There will be an inquiry; there had better be, to stop the assumption of yet another case of brutality against farm workers, although there's nothing in doubt—an accident, and all the facts fully admitted by Van der Vyver. He made a statement when he arrived at the police station with the dead man in his *bakkie*. Captain Beetge knows him well, of course; he gave him brandy. He was shaking, this big, calm, clever son of Willem Van der Vyver, who inherited the old man's best farm. The black was stone dead, nothing to be done for him. Beetge will not tell anyone that after the brandy Van der Vyver wept. He sobbed, snot running onto his hands, like a dirty kid. The captain was ashamed for him, and walked out to give him a chance to recover himself.

Marais Van der Vyver left his house at three in the afternoon to cull a buck from the family of kudu he protects in the bush areas of his farm. He is interested in wildlife and sees it as the farmers' sacred duty to raise game as well as cattle. As usual, he called at his shed to pick up Lucas, a twenty-year-old farmhand who had shown mechanical aptitude and whom Van der Vyver himself had taught to maintain tractors and other farm machinery. He hooted, and Lucas followed the familiar routine, jumping onto the back of the truck. He liked to travel standing up there, spotting game before his employer did. He would lean forward, bracing against the cab below him.

Van der Vyver had a rifle and .30 caliber ammunition beside him in the cab. The rifle was one of his father's, because his own was at the gunsmith's in town. Since his father died (Beetge's sergeant wrote "passed on") no one had used the rifle, and so when he took it from a cupboard he was sure it was not loaded. His father had never allowed a loaded gun in the house, he himself had been taught since childhood never to ride with a loaded weapon in a vehicle. But this gun was loaded. On a dirt track, Lucas thumped his fist on the cab roof three times to signal: look left. Having seen the white-ripple-marked flank of a kudu, and its fine horns raking through disguising bush, Van der Vyver drove rather fast over a pothole. The jolt fired the rifle. Upright, it was pointing straight through the cab roof at the head of Lucas. The bullet pierced the roof and entered Lucas's brain by way of his throat.

That is the statement of what happened. Although a man of such standing in the district, Van der Vyver had to go through the ritual of swearing that it was the truth. It has gone on record, and will be there in the archive of the local police station as long as Van der Vyver lives, and beyond that, through the lives of his children, Magnus, Helena, and Karel—unless things in the country get worse, the example of black mobs in the town spreads to the rural areas and the place is burned down as many urban police stations have been. Because nothing the government can do will appease the agitators and the whites who encourage them. Nothing satisfies them, in the cities: blacks can sit and drink in white hotels now, the Immorality Act has gone, blacks can sleep with whites . . . It's not even a crime anymore.

Van der Vyver has a high, barbed security fence round his farmhouse and garden which his wife, Alida, thinks spoils completely the effect of her artificial stream with its tree ferns beneath the jacarandas. There is an aerial soaring like a flagpole in the backyard. All his vehicles, including the truck in which the black man died, have aerials that swing their whips when the driver hits a pothole: they are part of the security system the farmers in the district maintain, each farm in touch with every other by radio, twenty-four hours out of twenty-four. It has already happened that infiltrators from over the border have mined remote farm roads, killing white farmers and their families out on their own property for a Sunday picnic. The pothole could have set off a land mine, and Van der Vyver might have died with his farm boy. When neighbors use the communications system to call up and say they are sorry about "that business" with one of Van der Vyver's boys, there goes unsaid: it could have been worse.

It is obvious from the quality and fittings of the coffin that the farmer has provided money for the funeral. And an elaborate funeral means a great deal to blacks; look how they will deprive themselves of the little they have, in their lifetime, keeping up payments to a burial society so they won't go in boxwood to an unmarked grave. The young wife is pregnant (of course) and another little one, a boy wearing red shoes several sizes too large, leans under her jutting belly. He is too young to understand what has happened, what he is witnessing that day, but neither whines nor plays about; he is solemn without knowing why. Blacks expose small children to everything, they don't protect them from the sight of fear and pain the way whites do theirs. It is the young wife who rolls her head and cries like a child, sobbing on the breast of this relative and that. All present work for Van der Vyver or are the families of those who work; in the weeding and harvest seasons, the women and children work for him too, carried at sunrise to the fields, wrapped in their blankets, on a truck, singing. The dead man's mother is a woman who can't be more than in her late thirties (they start bearing children at puberty), but she is heavily mature in a black dress, standing between her own parents, who were already working for old Van der Vyver when Marais, like their daughter, was a child. The parents hold her as if she were a prisoner or a crazy woman to be restrained. But she says nothing, does nothing. She does not look up; she does not look at Van der Vyver, whose gun went off in the truck, she stares at the grave. Nothing will make her look up; there need be no fear that she will look up, at him. His wife, Alida, is beside him. To show the proper respect, as for any white funeral, she is wearing the navy blue and cream hat she wears to church this summer. She is always supportive, although he doesn't seem to notice it; this coldness and reserve—his mother says he didn't mix well as a child—she accepts for herself but regrets that it has prevented him from being nominated, as he should be, to stand as the Party's parliamentary candidate for the district. He does not let her clothing, or that of anyone else gathered closely, make contact with him. He, too, stares at the grave. The dead man's mother and he stare at the grave in communication like that between the black man outside and the white man inside the cab the moment before the gun went off.

The moment before the gun went off was a moment of high excitement shared through the roof of the cab, as the bullet was to pass, between the young black man outside and the white farmer inside the vehicle. There were such moments, without explanation, between them, although often around the farm the farmer would pass the young man without returning a greeting, as if he did not recognize him. When the bullet went off what Van der Vyver saw was the kudu stumble in fright at the report and gallop away. Then he heard the thud behind him, and past the window saw the young man fall out of the vehicle. He was sure he had leapt up and toppled—in fright, like the buck. The farmer was almost laughing with relief, ready to tease, as he opened his door, it did not seem possible that a bullet passing through the roof could have done harm.

The young man did not laugh with him at his own fright. The farmer carried him in his arms, to the truck. He was sure, sure he could not be dead. But the young black man's blood was all over the farmer's clothes, soaking against his flesh as he drove.

How will they ever know, when they file newspaper clippings, evidence, proof, when they look at the photographs and see his face— guilty! guilty! they are right!—how will they know, when the police stations burn with all the evidence of what has happened now, and what the law made a crime in the past? How could they know that *they do not know*. Anything. The young black callously shot through the negligence of the white man was not the farmer's boy; he was his son.

Interpretations

1. From whose point of view is the story told? How and why does the author put the reader in an awkward position?

2. How does Van der Vyver's wife view her husband's emotional state?

3. Why will the captain not tell anyone that Van der Vyver wept? How does his weeping confirm or refute his wife's opinion of him?

4. What is ironic about the statement that "blacks can sleep with whites now"?

5. What important choices has Van der Vyver made in the past? What does he now face as a result?

Correspondences

1. Gordimer's protagonist assumes financial responsibility for the family of the young man he shot accidentally. How did this affect your view of him? (Would he have done this had he not also been his illegitimate son? Why or why not?) What does this story and the essays by Parks and Bonilla suggest about the *consequences* of choices?

2. To what extent is Gordimer's South Africa patriarchal? What is the evidence? How does her portrayal of patriarchy compare to that of Rodriguez in "To the Border"?

Applications

1. Write an essay analyzing the public and private lives of Van der Vyver. To what extent was his public life the result of a personal choice?

2. Study the life and career of one of the following South Africans: Nelson Mandela, Winnie Mandela, Nadine Gordimer, Athol Fugard, Stephen Biko, Bishop Desmond Tutu, or Donald Woods. Then write an analysis of the factors behind your subject's choice to fight apartheid.

Passport to Knowledge

Mark Mathabane

Mark Mathabane was born in 1960 in South Africa. His skill as a tennis player led to an athletic scholarship at a college in the United States. His first book, Kaffir Boy *(1986), from the which the following excerpt is taken, recounts some of his experiences growing up under the repressive system of apartheid; his second book,* Kaffir Boy in America *(1989), describes his life in the United States. Mathabane and his wife Gail have just published a third book,* Love in Black and White *(1992).*

TO LEARN TO EXPRESS my thoughts and feelings effectively in English became my main goal in life. I saw command of the English language as the crucial key with which to unlock doors leading into that wonderful world of books revealed to me through the reading of Robert Louis Stevenson's gripping tale of buried treasure, mutiny on the high seas, one-legged seamen and the old sea song that I could recite even in my dreams:

> Fifteen men on a dead man's chest
> Yo-ho-ho, and a bottle of rum.

My heart ached to explore more such worlds, to live them in the imagination in much the same way as I lived the folktales of my mother and grandmother. I reasoned that if I somehow kept improving my English and ingratiated Mrs. Smith by the fact, then possibly she would give me more books like *Treasure Island* each time Granny took me along. Alas, such trips were few and far between. I could not afford to skip school regularly; and besides, each trip did not yield a book. But I clung to my dream.

A million times I wondered why the sparse library at my tribal school did not carry books like *Treasure Island,* why most of the books we read had tribal points of view. I would ask teachers and would be told that under the Bantu Education law black children were supposed to acquire a solid foundation in tribal life, which would prepare them for a productive future in their respective homelands. In this way the dream of Dr. Verwoerd, prime minister of South Africa and the architect of Bantu Education, would be realised, for he insisted that "the native child must be taught subjects which will enable him to work with and among his own people; therefore there is no use misleading him by showing him the green pastures of European society, in which he is not allowed to graze. Bantu Education should not be used to create imitation Whites."

How I cursed Dr. Verwoerd and his law for prescribing how I should feel and think. I started looking toward the Smiths to provide me with the books about a different reality. Each day Granny came back from work around five in the afternoon, I would be the first to meet her at the gate, always with the same question, "Any books for me today?" Many times there weren't any. Unable to read new English books on a regular basis, I reread the ones I had over and over again, till the pages become dog-eared. With each reading each book took on new life, exposed new angles to the story, with the result that I was never bored.

My bleak vocabulary did not diminish my enthusiasm for reading. I constantly borrowed Mr. Brown's pocket-size dictionary to look up meanings of words, and would memorize them like arithmetic tables and write them in a small notebook. Sometimes I would read the dictionary. My pronunciation was appalling, but I had no way of finding out. I was amazed at the number of words in the English language, at the fact that a word could have different shades of meaning, or that certain words looked and sounded alike and yet differed greatly in meaning. Would I ever be able to learn all that?

At the same time I was discovering the richness of the English language I began imitating how white people talked, in the hope of learning proper pronunciation. My efforts were often hilarious, but my determination increased with failure. I set myself the goal of learning at least two new English words a day.

At this time Uncle Pietrus, on my father's side, had moved into our yard. A bachelor with some education, he read the *World* and the black edition of the *Star* every day. Each evening I would go to his shack to borrow the two papers. I often found him through with chores, and the two of us would sit and discuss the mainstay of black news: crime, sports (mainly boxing and soccer), murder stories (the staggering statistics and the gruesome ways through which blacks killed blacks) and the latest police raids and shebeen swoops.

On Mondays and Fridays we filled out Jackpots (crossword puzzles that paid cash prizes to winners). We never won anything, but my vocabulary benefitted from the exercise. I began looking for opportunities to use my improved vocabulary in conversation. But such opportunities were rare: all talk, all teaching, all thinking for that matter, at my school was in Tsonga. The only time I encountered English was during the English period, one of the shortest in school, devoted mainly to honing servanthood English. For lack of practise I soon forgot many of the words and had to relearn them, only to forget them again, only to relearn them. I refused to quit.

My love for reading removed me from the streets and curtailed my involvement in gangs. This infuriated the leaders of my gang, the Thirteenth Avenue Tomahawks. Friends within warned me that there was a plot afoot to teach me a lesson for not showing up at the gang's fights. The Thirteenth Avenue Tomahawks fought just about every week, against this or that street's gang, for reasons ranging from territorial disputes to harassment of each other's girlfriends.

One weekday afternoon while I was splitting wood in front of our house the leader of the Thirteenth Avenue Tomahawks, a sixteen-year-old delinquent named Jarvas—whose claim to notoriety was that he once stabbed a rival to death over a girl he later made pregnant and dumped—and several of his henchmen approached me. The Tomahawks were in the middle of a protracted, two-pronged war against rival gangs, the Mongols from Sixteenth Avenue and the Dirty Dozen from Eleventh Avenue.

"Are you still one of us?" Jarvas demanded, in a tone suggesting that he normally let his knife do the talking, but was doing me a favour by giving me a chance to exonerate myself.

My heart was no longer into gangs, but I replied, "Yes."

"Then why haven't you been in any of our recent fights?"

"I've been too busy."

"So busy you neglect your gang duties?" he sneered.

"I've had too much schoolwork."

"Oh, too much schoolwork, heh," he said, doffing his worn-out beret in mock salute. "Excuse us for bothering you, Professor, we didn't know you were that busy." At this, his cohorts, who were smoking several bottles of glue, laughed.

I kept silent, sensing that Jarvas was provoking me into saying something that might give him an excuse to stab me. I bore the stream of filth he and his cohorts spewed at me, for I knew that it was better to act a coward and live than to act a hero and end up six feet under.

"What have you to say, wimp?" Jarvas sneered. "Will you fight, or will you hide behind your mama's apron like a little girl?"

"I'll fight in the next fight," I said.

"Better be there," Jarvas said, "If you know what's good for you."

The group left, and I sank into despair. Just when things were beginning to turn around in my life, this had to happen.

The next fight was on Saturday. It was a hot day. The Tomahawks were locked in fierce combat against the Mongols. Traffic was at a standstill as the two gangs went at each other with every type of weapon imaginable: tomahawks, machetes, bottles, rocks, daggers, slingshots, crowbars.

I was in the middle row of the Tomahawk formation, slingshot in hand. I had been grazed several times by rocks and bottles, but fought on. Mothers called their sons home, but we paid no heed. Amidst whistling, yelling and cursing, something whizzed past me, barely missing my head, but struck a barrel-chested thirteen-year-old boy to my left. He clutched his face and shrieked. "The bastards. They've hurt my eye." A couple of us rushed to his side. Someone said, "Let go of your face and let's see." He removed his bloodied hand from his face. His right eye had been completely gouged out by a stone from a slingshot.

Blood spurted out from the socket, down his cheeks like giant tear-drops. There were no cars nearby, no phones, no means of getting him to the clinic. He might bleed to death, and he would be one-eyed for the rest of his life. Those thoughts numbed me. Then and there I decided to quit the gang, permanently.

On the way home, voices kept ringing in my head. Why do you fight when you don't want to? It could easily have been you with the gouged eye. Are you willing to pay such a price for conformity? Leave the gang, leave it now, while you still have both eyes, and your life; leave it now and be called a wimp for the rest of your life, if need be; but do not needlessly, recklessly and foolishly jeopardize your future.

I never again fought for any gang.

My leaving the gang, however, brought hostility and harassment. Jarvas warned me that my days were numbered, but I was resolved on quitting. Now an outcast and a marked man, I seldom travelled alone at night. During the day, I promptly came home after school and spent the rest of the day doing homework, reading and helping around the house. Occasionally, I would go out and play soccer with boys who did not belong to gangs.

My parents had known all along that I was involved with gangs and had said nothing, but when the harassment increased, I decided to tell them that I had quit gang life.

My mother, when she heard the full story behind my decision, heaved a deep sigh of relief and said, "You had two paths to choose from, just like every black boy in Alexandra: to become a *tsotsi,* or not to become a *tsotsi.* You chose the difficult way out. From now on, the going will be rough, for your *tsotsi* friends will try everything to make you change your mind. I hope you will remain firm in your decision. If you do, chances are you'll live to be old enough not to regret it."

My father in a typical remark said, "Watch out they don't kill you." He paused, then added, "Maybe it's about time I sent you to a school back in the homelands, where they'll make a warrior out of you."

Interpretations

1. Dr. Verwoerd's Bantu Education law assumed that learning should begin and end with one's own culture. Do you agree that the curriculum of the earliest grades, at least, should concentrate on one's own

culture, leaving until later years the study, if any, of other cultures? Or should schools from the beginning provide instruction in other cultures?

2. Perhaps the most important choice Mathabane makes in this selection is to leave the gang. Was it the right choice? What were its ramifications?

Correspondences

1. Mathabane and Rodriguez present contrasting attitudes toward their respective native tongues. Explain the reasons for their points of view. Who best expresses your thinking about language?

2. South Africa is the setting for the selections by Gordimer and Mathabane. Compare and contrast their portrayals of black life under apartheid.

Applications

1. Discuss Mathabane's attitude toward books. To what extent do you share his belief that language is power? What evidence can you offer?

2. Rose (Chapter 4) and Mathabane discuss gang life in their neighborhoods. What factors account for power and popularity? Speculate as to their social effects. How might they affect one's choices?

A Tale of Two Moralities

Peter Berger

Peter Ludwig Berger (b. 1929) was born in Vienna, Austria, and emigrated to the United States in 1946. He received his Ph.D. in 1954 from the New School for Social Research and has taught at several major universities, among them Brooklyn College of the City University of New York and Rutgers University. His publications include The Homeless Mind: Modernization and Consciousness *(1973),* Pyramids of Sacrifice: Political Ethics and Change *(1974), and* To Empower People: The Role of Mediating Structures in Public Policy *(1977). In the following selection, Berger examines some ethical and cultural dilemmas that commonly confront many Mexican immigrants in the United States.*

For more information about Mexican-Americans see the headnote on Rendón on page 163.

MANUELA KEEPS DREAMING about the village. She does not think about it very much in the daytime. Even when she thinks about Mexico, it is not usually about the village. In any case, during the day it is the brash, gleaming reality of California that dominates, its loud demand for full attention pushing into the background the old images and feelings. It is at night that the village comes back, reclaiming its power over Manuela. It is then as if she had never left it—or, worse, as if she must inevitably return to it.

It is often very hot in the village, though at night one may freeze. The earth is dry. Time moves very slowly, as the white clouds move through the brightly blue sky over the brown and arid hills. Time moves slowly in the faces of the people, too, and the faces too are brown and arid. Even the faces of the very young seem to hold old memories. The children do not smile easily. The day is measured by the halting motion of shadows over houses and trees. The years are mostly measured by calamities. The past is powerfully present, although there are few words for it. No one in the village speaks an Indian language, though everyone has Indian blood. Can the blood speak, without words? Do the dead speak from the earth? Somewhere in this blue sky and in these brown hills there are very old presences, more threatening than consoling. Some years ago the schoolteacher dug up some Indian artifacts and wanted to take them to the city, to sell them to a museum. Calamity struck at once, all over the village. The dead do not want to be disturbed, and they are dangerous.

The village is distant. Distant from what? Distant from everything, but most importantly distant from the places where time moves quickly and purposefully. There is no paved road, no telephone, no electricity. Even the schoolteacher only comes on two days of the week. He has two other villages to take care of, and he lives somewhere else. To get to the nearest bus station one rides on a donkey for three hours over footpaths of trampled dirt. Time and distance determine the world of the village, in fact and in Manuela's dreams. If she were to put it in one sentence, this world, she would have to say: It is very far away, and life there moves very slowly. On the maps the village is in the state of Guerrero, in a very specific location between Mexico City and the Pacific Ocean. In Manuela's dreams the village is located in the center of her self, deep down inside rather than out there somewhere.

Manuela was born in the village twenty-two years ago. Her mother died shortly afterward. Her father, already married to another woman with seven legitimate children, never acknowledged Manuela. Indeed, he has never spoken with her. She was raised by one of her mother's brothers, a man without land and much of the time without work, with a large family of his own that he barely managed to support. There was never any question about the family obligation to take care of Manuela; the only question at the time, lengthily discussed by her grandfather and the three uncles still living in the area, was which of the three would take the baby in. But this obligation did not greatly exceed supplying the bare necessities of life. There was never the slightest doubt about Manuela's status in her uncle's household as the unwanted bastard who took the food out of the mouths of her more deserving cousins—and she was told so in no uncertain terms on many occasions. If there was little food, she would be the hungriest. If there was hard work, she would be the one to do it. This does not mean that she received no affection. She was a very pretty, winsome child, and often people were kind to her. But she always knew that affection and kindness were not her right, were given to her gratuitously—and, by the same token, could be gratuitously taken away again. As a child Manuela wished for someone who would love her all the time, reliably, "officially." However, she was only dimly unhappy in her uncle's household, since she knew nothing else. She was often hungry, sometimes beaten. She did not have shoes until her tenth birthday, when her grandfather made her a present of a pair. This was also the first occasion when she went outside the village, accompanying her grandfather on a visit to the doctor in the nearest town.

Her grandfather and one of her uncles in the village were *ejidatários*, belonging to the minority that owned parcels of land under the village *ejido* (agricultural cooperative). Most of the time the uncle with whom she stayed worked on this land, too, though he would hire himself out for work elsewhere when there was an opportunity. When she was not working in the house or taking care of her little cousins, Manuela also worked in the fields or with the animals belonging to her family. After her tenth birthday she sometimes worked for outsiders, but she was expected to turn over the money she received for this. Sometimes she succeeded in keeping a few coins for herself, though she knew that she would be beaten if found out. She was allowed to go to school and, being very bright, she learned to read and write well. It was her brightness that attracted her grandfather, who was amused by her and took a liking to her (much to the annoyance of her cousins).

"Bad blood will show." "You will come to no good end, like your mother." Manuela must have heard this hundreds of times during her childhood. The prophecy was fulfilled when she was fifteen and made pregnant by the secretary of the *ejido,* one of the most affluent farmers in the village. When her condition could no longer be concealed, there was a terrible scene and her uncle threw her out of the house. Her grandfather, after slapping her a couple of times rather mildly, gave her the address of an aunt in Acapulco and enough money to pay her busfare there. It was thus that she left the village.

Manuela marveled at Acapulco and its astonishing sights, but, needless to say, she lived there in a world far removed from that experienced by the tourists. Her aunt, a gentle widow with two children and a maid's job in one of the big hotels, took Manuela in very warmly (at least in part because she could use some help in the house). Manuela's baby was born there, a healthy boy whom she named Roberto. Not much later Manuela also started to work outside the house.

A Mexican *campesino,* when he migrates, normally follows an itinerary taken before him by relatives and *compadres.* When he arrives, the latter provide an often intricate network of contacts that are indispensable for his adjustment to the new situation. They will often provide initial housing, they can give information and advice, and, perhaps most important, they serve as an informal labor exchange. Such a network awaited Manuela in Acapulco. In addition to the aunt she was staying with, there were two more aunts and an uncle with their respective families, including some twelve cousins of all ages. This family system, of course, was transposed to the city life from the village, but it took on a quite different character in the new context. Freed from the oppressive constraints of village life, the system, on the whole, was more benign. Manuela experienced it as such. Several of her cousins took turns taking care of little Roberto when Manuela started to work. Her aunt's "fiancé" (a somewhat euphemistic term), who was head clerk in the linen supply department of the hotel, found Manuela a job in his department. The uncle, through a *compadre* who was head waiter in another hotel, helped her get a job there as a waitress. It was this uncle, incidentally, who had gone further than any other member of the Acapulco clan, at least for a brief time. An intelligent and aggressive man, he worked himself up in the municipal sanitation department to the rank of inspector. Through a coup, the

details of which were shrouded in mystery but which were safely assumed by everyone to involve illegality of heroic proportions, Uncle
Pepe amassed the equivalent of about one thousand U.S. dollars in a few
months' time, a staggering sum in this ambience. With this money he set
out for Mexico City, ostensibly to look into a business proposition. In fact
he checked into one of the capital's finest hotels, made the rounds of
nightclubs and luxury brothels, and returned penniless but not overly
unhappy a month later. The clan has viewed him with considerable awe
ever since.

Manuela now had a fairly steady cash income, modest to be sure, but
enough to keep going. This does not mean, however, that she could keep
all of it for herself and her child. The family system operated as a social
insurance agency as well as a labor exchange, and there was never a
shortage of claimants. An aunt required an operation. An older cousin set
up business as a mechanic and needed some capital to start off. Another
cousin was arrested and a substantial *mordida* was required to bribe his
way out of jail. And then there were always new calamities back in the
village, requiring emergency transfers of money back there. Not least
among them was the chronic calamity of grandfather's kidney ailment,
which consumed large quantities of family funds in expensive and generally futile medical treatments.

Sometimes, at the hotel, Manuela did baby-sitting for tourists with
children. It was thus that she met the couple from California. They stayed
in Acapulco for a whole month, and soon Manuela took care of their little
girl almost daily. When they left the woman asked Manuela whether she
wanted a job as a maid in the States. "Yes," replied Manuela at once,
without thinking. The arrangements were made quickly. Roberto was put
up with a cousin. Uncle Pepe, through two trusted intermediaries, arranged for Manuela to cross the border illegally. Within a month she
arrived at the couple's address in California.

And now she has been here for over a year. California was even more
astonishing than Acapulco had been when she first left the village, but
now she had more time to explore this new world. She learned English
in a short time and, in the company of a Cuban girl who worked for a
neighbor, she started forays into the American universe, in ever-wider
circles from her employers' house. She even took bus trips to Hollywood
and San Francisco. For the first time in her life she slept in a room all by
herself. And, despite her regular payments for Roberto's keep, she started
to save money and put it in a bank account. Most important, she started
to think about her life in a new way, systematically. "What will become
of you when you go back?" asked the American woman one day.
Manuela did not know then, but she started to think. Carmelita, the
Cuban girl, discussed the matter with her many times—in exchange for
equal attention paid to her own planning exercises. Eventually, one
project won out over all the alternatives: Manuela would return to go to

commercial school, to become a bilingual secretary. She even started a typing course in California. But she would not return to Acapulco. She knew that, to succeed, she would have to remove herself from the family there. She would go to Mexico City, first alone, and then she would send for Roberto.

This last decision was made gradually. It was the letters that did it. Manuela, some months before, had mentioned the amount of money she had saved (a very large amount, by her standards, and enough to keep her and Roberto afloat for the duration of the commercial course). Then the letters started coming from just about everyone in the Acapulco clan. Most of the contents were family gossip, inquiries about Manuela's life in the States, and long expressions of affectionate feelings. There were frequent reminders not to forget her relatives, who took such good care of Roberto. Only gradually did the economic infrastructure emerge from all this: There was to be a *fiesta* at the wedding of a cousin, and could Manuela make a small contribution. The cousin who had been in jail was still to be tried, and there were lawyer's expenses. Uncle Pepe was onto the most promising business opportunity of his "long and distinguished career in financial activities" (his own words), and just three hundred American dollars would make it possible for him to avail himself of this never-to-recur opportunity—needless to say, Manuela would be a full partner upon her return. Finally, there was even a very formal letter from grandfather, all the way from the village, containing an appeal for funds to pay for a trip to the capital so as to take advantage of a new treatment that a famous doctor had developed there. It took a while for Manuela to grasp that every dollar of her savings had already been mentally spent by her relatives.

The choice before Manuela now is sharp and crystal-clear: She must return to Mexico—because she wants to, because of Roberto, and because the American authorities would send her back there sooner or later anyway. She can then return to the welcoming bosom of the family system, surrender her savings, and return to her previous way of life. Or she can carry through her plan in the face of family opposition. The choice is not only between two courses of action, but between two moralities. The first course is dictated by the morality of collective solidarity, the second by the morality of personal autonomy and advancement. Each morality condemns the other—as uncaring selfishness in the former case, as irresponsible disregard of her own potential and the welfare of her son in the latter. Poor Manuela's conscience is divided; by now she is capable of feeling its pangs either way.

She is in America, not in Mexico, and the new morality gets more support from her immediate surroundings. Carmelita is all for the plan, and so are most of the Spanish-speaking girls with whom Manuela has been going out. Only one, another Mexican, expressed doubt: "I don't know. Your grandfather is ill, and your uncle helped you a lot in the past.

Can you just forget them? I think that one must always help one's relatives." Manuela once talked about the matter with the American woman. "Nonsense," said the latter, "you should go ahead with your plan. You owe it to yourself and to your son." So this is what Manuela intends to do, very soon now. But she is not at ease with the decision. Every time another letter arrives from Mexico, she hesitates before opening it, and she fortifies herself against the appeals she knows to be there.

Each decision, as dictated by the respective morality, has predictable consequences: If Manuela follows the old morality, she will, in all likelihood, never raise herself or her son above the level she achieved in Acapulco—not quite at the bottom of the social scale, but not very far above it. If, on the other hand, she decides in accordance with the new morality (new for her, that is), she has at least a chance of making it up one important step on that scale. Her son will benefit from this, but probably no other of her relatives will. To take that step she must, literally, hack off all those hands that would hold her back. It is a grim choice indeed.

What will Manuela do? She will probably at least start out on her plan. Perhaps she will succeed. But once she is back in Mexico, the tentacles of the old solidarity will be more powerful. They will pull more strongly. It will be harder to escape that other village, the village of the mind within herself. The outcome of the struggle will decide whether the village will be Manuela's past or also her future. Outside observers should think very carefully indeed before they take sides in this contest.

Interpretations

1. What is Berger's purpose in telling this story?

2. What is your reaction to the main features of life in "the village"? Do you find them appealing? Why or why not?

3. As a result "of telling her relatives how much money she had saved," why is Manuela faced not just with two choices but two moralities? What are they? Have you ever faced these two moralities? Do you think you made the right choice? Why? If Manuela had not mentioned the amount of her savings in her letters, would she still be faced with this dilemma?

4. Berger gives us an opportunity to take sides in this "contest," but warns us too to think carefully beforehand. Which side do you take and why? To what extent do you share Manuela's sense of responsibility to family?

5. "A Tale of Two Moralities" is fiction. How can fiction sometimes be "truer" than nonfiction? Is such the case with this "tale"? How?

Correspondences

1. Manuela must choose between two moralities—her obligation to herself (the newfound morality of the United States) and her obligation to her family (the "old" morality of the Third World). What aspects of her choice are the most difficult? How does her choice compare to that of Glickman?

2. "The outcome of the struggle will decide whether the village will be Manuela's past or also her future." How will Manuela's personal and traditional associations influence her choice? Might she agree with Reid (Chapter 5) that "The landscapes of childhood are irreplaceable, since they have been the backdrop for so many epiphanies, so many realizations"? What epiphantes (see Glossary) and realizations did Manuela experience?

Applications

1. Watch the film *El Norte*. What does it add to your understanding of Manuela's "two moralities" and of the dangers involved in border crossings? What other insights did you gain?

2. Where does responsibility to family end and responsibility to oneself begin? How are your family's needs and expectations similar to or different from those of Manuela? Write an essay comparing family responsibilities in Manuela's culture(s) with those of most families in the United States.

The Impossible Became No Longer Unthinkable

Hana Weble

Hana Weble (b. 1917) was born in Czechoslovakia. She is a survivor of the Theresienstadt, Auschwitz, and Stutthof concentration camps. After the defeat of the Nazis in 1945, she returned to Czechoslovakia, where she remarried. In 1951, she and her husband, also a survivor of Auschwitz, emigrated to the United States. She has published several essays about her concentration camp experiences. This is how she describes her purpose in writing "The Impossible Became No Longer Unthinkable":

> *This piece is about choices made in the alien universe of the concentration camp. I feel compelled to bear witness at every possible opportunity, so that such madness as the Holocaust will not occur again. Since the responses of the Free World during that period were either silence or inaction resulting in the death of millions, I want to address especially the generation born after World War II. It is they who will be responsible for choices made in the future.*

Prague, the capital of Czechoslovakia, has been a cultural center of the Holy Roman Empire and then of the Austro-Hungarian Empire at least since the fourteenth century, but the nation of Czechoslovakia was born almost at the same time as Weble. A provisional government set up during World War I in 1914 proclaimed the new republic in 1918, a month before the end of World War I. It emerged from that war a stable democracy to soon enjoy recognition as an industrial and technological leader. However, in 1939 Hitler overran and dissolved Czechoslovakia, and he began to implement the "Final Solution"— systematic extermination of Jews. Czechoslovakia was liberated in May 1945 by Russian troops coming from the East and Allied troops coming from the West and Czechoslovakia was revived as a democratic republic. However, in 1948 the Communists seized power. A harsh period of Stalinist rule followed. All political opposition was suppressed except for a brief period of democratiza-

tion under Alexander Dubček in 1968 known as the "Prague Spring." When Warsaw Pact nations invaded Czechoslovakia seven months later and reimposed a hard-line Communist government, forty thousand Czechs fled. In 1989 a new chapter opened in Czechoslovakia's tumultuous history when street demonstrations and events in neighboring Poland, Hungary, and East Germany brought down the Communist government and chose as head of state Vaclav Havel, a distinguished playwright who had spent several years in prison for his outspoken opposition to the Soviet-dominated government.

IN MAY 1942, Anna, then 25 years old, together with her husband Peter and his elderly parents, was deported by the Germans from her home in Prague to the Ghetto Theresienstadt[1] in the northern part of Bohemia.

With this deportation their old world was demolished and a new, incomprehensible world was thrust upon them which uprooted and completely dislocated them from any habitual way of life.

The "Ghettoization" process of Anna and her family began immediately after their arrival, when they were separated and dispatched to various living quarters throughout the Ghetto. Anna was assigned to work in the Ghetto laundry, while Peter was assigned to the registration of new arrivals. Peter's parents, being over the working age limit, were mostly confined to their living places. After work, Peter, Anna, or both tried to visit them as often as possible. The young couple managed to warm their lonely existence either with some news which at the time was circulating in the Ghetto, or they all would pull out from the recesses of their memories some precious recollections from the past. [At] other times they would satisfy their empty stomachs by talking about the delicious meals they had eaten at home—the place they had loved and lost.

Gradually, life in the Ghetto took on a certain routine of fending off hunger and disease. With the constantly incoming transports, the average population of 35,000 swelled in the summer of 1942 to 50,000. The

---

[1]Theresienstadt before the war served as a garrison town with a capacity of about 3,500 soldiers housed in several barracks, scattered amidst some 200 houses. The town was built as a fortress almost three centuries ago by the Austrian Emperor Joseph the Second, who named it after his mother Maria Theresa.

The new history of Theresienstadt began in 1941, when the Nazi transformed the town into a Ghetto for the Jews deported there from the German occupied lands in Europe. By the end of that year, under the label "Resettlement," trains from all over Europe began to converge on the Ghettos and death camps. On the one hand, Jews were deported to Poland, which became a mass execution ground for them, on the other hand, the Nazis established a grotesque "Model Ghetto" in Theresienstadt where they practiced the greatest art of deception. They actually succeeded in keeping alive the concept of "The Settlement of the Jews," as they called it for the visits of foreign observers, in order to conceal from the world their plan of isolation, deportation and finally extermination of the European Jews.

barracks and houses were filled to overflowing and sanitary conditions worsened every day, causing a dysentery epidemic which added to the already unbearable situation.

In the height of the summer, the streets were dotted with the dead and dying. Soon also Peter's father became one of the victims. The family gathered in the dark, overcrowded room where a small bulb shed a dim pool of light on his body lying on the wooden floor. In spite of the room's stifling air, the skin of this kind man seemed to glow with relief and peace. The mourning scene lost its usual significance or rather assumed a different one. It was only Peter's mother, a tiny, pious woman, clutching in her gnarled fingers a worn-out prayer book, who submerged herself in silent prayer.[2]

Slowly the autumn colors blended into the monotonous landscape of the Ghetto and there was a shiver of the coming winter in the air. The transports, dispatched from Theresienstadt to the East in irregular intervals, became one of the most important and sinister features of the Ghetto life, which soon took on energy of its own only between the incoming and outgoing transports.

In December, Christmas bells were tolling "Peace on Earth" in the Christian world, while in the Jewish world in Theresienstadt, the ever-present threat of deportation to the extermination camps in Poland posed [sic] like a descending pendulum above the pit of the Ghetto. Whenever the summonses for the deportation were distributed, an ominous panic permeated the desperate population. Life almost ceased to exist and began to tick again only for those "lucky" ones who were, for the time being, permitted to still dwell in the misery of Theresienstadt.

When the pale March sun melted the last vestiges of snow, Anna's mother arrived in the Ghetto as well. Now the endless fearful expectation which accompanied every incoming transport was over. Anna met her mother in a dense concentration of bewildered people. Both tried to smile at each other through tears tinted with tenderness and sadness. But there was no time for tears in this merciless place. Soon her mother was led away together with a group of other women and assigned to a dwelling space in a barrack not too far away from Anna's.

The very next day Anna's mother was marched off in a group of working women to a part-time job as a cleaning person for the women's lavatories. Anna thought at first that it was remarkable how her mother, whose husband and son had been deported already in January, 1941, to Riga in Estonia, stoically adapted herself to the new, unfamiliar circumstances. However, within a very short time, Anna noticed with great concern how this once handsome woman who used to return from brisk morning walks in the countryside with gleaming red cheeks, had sud-

---

[2]Since the death of hundreds of inmates daily occurred in the Ghetto at that time, the event of one death became almost part of everyday life.

denly aged and how her almost wrinkle-free face had become shrunken and pale. She had loved nature and after her walks she would enthusiastically talk about the rising sun, birds, and flowers which had greeted her on her way. Then, Anna remembered her retreats to the "salon," as she called the room where she surrounded herself with books. Often she would recite poems by Goethe, Schiller, and Heine in German which Anna, to the annoyance of her mother, could not understand. "I hope you will learn German one day," she would say, "so you will be able to enjoy these classics!" It was ironic that for Anna's mother German literature was the source of ethical and moral inspiration which she faithfully transmitted to her children; many of her quotations became engraved in Anna's memory and formed a lasting link to her happy childhood.

It was almost a year since Anna, Peter, and his parents had arrived in Theresienstadt and two months after the arrival of her mother In the Ghetto, days sank into the past, washing away the hopes they cradled in their hearts. Things turned out very differently from what they expected.

One day in April, Anna was on her way to her mother. The sun was already sliding behind the arches of the courtyard, when she was about to enter the gate of the barrack. Suddenly, an SS man driving a tractor flashed out of the yard—and was gone. After the gray cloud of dust settled behind him, Anna, somewhat perturbed, spotted a group of people in one of the arches. Curiously she turned into the yard and headed toward them. Already from some distance she heard their agitated voices blaming the driver of the tractor for deliberately hitting the stricken man in their midst. With apprehension she joined the group of onlookers.

On the blood-stained cobblestones worn to smoothness by the feet of centuries was a torn leather coat shielding the crushed body of a man. Startled, Anna was about to lean forward when her body froze midway and her eyes signaled something awful, something so dark and chilling. . . . She looked down on the blood-covered body of—her Peter. "He is dead!" she gasped. But it took a while for her numbed senses to grasp the meaning of her words. The whole world sank before her eyes. . . .

In the semi-darkness of her room Peter's mother was waiting. Anna looked into the deeply lined face with a terrifying silence. It took more courage than she could command to produce some reassuring words. "Her only son is dead and his mother still lives," Anna contemplated; "she must be made whole if at all possible." With a great effort Anna produced a faint smile that was rather close to tears. But suddenly there was a new gravity in her face and tears, hot like molten iron brimmed over, and she began to tell the horrible truth. The color drained from Peter's mother's face leaving it as white as her hair. Her eyes looked as if all life had vanished out of them. With both hands she covered her face and muttered: "Dead? Peter dead? He can't be dead! All that can't be true!" Her voice broke, not her words only but the agony in her voice laid bare her torment.

Had the circumstances surrounding Peter's death been less horrifying, Anna might have recovered more quickly. But the nightmarish event of that day was seared deep in her memory. She missed Peter terribly; her mind turned again and again to the incredible fact that he was dead. Despite her own grief Anna also grieved for her mother-in-law. If Peter's dying could do this to her, what must it have done to his mother! With all her will, Anna tried to pour out love toward this devastated woman, even though his going had created a gap so huge that she herself did not know how they could go on without him.

A cluster of three broken women was all that was left. Weeks went by, then months before Anna could begin again to harness her energy toward their survival. She could not permit herself to dwell only on that awful past, since the tide of a new battle was closing in on them. For some reason during the next few months there were no transports leaving Theresienstadt, but on September 1, 1943, the illusion of safety abruptly ended and the deportations to the East resumed. The prisoners of the Ghetto did not know what the destination "East" really meant since information about Auschwitz, crematoria and gas chambers was still a well-guarded German secret.[3] However, even though the official version was that the transports were heading for some labor camps in the East, there was an uneasy foreboding in the air and everyone feared the worst.

In the evening of the first of September, the dreaded summonses were distributed throughout the Ghetto. This time Anna's mother was one of the recipients as well. Troubled, Anna inspected the fateful slip. Then she tried to read her mother's deep-seeing eyes resting intensely upon her. Never had she seen her mother crushed like this; nor could she face her mother-in-law's forsaken look. At that moment more than ever Anna felt that her life was no longer her own. Time was running out and a decision had to be made.

Hoping against hope that she might be able to give some assistance to her mother, Anna murmured more to herself. "I cannot let you go alone!" Then with a sense of guilt she looked at her mother-in-law who was visibly shaken. Her quivering chin produced a slow movement of her colorless lips: "I will go with you wherever you go; just don't leave me here alone," she pleaded with almost childlike fear. Anna blinked to hide her tears and her thoughts turned inward. How could she expose this fragile woman to the terrifying unknown awaiting her mother and her? Through the shadows of Anna's thoughts came the light of Peter's reassuring voice accompanied with a gentle smile. As she examined with tenderness the two solemn faces in front of her, a powerful urgency to struggle on together surged through her. She reached the decision that she herself, together with her mother-in-law, would voluntarily join her mother in the transport . . . And so the lonely group savored their last

[3]Auschwitz was one of many extermination camps in Poland.

evening in the Ghetto together, packing, and sharing the last fragile moments of anxiety and love.

In the morning of September 2, a heartbreaking procession of 5,000 deportees burdened with their pathetic belongings, a transport number swinging around their necks, were marched off toward the railroad station. Anna and her mother were among them while Peter's mother, upon Anna's suggestion, was waiting in her room in order to be spared the long hours of waiting in line.

Already in the distance, the loading of the prisoners could be seen and heard. There was pushing and screaming. Everyone was brutally forced into the prepared cattle cars. A cordon formed by gendarmes together with transport orderlies forcefully enclosed the swelling crowd. "This is the time I must get my mother-in-law," Anna thought to herself. But suddenly she felt something snap inside her instead. At that moment it became clear to her that she must do something, do it at once and do it quickly, or else. . . .

As if she were someone else, Anna removed the transport number from her and her mother's necks and let them slide to the ground. Then, she seized her mother's hand and urged her to follow her. The next moment a frantic jerk propelled them through the cordon of the guards and in the ensuing confusion, both of them escaped the perilous scene. Any minute they expected to be stopped: a cry an order, a blow on the head . . . Nothing. In order not to become conspicuous they now walked in slow, measured steps and lost themselves in the turmoil of the Ghetto.

Their wild escape ended in a deserted lumberyard on the periphery of the Ghetto. Terror stricken, they scanned the area around them. Perhaps the aroma of the freshly cut wood agitated their senses; in a frenzy they slipped, like two wild animals, behind a wall of piled up lumber. Still gasping for breath, they set their scanty luggage on the sawdust covered ground. Before long the mother's trembling legs gave way, and she slouched between the lumber behind and the suitcases in front of her.

Anna bent over her mother's recumbent body with an uneasy feeling. Only now did she realize what they had just done. A chill crept down her fingertips as she touched the curve of her mother's shoulder. "Everything will be all right. You just stay here until I come back to get you," she said with tough tenderness. It seemed that only the soothing tone of Anna's voice reached her mother's consciousness which had already succumbed to an irresistible sleep. Anna withdrew cautiously, leaving her mother in the protection of the strip of shade stretching alongside the wall of lumber.

As she moved anxiously off, she watched her mother fade away until she could hardly distinguish the frail shape blending into the wall of lumber behind her. Anna forced herself not to think, not to do anything but hasten forward on the dusty road toward the rampart above the deportation area. Finally, she reached the elevation from where she could follow the scene below, where the process of loading the "cargo" of Jews into the cattle cars was in full swing. There were panic, screams, blows! The cars filled up quickly and each time the heavy sliding doors were shut and the iron bars were pushed down with thuds into their slots. The fate of the victims was sealed. She could hear the frantic cries escaping through the small, barred windows in the upper corner of the cars. Anna agonized over the aching spasms of the travelers who would be spending many hours behind the steel doors of these "rolling coffins." And still, incredible as it might seem, she calculated that the faster the doors were to close, the closer the success of their escape would be. Her nerves overloaded, she was now only waiting for the last wagon to be closed. Entirely absorbed in the process of loading, a sort of callousness began to take hold of her.

At last, some frantic activities on the platform heralded the imminent departure of the train. Anna's hope began to grow and grew with each minute. Finally, the train began crackling and squealing as if panting for breath. The black locomotive was howling mournfully and flurries of furious puffs were rising toward the sky. The train jerked against the rails and crept forward, then the speed increased and finally it became a smoky streak in the distance. It was all over. . . .

Despite the situation, Anna felt a hysterical sensation of triumph. However, it did not last too long; soon the exuberant feeling changed into a nervous tremor. What about her mother in the lumberyard! Terror gripped her throat. So many hours had passed since she left her. Had she panicked? Had the Germans found her? She descended from the rampart as fast as she could.

The Ghetto was enveloped in darkness and silence. Anna looked around, her heart beating violently; at every step she glanced from the corner of her eyes at the shadowy passerby. She walked tightly along the pavement and up the dusty path toward the lumberyard. There she found her mother as she had left her. Anna's sagging courage was up again. "I just woke up a little while ago," her mother said with an angelic smile when she saw her daughter again. With a sigh of relief Anna looked into her shining eyes and full of thankfulness realized how the miracle of sleep had washed away the long hours of her mother's waiting.

Anna helped her mother struggle to her feet and both started on their way back. They eagerly inhaled again the Ghetto's dusty air on their way to Peter's mother's place. They found her still waiting, her prayer book open on her lap. She lifted her tired eyes and a twinkle of a smile passed over her exhausted face. Soon the fear subsided and the exhilaration from their reunion kindled new hope as they huddled in the dark room. That night before sinking into sleep, Anna reflected upon the miracle of prayer and the sleep that had blotted out from both mothers the horrors of that day.

However, on December 15th, and 18th, 1943 two transports, each with 2,500 prisoners, were scheduled to leave from Theresienstadt for Auschwitz. This time both mothers received summonses for the December 18th transport. "There is no way out this time," thought Anna "the September 'miracle' can not be repeated," Anna joined them voluntarily. On that day, the three of them became a part of the group of victims struggling behind the closed doors in one of the cattle cars of a long train heading for Auschwitz.

When Anna faced the peril that awaited them at the end of the arduous journey she began to perceive that Auschwitz was an orderly kingdom of the doomed. With all her remaining strength, she managed somehow to hold on to her two mothers as they were herded with the rest of the prisoners into the so-called "Family Camp" in Birkenau.[4] There they found themselves with people who came from Theresienstadt on the September, 1943, transport. They all looked debilitated, their gazes distant, their bodies starved.

"How will I be able to preserve the weak flicker of my mothers' lives amid such an inferno?" she asked herself bewildered and full of pain. Nevertheless, she was soon to find that they somehow managed to grapple with their day-to-day numbing existence. In the solitude of night, Anna thought back to the days in Theresienstadt, where she still could orchestrate an escape, while in Auschwitz everything was beyond her power of influence.

But not until the night of March 8th, 1944, could the three women really appreciate the true importance of their escape from the September, 1943, transport. On that dark, moonless night, events beyond any imagination took place: Without any warning, camp curfew was ordered and large commandos of SS guards with leashed dogs at their sides stormed the camp. They rounded up 4,000 of the original 5,000 men, women, and children, survivors of the September 1943, transport, from which Anna and her mothers had run away. They were cremated that same night in the gas chambers of Birkenau.

---

[4]"Family Camp" Birkenau was a part of the concentration camp Auschwitz which was known as the "Czech Family Camp." Its first inmates were 5,000 Jewish men, women and children who arrived there in September, 1943, from the concentration camp Theresienstadt in Czechoslovakia. Unlike all preceding transports, they were not subjected to the notorious selection upon arrival in which the fit were thumbed to the right and life and the unfit to the left and death in the gas chambers. Instead, under a new scheme ordered by the General Reich Security Authority in Berlin, the inmates were to be kept in this camp in a sort of isolation or quarantine of six months' duration, after which period those who were still able would be liquidated or, as it was called euphemistically, "subject to special treatment." In line with this plan, the night of the 8th of March, 1944, the surviving prisoners from the September transport were gassed, while the December transport from Theresienstadt (including Anna and her mothers) were to be quarantined for another three months before they would be gassed as well. However, when the end of that period arrived, the camp was not liquidated in its entirety, as described in the essay.

As long as the hope which could come from deep faith pulsated within the three women, survival still seemed possible. This event, however, shattered their remaining faith. "Faith in what? Was that what was also awaiting the December transport?" they asked themselves with trepidation. Auschwitz—a landscape so alienated from any culture ever known, seemed to be the end of the road for the three of them. They counted months, weeks, days until they too would have to follow the fate of the September transport.

Spring turned into summer. The sky became blue without joy, the sun became hot without pity for the doomed prisoners in Birkenau. On July 15th a wintry hush once again swept over the camp's population. A new selection! This time the old, the sick, and children, some accompanied by their mothers, were brutally forced into prepared trucks and transported to the crematoria, where they were, as the transport before them, destroyed with the Nazi "blitz" efficiency. A work force, formed from the younger and still somewhat able-bodied inmates, was transferred to other labor camps. The "Family Camp" in Birkenau was liquidated and so was Peter's mother. . . .

Anna, together with her mother, huddled in a cattle car again. They arrived in Stutthof, a desolate concentration camp in Prussia. There hard work, starvation, and disease again became their companions. In a few months Anna's mother aged several years. Even though her physical and mental endurance went beyond all limits given the circumstances, Anna noticed the unmistakable signs of her [mother's] imminent collapse. Helpless and in despair, she watched over her deteriorating state of health until one day in January, 1945, the mother succumbed.

Anna (miraculously) survived and so the impossible became no longer unthinkable.

Interpretations

1. Anna's plan was that all three women would leave the camp together. Instead she accomplished "the September miracle." Are you surprised at this accomplishment? Why? What is the most miraculous thing about it?

2. Explain the title. What was "the impossible"?

3. Most of this story deals with Anna's unsuccessful attempts to save the two older women. Was her own salvation merely a matter of chance? If so, does the account make a point about who may survive the death camps? What point?

4. From whose point of view is this story told? How do we know that? Why is this the natural choice of point of view?

Correspondences

1. "At that moment more than ever Anna felt that her life was no longer entirely her own. Time was running out and a decision had to be made." Why did Anna decide that she and her mother would not join the transport? Was her decision premeditated? What role did her mother and mother-in-law play in her choice? To what extent does Anna's choice also involve "two moralities"? How does her choice differ from Manuela's?

2. Review Lowell's perspective on choices (page 444) and discuss its application to Wehle's essay.

Applications

1. Although in many ways the Holocaust was "unthinkable," Wehle is asking her readers to think about it. What are some of the conclusions thinking might force on one who reads about the Holocaust?

2. One of Anna's mother's favorite quotations (from Goethe's *Faust*) was "A good man, driven by his dim impulses is always conscious of his right way." What does it mean? How does this apply to Wehle's essay?

No Sacrifice Too Great

Lev Tagayev

Born in Persia (in 1948) into what could have been a fairy-tale life, Lev Tagayev was named after and related to Lev Tolstoy. His father was a Russian Romanov prince, while his mother came from Armenian peasant stock. Coming to the United States as a child, he later served in the U.S. Army in Southeast Asia, and then ventured into a successful career in professional theatre. First as an actor, singer and dancer, and then as a lighting designer, stage manager, and company manager, he was blessed with the opportunity to work with some of the great artistic minds of our time: Alvin Ailey, Martha Graham, Bhaskar, Leonard Bernstein, Zuben Mehta, Jerome Robbins, and Luciano Pavarotti, to name a few. He founded, published, and edited his own arts newspaper and eventually became a pioneer in videographics and computer art. A painter, sculptor, poet, and playwright, his life's dream is to build a sculpture-home in the mountains of Lake Tahoe and spend the rest of his life teaching. He graduated from Queensborough Community College in June, 1992.

*It wasn't me that started that old crazy Asia war
But I was proud to go and do my patriotic chores.
Oh, I know, Ruby, that I'm not the man I used to be . . .
Mel Tillis, "Ruby," 1966*

There was a shield of silence around each and every soldier as the huge transport circled the Bien Hoa Air Terminal ready to land. Fear and apprehension were as much a part of the atmosphere as the cool chill of the wind sneaking through the cracks. Most "twinks" (soldiers that had never before seen combat) flew in on regular airliners, but as part of the elite Army Special Forces that were to be assigned to the various companies in Vietnam, we were consigned to military transports. It had been a long flight from San Diego with stopovers in Honolulu and Manila. Cold and quiet for the most part, the boisterousness died somewhere over the South China Sea. These were young men wondering if they would ever see their loved ones again. The bravado of their actions in Fort Bragg and Fort Jackson during advanced infantry training had transformed into the

496

deepest, richest form of paranoia. We knew that the only reason we were in Southeast Asia was to kill or be killed.

The set-down was a bumpy one and when the huge airship finally grinded to a halt with its screeching tires sending an ominous chemical reaction through my soul. Every one of us looked around to see into the eyes of the person standing next to him. We tried so hard to shed the fear, forcing the slightest smile which we hoped would hide the chattering teeth and shaking knees.

This was the beginning of our DEROS (Date of Exit of Return from Overseas). It would be one full year, 365 days of the Vietnam experience for each of us—that is, if we were lucky to survive that long. The order came for us to evacuate the aircraft in an orderly fashion, and in long columns, two abreast, we marched onto the airfield. As we began our trek into the world of war, we could see the war-weary grunts awaiting their turn to get onto the transport which we were exiting. As we marched past them, not one of them looked into our eyes. There was no more than ten feet between us—those who were at the end of their DEROS slowly lugged and shuffled their boots on the left with their heads held down, and we who were their replacements marched on the right with our heads held high. A few of us would say something or another to the exiting heros on their way stateside—"The World," as they called it—but there was never a response. Their eyes looked down, gazing in a cold, somber stare at the boots of the soldier in front of them, never looking up. Not able to raise their eyes, they did not want to take the memory of the face of those who might never return home. It wasn't until later that I fully understood that feeling. Only later could I understand what was going through the tortured minds of those I marched past on that first day "in country."

As I marched by those naked eyes on my way to Di An to be processed before I joined "C" Company in Lai Khe, I began to daydream about the recent past. It seemed like yesterday that I had anticipated graduating from high school. I could remember thinking there was only one week left to kiss goodbye to Brooklyn Technical High School in New York. I was older and much luckier than the other prospective graduates. It was quite an achievement to have a 96.5 average after three years of high school. Princeton, M.I.T., Northwestern and Cal. Tech were all willing to give me baseball scholarships. I had moved out of my mother's house when I was seventeen and all I ever wanted to do was play baseball professionally. The San Diego Padres had scouted me in high school and chose me as a sixth-round draft choice, and that was probably the direction I was going to take.

Then, just one week before graduation, on a Friday when my friends and I usually stayed up all night getting stoned and playing cards, my friend Michael's mother received that fateful, hand delivered telegram. Some no-faced Lieutenant delivered the message in a most apologetic way and tried to console her. I never read the letter, but I know it said something like, "We are sorry to inform you that your son, Thomas, is M.I.A. (Missing In Action)." Little did I know that star-crossed night how that simple news of woe would change and rearrange my whole life.

The news of his brother hit Michael hard that night and our regular card game had to be called off. We decided to go to a bar instead. Sorrow and tears led to anger and patriotic machismo and before I was sober again, I had enlisted in the Army, asking to be assigned to combat infantry in Vietnam.

They called Lai Khe "Rocket City." It held true to its name, for the moment the small convoy of trucks had reached inside the perimeter, someone yelled "incoming," and we were all scurrying to find cover and hide from the flurry of enemy fire. "Welcome to Vietnam," I thought. "With my luck, I'll probably die my first day here."

When the fireworks ended and I went through some further processing, I was directed to "C" Company barracks. On the top of the small building were the words "Big Charlie's Place," graphically designed like the head of the bunny rabbit used by *Playboy*. On the left side was a large sign with the Big Red One of the First Infantry Division and on the right a shield of the Black Lion of Cantigny, the sacred logo of the Second Battalion of the 28th Infantry Regiment. The motto of Charlie Company was "Duty First. No Mission Too Difficult. No Sacrifice Too Great." "Great," I pondered on those words, "No sacrifice too great. For the next year, if I'm lucky enough to survive, I have to coexist with a bunch of grunts that think 'no mission is too difficult, no sacrifice too great'."

I learned quickly that you don't make friends with anyone because it is hard to see your friends die. Day after day, through the mud and the rain fighting off mosquitos the size of hummingbirds. Mission after mission, constantly living with fear and leeches. Killing the enemy, man, woman or child, in order to survive so some mucky-muck General or politician could relish in the body counts. Always smelling the stench of death, American and Vietnamese, or the hellish scent of napalm and burning flesh, I survived. Or did I? What was once a youthful, intelligent man on the brink of his life that fateful night when Michael's brother was proclaimed M.I.A., is now a bitter, angry man.

I made my bed that day that I decided to enlist and I have had to sleep in it ever since. The only problem is that even over twenty years later, my sleep is filled with nightmarish dreams of severed limbs and shattered lives, and my days are filled with tears for the ones whom I was asked to kill and for those who died fighting next to me in a war we were not allowed to win. A war that was not lost on the battle fields of Vietnam, but rather, in the living rooms of Americans watching the six o'clock news.

Interpretations

1. Why are the downcast and unresponding troops on their way back to "The World" such a surprising and important feature of Tagayev's first day in Vietnam?

2. How appropriate to the essay is the introductory quotation?

3. What other choices besides Tagayev's decision to enlist does this essay mention? Does mention of these other choices add to or distract from Tagayev's presentation of his own "star-crossed night"?

4. Discuss the nonchronological, or flash-back, technique as used by Tagayev. Expanded treatment of what points or portions of this essay—if any—would increase its effectiveness?

Correspondences

1. Review Emerson's perspective on choices (page 444) and discuss its relevance to Tagayev's essay. In how many "experiments" was he involved? Analyze his attitude toward his "choice."

2. Contrast the factor of "enlisting" in the essays by Tagayev and Thanh. To what extent did politics influence their choices?

Applications

1. Analyze the tone of the essay including the significance of the title. What evidence best supports Tagayev's description of himself as "bitter" and "angry"?

2. "Sorrow and tears," "anger," and "patriotic machismo" are the causes of Tagayev's choice, as he now sees it. How would you evaluate the importance of these causes and how would you define the fourth? How important is a fifth possible cause—drinking?

A Train Ride

Hugo Lindo

Translated by
Elizabeth Gamble Miller

Hugo Lindo (b. 1917) is one of El Salvador's best-known poets and novelists. His concern for the political and sociological situation in his country is revealed in his novels, which include Justicia, señor Gobernador *published in 1960.*

As LEONARDO VILLENA strolled along the station platform toward the second-class cars, he inhaled the air with extraordinary gusto. There was always that special aroma of vapors that smelled of a trip. A small briefcase in his left hand was his only baggage. With his right hand he dug into the pocket of his jacket, and, reassured that his ticket was in place, he boarded the train.

The seats in the second-class car were hard, but that didn't seem to matter. He chose one next to a window and sought to entertain himself by looking out. At the moment there wasn't much scenery, unless that's what you would call the yellowed railroad ties piled high like a wall on either side of the tracks. The landscape would later change into meadows and woods, fields of sugar and corn, and little lakes dotted with coveys of wild ducks.

A heavy-set, bald-headed man took the seat beside him and made it immediately clear that he wanted to talk:

"Is your destination La Alianza?"

"No."

"San Esteban?"

"I'm really not going anywhere in particular."

The man was disconcerted, but only for a moment, and then he charged in again:

"Well, I am. I'm going to La Alianza. I've got a whole day of joggling up and down on this foul train. That's where my in-laws are waiting; they're taking care of my little boy while my wife is gone. She's in Miami picking up a few things (lowering his voice to a confidential tone)—contraband, you know."

Leonardo nodded his assent courteously and then directed his attention to lighting a cigarette and taking a deep, long draw.

"They notified me that he got sick, from one day to the next. He's seriously ill, and I have to go to him. I'm really worried, rather upset, you know. I wish the train was almost there."

Leonardo smiled to himself. Everything about the other passenger seemed to be a contradiction: he discussed his anguish with complete composure. He spoke very slowly while explaining his hurry. The man had piqued his interest. For his part he wouldn't try to be aloof or unsociable or to avoid the contact being offered. On the contrary, it was necessary for him to act naturally and even sympathetically. The fact was, he had started the day with a certain pensive disposition, and it was difficult to become engaged in dialogue. He would have to put forth a conscious effort to break down his own noncommunicative shell.

"You say you're not going anywhere in particular. I don't under-stand."

"I'm just taking a ride. I'll travel until about noon, get off wherever I am and take the next train going west."

"Oh, now I see!

The car had been filling up with passengers, who were putting their suitcases up, or down in between the seats, or in the passageway, push-ing and cursing under their breaths. An atmosphere of ill humor seemed to permeate the air. However, the bad humor around them didn't affect Leonardo Villena or his companion, for they were apparently in another world.

The train whistled, announcing its departure. The men heard the initial asthmatic chugs of the locomotive; that special odor of trains became stronger. They felt the first jerks, heard the squealing of the wheels, and the piles of railroad ties began to move backward, slowly.

"Do you travel like this very often, for pleasure?"

"Not frequently, but when I can. I like trains. Or I should say, I love trains."

"I don't. They bore me; they wear me out. But in a case like this. Just imagine. The poor child, seriously ill and without his mother or his father, depending on his aunts, and what can they do?"

"How old is the boy?" Leonardo asked, in an effort to appear inter-ested.

"Three years old, and an only child. He looks like his mother."

"So much the better!"

The man caught the joke right away and smiled:

"Absolutely! Much better!"

Leonardo's career successes were due to his innate understanding of psychology. He had studied an average amount since entering the uni-versity a few years previously. But he had an unusual gift for sizing up people, guessing their intentions, anticipating their actions, and not being caught by surprise. It seemed an appropriate moment to analyze his traveling companion.

As a matter of fact he was rather young. His weight and his baldness contributed to the impression of his being older. This was emphasized by his loose, careless way of dressing. But his small, sharp eyes belied the first impression: there was something about them, a certain innocence, the sign of a rural upbringing; they displayed no tension or malice.

Little by little, the train had picked up speed. The telephone posts sped by and the wires seemed to be suddenly separated and then again united behind the string of cars.

"Don Horacio!"

The greeting was unexpected and enthusiastic. Entering their coach from the second-class car in front of them was a woman. She would have been pretty if it hadn't been for her pronounced nose. Brunette, black eyes, straight hair, a bit fleshy, her appearance was, generally speaking, attractive, although somewhat common. Her only facial feature out of the ordinary was her nose, which made her uglier; however, it also gave her a certain mark of distinction and intelligence.

"Mariita!"

"Where are you bound for?"

Don Horacio—now Leonardo knew his name—repeated the story: the sick child, the absent mother, the aunts, the long tedious train ride, and above all, the concern for his son. The tremendous worry expressed with a placid face; the uncertain urgency spoken of calmly.

Leonardo Villena again tried to immerse himself in his thoughts, but now the woman had taken the seat directly in front of them and was carrying on a long conversation with Don Horacio. She spoke energetically, affectionately, and with exaggerated gestures. Oh, three-year-olds! So precious! So smart! Something new every minute! So adorable!

Mariita found no lack of expressions of affection for children. One might conclude that she belonged to a society for the protection of children. Villena was engaged in his own thoughts when, without warning, the woman threw a direct question at him:

"And you, sir, have you any children?"

"Yes, I have two."

"Oh, how lovely! How old are they? Are they pretty big now?"

"No. The older one is five. The younger is three."

"Little boys?"

"Yes, they are."

Leonardo thought Mariita was too forward, but his rearing obliged him to answer and not ignore her. Yes, his rearing, a vestige of the bourgeois "teachings" that he had been subjected to by his parents and professors and by the general environment. However, there seemed to be something else involved. It was as if that woman held a strange magnetism for him. She spoke, and he was compelled to pay attention. Besides, her words, though simple enough, carried an undercurrent of emotion that could not be ignored.

He was cognizant of the fact that he should not think about his own children. Certainly not with any emotion. The thought of his boys would of necessity be an inhibiting factor and could jeopardize his mission. No sentimentality, no familial sentimentalism. Nevertheless, it seemed that between them, Mariita and Don Horacio were determined to ruin his plans. He couldn't refrain from thinking of his children. When he had left, they were in bed and he had planted a kiss on each forehead. Fortunately, they were healthy. Because when Leonardito, the older one, caught the measles and was completely covered with bumps, his temperature had risen devilishly high. He had been so worried! Every few minutes he would call the doctor, who could do nothing but prescribe aspirin to lower the fever. Don Horacio, the poor devil, must be feeling the same disquietude, only with his temperament, or perhaps it was just a façade, his anxiety didn't show. But what the devil did he care about Don Horacio and Mariita and the children?

The train made its customary noises as it approached the station: it blew, whistled, screeched, rumbled, and finally pulled to a stop in front of the station shed at Las Palmas, a shed blackened by trains like all the others in the country, identical to the others in the Americas and even in the world.

One advantage, he said to himself: this interruption will cut off that woman's chitchat and put an end to this man's meddling. He noted his watch. It wasn't time to get off yet. The next station would be the one. But, because of the circumstances, perhaps it would be preferable.

He didn't reveal his intentions, but as he was moving toward the step in order to get off the train, the heavy-set man spied him and called out in a rather demanding voice that attracted everyone's attention:

"Mister! Mister! You're forgetting your valise!"

He thought quickly. If he ran, they would surely go through his briefcase and consequently his mission would fail. If on the other hand he stayed, there would still be time to think up something that would work.

"No, Don Horacio, I'm not leaving. I was just going to get a breath of fresh air."

It was difficult for him to hide his rage and frustration. Why had his seatmates turned out to be precisely these people with their inopportune interference that seemed destined to upset his plans? Like the best actor, he adopted the disguise of being pleasant and relaxed while he cursed his bad luck. He again took his seat and thanked the man for his trouble over the little baggage that he had.

So it was that the train renewed its journey with its tedious, isochronal rhythm, that the woman in a like manner resumed her chatter about children, their charms, their illnesses, the unsettling moments that await their elders, and he was forced to pay even closer attention because of the necessity for dissimulation.

And it was through the small door this attention had opened that the woman's words gradually crept in. With their intense power of suggestion, their incomparable emotional force and subjugating pathos, in spite of the simplicity and domesticity of the thoughts being expressed, her words convinced him: "Hypnotism or something of that order," thought Leonardo Villena for a moment. Just for a moment, because that thought couldn't occupy the same space being reclaimed by his home. The warm images emerged from behind that prominent nose through the strange voice of Mariita and those steady, unavoidable, demanding eyes that shone like precious stones. "Absurd," he thought instantly. And then again he saw Leonardito burning up with fever, his little head wet with perspiration lying on the pillow and moving about restlessly, just the way this fat man's son must be doing now in La Alianza—the son of his gentle traveling companion.

"Traveling companion"—something clicked in his memory as the phrase crossed his mind. Possible; he was not sure. He did begin to consider that at least for the moment his mission was inopportune. Rather than the government, its victims would be the anonymous train passengers. Perhaps even more than them, the injury would be to that unknown child, his traveling companion's son—the boy who might be Leonardito's traveling companion at some future date.

Exerting his willpower, he shook his head and succeeded in uttering one word, "foolishness," but the word was swallowed up in a great black tunnel mysteriously taking shape as he saw before him Mariita's eyes and, deep within, like a drop of gleaming water, the flash of innocence. He could not complete his mission.

Old houses with crumbling walls moved slowly across the train window. Cows were mooing. Wire fences etched stripes into the landscape. And then came the school yard with its children, lots of children, noisy children whose cries penetrated the railroad car. The train stopped moving and Leonardo found it the opportune moment to escape that diabolical pair. He grabbed his briefcase, muttering to himself the word "traitor," and made his way off the train.

Interpretations

1. When did you first become aware that Leonardo is no ordinary traveler? Cite the clearest indication of how extraordinary he is.

2. Horacio and Mariita never realize that Leonardo is no ordinary traveler. How does the story attempt to make plausible their lack of awareness?

3. What are Leonardo's outstanding character traits? Cite evidence of them.

4. Leonardo notices something contradictory about Horacio: "the tremendous worry" that Horacio expresses about his son is inconsistent with his "complete composure." What is ironic about Leonardo's observations, and what does this irony contribute to the story?

Correspondences

1. Review the Fanon quotation (page 444). How does it apply to Leonardo's choice in "A Train Ride"? What is the main factor behind this choice?

2. "Leonardo thought Mariita was too forward, but his rearing obliged him to answer and not ignore her. Yes, his rearing, a vestige of the bourgeois 'teachings' that he had been subjected to by his parents and professors and by the general environment." What personal and political choices does Lindo's traveler make? How do they compare with those of Matshoba's protagonists?

Applications

1. Leonardo makes what most would consider an honorable choice. Yet he refers to himself as a traitor. Write a journal entry explaining this contradiction.

2. Leonardo is a terrorist who chooses not to carry out his mission. Why? At what possible price? (To what extent is he aware of the possible consequences of his choice?)

ADDITIONAL WRITING TOPICS

1. Review the Frost quotation (page 444). What does it imply about the nature of choice? Under what circumstances might you make a similar choice? In an essay, analyze your reasons for a choice you would make to take "the road less traveled."

2. Using the selections by Mukherjee (Chapter 4) and by Thanh, Rodriguez, and Berger (this chapter) as a base, write an analysis of the price of being a refugee, migrant worker, or illegal alien in the United States.

3. According to the Yiddish proverb, "Troubles overcome are good to tell." How does this proverb apply to the selections by Glickman, Parks, and Wehle? To what extent did cultural factors affect their choices?

4. Paule Marshall (Chapter 3) sees language as both a refuge and a weapon. To what extent do Rendón (Chapter 3), Rodriguez, and Berger agree with her? (How real is the power of language? Does language define and shape people or vice versa?) Cite specific examples from this textbook and your own experience to support your point of view.

5. Each chapter in this textbook begins with a myth, a folktale, or a story that teaches a lesson. Collaborate with members of your group on composing a moralistic tale that, like "The Wise Daughter," teaches a moral lesson about choices.

6. View the videotape *Romero* and analyze the factors involved in this Salvadoran priest's decisions to fight terrorism in his own country.

7. Study the videotape *Au Revoir Les Enfants, Garden of the Finzi-Continis,* or *Weapons of the Spirit.* Analyze the nature of the choices or new choices presented. What do you conclude about the price of survival? The phenomenon of survivor guilt?

8. Thanh refers to the United States as "the promised land" in which he hopes to fulfill his dream. To what extent are the selections by Rodriguez and Berger also concerned with the "American dream"? Compare and contrast their dreams. How are they different from the original "American dream"? How do their dreams compare with yours?

9. Is culture, like nature, a limitation on freedom of choice, or does it allow more free play of individual wisdom and imagination? Do we increase our own choices to the degree that we free ourselves from culture? Limit your discussion to any three selections in this chapter.

CHAPTER 7

Aspirations

If "aspirations" sounds a little too grand for ordinary people on an ordinary day, substitute the word "ambitions" or "desires" or "dreams" or "wishes." Aspiration is perhaps more sustained than desire, for it implies more willingness to wait and to struggle, and it is a little less private than a wish.

Is there any limit to human aspirations? Probably not, but there are both natural and cultural limits to which aspirations can be realized. Some desires (perhaps not to be confused with aspirations) are antisocial and destructive. Law and government would be unnecessary if aspirations were never harmful, were never the results of greed and selfishness and intolerance. And many potentially beneficial aspirations are never realized because of fear or laziness or poor education or blind acceptance of unjust political and social systems.

Are our aspirations affected by our culture? Indeed they are. "The American Dream," for example, is more than a slogan adorning a T-shirt; it is a shorthand expression of a widespread belief among Americans that freedom, social justice, and improvement in material standards are desirable and possible for all. Some cultures may ignore or discourage aspirations. Some religions teach that human desire is the cause of all human suffering and that one's goal should be to eliminate desire. Some cultures encourage group but not individual aspirations; and some actively discourage individual aspirations: "The nail that sticks up gets hammered down," they point out. Americans do not often use that proverb. In the United States there is a widespread belief that aspirations can benefit both the individual and the society. Ralph Lamberti's tribute to Rachel Asrelsky is a case in point. Although Asrelsky's life was cut short, it was fulfilling both to herself and to those around her.

Some voices in this chapter echo the typically American desire for upward mobility (Villarreal). Others plead for respect for other cultures (Ford), and for respect and opportunity for minorities (Reed, Pipolo, Lorde, Villarreal, Johnson).

Most of the hopes and dreams in the selections of this chapter are collective or communal. Hiawatha, who lived in the sixteenth century and whose story now contains legendary elements, had a vision of uniting five warring Iroquois tribes so that against a common enemy they could contribute their strengths to a common multicultural tribe. Four centuries later, Ishmael Reed envisions an America in which "blurring of cultural styles" is accepted and the contributions to civilization of non-European peoples are considered on a par with those of Europe. He asserts that "the United States is unique in the world: The world is here."

Student Isabel Pipolo, aspiring to help her "neighbor," describes how as a high school student in New York City she was initially "ecstatic" to be given the assignment to tutor a grammar-school student, only to find that she had underestimated the job. And for the morale of their whole family, Audre Lorde's immigrant parents aspired to escape confrontation with racism in North America. The aspirations of Jay Ford also evidence a combining of the personal and the social. In "20/20 Hindsight," Ford recounts the effects of a sojourn in Kenya on his sense of identity and his hope that Americans can learn from Kenyans how better to value simple human relationships.

Mexican-American Richard Rubio's aspirations seem more private. The ambitions of twelve-year-old Richard (in José Antonio Villarreal's novel *Pocho*) are very personal, even rebellious. Nevertheless, they are influenced by a general *norteamericano* attitude toward individualism. Richard learns that "everything had another way to it if only you looked hard enough," that "what people thought was honorable was not important, because he was the important guy," that "he would never succumb to foolish social pressures again." And although Richard is a "nail" willing to be hammered in the boxing ring on the way to his goals, he is not willing to be relegated to some immigrant limbo.

PERSPECTIVES

Out of poverty, poetry;
Out of suffering, song.

Mexican saying

Civilization progresses at the expense of individual
happiness.

Sigmund Freud

The greatest mystery is not that we have been flung at
random among the profusion of the earth and the
galaxy of the stars, but that in this prison we can
fashion images of ourselves sufficiently powerful to deny
our nothingness.

André Malraux

Where young boys plan for what they will achieve and
attain, young girls plan for whom they will achieve and
attain.

Charlotte Perkins Gilman

A little madness in the Spring
Is wholesome even for the king.

Emily Dickinson

Possibility is the oldest American story. Head west for
freedom and the chance of inventing a spanking new
life for yourself. Our citizens are always leaping the
traces when their territory gets too small and cramped.

William Kittredge

Only the liberation of the natural capacity for love in
human beings can master their sadistic destructiveness.

William Reich

The greatest use of life is to spend it on something that will outlast it.

William James

I have a dream that my four little children will one day live in a nation where they will not be judged by the color of their skin but by the content of their character.

Martin Luther King, Jr.

I don't know the key to success, but the key to failure is trying to please everybody.

Bill Cosby

Nothing is as real as a dream. The world can change around you, but your dream will not. Your life may change, but your dream doesn't have to. Responsibilities need not erase it. Duties need not obscure it. Your spouse and children need not get in its way, because the dream is within you. No one can take your dream away. . . . The only way that your dream can die is if you kill it yourself . . . If you hold onto it, you may grow old, but you will never be old. And that, ladies and gentlemen, is the ultimate success.

Tom Clancy

A world with no limits is a world of perpetual misery.

Eviatan Zerubavel

. . . Satisfaction is a lowly thing, how pure a thing is joy.

Marianne Moore

. . . tolerance, as we have still to learn, is the most fundamental of all human wisdoms.

John Fowles

I call people rich when they're able to meet the requirements of their own imagination.

Henry James

Learning to read books—or pictures, or films—is not just a matter of acquiring information from texts, it is a matter of learning to read and write the texts of our lives.

Robert Scholes

Applications

1. Write a journal entry on Dickinson's perspective. What does she mean by madness? What does madness have to do with aspirations?

2. What are aspirations? How do they differ from dreams, hopes, goals, or convictions? How do they differ in connotation and applicability? Discuss these words in your group.

Hiawatha,
the Great Unifier

Iroquois Myth

*Hiawatha (b. about 1570), a member of the Mohawk tribe, is
credited with forming the League of Five Nations, also known as
the Iroquois Confederacy (the Mohawk, Oneida, Onondaga,
Cayuga, and Seneca tribes). After later addition of the Tuscaro-
ras, the confederacy became known as the League of Six Nations.
In the seventeenth century—at the height of their power—the
Iroquois inhabited a large part of New York state and controlled
an area bounded by the Kennebec, the Ottawa, the Illinois, and
the Tennessee rivers. Their articles of confederation evoked admiration in their time, in particular by Benjamin Franklin.*

THE SLUMBER OF Ta-ren-ya-wa-gon, Upholder of Heavens, was disturbed
by a great cry of anguish and woe. He looked down from his abode to
earth and saw human beings moaning with terror, pursued by horrifying
monsters and cruel, man-devouring giants. Turning himself into a mortal,
Ta-ren-ya-wa-gon swiftly descended to earth and, taking a small girl by
the hand, told the frightened humans to follow him. By trails known only
to him, he led the group of shivering refugees to a cave at the mouth of
a great river, where he fed them and told them to sleep.

After the people had somewhat recovered under his protection,
Ta-ren-ya-wa-gon again took the little girl by the hand and led them
toward the rising sun. The band traveled for many days until they came
to the confluence of two mighty rivers whose waters, white with spray,
cascaded over tremendous rocks. There Ta-ren-ya-wa-gon halted and
built a longhouse for himself and his people.

For years they lived there, content and growing fat, their children
turning into strong men and handsome women. Then Ta-ren-ya-wa-gon,
the Sky Upholder became mortal, gathered the people around him and
spoke: "You, my children, must now spread out and become great nations. I will make your numbers like the leaves of a forest in summertime,
like pebbles on the shore of the great waters." And again he took one
little girl by the hand and walked toward the setting sun, all the people
following him.

After a long journey they came to the banks of a beautiful river.
Ta-ren-ya-wa-gon separated a few families from the rest and told them to

512

build a longhouse at that spot and found a village. "You shall be known by the name of Te-ha-wro-gah, Those-of-Divided-Speech," he told them, and they grew into the Mohawk tribe. And from the moment he had named them, their language changed and they could no longer understand the rest of the people.

To the Mohawks Ta-ren-ya-wa-gon gave corn, beans, squash, and tobacco, together with dogs to help them hunt game. He taught them how to plant and reap and pound corn into meal. He taught them the ways of the forest and the game, for in that long-ago time, people did not yet know all these things. When he had fully instructed them and given them the necessities of life, Ta-ren-ya-wa-gon again took one little girl by the hand and traveled with the remaining people toward the sunset.

After a long journey they halted in a beautiful well-watered valley surrounded by forests, and he commanded another group to build their village at that spot. He gave them what was necessary for life, taught them what they needed to know, and named them Ne-ha-wre-ta-go, the Big-Tree people, for the great forests surrounding them. And these people, who grew into the Oneida nation, also spoke a tongue of their own as soon as he had named them.

Then once more Ta-ren-ya-wa-gon took a little girl's hand and wandered on, always toward the setting sun, and the rest of the people followed him. They came to a big mountain which he named O-nun-da-ga-o-no-ga. At its foot he commanded some more families to build a longhouse, and he gave them the same gifts and taught them the same things that he had the others. He named them after the mountain towering above them and also gave them a speech of their own. And these people became the Onondaga nation.

Again with a small girl at his side, Ta-ren-ya-wa-gon wandered on, leading the people to the shores of a lake sparkling in the sun. The lake was called Go-yo-gah, and here still another group built their village, and they became the Cayugas.

Now only a handful of people were left, and these Ta-ren-ya-wa-gon led to a lake by a mountain called Ga-nun-da-gwa. There he settled them, giving them the name of Te-ho-ne-noy-hent—Keepers of the Door. They too received a language of their own and grew into the mighty Seneca nation.

There were some among the people who were not satisfied with the places appointed to them by the Upholder of Heavens. These wandered on toward the setting sun until they came to a river greater than all others, a river known as the Mississippi. They crossed it on a wild grapevine that formed a bridge from bank to bank, and after the last of them had crossed over, the vine tore asunder. None could ever return, so that this river divided the western from the eastern human beings.

To each nation the Upholder of Heavens gave a special gift. To the Senecas he gave such swift feet that their hunters could outrun the deer.

To the Cayugas he gave the canoe and the skill to guide it through the most turbulent waters. To the Onondagas he gave the knowledge of eternal laws and the gift to fathom the wishes of the Great Creator. To the Oneidas he gave skills in making weapons and weaving baskets, while to the Mohawks he gave bows and arrows and the ability to guide the shafts into the hearts of their game and their enemies.

Ta-ren-ya-wa-gon resolved to live among the people as a human being. Having the power to assume any shape, he chose to be a man and took the name of Hiawatha. He chose to live among the Onondagas and took a beautiful young woman of that tribe for his wife. From their union came a daughter, Mni-haha, who surpassed even her mother in beauty and womanly skills. Hiawatha never ceased to teach and advise, and above all he preached peace and harmony.

Under Hiawatha the Onondagas became the greatest of all tribes, but the other nations founded by the Great Upholder also increased and prospered. Traveling in a magic birchbark canoe of dazzling whiteness, which floated above waters and meadows as if on an invisible bird's wings, Hiawatha went from nation to nation, counseling them and keeping man, animal, and nature in balance according to the eternal laws of the manitous.[1] So all was well and the people lived happily.

But the law of the universe is also that happiness alternates with sorrow, life with death, prosperity with hardship, harmony with disharmony. From out of the north beyond the Great Lakes came wild tribes, fierce, untutored nations who knew nothing of the eternal law; peoples who did not plant or weave baskets or fire clay into cooking vessels. All they knew was how to prey on those who planted and reaped the fruits of their labor. Fierce and pitiless, these strangers ate their meat raw, tearing it apart with their teeth. Warfare and killing were their occupation. They burst upon Hiawatha's people like a flood, spreading devastation wherever they went. Again the people turned to Hiawatha for help. He advised all the nations to assemble and wait his coming.

And so the five tribes came together at the place of the great council fire, by the shores of a large and tranquil lake where the wild men from the north had not yet penetrated. The people waited for Hiawatha one day, two days, three days. On the fourth day his gleaming-white magic canoe appeared, floating, gliding above the mists. Hiawatha sat in the stern guiding the mystery canoe, while in the bow was his only child, his daughter.

The sachems, elders, and wise men of the tribes stood at the water's edge to greet the Great Upholder. Hiawatha and his daughter stepped ashore. He greeted all he met as brothers and spoke to each in his own language.

Suddenly there came an awesome noise, a noise like the rushing of a hundred rivers, like the beating of a thousand giant wings. Fearfully the

---

[1] In Algonquian (and related) tribes, a personal totem discovered through a dream.

people looked upward. Out of the clouds, circling lower and lower, flew the great mystery bird of the heavens, a hundred times as big as the largest eagles, and whenever he beat his wings he made the sound of a thousand thunderclaps. While the people cowered, Hiawatha and his daughter stood unmoved. Then the Great Upholder laid his hands upon his daughter's head in blessing, after which she said calmly, "Farewell, my father." She seated herself between the wings of the mystery bird, who spiraled upwards and upwards into the clouds and at last disappeared into the great vault of the sky.

The people watched in awe, but Hiawatha, stunned with grief, sank to the ground and covered himself with the robe of a panther. Three days he sat thus in silence, and none dared approach him. The people wondered whether he had given his only child to the manitous above as a sacrifice for the deliverance of his people. But the Great Upholder would never tell them, would never speak of his daughter or of the mystery bird who had carried her away.

After having mourned for three days, Hiawatha rose on the morning of the fourth and purified himself in the cold, clear waters of the lake. Then he asked the great council to assemble. When the sachems,[2] elders, and wise men had seated themselves in a circle around the sacred fire, Hiawatha came before them and said:

> What is past is past; it is the present and the future which concern us. My children, listen well, for these are my last words to you. My time among you is drawing to the end.
>
> My children, war, fear, and disunity have brought you from your villages to this sacred council fire. Facing a common danger, and fearing for the lives of your families, you have yet drifted apart, each tribe thinking and acting only for itself. Remember how I took you from one small band and nursed you up into many nations. You must reunite now and act as one. No tribe alone can withstand our savage enemies, who care nothing about the eternal law, who sweep upon us like the storms of winter, spreading death and destruction everywhere.
>
> My children, listen well. Remember that you are brothers, that the downfall of one means the downfall of all. You must have one fire, one pipe, one war club.

Hiawatha motioned to the five tribal firekeepers to unite their fires with the big sacred council fire, and they did so. Then the Great Upholder sprinkled sacred tobacco upon the glowing embers so that its sweet fragrance enveloped the wise men sitting in the circle. He said:

---

[2]A member of the fifty-member council of the Iroquois league.

Onondagas, you are a tribe of mighty warriors. Your strength is like that of a giant pine tree whose roots spread far and deep so that it can withstand any storm. Be you the protectors. You shall be the first nation.

Oneida, your men are famous for their wisdom. Be you the counselors of the tribes. You shall be the second nation.

Seneca, you are swift of foot and persuasive in speech. Your men are the greatest orators among the tribes. Be you the spokesmen. You shall be the third people.

Cayuga, you are the most cunning. You are the most skilled in the building and managing of canoes. Be you the guardians of our rivers. You shall be the fourth nation.

Mohawk, you are foremost in planting corn and beans and in building longhouses. Be you the nourishers.

You tribes must be like the five fingers of a warrior's hand joined in gripping the war club. Unite as one, and then your enemies will recoil before you back into the northern wastes from whence they came. Let my words sink deep into your hearts and minds. Retire now to take counsel among yourselves, and come to me tomorrow to tell me whether you will follow my advice.

On the next morning the sachems and wise men of the five nations came to Hiawatha with the promise that they would from that day on be as one nation. Hiawatha rejoiced. He gathered up the dazzling white feathers which the great mystery bird of the sky had dropped and gave the plumes to the leaders of the assembled tribes. "By these feathers," he said, "you shall be known as the Ako-no-shu-ne, the Iroquois." Thus with the help of Hiawatha, the Great Unifier, the mighty League of the Five Nations was born, and its tribes held sway undisturbed over all the land between the great river of the west and the great sea of the east.

The elders begged Hiawatha to become the chief sachem of the united tribes, but told them: "This can never be, because I must leave you. Friends and brothers, choose the wisest women in your tribes to be the future clan mothers and peacemakers, let them turn any strife arising among you into friendship. Let your sachems be wise enough to go to such women for advice when there are disputes. Now I have finished speaking. Farewell."

At that moment there came to those assembled a sweet sound like the rush of rustling leaves and the song of innumerable birds. Hiawatha stepped into his white mystery canoe, and instead of gliding away over the waters of the lake, it rose slowly into the sky and disappeared into the clouds. Hiawatha was gone, but his teachings survive in the hearts of the people.

Interpretations

1. What is the purpose of this legend? What aspiration does it embody? Was the goal achieved in Iroquois history? How do we know?

2. What are Hiawatha's outstanding character traits? How are they best revealed?

3. Why do you think Ta-ren-ya-wa-gon, before he led a migration, always took along a small girl "by the hand"? (What does this act reveal about his character and his purpose? How might she relate to Hiawatha's daughter Mni-haha?)

4. The provocation for unifying the Five Nations is the incursion of "wild" tribes from the North. Why are they considered wild? What is Hiawatha's attitude toward warfare?

5. Why do you think Ta-ren-ya-wa-gon/Hiawatha separated and then united the people instead of leaving them united as they were in the beginning?

The Brahman
and the Pot of Rice

Indian Folk Tale

"The Brahman and the Pot of Rice" is an ancient Indian story attributed to Buddha. Milton Rugoff introduces the origins of this fable in his A Harvest of World Folk Tales.

> *India may not have been, as certain scholars once thought, the original fountain of fable, but certainly no civilization of antiquity can boast richer collections of story. Among the richest and oldest collections—scenes from it appear on a monument in Central India that dates back to the third century* B.C.—*is the* Iataka, *a gathering of more than five hundred tales reputed to have been drawn by Buddha from his experiences in previous incarnations, when he was preparing to become Buddha. The tales are intended, as the concluding comment of each insists, to be instructive. Even though the moral sometimes seems farfetched or forced, the stories themselves are usually well and interestingly told, and many of them have become in one form or another among the most popular the world over.*

THERE LIVED IN a certain place a Brahman, whose name was Svabhavakripana, which means a born miser. He had collected a quantity of rice by begging, and after having dined off it, he filled a pot with what was left over. He hung the pot on a peg on the wall, placed his couch beneath, and looking intently at it all the night, he thought, "Ah, that pot is indeed brimful of rice. Now if there should be a famine, I should certainly make a hundred rupees by it. With this I shall buy a couple of goats. They will have young ones every six months, and thus I shall have a whole herd of goats. Then with the goats I shall buy cows. As soon as they have calved, I shall sell the calves. Then with the cows I shall buy buffaloes; with the buffaloes, mares. When the mares have foaled, I shall have plenty of horses; and when I sell them, plenty of gold. With that gold I shall get a house with four wings. And then a Brahman will come to my house and will give me his beautiful daughter, with a large dowry. She will have a son, and I shall call him Somasarman. When he is old enough to be danced on his father's knee, I shall sit with a book at the back of the stable, and while I am reading the boy will see me, jump from his mother's lap, and run toward me to be danced on my knee. He will come too near the horse's hoof, and full of anger I shall call to my wife, 'Take the baby, take him!' But she, distracted by some domestic work, does not hear me. Then I get up, and give her such a kick with my foot."

While he thought this, he gave a kick with his foot and broke the pot. All the rice fell over him and made him quite white.

Therefore I say, "He who makes foolish plans for the future will be white all over, like the father of Somasarman."

Interpretations

1. How did you react to the concluding statement? Did you anticipate it or were you surprised? Why do you think the storyteller considers the Brahman "foolish"—because of the quantity or the quality of his wishes? Are all his aspirations foolish? If not, which are?

2. Do you think this "panicked litany" could have been stopped earlier or later, or is it important to end it just at the point where the Brahman aspires to kick his wife? Why?

3. What details or aspects of the fable are most influential in setting its tone?

4. What changes would have to be made in the fable to adapt it to American culture?

Correspondences

1. Review the Gilman quotation (page 509). Can you think of any examples to support it? Then review the last two paragraphs of Hiawatha's teachings. What do his admonitions suggest about his attitude towards and his aspirations for women? To what extent would Gilman "approve"?

2. Compare Hiawatha's ethics with those of the Brahman. What factors account for differences in their aspirations?

Applications

1. Is it important to have a code of ethics? On what should such a code be based? Write an essay on three moral principles in which you believe.

2. Write a journal entry on your most *painful* choice and its relationship to your aspirations.

America:
The Multicultural Society

Ishmael Reed

*Ishmael Reed (b. 1938) was raised and educated in Buffalo,
New York, and now lives in Oakland, California. He has taught
at Yale, Harvard, and Dartmouth, and currently teaches at the
University of California at Berkeley. His publications include
the novels* The Free-Lance Pallbearers *(1967),* Mumbo Jumbo
(1978), and Reckless Eyeballing *(1986), and two essay collections—*Shrovetide in Old New Orleans *(1979) and* Writin' Is
Fightin' *(1988).*

*At the annual Lower East Side Jewish Festival yesterday, a
Chinese woman ate a pizza slice in front of Ty Thuan Duc's
Vietnamese grocery store. Beside her a Spanish-speaking
family patronized a cart with two signs: "Italian Ices" and
"Kosher by Rabbi Alper." And after the pastrami ran out,
everybody ate knishes.*

New York Times, June 23, 1983

On the day before Memorial Day, 1983, a poet called me to describe a
city he had just visited. He said that one section included mosques, built
by the Islamic people who dwelled there. Attending his reading, he said,
were large numbers of Hispanic people, forty thousand of whom lived in
the same city. He was not talking about a fabled city located in some
mysterious region of the world. The city he'd visited was Detroit.

A few months before, as I was leaving Houston, Texas, I heard it
announced on the radio that Texas's largest minority was Mexican-American, and though a foundation recently issued a report critical of bilingual
education, the taped voice used to guide the passengers on the air trams
connecting terminals in Dallas Airport is in both Spanish and English. If
the trend continues, a day will come when it will be difficult to travel
through some sections of the country without hearing commands in both
English and Spanish; after all, for some western states, Spanish was the
first written language and the Spanish style lives on in the western way
of life.

Shortly after my Texas trip, I sat in an auditorium located on the campus of the University of Wisconsin at Milwaukee as a Yale professor—whose original work on the influence of African cultures upon those of the Americas has led to his ostracism from some monocultural intellectual circles—walked up and down the aisle, like an old-time southern evangelist, dancing and drumming the top of the lectern, illustrating his points before some serious Afro-American intellectuals and artists who cheered and applauded his performance and his mastery of information. The professor was "white." After his lecture, he joined a group of Milwaukeeans in a conversation. All of the participants spoke Yoruban, though only the professor had ever traveled to Africa.

One of the artists told me that his paintings, which included African and Afro-American mythological symbols and imagery, were hanging in the local McDonald's restaurant. The next day I went to McDonald's and snapped pictures of smiling youngsters eating hamburgers below paintings that could grace the walls of any of the country's leading museums. The manager of the local McDonald's said, "I don't know what you boys are doing, but I like it," as he commissioned the local painters to exhibit in his restaurant.

Such blurring of cultural styles occurs in everyday life in the United States to a greater extent than anyone can imagine and is probably more prevalent than the sensational conflict between people of different backgrounds that is played up and often encouraged by the media. The result is what the Yale Professor, Robert Thompson, referred to as a cultural bouillabaisse,[1] yet members of the nation's present educational and cultural Elect still cling to the notion that the United States belongs to some vaguely defined entity they refer to as "Western civilization," by which they mean, presumably, a civilization created by the people of Europe, as if Europe can be viewed in monolithic terms. Is Beethoven's Ninth Symphony, which includes Turkish marches, a part of Western civilization, or the late nineteenth- and twentieth-century French paintings, whose creators were influenced by Japanese art? And what of the cubists, through whom the influence of African art changed modern painting, or the surrealists, who were so impressed with the art of the Pacific Northwest Indians that, in their map of North America, Alaska dwarfs the lower forty-eight in size?

Are the Russians, who are often criticized for their adoption of "Western" ways by Tsarist dissidents in exile, members of Western civilization? And what of the millions of Europeans who have black African and Asian ancestry, black Africans having occupied several countries for hundreds of years? Are these "Europeans" members of Western civilization, or the Hungarians, who originated across the Urals[2] in a place called Greater Hungary, or the Irish, who came from the Iberian Peninsula?

[1]Fish soup

[2]Mountain system in USSR, traditional boundary between Europe and Asia.

Even the notion that North America is part of Western civilization because our "system of government" is derived from Europe is being challenged by Native American historians who say that the founding fathers, Benjamin Franklin especially, were actually influenced by the system of government that had been adopted by the Iroquois hundreds of years prior to the arrival of large numbers of Europeans.

Western civilization, then, becomes another confusing category like Third World, or Judeo-Christian culture, as man attempts to impose his small-screen view of political and cultural reality upon a complex world. Our most publicized novelist recently said that Western civilization was the greatest achievement of mankind, an attitude that flourishes on the street level as scribbles in public restrooms: "White Power," "Niggers and Spics Suck," or "Hitler was a prophet," the latter being the most telling, for wasn't Adolph Hitler the archetypal monoculturalist who, in his pig-headed arrogance, believed that one way and one blood was so pure that it had to be protected from alien strains at all costs? Where did such an attitude, which has caused so much misery and depression in our national life, which has tainted even our noblest achievements, begin? An attitude that caused the incarceration of Japanese-American citizens during World War II, the persecution of Chicanos and Chinese-Americans, the near-extermination of the Indians, and the murder and lynchings of thousands of Afro-Americans.

Virtuous, hardworking, pious, even though they occasionally would wander off after some fancy clothes, or rendezvous in the woods with the town prostitute, the Puritans are idealized in our schoolbooks as "a hardy band" of no-nonsense patriarchs whose discipline razed the forest and brought order to the New World (a term that annoys Native American historians). Industrious, responsible, it was their "Yankee ingenuity" and practicality that created the work ethic. They were simple folk who produced a number of good poets, and they set the tone for the American writing style, of lean and spare lines, long before Hemingway. They worshiped in churches whose colors blended in with the New England snow, churches with simple structures and ornate lecterns.

The Puritans were a daring lot, but they had a mean streak. They hated the theater and banned Christmas. They punished people in a cruel and inhuman manner. They killed children who disobeyed their parents. When they came in contact with those whom they considered heathens or aliens, they behaved in such a bizarre and irrational manner that this chapter in the American history comes down to us as a late-movie horror film. They exterminated the Indians, who taught them how to survive in a world unknown to them, and their encounter with the calypso culture of Barbados resulted in what the tourist guide in Salem's Witches' House refers to as the Witchcraft Hysteria.

The Puritan legacy of hard work and meticulous accounting led to the establishment of a great industrial society; it is no wonder that the

American industrial revolution began in Lowell, Massachusetts, but there was the other side, the strange and paranoid attitudes toward those different from the Elect.

The cultural attitudes of that early Elect continue to be voiced in everyday life in the United States: the president of a distinguished university, writing a letter to the *Times,* belittling the study of African civilizations; the television network that promoted its show on the Vatican art with the boast that this art represented "the finest achievements of the human spirit." A modern up-tempo state of complex rhythms that depends upon contacts with an international community can no longer behave as if it dwelled in a "Zion Wilderness"[3] surrounded by beasts and pagans.

When I heard a schoolteacher warn the other night about the invasion of the American educational system by foreign curriculums, I wanted to yell at the television set, "Lady, they're already here." It has already begun because the world is here. The world has been arriving at these shores for at least ten thousand years from Europe, Africa, and Asia. In the late nineteenth and early twentieth centuries, large numbers of Europeans arrived, adding their cultures to those of the European, African, and Asian settlers who were already here, and recently millions have been entering the country from South America and the Caribbean, making Yale professor Bob Thompson's bouillabaisse richer and thicker.

One of our most visionary politicians said that he envisioned a time when the United States could become the brain of the world, by which he meant the repository of all of the latest advanced information systems. I thought of that remark when an enterprising poet friend of mine called to say that he had just sold a poem to a computer magazine and that the editors were delighted to get it because they didn't carry fiction or poetry. Is that the kind of world we desire? A humdrum homogeneous world of all brains and no heart, no fiction, no poetry; a world of robots with human attendants bereft of imagination, of culture? Or does North America deserve a more exciting destiny? To become a place where the cultures of the world crisscross. This is possible because the United States is unique in the world: The world is here.

Interpretations

1. "Such blurring of cultural styles occurs in everyday life in the United States . . . " What do you think Reed means by "blurring"? Do you think Reed would prefer cultural identities to be lost, blurred, or "melted" (as in "melting pot")—or retained and respected? Cite evidence for your position.

[3]Variously, a hill in Jerusalem, the Jewish people or homeland, Judaism.

2. What is the purpose of this essay? Is it to argue that "Western civilization" is a vague concept or entity? Is it to state that cultural blurring is already occurring in the United States ("Lady, [foreign curricula] are already here")? Is it to argue that such blurring should be encouraged ("a more exciting destiny")? Or is it some other purpose? Where is his purpose most clearly indicated?

3. What is your reaction to Reed's depiction of the Puritans? Just how important were the Puritans in establishing American "aspirations"?

4. The last paragraph of this essay contends that the United States should lead the world not only in brains but also in imagination. Is this a new idea or a continuation of an earlier one? How might this type of leadership be accomplished? How effective is this concluding paragraph?

Correspondences

1. Why, according to Reed, are categories like "Western civilization, . . . Third World, or Judeo-Christian culture" reflections of "man's attempts to impose his small-screen view of political and cultural reality upon a complex world"? What evidence from other ethnic groups does Reed offer to support his thesis? Which writers in this anthology can you imagine agreeing with him? Who are most likely to disagree? Offer evidence to support your choices.

2. Review Reed's assessment of the positive and negative aspects of the Puritan legacy. How does it compare with that of Novak (Chapter 5)? To what extent do you agree with the views of either or both?

Applications

1. What is cultural assimilation as opposed to cultural "crisscrossing" (Reed's term)? Define each and cite examples that clearly illustrate how they differ.

2. Yale professor Robert Thompson refers to the blending of cultural styles as a "cultural bouillabaisse." What cultural contribution of your ethnic group(s) do you value most? (How does it enrich the "bouillabaisse"?)

For My Indian Daughter

Lewis P. Johnson

Lewis P. Johnson (b. 1935) was raised in Harbor Springs, Michigan, where his great-grandfather was the last official chief of the Potawatomi Ottawas. A surveyor by profession, Johnson is currently working on a study of the Indian approaches to interpretive dreams. In "For My Indian Daughter," Johnson portrays his personal odyssey towards greater ethnic pride and cultural awareness.

According to tradition, the Ottawas, the Ojibway, and the Potawatomi were originally one tribe living north of the Great Lakes. After the Ottawas separated they were active in the Indian Wars as allies of the French. After joining the Huron at Mackinaw in Michigan (adjacent to the area of Johnson's hometown of Harbor Springs and nearby Burt Lake), the Ottawa dispersed over a wide area. When first encountered by whites (in the seventeenth century), the Potawatomi lived mainly near the mouth of the Green Bay in Wisconsin. By the end of the century, they had settled along both sides of the southern end of Lake Michigan. The majority of the tribe still lives in Michigan.

MY LITTLE GIRL is singing herself to sleep upstairs, her voice mingling with the sounds of the birds outside in the old maple trees. She is two and I am nearly 50, and I am very taken with her. She came along late in my life, unexpected and unbidden, a startling gift.

Today at the beach my chubby-legged, brown-skinned daughter ran laughing into the water as fast as she could. My wife and I laughed watching her, until we heard behind us a low guttural curse and then an unpleasant voice raised in an imitation war whoop.

I turned to see a fat man in a bathing suit, white and soft as a grub, as he covered his mouth and prepared to make the Indian war cry again. He was middle-aged, younger than I, and had three little children lined up next to him, grinning foolishly. My wife suggested we leave the beach, and I agreed.

I knew the man was not unusual in his feelings against Indians. His beach behavior might have been socially unacceptable to more civilized whites, but his basic view of Indians is expressed daily in our small town, frequently on the editorial pages of the county newspaper, as white people speak out against Indian fishing rights and land rights, saying in essence, "Those Indians are taking our fish, our land." It doesn't matter to them that we were here first, that the U.S. Supreme Court has ruled in our favor. It matters to them that we have something they want, and they hate us for it. Backlash is the common explanation of the attacks on Indians, the bumper stickers that say, "Spear an Indian, Save a Fish," but I know better. The hatred of Indians goes back to the beginning when white people came to this country. For me it goes back to my childhood in Harbor Springs, Michigan.

Theft

Harbor Springs is now a summer resort for the very affluent, but a hundred years ago it was the Indian village of my Ottawa ancestors. My grandmother, Anna Showanessy, and other Indians like her, had their land there taken by treaty, by fraud, by violence, by theft. They remembered how whites had burned down the village at Burt Lake in 1900 and pushed the Indians out. These were the stories in my family.

When I was a boy my mother told me to walk down the alleys in Harbor Springs and not to wear my orange football sweater out of the house. This way I would not stand out, not be noticed, and not be a target.

I wore my orange sweater anyway and deliberately avoided the alleys. I was the biggest person I knew and wasn't really afraid. But I met my comeuppance when I enlisted in the U.S. Army. One night all the men in my barracks gathered together and, gang-fashion, pulled me into the shower and scrubbed me down with rough brushes used for floors, saying, "We won't have any dirty Indians in our outfit." It is a point of irony that I was cleaner than any of them. Later in Korea I learned how to kill, how to bully, how to hate Koreans. I came out of the war tougher than ever and, strangely, white.

I went to college, got married, lived in La Porte, Indiana, worked as a surveyor and raised three boys. I headed Boy Scout groups, never thinking it odd when the Scouts did imitation Indian dances, imitation Indian lore.

One day when I was 35 or thereabouts I heard about an Indian powwow. My father used to attend them and so with great curiosity and a strange joy at discovering a part of my heritage, I decided the thing to do to get ready for this big event was to have my friend make me a spear in his forge. The steel was fine and blue and iridescent. The feathers on the shaft were bright and proud.

In a dusty state fairground in southern Indiana, I found white people dressed as Indians. I learned they were "hobbyists," that is, it was their hobby and leisure pastime to masquerade as Indians on weekends. I felt ridiculous with my spear, and I left.

It was years before I could tell anyone of the embarrassment of this weekend and see any humor in it. But in a way it was that weekend, for all its silliness, that was my awakening. I realized I didn't know who I was. I didn't have an Indian name. I didn't speak the Indian language. I didn't know the Indian customs. Dimly I remembered the Ottawa word for dog, but it was a baby word, *kahgee,* not the full word, *muhkahgee,* which I was later to learn. Even more hazily I remembered a naming ceremony (my own). I remembered legs dancing around me, dust. Where had that been? Who had I been? "Suwaukquat," my mother told me when I asked, "where the tree begins to grow."

That was 1968, and I was not the only Indian in the country who was feeling the need to remember who he or she was. There were others. They had powwows, real ones, and eventually I found them. Together we researched our past, a search that for me culminated in the Longest Walk, a march on Washington in 1978. Maybe because I now know what it means to be Indian, it surprises me that others don't. Of course there aren't very many of us left. The chances of an average person knowing an average Indian in an average lifetime are pretty slim.

Circle

Still, I was amused one day when my small, four-year-old neighbor looked at me as I was hoeing in my garden and said, "You aren't a real Indian, are you?" Scotty is little, talkative, likable. Finally I said, "I'm a real Indian." He looked at me for a moment and then said, squinting into the sun, "Then where's your horse and feathers?" The child was simply a smaller, whiter version of my own ignorant self years before. We'd both seen too much TV, that's all. He was not to be blamed. And so, in a way, the moronic man on the beach today is blameless. We come full circle to realize other people are like ourselves, as discomfiting as that may be sometimes.

As I sit in my old chair on my porch, in a light that is fading so the leaves are barely distinguishable against the sky, I can picture my girl asleep upstairs. I would like to prepare her for what's to come, take her each step of the way saying, there's a place to avoid, here's what I know about this, but much of what's before her she must go through alone. She must pass through pain and joy and solitude and community to discover her own inner self that is unlike any other and come through that passage to the place where she sees all people are one, and in so seeing may live her life in a brighter future.

Interpretations

1. What audience besides his daughter is Johnson writing for? Cite evidence. Why do you suppose he waited until he was nearly fifty and had a daughter—he has three other children, boys—to express these thoughts?

2. "I didn't know who I was." What do we have to know about ourselves before we know who we are? How important is ancestry to a sense of identity? What should be our attitude toward our ancestry—or ancestries?

3. Until he asked his mother, Johnson did not know his Indian name, Suwaukquat. Why do you suppose she withheld it? How do you think you would feel to discover that you had another name? Why?

4. What was involved in Johnson's "finding himself"? Why must such a search be conducted with others? How did white society delay the search and make it difficult?

5. How does the return to the "moronic man on the beach" in the conclusion sum up what Johnson has to say? How does the tone of the image change in the conclusion (even though the man is still called "moronic")? How does the description—in both the introduction and the conclusion—of his daughter, the maples, and the birds affect the tone of the essay as a whole?

Correspondences

1. Review the King quotation (page 510). How does it apply to "For My Indian Daughter"? What judgment of the United States is implied in each father's dreams?

2. Who prompts Johnson to explore his cultural heritage? How has that experience affected his aspirations? Which other writers in this chapter undergo a similar experience? With what effect?

Applications

1. "We come full circle to realize other people are like ourselves, as discomfiting as that may be sometimes." To what extent do you agree with Johnson?

2. Write a journal entry on a part of your cultural heritage you might someday want to share with your children.

The Fourth of July

Audre Lorde

Audre Lorde (b. 1934) is from New York City. She was educated at Hunter College and Columbia University, and has taught at various colleges of the City University of New York. She has been a professor of English at Hunter College since 1981. Her publications include Between Ourselves *(1976) and* Chosen Poems *(1982). In the following excerpt from her autobiography* Zami: A New Spelling of My Name *(1982), Lorde compares her expectations as an African-American with those of her African-Caribbean immigrant parents. Audre Lorde has been named official State Poet of New York State (in 1991).*

THE FIRST TIME I went to Washington, D.C., was on the edge of the summer when I was supposed to stop being a child. At least that's what they said to us all at graduation from the eighth grade. My sister Phyllis graduated at the same time from high school. I don't know what she was supposed to stop being. But as graduation presents for us both, the whole family took a Fourth of July trip to Washington, D.C., the fabled and famous capital of our country.

It was the first time I'd ever been on a railroad train during the day. When I was little, and we used to go to the Connecticut shore, we always went at night on the milk train, because it was cheaper.

Preparations were in the air around our house before school was even over. We packed for a week. There were two very large suitcases that my father carried, and a box filled with food. In fact, my first trip to Washington was a mobile feast; I started eating as soon as we were comfortably ensconced in our seats, and did not stop until somewhere after Philadelphia. I remember it was Philadelphia because I was disappointed not to have passed by the Liberty Bell.

My mother had roasted two chickens and cut them up into dainty bite-size pieces. She packed slices of brown bread and butter and green pepper and carrot sticks. There were little violently yellow iced cakes with scalloped edges called "marigolds," that came from Cushman's Bakery. There was a spice bun and rock-cakes from Newton's, the West Indian bakery across Lenox Avenue from St. Mark's School, and iced tea in a wrapped mayonnaise jar. There were sweet pickles for us and dill pickles for my father, and peaches with the fuzz still on them, individually wrapped to keep them from bruising. And, for neatness, there were piles of napkins and a little tin box with a washcloth dampened with rosewater and glycerine for wiping sticky mouths.

I wanted to eat in the dining car because I had read all about them, but my mother reminded me for the umpteenth time that dining car food always cost too much money and besides, you never could tell whose hands had been playing all over that food, nor where those same hands had been just before. My mother never mentioned that Black people were not allowed into railroad dining cars headed south in 1947. As usual, whatever my mother did not like and could not change, she ignored. Perhaps it would go away, deprived of her attention.

I learned later that Phyllis's high school senior class trip had been to Washington, but the nuns had given her back her deposit in private, explaining to her that the class, all of whom were white, except Phyllis, would be staying in a hotel where Phyllis "would not be happy," meaning, Daddy explained to her, also in private, that they did not rent rooms to Negroes. "We will take among-you to Washington, ourselves," my father had avowed, "and not just for an overnight in some measly fleabag hotel."

American racism was a new and crushing reality that my parents had to deal with every day of their lives once they came to this country. They handled it as a private woe. My mother and father believed that they could best protect their children from the realities of race in america and the fact of american racism by never giving them name, much less discussing their nature. We were told we must never trust white people, but *why* was never explained, nor the nature of their ill will. Like so many other vital pieces of information in my childhood, I was supposed to know without being told. It always seemed like a very strange injunction coming from my mother, who looked so much like one of those people we were never supposed to trust. But something always warned me not to ask my mother why she wasn't white, and why Auntie Lillah and Auntie Etta weren't, even though they were all that same problematic color so different from my father and me, even from my sisters, who were somewhere in-between.

In Washington, D.C., we had one large room with two double beds and an extra cot for me. It was a back-street hotel that belonged to a friend of my father's who was in real estate, and I spent the whole next day after Mass squinting up at the Lincoln Memorial where Marian Anderson had sung after the D.A.R. refused to allow her to sing in their auditorium because she was Black. Or because she was "Colored," my father said as he told us the story. Except that what he probably said was "Negro," because for his times, my father was quite progressive.

I was squinting because I was in that silent agony that characterized all of my childhood summers, from the time school let out in June to the end of July, brought about by my dilated and vulnerable eyes exposed to the summer brightness.

I viewed Julys through an agonizing corolla of dazzling whiteness and I always hated the Fourth of July, even before I came to realize the travesty such a celebration was for Black people in this country.

My parents did not approve of sunglasses, nor of their expense.

I spent the afternoon squinting up at monuments to freedom and past presidencies and democracy, and wondering why the light and heat were both so much stronger in Washington, D.C., than back home in New York City. Even the pavement on the streets was a shade lighter in color than back home.

Late that Washington afternoon my family and I walked back down Pennsylvania Avenue. We were a proper caravan, mother bright and father brown, the three of us girls step-standards in-between. Moved by our historical surroundings and the heat of the early evening, my father decreed yet another treat. He had a great sense of history, a flair for the quietly dramatic and the sense of specialness of an occasion and a trip.

"Shall we stop and have a little something to cool off, Lin?"

Two blocks away from our hotel, the family stopped for a dish of vanilla ice cream at a Breyer's ice cream and soda fountain. Indoors, the soda fountain was dim and fan-cooled, deliciously relieving to my scorched eyes.

Corded and crisp and pinafored, the five of us seated ourselves one by one at the counter. There was I between my mother and father, and my two sisters on the other side of my mother. We settled ourselves along the white mottled marble counter, and when the waitress spoke at first no one understood what she was saying, and so the five of us just sat there.

The waitress moved along the line of us closer to my father and spoke again. "I said I kin give you to take out, but you can't eat here. Sorry." Then she dropped her eyes looking very embarrassed, and suddenly we heard what it was she was saying all at the same time, loud and clear.

Straight-backed and indignant, one by one, my family and I got down from the counter stools and turned around and marched out of the store, quiet and outraged, as if we had never been Black before. No one would answer my emphatic questions with anything other than a guilty silence. "But we hadn't done anything!" This wasn't right or fair! Hadn't I written poems about Bataan and freedom and democracy for all?

My parents wouldn't speak of this injustice, not because they had contributed to it, but because they felt they should have anticipated it and avoided it. This made me even angrier. My fury was not going to be acknowledged by a like fury. Even my two sisters copied my parents' pretense that nothing unusual and anti-american had occurred. I was left to write my angry letter to the president of the united states all by myself, although my father did promise I could type it out on the office typewriter next week, after I showed it to him in my copybook diary.

The waitress was white, and the counter was white, and the ice cream I never ate in Washington, D.C., that summer I left childhood was white, and the white heat and the white pavement and the white stone monuments of my first Washington summer made me sick to my stomach for the whole rest of that trip and it wasn't much of a graduation present after all.

Interpretations

1. How do Lorde's descriptions of elaborate picnic food, the pretexts for avoiding of the dining car, and the story of Phyllis's exclusion from her senior class trip increase the impact of the final event of the essay?

2. Where does Lorde reveal how she feels about her parents' general policy of trying to "anticipate and avoid" racial prejudice? In similar circumstances would you feel the same way as Lorde? Why or why not?

3. The tone of the sentence (in the first paragraph) "I don't know what she was supposed to stop being" is somewhat ironic. Find other passages in a similar tone. Is this also the tone of the last paragraph? What is the essay's prevailing tone?

Correspondences

1. What is ironic about the date of Lorde's graduation trip? What incidents occur that contribute to the irony? Compare the author's experience with that of Parks (Chapter 6).

2. Compare the effects of stereotyping in the selections by Johnson and Lorde. How might stereotyping affect aspirations?

Applications

1. "As usual, whatever my mother did not like and could not change, she ignored. Perhaps it would go away, deprived of her attention." Is it better to ignore unpleasant realities or to confront them? Which attitude is more likely to nurture aspirations? Explain your answer.

2. View a video of *Born on the Fourth of July* and write an analysis of the importance of that date in Lorde's essay and Stone's film.

Tolerance

E. M. Forster

E. M. Forster (1879–1970) was an English novelist, short-story writer, and essayist. He wrote six novels, all of which deal with the class concerns of his era, among them Where Angels Fear to Tread *(1905),* A Room with a View *(1908),* Howard's End *(1910), and his best-known novel,* A Passage to India *(1924). He wrote seven books of literary criticism, and in 1951 published a collection of sociological essays entitled* Two Cheers for Democracy, *from which the following essay is taken.*

EVERYBODY IS TALKING about reconstruction. Our enemies have their schemes for a new order in Europe, maintained by their secret police, and we on our side talk of rebuilding London or England, or western civilisation, and we make plans how this is to be done. Which is all very well, but when I hear such talk, and see the architects sharpening their pencils and the contractors getting out their estimates, and the statesmen marking out their spheres of influence and everyone getting down to the job, a very famous text occurs to me: "Except the Lord build the house, they labour in vain who build it." Beneath the poetic imagery of these words lies a hard scientific truth, namely, unless you have a sound attitude of mind, a right psychology, you cannot construct or reconstruct anything that will endure. The text is true, not only for religious people, but for workers whatever their outlook, and it is significant that one of our historians, Dr. Arnold Toynbee, should have chosen it to preface his great study of the growth and decay of civilisations. Surely the only sound foundation for a civilisation is a sound state of mind. Architects, contractors, international commissioners, marketing boards, broadcasting corporations will never, by themselves, build a new world. They must be inspired by the proper spirit, and there must be the proper spirit in the people for whom they are working. For instance, we shall never have a beautiful new London until people refuse to live in ugly houses. At present, they don't mind; they demand comfort, but are indifferent to civic beauty; indeed they have no taste. I live myself in a hideous block of flats, but I can't say it worries me, and until we are worried, all schemes for reconstructing London beautifully must automatically fail.

What though is the proper spirit? We agree that the basic problem is psychological, that the Lord must build if the work is to stand, that there must be a sound state of mind before diplomacy or economics or trade-conferences can function. But what state of mind is sound? Here we may differ. Most people, when asked what spiritual quality is needed to rebuild civilisation, will reply "Love." Men must love one another, they say; nations must do likewise, and then the series of cataclysms which is threatening to destroy us will be checked.

Respectfully but firmly, I disagree. Love is a great force in private life; it is indeed the greatest of all things: but love in public affairs does not work. It has been tried again and again: by the Christian civilisations of the Middle Ages, and also by the French Revolution, a secular movement which reasserted the Brotherhood of Man. And it has always failed. The idea that nations should love one another, or that business concerns or marketing boards should love one another, or that a man in Portugal should love a man in Peru of whom he has never heard—it is absurd, unreal, dangerous. It leads us into perilous and vague sentimentalism. "Love is what is needed," we chant, and then sit back and the world goes on as before. The fact is we can only love what we know personally. And we cannot know much. In public affairs, in the rebuilding of civilisation, something much less dramatic and emotional is needed, namely, tolerance. Tolerance is a very dull virtue. It is boring. Unlike love, it has always had a bad press. It is negative. It merely means putting up with people, being able to stand things. No one has ever written an ode to tolerance, or raised a statue to her. Yet this is the quality which will be most needed after the war. This is the sound state of mind which we are looking for. This is the only force which will enable different races and classes and interests to settle down together to the work of reconstruction.

The world is very full of people—appallingly full; it has never been so full before, and they are all tumbling over each other. Most of these people one doesn't know and some of them one doesn't like; doesn't like the colour of their skins, say, or the shapes of their noses, or the way they blow them or don't blow them, or the way they talk, or their smell, or their clothes, or their fondness for jazz or their dislike of jazz, and so on. Well, what is one to do? There are two solutions. One of them is the Nazi solution. If you don't like people, kill them, banish them, segregate them, and then strut up and down proclaiming that you are the salt of the earth. The other way is much less thrilling, but it is on the whole the way of the democracies, and I prefer it. If you don't like people, put up with them as well as you can. Don't try to love them: you can't, you'll only strain yourself. But try to tolerate them. On the basis of that tolerance a civilised future may be built. Certainly I can see no other foundation for the post-war world.

For what it will most need is the negative virtues: not being huffy, touchy, irritable, revengeful. I have lost all faith in positive militant ideals; they can so seldom be carried out without thousands of human beings getting maimed or imprisoned. Phrases like "I will purge this nation," "I will clean up this city," terrify and disgust me. They might not have mattered when the world was emptier: they are horrifying now, when one nation is mixed up with another, when one city cannot be organically separated from its neighbours. And, another point: reconstruction is unlikely to be rapid. I do not believe that we are psychologically fit for it, plan the architects never so wisely. In the long run, yes, perhaps: the history of our race justifies that hope. But civilisation has its mysterious regressions, and it seems to me that we are fated now to be in one of them, and must recognise this and behave accordingly. Tolerance, I believe, will be imperative after the establishment of peace. It's always useful to take a concrete instance: and I have been asking myself how I should behave if, after peace was signed, I met Germans who had been fighting against us. I shouldn't try to love them: I shouldn't feel inclined. They have broken a window in my little ugly flat for one thing. But I shall try to tolerate them, because it is common sense, because in the post-war world we shall have to live with Germans. We can't exterminate them, any more than they have succeeded in exterminating the Jews. We shall have to put up with them, not for any lofty reason, but because it is the next thing that will have to be done.

I don't then regard tolerance as a great eternally established divine principle, though I might perhaps quote "In My Father's House are many mansions" in support of such a view. It is just a makeshift, suitable for an overcrowded and overheated planet. It carries on when love gives out, and love generally gives out as soon as we move away from our home and our friends, and stand among strangers in a queue for potatoes. Tolerance is wanted in the queue; otherwise we think, "Why will people be so slow?"; it is wanted in the tube, or "Why will people be so fat?"; it is wanted at the telephone, or "Why are they so deaf?" or conversely, "Why do they mumble?" It is wanted in the street, in the office, at the factory, and it is wanted above all between classes, races, and nations. It's dull. And yet it entails imagination. For you have all the time to be putting yourself in someone else's place. Which is a desirable spiritual exercise.

This ceaseless effort to put up with other people seems tame, almost ignoble, so that it sometimes repels generous natures, and I don't recall many great men who have recommended tolerance. St. Paul certainly did not. Nor did Dante. However, a few names occur. Going back over two thousand years, and to India, there is the great Buddhist Emperor Asoka, who set up inscriptions recording not his own exploits but the need for mercy and mutual understanding and peace. Going back about four hundred years, to Holland, there is the Dutch scholar Erasmus, who stood apart from the religious fanaticism of the Reformation and was abused by both parties in consequence. In the same century there was the Frenchman Montaigne, subtle, intelligent, witty, who lived in his quiet country house and wrote essays which still delight and confirm the civilised. And England: there was John Locke, the philosopher; there was Sydney Smith, the Liberal and liberalising divine; there was Lowes Dickinson, writer of

A Modern Symposium, which might be called the Bible of Tolerance. And Germany—yes, Germany: there was Goethe. All these men testify to the creed which I have been trying to express: a negative creed, but necessary for the salvation of this crowded jostling modern world.

Two more remarks. First it is very easy to see fanaticism in other people, but difficult to spot in oneself. Take the evil of racial prejudice. We can easily detect it in the Nazis; their conduct has been infamous ever since they rose to power. But we ourselves—are we guiltless? We are far less guilty than they are. Yet is there no racial prejudice in the British Empire? Is there no colour question? I ask you to consider that, those of you to whom tolerance is more than a pious word. My other remark is to forestall a criticism. Tolerance is not the same as weakness. Putting up with people does not mean giving in to them. This complicates the problem. But the rebuilding of civilisation is bound to be complicated. I only feel certain that unless the Lord builds the house, they will labour in vain who build it. Perhaps, when the house is completed, love will enter it, and the greatest force in our private lives will also rule in public life.

Interpretations

1. To what extent do you agree with Forster that "Except the Lord build the house" can be interpreted to mean "unless you have a sound attitude of mind"? What are the intermediate steps in this interpretation?

2. Forster bases his rejection of love as the state-of-mind-we-are-looking-for on the problem that "we can only love what we know personally." Is this true, and if so, is it sufficient to disqualify love as the solution?

3. How would your college, home town, state, or nation be different if people, instead of calling for a clean-up or purge, tried tolerance? Is Forster calling for the tolerance of ideas, of programs, of behavior or misbehavior, or just of other people?

4. What imagination is needed in order for people to have tolerance? Can you give an example close to home of tolerance based on imagination? Are tolerant people, as Forster keeps saying, really duller and less noble than fanatics?

Correspondences

1. Apply Zerubavel's perspective on limits (page 510) to Forster's essay on "tolerance." Discuss its relevance to Forster's distinctions between

love and tolerance. To what extent do you agree that limits contribute to personal happiness?

2. According to Forster tolerance "is the only force which will enable different races and classes and interests to settle down together to do the work of reconstruction." Justify his thesis by applying it to the selections by Lorde or Johnson. Evaluate the part to be played by tolerance just "putting up with people" in solving problems of racial prejudice in the United States.

Applications

1. Consult a dictionary or thesaurus on the various meanings of *fanaticism*. Discuss the implications of Forster' s thesis that "it is very easy to see fanaticism in other people, but difficult to spot in oneself."

2. Forster thinks that aspiring to love strangers and whole groups of people is fruitless, but that aspiring to tolerance, a less noble and demanding virtue, might be fruitful. Do you think that aspiring too high can be self-defeating? Is it better not to aspire at all than to aspire too high? Do we choose our aspirations or are they thrust upon us?

Learning to Teach

Isabel L. Pipolo

Isabel Pipolo was born and raised in New York City. She attended Stuyvesant High School, in Manhattan, and is now a sophomore at Cornell University in Ithaca, New York. She spends her free time deciding on a major and battling the Ithaca weather. She is proud to be making her publishing debut.

STUYVESANT HIGH SCHOOL is renowned as being a math and science high school, but after practically living there for four years, I can honestly say that I received the most well-rounded liberal arts education one could ever hope for. This wasn't only because of the kinds of courses available, but also because of the opportunity to connect one's learning to the life of the city around us.

In my junior year, for instance, I worked in a psychology internship program teaching poor grammar-school children from the neighborhood to read and write. In this program a group of Stuyvesant students would go to a nearby grammar school and sit with individual children, helping them with reading and math for two hours each day. At the start of the program I was ecstatic. It seemed like a wonderful opportunity not only to learn more about children and teaching, but also to really make a difference in someone's life. These adorable eight-year-olds seemed to cry out for our attention. They needed us; they wanted role models and we wanted to fulfill their ideals.

My child's name was Tamika. She was an affectionate black girl who lived with her grandmother and younger sister in one of the worst inner city neighborhoods in New York. Tamika and her sister (who was six) walked to and from school through a neighborhood that I would refuse to walk through alone at three o'clock in the afternoon.

From the little I could gather about Tamika's home life, her mother had disappeared suddenly when she was very young; she never even mentioned a father. I never met her grandmother, but sometimes I suspected that Tamika was mistreated at home because she occasionally came to school with bruises on her face and arms, which she refused to discuss. One day her sister was absent and when I asked her teacher about it, she became flustered and told me not to ask. Tamika told me that she wasn't allowed to tell me the reason. Since it really upset her, I didn't pursue the topic, but the incident only increased my suspicion that Tamika's grandmother was not the ideal parent.

I wanted to make an impact on this girl's life—to be her foster mother, to love her and take care of her. I wanted to open her eyes to the world of education and learning and make a lasting impression on her mind. I wanted to be able to change the course of her life just by caring for her for a few months.

Of course, these wishes were unrealistic. One person could not possibly make that much of a change in a mere fifteen weeks. Tamika was friendly and loving and seemed to enjoy being with me. She wrote little notes and drew pictures for me and always seemed happy to see me. Nevertheless, she continued to be the same hyperactive, restless girl that she was at the beginning. She was easily distracted and often if I insisted that we do her schoolwork, she would burst into tears or run screaming from the room. She had no interest in reading or math or in anything having to do with school. Eight years of bad habits could not be corrected in a few weeks, especially not by someone with minimal training in child psychology.

I soon realized that I really could not single-handedly make a big difference in Tamika's life simply by being a big sister for four and a half months, and that any such hopes that such an internship program could work that quickly were idealistic. Simply because a group of super smart, well-intentioned Stuyvesant students set their minds to the task, there was no guarantee that it could happen.

Tamika came to symbolize something in the society that I had trouble dealing with. Her problem, multiplied by the hundreds of thousands of students in the public school system, became overwhelming. These feelings were so strong that sometimes when in her neighborhood, I found myself wishing to be back in my safe, suburban, middle-class American home, where life was simple and easy. I was frustrated and confused, but also disappointed and bitter because if we—i.e., Stuyvesant students—were supposedly the "cream of the crop," as our principal so loved to call us, and we couldn't make a difference, then who could?

My experience with Tamika helped me to realize that changing the world would take a lot more than I had bargained for. For a program of this kind to succeed, more people need to devote more time and energy to it. Trying to correct eight years of ineffective education and inadequate parenting requires a commitment by society in general, not just a few enthusiastic teenagers enrolled in a psychology elective in a local high school. Reading and math are certainly important to every child's education, but it is difficult, if not impossible to teach these when the child does not have a basic sense of security and self-confidence. It is even more important, therefore, to teach children to care about themselves, for it is this that will give them the confidence they need to learn other skills, to succeed, and to have a happy life.

Interpretations

1. Pipolo comes to feel that the problem "requires a commitment by society in general." Does that mean that there is nothing individuals can do, acting alone, to help people like Tamika?

2. How typical is Pipolo's frustrating effort to help a less fortunate neighbor? Where can further information to be obtained on the success rate of such volunteer (or semi-volunteer) teaching programs? What examples of success in this area can you provide?

3. What changes in the program might lead to greater success in the future? (A class period shorter than two hours? Students younger than eight years? More selectivity in students? More involvement with the students' families?)

Correspondences

1. "She had no interests in reading or math or in anything having to do with school. Eight years of bad habits could not be corrected in a few weeks, especially not by someone with minimal training in child psychology." Compare Pipolo's experience with those of the vocational-education kids described by Mike Rose (Chapter 4). To what extent do you agree that a societal commitment is necessary to improve public education in the United States?

2. Pipolo and Lorde are forced to modify their aspirations. Analyze their experiences and evaluate what they learned from lowering their expectations.

Applications

1. "Reading and math are certainly important to every child's education, but it is difficult, if not impossible, to teach these when the child does not have a basic sense of security and self-confidence." What role can you imagine society playing in creating a situation in which Tamika would gain "a sense of security and self-confidence"?

2. Discuss Henry James's perspective (page 510). How do you define "imagination"? Is it possible to meet its "requirements"? Why or why not?

Balthazar's Marvelous Afternoon

Gabriel García Márquez

Gabriel García Márquez was born in 1928 in a small town on the Caribbean Coast of Colombia. He studied law at the National University in Bogotá and at the University of Cartagena. He worked as a journalist in Bogotá and in Cuba for the government of Fidel Castro (1959 – 1961). He was living in Mexico City when he wrote his masterpiece One Hundred Years of Solitude *(1967), which has been translated into over thirty languages. While living in Barcelona (1967–1975) he wrote* The Incredible and Sad Tale of Innocent Erendira and Her Heartless Grandmother *(1972) and* The Autumn of the Patriarch *(1975). Since the late 1970s he has maintained residences in both Mexico and Colombia. He was awarded the Nobel Prize for literature in 1982. His most recent novel is* Love in the Time of Cholera *(1985).*

García Márquez' native Colombia at the northwest corner of South America has a varied topography: three separate Andean ranges traverse the country, and out of one of these ranges flows the Magdalena River north to the Caribbean Sea through the rich alluvial plain where García Márquez was born. Spain conquered the native tribes in the 1530s and ruled the country as New Granada for three centuries. Events and personalities of a civil war in the early years of this century, which García Márquez' grandmother remembered vividly, provided the basis for his fictional Macondo, the locale of One Hundred Years of Solitude *and many other of his stories. More recently Colombia has been torn by violence between drug traffickers and the government, which in 1989 stepped up efforts to eradicate the drug trade, prompting a wave of retaliatory killings, including the assassination of three presidential candidates.*

THE CAGE WAS finished. Balthazar hung it under the eave, from force of habit, and when he finished lunch everyone was already saying that it was the most beautiful cage in the world. So many people came to see it that a crowd formed in front of the house, and Balthazar had to take it down and close the shop.

"You have to shave," Ursula, his wife, told him. "You look like a Capuchin."

"It's bad to shave after lunch," said Balthazar.

He had two weeks' growth, short, hard, and bristly hair like the mane of a mule, and the general expression of a frightened boy. But it was a false expression. In February he was thirty; he had been living with Ursula for four years, without marrying her and without having children, and life had given him many reasons to be on guard but none to be frightened. He did not even know that for some people the cage he had just made was the most beautiful one in the world. For him, accustomed to making cages since childhood, it had been hardly any more difficult than the others.

"Then rest for a while," said the woman. "With that beard you can't show yourself anywhere."

While he was resting, he had to get out of his hammock several times to show the cage to the neighbors. Ursula had paid little attention to it until then. She was annoyed because her husband had neglected the work of his carpenter's shop to devote himself entirely to the cage, and for two weeks had slept poorly, turning over and muttering incoherencies, and he hadn't thought of shaving. But her annoyance dissolved in the face of the finished cage. When Balthazar woke up from his nap, she had ironed his pants and a shirt; she had put them on a chair near the hammock and had carried the cage to the dining table. She regarded it in silence.

"How much will you charge?" she asked.

"I don't know," Balthazar answered. "I'm going to ask for thirty pesos to see if they'll give me twenty."

"Ask for fifty," said Ursula. "You've lost a lot of sleep in these two weeks. Furthermore, it's rather large. I think it's the biggest cage I've ever seen in my life."

Balthazar began to shave.

"Do you think they'll give me fifty pesos?"

"That's nothing for Mr. Chepe Montiel, and the cage is worth it," said Ursula. "You should ask for sixty."

The house lay in the stifling shadow. It was the first week of April and the heat seemed less bearable because of the chirping of the cicadas. When he finished dressing, Balthazar opened the door to the patio to cool off the house, and a group of children entered the dining room.

The news had spread. Dr. Octavio Giraldo, an old physician, happy with life but tired of his profession, thought about Balthazar's cage while he was eating lunch with his invalid wife. On the inside terrace, where they put the table on hot days, there were many flowerpots and two cages with canaries. His wife liked birds, and she liked them so much that she hated cats because they could eat them up. Thinking about her, Dr. Giraldo went to see a patient that afternoon, and when he returned he went by Balthazar's house to inspect the cage.

There were a lot of people in the dining room. The cage was on display on the table: with its enormous dome of wire, three stories inside, with passageways and compartments especially for eating and sleeping and swings in the space set aside for the birds' recreation, it seemed like a small-scale model of a gigantic ice factory. The doctor inspected it carefully, without touching it, thinking that in effect the cage was better than its reputation, and much more beautiful than any he had ever dreamed of for his wife.

"This is a flight of the imagination," he said. He sought out Balthazar among the group of people and, fixing his maternal eyes on him, added, "You would have been an extraordinary architect."

Balthazar blushed.

"Thank you," he said.

"It's true," said the doctor. He was smoothly and delicately fat, like a woman who had been beautiful in her youth, and he had delicate hands. His voice seemed like that of a priest speaking Latin. "You wouldn't even need to put birds in it," he said, making the cage turn in front of the audience's eyes as if he were auctioning it off, "It would be enough to hang it in the trees so it could sing by itself." He put it back on the table, thought a moment, looking at the cage, and said:

"Fine, then I'll take it."

"It's sold," said Ursula.

"It belongs to the son of Mr. Chepe Montiel," said Balthazar. "He ordered it specially."

The doctor adopted a respectful attitude.

"Did he give you the design?"

"No," said Balthazar. "He said he wanted a large cage, like this one, for a pair of troupials."

The doctor looked at the cage.

"But this isn't for troupials."

"Of course it is, Doctor," said Balthazar, approaching the table. The children surrounded him. "The measurements are carefully calculated," he said, pointing to the different compartments with his forefinger. Then he struck the dome with his knuckles, and the cage filled with resonant chords.

"It's the strongest wire you can find, and each joint is soldered outside and in," he said.

"It's even big enough for a parrot," interrupted one of the children.

"That it is," said Balthazar.

The doctor turned his head.

"Fine, but he didn't give you the design," he said. "He gave you no exact specifications, aside from making it a cage big enough for troupials. Isn't that right?"

"That's right," said Balthazar.

"Then there's no problem," said the doctor. "One thing is a cage big enough for troupials, and another is this cage. There's no proof that this one is the one you were asked to make."

"It's this very one," said Balthazar, confused. "That's why I made it." The doctor made an impatient gesture.

"You could make another one," said Ursula, looking at her husband. And then, to the doctor: "You're not in any hurry."

"I promised it to my wife for this afternoon," said the doctor.

"I'm very sorry, Doctor," said Balthazar, "but I can't sell you something that's sold already."

The doctor shrugged his shoulders. Drying the sweat from his neck with a handkerchief, he contemplated the cage silently with the fixed, unfocused gaze of one who looks at a ship which is sailing away.

"How much did they pay you for it?"

Balthazar sought out Ursula's eyes without replying.

"Sixty pesos," she said.

The doctor kept looking at the cage. "It's very pretty." He sighed. "Extremely pretty." Then, moving toward the door, he began to fan himself energetically, smiling, and the trace of that episode disappeared forever from his memory.

"Montiel is very rich," he said.

In truth, José Montiel was not as rich as he seemed, but he would have been capable of doing anything to become so. A few blocks from there, in a house crammed with equipment, where no one had ever smelled a smell that couldn't be sold, he remained indifferent to the news of the cage. His wife, tortured by an obsession with death, closed the doors and windows after lunch and lay for two hours with her eyes opened to the shadow of the room, while José Montiel took his siesta. The clamor of many voices surprised her there. Then she opened the door to the living room and found a crowd in front of the house, and Balthazar with the cage in the middle of the crowd, dressed in white, freshly shaved, with that expression of decorous candor with which the poor approach the houses of the wealthy.

"What a marvelous thing!" José Montiel's wife exclaimed, with a radiant expression, leading Balthazar inside. "I've never seen anything like it in my life," she said, and added, annoyed by the crowd which piled up at the door:

"But bring it inside before they turn the living room into a grandstand."

Balthazar was no stranger to José Montiel's house. On different occasions, because of his skill and forthright way of dealing, he had been called in to do minor carpentry jobs. But he never felt at ease among the rich. He used to think about them, about their ugly and argumentative wives, about their tremendous surgical operations, and he always experienced a feeling of pity. When he entered their houses, he couldn't move without dragging his feet.

"Is Pepe home?" he asked.

He had put the cage on the dining-room table.

"He's at school," said José Montiel's wife. "But he shouldn't be long," and she added, "Montiel is taking a bath."

In reality, José Montiel had not had time to bathe. He was giving himself an urgent alcohol rub, in order to come out and see what was going on. He was such a cautious man that he slept without an electric fan so he could watch over the noises of the house while he slept.

"Adelaide!" he shouted. "What's going on?"

"Come and see what a marvelous thing!" his wife shouted.

José Montiel, obese and hairy, his towel draped around his neck, appeared at the bedroom window.

"What is that?"

"Pepe's cage," said Balthazar.

His wife looked at him perplexedly.

"Whose?"

"Pepe's," replied Balthazar. And then, turning toward José Montiel, "Pepe ordered it."

Nothing happened at that instant, but Balthazar felt as if someone had just opened the bathroom door on him. José Montiel came out of the bedroom in his underwear.

"Pepe!" he shouted.

"He's not back," whispered his wife, motionless.

Pepe appeared in the doorway. He was about twelve, and had the same curved eyelashes and was as quietly pathetic as his mother.

"Come here," José Montiel said to him. "Did you order this?"

The child lowered his head. Grabbing him by the hair, José Montiel forced Pepe to look him in the eye.

"Answer me."

The child bit his lip without replying.

"Montiel," whispered his wife.

José Montiel let the child go and turned toward Balthazar in a fury. "I'm very sorry, Balthazar," he said. "But you should have consulted me before going on. Only to you would it occur to contract with a minor." As he spoke, his face recovered its serenity. He lifted the cage without looking at it and gave it to Balthazar.

"Take it away at once, and try to sell it to whomever you can," he said. "Above all, I beg you not to argue with me." He patted him on the back and explained, "The doctor has forbidden me to get angry."

The child had remained motionless, without blinking, until Balthazar looked at him uncertainly with the cage in his hand. Then he emitted a gutteral sound, like a dog's growl, and threw himself on the floor screaming.

José Montiel looked at him, unmoved, while the mother tried to pacify him. "Don't even pick him up," he said. "Let him break his head on the floor, and then put salt and lemon on it so he can rage to his heart's content." The child was shrieking tearlessly while his mother held him by the wrists.

"Leave him alone," José Montiel insisted.

Balthazar observed the child as he would have observed the death throes of a rabid animal. It was almost four o'clock. At that hour, at his house, Ursula was singing a very old song and cutting slices of onion.

"Pepe," said Balthazar.

He approached the child, smiling, and held the cage out to him. The child jumped up, embraced the cage which was almost as big as he was, and stood looking at Balthazar through the wirework without knowing what to say. He hadn't shed one tear.

"Balthazar," said José Montiel softly. "I told you already to take it away."

"Give it back," the woman ordered the child.

"Keep it," said Balthazar. And then, to José Montiel: "After all, that's what I made it for."

José Montiel followed him into the living room.

"Don't be foolish, Balthazar," he was saying, blocking his path. "Take your piece of furniture home and don't be silly. I have no intention of paying you a cent."

"It doesn't matter," said Balthazar. "I made it expressly as a gift for Pepe. I didn't expect to charge anything for it."

As Balthazar made his way through the spectators who were blocking the door, José Montiel was shouting in the middle of the living room. He was very pale and his eyes were beginning to get red.

"Idiot!" he was shouting. "Take your trinket out of here. The last thing we need is for some nobody to give orders in my house. Son of a bitch!"

In the pool hall, Balthazar was received with an ovation. Until that moment, he thought that he had made a better cage than ever before, that he'd had to give it to the son of José Montiel so he wouldn't keep crying, and that none of these things was particularly important. But then he realized that all of this had a certain importance for many people, and he felt a little excited.

"So they give you fifty pesos for the cage."

"Sixty," said Balthazar.

"Score one for you," someone said. "You're the only one who has managed to get such a pile of money out of Mr. Chepe Montiel. We have to celebrate."

They bought him a beer, and Balthazar responded with a round for everybody. Since it was the first time he had ever been out drinking, by dusk he was completely drunk, and he was talking about a fabulous project of a thousand cages, at sixty pesos each, and then of a million cages, till he had sixty million pesos. "We have to make a lot of things to sell to the rich before they die," he was saying, blind drunk. "All of them are sick, and they're going to die. They're so screwed up they can't even get angry any more." For two hours he was paying for the jukebox, which played without interruption. Everybody toasted Balthazar's health, good luck, and fortune, and the death of the rich, but at mealtime they left him alone in the pool hall.

Ursula had waited for him until eight, with a dish of fried meat covered with slices of onion. Someone told her that her husband was in the pool hall, delirious with happiness, buying beer for everyone, but she didn't believe it, because Balthazar had never got drunk. When she went to bed, almost at midnight, Balthazar was in a lighted room where there were little tables, each with four chairs, and an outdoor dance floor, where the plovers were walking around. His face was smeared with rouge, and since he couldn't take one more step, he thought he wanted to lie down with two women in the same bed. He had spent so much that he had had to leave his watch in pawn, with the promise to pay the next day. A moment later, spread-eagled in the street, he realized that his shoes were being taken off, but he didn't want to abandon the happiest dream of his life. The women who passed on their way to five-o'clock Mass didn't dare look at him, thinking he was dead.

Interpretations

1. Discuss the significance of Balthazar's two-week growth of beard.

2. Why, if not for money, did Balthazar make the cage? What is the significance of the fact that "he did not even know that for some people the cage he had just made was the most beautiful one on the world"? Why, after a life of sobriety, does he get drunk?

3. "We have to make a lot of things to sell to the rich before they die." In reality, Balthazar didn't sell the thing he made. Why not? What is the significance of his giving it away? Is it fair or just that Pepe should end up possessing the cage? Explain your answer.

4. What status does Balthazar's ability to make the world's biggest or most beautiful cage bestow on him?

5. A strong clue to the meaning of the story may be the contrast between the two characters Balthazar and Montiel. How are they different?

Correspondences

1. Apply Moore's perspective (page 510) to Balthazar's adventure. To what extent did he experience "joy"? Should he have settled for satisfaction? Explain your answer.

2. Review James's perspective (page 510) and discuss its application to García Márquez' short story.

Applications

1. Balthazar values creativity and elevates his carpentry to an art. Compare your creative experiences with theirs. Should creativity be considered a luxury or a necessity? What is its connection to aspirations?

2. Analyze García Márquez' narrative style. To what extent does the narrator comment on the actions of his characters or examine their motives? Does he approve or disapprove of Balthazar? How do you know?

Rachel Maria Asrelsky

Ralph J. Lamberti

Ralph J. Lamberti is a former borough president of Staten Island, New York. The selection which follows is his memorial eulogy to Rachel Maria Asrelsky.

IN A FEW MINUTES we'll be hearing "The Trumpet Shall Sound" by Handel. Rachel had said that she wanted that aria performed at her wedding. Not that Rachel was contemplating marriage. She wasn't even engaged. Indeed, marriage, I think, had little to do with it. Rather, her selection of an aria years in advance of her wedding was a function of her energy.

Only Rachel, and that handful of endlessly buoyant people like her, could have requested wedding music long before she accepted someone's hand in matrimony. Her energy required that if she liked a piece of music, it could not be allowed to pass but be held onto and scheduled for use in her boundless future.

Some of us may drift through time and space. Not Rachel. She steamed full throttle, filling every place and every moment she occupied with her energy. And what energy it was.

When God made Rachel, He, or as Rachel might say, She, created a whirlwind.

On the program, you'll note Rachel's middle name. It is not pronounced Maria. She pronounced it More-riah. As in, "Call the Wind Moriah."

It was apt. She had the energy of a full gale.

I first encountered it in 1984 in San Francisco. I was a delegate to the national Democratic Party Convention. My wife, Sue, and I were waiting for a trolley when out of nowhere appeared cousin Rachel. Her energy could knock you over.

In less than 24 hours, I had secured for her a visitor's pass, and she was on the convention floor politiking relentlessly by day, attending political dinners by night. She was only 16, and visiting friends in San Francisco.

But already by that time, travelling and sightseeing had become a passion for her, a passion that only increased through the years.

She was the ultimate sightseer. This past October, she declined a second visit to her beloved Capri because she felt obliged to travel to southern Italy and poke around a Greek temple.

As her host family in Italy said of her: "Most students come to Italy to study art; Rachel came to study Italy."

But she was no idle tourist. Beneath the torrent of energy that was her outward life there was deep inside her, a pool of such stillness and depth that in talking and confiding to her others became calm and derived strength. In her depths, they could see themselves with a fiercer clarity.

From her days at Stuyvesant High School and then at Grinnell College, Rachel was psychiatrist, counsellor, confessor and advisor to many. There was a certitude to her that her energy complemented, and it drew people who sought help from their own insecurities.

And she had help to offer. Her strength and determination were always evident. You experienced them directly as soon as you conversed with her. You inferred them quickly by simply observing her.

No one, I found myself thinking, could go off in so many directions, and achieve so much, unless she was motivated by clear direction and mature understanding.

This clarity and maturity were evident in the small things she did as in the big things.

She had written a research paper for the Grinnell Anthropology Department that was valued so highly by the faculty as a piece of original scholarship, that she was urged to pursue her work and have the paper published. The same zeal left Hope and Arnold just a tiny bit exhausted when Rachel returned to Iowa after a semester break. After she had cooked her way through vacation and urged Hope to change her hairstyle, or buy that new dress, or rearrange the furniture, or read this wonderful book, or see that play, or try this recipe.

Throughout the western world, in the homes of people for whom Rachel cooked—and she loved to cook—there are at this moment dozens of little bottles of obscure spices and herbs. They are part of her legacy.

"How could you," she would ask her hosts with that charming and maddening combination of sweetness and iron determination that were Rachel's, "cook without fresh dill? Let me run out and get some." And she would, leaving her hosts baffled and amused and better educated on the subject of cooking.

Cooking was a passion with her, or rather a manifestation of a deeper passion for life, for experience. She had a wicked sense of humor, which this place and this occasion suggest I do not fully ventilate, but let me say that her humor issued from a life force of such intensity that it was as irrepressible in her as it was hilarious for us. To Rachel, life was great fun. It was not, however, a game.

One summer, she worked at the state office of the Public Employees Federation. During this time, she became appalled at the waste of good food from luncheons.

It was characteristic of Rachel that she contacted Trinity Episcopal Church to see if they'd be interested in taking the uneaten food for their feeding ministry. They were. And she arranged it. And the food that would have been wasted went to feed the hungry.

In between feeding the destitute and writing scholarly papers, she studied ballroom dancing, self defense, photography, drawing, jewelry making . . . the list goes on. When she was a little girl, her father took her to a museum.

At the end of the trip she noted, "Museums are places with little pieces of the world." It was not only an astute comment but almost an inspiration for the rest of her life. Those little pieces she had observed in the museum inspired her to seek the big pieces, to travel, to learn, to experience.

These were not superficial impulses, because they were harnessed by something deep within her, something rare and profound—the capacity of the saints to take the data of experience, transmute it into knowledge and distill the knowledge into wisdom.

And others found that wisdom in her and sought her advice constantly. For she brought to anyone's problems—ranging from their romantic and sexual fears to courses they should take to how they might rearrange their dormitory rooms—a force and commitment, an insight and integrity, which leads us to only one word in describing it: love.

Love is not something like knowledge. It need not first be accumulated to be imparted. It has only to be given. Always it must be given. And the more it is given, the more there is to give.

Rachel knew that in her very depths. Her love was true because it was given so freely and because it still goes on.

She touched many lives in ways that will never end. She uplifted; she inspired; she gave. When thinking about her it is easy to believe in immortality. Rachel's spirit is endless. She is the whirlwind.

God gave her to us, and Rachel gave us her love. We'll certainly go mad thinking about what she might have been, and she wouldn't have liked that.

So for me I shall remember what was, and value the love that she gave and which rolls through our lives now and forever. Handel's "The Trumpet Shall Sound" is Rachel's song.

It is triumph, it is passion, it is love, and it is our great good fortune that in our lives, in our time, she was there to play it for us.

Interpretations

1. What was Rachel's attitude toward other cultures? Why does the author think Rachel had the potential to be a successful student of cultures? (What were her aspirations?)

2. The author introduces humor into his eulogy. Where? How does humor honor the memory of Rachel?

3. How do you interpret Lamberti's statement that life to Rachel was "great fun" but not "a game"? What evidence from the eulogy suggests that this is true? What does the subject of food contribute to this characterization of Rachel?

4. Look up the words to Handel's aria from *The Messiah,* "The Trumpet Shall Sound," the central idea of which is death and resurrection. What attitude toward death does the aria express? How is this attitude in tune with Rachel's approach to life and to marriage?

5. "Rachel's spirit is endless." Of what significance is the author's use of Rachel's middle name and the etymology of the word *spirit* (breath, wind) to embody important aspects of Rachel's personality and unify his composition?

Correspondences

1. Review the James quotation (page 510). How does it apply to the memorial tribute to Rachel Asrelsky? (What kind of legacy did she leave?)

2. Pipolo and Asrelsky both graduated from Stuyvesant High School. To what extent did this factor influence their aspirations?

Applications

1. Discuss how a favorite museum or library has shaped your aspirations.

2. "Love is not something like knowledge. It need not first be accumulated to be imparted. It has only to be given." Write a journal entry on the aspect of Rachel's sharing that impressed you most. What does it convey about her aspirations?

20/20 Hindsight

Jay Ford

Jay Ford (b. 1969) was raised and educated in New York City. He graduated from Wesleyan University, majoring in African-American history. In his junior year, he studied for one semester in Kenya as part of an international exchange program. His essay "20/20 Hindsight" is an account of what he learned there—about himself and Kenyan culture.

Kenya, located on the eastern coast of Africa with a population of twenty-three million, is slightly smaller in area than Texas. Kenya won independence from Great Britain in 1963, has until recently had a relatively free political life, and has shown steady growth in industry and agriculture. The official language is Swahili. The Kikuyu account for twenty-one percent of the population and are the largest of Kenya's many ethnic groups. Thirty-eight percent of Kenyans are Protestant, twenty-six percent Roman Catholic, and six percent Muslim. Tourists and other visitors account for $355 million of Kenya's annual budget of $2 billion.

BORN INTO A middle class African-American family on the upper west side of Manhattan, I have spent most of my life chasing the (white) American dream. Absorbing the rhetoric brewed by the media, school curricula, and, more important, my teachers, I was graduated from high school with the goal of travelling to Europe, achieving a college degree, becoming a corporate lawyer and, eventually, marrying a spouse who would be most likely white or a light-skinned black. We would have two homes and probably three children. This was my rough sketch of my future, one with which I was satisfied. I would be a success and this was very important because I clearly represent what W. E. B. DuBois coined as the "talented tenth." Therefore, I had a responsibility to my people to succeed, to vanquish the disabilities associated with my color and earn my place in white America, my America.

In starting off on my journey to success, I met my first obstacle as I neared the end of my sophomore year in college. The student body had taken over the administration building in hopes of persuading the University to divest monies invested in corporations in South Africa. A meeting between the students and the administration had been arranged during which the administration had thoroughly explained its position on divestment. Now it was the students' turn to respond. As student after student approached the microphone, explaining what he/she believed to be the most important reasons for disinvesting, an unsettling feeling began to overwhelm me. Although all of the explanations were more than legitimate reasons to disinvest, none of them had touched my personal reasons for protesting the University is position on divestment.

When it was my turn, I did not actually know what I wanted to say, but I was determined to say something. "My name is Julius J. Ford. I am an Afro-American. Inherent in my title is the word African, meaning "of Africa." My ancestry is from Africa. Africans are therefore my people, my history. So as long as you continue to oppress my people through violence or investment or silence, you oppress me. And as long as you oppress me, I will fight you! I will fight you!" As I returned to my seat, my friend leaned over, patted me on the back and said, "That was great, I never really knew you felt that way." I turned to him and said, "Neither did I."

It was this event that made me question myself. How could I be satisfied with my sketch of success when it had no background or depth? Why had I not felt this strongly about Africa or Africans before? Why was I more attracted to women who possessed European features (straight hair, light skin, thin nose) than those who possessed African features? Why did I feel that Europe was so great and Africa so primitive? Why did I choose to call myself an African-American when I knew virtually nothing about Africa? These questions would trouble my soul for the remainder of the year. In fact, they would push me to apply to a student exchange program in East Africa, Kenya.

Called "An Experiment in International Living," the program would offer me travel throughout the country, during which time I would live in both rural and urban areas, in both huts and hotels, for approximately four months from February through mid-May, 1989. I would be equipped with two academic directors with numerous university and government contacts and ensured a variety of learning opportunities, as I would stay with native families and be allowed to venture off on my own.

Even though this program seemingly presented an optimum opportunity to find answers to all my pending questions, I was still apprehensive about my decision to go. But, perhaps if there was one specific incident that canceled any wavering on my part, it was that Friday afternoon at drama class. On Fridays, I taught drama to about twenty 9–14-year-old kids from predominantly black families with low incomes at a community center about twenty minutes from my college. On this particular day I had decided to ask the class what they thought about my taking a trip to Africa. They shot off these responses: "Why would you want to go to Africa to get even blacker than you are now?", "Why don't you take a trip somewhere nice like Paris, London, Rome?", "But they say in Africa every one is backwards, they can't teach you anything," "People are so black and ugly there." And, although some of the comments from the children were said specifically to make the other children laugh, many of them were exemplifications of how our educational system and other forms of external social propaganda affect a black child's mind.

When I first arrived in Kenya, we stayed in its capital city, Nairobi. Surprisingly enough, my first impression of Nairobi was that it was just like any American city: skyscrapers, movie theatres, discos, and crime. In fact, I was a bit disappointed, feeling that I had travelled fifteen hours in a Pan Am jet just to come back to New York City. But upon more detailed observation, I realized that this city was quite different from any other I had visited before. This city was black and, when I say black, I'm not talking your coffee-colored Atlanta, Oakland, Harlem black people. I mean black! I mean when you were small and used to play games and chose to embarrass the darkest kid on the block by calling him "midnight," "shadow," and "teeth black."

But the lesson to be learned in Nairobi was that all shades of black were equally attractive and the small children did not penalize attractiveness according to shade of skin, or length of hair, or size of nose. Furthermore, being in a black city, knowing I was in a mostly black country that sits on a predominantly black continent, enhanced my confidence and hence my actions. For the first time in my life I felt as though I could do anything, fit in anywhere, be welcomed by everyone because of my color. This was the feeling I had often assumed blacks felt during the Twenties, the period of the Harlem Renaissance. It was wonderful! I would go for days without being aware of my color. It did not seem to matter.

It was only a few weeks into the program, however, when I began to notice racial insecurities developing within my peer group (of twenty-four I was the only black). As many as half a dozen of the other students declared that they had begun to view black children as more beautiful than white, that black women and black features were more pleasing to the eye than white ones. Others simply segregated themselves from the black society as much as possible, refusing to stay with families without another white person present. Perhaps, then, inherent in the role of minority come feelings of inferiority, a certain lack of confidence, insecurity.

Because there is much tribalism in Kenya, the first title I had to drop was African-American. When people around me refer to themselves as Masai or Kikuyu as opposed to Kenyan or East African, then how could I refer to myself as an African? Furthermore, the language I spoke, my values, morals and education were not African. So this put me in an awkward position. No one could question my ancestry as African because of my color, so I enjoyed most benefits of majority status. Yet, to many Kenyans, I was much more similar to a white American than an African so there was a wide gap between us.

It was here I realized that to be an accepted descendant of Africa I had a lot of work to do. I needed to learn a new language and a new culture. I needed to assimilate, and I figured that that shouldn't be too hard as I had twenty years of experience in that in the United States. But, the difference between my American and Kenyan assimilations is that in Kenya it seemed to be welcomed if not encouraged by the majority. The more knowledge I attained of Kenya and the more I left my English at home and spoke Swahili or another tribal language, the more cultural doors opened to me. For example, as I became increasingly familiar with Gidiam tribal customs and my use of Kiswahili improved, I was able to travel along the coast for days never I worrying about food or lodging. I was often given the opportunity to sit and discuss with elders, and take part in tribal ceremonies and had responsibilities bestowed on me by elder men, *Mzees,* or my temporary *Mama.* In fact, toward the end of my trip, when travelling alone, it was often difficult for me to convince people that I was African-American. They would tell me, *"Una toka Africa qwa sababo una weza kusema Kiswahili na una famhamu Africa life"* (You are from Africa because you are able to speak Kiswahili and you understand African life). The more I learned, the more comfortable I was with the title African-American.

I also took more pride in myself. Here it was important to learn that the black empowerment was not from sheer numbers, it was from the fact that the blacks in Africa possess a communal sense of self, a shared past that is to never be forgotten, that has passed through generations, and is used as a reference for modern-day experiences. An exemplification of this concept is the way in which Kenyans and Africans in general treat their elderly. In Kenya you are told that you never grow to equal your parents' authority or knowledge. Your elders will forever be your elders and respected as such. In Kenya, elderly people are cherished not forgotten.

As we visited small villages in the areas of Kisumu, Nakru, and on the coast, villages which by American standards were far below the poverty line, we were welcomed with feasts of foods, drinks, people and music. To them we were guests paying them the honor of visitation. Even on a more individual level, most Kenyan families were extraordinarily hospitable. To be welcomed into a stranger's home and be offered food, wine, and a bed for an unlimited number of days is shocking to Americans and even more so to a New Yorker.

This humanistic view was very difficult to adapt to because it affected every level of Kenyan society. For example, Kenyans have a very limited concept of personal space (but in a country with a population growth rate of 4.3 percent that is quite understandable). So it was often difficult for me to discover that my four newly acquired brothers were also my newly acquired bedmates, to change money at the bank while the people behind me were looking over my shoulder examining my passport and money exchange papers, and, to learn not to tell your family that you would like to be left alone because crazy people stay by themselves.

Also, Americans are lost outside of a linear society. We are taught from kindergarten to stay in line. Order for us is symbolically represented by the line, and we therefore choose to see all other forms of non-linear collective activity as chaotic. Kenyans, however, do not have this same view of order. They choose to mass together, aggressively seeking out their desires and bringing new meaning to the words "organized chaos." Mobs catch buses, herds are seen at ticket counters, and, unfortunately, until your adjustment period is complete, you stand apart from the chaos, "jaw dropped," staring at the stampede of people. As a result, you do not obtain a ticket or get on the bus.

This conception of order plus the Kenyan view of personal space make for exciting moments in the public sphere. For example, there is a type of Kenyan public transportation called *matatus*. Matatus are small privately owned minivans that serve as buses for local citizens. To ride a matatu is like taking the most crowded New York City subway car during rush hour, placing that car on Broadway, and allowing a taxicab driver to control the wheel. Matatus do not actually stop at designated bus stops; in fact, they do not actually stop at all. Instead, they simply slow down and those who need to get off push and shove their way to the front of the van and jump out. And as for those who wish to board, they simply chase the matatu down and shove and push their way onto the van. As with circus clown cars, there is always room for one more.

Another linear concept I was introduced to was time. In rural areas there would sometimes be days when we would have no activities planned. It was at these moments when I would curse my directors for poor planning. But I was soon to learn that doing nothing was not necessarily wasted time. This time to think, relax, conversationalize was most important for a peaceful state of mind. I finally understood that it is not imperative even in America to eat breakfast, read the paper in the street while you are running to the subway, or to work two jobs just to pay off your life insurance bill. Here there was not "so much to do and so little time"; here there was a great deal to do but also the belief that that which is supposed to get done will get done in time.

For example, during the last month of my stay in Kenya I visited a small farm in Kisumu Kaubu, Uganda, with a woman and her three sons. I was only to stay for a day and one night. I had come to visit just prior to the time the rains were expected, so I had assumed that the family was going to spend very little time relaxing with me because it was imperative that the soil and seeds for the year be prepared for the rains which could come at any moment.

However, once I arrived, we did very little field work. We talked instead—about the history of her people, about America, and about American perceptions of Kenya. Of course this was hard work since their

English was very limited and my Swahili is fair at best. And as the day crept on to the night, I asked her how she could afford to give her attentions to me when the threat of the rains could come at any day now. *"Pole Pole, bwana,"* she replied (We have not neglected our work to the fields. We have only delayed our work so to welcome our new son, who by joining us will ease our workload). I then asked her, "But, Mama, it is already 11:00 and I leave tomorrow at 9:00." She replied, "Don't worry, bwana, we start to work the cattle (plow) at 2:00 A.M. Good night."

It seemed as though Kenyan culture chose to be humanistic rather than materialistic. The value placed on human life and interaction is much greater than in the States. To shake hands, to share a meal or even your home with a foreigner is an honor, not a burden. And, for you as a guest to turn down that hand, meal, or bed is an insult. How wonderfully strange to travel to a foreign land where people who can hardly understand what language you speak are ready to take you home and make you part of the family. They wouldn't last too long in New York, I thought.

In most places in Kenya, it was common knowledge for one to know his/her environment. People could name the types of trees along the roads, tell you animals indigenous to the area, and explain which types of soil were best for growing specific crops. They could tell you the staple foods of different parts of Kenya *or* even the U.S. In fact, their world geography was superior to that of most American college students. Access to information, whether at home or in schools, was a privilege to be appreciated by those involved and then passed down to younger generations orally. I wonder why I did not feel this way. My country offers more educational opportunities than any other in the world and yet seldom are these opportunities fully exploited. American students go to school, but they do not go to learn. They go to get A's and move up economically. They go to play the game, the educational game of success that I like to refer to as DT (Diploma Training), a process that verifies one's intelligence by certificate as opposed to action or common sense.

Furthermore, along with this overwhelming appreciation for knowledge, Kenyans show reverence for everyday simplicities which we in America take for granted: the appreciation for candlelight, running water, a toilet with a seat cover, a long hot shower every day. Learning to live is to stay in Kenya and survive with twenty-three other people living mostly off rain water, sleeping in huts, and eating many fruits and vegetables with only the occasional beef meal. I felt as though Kenya taught me a new dimension of life, a rebirth of sorts. It put objectives, time, goals, values into a new perspective. It did not tell me, "Please be aware of how much water you use because a drought warning is in effect." It gave me a gallon of water and told me to drink and bathe for an undetermined period. It did not tell me of the beauties of nature, rather it revealed them to me by greeting me in the morning with the sights of Mt. Kenya, Kilimanjaro, and Lake Victoria. I saw no need for National Geographic or wildlife television, for when it wanted to introduce me to animals, a monkey, leopard, or family of raccoons would become my fellow pedestrians. There was no urge to tell me of the paradox of zoos when it could show me national parks with hundreds of acres of land.

In Kenya I felt more free than I have ever felt before. The only thing holding me captive was the earth which would grow the food, the sky which would quench the earth of its thirst, and the sun which would warm and help all things to grow. But these masters were sure to give back all that you have put in. When you worked hard, your rewards were great and if you chose to relax so would your crop and cattle. And with a give-and-take relationship like this, one learns that it is okay to take time, time for others, for oneself, time to enjoy and appreciate all that life and earth offer. Some choose to call this type of relationship religion, a covenant with the Lord and her divinity (sky, earth, and animals and I will not deny that there was a strong sense of God or Allah or Sa or Buddha).

A forest burning to the ground germinates the soil, allowing new life to grow. The omnipotence of nature—floods, lightning, hurricanes, earthquakes, the beauty of a cheetah or giraffe running, an open field, the sky, the mountains, the sea—is overwhelming and foreign to me living so long in a concrete jungle. When all of this engulfed me and I took the time to embrace it, I became convinced that there exists a master craftsperson of this creation, that there exists a God.

Kenya has more than (just) given me a new perception of the world; Kenya has widened my world view. I now realize that there are other significant cultures in the world besides a western one. I no longer think of the world in First, Second, and Third World terms. There are aspects of Kenyan values which should be regarded as more First World than American: humanistic sentiments, importance of family, pride of ancestry, appreciation and respect for other peoples' differences.

Also, whereas I ventured off to Kenya to learn about a new culture and its new people, I found that most of the more important discoveries and evaluations were about myself. Upon leaving Kenya I feel that I have grown more confident about my African-Americanness, my perceptions of the world around me, and my expectation of 21/21 vision and beyond. I do not believe I could have gone anywhere else on earth and been as personally challenged.

Interpretations

1. Was the author wrong to assume that the aspirations of "white America" should or could also be the aspirations of a black American? Why? To what extent are the aspirations ("rhetoric") he mentions in the first paragraph misguided? Why? How does the speech made

before students and administration relate to these aspirations and the identity crisis raised by the label "African-American"?

2. What does the title mean? What is the author scrutinizing with 20/20 hindsight? How successfully does he combine the story of an identity crisis with cultural commentary? Support your conclusion.

3. What did the author's young drama-class students teach him about attitudes of American blacks toward Africa? How does this attitude contrast with what he found among children in Nairobi? How reliable are children's conversation and vocabulary as indicators of widespread but unconscious attitudes?

4. "Perhaps . . . inherent in the role of minority come feelings of inferiority. . . ." Can you offer evidence from your own life that supports or refutes this idea? Does the author's evidence (the white group's behavior in Kenya) convince you? How does this idea relate to Ford's later assertion that "black empowerment [in Africa] was not from sheer numbers" but from long and rich cultural traditions?

Correspondences

1. Review the Cosby quotation (page 510). How does it apply to Ford's essay? How did Ford's education in the United States affect his aspirations? What modifications did he make as a result of his semester in Kenya?

2. Ford's semester in Kenya also changed his cultural perspective: "I no longer think of the world in First, Second, and Third World terms." What evidence does he cite? How does his point of view compare to that of Reed in "America: The Multinational Society"?

Applications

1. "American students go to school, but they do not go to learn. They go to get A's and move up economically." Is this an accurate assessment of the aspirations of American college students? Write an essay attacking or defending Ford's point of view.

2. "In Kenya, elderly people are cherished not forgotten." How might such an attitude affect social and cultural aspirations? How does it compare to prevailing attitudes towards older people in the United States?

Richard's Discovery

José Antonio Villarreal

José Antonio Villarreal (b. 1924), the son of a Mexican immi-
grant, was born and grew up in California. He received his
degree from the University of California in 1950 and spent four
years in the U.S. Navy. "Richard's Discovery" is from the novel
Pocho *(1959), the first known Chicano novel acquired by a*
major publisher (Doubleday). His subsequent novels include
The Fifth Horseman *(1974) and* Clemente Chacón *(1984). The*
main character in "Richard's Discovery" lives in California and,
like his creator, is very conscious of his Mexican heritage.

For information on Mexico, see the headnote to Gary Soto,
Chapter 4.

THE WORLD of Richard Rubio was becoming too much for him. He felt that
time was going by him in an overly accelerated pace, because he was not
aware of days but of weeks and, at times, even months. And he lived in
dread that suddenly he should find himself old and ready to die before
he could get from life the things it owed him. He was approaching his
thirteenth year, and thought of his friend Joe Pete Manöel, though not
forgotten, did not hurt as much. For the most part, he lost himself in
dreams or spent hours reading everything he could find, indiscriminate
in his choice through his persevering desire to learn. Now, after work, he
was a familiar figure in the town library, and later, when the vacation
ended, he continued the practice, for by then the meager library at school
provided little for him. Yet he was disturbed by the thought that now,
while he was young and strong in body, his wanderings should be
physical. Imagination would do only when he became old and incapable
of experiencing actual adventure.

At school, Richard was the favorite of his teachers because his old-
country manners made him most courteous in contrast to the other students.
He was also a good student, and stood near the top of his class without
seemingly trying. His teachers encouraged his reading, but unfortunately
did not direct it, and he became increasingly complex in his moods.

It was natural that in his frantic hunger for reading he went through
books he did not understand. A friend of his father had a few Spanish
novels, and he read a simplified "Quixote"[1] and made several attempts at

---

[1]Don Quixote, satirical, chivalric romance by Spanish author Miguel Cervantes (1605–1615).

Ibáñez,[2] but for the first time in his life he found reading to be actual work. So he limited his Spanish reading to the newspaper he received in the mail from Los Angeles. With determination, he followed Tom Jones and Dr. Pangloss[3] through their various complicated adventures. From *Gone with the Wind,* he emerged with tremendous respect and sympathy for the South and its people. And when the Dust Bowl families who had begun trickling into the valley arrived in increasing numbers, he was sad. They represented the South to him, and he mourned that the once proud could come to such decay.

When the boy fell asleep over a book, his father blew out the coal-oil lamp and tenderly put him to bed. Only when riding out in the country lanes was Richard forbidden to read. Twice his father threw his books out the window of the car. "Look!" he would say. "Look at the world around you, burro!" And the boy would think, What a funny one the old man is!

Indeed, the father was a paradox.

Richard went into the barn that was used to house the town's garbage wagons. Today the barn was empty of equipment and full of young guys and a few older people. Over at one end of the building stood a huge ring. It had two ropes, instead of three, and the posts were big iron pipes wrapped in burlap. There were two kids going at it pretty hard, and suddenly one of them put his hands to his mouth and stood transfixed in the center of the ring. The other one jumped around, throwing punches that either missed his opponent completely or landed on his shoulders or the top of his head. The puncher was too anxious, and the one who couldn't believe his mouth was bleeding got away, and then the bell rang.

Two other guys jumped into the ring then, and started dancing around and flexing like professionals, blowing snot all over the place, and then this local guy who was doing pretty good in the game up in the City jumped in there to do the announcing, and another guy who was already in there was the referee.

He noticed that the announcer's face was a little bumpy already, and he was already talking through his nose from fighting pro. He was a little guy and he moved around funny—real jerky, like the old silent movies—and somebody said there goes the next flyweight champ, which meant he would be the Filipino champion, since they were the only flyweights around. Richard could tell already he would not even be champ of Santa Clara, but he did not say anything, because people in small towns are funny about things like that—they think they have the best of everything.

While the two guys were fighting, Thomas Nakano came over to him. He was wearing only pants, and they were rolled up to his knees and he was barefooted.

---

[2]Vincente Blasco Ibáñez (1867–1928), Spanish novelist, journalist, and politician.

[3] *Tom Jones,* English novel by Henry Fielding (1707–1754). Dr. Pangloss, character in *Candide,* a novel by Voltaire (1694–1778).

"You gonna fight, Thomas?" asked Ricky.

"I can't find nobody who's my size and wants to fight me," Thomas said, sounding disappointed.

Richard felt his stomach begin to get funny, because he knew what was coming. "Don't look at me, Punchie," he said, trying to make a little joke out of it, but nobody laughed and it was real quiet.

"Aw, come on, Richard." He was begging him to let him hit him. "Come on, you're just my size. I'll fight anybody, only they won't let ya less'n you're the same size as the other guy."

He said no he would not, but he felt sorry for Thomas because he wanted someone to fight with him so bad. And then the guys were finished in the ring, and somebody called Thomas and asked him if he had a partner yet. He said no, but by then even guys Richard didn't know were trying to talk him into fighting him, and the pro came over, and in the end he was up in the ring shaking, because he didn't want any of these people to see him look bad. He thought back to the pictures in *Ring Magazine* and tried to imitate the poses, but before he could really decide which he liked best, Thomas was all over him. He kind of clinched and said, "What the hell you trying to do, you crazy bastard?" And Thomas said, "Don't worry—I'll take it easy," and Richard felt pretty good about then, because Thomas was his buddy and he would take it easy on him. But as they pulled away from each other, Thomas clouted him on the mouth when he wasn't looking, and Richard's head felt suddenly numb. Then Thomas was hitting him all over the place, like nobody's business— in the ribs, the stomach, and even his back sometimes, and the gloves were feeling like great big pillows on Richard's hands. It was the longest round in the history of boxing, and Thomas pissed him off. *My friend— one of the gang!* So he thought and thought, and finally, when they were apart one time, he dropped his hands and moved toward Thomas, look- ing real sadlike right into his eyes, as if to say, *Go ahead, kill me.* Thomas stopped also, and a funny what-the-hell's-going-on? look came to his face, and when Richard knew he was relaxed good, he brought one up from the next neighborhood and clipped him good right on the ear. Thomas spun clean around and started to walk away; then he walked in a circle and the son of a bitch was smiling, but he walked right past Richard and around the other side again, and all Richard could do was stand there and look at the crooked little legs that were browner than his. Then he heard everybody hollering for him to go after Thomas, and he thought he might as well, so he followed him around, but Thomas wouldn't stand still. So finally he grabbed him and turned him around, and Thomas stood there grinning, and his eyes were almost closed, because his eyelids were almost together anyway. Richard couldn't hit him when he was smiling at him like that. He smiled back at him, and then the bell rang.

Richard couldn't help laughing at Thomas's grin, but suddenly he stopped, because the bell rang again and he knew he was in for it. Right away, Thomas hit him in the stomach, and Richard bent right over, and there it was—he just kept right on going, and landed on his head and took the count there curled up like a fetus. He didn't have to fight any more, and Thomas was very happy as he helped him up, and Thomas kept saying how he was like Fitzsimmons and that his Sunday punch was a right to the solar plexus. "I hit you in the solar plexus, Richard," he said over and over again, but Richard wasn't really listening to him, because he was sneaking looks at the people, and finally decided he had made it look pretty good.

The referee and the professional came over to see him. "Nice faking, kid," said the referee. "How'd ya like to be a fighter?"

"Uh-uh," he said, pulling at the laces with his teeth. The man took his gloves off.

"You don't know how to fight, but you got a punch for a kid and you're smart," he said.

"I not only can't fight, but I'm scared to fight, so you don't want me," he said.

"How old are ya, kid?"

"I'll be thirteen soon."

"I thought you was older," he said. "But, hell, I can teach ya a lot, and in a year I can put you in smokers. Make five or ten bucks a night that way."

"Not me, Mister. I don't need five or ten bucks."

"How about me?" said Thomas. "I'm the guy that won. You saw me hit him in the solar plexus." Now Richard knew why Thomas had been so anxious to fight.

"Yeah, I can use you, too," said the man, "but I want this other kid."

"Oboyoboy!" said Thomas. He had a trade now.

"How about it, kid?" asked the man. "I'm giving ya the chance of your life—it's the only way people of your nationality can get ahead."

"I'm an American," said Richard.

"All right, you know what I mean. Mexicans don't get too much chance to amount to much. You wanna pick prunes the rest of your life?" Richard didn't say anything, and he said, "Look, I'll go talk it over with your old man, and I'll bet he'll agree with me. I'll bet he knows what's good for you."

"You better not do that, Mister. You don't know my old man. He's already been in jail for knifing three guys."

Richard could tell he was dumb, and, like a lot of people, believed that Mexicans and knives went together. He thought he had finished with him, but the man said, "All right, we won't tell 'im anything, and when you start bringing money home, he'll come and see *me.*"

"Listen," Richard said. "He'll come and see you all right, but it won't make any difference. My old man don't feel about money the way some people do. So leave me alone, why don't you?"

But the man kept insisting, and said, "I gotta line up a smoker for the Eagles, and if you and the Jap kid here put 'em on, I'll give ya each a fin.[4] Then, when your old man sees the dough, he'll be in the bag. What do you say?"

"Okay with me," said Thomas, "but don't call me no Jap." Richard was walking away by then, and the man followed him. "I'll give ya seven-fifty and the Jap a fin."

"No, thanks." He kept walking. They would never be able to make him do anything like that. He was sure he could be no more than a punching bag, because, hell, everybody in the neighborhood could beat him, and besides he was afraid.

The guys caught up to him, but he wasn't talking. He thought how funny the guy back there was—the fight manager. He felt that the manager was the kid and he was the grownup. *Amount to something!* Jesus! Everybody was telling him what he should make of himself these days, and they all had the same argument, except that this guy was thinking of himself. At least the little old lady who was so nice and let him read the Horatio Alger books was thinking of him when she told him he should work hard to be a gardener and someday he could work on a rich person's estate; she was sure he would be successful at that because she had known of some Mexicans who held very fine places like that. . . . Funny about her, how the Horatio Alger books meant as much to her as the Bible meant to Protestants. . . . And the adviser in the high school, who had insisted he take automechanics or welding or some shop course, so that he could have a trade and be in a position to be a good citizen, because he was Mexican, and when he had insisted on preparing himself for college, she had smiled knowingly and said he could try those courses for a week or so, and she would make an exception and let him change his program to what she knew was better for him. She'd been eating crow ever since. What the hell makes people like that, anyway? Always worried about his being Mexican and he never even thought about it, except sometimes, when he was alone, he got kinda funnyproud about it.

As he walked toward home with the guys, he thought about the things he had just discovered. He would never really be afraid again. Like with hitting Thomas and ending the fight the way he did; funny he had never thought about that before—the alternative. Everything had another way to it, if only you looked hard enough, and he would never be ashamed again for doing something against the unwritten code of honor. Codes of honor were really stupid—it amazed him that he had just learned this—and what people thought was honorable was not important, because he was the important guy. No matter what he did and who was affected by his actions, in the end it came back to him and his feelings. He was himself, and everything else was there because

[4.] Five-dollar bill.

he was *himself,* and it wouldn't be there if he were not himself, and then, of course, it wouldn't matter to him. He had the feeling that *being* was important, and he *was*—so he knew that he would never succumb to foolish social pressures again. And if he hurt anyone, it would be only if he had no choice, for he did not have it in him to hurt willingly.

He thought of Thomas's face in the ring, and began to laugh at the silliness of his grin, and then he laughed louder and louder, about the fight manager and all the people who tried to tell him how to live the good life, and then laughed about the guys with him, because they were laughing like crazy, too, and the sad bastards did not know what the hell they were laughing about.

Interpretations

1. Richard "mourned" the people of the Dust Bowl. What trait does this reaction to reading show? How does this same trait land him in the ring with Thomas?

2. Take note of all the references to Richard's father. What conclusions can you reach about the kind of man he is and why? How does he influence Richard?

3. "[Boxing's] the only way people of your nationality can get ahead." What's the best evidence that Richard doesn't believe this statement and intends to disprove it?

4. "Codes of honor were really stupid. . . ." What specific rule does Richard break in order to end the fight? Do you agree that he has "just learned" something important? about what? What will happen if Richard goes through life applying this lesson?

5. What is Richard's "discovery"?

Correspondences

1. "Mexicans don't get too much chance to amount to much. You wanna pick prunes the rest of your life?" Who besides the referee tries to stereotype Richard? Who among them should have known better? How does Richard respond to their attempts? Compare his response to that of Wright (Chapter 3). How do you account for the difference?

2. Review Kittredge's quotation (page 509). What does he mean by "possibility"? What possibilities does Richard become aware of in himself?

Applications

1. Richard vows never to "succumb to foolish social pressures again." Are such social pressures usually negative? Is it easy to resist them? Write an essay analyzing how they might affect aspirations.

2. "Only when riding out in the country lanes was Richard forbidden to read. Twice his father threw his books out the window of the car. 'Look!' He would say. Look at the world around you, burro!" What have you learned from "looking at the world around you"? How has such looking influenced your dreams or helped to shape your convictions? Respond to these questions in a journal entry.

ADDITIONAL WRITING TOPICS

1. As a result of his semester in Africa, Ford writes: "There are aspects of Kenyan values which should be regarded as more First World than American; humanistic sentiments, importance of family, pride of ancestry, appreciation and knowledge of natural surroundings and respect for other peoples' differences." In which other selections in this anthology are these values variously expressed? Are these values, as Ford implies, more characteristic of Third World cultures than of Americans? Write an essay attacking or defending Ford's point of view; use examples from selections in this and other chapters as evidence.

2. Review the Freud quotation (page 509). What does it mean? Cite examples from selections in this or in other chapters to support or refute it. Attack or defend the quotation using evidence from the selections and your own experience.

3. ". . . does North America deserve a more exciting destiny? To become a place where the cultures of the world crisscross. This is possible because the United States is unique in the world: The world is here." Is Reed's wish feasible? Given the history of racism to which African-Americans have been subjected in the United States, how do you account for his optimism? Is it possible to create a United States without bigotry? What factors would have to change? Write an essay responding to these questions. Avoid sentimentality and superficial generalizations.

4. Review the Mexican saying on page 509. What does it mean? How might it affect aspirations? In a 500-word essay, explain its application to any three selections in this chapter.

5. The King quotation on page 510 is taken from his "I Have a Dream" speech, delivered on August 28, 1963, during the now historical civil rights march on Washington. There he describes his dream as "being deeply rooted in the American dream." Read this speech and then write your definition of the American Dream, supporting it with specific examples from experience, observation, and prior knowledge.

6. Several selections in this anthology focus on the experiences of Native Americans. Review these selections and write an analysis of what you learned about Native-American interactions and aspirations.

7. As college campuses become more ethnically diverse, how might administrations, faculty, staff, and students work together to create a

climate of inclusiveness that enhances educational and social interactions and personal and cultural aspirations? As a member of a
group, interview a cross-section of the college community on this
issue. What suggestions did they make? What responsibilities were
they willing to assume? Write a summary of your findings for your
campus or local newspaper.

8. ". . . tolerance, as we have still to learn, is the most fundamental of
human wisdoms." Consult a dictionary or thesauraus on the various
connotations of *tolerance* and analyze its effects on the aspirations in
the selections by Ford, Forster, Johnson or Lorde.

RHETORICAL GLOSSARY

Abstract   Without physical, tangible existence in itself; a concept as opposed to an object. A "child" is a concrete object that our senses can perceive, but "childishness" is an abstract quality. *See* "Concrete."

Analogy   A comparison that points out a resemblance between two essentially different things. Sleep and death are analogous, although certainly not identical. Often an analogy is drawn to explain simply and briefly something that is complex or abstract by pointing out one way in which it resembles something that is simpler or more concrete. To explain how the mind processes and stores information in its memory, an analogy might be drawn to the way in which a bank processes and stores deposits.

Antonym   A word of opposite meaning from another word. "Good" is an antonym of "bad." *See* "Synonym."

Argumentation   In persuasive essays, a unit of discourse meant to prove a point or to convince; the process of proving or persuading.

Audience   A work's intended readership, the author's perception of which directly affects style and tone. As a rule, the more limited or detailed the subject matter, the more specific the audience. An author may write more technically if the intended audience is composed of specialists in the field and may write less technically if the writing is for the general public.

Cause and Effect   A type of exposition used primarily to answer the questions "Why did this occur?" and "What will happen next?" The structure of a cause-and-effect essay is a series of events or conditions, the last of which (the effect) cannot occur without the preceding ones (causes). When you write a cause-and-effect essay, it is helpful to keep chronology clearly in mind: remember, causes always create effects and effects are derived from causes.

Cliché   An expression so overused that it has lost its ability to convey a sharp image or fresh idea. Clichés, such as "busy as a bee," diminish clarity and precision. Familiarity reduces them to little more than vague generalizations.

Coherence   The sense of connection and interrelationship present among the parts of a work. In a coherent piece of writing each sentence leads reasonably to the next sentence, and each paragraph follows reasonably from the preceding paragraph. A lack of coherence is evident when gaps are left between parts. The reader of a poorly written essay might begin to ask, "Why does the writer say this here?" or "How did the writer get to this idea from the preceding idea?" *See* "Transition" and "Unity."

Colloquialism   A conversational or folksy word or phrase deemed inappropriate in formal writing. Using colloquialisms ("booze" for "whiskey" or "loosen up" for "relax") imparts a less dignified, less studied quality to one's writing. *See* "Slang."

Comparison and Contrast   A type of exposition that states or suggests similarities and differences between two or more things. Two types of organization for comparison and contrast essays are point by point and subject by subject.

Conclusion   A summing up or restatement of the writer's thesis. A strong conclusion imparts a sense of completion and finality to a piece of writing. The conclusion may be no more than a sentence in a short essay; it may be many paragraphs in a long report. A short conclusion may restate the writer's thesis in a memorable way, place the specific topic being discussed within or against a broader framework, or suggest answers to questions raised in the essay. A summary of the writer's main points may be effective as the conclusion to a long paper, but in a short essay it will seem unnecessarily repetitious.

Concrete   Specific and tangible as opposed to general and abstract. "Wealth" is an abstract concept of which "gold" is a concrete form. The use of concrete details, examples, and illustrations is a key to clear and effective writing. *See* "Abstract."

Connotation   The implication(s) and overtones, qualities, feelings, and ideas a word suggests. Connotation goes beyond literal meaning or dictionary definition. "Sunshine" denotes the light rays of the sun, but connotes warmth, cheer, happiness, and even prosperity. *See* "Denotation."

Definition   A type of exposition that explains the meaning of a word or concept by bringing its characteristics into sharp focus. An **extended definition** explores the feelings and ideas you attach to a word. Extended definitions are suited to words with complex meanings, words that are subject to interpretation, or words that evoke strong reactions. Such definitions are an appropriate basis for organizing exposition. A **dictionary definition** places a word in a class with similar items but also differentiates it from members of the same class.

Denotation   The literal meaning of a word as defined in a dictionary. *See* "Connotation."

Description   A method of paragraph development that conveys sensory experience through one or more of the five senses: sight, hearing, touch, taste, and smell. Description is generally either objective or subjective and can be organized in three broad categories: spatial, chronological, or dramatic. *See* "Mode."

Diction   The writer's choice of words. Writers are said to employ proper diction when the words they choose to express their ideas are accurate and appropriate; that is, when what they write says exactly what they mean. Poor diction stems from choosing words whose denotation does not accurately convey the author's intended meaning or from choosing words regarded as inappropriate because they are nonstandard ("ain't"), colloquial, or obsolete.

Epiphany   A moment of insight for a character, often resulting in a turning point.

Exposition   A mode or form of discourse that conveys information, gives directions, or explains an idea that is difficult to understand.

Figure of Speech   An imaginative phrase and comparison that is not meant to be taken literally. "He ran as fast as the wind" is a figure of speech known as a simile. See "Analogy," "Hyperbole," "Metaphor," "Personification," "Simile," and "Understatement."

Generalization   A broad statement, idea, or principle that holds a common truth. Despite many possible exceptions, it is generally true that a soldier's job is to go to war. Writing that relies too much on generalization is likely to be vague and overly abstract. *See* "Specificity."

Hyperbole   Obvious exaggeration, an extravagant statement, intentionally designed to give the reader a memorable image. A fisherman who brags that the one that got away was "big as a whale" almost certainly is speaking hyperbolically. *See* "Understatement."

Image   In writing, an image is a picture drawn with words, a reproduction of persons, objects, or sensations that are perceived through sight, sound, touch, taste, or smell. Often an image is evoked to visually represent an idea. *See* "Symbol."

Impressionistic   Depicting a scene, emotion, or character so that it evokes subjective or sensory impressions. An impression is an effect produced upon the mind or emotions. The more writing emphasizes the effects on the writer of scenes, persons, and ideas, the more impressionistic, and hence the less objective, it will be. *See* "Objectivity" and "Subjectivity."

Induction   The process by which one draws a generalized conclusion from specifics. If it is a fact that a high percentage of people who die from lung cancer each year also smoke cigarettes, one might safely induce that cigarette smoking is a contributing factor in the disease. *See* "Deduction."

Introduction   An introduction sets forth the writer's thesis or major themes and establishes tone (attitude toward one's subject), and—particularly in a long paper— suggests an organizational plan. The introduction, or opening, of an essay should capture the reader's attention and interest. Like the conclusion, it may be no more than a sentence or it may be many paragraphs.

Irony   The undermining or contradicting of someone's expectations. Irony may be either verbal or dramatic. **Verbal irony**   arises from a discrepancy, sometimes intentional and sometimes not, between what is said and what is meant, as when a dog jumps forward to bite you, and you say, "What a friendly dog!" **Dramatic irony**   arises from a discrepancy between what someone expects to happen and what does happen; for example, if the dog that seemed so unfriendly to you saves your life. *See* "Sarcasm" and "Satire."

Jargon   The specialized language of a trade, profession, or other socioeconomic group. Truck drivers employ a jargon on their citizen's band radios that sounds like gibberish to most people. Writing that employs contextless jargon is inappropriate.

Journal   A daily written record of ideas, memories, experiences, or dreams. A journal can be used for prewriting and as a source for formal writing.

Journalism   The profession of writing for newspapers, magazines, wire services, and radio and television. Journalistic writing emphasizes objectivity and factual reportage; the work of editorial writers, columnists, and feature writers often is a more subjective form of reportage.

Literal   The ordinary or primary meaning of a word or expression. Dwelling on literal meaning can promote erroneous thinking. The sentence "Childhood is a time of sunshine" should be read figuratively, not literally. (The sun does not always shine during childhood; rather, childhood is a happy time.)

Metaphor   A figure of speech in which, through an implied comparison, one object is identified with another and some qualities of the first object are ascribed to the second. *See* "Simile."

Mode   A conventional form or usage. Writing includes four customary modes of discourse: description, narration, exposition, and persuasion (argumentation).

Narration   A narrative essay is a story with a point; narration is the technique used to tell the story. When writing a narrative essay, pay close attention to point of view, pacing, chronology, and transitions.

Objectivity   Freedom from personal bias. A report about a scientific experiment is objective insofar as facts in it are explained without reference to the writer's feelings about the experiment. But not even the most factual piece of writing is completely uncolored by the writer's attitudes and impressions. Objectivity is best thought of as a matter of degree, increasing in direct proportion with the writer's distance from the work. *See* "Subjectivity."

Paradox   A statement that sounds self-contradictory, even absurd, and yet expresses a truth. It is paradoxical, though nonetheless true, to say that one person can simultaneously feel both love and hatred for another person.

Parallel Structure   The association of ideas phrased in parallel ways, thus giving a piece of writing balance and proportion. "He loves wine, women, and singing" lacks parallelism. "He loves wine, women, and song" is parallel; the verbal noun "singing" interrupts the series of nouns.

Personification   A figure of speech in which abstract concepts or inanimate objects are represented as having human qualities or characteristics. To write that "death rides a pale horse," for example, is to personify death.

Persuasion   The art of moving someone else to act in a desired way or to believe in a chosen idea. Logic and reason are important tools of persuasion. Equally effective may be an appeal either to the emotions or to the ethical sensibilities.

Point of View   The vantage point from which an author writes. In expository prose, an author may adopt a first-person or a third-person point of view. *See* "Style" and "Tone."

Sarcasm   An expression of ridicule, contempt, or derision. Sarcastic remarks are nasty or bitter in tone and often characterized by irony that is meant to hurt. You might express your displeasure with those who have given you a hard time by sarcastically thanking them for their help. *See* "Irony."

Satire   A genre of writing that makes various use of irony, sarcasm, ridicule, and broad humor in order to expose, denounce, or reform. Satires dwell on the follies and evils of human beings and institutions. The satirist's tone may range from amusement and gentle mockery to harsh contempt and moral indignation.

Simile   A figure of speech including *like* or *as* and stating a direct, explicit comparison between two things: he ate *like* a pig; her heart felt light *as* a feather. *See* "Metaphor."

Slang   Colloquialisms and jargon are deemed inappropriate in formal writing. Whether a word or phrase is considered colloquial or slang is often a matter of personal taste. Also, slang often gains acceptance in time. A word such as *uptight,* once considered slang by cultivated people, is now an acceptable colloquialism. *See* "Colloquialism" and "Jargon."

Specificity   Precision, particularity, concreteness. Specificity, like generalization, is a matter of degree; the word *horse* is more specific than *animal* but more general than *stallion*. *See* "Generalization."

Style   The "fingerprint," the identifying mark, of a writer—both as an individual and as a representative of his or her age and culture. An author's style is the product of the diction employed, sentence structure and organization, and the overall form and tone in which thoughts are expressed. Style is variously described, depending on the analyzer's purpose. It may be simple or complex, forthright or subtle, colloquial or formal; modern or classical, romantic or realistic, "logical" or poetic. It may be anything, in short, that reflects the writer's personality, background, and talent. See "Point of View" and "Tone."

Subjectivity   The personal element in writing. The more subjective a piece of writing, the more it is likely to be focused on the writer's opinions and feelings. *See* "Objectivity."

Syllogism   A highly formal three-part form of deductive logic. The syllogist argues that if a generalization (major premise) is true and a specific case of the generalization (minor premise) is also true, then any conclusion reached is necessarily true. If the major premise is "smoking causes cancer" and the minor premise is "John Doe smokes," then the conclusion is "John Doe will contract lung cancer." Syllogisms often sound logical, but are not true because one or both premises are faulty. *See* "Deduction."

Symbol   Something that stands for something else. An eagle is a conventional symbol of the United States. Any word, image, or description, any name, character, or action that has a range of meanings and associations beyond its literal denotation may be symbolic, depending on who is interpreting it and the context in which it appears. The word *eagle,* therefore, may bring to mind different images or ideas; it may connote freedom or power or solitude.

Synonym   One of two or more words having approximately the same meaning. "Happiness" and "joy" are synonyms. *See* "Antonym. "

Tautology   Inherent or pointless repetition. To write that a person was treated with "cruel inhumanity" is tautological: inhumanity is always cruel.

Thesis   The main idea or theme of an essay. In expository prose, the writer usually states the thesis clearly in the introduction. The thesis statement should establish point of view, the primary point(s) intended for discussion, and the writer's attitude toward it.

Tone   Tone of voice; an author's attitude toward his or her subject, and, at times, audience. Tone is caught in the "sound" of a piece of writing. The tone of an essay may be angry, resigned, humorous, serious, sentimental, mocking, ironic, sarcastic, satirical, reasoning, emotional, philosophic—anything, in short, that echoes the voice of the author. One tone may predominate or many tones ("overtones"?) may be heard in any work. *See* "Style."

Topic Sentence   The sentence in a paragraph that states clearly the main theme or point of the paragraph.

Transition   A bridge between one point or topic or idea and another. The logical movement from sentence to sentence and paragraph to paragraph should be easy to follow if a piece of writing is coherent. This logic is often emphasized by means of transitional expressions such as *therefore, hence, similarly, however, but, furthermore, also,* and *for example. See* "Coherence."

Understatement   An obvious downplaying or underrating of something. It is the opposite of hyperbole, although use of either may create a memorable image or an ironic effect. To say that "after they ate the apple, Adam and Eve found life a bit tougher," is to understate their condition. *See* "Hyperbole."

Unity   The basic focus or theme that permeates a piece of writing, thus lending the piece a sense of wholeness and completeness. The words and sentences and paragraphs, the images and ideas, the explanations and examples, the characters and actions, the descriptions and arguments—all should be relevant to the overriding purpose or point of a work. *See* "Coherence."

GEOGRAPHICAL INDEX

NEAR EAST

SOUTH AMERICA

UNITED STATES

UNITED STATES: ETHNIC GROUPS

AFRICAN-AMERICAN

CARIBBEAN-AMERICAN

CHINESE-AMERICAN

EASTERN EUROPEAN-AMERICAN

IRISH-INDIAN-AMERICAN

IRISH-ITALIAN-AMERICAN

ITALIAN-AMERICAN

Pages 10–16 From *The Good Times* by Russell Baker. Copyright © 1989 by Russell Baker. By permission of William Morrow & Company, Inc.

Pages 18–23 Excerpts from *The Great Chinese Revolution* by John King Fairbank. Copyright © 1986 by John King Fairbank. Reprinted by permission of HarperCollins Publishers.

Pages 25–30 From *The Complete Grimm's Fairy Tales* by Jacob Ludwig Karl Grimm and Wilhelm Karl Grimm. Copyright 1944 by Pantheon Books, Inc. and renewed 1972 by Random House, Inc. Reprinted by permission of Pantheon Books, a division of Random House, Inc.

Pages 32–34 "The Algonquin Cinderella" from *World Tales* by Indries Shah, copyright © 1979 by Technographia, S.A. and Harcourt Brace Jovanovich, Inc., reprinted by permission of Harcourt Brace Jovanovich, Inc.

Pages 36–40 Reprinted by permission of The University of New Mexico Press. First published in *The Reporter*, 26 January 1967. Reprinted from *The Way to Rainy Mountain*, © 1969, The University of New Mexico Press.

Pages 46–52 From *A Woman of Egypt* by Jehan Sadat. Copyright © 1987 by Simon and Schuster, Inc. Reprinted by permission of Simon and Schuster.

Pages 54–57 Reprinted with permission of Yael Yarimi.

Pages 59–60 Reprinted with permission of Andrew Rein.

Pages 61–66 From *The Blindfold Horse* by Shusha Guppy. Copyright © 1988 by Shusha Guppy. Reprinted by permission of Beacon Press.

Pages 68–75 From *The Lottery* by Shirley Jackson. Copyright © 1948, 1949 by Shirley Jackson. Renewal Copyright © 1976, 1977 by Lawrence Hyman, Barry Hyman, Mrs. Sarah Webster and Mrs. Joanne Schnurer. Reprinted by permission of Farrar, Straus & Giroux, Inc.

Pages 76–83 Copyright © 1987 by Gish Jen. First published in *Nimrod*, Fall/Winter 1987 issue. All rights reserved. Reprinted by permission of the author.

Pages 85–88 Reprinted with permission of Joan Ackermann.

Pages 90–92 Copyright © 1988 by The New York Times Company. Reprinted by permission. This column first appeared in the December 11, 1988 issue of *The New York Times*.

Page 104 From *The New English Bible*, © The Delegates of the Oxford University Press and The Syndics of the Cambridge University Press 1961, 1970. Reprinted by permission.

Pages 106–115 From "Can the American Family Survive?" by Margaret Mead. Reprinted with permission of William Morrow & Co., Inc., from *Aspects of the Present* by Margaret Mead and Rhoda Metraux. Copyright © 1980 by Mary Catherine Bateson Kassarjian and Rhoda Metraux.

Pages 117–126 Copyright © 1987 by The New York Times Company. Reprinted by permission. This column first appeared in the April 5, 1987 *New York Times Magazine*.

Pages 128–132 From *Soviet Women: Walking the Tightrope* by Francine du Plessix Gray. Copyright © 1990 by Francine du Plessix Gray. Originally in The New Yorker Magazine. Used by permission of Doubleday, a division of Bantam Doubleday Dell Publishing Group, Inc.

Pages 134–138 From *Black Elk Speaks* by John G. Neihardt, copyright 1932, 1959, 1988, etc. Published by the University of Nebraska Press. Reprinted by permission.

Pages 140–149 "El Doctor" by Julia Alvarez. Copyright © 1982 by Julia Alvarez. First appeared in *Revista Chicano-Riqueña*, Summer 1982. Reprinted by permission of the author.

Pages 151–156 "Quintana", from *Quintana & Friends* by John Gregory Dunne. Copyright © 1961, 1965, 1966, 1967, 1969, 1970, 1971, 1973, 1974, 1976, 1977, 1978 by John Gregory Dunne. Used by permission of the publisher, Dutton, an imprint of New American Library, a Division of Penguin Books USA Inc.

Pages 157–158 Reprinted with permission of Danit Wehle.

Pages 160–161 Reprinted with permission of Paul Cohen.

Pages 163–169 From *A Woman of Egypt* by Jehan Sadat. Copyright © 1987 by Simon and Schuster, Inc. Reprinted by permission of Simon and Schuster.

Pages 171–176 From *The Woman Warrior: Memoirs of a Girlhood among Ghosts* by Maxine Hong Kingston. Copyright © 1975, 1976 by Maxine Hong Kingston. Reprinted by permission of Alfred A. Knopf, Inc.

Pages 178–183 Copyright © 1990 by Amy Tan. First published in *Threepenny Review*.

Pages 184–188 Reprinted with permission of Grove Weidenfeld, from *A Pack of Cards*. Copyright © 1984 by Penelope Lively.

Pages 195–196 From *Indian Legends from the Northern Rockies*, by Ella E. Clark. Copyright © 1966 by the University of Oklahoma Press.

Pages 198–201 Reprinted with the permission of Macmillan Publishing Company from *Chicano Manifesto* by Armando B. Rendón. Copyright © 1971 by Armando B. Rendón.

Pages 203–205 Reprinted with permission of Norman Cousins, *Saturday Review*. This editorial first appeared in the *Saturday Review* of May 10, 1952.

Pages 207–214 Reprinted with permission of the author. Copyright © 1983 by Paule Marshall. This excerpt first appeared in *The New York Times* of January 9, 1983.

Pages 216–223 "Discovering Books" from *Black Boy* by Richard Wright. Copyright 1937, 1942, 1944, 1945 by Richard Wright. Reprinted by permission of HarperCollins Publishers.

Pages 225–231 From *Gorilla, My Love* by Toni Cade Bambara. Copyright © 1972 by Toni Cade Bambara. Reprinted by permission of Random House, Inc.

Pages 233–237 From "The Stolen Party," by Liliana Heker (1982), in *Other Fires: Short Fiction by Latin American Women*, edited by Alberto Manguel. Translation copyright © 1986 by Alberto Manguel. Reprinted by permission of Clarkson N. Potter, Inc., a division of Crown Publishers, Inc.

Pages 239–241 Reprinted with permission of Gretel Ehrlich.

Pages 243–244 Reprinted with permission of Doris Viloria.

Pages 246–249 Reprinted with permission of The Free Press, a Division of Macmillan, Inc. from *Lives on the Boundary: The Struggles and Achievements of America's Underprepared* by Mike Rose. Copyright © 1989 by Mike Rose.

Pages 251–254 Sophronia Liu, "So Tsi-fai." Originally appeared in *Hurricane Alice*, vol. 2, no. 4 (Fall 1986). Copyright © 1986 by Sophronia Liu. Reprinted by permission of the author.

Pages 261–262 From *The New English Bible*, © The Delegates of the Oxford University Press and The Syndics of the Cambridge University Press 1961, 1970. Reprinted by permission.

Page 263 Reproduced by permission of the American Folklore Society from the *Journal of American Folklore*, 1936. Not for sale or further reproduction.

Pages 265–269 Copyright 1981 Time Warner Inc. Reprinted by permission.

Pages 271–275 "Choosing a Dream: Italians in Hell's Kitchen" by Mario Puzo, from *The Immigrant Experience* by Thomas C. Wheeler. Copyright 1971. Used by permission of Doubleday, a division of Bantam Doubleday Dell Publishing Group, Inc.

Pages 277–281 William Ouchi, *Theory Z*, © 1981. Reprinted with permission of Addison-Wesley Publishing Company.

Pages 283–290 Reprinted by permission of Russell & Volkening as agents for the author. Copyright © 1946 by Ann Petry, renewed in 1974 by Ann Petry. This story first appeared in *Crisis* magazine.

Pages 292–294 Reprinted with permission of Steve Olson.

Pages 296–303 Excerpt from *The Dark Child* by Camara Laye. Copyright © 1954 by Camara Laye. Renewal copyright © 1982 by Camara Laye. Reprinted by permission of Farrar, Straus and Giroux, Inc.

Pages 305–309 Reprinted with permission of Rachel Jones. This article first appeared in the June 19, 1988 issue of the *St. Petersburg Times*.

Pages 311–317 Reprinted from *The Massachusetts Review*, © 1989 *The Massachusetts Review*, Inc.

Pages 319–320 Reprinted with permission of Michael Gnolfo.

Pages 322–323 Reprinted with permission of Sharon Y. Friedner.

Pages 325–329 Reprinted with permission of Strawberry Hill Press, from *Living Up the Street*, copyright 1985, Gary Soto. Published by Strawberry Hill Press.

Pages 331–339 From *[The] Middleman and Other Stories* by Bharati Mukherjee. Reprinted by permission of Grove Weidenfeld, a division of Wheatland Corporation. Copyright © 1988 by Bharati Mukherjee.

Pages 341–345 From *The Promised Land* by Nicholas Lemann. Copyright © 1990 by Nicholas Lemann. Reprinted by permission of Alfred A. Knopf, Inc.

Pages 357–358 Introduction from *A Harvest of World Folk Tales,* edited by Milton Rugoff. The Viking Press, 1949. Story originally from *The Exempla of the Rabbis,* by Moses Gaster. Copyright © 1924 by The Asia Publishing Co.

Pages 359–362 Reprinted by permission of Georges Borchardt, Inc. for the author. Copyright © 1984 by Richard Rodriguez. This essay was first published in the March 1984 issue of *Harper's*.

Pages 364–371 Reprinted from the *Georgia Review* (1991) with permission of the Arte Publico Press.

Pages 373–378 Reprinted with permission of Juliet E. Wright.

Pages 380–385 From *The Rise of the Unmeltable Ethnics,* by Michael Novak. Reprinted by permission of Sterling Lord Literistic, Inc. Copyright © 1972 by Michael Novak.

Pages 387–390 Reprinted with permission of Brent Staples.

Pages 392–396 Reprinted with permission of Jim Fusilli.

Pages 397–398 Reprinted with permission of Brian E. Delaney.

Pages 400–404 Excerpt from *The Koreans: Passion and Grace,* copyright © 1988 by Russell Warren Howe, reprinted by permission of Harcourt Brace Jovanovich, Inc.

Pages 406–416 Reprinted by permission of Harriet Wasserman Literary Agency, Inc., as agents for author. Copyright © 1972 by Ruth Prawer Jhabvala.

Pages 417–421 "A Few Pointers" by James Fallows. From the *Atlantic Monthly* (November 1989). Used by permission of the author.

Pages 423–427 Reprinted with permission of Alastair Reid. This article first appeared in *The New Yorker*.

Pages 429–437 "Call Me Not a Man," by Mtutuzeli Matshoba © 1979 by Ravan Press.

Pages 447–450 Reprinted with permission of Marshall Glickman.

Pages 452–454 Reprinted by permission of the Rosa Parks Institute, Detroit, Michigan.

Pages 456–461 Reprinted from *The Far East Comes Near: Autobiographical Accounts of Southeast Asian Students in America,* Lucy Nguyen-Hong-Nhiem and Joel Martin Halpern, eds. (Amherst: University of Massachusetts Press, 1989), copyright © 1989 by The University of Massachusetts Press.

Pages 463–467 Reprinted by permission of Georges Borchardt, Inc. for the author. Copyright © 1988 by Richard Rodriguez. This essay was first published in *Aperture* (1988).

Pages 469–473 "The Moment Before the Gun Went Off" from *Jump* by Nadine Gordimer. Copyright © 1991 by Felix Licensing B. V. Reprinted by permission of Farrar, Straus & Giroux, Inc.

Pages 474–477 Reprinted with the permission of Macmillan Publishing Company from *Kaffir Boy* by Mark Mathabane. Copyright © 1986 by Mark Mathabane.

Pages 479–484 Excerpts from *Pyramids of Sacrifice* by Peter L. Berger. Copyright © 1975 by Basic Books, Inc. Reprinted by permission of Basic Books, a division of HarperCollins Publishers.

Pages 486–494 Reprinted with permission of Hana Wehle.

Pages 496–498 Reprinted with permission of Lev Tagayev.

Pages 500–504 From "A Train Ride" by Hugo Lindo. Translated by Elizabeth Gamble Miller. Copyright © 1988 by City Lights Books. Reprinted by permission of City Lights Books.

Pages 512–516 From *American Indian Myths and Legends* by Richard Erdoes and Alfonso Ortiz. Copyright © 1984 by Richard Erdoes and Alfonso Ortiz. Reprinted by permission of Pantheon Books, a division of Random House, Inc.

Pages 520–523 Reprinted with the permission of Atheneum Publishers, an imprint of Macmillan Publishing Company, from *Writin' Is Fightin'* by Ishmael Reed. Copyright © by Ishmael Reed.

Pages 525–527 From "My Turn" column by Lewis P. Johnson, *Newsweek* magazine, September 5, 1983. Reprinted by permission of *Newsweek*.

Pages 529–532 Excerpt from *Zami*, pages 68–71, copyright © 1982 by Audre Lorde. Published by The Crossing Press, Freedom, Calif. 95019. Reprinted with permission of the publisher.

Pages 533–536 "Tolerance" from *Two Cheers for Democracy*, copyright © 1951 by E. M. Forster and renewed 1979 by Donald Parry, reprinted by permission of Harcourt Brace Jovanovich, Inc.

Pages 538–539 Reprinted with permission of Isabel L. Pipolo.

Pages 541–547 "Balthazar's Marvelous Afternoon" from *No One Writes to the Colonel* by Gabriel García Márquez. English translation copyright © 1968 by Harper & Row, Publishers, Inc. Reprinted by permission of HarperCollins Publishers.

Pages 549–551 Reprinted with permission of Ralph J. Lamberti from a memorial tribute to Rachel Maria Asrelsky, January 16, 1989.

Pages 553–559 Reprinted with permission of Julius J. Ford.

Pages 561–566 From *Pocho* by José Antonio Villarreal. Copyright © 1959 by José Antonio Villarreal. Used by permission of Doubleday, a division of Bantam Doubleday Dell Publishing Group, Inc.